P9-DGQ-649

CLYMER®

KAWASAKI
NINJA ZX900-1100 • 1984-2001

The world's finest publisher of mechanical how-to manuals

PRIMEDIA
Business Magazines & Media

P.O. Box 12901, Overland Park, Kansas 66282-2901

629.287
SCO

Copyright ©2002 PRIMEDIA Business Magazines & Media Inc.

FIRST EDITION
First Printing November, 1989
Second Printing October, 1990
Third Printing April, 1992

SECOND EDITION
Updated by Ed Scott to include 1988-1993 models
First Printing May, 1994
Second Printing March, 1996
Third Printing August, 1997
Fourth Printing September, 1999

THIRD EDITION
First Printing April, 2002

Printed in U.S.A.

CLYMER and colophon are registered trademarks of PRIMEDIA Business Magazines & Media Inc.

ISBN: 0-89287-825-8

Library of Congress: 2002102819

AUTHOR: Ed Scott

TECHNICAL PHOTOGRAPHY: Ron Wright and Ed Scott

TECHNICAL ILLUSTRATIONS: Steve Amos, Mitzi McCarthy and Robert Caldwell

ASSISTANCE: Curt Jordan, Jordan Engineering, Santa Ana, California

TOOLS AND EQUIPMENT: K&L Supply Co. (www.klsupply.com)

COVER: Mark Clifford, Mark Clifford Photography, Los Angeles, California

CONTENTS

QUICK REFERENCE DATA

MAINTENANCE AND TUNE-UP TIGHTENING TORQUES

Item	N•m	ft.-lb.
Oil drain plugs	29	22
Oil filter bolt	20	14.5
Spark plug	14	10
Valve tappet locknut (1984-1987)	25	18
Upper fork tube pinch bolts		
1984-1987	21	15
1988-on	28	21
Fork cap		
ZX900		
1984	23	16.5
1985-1986	25	18
ZX1000, ZX1100	23	16.5
Rear axle nut		
1984-1987	88	65
1988-on	108	80
Chain adjuster pinch bolts		
ZX900	32	24
ZX1000, ZX1100	39	29
Steering stem nut	39	29
Torque link nuts		
ZX1000 (1986-1987)	29	22
ZX1000 (1988-1990), ZX1100	25	18

TIRES AND TIRE PRESSURE (ZX900)*

Tire size	Pressure	Tire wear limit
Front-110/90 V16	32 psi (2.25 kg/cm^2)	1 mm (1/32 in.)
Rear-130/90 V16	36 psi (2.5 kg/cm^2)	3 mm (1/8 in.)
*Check tire pressure when cold.		

TIRES AND TIRE PRESSURE (ZX1000)*

Tire size	Pressure	Tire wear limit
1984-1987		
U.S. and Canadian		
Front-128/80 V16	36 psi (2.50 kg/cm^2)	1 mm (1/32 in.)
Rear-150/80 V16	41 psi (2.90 kg/cm^2)	2 mm (3/32 in.)
Other than U.S. and Canadian		
Front-128/80 V16	36 psi (2.50 kg/cm^2)	1 mm (1/32 in.)
Rear-150/80	36 psi (2.5 kg/cm^2)**	2 mm (3/32 in.)
1988-on		
Front		
120/70 VR17-V280	36 psi (2.5 kg/cm^2)	1 mm (1/32 in.)
Rear		
160/60 VR18-V280		
Under 80 mph (130 km/h)	41 psi (2.9 kg/cm^2)	2 mm (3/32 in.)
Over 80 mph (130 km/h)	41 psi (2.9 kg/cm^2)	3 mm (1/8 in.)

*Check tire pressure when cold.
**Kawasaki recommends to set rear tire pressure @ 41 psi (2.90 kg/cm^2) when vehicle speeds exceed 130 mph (210 km/h). When using your vehicle for racing purposes, consult with the tire manufacturer for additional tire information.

TIRES AND TIRE PRESSURE (ZX1100)*

Tire size	Pressure	Tire wear limit
Front 　120/70 ZR17	41 psi (2.9 kg/cm2)	1 mm (1/32 in.)
Rear 　180/55 ZR17		
Under 80 mph (130 km/h)	41 psi (2.9 kg/cm2)	2 mm (3/32 in.)
Over 80 mph (130 km/h)	41 psi (2.9 kg/cm2)	3 mm (1/8 in.)

RECOMMENDED LUBRICANTS AND FLUIDS

Engine oil	SAE 10W40, 10W50, 20W40, 20W50 rated SE, SF or SG
Front fork oil	SAE 10W20
Brake fluid	DOT 4
Clutch hydraulic fluid	DOT 4
Fuel	87 pump octale (RON + MON)/2 　91 Research octane (RON)
Battery	Distilled water
Cooling system	Permanent type antifreeze compounded 　for aluminum engines and radiators

ENGINE OIL CAPACITY

	Liter	U.S. qt.
Without filter change		
ZX900	2.6	2.7
ZX1000, ZX1100	3.5	3.7
With filter change		
ZX900	3.0	3.2
ZX1000, ZX1100	4.0	4.2

FRONT FORK OIL CAPACITY AND OIL LEVEL

Model	Change cc (oz.)	Rebuild cc (oz.)	Oil level mm (in.)
ZX900	273 (9.23)	317-325 (10.72-11.00)	332-336 13.071-13.228)
ZX1000			
1984-1987	295 (9.97)	344-352 (11.63-11.90)	377-381 (14.84-15.00)
1988-1990	360 (12.17)	415-423 (14.03-14.30)	128-132* (5.0-5.19)
ZX1100 C1-4	390 (13.18)	454-462 (15.35-15.62)	147-151* (5.78-5.94)
ZX1100 D1-9	410 (13.86)	461-469 (15.59-15.86)	131-135* (5.15-5.31)

* Fork assembly fully compressed.

COOLING SYSTEM SPECIFICATIONS

Capacity	
ZX900	2.0 L (2.1 U.S. qt.)
ZX1000	3.1 L (3.3 U.S. qt.)
Coolant ratio	50% soft water:50% coolant
Radiator cap	0.95-1.25 kg/cm^2 (14-18 psi)
Thermostat	
Opening temperature	80-84° C (176-183° F)
Valve operating lift	Not less than 8 mm (5/16 in.) @ 95° C (203° F)

FRONT FORK AIR PRESSURE (1984-1987)*

	kg/cm^2	psi
Standard		
ZX900	0.6	8.5
ZX1000	0.5	7.1
Usable range		
ZX900	0.5-0.7	7.1-10.0
ZX1000	0.4-0.6	5.7-85
Maximum	2.50	36

*The 1988-on models are not equipped with air pressurized front forks.

REAR SHOCK ABSORBER AIR PRESSURE (ZX900)

Road/load conditions	kg/cm^2	psi
Good/light	0	0
Bad/heavy	3.5	35

REAR SHOCK ABSORBER AIR PRESSURE (ZX1000)

	kg/cm^2	psi
1986-1987		
Recommended	0.5	7.1
Maximum	1.5	21
1988-1990		
Recommended	0-1.0	0-14
Maximum	1.0	14

REAR SHOCK ABSORBER DAMPING ADJUSTMENT

Adjuster position	Load	Road	Speed
1	Light	Good	Slow
2			
3			
4	Heavy	Rough	High

TUNE-UP SPECIFICATIONS

Spark plug gap	0.7-0.8 mm (0.028-0.031 in.)
Valve clearance (cold)	
1984-1987	
Intake	0.13-0.18 mm (0.005-0.007 in.)
Exhaust	0.18-0.23 mm (0.007-0.009 in.)
1988-on	
Intake	0.13-0.19 mm (0.005-0.007 in.)
Exhaust	0.18-0.24 mm (0.007-0.009 in.)
Idle speed	
ZX900	1,000 100 rpm
ZX1000 (1984-1987)	
U.S. 49-state	1,000 100 rpm
California	1,200 100 rpm
Canada and Europe	1,000 100 rpm
ZX1000 (1988-1990), ZX1100	1,000 50 rpm
Compression*	
ZX900	9.9 2.1 kg/cm2 (140 31 psi)
ZX1000	
1986-1987	10.7 2.1 kg/cm2 (152 33 psi)
1988-1990	8.8-13.5 kg/cm2 (125-192 psi)
ZX1100	9.0-13.8 kg/cm2 (128-196 psi)

*Compression readings listed are for stock engines. If your engine is equipped with non-stock camshafts or pistons, these compression figures cannot be used as references; ask the camshaft or piston manufacturer for new compression numbers.

SPARK PLUGS

	Standard riding	High speed riding	Low speed riding
1984-1987			
U.S. and Italy	NGK D9EA	NGK D9EA	NGK D8EA
	ND X27ES-U	ND X27ES-U	ND X24EX-U
Canada	NGK DR8ES	NGK DR8ES	NGK DR9ES-L
	ND X27ESR-U	ND X27ESR-U	ND X24ESR-U
All Europe	NGK DR8ES	NGK DR8ES	NGK DR8ES-L
except Italy	ND X27ES-U	ND X27ES-U	ND X24ES-U
1988-on			
U.S.	NGK C9E, ND U27ES-N —		—
All other	NGK CR9E, ND U27ESR-N —		—

CLYMER®

KAWASAKI

NINJA ZX900-1100 • 1984-2001

NOTE: If you own a 1988 or later model, first check the Supplement at the back of this book for any new service information.

CHAPTER ONE

GENERAL INFORMATION

This detailed, comprehensive manual covers 1984-1986 Kawasaki ZX900 and 1986-1987 ZX1000 Ninja models.

Troubleshooting, tune-up, maintenance and repair are not difficult, if you know what tools and equipment to use and what to do. Anyone of average intelligence and with some mechanical ability can perform most of the procedures in this manual.

The manual is written simply and clearly enough for owners who have never worked on a motorcycle, but is complete enough for use by experienced mechanics.

Some of the procedures require the use of special tools. Using an inferior substitute tool for a special tool is not recommended as it can be dangerous to you and may damage the part.

Table 1 lists model coverage with engine and frame serial numbers.

Metric and U.S. standards are used throughout this manual. Metric to U.S. conversion is given in **Table 2**.

MANUAL ORGANIZATION

This chapter provides general information and discusses equipment and tools useful both for preventive maintenance and troubleshooting.

Chapter Two provides methods and suggestions for quick and accurate diagnosis and repair of problems. Troubleshooting procedures discuss typical symptoms and logical methods to pinpoint the trouble.

Chapter Three explains all periodic lubrication and routine maintenance necessary to keep your Kawasaki operating well. Chapter Three also includes recommended tune-up procedures, eliminating the need to constantly consult other chapters on the various assemblies.

Subsequent chapters describe specific systems such as the engine, clutch, transmission, fuel, exhaust, suspension, steering, brakes and fairing. Each chapter provides disassembly, repair, and assembly procedures in simple step-by-step form. If a repair is impractical for a home mechanic, it is so indicated. It is usually faster and less expensive to take such repairs to a dealer or competent repair shop. Specifications concerning a particular system are included at the end of the appropriate chapter.

NOTES, CAUTIONS AND WARNINGS

The terms NOTE, CAUTION and WARNING have specific meanings in this manual. A NOTE provides additional information to make a step or procedure easier or clearer. Disregarding a NOTE could cause inconvenience, but would not cause damage or personal injury.

A CAUTION emphasizes areas where equipment damage could occur. Disregarding a CAUTION could cause permanent mechanical damage; however, personal injury is unlikely.

A WARNING emphasizes areas where personal injury or even death could result from negligence. Mechanical damage may also occur. WARNINGS *are to be taken seriously*. In some cases, serious injury and death has resulted from disregarding similar warnings.

SAFETY FIRST

Professional mechanics can work for years and never sustain a serious injury. If you observe a few rules of common sense and safety, you can enjoy many safe hours servicing your own machine. If you ignore these rules you can hurt yourself or damage the equipment.

1. Never use gasoline as a cleaning solvent.
2. Never smoke or use a torch in the vicinity of flammable liquids, such as cleaning solvent, in open containers.
3. If welding or brazing is required on the machine, remove the fuel tank and rear shock to a safe distance, at least 50 feet away. Welding on a gas tank requires special safety precautions and must be performed by someone skilled in the process. Do not attempt to weld or braze a leaking gas tank.
4. Use the proper sized wrenches to avoid damage to fasteners and injury to yourself.
5. When loosening a tight or stuck nut, be guided by what would happen if the wrench should slip. Be careful; protect yourself accordingly.
6. When replacing a fastener, make sure to use one with the same measurements and strength as the old one. Incorrect or mismatched fasteners can result in damage to the vehicle and possible personal injury. Beware of fastener kits that are filled with cheap and poorly made nuts, bolts, washers and cotter pins. Refer to *Fasteners* in this chapter for additional information.
7. Keep all hand and power tools in good condition. Wipe greasy and oily tools after using them. They are difficult to hold and can cause injury. Replace or repair worn or damaged tools.
8. Keep your work area clean and uncluttered.
9. Wear safety goggles during all operations involving drilling, grinding, the use of a cold chisel or anytime you feel unsure about the safety of your eyes. Safety goggles should also be worn anytime compressed air is used to clean a part.
10. Keep an approved fire extinguisher nearby. Be sure it is rated for gasoline (Class B) and electrical (Class C) fires.

11. When drying bearings or other rotating parts with compressed air, never allow the air jet to rotate the bearing or part; the air jet is capable of rotating them at speeds far in excess of those for which they were designed. The bearing or rotating part is very likely to disintegrate and cause serious injury and damage.

SERVICE HINTS

Most of the service procedures covered are straightforward and can be performed by anyone reasonably handy with tools. It is suggested, however, that you consider your own capabilities carefully before attempting any operation involving major disassembly of the engine or transmission.

1. "Front," as used in this manual, refers to the front of the motorcycle; the front of any component is the end closest to the front of the motorcycle. The "left-" and "right-hand" sides refer to the position of the parts as viewed by a rider sitting on the seat facing forward. For example, the throttle control is on the right-hand side. These rules are simple, but confusion can cause a major inconvenience during service.
2. Whenever servicing the engine or transmission, or when removing a suspension component, the bike should be secured in a safe manner. If the bike is to be parked on its sidestand, check the stand to make sure it is secure and not damaged. Block the front and rear wheels if they remain on the ground. If the bike is on its center stand, a small hydraulic jack and a block of wood can be used to raise the chassis. If the transmission is not going to be worked on and the drive chain is connected to the rear wheel, shift the transmission into first gear.
3. Disconnect the negative battery cable when working on or near the electrical, clutch or starter systems and before disconnecting any wires. On most batteries, the negative terminal will be marked with a minus (-) sign and the positive terminal with a plus (+) sign.
4. When disassembling a part or assembly, it is a good practice to tag the parts for location and mark all parts which mate together. Small parts, such as bolts, can be identified by placing them in plastic sandwich bags. Seal the bags and label them with masking tape and a marking pen. When reassembly will take place immediately, an accepted practice is to place nuts and bolts in a cupcake tin or egg carton in the order of disassembly.
5. Finished surfaces should be protected from physical damage or corrosion. Keep gasoline and brake fluid off painted surfaces.

6. Use penetrating oil on frozen or tight bolts, then strike the bolt head a few times with a hammer and punch (use a screwdriver on screws). Avoid the use of heat where possible, as it can warp, melt or affect the temper of parts. Heat also ruins finishes, especially paint and plastics.

7. Keep flames and sparks away from a charging battery or flammable fluids and do not smoke near them. It is a good idea to have a fire extinguisher handy in the work area. Remember that many gas appliances in home garages (water heater, clothes drier, etc.) have pilot lights.

8. No parts removed or installed (other than bushings and bearings) in the procedures given in this manual should require unusual force during disassembly or assembly. If a part is difficult to remove or install, find out why before proceeding.

9. Cover all openings after removing parts or components to prevent dirt, small tools, etc. from falling in.

10. Read each procedure *completely* while looking at the actual parts before starting a job. Make sure you *thoroughly* understand what is to be done and then carefully follow the procedure, step by step.

11. Recommendations are occasionally made to refer service or maintenance to a Kawasaki dealer or a specialist in a particular field. In these cases, the work will be done more quickly and economically than if you performed the job yourself.

12. In procedural steps, the term "replace" means to discard a defective part and replace it with a new or exchange unit. "Overhaul" means to remove, disassemble, inspect, measure, repair, reassemble and install major systems or parts.

13. Some operations require the use of a hydraulic press. It would be wiser to have these operations performed by a shop equipped for such work, rather than to try to do the job yourself with makeshift equipment that may damage your machine.

14. Repairs go much faster and easier if your machine is clean before you begin work. There are many special cleaners on the market, like Bel-Ray Degreaser, for washing the engine and related parts. Follow the manufacturer's directions on the container for the best results. Clean all oily or greasy parts with cleaning solvent as you remove them.

WARNING
Never use gasoline as a cleaning agent. It presents an extreme fire hazard and can be explosive under certain conditions. Be sure to work in a

well-ventilated area when using cleaning solvent. Keep a fire extinguisher, rated for gasoline fires, handy in any case.

15. Much of the labor charges for repairs made by dealers are for the time involved during in the removal, disassembly, assembly, and reinstallation of other parts in order to reach the defective part. It is frequently possible to perform the preliminary operations yourself and then take the defective unit to the dealer for repair at considerable savings.

16. If special tools are required, make arrangements to get them before you start. It is frustrating and time-consuming to get partly into a job and then be unable to complete it.

17. Make diagrams (or take a Polaroid picture) wherever similar-appearing parts are found. For instance, crankcase bolts are often not the same length. You may think you can remember where everything came from—but mistakes are costly. There is also the possibility that you may be sidetracked and not return to work for days or even weeks—in which the time carefully laid out parts may have become disturbed.

18. When assembling parts, be sure all shims and washers are replaced exactly as they came out.

19. Whenever a rotating part butts against a stationary part, look for a shim or washer. Use new gaskets if there is any doubt about the condition of the old ones. A thin coat of oil on non-pressure type gaskets may help them seal more effectively.

20. If it is necessary to make a gasket, and you do not have a suitable old gasket to use as a guide, apply engine oil to the gasket surface of the part. Then place the part on the new gasket material and press the part slightly. The oil will leave a very accurate outline on the gasket material that can be cut around.

21. Heavy grease can be used to hold small parts in place if they tend to fall out during assembly. However, keep grease and oil away from electrical and brake components.

22. A carburetor is best cleaned by spraying the orifices and jets with aerosol carburetor cleaner. Soaking the carburetor in commercial carburetor cleaner often results in more damage than good; never soak gaskets and rubber parts in these cleaners. Never use wire to clean out jets and air passages. They are easily damaged. Use compressed air to blow out the carburetor only if the float has been removed first.

23. Take your time and do the job right. Do not forget that a newly rebuilt engine must be broken in just like a new one.

TORQUE SPECIFICATIONS

Torque specifications throughout this manual are given in Newton-meters (N•m) and foot-pounds (ft.-lb.).

Table 3 lists general torque specifications for nuts and bolts that are not listed in the respective chapters. To use the table, first determine the size of the nut or bolt. **Figure 1** and **Figure 2** show how this is done.

FASTENERS

The materials and designs of the various fasteners used on your Kawasaki are not arrived at by chance or accident. Fastener design determines the type of tool required to work the fastener. Fastener material is carefully selected to decrease the possibility of physical failure.

Nuts, bolts and screws are manufactured in a wide range of thread patterns. To join a nut and bolt, the diameter of the bolt and the diameter of the hole in the nut must be the same. It is just as important that the threads on both be properly matched.

The best way to tell if the threads on 2 fasteners are matched is to turn the nut on the bolt (or the bolt into the threaded hole in a piece of equipment) with fingers only. Be sure both pieces are clean. If much force is required, check the thread condition on each fastener. If the thread condition is good but the fasteners jam, the threads are not compatible. A thread pitch gauge can also be used to determine pitch. Kawasaki motorcycles are manufactured with ISO (International Organization for Standardization) metric fasteners. The threads are cut differently than those of American fasteners (**Figure 3**).

Most threads are cut so that the fastener must be turned clockwise to tighten it. These are called right-hand threads. Some fasteners have left-hand threads; they must be turned counterclockwise to be tightened. Left-hand threads are used in locations where normal rotation of the equipment would tend to loosen a right-hand threaded fastener.

ISO Metric Screw Threads

ISO (International Organization for Standardization) metric threads come in 3 standard thread sizes: coarse, fine and constant pitch. The ISO coarse pitch is used for most all common fastener applications. The fine pitch thread is used on certain precision tools and instruments. The constant pitch thread is used

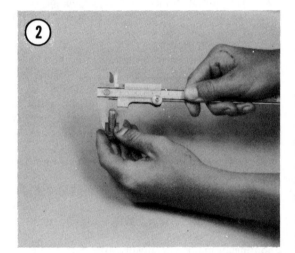

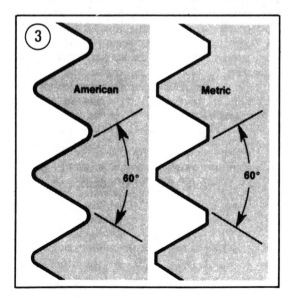

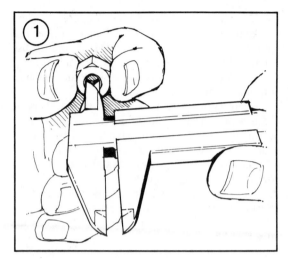

mainly on machine parts and not for fasteners. The constant pitch thread, however, is used on all metric thread spark plugs.

ISO metric threads are specified by the capital letter M followed by the diameter in millimeters and the pitch (or the distance between each thread) in millimeters separated by the sign ×. For example a M8×1.25 bolt is one that has a diameter of 8 millimeters with a distance of 1.25 millimeters between each thread. The measurement across 2 flats on the head of the bolt indicates the proper wrench size to be used. **Figure 2** shows how to determine bolt diameter.

Machine Screws

There are many different types of machine screws. **Figure 4** shows a number of screw heads

requiring different types of turning tools. Heads are also designed to protrude above the metal (round) or to be slightly recessed in the metal (flat). See **Figure 5**.

Bolts

Commonly called bolts, the technical name for these fasteners is cap screw. Metric bolts are described by the diameter and pitch (or the distance between each thread). For example a M8×1.25 bolt is one that has a diameter of 8 millimeters with a distance of 1.25 millimeters between each thread. The measurement across 2 flats on the head of the bolt indicates the proper wrench size to be used. **Figure 2** shows how to determine bolt diameter.

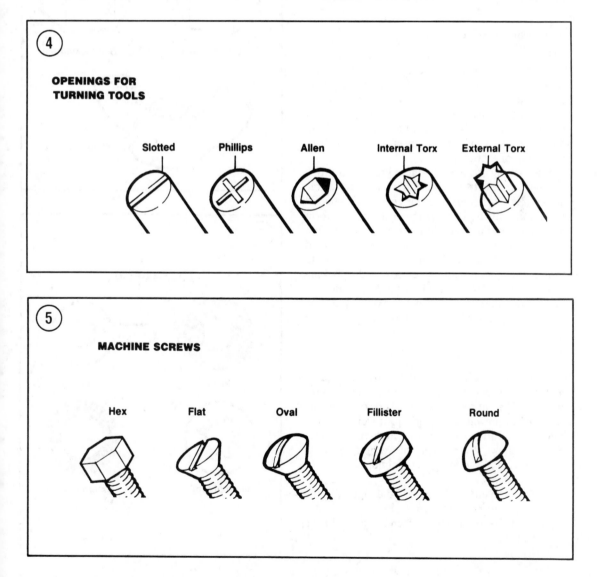

(4)

OPENINGS FOR TURNING TOOLS

Slotted Phillips Allen Internal Torx External Torx

(5)

MACHINE SCREWS

Hex Flat Oval Fillister Round

Nuts

Nuts are manufactured in a variety of types and sizes. Most are hexagonal (6-sided) and fit on bolts, screws and studs with the same diameter and pitch.

Figure 6 shows several types of nuts. The common nut is generally used with a lockwasher. Self-locking nuts have a nylon insert which prevents the nut from loosening; no lockwasher is required. Wing nuts are designed for fast removal by hand. Wing nuts are used for convenience in non-critical locations.

To indicate the size of a metric nut, manufacturers specify the diameter of the opening and the thread pitch. This is similar to bolt specifications, but without the length dimension. The measurement across 2 flats on the nut indicates the proper wrench size to be used.

Self-locking Fasteners

Several types of bolts, screws and nuts incorporate a system that develops an interference between the bolt, screw, nut or tapped hole threads. Interference is achieved in various ways: by distorting threads, coating threads with dry adhesive or nylon, distorting the top of an all-metal nut, using a nylon insert in the center or at the top of a nut, etc.

Self-locking fasteners offer greater holding strength and better vibration resistance. Some self-locking fasteners can be reused if in good condition. Others, like the nylon insert nut, form an initial locking condition when the nut is first installed; the nylon forms closely to the bolt thread pattern, thus reducing any tendency for the nut to loosen. When the nut is removed, the locking efficiency is greatly reduced. For greatest safety, it is recommended that you install new self-locking fasteners whenever they are removed.

Washers

There are 2 basic types of washers: flat washers and lockwashers. Flat washers are simple discs with a hole to fit a screw or bolt. Lockwashers are designed to prevent a fastener from working loose due to vibration, expansion and contraction. **Figure 7** shows several types of washers. Washers are also used in the following functions:

    a. As spacers.
    b. To prevent galling or damage of the equipment by the fastener.
    c. To help distribute fastener load during torquing.
    d. As seals.

Note that flat washers are often used between a lockwasher and the part to provide a smooth bearing surface. This allows the fastener to be turned easily with a tool and also prevent damage to the part.

Cotter Pins

Cotter pins (**Figure 8**) are used to secure special kinds of fasteners. The threaded stud must have a hole in it; the nut or nut lock piece has castellations

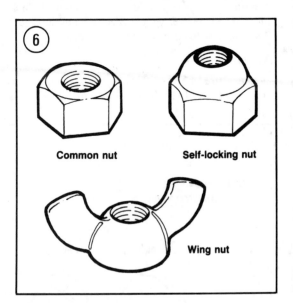

Common nut   Self-locking nut

Wing nut

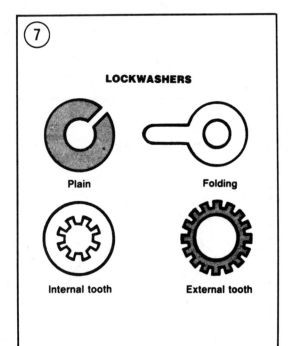

LOCKWASHERS

Plain   Folding

Internal tooth   External tooth

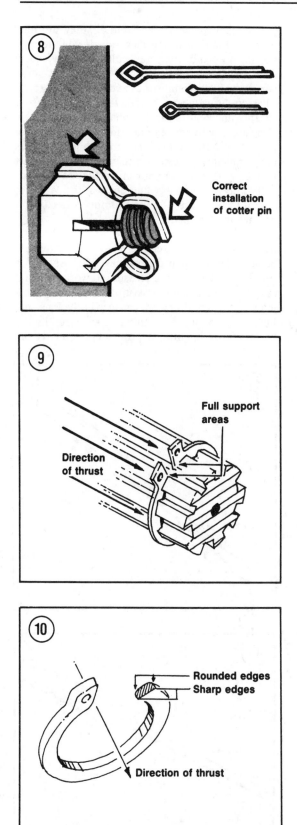

8

Correct
installation
of cotter pin

9

Full support
areas

Direction
of thrust

10

Rounded edges
Sharp edges

Direction of thrust

around which the cotter pin ends wrap. Cotter pins should not be reused after removal.

Snap Rings

Snap rings can be internal or external design. They are used to retain items on shafts (external type) or within tubes (internal type). In some applications, snap rings of varying thicknesses are used to control the end play of parts assemblies. These are often called selective snap rings. Snap rings should be replaced during installation, as removal weakens and deforms them.

Two basic styles of snap rings are available: machined and stamped snap rings. Machined snap rings (**Figure 9**) can be installed in either direction (shaft or housing) because both faces are machined, thus creating two sharp edges. Stamped snap rings (**Figure 10**) are manufactured with one sharp edge and one rounded edge. When installing stamped snap rings in a thrust situation (transmission shafts, fork tubes, etc.), the sharp edge must face away from the part producing the thrust. When installing snap rings, observe the following:

a. Compress or expand snap rings only enough to install them.

b. After the snap ring is installed, make sure it is completely seated in its groove.

LUBRICANTS

Periodic lubrication assures long life for any type of equipment. The *type* of lubricant used is just as important as the lubrication service itself, although in an emergency the wrong type of lubricant is better than none at all. The following paragraphs describe the types of lubricants most often used on motorcycle equipment. Be sure to follow the manufacturer's recommendations for lubricant types.

Generally, all liquid lubricants are called "oil." They may be mineral-based (including petroleum bases), natural-based (vegetable and animal bases), synthetic-based or emulsions (mixtures). "Grease" is an oil to which a thickening base has been added so that the end product is semi-solid. Grease is often classified by the type of thickener added; lithium soap is commonly used.

Engine Oil

Oil for motorcycle and automotive engines is graded by the American Petroleum Institute (API) and the Society of Automotive Engineers (SAE) in several categories. Oil containers display these ratings on the top or label.

API oil grade is indicated by letters; oils for gasoline engines are identified by an "S". The engines covered in this manual require SE or SF graded oil.

Viscosity is an indication of the oil's thickness. The SAE uses numbers to indicate viscosity; thin oils have low numbers while thick oils have high numbers. A "W" after the number indicates that the viscosity testing was done at low temperature to simulate cold-weather operation, such as SAE 10W.

Multi-grade oils (for example 10W-40) are less viscous (thinner) at low temperatures and more viscous (thicker) at high temperatures. This allows the oil to perform efficiently across a wide range of engine operating conditions. The lower the number, the better the engine will start in cold climates. Higher numbers are usually recommended for engines running in hot weather conditions.

Grease

Greases are graded by the National Lubricating Grease Institute (NLGI). Greases are graded by number according to the consistency of the grease; these range from No. 000 to No. 6, with No. 6 being the most solid. A typical multipurpose grease is NLGI No. 2. For specific applications, equipment manufacturers may require grease with an additive such as molybdenum disulfide (MOS2).

PARTS REPLACEMENT

Kawasaki makes frequent changes during a model year, some minor, some relatively major. When you order parts from the dealer or other parts distributor, always order by engine and frame numbers. Write the numbers down and carry them with you. Compare new parts to old before purchasing them. If they are not alike, have the parts manager explain the difference to you. Some newer parts may be retrofitted onto earlier production models, but be sure before leaving the dealer.

BASIC HAND TOOLS

Many of the procedures in this manual can be carried out with simple hand tools and test equipment familiar to the average home mechanic. Keep your tools clean and in a tool box. Keep them organized with the sockets and related drives together, the open-end and combination wrenches together, etc. After using a tool, wipe off dirt and grease with a clean cloth and return the tool to its correct place.

Top quality tools are essential; they are also more economical in the long run. If you are now starting to build your tool collection, stay away from the "advertised specials" featured at some parts houses, discount stores and chain drug stores. These are usually a poor grade tool that can be sold cheaply and that is exactly what they are—*cheap*. They are usually made of inferior material, and are thick, heavy and clumsy. Their rough finish makes them difficult to clean and they usually don't last very long. If it is ever your misfortune to use such tools, you will probably find out that the wrenches do not fit the heads of bolts and nuts correctly and damage the fastener.

Quality tools are made of alloy steel and are heat treated for greater strength. They are lighter and better balanced than cheap ones. Their surface is smooth, making them a pleasure to work with and easy to clean. The initial cost of good quality tools may be more but they are cheaper in the long run. Don't try to buy everything in all sizes in the beginning; do it a little at a time until you have the

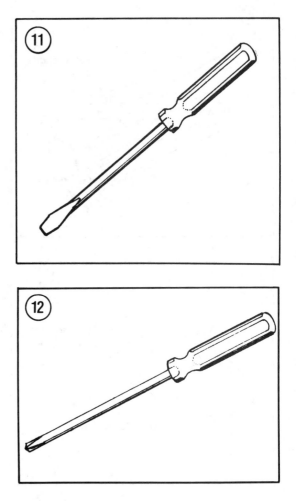

necessary tools. To sum up tool buying, "...the bitterness of poor quality lingers long after the sweetness of low price has faded."

The following tools are required to perform virtually any repair job. Each tool is described and the recommended size given for starting a tool collection. Additional tools and some duplicates may be added as you become familiar with the vehicle. Kawasaki motorcycles are built with metric standard fasteners—so if you are starting your collection now, buy metric sizes.

Screwdrivers

The screwdriver is a very basic tool, but if used improperly it will do more damage than good. The slot on a screw has a definite dimension and shape. A screwdriver must be selected to conform with that shape. Use a small screwdriver for small screws and a large one for large screws or the screw head will be damaged.

Two basic types of screwdriver are required: common (flat-blade) screwdrivers (**Figure 11**) and Phillips screwdrivers (**Figure 12**).

Screwdrivers are available in sets which often include an assortment of common and Phillips blades. If you buy them individually, buy at least the following:

  a. Common screwdriver—5/16×6 in. blade.
  b. Common screwdriver—3/8×12 in. blade.
  c. Phillips screwdriver—size 2 tip, 6 in. blade.

Use screwdrivers only for driving screws. Never use a screwdriver for prying or chiseling metal. Do not try to remove a Phillips or Allen head screw with a common screwdriver (unless the screw has a combination head that will accept either type); you can damage the head so that the proper tool will be unable to remove it.

Keep screwdrivers in the proper condition and they will last longer and perform better. Always keep the tip of a common screwdriver in good condition. **Figure 13** shows how to grind the tip to the proper shape if it becomes damaged. Note the symmetrical sides of the tip.

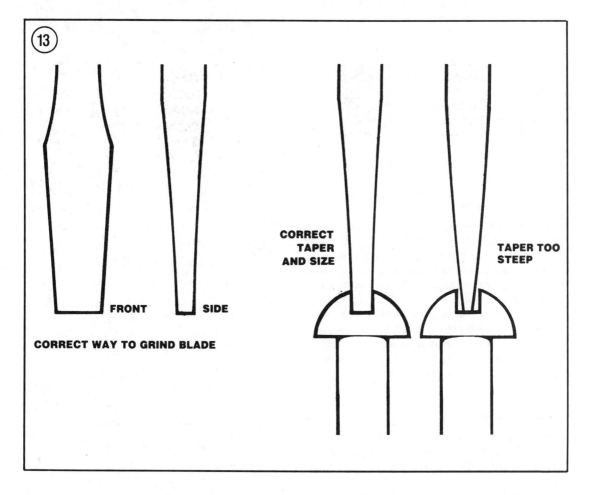

(13)

FRONT SIDE

CORRECT WAY TO GRIND BLADE

CORRECT TAPER AND SIZE

TAPER TOO STEEP

Pliers

Pliers come in a wide range of types and sizes. Pliers are useful for cutting, bending and crimping. They should never be used to cut hardened objects or to turn bolts or nuts. **Figure 14** shows several pliers useful in motorcycle repairs.

Each type of pliers has a specialized function. Gas pliers are general purpose pliers and are used mainly for holding things and for bending. Vise Grips are used as pliers or to hold objects very tightly like a vise. Needlenose pliers are used to hold or bend small objects. Channel lock pliers can be adjusted to hold various sizes of objects; the jaws remain parallel to grip round objects such as pipe or tubing. There are many more types of pliers.

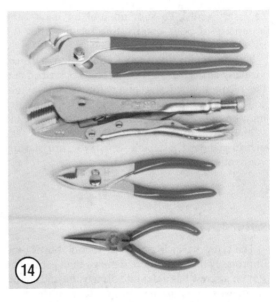

Box, Open-end Combinations Wrenches

Box and open-end wrenches are available in sets or separately in a variety of sizes. The size number stamped near the end refers to the distance between 2 parallel flats on the hex head bolt or nut.

Box wrenches are usually superior to open-end wrenches (**Figure 15**). Open-end wrenches grip the nut on only 2 flats. Unless a wrench fits well, it may slip and round off the points on the nut. The box wrench grips on all 6 flats. Both 6-point and 12-point openings on box wrenches are available. The 6-point gives superior holding power; the 12-point works better in tight confines.

Combination wrenches which are open on one side and boxed on the other are also available. Both ends are the same size. See **Figure 16.**

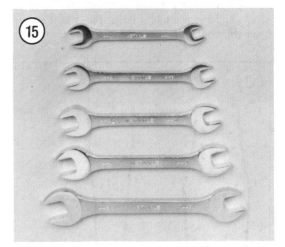

Adjustable Wrenches

An adjustable wrench can be adjusted to fit a variety of nuts or bolt heads (**Figure 17**). They are directional; always position the wrench so its solid (non-moving) jaw is applying most of the force. Using it improperly can cause it to loosen and slip, causing damage to the nut and injury to your knuckles. Use an adjustable wrench only when other wrenches are not available.

Adjustable wrenches come in sizes ranging from 4-18 in. overall. A 6 or 8 in. wrench is recommended as an all-purpose wrench.

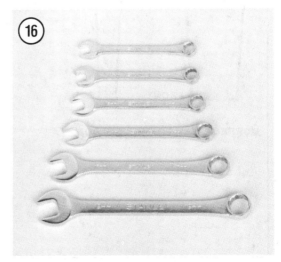

Socket Wrenches

This type is undoubtedly the fastest, safest and most convenient to use. Sockets which attach to a ratchet handle (**Figure 18**) are available with

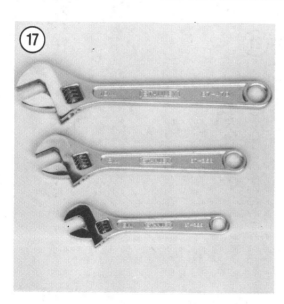

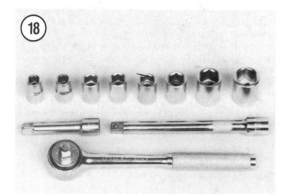

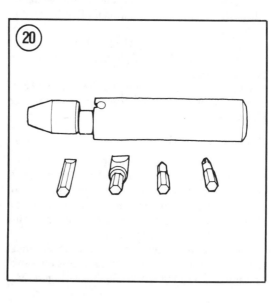

6-point or 12-point openings and 1/4, 3/8, 1/2 and 3/4 inch drives. The drive size indicates the size of the square hole which mates with the ratchet handle. 6-point sockets are much stronger and have an increased service life compared to 12-point sockets.

Torque Wrench

A torque wrench (**Figure 19**) is used with a socket to measure how tightly a nut or bolt is installed. They come in a wide price range and with either 3/8 or 1/2 in. square drive. The drive size indicates the size of the square drive which mates with the socket.

Impact Driver

This tool makes removal of tight fasteners easy and eliminates damage to bolts and screw slots. Impact drivers and interchangeable bits (**Figure 20**) are available at most large hardware and motorcycle dealers. Sockets can also be used with a hand impact driver. However, make sure the socket is designed for impact use. Do not use regular hand type sockets, as they may shatter.

Hammers

The correct hammer is necessary for repairs. Use only a hammer with a face (or head) of rubber or plastic or the soft-faced type that is filled with buckshot. These are sometimes necessary in engine teardowns. *Never* use a metal-faced hammer, as severe damage will result in most cases. You can always produce the same amount of force with a soft-faced hammer.

Feeler Gauge

This tool has both flat and wire measuring gauges and is used to measure various clearances and spark plug gap. See **Figure 21**. Wire gauges are used to measure spark plug gap; flat gauges are used for all other measurements.

Vernier Caliper

This tool is invaluable when reading inside, outside and depth measurements to close precision. The vernier caliper can be purchased from large dealers or mail order houses. See **Figure 22**.

Special Tools

A few special tools may be required for major service. These are described in the appropriate chapters and are available either from Kawasaki dealers or other manufacturers as indicated.

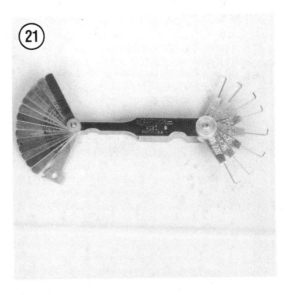

TEST EQUIPMENT

Voltmeter, Ammeter and Ohmmeter (Multimeter)

A good voltmeter is required for testing ignition and other electrical systems. Voltmeters are available with analog meter scales or digital readouts. An instrument covering 0-20 volts is satisfactory. It should also have a 0-2 volt scale for testing individual contacts where voltage drops are much smaller. Accuracy should be ± 1/2 volt.

An ohmmeter measures electrical resistance. This instrument is useful in checking continuity (for open and short circuits) and testing lights. A self-powered 12-volt test light can often be used in its place.

The ammeter measures electrical current. These are useful for checking battery starting and charging currents.

Some manufacturers combine the 3 instruments into one unit called a multimeter or VOM. See **Figure 23**.

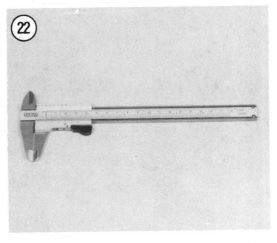

Compression Gauge

An engine with low compression cannot be properly tuned and will not develop full power. A compression gauge measures the amount of pressure present in the engine's combustion chambers during the compression stroke. This indicates general engine condition.

The Kawasaki models described in this manual require the use of a screw-in compression gauge that threads into the spark plug holes (**Figure 24**).

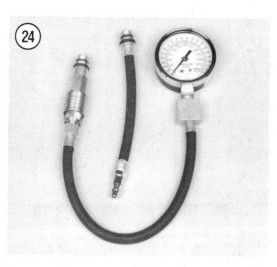

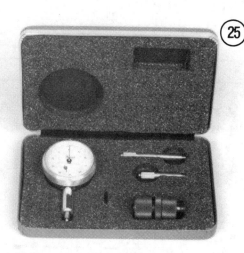

Dial Indicator

Dial indicators (**Figure 25**) are precision tools used to check dimension variations on machined parts such as transmission shafts and axles and to check crankshaft and axle shaft end play. Dial indicators are available with various dial types for different measuring requirements.

Strobe Timing Light

This instrument is necessary for checking ignition timing. By flashing a light at the precise instant the spark plug fires, the position of the timing mark can be seen. The flashing light makes a moving mark appear to stand still opposite a stationary mark.

Suitable lights range from inexpensive neon bulb types to powerful xenon strobe lights. See **Figure 26**. A light with an inductive pickup is recommended to eliminate any possible damage to ignition wiring.

Portable Tachometer

A portable tachometer is necessary for tuning. See **Figure 27**. Ignition timing and carburetor adjustments must be performed at the specified idle speed. The best instrument for this purpose is one with a low range of 0-2,000 rpm and a high range of 0-8,000 rpm. The instrument should be capable of detecting changes of 25 rpm on the low range.

Expendable Supplies

Certain expendable supplies are also required. These include grease, oil, gasket cement, shop rags

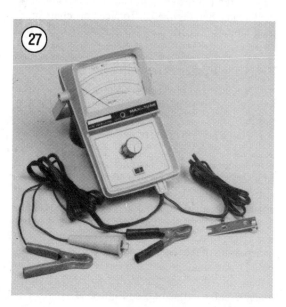

and cleaning solvent. Ask your dealer for the special locking compounds, silicone lubricants and lube products which make vehicle maintenance simpler and easier. Cleaning solvent is available at some service stations.

MECHANIC'S TIPS

Removing Frozen Nuts and Screws

When a fastener rusts and cannot be removed, several methods may be used to loosen it. First, apply penetrating oil such as Liquid Wrench or WD-40 (available at hardware or auto supply stores). Apply it liberally and let it penetrate for 10-15 minutes. Rap the fastener several times with a small hammer; do not hit it hard enough to cause damage. If an impact driver is available, use it now. Reapply the penetrating oil if necessary.

For frozen screws, apply penetrating oil as described, then insert a screwdriver in the slot and rap the top of the screwdriver with a hammer. This loosens the rust so the screw can be removed in the normal way. If an impact driver is available, use it now. If the screw head is too chewed up to use this method, grip the head with Vise Grips and twist the screw out.

Avoid applying heat unless specifically instructed, as it may melt, warp or remove the temper from parts.

Remedying Stripped Threads

Occasionally, threads are stripped through carelessness or impact damage. Often the threads can be cleaned up by running a tap (for internal threads on nuts) or die (for external threads on bolts) through the threads. See **Figure 28**. To clean or repair spark plug threads, a spark plug tap can be used (**Figure 29**).

Removing Broken Screws or Bolts

When the head breaks off a screw or bolt, several methods are available for removing the remaining portion.

If a large portion of the remainder projects out, try gripping it with Vise Grips. If the projecting portion is too small, file it to fit a wrench or cut a slot in it to fit a screwdriver. See **Figure 30**.

If the head breaks off flush, first try to use a small chisel and hammer to remove it by tapping it counterclockwise with the chisel. If that doesn't work, use a screw extractor. To do this, centerpunch the exact center of the remaining portion of the screw or bolt. Drill a small hole in the screw and tap the extractor into the hole. Back the screw out with a wrench on the extractor. See **Figure 31**.

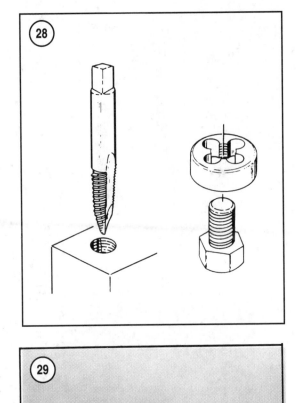

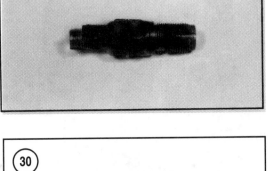

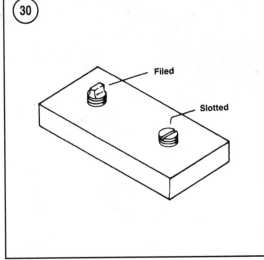

(31)

1

REMOVING BROKEN SCREWS AND BOLTS

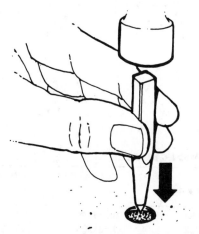

1. Center punch broken stud

2. Drill hole in stud

3. Tap in screw extractor

4. Remove broken stud

Table 1 ENGINE SERIAL NUMBERS

Year and model	Engine serial No. (start to finish)
1984 ZX900-A1	ZX900AE000001-ZX900AE019000
1985 ZX900-A2	ZX900AE019001-ZX900AE040000
1986 ZX900-A3	ZX900AED40001-*
1986 ZX1000-A1	ZXT00AE000001-ZXT00AE021000
1987 ZX1000-A2	ZXT00AE021001-*

*Not available at time of publication.

Table 2 DECIMAL AND METRIC EQUIVALENTS

Fractions	Decimal in.	Metric mm	Fractions	Decimal in.	Metric mm
1/64	0.015625	0.39688	33/64	0.515625	13.09687
1/32	0.03125	0.79375	17/32	0.53125	13.49375
3/64	0.046875	1.19062	35/64	0.546875	13.89062
1/16	0.0625	1.58750	9/16	0.5625	14.28750
5/64	0.078125	1.98437	37/64	0.578125	14.68437
3/32	0.09375	2.38125	19/32	0.59375	15.08125
7/64	0.109375	2.77812	39/64	0.609375	15.47812
1/8	0.125	3.1750	5/8	0.625	15.87500
9/64	0.140625	3.57187	41/64	0.640625	16.27187
5/32	0.15625	3.96875	21/32	0.65625	16.66875
11/64	0.171875	4.36562	43/64	0.671875	17.06562
3/16	0.1875	4.76250	11/16	0.6875	17.46250
13/64	0.203125	5.15937	45/64	0.703125	17.85937
7/32	0.21875	5.55625	23/32	0.71875	18.25625
15/64	0.234375	5.95312	47/64	0.734375	18.65312
1/4	0.250	6.35000	3/4	0.750	19.05000
17/64	0.265625	6.74687	49/64	0.765625	19.44687
9/32	0.28125	7.14375	25/32	0.78125	19.84375
19/64	0.296875	7.54062	51/64	0.796875	20.24062
5/16	0.3125	7.93750	13/16	0.8125	20.63750
21/64	0.328125	8.33437	53/64	0.828125	21.03437
11/32	0.34375	8.73125	27/32	0.84375	21.43125
23/64	0.359375	9.12812	55/64	0.859375	21.82812
3/8	0.375	9.52500	7/8	0.875	22.22500
25/64	0.390625	9.92187	57/64	0.890625	22.62187
13/32	0.40625	10.31875	29/32	0.90625	23.01875
27/64	0.421875	10.71562	59/64	0.921875	23.41562
7/16	0.4375	11.11250	15/16	0.9375	23.81250
29/64	0.453125	11.50937	61/64	0.953125	24.20937
15/32	0.46875	11.90625	31/32	0.96875	24.60625
31/64	0.484375	12.30312	63/64	0.984375	25.00312
1/2	0.500	12.70000	1	1.00	25.40000

Table 3 GENERAL TORQUE SPECIFICATIONS

Thread diameter	N·m	ft.-lb.
5 mm	3.4-4.9	30-43 in.-lb.
6 mm	5.9-7.8	52-69 in.-lb.
8 mm	14-19	10.0-13.5
10 mm	25-39	19-25
12 mm	44-61	33-45
14 mm	73-98	54-72
16 mm	115-155	83-115
18 mm	165-225	125-165
20 mm	225-325	165-240

NOTE: If you own a 1988 or later model, first check the Supplement at the back of this book for any new service information.

CHAPTER TWO

TROUBLESHOOTING

Diagnosing mechanical problems is relatively simple if you use orderly procedures and keep a few basic principles in mind.

The troubleshooting procedures in this chapter analyze typical symptoms and show logical methods of isolating causes. These are not the only methods. There may be several ways to solve a problem, but only a systematic approach can guarantee success.

Never assume anything. Do not overlook the obvious. If you are riding along and the bike suddenly quits, check the easiest, most accessible problem spots first.

If nothing obvious turns up in a quick check, look a little further. Learning to recognize and describe symptoms will make repairs easier for you or a mechanic at the shop. Describe problems accurately and fully. Saying that "it won't run" isn't the same thing as saying "it quit at high speed and won't start," or that "it sat in my garage for 3 months and then wouldn't start."

Gather as many symptoms as possible to aid in diagnosis. Note whether the engine lost power gradually or all at once. Remember that the more complicated a machine is, the easier it is to troubleshoot because symptoms point to specific problems.

After the symptoms are defined, areas which could cause problems are tested and analyzed. Guessing at the cause of a problem may provide the solution, but it can easily lead to frustration, wasted time and a series of expensive, unnecessary parts replacements.

You do not need fancy equipment or complicated test gear to determine whether repairs can be attempted at home. A few simple checks could save a large repair bill and lost time while the bike sits in a dealer's service department. On the other hand, be realistic and don't attempt repairs beyond your abilities. Service departments tend to charge heavily for putting together a disassembled engine that may have been abused. Some won't even take on such a job—so use common sense and don't get in over your head.

Electrical test specifications are listed in **Table 1** (end of chapter).

OPERATING REQUIREMENTS

An engine needs 3 basics to run properly: correct fuel/air mixture, compression and a spark at the correct time. If one or more are missing, the engine will not run. Four-stroke engine operating principles are described under *Engine Principles* in

Chapter Four. The electrical system is the weakest link of the 3 basics. More problems result from electrical breakdowns than from any other source. Keep that in mind before you begin tampering with carburetor adjustments and the like.

If the machine has been sitting for any length of time and refuses to start, check and clean the spark plugs and then look to the gasoline delivery system. This includes the fuel tank, fuel shutoff valve and fuel line to the carburetor. Gasoline deposits may have formed and gummed up the carburetor jets and air passages. Gasoline tends to lose its potency after standing for long periods. Condensation may contaminate the fuel with water. Drain the old fuel (fuel tank, fuel lines and carburetors) and try starting with a fresh tankful.

TROUBLESHOOTING INSTRUMENTS

Chapter One lists the instruments needed and instruction on their use.

STARTING THE ENGINE

When experiencing engine starting troubles, frustration can cause the most experienced rider to forget basic engine starting procedures.

NOTE
Never operate the electric starter for more than 5 seconds at a time. Wait approximately 15 seconds between starting attempts.

Starting Notes

1. The electric starter can operate when the transmission is in gear and the clutch disengaged.
2. Shift the transmission into NEUTRAL, turn the fuel valve to ON and push the engine stop switch to RUN.
3. The engine is now ready to start. Refer to the starting procedure in this section that pertains to the temperature that exists with your engine.

CAUTION
If the engine is idled at a fast speed for 5 minutes or more and/or the throttle is snapped on and off rapidly at normal air temperatures, the exhaust pipes may discolor. Excessive use of the choke may cause a rich mixture and result in piston and cylinder wall scuffing.

CAUTION
Once the engine starts, the red oil pressure warning light should go off in a few seconds. If the light stays on

longer than a few seconds, immediately stop the engine. Check the engine oil level as described in Chapter Three and correct if necessary. If the oil level is okay, the oil pressure is too low. Check the oiling system and correct the problem before starting the engine. Severe engine damage will occur if the engine is run with low oil pressure.

**Starting Procedure
(Cold Engine With Normal Air Temperature)**

Normal air temperature is considered to be between 50-95° F (10-35° C).
1. Perform the procedures under *Starting Notes*.
2. Install the ignition key and turn the ignition switch to ON.
3. Pull the choke lever to the fully open position.
4. Operate the starter button and start the engine. Do not open the throttle.

NOTE
When a cold engine is started with the throttle open and the choke open, a lean mixture will result and cause hard starting.

5. With the engine running, operate the choke lever as required to keep the engine idle at 1,500-2,500 rpm.
6. After approximately 30 seconds, push the choke lever to the fully closed position. If the idling is rough, open the throttle to help warm the engine.

**Starting Procedure
(Cold Engine With Low Air Temperature)**

Low air temperature is considered to be 50° F (10° C) or lower.
1. Perform the procedures under *Starting Notes*.
2. Install the ignition key and turn the ignition switch to ON.
3. Pull the choke lever to the fully open position.
4. Operate the starter button and start the engine. Do not open the throttle when pressing the starter button.
5. Once the engine is running, open the throttle slightly to help warm the engine. Continue warming the engine until the choke can be turned to the fully closed position and the engine responds to the throttle cleanly.

**Starting Procedure
(Warm Engine and/or High Air Temperature)**

High air temperature is considered to be 95° F (35° C) or higher.

1. Perform the procedures under *Starting Notes*.
2. Install the ignition key and turn the ignition switch to ON.
3. Operate the starter button, open the throttle slightly and start the engine.

Starting Procedure
(Flooded Engine)

If the engine does not start after a few attempts it may be flooded. If the smell of gasoline is present, you can be sure it is flooded. To start a flooded engine, perform the following.
1. Perform the procedures under *Starting Notes*.
2. Install the ignition key and turn the ignition switch to ON.
3. Push the choke lever to the closed position.
4. Open the throttle grip completely and push the starter button and crank the engine.

EMERGENCY
TROUBLESHOOTING

When the bike is difficult to start, or won't start at all, it doesn't help to wear down the battery using the electric starter. Check for obvious problems even before getting out your tools. Go down the following list step by step. Do each one; you may be embarrassed to find the engine stop switch off, but that is better than wearing down the battery. If the bike still will not start, refer to the appropriate troubleshooting procedures which follows in this chapter.
1. Is there fuel in the tank? Open the filler cap and rock the bike. Listen for fuel sloshing around.

> *WARNING*
> *Do not use an open flame to check in the tank. A serious explosion is certain to result.*

2. Is the fuel supply valve in the ON position? If necessary, turn the valve to the RES position to be sure you get the last remaining gas.
3. Make sure the engine stop switch (**Figure 1**) is not stuck in the OFF position or that the wire is not broken and shorting out. Test the switch as described under *Switches* in Chapter Eight.
4. Are the spark plug wires on tight? Remove the fuel tank as described in Chapter Seven. Push all 4 spark plug caps on and slightly rotate them to clean the electrical connection between the plug and the connector.
5. Is the choke lever (**Figure 2**) in the right position?

ENGINE STARTING

An engine that refuses to start or is difficult to start is very frustrating. More often than not, the problem is very minor and can be found with a simple and logical troubleshooting approach.

The following items will help isolate engine starting problems.

Engine Fails to Start

Perform the following spark test to determine if the ignition system is operating properly.
1. Remove the fuel tank as described in Chapter Seven.
2. Remove one of the spark plug caps (**Figure 3**) and remove the spark plug.
3. Connect the spark plug wire and connector to the spark plug and touch the spark plug base to a

good ground like the engine cylinder head. Position the spark plug so you can see the electrodes, but away from the spark plug hole in the cylinder head.

WARNING
During the next step, do not hold the spark plug, wire or connector with fingers or a serious electrical shock may result. If necessary, use a pair of insulated pliers to hold the spark plug or wire. The high voltage generated by the ignition system could produce serious or fatal shocks.

4. Crank the engine over with the starter. A fat blue spark should be evident across the spark plug electrodes.

NOTE
*If the starter does not operate or if the starter motor rotates but the engine does not turn over, refer to **Engine Will Not Crank** in this section.*

5. If the spark is good, check for one or more of the following possible malfunctions:
   a. Obstructed fuel line or fuel filter.
   b. Low compression.
6. If the spark is not good, check for one or more of the following:
   a. Loose electrical connections.
   b. Dirty electrical connections.
   c. Loose or broken ignition coil ground wire.
   d. Broken or shorted high tension lead to the spark plug(s).
   e. Discharged battery.
   f. Disconnected or damaged battery connection.
   g. IC igniter malfunction.

h. Neutral, starter lockout or sidestand switch malfunction.
i. Ignition or engine stop switch malfunction.
j. Blown fuse.

Engine is Difficult to Start

Check for one or more of the following possible malfunctions:
   a. Fouled spark plug(s).
   b. Improperly adjusted choke.
   c. Intake manifold air leak.
   d. Contaminated fuel system.
   e. Improperly adjusted carburetor.
   f. Weak ignition unit.
   g. Weak ignition coil(s).
   h. Poor compression.
   i. Engine and transmission oil too heavy.

Engine Will Not Crank

Check for one or more of the following possible malfunctions:
   a. Blown fuse.
   b. Discharged battery.
   c. Defective starter motor.
   d. Starter lockout or neutral switch malfunction.
   e. Engine stop switch malfunction.
   f. Defective starter motor button and contact.
   g. Seized or broken piston(s).
   h. Seized crankshaft bearings.
   i. Broken connecting rod.

Starter Motor Turns but
Engine Doesn't Turn Over

Defective starter motor clutch.

ENGINE PERFORMANCE

In the following checklist, it is assumed that the engine runs, but is not operating at peak performance. This will serve as a starting point from which to isolate a performance malfunction.

Engine Will Not Idle

   a. Carburetor incorrectly adjusted.
   b. Improperly adjusted choke (engine dies when throttle is closed).
   c. Valve clearance incorrect.
   d. Fouled or improperly gapped spark plug(s).
   e. Obstructed fuel line or fuel shutoff valve.
   f. Obstructed fuel filter.
   g. Ignition timing incorrect due to defective ignition component(s).
   h. Leaking head gasket.

Engine Misses at High Speed

a. Fouled or improperly gapped spark plugs.
b. Dirty air cleaner.
c. Clogged carburetor jets.
d. Obstructed fuel line or fuel shutoff valve.
e. Obstructed fuel filter.
f. Ignition timing incorrect due to defective ignition component(s).
g. Weak ignition coil(s).
h. Air suction valve malfunction (U.S. models).

Engine Overheating

a. Incorrect carburetor adjustment or jet selection.
b. Ignition timing retarded due to defective ignition component(s).
c. Improper spark plug heat range.
d. Incorrect coolant level.
e. Oil level low.
f. Oil not circulating properly.
g. Heavy engine carbon deposits.
h. Dragging brake(s).
i. Clutch slipping.
j. Cooling system malfunction (see below).

Engine Overheating (Cooling System Malfunction)

Note the above, then proceed with the following items:

a. Clogged radiator.
b. Worn or damaged radiator cap.
c. Damaged thermostat.
d. Water pump worn or damaged.
e. Fan relay malfunction.
f. Thermostatic fan switch malfunction.
g. Damaged fan blade(s).

Smoky (Black) Exhaust and Engine Runs Roughly

a. Clogged air filter element.
b. Carburetor adjustment incorrect—mixture too rich.
c. Choke not operating correctly.
d. Water or other contaminants in fuel.
e. Spark plugs fouled.
f. Ignition coil defective.
g. IC igniter or pickup coil defective.
h. Loose or defective ignition circuit wire.
i. Short circuit from damaged wire insulation.
j. Loose battery cable connection.
k. Valve timing incorrect.

Engine Loses Power at Normal Riding Speed

a. Carburetor incorrectly adjusted.
b. Engine overheating.
c. Ignition timing incorrect due to defective ignition component(s).
d. Incorrectly gapped spark plugs.
e. Obstructed muffler.
f. Dragging brake(s).

Engine Lacks Acceleration

a. Carburetor mixture too lean.
b. Clogged fuel line.
c. Ignition timing incorrect due to defective ignition component(s).
d. Dragging brake(s).
e. Slipping clutch.

ENGINE NOISES

Often the first evidence of an internal engine problem is a strange noise. That knocking, clicking or tapping sound which you never heard before may be warning you of impending trouble.

While engine noises can indicate problems, they are difficult to interpret correctly; inexperienced mechanics can be seriously misled by them.

Professional mechanics often use a special stethoscope (which looks like a doctor's stethoscope) for isolating engine noises. You can do nearly as well with a "sounding stick" which can be an ordinary piece of doweling, a length of broom handle or a section of small hose. By placing one end in contact with the area to which you want to listen and the other end near your ear, you can amplify sounds emanating from that area. The first time you do this, you may be horrified at the strange sounds coming from even a normal engine. If you can, have an experienced friend or mechanic help you sort out the noises.

Consider the following when troubleshooting engine noises:

1. *Knocking or pinging during acceleration*— Caused by using a lower octane fuel than recommended. May also be caused by poor fuel quality. Pinging can also be caused by a spark plug of the wrong heat range or carbon build-up in the combustion chamber(s). Refer to *Correct Spark Plug Heat Range* and *Compression Test* in Chapter Three.

2. *Slapping or rattling noises at low speed or during acceleration*—May be caused by piston slap, i.e., excessive piston-cylinder wall clearance.

NOTE
Piston slap is easier to detect when the engine is cold and before the pistons have expanded. Once the engine has warmed up, piston expansion reduces piston-to-cylinder clearance.

3. *Knocking or rapping while decelerating—* Usually caused by excessive rod bearing clearance.
4. *Persistent knocking and vibration—* Usually caused by worn main bearing(s).
5. *Rapid on-off squeal—* Compression leak around cylinder head gasket or spark plug(s).
6. *Valve train noise—* Check for the following:
   a. Valves adjusted incorrectly.
   b. Loose valve adjuster.
   c. Valve sticking in guide.
   d. Low oil pressure.
   e. Damaged rocker arm or shaft. Rocker arm may be binding on shaft.

ENGINE LUBRICATION

An improperly operating engine lubrication system will quickly lead to engine seizure. The engine oil level should be checked weekly and topped up, as described in Chapter Three. Oil pump service is described in Chapter Four.

Oil Consumption High or Engine Smokes Excessively

   a. Worn valve guides.
   b. Worn or damaged piston rings.

Excessive Engine Oil Leaks

   a. Clogged air cleaner breather hose.
   b. Loose engine parts.
   c. Damaged gasket sealing surfaces.

EXCESSIVE EXHAUST SMOKE

Black Smoke

   a. Clogged air cleaner.
   b. Incorrect carburetor float level (too high).
   c. Choke stuck open.
   d. Incorrect main jet (too large).

White Smoke

   a. Worn valve guide.
   b. Worn valve oil seal.
   c. Worn piston oil ring.
   d. Excessive cylinder and/or piston wear.
   e. Engine oil level too high.

Brown Smoke

   a. Incorrect main jet (too small).
   b. Incorrect carburetor fuel level (too low).
   c. Loose or damaged air cleaner housing ducting.
   d. Air cleaner element not sealing properly.

CLUTCH

The three basic clutch troubles are:
   a. Clutch noise.
   b. Clutch slipping.
   c. Improper clutch disengagement or dragging.

All clutch troubles, except adjustments, require partial clutch disassembly to identify and cure the problem. The troubleshooting chart in **Figure 4** lists clutch troubles and checks to make. Refer to Chapter Five for clutch service procedures.

TRANSMISSION

The basic transmission troubles are:
   a. Excessive gear noise.
   b. Difficult shifting.
   c. Gears pop out of mesh.
   d. Incorrect shift lever operation.

Transmission symptoms are sometimes hard to distinguish from clutch symptoms. The troubleshooting chart in **Figure 5** lists transmission troubles and checks to make. Refer to Chapter Six for transmission service procedures. Be sure that the clutch is not causing the trouble before working on the transmission.

ELECTRICAL TROUBLESHOOTING

This section describes the basics of electrical troubleshooting, how to use test equipment and the basic test procedures with the various pieces of test equipment.

Electrical troubleshooting can be very time consuming and frustrating without proper knowledge and a suitable plan. Refer to the wiring diagrams at the end of the book and at the individual system diagrams included with the charging system, ignition system and starting system sections in this chapter. Wiring diagrams will help you determine how the circuit should work by tracing the current paths from the power source through the circuit components to ground. Also check any circuits that share the same fuse, ground or switch, etc. If the other circuits work properly, the shared wiring is okay and the cause must be in the wiring used only by the suspect circuit. If all related circuits are faulty at the same time the probable cause is a poor ground connection or a blown fuse(s).

As with all troubleshooting procedures, analyze typical symptoms in a systematic procedure. Never assume anything and don't overlook the obvious like a blown fuse or an electrical connector that has separated. Test the simplest and most obvious cause first and try to make tests at easily accessible points on the bike.

Preliminary Checks and Precautions

Prior to starting any electrical troubleshooting procedure perform the following:

a. Check the individual fuse(s) for each circuit; make sure it is not blown. Replace if necessary. Refer to *Junction Box and Fuses* in Chapter Eight.

b. Inspect the battery. Make sure it is fully charged, the electrolyte level is correct and that the battery leads are clean and securely attached to the battery terminals. Refer to *Battery* in Chapter Three.

c. Disconnect each electrical connector in the suspect circuit and check that there are no bent metal pins on the male side of the electrical connector (**Figure 6**). A bent pin will not connect to its mating receptacle in the female end of the connector, causing an open circuit.

d. Check each female end of the connector. Make sure that the metal terminal on the end of each wire (**Figure 7**) is pushed all the way into the plastic connector. If not, carefully push them in with a narrow, flat-blade screwdriver.

e. Check all electrical wires where they enter the individual metal terminals in both the male and female plastic connector.

f. Make sure all electrical terminals within the connector are clean and free of corrosion.

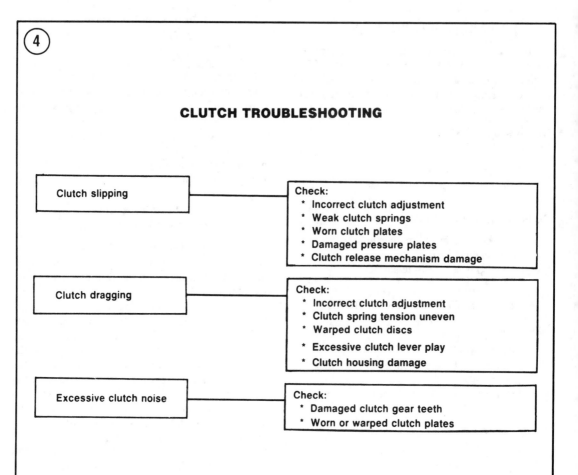

④

CLUTCH TROUBLESHOOTING

Clutch slipping — Check:
* Incorrect clutch adjustment
* Weak clutch springs
* Worn clutch plates
* Damaged pressure plates
* Clutch release mechanism damage

Clutch dragging — Check:
* Incorrect clutch adjustment
* Clutch spring tension uneven
* Warped clutch discs
* Excessive clutch lever play
* Clutch housing damage

Excessive clutch noise — Check:
* Damaged clutch gear teeth
* Worn or warped clutch plates

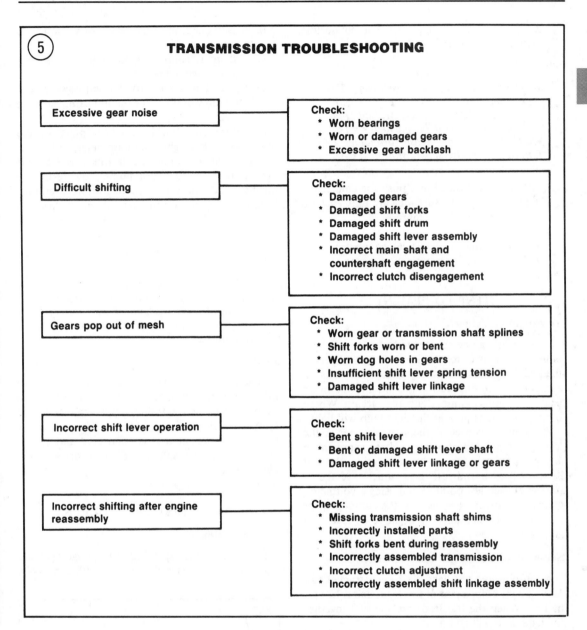

⑤ TRANSMISSION TROUBLESHOOTING

| Excessive gear noise | Check:
* Worn bearings
* Worn or damaged gears
* Excessive gear backlash |

| Difficult shifting | Check:
* Damaged gears
* Damaged shift forks
* Damaged shift drum
* Damaged shift lever assembly
* Incorrect main shaft and countershaft engagement
* Incorrect clutch disengagement |

| Gears pop out of mesh | Check:
* Worn gear or transmission shaft splines
* Shift forks worn or bent
* Worn dog holes in gears
* Insufficient shift lever spring tension
* Damaged shift lever linkage |

| Incorrect shift lever operation | Check:
* Bent shift lever
* Bent or damaged shift lever shaft
* Damaged shift lever linkage or gears |

| Incorrect shifting after engine reassembly | Check:
* Missing transmission shaft shims
* Incorrectly installed parts
* Shift forks bent during reassembly
* Incorrectly assembled transmission
* Incorrect clutch adjustment
* Incorrectly assembled shift linkage assembly |

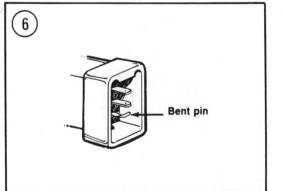

⑥ Bent pin

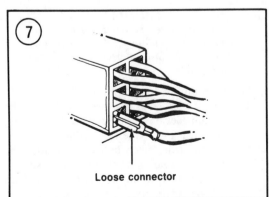

⑦ Loose connector

Clean, if necessary, and pack the connectors with a dielectric grease.

> *NOTE*
> *Connectors can be serviced by disconnecting them and cleaning with electrical contact cleaner. Multiple pin connectors should be packed with a dielectric silicone grease (available at most automotive supply stores).*

g. After all is checked out, push the connectors together and make sure they are fully engaged and locked together (**Figure 8**).

h. Never pull on the electrical wires when disconnecting an electrical connector—pull only on the connector plastic housing.

TEST EQUIPMENT

Test Light or Voltmeter

A test light can be constructed of a 12-volt light bulb with a pair of test leads carefully soldered to the bulb. To check for battery voltage (12 volts) in a circuit, attach one lead to ground and the other lead to various points along the circuit. Where battery voltage is present the light bulb will light.

A voltmeter is used in the same manner as the test light to find out of battery voltage is present in any given circuit. The voltmeter, unlike the test light, will also indicate how much voltage is present at each test point. When using a voltmeter, attach the positive (+) lead to the component or wire to be checked and the negative (-) lead to a good ground.

Self-powered Test Light and Ohmmeter

A self-powered test light can be constructed of a 12-volt light bulb, a pair of test leads and a 12-volt battery. When the test leads are touched together the light bulb will go on.

> *CAUTION*
> *Never use a self-powered test light on circuits that contain solid-state devices. The solid-state devices may be damaged.*

Use a self-powered test light as follows:

a. Touch the test leads together to make sure the light bulb goes on. If not, correct the problem prior to using it in a test procedure.

b. Disconnect the bike's battery or remove the fuse(s) that protects the circuit to be tested.

c. Select 2 points within the circuit where there should be continuity.

d. Attach one lead of the self-powered test light to each point.

e. If there is continuity, the self-powered test light bulb will come on.

f. If there is no continuity, the self-powered test light bulb will *not* come on, indicating an open circuit.

An ohmmeter can be used in place of the self-powered test light. The ohmmeter, unlike the test light, will also indicate how much resistance is present between each test point. Low resistance means good continuity in a complete circuit. Before using an ohmmeter, it must first be calibrated. This is done by touching the leads together and turning the ohms calibration knob until the meter reads "zero."

> *CAUTION*
> *An ohmmeter must never be connected to any circuit which has power applied to it. Always disconnect the battery negative lead before using the ohmmeter.*

Jumper Wire

When using a jumper wire always install an inline fuse/fuse holder (available at most auto supply stores or electronic supply stores) to the jumper wire. Never use a jumper wire across any load (a component that is connected and turned on). This would result in a direct short and will blow the fuse(s).

BASIC TEST PROCEDURES

Voltage Testing

Unless otherwise specified, all voltage tests are made with the electrical connector still *connected*.

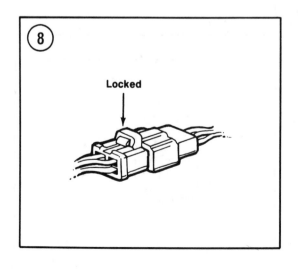

(8)

Locked

Insert the test leads into the backside of the connector and make sure the test lead touches the electrical wire or metal connector within the connector. If the test lead only touches the wire insulation, you will get no reading.

Always check both sides of the connector as one side may be loose or corroded thus preventing electrical flow through the connector. This type of test can be performed with a test light or a voltmeter. A voltmeter will give the best results.

NOTE
If using a test light, it doesn't make any difference which test lead is attached to ground.

1. Attach one test lead (negative, if using a voltmeter) to a good ground (bare metal). If necessary, scrape away paint from the frame or engine (retouch later with paint). Make sure the part used for ground is not insulated with a rubber gasket or rubber grommet.
2. Attach the other test lead (positive, if using a voltmeter) to the point (electrical connector, etc.) you want to check.
3. Turn the ignition switch to the ON position. If using a test light, the test light will come on if voltage is present. If using a voltmeter, note the voltage reading. The reading should be within 1 volt of battery voltage (12 volts). If the voltage is 11 volts or less there is a problem in the circuit.

Voltage Drop Test

A voltage drop of 1 volt means there is a problem in the circuit. All components within the circuit are designed for low resistance in order to conduct electricity within a minimum loss of voltage.
1. Connect the voltmeter positive test lead to the end of the wire or switch closest to the battery.
2. Connect the voltmeter negative test lead to the other end of the wire or switch.
3. Turn the components on in the circuit.
4. The voltmeter should indicate 12 volts. If there is a drop of 1 volt or more, there is a problem within the circuit.
5. Check the circuit for loose or dirty connections within electrical connector(s).

Continuity Test

A continuity test is made to determine if the circuit is complete with no opens in either the electrical wires or components within that circuit.

Unless otherwise specified, all continuity tests are made with the electrical connector still *connected*. Insert the test leads into the backside of

the connector and make sure the test lead touches the electrical wire or metal connector within the connector. If the test lead only touches the wire insulation you will get a false reading.

Always check both sides of the connectors as one side may be loose or corroded thus preventing electrical flow through the connector. This type of test can be performed with a self-powered test light or an ohmmeter. An ohmmeter will give the best results.

If using an ohmmeter, calibrate the meter by touching the leads together and turning the ohms calibration knob until the meter reads "zero." This is necessary in order to get accurate results.
1. Disconnect the battery negative lead.
2. Attach one test lead (test light or ohmmeter) to one end of the part of the circuit to be tested.
3. Attach the other test lead to the other end of the part of the circuit to be tested.
4. The self-powered test light will come on if there is continuity. The ohmmeter will indicate either low or no resistance (which means good continuity in a complete circuit) or infinite resistance (which means an open circuit).

Testing For a Short
With a Self-powered Test Light
or Ohmmeter

This test can be performed with either a self-powered test light or an ohmmeter.
1. Disconnect the battery negative lead.
2. Remove the blown fuse from the fuse panel.
3. Connect one test lead of the test light or ohmmeter to the negative side of the fuse terminal in the fuse panel.
4. Connect the other test lead to a good ground (bare metal). If necessary, scrape away paint from the frame or engine (retouch later with paint). Make sure the part used for a ground is not insulated with a rubber gasket or rubber grommet.
5. With the self-powered test light or ohmmeter attached to the fuse terminal and ground, wiggle the wiring harness relating to the suspect circuit at 6 in. intervals. Start next to the fuse panel and work your way away from the fuse panel. Watch the self-powered test light or ohmmeter as you progress along the harness.
6. If the test light blinks or the needle on the ohmmeter moves, there is a short-to-ground at that point in the harness.

Testing For a Short
With a Test Light or Voltmeter

This test can be performed with either a test light or voltmeter.

1. Remove the blown fuse from the fuse panel.

2. Connect the test light or voltmeter across the fuse terminals in the fuse panel. Turn the ignition switch on and check for battery voltage (12 volts).

3. With the test light or voltmeter attached to the fuse terminals, wiggle the wiring harness relating to the suspect circuit at 6 in. intervals. Start next to the fuse panel and work your way away from the fuse panel. Watch the test light or voltmeter as you progress along the harness.

4. If the test light blinks or the needle on the voltmeter moves, there is a short-to-ground at that point in the harness.

CHARGING SYSTEM TROUBLESHOOTING

The charging system consists of the battery, main fuse, main switch, alternator and the rectifier/regulator assembly. See **Figure 9** (ZX900) or **Figure 10** (ZX1000).

Whenever the charging system is suspected of trouble, make sure the battery is fully charged before testing further. Clean and test the battery as described under *Battery* in Chapter Three. If the battery is in good condition, test the charging system as follows.

Potential charging system troubles are:

a. Discharged battery (starter will not turn).

b. Overcharged battery (battery electrolyte level is low).

c. Alternator noise.

If any of the conditions in "a" or "b" are experienced, first perform the *Wiring Inspection* procedure in Chapter Eight. This will help to locate and repair wiring problems that may be causing the charging system troubles. If the wiring is okay, perform the one of the following procedures that best describes your bike's condition.

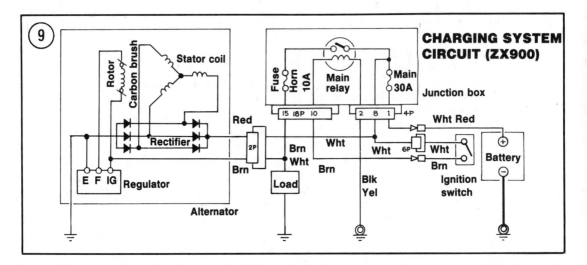

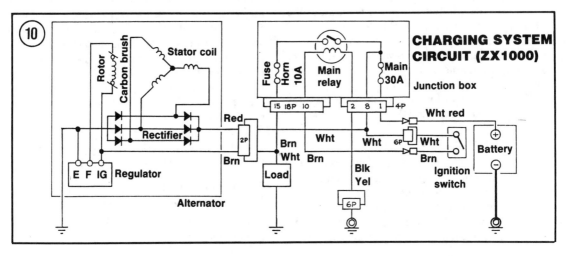

Test 1: Battery Discharged

If your bike's battery is discharged (starter will not turn), perform the following.

1. Park the vehicle on its center stand. Remove the seat.

2. Refer to the charging system schematic in **Figure 9** (ZX900) or **Figure 10** (ZX1000) and check all connections to make sure they are clean and tight. Check the wiring for fraying or other damage. Electrical connections should be cleaned with electrical contact cleaner and reconnected.

NOTE
Do not disconnect either the positive or negative battery cables. They are to remain in the circuit as is.

3. Test the battery as described in Chapter Three under *Battery*. Once the battery charge is correct, proceed to Step 4. If the battery will not charge properly, install a good battery that is fully charged. Do not perform the following steps with a discharged battery.

4. Connect a voltmeter to the battery terminals. Connect the positive voltmeter lead to the positive battery terminal. Connect the negative voltmeter lead to the negative battery terminal. Start the engine. The voltage should be 13.5 or more. Interpret results in Step 5.

5A. *Less than 13.5 volts:* Remove the alternator cover (**Figure 11**) and connect a jumper wire between the regulator F terminal and ground (**Figure 12**). Then connect a voltmeter to the battery terminals. Start the engine and allow it to idle. Note the voltage reading and interpret results as follows:

    a. 13.5 volts or higher: Check the regulator as described in Chapter Eight.

    b. Less than 13.5 volts: Check the alternator carbon brushes and slip rings as described in Chapter Eight. Also check the rectifier, stator coil and rotor coil as described in Chapter Eight.

Test 2: Overcharged Battery

If your bike's battery is being overcharged (battery electrolyte level drops fast), perform the following:

    a. Test the regulator as described in Chapter Eight.

    b. Test the rotor as described in Chapter Eight.

Test 3: Alternator Noise

Disassemble the alternator as described under *Alternator Disassembly/Reassembly* in Chapter Eight. Check each ball bearing for excessive wear or damage by turning the inner bearing race by hand. Replace any worn or damaged bearing. If the bearings are okay, check all alternator components for loose or missing mounting bolts. Also check for damaged component mounting brackets. Replace damaged parts as required.

IGNITION SYSTEM

The ignition system is a breakerless type. See **Figure 13** (ZX900) or **Figure 14** (ZX1000). Most problems involving failure to start, poor driveability or rough running are caused by trouble in the ignition system.

Note the following symptoms:

a. Engine misses.

b. Stumbles on acceleration (misfiring).

c. Loss of power at high speed (misfiring).

d. Hard starting (or failure to start).

e. Rough idle.

Most of the symptoms can also be caused by a carburetor that is improperly adjusted. But considering the law of averages, the odds are far better that the source of the problem will be found in the ignition system rather than the fuel system. The following basic tests are designed to quickly pinpoint and isolate problems in the ignition system.

Precautions

Remember, by performing tests incorrectly, you can damage components that are working properly. When troubleshooting the ignition system, several precautions should be observed to avoid damage to the ignition system.

1. Do not reverse the battery connections. This reverses polarity and can damage the rectifier/regulator or CDI unit.

2. Do not "spark" the battery terminals with the battery cable connections to check polarity.

3. Do not disconnect the battery cables with the engine running.

4. Do not crank the engine when the CDI unit is not grounded to the engine.

5. Do not touch or disconnect any ignition components when the engine is running, while the ignition switch is ON or while the battery cables are connected.

Troubleshooting Preparation

Usually, ignition trouble is due to connector or wiring damage and not because of component failure. Perform the following checks before testing individual components.

1. Check the wiring harness and all plug-in connections to make sure that all terminals are free of corrosion, all connectors are tight and the wiring insulation is in good condition.

2. Make sure that all ground wires are properly connected and that the connections are clean and tight.

NOTE
*Refer to **Figure 13** or **Figure 14** for component-to-ground connections.*

3. Check all electrical components that are grounded to the engine for a good ground.

4. Check all wiring for disconnected wires and short or open circuits.

5. Check the fuse(s) to make sure it is not defective.

6. Make sure there is an adequate supply of fresh fuel in the fuel tank.

7. Check the battery condition. Clean terminals and recharge battery, if necessary. Refer to *Battery* in Chapter Three.

8. Check spark plug cable routing. Make sure the cables are properly connected to their respective spark plugs.

9. Remove all spark plugs, keeping them in order. Check the condition of each plug. See *Reading Spark Plugs* in Chapter Three.

10. Perform the *Ignition Spark Test* in this chapter.

Ignition Spark Test

Perform the following spark test to determine if the ignition system is firing the spark plugs.

1. Remove the fuel tank as described in Chapter Seven.

2. Remove one of the spark plugs.

3. Connect the spark plug wire and connector to the spark plug and touch the spark plug base to a good ground like the engine cylinder head. Position the spark plug so you can see the electrodes, but away from the spark plug hole in the cylinder head.

WARNING
During the next step, do not hold the spark plug, wire or connector or a serious electrical shock may result. If necessary, use a pair of insulated pliers to hold the spark plug or wire. The high voltage generated by the ignition system could produce serious or fatal shocks.

4. Crank the engine over with the starter. A fat blue spark should be evident across the spark plug electrodes.

5A. If a spark is obtained in Step 4, the problem is not in the coil, but there may be a problem in the breakerless ignition. Proceed with the following tests. Also, check the fuel system and spark plugs.

5B. If no spark is obtained, proceed with the following tests.

Testing

Test procedures for troubleshooting the ignition system for are found in the diagnostic chart in **Figure 15**. A multimeter, as described in Chapter One, is required to perform the test procedures.

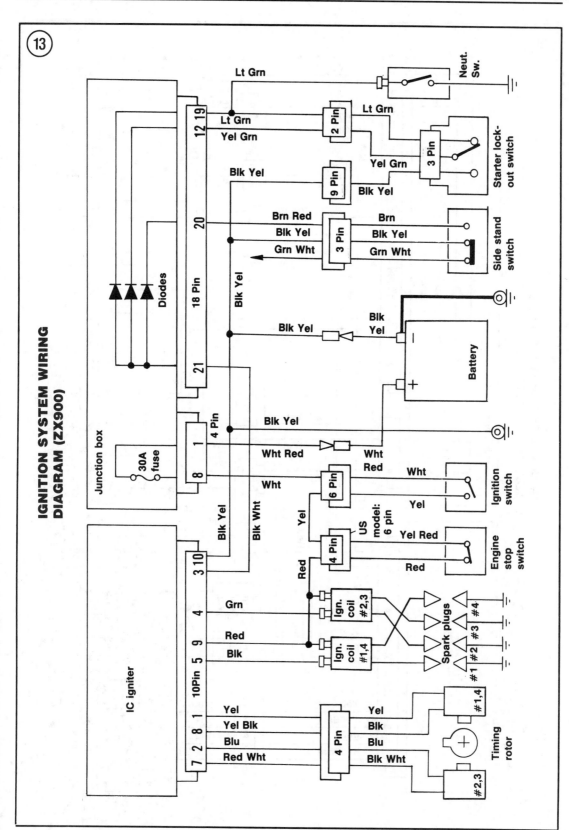

IGNITION SYSTEM WIRING DIAGRAM (ZX900)

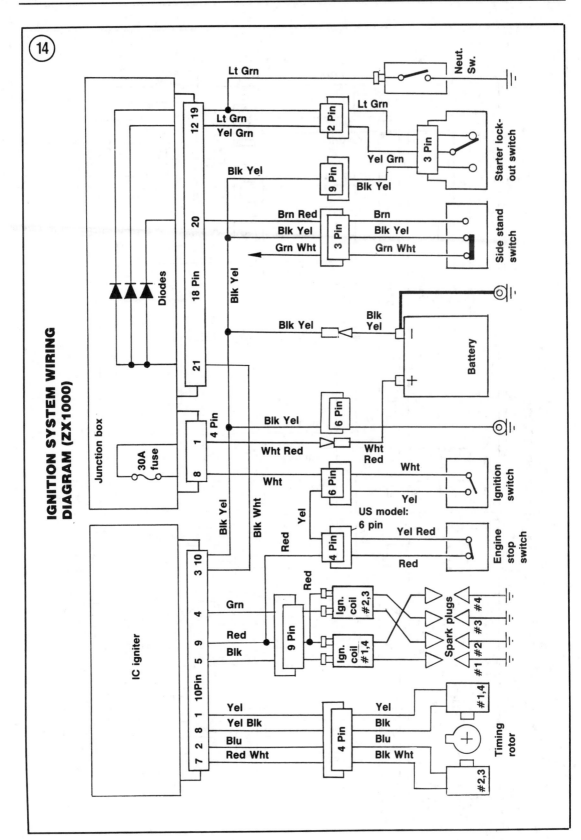

IGNITION SYSTEM WIRING DIAGRAM (ZX1000)

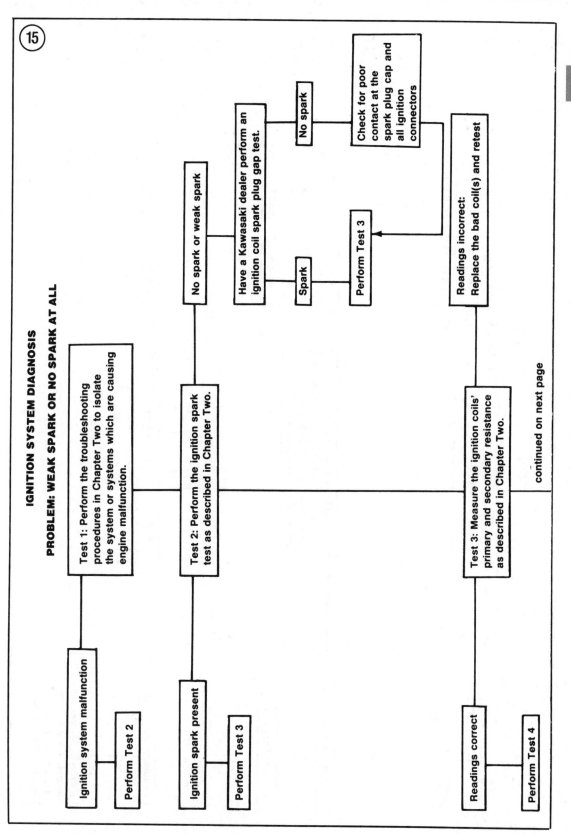

⑮

IGNITION SYSTEM DIAGNOSIS

PROBLEM: WEAK SPARK OR NO SPARK AT ALL

Test 1: Perform the troubleshooting procedures in Chapter Two to isolate the system or systems which are causing engine malfunction.

Ignition system malfunction

Perform Test 2

Test 2: Perform the ignition spark test as described in Chapter Two.

Ignition spark present

Perform Test 3

No spark or weak spark

Have a Kawasaki dealer perform an ignition coil spark plug gap test.

No spark

Check for poor contact at the spark plug cap and all ignition connectors

Spark

Perform Test 3

Test 3: Measure the ignition coils' primary and secondary resistance as described in Chapter Two.

Readings correct

Perform Test 4

Readings incorrect: Replace the bad coil(s) and retest

continued on next page

2

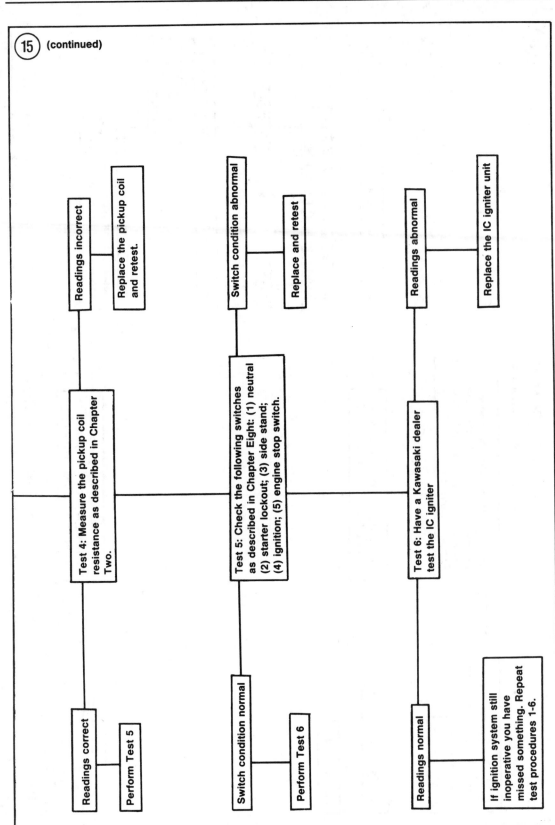

(15) (continued)

Test 4: Measure the pickup coil resistance as described in Chapter Two.

Readings incorrect

Replace the pickup coil and retest.

Readings correct

Perform Test 5

Test 5: Check the following switches as described in Chapter Eight: (1) neutral (2) starter lockout; (3) side stand; (4) ignition; (5) engine stop switch.

Switch condition abnormal

Replace and retest

Switch condition normal

Perform Test 6

Test 6: Have a Kawasaki dealer test the IC igniter

Readings abnormal

Replace the IC igniter unit

Readings normal

If ignition system still inoperative you have missed something. Repeat test procedures 1-6.

Before beginning actual troubleshooting, read the entire test procedure (**Figure 15**). When required, the diagnostic chart will refer you to a certain procedure for testing.

Pickup Coil Testing

The pickup coils are mounted on the left-hand side of the engine (**Figure 16**).

1. Disconnect the pickup coil connector.
2. Use an ohmmeter on R×100 to measure the pickup coil resistance between the following terminals:
   a. Pickup coil for No. 2 and No. 3 cylinders: Black/white to blue.

b. Pickup coil for No. 1 and No. 4 cylinders: Black to yellow.
3. The correct resistance is 390-590 ohms.
4. Replace the pickup coil(s) if it does not meet the test specifications. Refer to *Pickup Coil Removal/Installation* in Chapter Eight.
5. Test the pickup coil for shorting to ground as follows:
   a. Switch an ohmmeter to the R×100 scale.
   b. Connect one ohmmeter lead to ground and the other lead to one of the pickup coil connector leads. Repeat for each lead.
   c. The ohmmeter should read infinity.
   d. If any reading other than infinity was obtained, the pickup coil is shorted to ground and must be replaced.

Ignition Coil Testing

The following describes ignition coil static testing procedures. If the coils test okay and you're still experiencing ignition related troubles, remove the coils and have a Kawasaki dealer perform a 3-point arc test. The arc test is the most accurate way to determine ignition coil condition. If ignition coil replacement is required, you should look into installing aftermarket coils available from various distributors and manufacturers.

Refer to **Figure 17** for this procedure.

1. Remove the ignition coils as described in Chapter Eight.
2. Measure the coil primary resistance using an ohmmeter set at R×1. Measure between the coil's

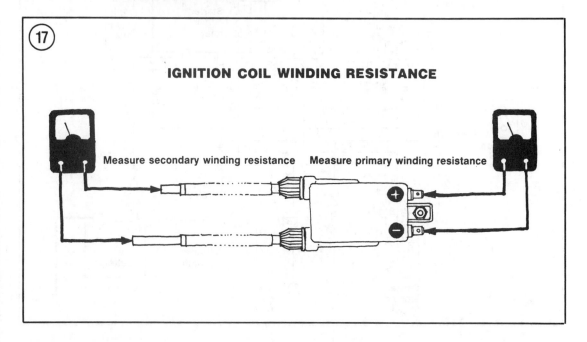

IGNITION COIL WINDING RESISTANCE

Measure secondary winding resistance   Measure primary winding resistance

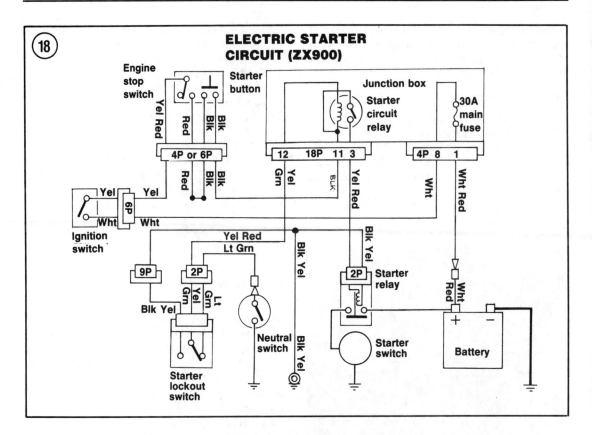

ELECTRIC STARTER CIRCUIT (ZX900)

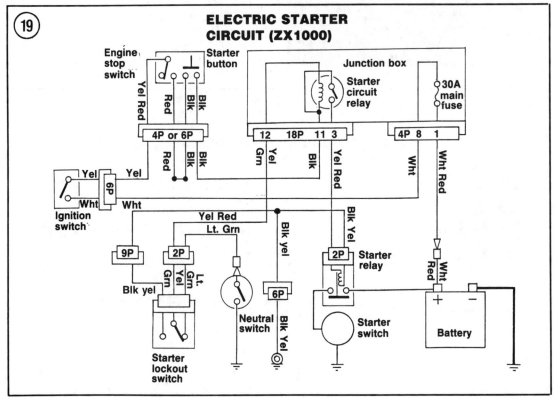

ELECTRIC STARTER CIRCUIT (ZX1000)

primary terminals as shown in **Figure 17**. The correct primary resistance is listed in **Table 1**.

3. Measure the secondary resistance using an ohmmeter set at R×100. Measure between the coil's secondary spark plug leads (**Figure 17**). The correct secondary resistance is listed in **Table 1**.

4. Replace the ignition coil(s) if it doesn't test within the specifications in **Table 1**. See *Ignition Coil Removal/Installation* in Chapter Eight.

Switches

Test the following switches as described under *Switches* in Chapter Eight:
- a. Neutral switch.
- b. Starter lockout switch.
- c. Side stand switch.
- d. Ignition switch.
- e. Engine stop switch.

IC Igniter Check

A special Kawasaki tester is necessary to check out the IC igniter. Refer the IC igniter to your Kawasaki dealer or a qualified specialist for this testing.

STARTING SYSTEM

The starting system is shown in **Figure 18** (ZX900) and **Figure 19** (ZX1000).

The four basic starter troubles are:
- a. Starter does not turn.
- b. Starter turns too slowly; engine will not start.
- c. Starter turns continuously.
- d. Starter turns; engine does not turn.

The troubleshooting chart in **Figure 20** lists starter troubles and checks to make. Refer to Chapter Eight for starter service procedures.

ELECTRICAL PROBLEMS

If bulbs burn out frequently, the cause may be excessive vibration, loose connections that permit sudden current surges, or the installation of the wrong type of bulb.

Most light and ignition problems are caused by loose or corroded ground connections. Check these prior to replacing a bulb or electrical component.

EXCESSIVE VIBRATION

Usually this is caused by loose engine mounting hardware. If not, it can be difficult to find without disassembling the engine. High speed vibration may be due to a bent axle shaft or loose or faulty suspension components. Vibration can also be caused by the following conditions:
- a. Broken frame.
- b. Worn drive chain.
- c. Improperly balanced wheels.
- d. Defective or damaged wheels.
- e. Defective or damaged tires.
- f. Internal engine wear or damage.

Symptom	Probable Cause	Remedy	(20)
Starter does not turn	Low battery	Recharge battery	
	Worn brushes	Replace brushes	
	Defective relay	Repair or replace	
	Defective switch	Repair or replace	
	Defective wiring connection	Repair wire or clean connection	
	Internal short circuit	Repair or replace defective component	
Starter action is weak	Low battery	Recharge battery	
	Pitted relay contacts	Clean or replace	
	Worn brushes	Replace brushes	
	Defective connection	Clean and tighten	
	Short circuit in commutator	Replace armature	
Starter runs continuously	Stuck relay	Replace relay	
Starter turns but does not crank engine	Defective starter clutch	Replace starter clutch	

CARBURETOR TROUBLESHOOTING

Basic carburetor troubleshooting procedures are found in **Figure 21**.

FRONT SUSPENSION AND STEERING

Poor handling may be caused by improper tire pressure, a damaged or bent frame or front steering components, worn wheel bearings or dragging brakes. Possible causes of suspension and steering malfunctions are listed below.

Irregular or Wobbly Steering

a. Loose axle nuts.
b. Loose or worn steering head bearings.
c. Excessive wheel hub bearing play.
d. Damaged wheel.
e. Unbalanced wheel assembly.
f. Incorrect wheel alignment.
g. Bent or damaged steering stem or frame (at steering neck).
h. Tire incorrectly seated on rim.
i. Excessive loading from non-standard equipment.
j. Damaged fairing assembly.
k. Loose fairing mounts or brackets.

Stiff Steering

a. Low front tire air pressure.
b. Bent or damaged steering stem or frame (at steering neck).
c. Steering head bearings too tight.

d. Improperly routed control cables or brake hose.

Stiff or Heavy Fork Operation

a. Incorrect fork springs.
b. Incorrect fork oil viscosity.
c. Excessive amount of fork oil.
d. Damaged fork tubes or sliders.
e. Anti-dive incorrectly adjusted.
f. Anti-dive unit malfunction.

Poor Fork Operation

b. Worn or damaged fork tubes or sliders.
a. Fork oil level low due to leaking fork seals.
c. Contaminated fork oil.
d. Worn fork springs.
e. Heavy loading from non-standard equipment.
f. Anti-dive unit malfunction.

Poor Rear Shock Absorber Operation

a. Damper unit leaking.
b. Incorrect rear shock adjustment.
c. Heavy loading from non-standard equipment.
d. Incorrect loading.

BRAKE PROBLEMS

Sticking disc brakes may be caused by a stuck piston(s) in a caliper assembly, warped pad shim(s) or improper rear brake adjustment. See **Figure 22** for disc brake troubles and checks to make.

Figure 22 and Table 1 are on the following pages.

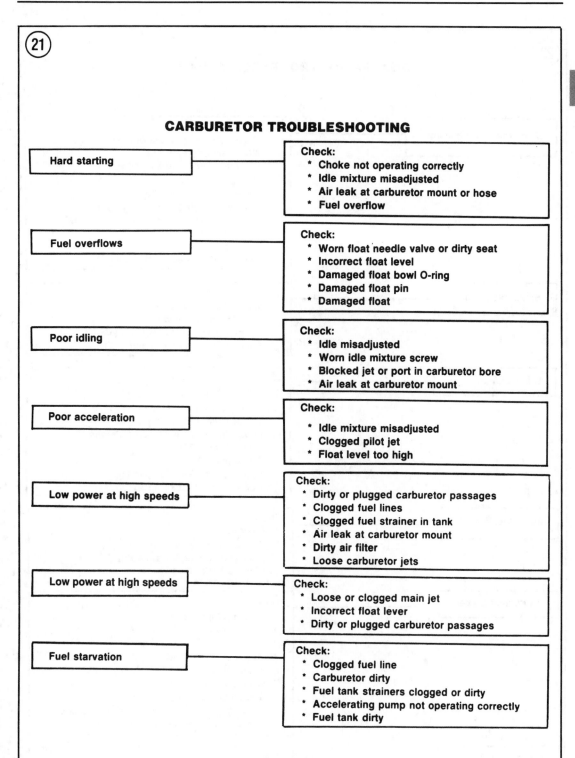

(21)

CARBURETOR TROUBLESHOOTING

Hard starting	Check:
	* Choke not operating correctly
	* Idle mixture misadjusted
	* Air leak at carburetor mount or hose
	* Fuel overflow

Fuel overflows	Check:
	* Worn float needle valve or dirty seat
	* Incorrect float level
	* Damaged float bowl O-ring
	* Damaged float pin
	* Damaged float

Poor idling	Check:
	* Idle misadjusted
	* Worn idle mixture screw
	* Blocked jet or port in carburetor bore
	* Air leak at carburetor mount

Poor acceleration	Check:
	* Idle mixture misadjusted
	* Clogged pilot jet
	* Float level too high

Low power at high speeds	Check:
	* Dirty or plugged carburetor passages
	* Clogged fuel lines
	* Clogged fuel strainer in tank
	* Air leak at carburetor mount
	* Dirty air filter
	* Loose carburetor jets

Low power at high speeds	Check:
	* Loose or clogged main jet
	* Incorrect float lever
	* Dirty or plugged carburetor passages

Fuel starvation	Check:
	* Clogged fuel line
	* Carburetor dirty
	* Fuel tank strainers clogged or dirty
	* Accelerating pump not operating correctly
	* Fuel tank dirty

2

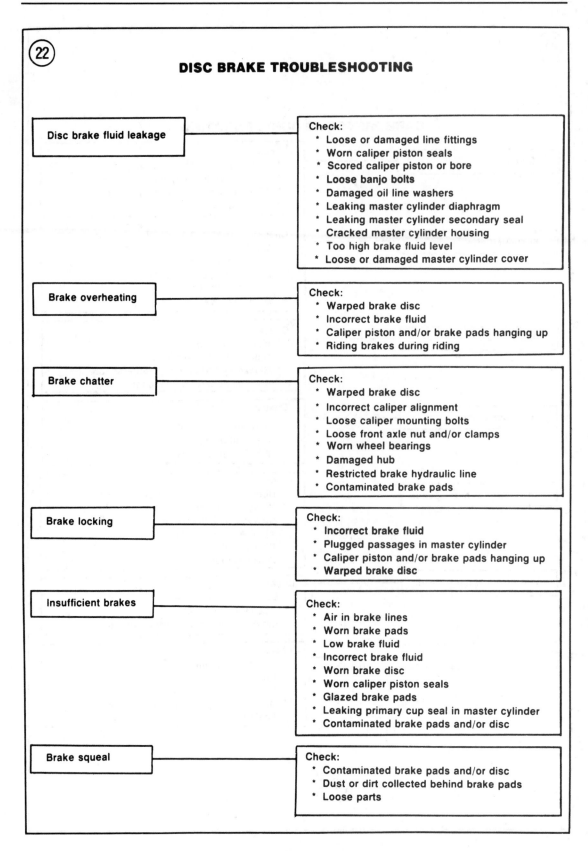

㉒

DISC BRAKE TROUBLESHOOTING

Disc brake fluid leakage

Check:
* Loose or damaged line fittings
* Worn caliper piston seals
* Scored caliper piston or bore
* Loose banjo bolts
* Damaged oil line washers
* Leaking master cylinder diaphragm
* Leaking master cylinder secondary seal
* Cracked master cylinder housing
* Too high brake fluid level
* Loose or damaged master cylinder cover

Brake overheating

Check:
* Warped brake disc
* Incorrect brake fluid
* Caliper piston and/or brake pads hanging up
* Riding brakes during riding

Brake chatter

Check:
* Warped brake disc
* Incorrect caliper alignment
* Loose caliper mounting bolts
* Loose front axle nut and/or clamps
* Worn wheel bearings
* Damaged hub
* Restricted brake hydraulic line
* Contaminated brake pads

Brake locking

Check:
* Incorrect brake fluid
* Plugged passages in master cylinder
* Caliper piston and/or brake pads hanging up
* Warped brake disc

Insufficient brakes

Check:
* Air in brake lines
* Worn brake pads
* Low brake fluid
* Incorrect brake fluid
* Worn brake disc
* Worn caliper piston seals
* Glazed brake pads
* Leaking primary cup seal in master cylinder
* Contaminated brake pads and/or disc

Brake squeal

Check:
* Contaminated brake pads and/or disc
* Dust or dirt collected behind brake pads
* Loose parts

Table 1 ELECTRICAL TEST SPECIFICATIONS

Alternator	
Output	25 amps @ 6,000 rpm, 14 volts
Stator coil resistance	Less than 1.0 ohms
Rotor coil resistance	Approximately 4 ohms
Ignition system	
Pickup coil resistance	
ZX900	390-590 ohms
ZX1000	400-490 ohms
Pickup coil air gap	0.5-0.9 mm (0.019-0.035 in.)
Ignition coil	
Secondary resistance	10,000-16,000 ohms
Primary resistance	1.8-2.8 ohms

2

NOTE: If you own a 1988 or later model, first check the Supplement at the back of this book for any new service information.

CHAPTER THREE

PERIODIC LUBRICATION, MAINTENANCE AND TUNE-UP

Your bike can be cared for by two methods: preventive and corrective maintenance. Because a motorcycle is subjected to tremendous heat, stress and vibration—even in normal use—preventive maintenance prevents costly and unexpected corrective maintenance. When neglected, any bike becomes unreliable and actually dangerous to ride. When properly maintained, your Kawasaki is one of the most reliable bikes available and will give many miles and years of dependable, fast and safe riding. By maintaining a routine service schedule as described in this chapter, costly mechanical problems and unexpected breakdowns can be prevented.

The procedures presented in this chapter can be easily performed by anyone with average mechanical skills. **Table 1** is a suggested factory maintenance schedule. **Table 2** lists tightening torques for certain components serviced in this chapter. **Tables 1-15** are located at the end of this chapter.

ROUTINE CHECKS

The following simple checks should be carried out before each ride.

Engine Oil Level

Refer to *Engine Oil Level Check* under *Periodic Lubrication* in this chapter.

Coolant Level

Check the coolant level when the engine is cool.
1. Park the motorcycle on the center stand.
2. Check the level through the level gauge in the coolant reservoir tank. The level should be between the FULL and LOW marks. See **Figure 1** (ZX900) or **Figure 2** (ZX1000).
3. If necessary, add coolant to the reservoir tank (not to the radiator) so the level is to the FULL mark. Add coolant as follows:
   a. *ZX900:* Remove the left-hand side cover to gain access to the reservoir tank (**Figure 1**).
   b. *ZX1000:* Remove the cover (**Figure 2**). Then add coolant to the tank (**Figure 3**).

General Inspection

1. Examine the engine for signs of oil or fuel leakage.

NOTE
If you are experiencing an oil leak somewhere on the engine, remove the lower fairing as described in Chapter Thirteen. Then place a large piece of cardboard underneath the engine. The cardboard may help you to locate the leak as well as determine the severity of the leak. If the leak is small, it may be necessary to leave the cardboard underneath the engine overnight.

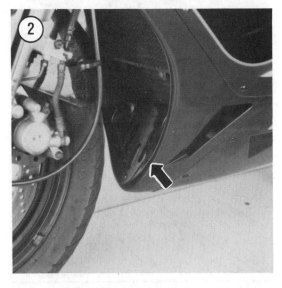

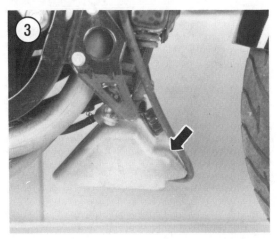

2. Check the tires for embedded stones. Pry them out with your ignition key.
3. Make sure all lights work.

NOTE
At least check the brake light. It can burn out anytime. Motorists can not stop as quickly as you and need all the warning you can give.

Tire Pressure

Tire pressure must be checked with the tires cold. Correct tire pressure depends on the load you are carrying. See **Table 3** (ZX900) or **Table 4** (ZX1000). Refer to *Tires* in this chapter.

Battery

The battery must be removed to check the electrolyte level. For complete details see *Battery Removal/Installation and Electrolyte Level Check* in this chapter.

Lights and Horn

With the engine running, check the following.
1. Pull the front brake lever and check that the brake light comes on.
2. Push the rear brake pedal and check that the brake light comes on soon after you have begun depressing the pedal.
3A. *U.S. and Canadian models:* With the engine running, check to see that the headlight and taillight are on.
3B. *All except U.S. and Canadian models:* With the engine running, check the headlight and taillight operation by operating the headlight switch.
the high and low positions, and check to see that both headlight elements are working.
5. Push the turn signal switch to the left position and the right position and check that all 4 turn signal lights are working.
6. Push the horn button and note that the horn blows loudly.
7. If the horn or any light failed to work properly, refer to Chapter Eight.

MAINTENANCE INTERVALS

The services and intervals shown in **Table 1** are recommended by the factory. Strict adherence to these recommendations will insure long life from your Kawasaki. If the bike is run in an area of high humidity, the lubrication services must be done more frequently to prevent possible rust damage.

For convenience when maintaining your motorcycle, most of the services listed in **Table 1** are described in this chapter. Those procedures which require more than minor disassembly or adjustment are covered elsewhere in the appropriate chapter. The Table of Contents and Index can help you locate a particular service procedure.

TIRES

Tire Pressure

Tire pressure should be checked and adjusted to accommodate rider and luggage weight. A simple, accurate gauge (**Figure 4**) can be purchased for a few dollars and should be carried in your motorcycle tool kit. The appropriate tire pressures are shown in **Table 3** (ZX900) and **Table 4** (ZX1000).

> *NOTE*
> *After checking and adjusting the air pressure, make sure you reinstall the air valve cap (**Figure 5**). The cap prevents small pebbles and/or dirt from collecting in the valve stem. This could allow air leakage or result in incorrect tire pressure readings.*

Tire Inspection

The likelihood of tire failure increases with tread wear. It is estimated that the majority of all tire failures occur during the last 10% of usable tread wear. Check tire tread for excessive wear, deep cuts, embedded objects such as stones, nails, etc.

Check also for high spots that indicate internal tire damage. Replace tires that show high spots or swelling. If you find a nail in a tire, mark its location with a light crayon before pulling it out. This will help locate the hole for repair. Refer to *Tubeless Tires and Tubeless Tire Changing* in Chapter Ten.

Measure tread wear at the center of the tire with a tread depth gauge (**Figure 6**) or small ruler. Because tires sometimes wear unevenly, measure wear at several points. **Table 3** and **Table 4** list tread wear limits for stock tires.

Rim Inspection

Frequently inspect the wheel rims. If a rim has been damaged it might have been knocked out of alignment. Improper wheel alignment can cause severe vibration and result in an unsafe riding condition. If the rim portion of an alloy wheel is damaged the wheel must be replaced as it cannot be repaired.

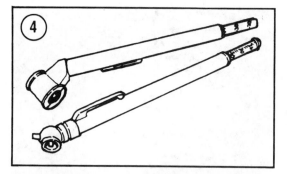

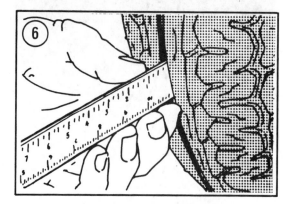

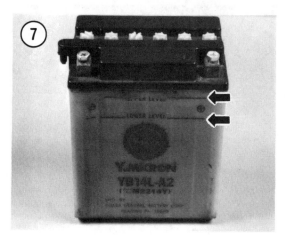

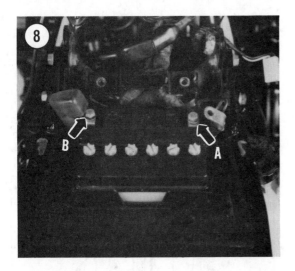

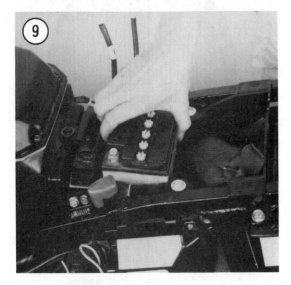

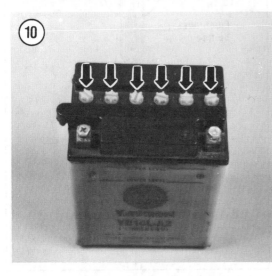

BATTERY

CAUTION
If it becomes necessary to remove the battery vent tube when performing any of the following procedures, make sure to route the tube correctly during installation to prevent acid fumes and droplets discharged from the battery from spilling on the drive chain, swing arm or other parts. In addition, make sure the battery vent tube is not pinched. A pinched or kinked tube would allow high pressure to accumulate in the battery and could cause the battery to burst. If the tube is pinched or otherwise damaged, install a new tube.

Removal/Installation and Electrolyte Level Check

The battery is the heart of the electrical system. It should be checked and serviced as indicated in **Table 1**. Most electrical system troubles can be attributed to neglect of this vital component.

In order to correctly service the electrolyte level it is necessary to remove the battery from the frame. The electrolyte level should be maintained between the two marks on the battery case (**Figure 7**). If the electrolyte level is low, it's a good idea to completely remove the battery so that it can be thoroughly cleaned, serviced and checked.

1. Remove the seat.
2. Remove the battery cover.
3. Disconnect the negative battery cable (A, **Figure 8**) from the battery.
4. Disconnect the positive battery cable (B, **Figure 8**).
5. Disconnect the battery vent tube.
6. Lift the battery (**Figure 9**) out of the battery box and remove it.

WARNING
Protect your eyes, skin and clothing. If electrolyte gets into your eyes, flush your eyes thoroughly with clean water and get prompt medical attention.

CAUTION
Be careful not to spill battery electrolyte on painted or polished surfaces. The liquid is highly corrosive and will damage the finish. If it is spilled, wash it off immediately with soapy water and thoroughly rinse with clean water.

7. Remove the caps (**Figure 10**) from the battery cells and add distilled water. Never add electrolyte (acid) to correct the level. Fill only to the upper battery level mark (**Figure 7**).

8. After the level has been corrected and the battery allowed to stand for a few minutes, check the specific gravity of the electrolyte in each cell with a hydrometer (**Figure 11**). Follow the manufacturer's instructions for reading the instrument. See *Battery Testing* in this chapter.

9. After the battery has been refilled, recharged or replaced, install it by reversing these removal steps.

Testing

Hydrometer testing is the best way to check battery condition. Use a hydrometer with numbered graduations from 1.100 to 1.300 rather than one with just color-coded bands. To use the hydrometer, squeeze the rubber ball, insert the tip into the cell and release the ball. Draw enough electrolyte to float the weighted float inside the hydrometer. Note the number in line with the electrolyte surface; this si the specific gravity for this cell. Return the electrolyte to the cell from which it came. See **Figure 11**.

The specific gravity of the electrolyte in each battery cell is an excellent indication of that cell's condition (**Table 5**). A fully charged cell will read 1.260-1.280 while a cell in good condition reads from 1.230-1.250 and anything below 1.140 is discharged.

> *NOTE*
> *Specific gravity varies with temperature. For each 10° that electrolyte temperature exceeds 80° F, add 0.004 to reading indicated on hydrometer. Subtract 0.004 for each 10° below 80° F.*

> *NOTE*
> *When measuring specific gravity, if the difference between the highest and lowest cell reading is more than 0.050, the battery must be replaced.*

If the cells test in the poor range, the battery requires recharging. The hydrometer is useful for checking the progress of the charging operation. **Table 5** shows approximate state of charge.

> *NOTE*
> *If a hydrometer is not available, the battery can be tested with a voltmeter. First, however, the battery surface charge must be removed. This is done to obtain more accurate readings. The surface charge can be removed by turning on the headlight for approximately 3 minutes (without the engine running). Then turn the headlight off and attach a voltmeter across the bat-*

tery terminals. The battery should read 12.30 volts or higher. If the reading is below this level, the battery requires charging.

Battery Draw Test

The battery draw test is useful in that it records battery voltage under working conditions. A voltmeter is required for this test.

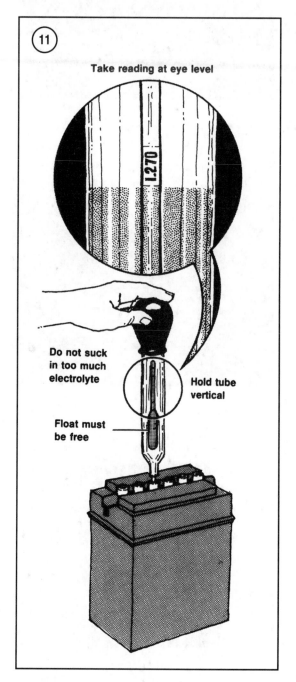

Take reading at eye level

1.270

Do not suck in too much electrolyte

Hold tube vertical

Float must be free

1. Attach a voltmeter across the battery terminals.
2. Turn on the ignition and headlight.
3. Observe the voltmeter readings. Interpret results as follows:
   a. 11.2 volts or higher: Battery is in good condition.
   b. 11.2 to 10 volts: Battery requires charging.
   c. Below 10 volts: Test battery condition with a hydrometer.
4. Turn the ignition off and remove the voltmeter.

Charging

CAUTION
Always remove the battery from the motorcycle before connecting charging equipment.

WARNING
During charging, highly explosive hydrogen gas is released from the battery. The battery should be charged only in a well-ventilated area, and open

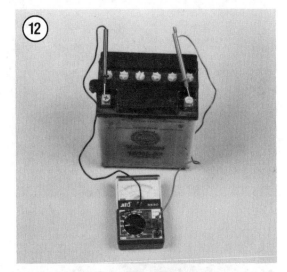

flames and cigarettes should be kept away. Never check the charge of the battery by arcing (connecting metal) across the terminals; the resulting spark can ignite the hydrogen gas.

1. Remove the battery from the motorcycle as described in this chapter.
2. Connect the positive (+) charger lead to the positive battery terminal and the negative (-) charger lead to the negative battery terminal.
3. Remove all vent caps from the battery, set the charger at 12 volts, and switch it on. If the output of the charger is variable, it is best to select a low setting—1 1/2 to 2 amps.

CAUTION
The electrolyte level must be maintained at the upper level during the charging cycle. Check and refill as necessary.

4. After the battery has been charged for about 8 hours, turn the charger off, disconnect the leads and check the specific gravity. It should be within the limits specified in **Table 5**. If it is, and remains stable for one hour, the battery is charged.
5. Check battery voltage with a voltmeter (**Figure 12**). Voltage should be 12-13 volts.
6. To ensure good electrical contact, cables must be clean and tight on the battery's terminals. If the cable terminals are badly corroded, even after performing the above cleaning procedures, the cables should be disconnected, removed from the bike and cleaned separately with a wire brush and a baking soda solution. After cleaning, apply a very thin coating of petroleum jelly (Vaseline) to the battery terminals before reattaching the cables. After connecting the cables, apply a light coating to the connections also—this can prevent future corrosion.

New Battery Installation

When replacing the old battery with a new one, be sure to charge it completely (specific gravity, 1.260-1.280) before installing it in the bike. Failure to do so, or using the battery with a low electrolyte level will permanently damage the battery.

PERIODIC LUBRICATION

Engine Oil Level Check

Engine oil level is checked through the inspection window on the left-hand side (**Figure 13**).
1. Start the engine and let it reach normal operating temperature.

2. Stop the engine and allow the oil to settle.

3. Park the bike so that it is off the center stand and level.

> *NOTE*
> *You can check the oil level with the bike on the center stand if you place a wooden block under the front wheel so that front and rear wheels are equal distance off the ground.*

4. The oil level should be between the maximum and minimum window marks (**Figure 13**). If necessary, remove the oil fill cap (**Figure 14**) and add the recommended oil (**Table 6**) to raise the oil to the proper level. Do not overfill.

Engine Oil and Filter Change

The factory-recommended oil and filter change interval is specified in **Table 1**. This assumes that the motorcycle is operated in moderate climates. The time interval is more important than the mileage interval because combustion acids, formed by gasoline and water vapor will contaminate the oil even if the motorcycle is not run for several months. If a motorcycle is operated under dusty conditions, the oil will get dirty more quickly and should be changed more frequently than recommended. Use only a detergent oil with an API classification of SE or SF. The classification is stamped on the container (**Figure 15**). Try always to use the same brand of oil. Use of oil additives is not recommended. Refer to **Table 6** for correct weight of oil to use.

To change the engine oil and filter you will need the following:

   a. Drain pan.
   b. Funnel.
   c. Can opener or pour spout.
   d. Wrench or socket to remove drain plugs.
   e. Oil (see **Table 7**).
   f. Oil filter element.

There are a number of ways to discard the used oil safely. The easiest way is to pour it from the drain pan into a gallon plastic bottle for disposal.

> *NOTE*
> *Some service stations and oil retailers will accept your used oil for recycling. Do not discard oil in your household trash or pour it onto the ground.*

1. Place the motorcycle on the center stand.

2. Remove the lower fairing as described under *Lower Fairing Removal/Installation* in Chapter Thirteen.

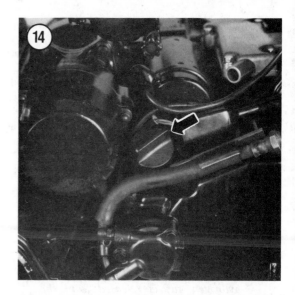

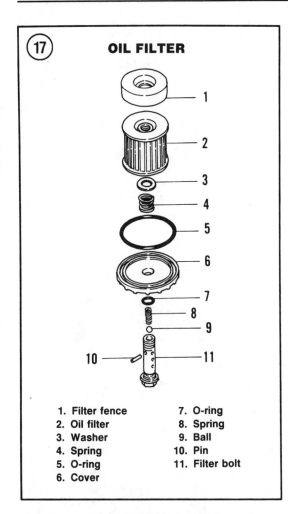

OIL FILTER

1. Filter fence
2. Oil filter
3. Washer
4. Spring
5. O-ring
6. Cover
7. O-ring
8. Spring
9. Ball
10. Pin
11. Filter bolt

3. Start the engine and run it until it is at normal operating temperature, then turn it off.

4. Place a drip pan under the crankcase and remove the 2 drain plugs (A, **Figure 16**).

NOTE
Figure 16 shows the drain plugs with the engine removed for clarity.

5. Replace the oil filter (**Figure 17**) as follows:

CAUTION
The oil filter mounting bolt is made of soft material. To prevent damaging the bolt head, always loosen the bolt with a socket or box-end wrench. Do not use an adjustable wrench.

a. Unscrew the filter mounting bolt from underneath the engine (B, **Figure 16**) and lower the filter assembly.

b. Remove the filter fence (**Figure 18**).

c. Hold the filter and turn the mounting bolt to remove the filter (**Figure 19**). Discard the oil filter.

d. Remove the washer (**Figure 20**) and spring (**Figure 21**).

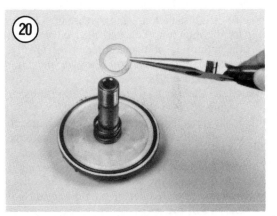

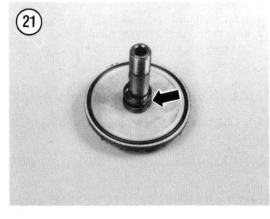

e. Pull the mounting bolt (**Figure 22**) out of the filter cover.

f. Inspect the filter cover (**Figure 23**) and mounting bolt (**Figure 24**) O-rings. Replace the O-rings if deformed, cracked or if the filter cover leaked previously.

g. Clean the filter cover and oil fence of all oil residue.

h. The oil filter bypass valve is located in the mounting bolt. Clean the mounting bolt in solvent and check the bypass valve assembly for damage. Check the mounting bolt hex head for damage that could make further removal of the bolt difficult. Replace the bolt if necessary.

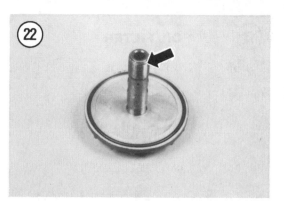

NOTE
To remove the bypass valve, drive the retaining pin out of the mounting bolt. Remove the spring and the bypass valve steel ball. If necessary, replace the mounting bolt and the bypass valve components as an assembly.

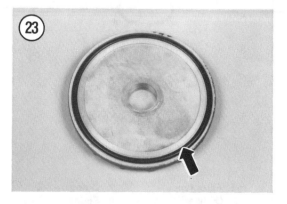

i. Wipe the crankcase gasket surface with a clean, lint-free cloth.

j. To ease installation, lightly grease the O-rings for the mounting bolt and filter cover. With the mounting bolt and filter cover O-rings installed, insert the bolt through the filter cover (**Figure 22**).

k. Slide the spring (**Figure 21**) and washer (**Figure 20**) over the mounting bolt.

l. Make sure there is a rubber washer (**Figure 25**) on both sides of the oil filter. Lightly grease the rubber washer to ease installation.

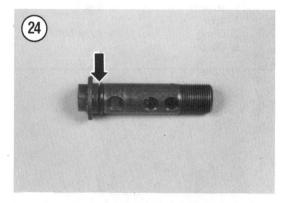

m. Install the oil filter (**Figure 19**) by turning it onto the mounting bolt. Make sure the rubber washers on both sides of the oil filter do not dislodge or tear.

n. Install the filter fence over the oil filter (**Figure 18**).

o. Install the oil filter assembly (B, **Figure 16**) into the oil pan. Tighten the mounting bolt to the torque specifications in **Table 2**.

CAUTION
The mounting bolt is made of soft material. To prevent damaging the hex head, always tighten the bolt with a socket or box-end wrench. Do not use an adjustable wrench. Do not overtighten the mounting bolt.

6. Replace the oil drain plug gaskets if necessary.

7. Install the 2 oil drain plugs (A, **Figure 16**) and gasket and tighten to the torque specifications in **Table 2**.

8. Remove the oil filler cap (**Figure 14**) and fill the crankcase with the correct weight (**Table 6**) and quantity of oil (**Table 7**).

9. Screw in the oil filler cap securely.

10. Start the engine; the oil pressure warning light should go out within 1-3 seconds. If it stays on, shut off the engine immediately and locate the problem. Do not run the engine with the oil warning light on.

11. Let the engine run at moderate speed and check for leaks.

12. Turn the engine off and allow the oil to settle. Then check for correct oil level as described under *Engine Oil Level Check* in this chapter. Adjust if necessary.

13. Reinstall the lower fairing assembly as described in Chapter Thirteen.

Front Fork Oil Change

1. Place the bike on the center stand.

2. Remove the air valve caps.

3A. *ZX900:* Depress the valve stem with a screwdriver on the right-hand fork tube (**Figure 26**) to release all air from both fork tubes.

3B. *ZX1000:* Depress the valve stem (**Figure 26**) with a screwdriver to release all air from the right fork tube. Repeat for the other side.

> *WARNING*
> *Always bleed off all air pressure; failure to do so may cause personal injury when disassembling the fork.*

4. Place a drain pan beside one fork tube and remove the drain screw (**Figure 27**). Allow the oil to drain until it stops. Then with both of the bike's wheels on the ground, apply the front brake and push down on the front end and allow it to return. Repeat to remove as much oil as possible.

> *WARNING*
> *Do not allow the fork oil to come in contact with any of the brake components.*

5. Install the drain screw (**Figure 27**).

6. Repeat Steps 3 and 4 for the opposite side.

7. Place the bike onto its center stand. Support the bike so that the front wheel clears the ground. It may be necessary to remove the lower fairing before you can place blocks of wood or a jack under the frame.

8. Remove the handlebar Allen bolts and lift the left- and right-hand handlebar (**Figure 28**) off of the

steering stem. It is not necessary to disconnect the control cables.

9. Working on one fork tube only, perform the following:

    a. Loosen the fork's upper pinch bolt (A, **Figure 29**).

    b. Slowly loosen and remove the fork cap (B, **Figure 29**).

    c. Lift the fork spring (**Figure 30**) out of the fork tube. Place the fork spring on some clean newspapers to keep from making a mess.

10. Fill the fork tube with slightly less than the specified quantity of oil (**Table 8**). **Table 6** lists the recommended fork oil to use.

> *NOTE*
> *In order to measure the correct amount of fluid, use a baby bottle. These bottles have measurements in cubic centimeters (cc) and fluid ounces (oz.) imprinted on the side.*

> *NOTE*
> *The amount of oil poured in is not as accurate a measurement as the actual level of the oil. You may have to add more oil later in this procedure.*

11. After filling the fork tube, slowly pump the forks up and down to distribute the oil throughout the fork damper.

> *NOTE*
> *Step 12 is performed with the fork tubes fully extended and the front wheel off the ground.*

12. Measure the distance from the top of the fork tube to the surface of the oil (**Figure 31**) with an oil level gauge or ruler.

13. Add oil, if required, to bring the level up to the oil level specifications (**Table 8**). Do not overfill.

> *CAUTION*
> *An excessive amount of oil can cause a hydraulic locking of the forks during compression, destroying the oil seals.*

> *NOTE*
> *Install the fork spring in Step 14 so that the closer wound coils face toward the top of the fork.*

14. Reinstall the fork spring and fork cap. Tighten the fork cap to the tightening torque in **Table 2**.

15. Repeat Steps 9-14 for the opposite side.

16. Fill the forks with air as described under *Front Fork Air Adjustment* in this chapter.

17. Install the left- and right-hand handlebars onto the upper fork clamp. Install the Allen bolts

(**Figure 28**) and tighten to the torque specifications in **Table 2**.

18. Tighten the upper fork tube pinch bolts to the torque specifications in **Table 2**.

19. Road test the bike and check for oil and air leaks.

Control Cables

The choke and throttle cables should be lubricated at the intervals specified in **Table 1**. At this time, they should also be inspected for fraying, and the cable sheath should be checked for chafing. The cables are relatively inexpensive and should be replaced when found to be faulty.

They can be lubricated with a cable lubricant and a cable lubricator available at most motorcycle dealers.

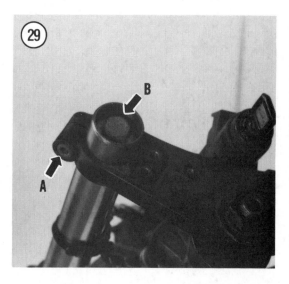

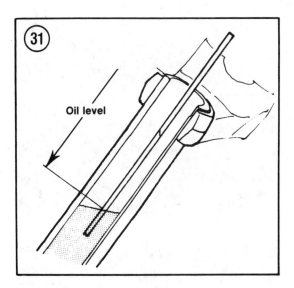

Oil level

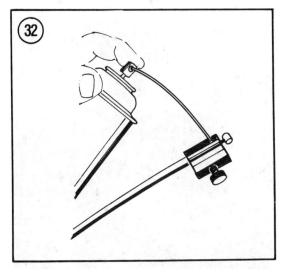

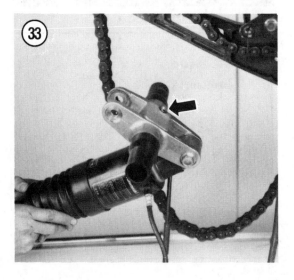

NOTE
The main cause of cable breakage or cable stiffness is improper lubrication. Maintaining the cables as described in this section will assure long service life.

1. Disconnect the choke cable from the left-hand handlebar. Label and then disconnect the throttle cable(s) from the throttle grip.

NOTE
To service the throttle cable(s), it is necessary to remove the screws that clamp the housing together to gain access to the cable ends.

2. Attach a cable lubricator (**Figure 32**) to the cable following the manufacturer's instructions.
3. Insert the nozzle of the lubricant can into the lubricator, press the button on the can and hold it down until the lubricant begins to flow out of the other end of the cable.

NOTE
Place a shop cloth at the end of the cable(s) to catch all excess lubricant that will flow out.

NOTE
If lubricant does not flow out the end of the cable, check the entire cable for fraying, bending or other damage. Replace damaged cables.

4. Remove the lubricator, reconnect and adjust the cable(s) as described in this chapter. Refer to:
   a. *Throttle Cable Adjustment.*
   b. *Choke Cable Adjustment.*

Swing Arm Bearings Lubrication

The rear swing arm needle bearings should be cleaned in solvent and lubricated with a molybdenum disulfide grease at the intervals specified in **Table 1**. The swing arm must be removed to service the needle bearings. Refer to Chapter Eleven.

Uni-Trak Linkage Lubrication

The Uni-Trak tie-rod and connecting rod needle bearings should be cleaned in solvent and lubricated with molybdenum disulfide grease at the intervals specified in **Table 1**. The Uni-Trak linkage must be removed to service the needle bearings. Refer to Chapter Eleven.

NOTE
*On ZX1000 models, a grease nipple is installed on the rocker arm (**Figure 33**). To gain access to the grease nipple, it is necessary to remove the battery.*

Speedometer Cable Lubrication

Lubricate the speedometer cable every year or whenever needle operation is erratic.

> *NOTE*
> *It is necessary to remove the windshield and part of the upper fairing to gain access to the back of the speedometer. See Chapter Thirteen for removal procedures.*

1. Unscrew the end of the speedometer cable at the back of the speedometer (**Figure 34**) and at the front wheel (**Figure 35**), then remove the cable.
2. Pull the cable from the sheath.
3. If the grease is contaminated, thoroughly clean off all old grease.
4. Thoroughly coat the cable with a good grade of multipurpose grease and reinstall into the sheath.
5. Make sure the cable is correctly seated into the speedometer drive unit.

Wheel Bearings
Inspection/Lubrication

Worn wheel bearings cause excessive wheel play that result in vibration and other steering troubles. Sealed bearings do not require periodic lubrication. Non-sealed bearings require periodic cleaning and lubrication. Refer to *Front Hub* in Chapter Ten and *Rear Hub* in Chapter Eleven.

Speedometer Gear Lubrication

Refer to *Speedometer Gear Lubrication* in Chapter Ten.

Steering Stem Lubrication

Refer to *Steering Head* in Chapter Ten.

Drive Chain Lubrication

Kawasaki recommends SAE 90 gear oil for chain lubrication; it is less likely to be thrown off the chain than lighter oils. Many commercial drive chain lubricants are also available that do an excellent job.

> *NOTE*
> *If the drive chain is very dirty, remove and clean it as described under **Drive Chain Cleaning** in Chapter Eleven before lubricating it as described in this procedure.*

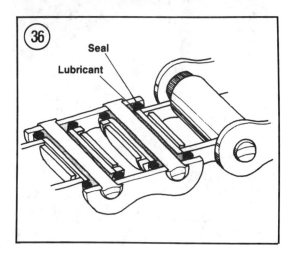

Seal

Lubricant

CAUTION
*The factory drive chain is equipped with O-rings between the side plates (**Figure 36**) that seal lubricant between the pins and bushings. To prevent damaging these O-rings, use only kerosene or diesel oil for cleaning. Do not use gasoline or other solvents that will cause the O-rings to swell or deteriorate. Refer to cleaning procedures in Chapter Eleven.*

1. Place the bike on the center stand.
2. Oil the bottom chain run with SAE 90 gear oil or a commercial chain lubricant *recommended for O-ring use*. Concentrate on getting the oil down between the side plates of the chain links and onto the O-rings (**Figure 36**).
3. Rotate the chain and continue until the entire chain has been lubricated.
4. Ride the bike a short distance. Then wipe off any oil that was slung off from the chain.

PERIODIC MAINTENANCE

Drive Chain Free Play

NOTE
As drive chains stretch and wear in use, the chain will become looser. The chain must be checked and adjusted as necessary.

1. Place the motorcycle on the center stand.
2. Turn the rear wheel and check the chain slack for its tightest point. Mark this spot and turn the wheel so that the mark is located on the lower chain run, midway between both drive sprockets. Check and adjust the drive chain as follows.
3. With thumb and forefinger, lift up and press down the chain at that point, measuring the distance the chain moves vertically.
4. The drive chain should have approximately 35-40 mm (1 3/8-1 9/16 in.) of vertical travel at midpoint (**Figure 37**). If necessary, adjust the chain as follows.
5A. *ZX900:* Perform the following:
   a. Loosen the locknut and loosen the collar fixing bolt (A, **Figure 38**).
   b. Loosen the brake caliper fixing bolt (B, **Figure 38**).
5B. *ZX1000:* Loosen the torque link nut (**Figure 39**).
6. Loosen the left- and right-hand chain adjuster pinch bolts (**Figure 40**).

7. Insert an Allen wrench into the hexagonal hole in the chain adjuster (A, **Figure 41**).

8. Rotate the chain adjusters equally until the drive chain free play (Step 4) is correct.

NOTE
Check the drive chain alignment, as described in this chapter, before tightening all the fasteners.

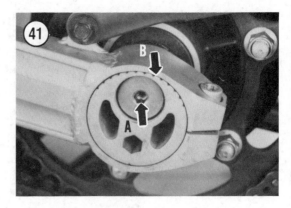

9. Tighten the chain adjuster pinch bolts (**Figure 40**) to the torque specification in **Table 2**.

10A. *ZX900:* Perform the following:

  a. Tighten the brake caliper fixing bolt (B, **Figure 38**).

  b. Tighten the collar fixing bolt and tighten its locknut (A, **Figure 38**).

  c. Tighten all bolts and nuts securely.

10B. *ZX1000:* Tighten the torque link nut to 29 N•m (22 ft.-lb.).

11. Check the drive chain alignment as described in this chapter.

NOTE
Drive chain replacement is described in Chapter Eleven.

Drive Chain Alignment

1. Check and adjust the drive chain free play as described in this chapter before checking alignment.

2. Alignment is checked by observing the swing arm marks (B, **Figure 41**) on both sides of the swing arm. If necessary, perform the following.

3. Remove the retaining rings (**Figure 42**).

4. *ZX1000:* Loosen the torque link nut (**Figure 39**).

5. Loosen the axle nut (**Figure 43**).

6. Loosen the left- and right-hand chain adjuster pinch bolts (**Figure 40**).

7. Turn the chain adjuster(s) (**Figure 44**) to align the left- and right-hand mark (B, **Figure 41**) on both sides of the swing arm.

8. Tighten the chain adjuster pinch bolts (**Figure 40**) to the torque specification in **Table 2**.

9. Tighten the axle nut to the torque specification in **Table 2**.

10. *ZX1000:* Tighten the torque link nut to 29 N•m (22 ft.-lb.).

11. Reinstall the retaining rings (**Figure 42**).

12. Check rear wheel alignment by sighting along the chain as it runs over the rear sprocket. It should not appear to bend sideways. See **Figure 45**.

13. Recheck chain play.

Disc Brake Inspection

The hydraulic brake fluid in the disc brake master cylinders should be checked every month.

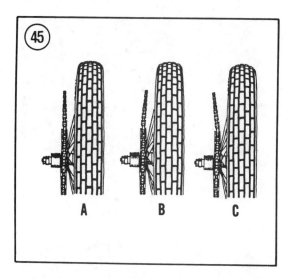

The disc brake pads should be checked at the intervals specified in **Table 1**. Replacement is described under *Brake Pad Replacement* in Chapter Twelve.

Disc Brake Fluid Level Inspection

1. Place the bike on its center stand.
2. Turn the handlebars so that the front master cylinder is level.
3. The brake fluid must be between the upper and lower level lines. See **Figure 46** (front) or **Figure 47** (rear).

Adding Brake Fluid

1. Clean the outside of the reservoir cap thoroughly with a dry rag and remove the reservoir cap. Remove the diaphragm under the cap.
2. The fluid level in the reservoir should be up to the upper level line. Add fresh DOT 4 brake fluid as required.

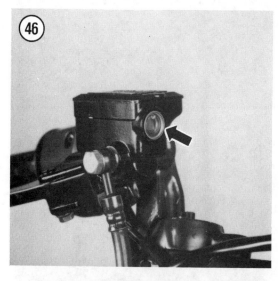

> *WARNING*
> *Use brake fluid clearly marked DOT 4 only and specified for disc brakes. Others may vaporize and cause brake failure. Do not intermix different brands or types of brake fluid as they may not be compatible. Do not intermix a silicone based (DOT 5) brake fluid as it can cause brake component damage leading to brake system failure.*

> *CAUTION*
> *Be careful not to spill brake fluid on painted or plated surfaces as it will destroy the surface. Wash immediately with soapy water and thoroughly rinse it off.*

3. Reinstall all parts. Make sure the cap is tightly secured.

> *NOTE*
> *If the brake fluid was so low as to allow air in the hydraulic system, the brakes will have to be bled. When air enters the system, the brake feels soft or spongy. Refer to **Bleeding the System** in Chapter Twelve.*

Disc Brake Lines and Seals

Check brake lines between the master cylinder and the brake caliper. If there is any leakage, tighten the connections and bleed the brakes as described in Chapter Twelve. If this does not stop the leak or if a line is obviously damaged, cracked, or chafed, replace the line and seals and bleed the brake.

Disc Brake Pad Inspection

Inspect the disc brake pads for wear according to the maintenance schedule.

1. Apply the front or rear brake.
2. Shine a light between the caliper and the disc and inspect the brake pads.
pads.
3. If either pad measures 1 mm (1/32 in.) or less, replace both pads as a set.

> *NOTE*
> *If it is difficult to observe the thickness and condition of the brake pads, remove them as described under **Brake Pad Replacement** in Chapter Twelve.*

4. Replace brake pads as described in Chapter Twelve.

Disc Brake Fluid Change

Every time you remove the reservoir cap a small amount of dirt and moisture enters the brake fluid. The same thing happens if a leak occurs or when any part of the hydraulic system is loosened or disconnected. Dirt can clog the system and cause unnecessary wear. Water in the fluid vaporizes at high temperatures, impairing the hydraulic action and reducing brake performance.

To change brake fluid while minimizing the need for air bleeding, do as follows: attach a clear hose to the air bleed valve (**Figure 48** or **Figure 49**). Insert the opposite end of the hose into a clear, clean container (**Figure 50**). Pump the lever or pedal to drain the reservoir while watching the reservoir's fluid level. Add new brake fluid to the reservoir before it drops below the low line. Keep pumping (and adding fluid) until the fluid coming through the hose is clear and clean. Now the system must be bled of any air. Refer to *Bleeding the System* in Chapter Twelve.

> *WARNING*
> *Use brake fluid clearly marked DOT 4 only and specified for disc brakes. Others may vaporize and cause brake failure. Do not intermix different brands or types of brake fluid as they may not be compatible. Do not intermix a silicone based (DOT 5) brake fluid as it can cause brake component damage leading to brake system failure.*

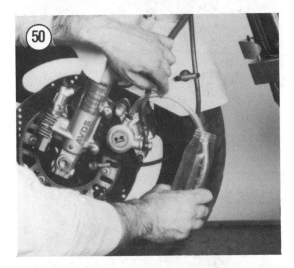

Front Brake Lever Adjustment

Periodic adjustment of the front disc brake is not required because disc pad wear is automatically

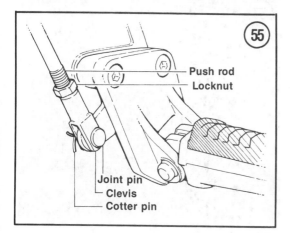

compensated. If there is excessive play in the front brake lever, check the fluid level and also check the front brake lever pivot hole and bolt for excessive wear. Add fluid or replace worn parts.

Rear Brake Pedal Height Adjustment (ZX900)

1. Place the motorcycle on the center stand.
2. Check to be sure the brake pedal is in the at-rest position.
3. The correct height position is 29-39 mm (1 5/32-1 17/32 in.) below the top of the footpeg (**Figure 51**). To adjust, proceed to Step 4.
4. Remove the right-hand footpeg bracket (**Figure 52**) as described in Chapter Thirteen.
5. Loosen the locknut (A, **Figure 53**). Turn the adjusting nut (B, **Figure 53**) in or out to adjust the brake pedal height.
6. Temporarily install the right-hand footpeg bracket and check the adjustment. Repeat until the adjustment is correct.
7. Check the brake light switch adjustment as described in this chapter.
8. Install the right-hand footpeg bracket as described in Chapter Thirteen.

Rear Brake Pedal Height Adjustment (ZX1000)

1. Place the motorcycle on the center stand.
2. Check to be sure the brake pedal is in the at-rest position.
3. The correct height position is approximately 37 mm (1 15/32 in.) below the top of the footpeg (**Figure 54**). To adjust, proceed to Step 4.
4. Referring to **Figure 55**, perform the following:
   a. Loosen the pushrod locknut.
   b. Remove the cotter pin.
   c. Slide the joint pin out of the clevis.
   d. Pull the clevis out of its pivot position.
   e. Turn the clevis as required to adjust the brake pedal position.
   f. Reverse to install the clevis. Install a new cotter pin.
5. Recheck the brake pedal position.
6. Check the brake light switch adjustment as described in this chapter.

Rear Brake Light Switch Adjustment

1. Turn the ignition switch to the ON position.
2. Depress the brake pedal. The brake light should come on after the brake pedal is depressed approximately 10 mm (13/32 in.). If necessary, adjust as follows.

3. *ZX900:* Remove the right-hand side cover as described in Chapter Thirteen.

4. See **Figure 56** (ZX900) or **Figure 57** (ZX1000). To make the light come on earlier, hold the switch body and turn the adjusting locknut to move the switch body *up*. Move the switch body *down* to delay the light. Tighten the locknut.

5. Check that the brakelight comes on when the pedal is depressed and goes off when the pedal is released. Readjust, as necessary.

NOTE
Figure 57 shows the right-hand side cover on ZX1000 models removed for clarity. It is not necessary to remove the side cover to adjust the rear brake light switch.

5. *ZX900:* Reinstall the side cover as described in Chapter Thirteen.

Clutch Fluid Level Check

The clutch is hydraulically operated and requires no routine adjustment. The system uses DOT 4 brake fluid.

The fluid in the clutch master cylinder should be checked weekly or whenever the level drops, whichever comes first. Bleeding the clutch system and servicing clutch components are covered in Chapter Five.

CAUTION
If the clutch operates correctly when the engine is cold or in cool weather, but operates erratically (or not at all) after the engine warms up or in hot weather, there is air in the hydraulic line and the clutch must be bled. Refer to Chapter Five.

The fluid level in the reservoir should be between the upper and lower lever marks on the reservoir window (**Figure 58**). The fluid level must be corrected by adding fresh DOT 4 brake fluid.

1. Park the bike on level ground and turn the handlebars so the master cylinder reservoir is level.

2. Clean any dirt from the area around the top cover prior to removing the cover.

3. Remove the top cover and diaphragm. Add brake fluid until the level is between the lower and upper lines on the reservoir window. Use fresh DOT 4 brake fluid from a sealed container.

WARNING
Only use brake fluid from a sealed container clearly marked DOT 4. Do not intermix different brands or types of

brake fluid as they may not be compatible. Do not intermix a silicone based (DOT 5) fluid as it can cause clutch component damage leading to clutch release system failure.

CAUTION
Be careful when handling hydraulic fluid. Do not spill it on painted or plated surfaces as it will destroy the surface. Wash the area immediately with soapy water and thoroughly rinse it off.

4. Reinstall the diaphragm and the top cover. Tighten the screws securely.

Clutch Hydraulic Lines

Check clutch lines between the master cylinder and the clutch slave cylinder. If there is any

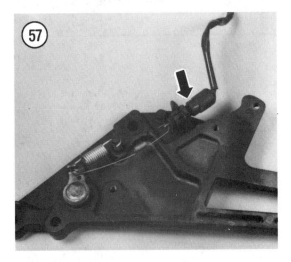

leakage, tighten the connections and bleed the clutch as described under *Bleeding the Clutch* in Chapter Five. If this does not stop the leak or if a clutch line is obviously damaged, cracked or chafed, replace the clutch line and bleed the system.

Throttle Cable Adjustment

Always check the throttle cable(s) before you make any carburetor adjustments. Too much free play causes delayed throttle response; too little free play will cause unstable idling.

Check the throttle cable(s) from grip to carburetors. Make sure they are not kinked or chafed. Replace them if necessary.

Make sure that the throttle grip rotates smoothly from fully closed to fully open. Check at center, full left, and full right position of steering.

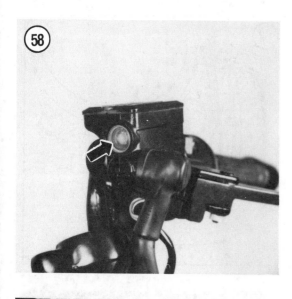

Check free play at the throttle grip flange. Kawasaki specifies about 2-3 mm (1/8 in.). If adjustment is required proceed as follows.

WARNING
If idle speed increases when the handlebar is turned to right or left, check throttle cable routing. Do not ride the motorcycle in this unsafe condition.

1A. *1984-1985:* Perform the following:
 a. Remove the seat and fuel tank. See Chapter Seven.
 b. Loosen the throttle cable adjuster locknut located in the middle of the cable.
 c. Turn the adjuster until the throttle grip free play is correct. Tighten the locknut.
1B. *1986-on:* Perform the following:
 a. Loosen the accelerator cable (outer) locknut at the handlebar and turn the adjuster until the correct amount of free play at the throttle grip is obtained. Tighten the locknut.
 b. If the correct throttle grip free play cannot be obtained by performing sub-step a, proceed with sub-step c.
 c. Remove the fuel tank as described in Chapter Seven.
 d. Loosen both cable locknuts at the carburetors (**Figure 59**) to obtain as much slack in the throttle grip as possible.
 e. Close the throttle grip and lengthen the decelerator cable adjusting nut (B, **Figure 59**) until its inner cable becomes tight. Tighten the locknut.
 f. Lengthen the accelerator adjusting nut (A, **Figure 59**) until the correct free play is obtained at the throttle grip. Tighten the locknut.
2. Operate the throttle grip a few times. Then check that the throttle linkage rests against the idle adjusting screw when the throttle grip is closed.
3. The throttle grip should now be adjusted correctly. If not, the throttle cables may be stretched and should be replaced.
4. Reinstall the fuel tank after completing the adjustment.
5. Park the motorcycle on its center stand. Sit on the seat and start the engine. Then lean back so that the front wheel clears the ground. Turn the handlebars from right to left to check for abnormal idle speed variances due to improper cable routing.

WARNING
If idle speed increases when the handlebar is turned to right or left, check throttle cable routing. Do not ride the motorcycle in this unsafe condition.

Choke Cable Adjustment

1A. *ZX900:* Perform the following:
   a. Remove the fuel tank as described in this chapter.
   b. Push the choke lever (**Figure 60**) to its released position.
   c. Locate the cable adjuster at the middle of the cable.
   d. Pull the cable in-and-out at the adjuster. Measure cable travel at this point. The free play should be 2-3 mm (1/8 in.).
   e. If necessary, adjust the choke cable at the carburetor (**Figure 61**). Loosen the cable clamp and reposition the cable. Tighten the clamp and recheck the free play.

1B. *ZX1000:* Pull the choke lever until the starter lever contacts the starter plunger at the carburetor. See **Figure 62**.
   a. The distance the choke lever traveled in sub-step a is choke cable play.
   b. The correct amount of choke lever play is 2-3 mm (1/8 in.).
   c. If the choke lever play is incorrect, proceed with sub-step e.
   d. Remove the fuel tank as described in Chapter Seven.
   e. Locate the choke cable midline adjuster (**Figure 63**) and loosen the locknut. Turn the adjuster until the correct amount of choke lever play is obtained. Tighten the locknut and recheck the adjustment.

2. Reinstall the fuel tank.

Fuel Valve/Filter

At the intervals specified in **Table 1**, remove and drain the fuel tank. Remove the fuel shutoff valve and clean it of all dirt and debris. Replace worn or damaged O-rings and gaskets. Refer to *Fuel Valve* in Chapter Seven.

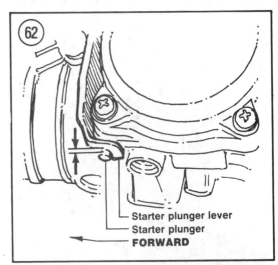

Fuel and Vacuum Line Inspection

Inspect the condition of all fuel and vacuum lines for cracks or deterioration; replace if necessary. Make sure the hose clamps are in place and holding securely.

Exhaust System

Check for leakage at all fittings. Tighten all bolts and nuts; replace any gaskets as necessary. Refer to *Exhaust System* in Chapter Seven.

Air Cleaner

A clogged air cleaner can decrease the efficiency and life of the engine. Never run the bike without the air cleaner installed; even minute particles of dust can cause severe internal engine wear.

The service intervals specified in **Table 1** should be followed with general use. However, the air cleaner should be serviced more often if the bike is ridden in dusty areas.

ZX900

Refer to **Figure 64** for this procedure.
1. Remove the left-hand side cover.
2. Remove the 2 Phillips screws and remove the side cover (**Figure 64**).
3. Remove the air filter by pulling on the holder.
4. Inspect the air filter element for tears or other damage that would allow unfiltered air to pass into the engine. Check the sponge gasket on the element for tears. Replace the element if necessary.
5. Clean the air filter as follows:
   a. Clean the element in solvent to remove oil and dirt. When cleaning the element, insert the element into the solvent bath so that only the outside of the element is soaking in the solvent. This will prevent the solvent from contaminating the inside of the element. After cleaning the outer element, pour clean solvent inside the element and allow it to drain through the element.

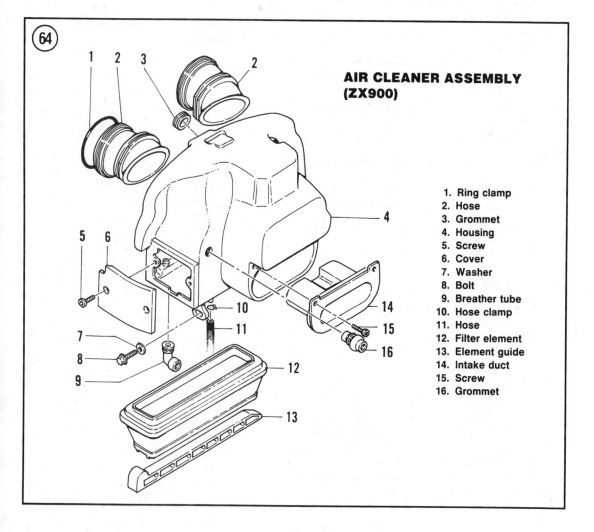

AIR CLEANER ASSEMBLY (ZX900)

1. Ring clamp
2. Hose
3. Grommet
4. Housing
5. Screw
6. Cover
7. Washer
8. Bolt
9. Breather tube
10. Hose clamp
11. Hose
12. Filter element
13. Element guide
14. Intake duct
15. Screw
16. Grommet

b. Dry the element with compressed air. Direct the compressed air from the inside of the element to the outside. If compressed air is not available, allow the element to air dry.

c. When the element is dry, saturate a clean lint-free towel with SAE 30 weight oil. Apply oil to the outside of the element by tapping the element with the oil soaked towel. Allow the element to sit on some clean newspapers to soak up any excess oil.

6. See **Figure 65**. Install the element into the housing without the holder. Push the element up against the filter housing. Then slide the holder (with the chamfered side facing up) into the element.

7. Install the filter side cover. Secure with the 2 Phillips screws.

8. Install the right-hand side cover.

ZX1000

Refer to **Figure 66** for this procedure.

1. Remove the fuel tank.
2. Remove the air filter cover screws and remove the cover (**Figure 67**).
3. Remove the air filter element (**Figure 68**).
4. Cover the air filter housing opening (**Figure 69**).
5. Clean the air filter as follows:

a. Clean the element in solvent to remove oil and dirt.

b. Dry the element with compressed air. Direct the compressed air from the inside of the element to the outside. If compressed air is not available, allow the element to air dry.

c. When the element is dry, saturate a clean lint-free towel with SAE 30 weight oil. Apply oil to the outside of the element by tapping the element with the oil soaked towel.

6. Reverse to install the air filter element.

Air Suction Valve
(U.S. Models)

Refer to *Air Suction System (U.S. Models)* in Chapter Seven for complete inspection and service procedures.

Steering Play

The steering head should be checked for looseness at the intervals specified in **Table 1** or whenever the following symptoms or conditions exist:

a. The handlebars vibrate more than normal.

b. The front forks make a clicking or clunking noise when the front brake is applied.

c. The steering feels tight or slow.

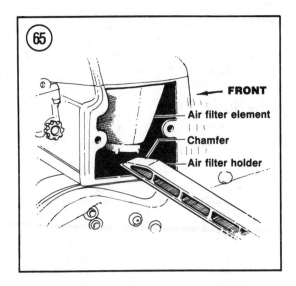

(65)

← FRONT
Air filter element
Chamfer
Air filter holder

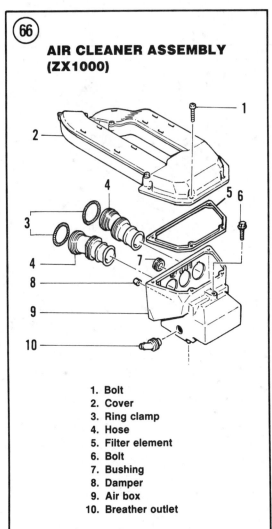

(66)

AIR CLEANER ASSEMBLY (ZX1000)

1. Bolt
2. Cover
3. Ring clamp
4. Hose
5. Filter element
6. Bolt
7. Bushing
8. Damper
9. Air box
10. Breather outlet

d. The motorcycle does not want to steer straight on level road surfaces.

Inspection

1. Prop up the motorcycle so that the front tire clears the ground.
2. Remove the upper and lower fairings. See Chapter Thirteen.
3. Center the front wheel. Push lightly against the left handlebar grip to start the wheel turning to the right, then let go. The wheel should continue turning under its own momentum until the forks hit their stop.
4. Center the wheel, and push lightly against the right handlebar grip.
5. If, with a light push in either direction, the front wheel will turn all the way to the stop, the steering adjustment is not too tight.

> *WARNING*
> *If idle speed changes when the handlebars turn, the throttle cable is misrouted through the frame. Do not ride the bike in this unsafe condition.*

6. If the front wheel would not turn all the way to the stop, the steering is too tight. Adjust the steering as described in this chapter.
7. Center the front wheel and kneel in front of it. Grasp the bottoms of the 2 front fork slider legs. Try to pull the forks toward you, and then try to push them toward the engine. If no play is felt, the steering adjustment is not too loose.
8. If the steering adjustment is too tight or too loose, adjust it as described in this chapter.

Adjustment

1. Prop up the motorcycle so that the front tire clears the ground.
2. Remove the upper and lower fairings. See Chapter Thirteen.
3. Remove the fuel tank.
4. Remove the steering stem head cover (**Figure 70**).

5. Loosen the lower front fork steering stem bolts.

6. Loosen the steering stem nut (A, **Figure 71**).

7. Loosen or tighten the steering stem locknut (B, **Figure 71**) less than 1/8 turn at a time.

8. Recheck the steering as described under *Inspection* in this chapter.

9. Tighten the steering stem nut to the torque specification in **Table 2**.

10. Tighten the lower front fork steering bolts.

11. Recheck the steering.

12. Perform Steps 6-9 until the adjustment is correct.

13. Install the steering stem head cover, fuel tank and fairings.

Cooling System Inspection

At the intervals indicated in **Table 1**, the following items should be checked. If you do not have the test equipment, the tests can be done by a Kawasaki dealer, radiator shop or service station.

> *WARNING*
> *Do not remove the radiator cap when the engine is hot.*

1. Have the radiator cap pressure tested (**Figure 72**). The specified radiator cap relief pressure is 0.75-1.05 kg/cm^2 (11-15 psi). The cap must be able to sustain this pressure for 6 seconds. Replace the radiator cap if it does not hold pressure or if the relief pressure is too high or too low.

2. Leave the radiator cap off and have the entire cooling system pressure tested (**Figure 73**). The entire cooling system should be pressurized up to, but not exceeding, 1.05 kg/cm^2 (15 psi). The system must be able to sustain this pressure for 6 seconds. Replace or repair any components that fail this test.

> *CAUTION*
> *If test pressures exceed specifications the radiator may be damaged.*

3. Test the specific gravity of the coolant with an antifreeze tester (**Figure 74**) to ensure adequate

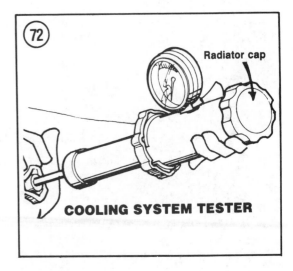

Radiator cap

COOLING SYSTEM TESTER

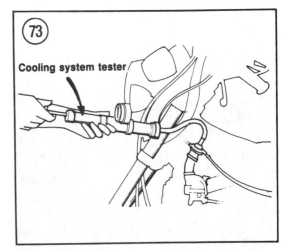

Cooling system tester

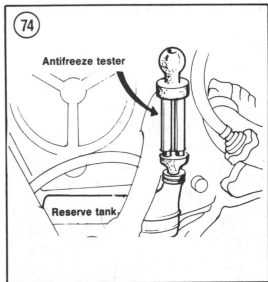

Antifreeze tester

Reserve tank

temperature and corrosion protection. Never let the mixture become less than 43% antifreeze or corrosion protection will be impaired. **Table 9** lists suggested water/coolant ratio.

4. Check all cooling system hoses for damage or deterioration. Replace any hose that is questionable. Make sure all hose clamps are tight.

5. Carefully clean any road dirt, bugs, mud, etc. from the radiator core. Use a whisk broom, compressed air or low-pressure water. If the radiator has been hit by a small rock or other item, *carefully* straighten out the fins with a screwdriver.

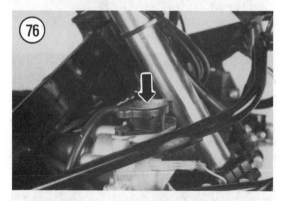

Coolant Change

The cooling system should be completely drained and refilled at the interval indicated in **Table 1**.

CAUTION
Use only a high quality ethylene glycol antifreeze specifically labeled for use with aluminum engines. Do not use an alcohol-based antifreeze.

In areas where freezing temperatures occur, add a higher percentage of antifreeze to protect the system to temperatures far below those likely to occur. **Table 9** lists the recommended amount of antifreeze for protection. The following procedure must be performed when the engine is cool.

WARNING
The EPA has classified ethylene glycol as a toxic waste. Do not drain the coolant into a sewer or storm drain. Dispose of it as you would used motor oil.

CAUTION
Coolant can stain concrete and harm plants. Do not drain the coolant onto a driveway or planted area.

CAUTION
Be careful not to spill antifreeze on painted surfaces as it will destroy the surface. Wash immediately with soapy water and rinse thoroughly with clean water.

1. Place the bike on the center stand.
2. Remove the lower fairing. See Chapter Thirteen.

WARNING
Do not remove the radiator cap when the engine is hot.

3. Remove the radiator cap. See **Figure 75** (ZX900) or **Figure 76** (ZX1000).
4. Place a drain pan under the front radiator pipe. Remove the drain plug from the water pipe (**Figure 77**) and drain coolant from the engine and radiator.

NOTE
Steps 5-7 describe procedures required to drain coolant from the cylinder block. Under normal engine operating conditions, draining the cylinder block is not required. However, if the coolant was contaminated or if the engine is

experiencing cooling problems, draining the cylinder block is recommended.

5. Remove the radiator as described in Chapter Nine.

6. Remove the exhaust pipes as described in Chapter Seven.

7. Remove the water pipes from the cylinder block (**Figure 78**). Then remove the 2 cylinder block drain bolts (located behind the water pipes) and drain the cylinder block.

8. Remove the coolant reservoir tank and drain the coolant. See **Figure 79** (ZX900) or **Figure 80** (ZX1000). Reinstall the reservoir tank.

9. Install all parts removed in Steps 5-8.

10. Reinstall the drain screw and sealing washer on the water pipe.

11. Fill the radiator. Add coolant through the radiator filler neck. Use the recommended mixture of antifreeze and distilled water (**Table 9**).

12. Bleed air from the cooling system as follows:

   a. Remove the radiator cap (if installed).

   b. Loosen the air bleed bolt on top of the water pump (**Figure 81**).

NOTE
Figure 81 shows the water pump with the engine partially disassembled. The engine need not be disassembled to perform this procedure.

   c. When the air bleed bolt is loosened, a combination of air and coolant should flow out of the hole. Allow the coolant to drain until only coolant flows out of the hole.

   d. Tighten the air bleed bolt (**Figure 81**).

13. After bleeding the cooling system, fill the radiator to the filler neck.

14. Refill the coolant reservoir tank. See **Figure 79** or **Figure 80**.

15. Install the radiator cap. Turn the radiator cap clockwise to the first stop. Then push the cap down and turn it clockwise until it stops.

16. Start the engine and let it run at idle speed until the engine reaches normal operating temperature. Make sure there are no air bubbles in the coolant and that the coolant level stabilizes at the correct level. Add coolant as necessary.

17. Test ride the bike and readjust the coolant level in the reservoir tank if necessary.

Front Suspension Check

1. Apply the front brake and pump the fork up and down as vigorously as possible. Check for smooth operation and check for any oil leaks.

2. Make sure the upper and lower steering stem bolts are tight.

3. Check that the axle nut is tight.

4. Check that the front axle pinch bolts are tight.

WARNING
If any of the previously mentioned bolts and nuts are loose, refer to Chapter Ten for correct procedures and torque specifications.

Rear Suspension Check

1. Place the bike on the center stand.

2. Push hard on the rear wheel sideways to check for side play in the swing arm bearings.

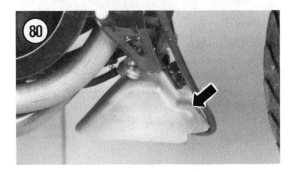

3. If any play is felt, remove the fairings and check the tightness of all suspension mounting bolts.

> *WARNING*
> *If any of the previously mentioned nuts or bolts are loose, refer to Chapter Eleven for correct procedures and torque specifications.*

Nuts, Bolts and Other Fasteners

Constant vibration can loosen many fasteners on a motorcycle. Check the tightness of all fasteners, especially those on:
   a. Engine mounting hardware.
   b. Engine crankcase covers.

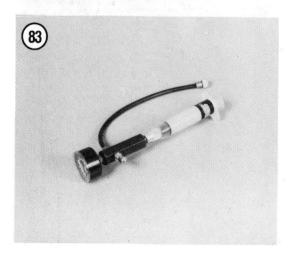

   c. Handlebars and front forks.
   d. Gearshift lever.
   e. Sprocket bolts and nuts.
   f. Brake pedal and lever.
   g. Exhaust system.
   h. Lighting equipment.

SUSPENSION ADJUSTMENT

Front Fork Air Adjustment

Both the fork springs and air pressure support the motorcycle and rider. Air pressure should be measured with the forks at normal room temperature.

The air pressure can be varied to suit the load and your ride preference. Don't use a high-pressure hose or bottle to pressurize the forks. A tire pump is a lot closer to the scale you need. Note the following when adjusting the front fork air pressure:
   a. Increase air pressure for heavy loads.
   b. If the suspension is too hard, reduce air pressure.
   c. If the suspension is too soft, increase air pressure.
1. Support the bike with the front wheel off the ground.

> *NOTE*
> *ZX900 models are equipped with one air valve (**Figure 82**) that supplies air pressure to both fork tubes. ZX1000 models have a single air valve installed in each fork tube.*

2. Remove the air valve cap(s).
3. Connect a pump (**Figure 83**) to the valve and pump the forks to about 20 psi.

> *CAUTION*
> *Do not exceed 36 psi or the fork seals will be damaged.*

4. Slowly bleed off the pressure to reach the desired value. The standard pressure is listed in **Table 10**.

> *NOTE*
> *Each application of a pressure gauge bleeds off some air pressure in the process of applying and removing the gauge.*

5. Install the valve cap(s).

Anti-dive Adjustment

The anti-dive system can be adjusted for different road and riding conditions by turning the adjuster ring (**Figure 84**) at the bottom of the anti-dive unit. The anti-dive adjusters on each fork tube can be set to one of the following positions:

    a. Position 1: Weak.

    b. Position 2: Moderate.

    c. Position 3: Strong.

When adjusting the anti-dive, note the following:

    a. The numbers on the adjuster (**Figure 85**) indicate the different numbered positions.

    b. Align the desired adjuster number with the triangle index mark on the fork tube (**Figure 85**).

    c. Turn the adjuster until it clicks into position.

    d. Turn both adjusters to the same numbered position.

> *WARNING*
> *If the anti-dive adjusters are not set to the same numbered position, front suspension operation may become uncertain and unstable.*

Rear Shock Absorber Adjustment

The Uni-Trak rear shock absorber is equipped with air pressure and damping adjustments.

Air pressure

Air pressure should be measured with the shock at normal room temperature.

The air pressure can be varied to suit the load and your ride preference. Don't use a high-pressure hose or bottle to pressurize the shock. A tire pump is a lot closer to the scale you need. Note the following when adjusting the rear shock air pressure:

    a. Increase air pressure for heavy loads.

    b. If the suspension is too hard, reduce air pressure.

    c. If the suspension is too soft, increase air pressure.

1. Support the bike on the center stand with the rear wheel off the ground.

2. Remove the left-hand side cover.

3. Remove the air valve cap. See A, **Figure 86** (ZX900) or A, **Figure 87** (ZX1000).

4. Connect a pump to the valve and pump the shock to about 30 psi.

> *CAUTION*
> *Do not exceed 71 psi or the shock absorber oil seal will be damaged.*

5. Slowly bleed off the pressure to reach the desired value. Suggested pressure ranges with varying load settings are listed in **Table 11** (ZX900) and **Table 12** (ZX1000).

> *NOTE*
> *Each application of a pressure gauge bleeds off some air pressure in the process of applying and removing the gauge.*

6. Install the air valve cap.

Damping adjustment

The damping can be adjusted to 4 different positions to best suit riding, load and speed conditions. **Table 13** lists adjuster positions in relation to various road and riding conditions.

1A. *ZX900:* The damping is changed by pushing or pulling the shock absorber damper stick (B, **Figure 86**) to the desired numbered position that corresponds to the adjuster positions in **Table 13**.

1B. *ZX1000:* The damping is changed by turning the adjuster dial (B, **Figure 87**) to the desired numbered position that corresponds to the adjuster positions in **Table 13**. The dial will click as each position is located.

2. Test ride the bike.

TUNE-UP

A complete tune-up restores performance and power that is lost due to normal wear and deterioration of engine parts. Because engine wear

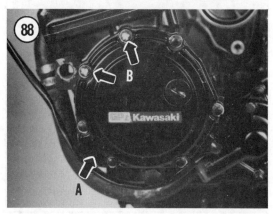

occurs over a combined period of time and mileage, the engine tune-up should be performed at the intervals specified in **Table 1**. More frequent tune-ups may be required if the bike is ridden primarily in stop-and-go traffic.

Table 14 lists tune-up specifications.

Before starting a tune-up procedure, make sure to have all the necessary new parts on hand.

Because different systems in an engine interact, the procedures should be done in the following order:

   a. Clean or replace the air cleaner element.
   b. Adjust valve clearances.
   c. Check engine compression.
   d. Check or replace the spark plugs.
   e. Check the ignition timing.
   f. Synchronize carburetors and set idle speed.

Tools

To perform a tune-up on your Kawasaki, you will need the following tools:

   a. Spark plug wrench.
   b. Socket wrench and assorted sockets.
   c. Flat feeler gauge.
   d. Compression gauge.
   e. Spark plug wire feeler gauge and gapper tool.
   f. Ignition timing light.
   g. Carburetor synchronization tool—to measure manifold vacuum.

Air Cleaner Element

The air cleaner element should be cleaned or replaced prior to doing other tune-up procedures. Refer to *Air Cleaner Removal/Installation* in this chapter.

Valve Clearance

CAUTION
Valve clearance check and adjustment
must be performed with the engine cold.

1. Place the motorcycle on the center stand.
2. Remove the cylinder head cover. Refer to *Cylinder Head Cover Removal/Installation* in Chapter Four.
3. Remove the spark plugs as described in this chapter. This will make it easier to turn the engine by hand.

NOTE
Place an oil pan underneath the pickup
coil cover.

4. Remove the pickup coil cover (A, **Figure 88**) from the left-hand side.

NOTE
The pistons are numbered 1-4, starting with the left piston and counting left-to-right.

NOTE
*Steps 5 and 7 describe camshaft positioning for adjusting valve clearance. Camshaft sprocket positioning is viewed from the left-hand side (**Figure 89**). The correct valve clearance is listed in **Table 14**. The clearance is measured correctly when there is a slight drag on the feeler gauge when it is inserted and withdrawn.*

5. Use the crankshaft nut (**Figure 90**) to turn the crankshaft counterclockwise until the "T" mark on the rotor is aligned with the crankcase TDC mark (**Figure 91**). The timing marks on the cam sprockets (**Figure 89**) should be as shown on **Figure 92**. If not, turn the crankshaft one full turn counterclockwise. Now, the rotor and TDC marks should be aligned (again) and the cam timing marks at 9 o'clock (EX) and 3 o'clock (IN). Adjust the following valves:

   a. No. 4 cylinder intake and exhaust valves.

   b. No. 2 cylinder intake valves.

   c. No. 3 cylinder exhaust valves.

6. See **Figure 93**. Adjust by loosening the adjuster locknut (**Figure 94**) and turning the adjuster as required to get the proper clearance. Hold the adjuster steady and tighten the locknut securely. Check that the locknut is tightened securely.

7. Turn the crankshaft (**Figure 90**) one full turn clockwise. The "T" mark should once again be aligned with the crankcase TDC mark (**Figure 91**). The timing marks on the cam sprocket should be as shown in **Figure 95**: EX at 3 o'clock and IN at 9 o'clock. Adjust the following valves:

   a. No. 1 cylinder intake and exhaust valves.

   b. No. 3 cylinder intake valves.

   c. No. 2 cylinder exhaust valves.

8. Repeat Step 6 for adjustment procedure.

9. Reinstall the spark plugs.

10. Reinstall the pickup coil cover. Apply Loctite 242 (blue) onto the bolts indicated in B, **Figure 88**.

11. Install the cylinder head cover. Refer to *Cylinder Head Cover Removal/Installation* in Chapter Four.

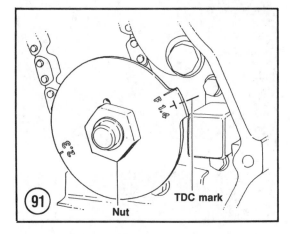

Compression Test

At every tune-up, check cylinder compression. Record the results and compare them at the next check. A running record will show trends in

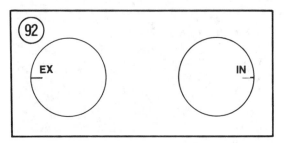

deterioration so that corrective action can be taken before complete failure.

The results, when properly interpreted, can indicate general cylinder, piston ring and valve condition.

NOTE
The valves must be properly adjusted to prevent incorrect clearance from adversely affecting the results of this test.

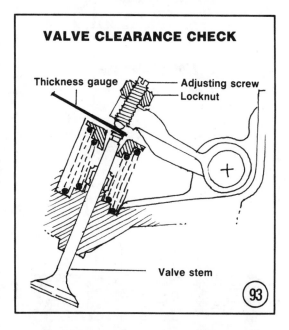

VALVE CLEARANCE CHECK

Thickness gauge — Adjusting screw — Locknut

Valve stem

93

94

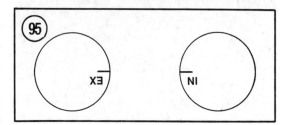

95

1. Warm the engine to normal operating temperature. Ensure that the choke valve is completely open.
2. Remove the spark plugs as described in this chapter.

NOTE
A screw-in type compression gauge will be required for this procedure.

3. Connect the compression gauge to one cylinder following manufacturer's instructions.
4. Hold the throttle open and crank the engine over until there is no further rise in pressure.

NOTE
It should not take more than five or six engine revolutions to reach maximum pressure. If it takes more than six revolutions, there is probably excessive wear on some of the critical components.

5. Record the reading, then remove the gauge.
6. Repeat Steps 3-5 for the other cylinders.
7. When interpreting the results, actual readings are not as important as the difference between the readings. Standard compression pressure is specified in Table 14. Greater differences indicate worn or broken rings, leaky or sticky valves, blown head gasket or a combination of all.

If compression reading does not differ between cylinders by more than 10 psi, the rings and valves are in good condition.

If a low reading (10% or more) is obtained on one of the cylinders, it indicates valve or ring trouble. To determine which, pour about a teaspoon of engine oil through the spark plug hole onto the top of the piston. Turn the engine over once to distribute the oil, then take another compression test and record the reading. If the compression increases significantly, the valves are good but the rings are defective on that cylinder. If compression does not increase, the valves require servicing.

NOTE
If the compression is low, the engine cannot be tuned to maximum performance. The worn parts must be replaced and the engine rebuilt.

Correct Spark Plug Heat Range

Spark plugs are available in various heat ranges that are hotter or colder than the spark plugs originally installed at the factory.

Select plugs in a heat range designed for the loads and temperature conditions under which the engine will operate. Using incorrect heat ranges, however, can cause piston seizure, scored cylinder walls or damaged piston crowns.

In general, use a hotter plug for low speeds, low loads and low temperatures. Use a colder plug for high speeds, high engine loads and high temperatures.

> *NOTE*
> *In areas where seasonal temperature variations are great, a "two-plug system"—a cold plug for hard summer riding and a hot plug for slower winter operation—may prevent spark plug and engine problems.*

The reach (length) of a plug is also important. A longer than normal plug could interfere with the valves and pistons, causing permanent and severe damage (**Figure 96**). The standard heat range spark plugs are listed in **Table 15**.

Spark Plug Removal/Cleaning

1. Remove the fuel tank as described in Chapter Seven.
2. Grasp the spark plug cap (**Figure 97**) as near to the plug as possible and pull it off the plugs.

> *CAUTION*
> *If you pull the spark plug lead, you could do permanent damage to the spark plug cap.*

> *WARNING*
> *Make sure to wear safety glasses when performing Step 3.*

3. Blow away any dirt that has accumulated in the spark plug wells.

> *CAUTION*
> *The dirt could fall into the cylinders when the plugs are removed, causing serious engine damage.*

4. Remove the spark plugs with a spark plug wrench.

> *NOTE*
> *If plugs are difficult to remove, apply penetrating oil, like WD-40 or Liquid Wrench, around base of plugs and let it soak in (about 10-20 minutes).*

5. Inspect spark plug carefully. Look for plugs with broken center porcelain, excessively eroded electrodes, and excessive carbon or oil fouling. Replace such plugs. See **Figure 98**.

> *NOTE*
> *Spark plug cleaning with the use of a sand-blast type device is not*

recommended. While this type of cleaning is thorough, the plug must be perfectly free of all abrasive cleaning material when done. If not, it is possible for the cleaning material to fall into the engine during operation and cause damage.

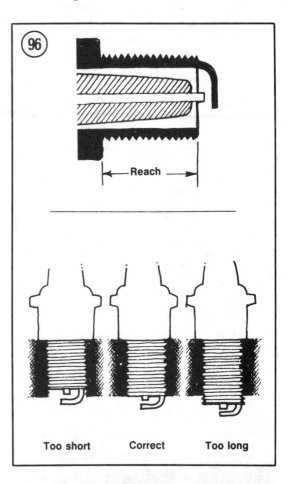

Reach

Too short   Correct   Too long

98

SPARK PLUG CONDITION

NORMAL

- Identified by light tan or gray deposits on the firing tip.
- Can be cleaned.

GAP BRIDGED

- Identified by deposit buildup closing gap between electrodes.
- Caused by oil or carbon fouling. If deposits are not excessive, the plug can be cleaned.

OIL FOULED

- Identified by wet black deposits on the insulator shell bore and electrodes.
- Caused by excessive oil entering combustion chamber through worn rings and pistons, excessive clearance between valve guides and stems, or worn or loose bearings. Can be cleaned. If engine is not repaired, use a hotter plug.

CARBON FOULED

- Identified by black, dry fluffy carbon deposits on insulator tips, exposed shell surfaces and electrodes.
- Caused by too cold a plug, weak ignition, dirty air cleaner, too rich a fuel mixture, or excessive idling. Can be cleaned.

LEAD FOULED

- Identified by dark gray, black, yellow, or tan deposits or a fused glazed coating on the insulator tip.
- Caused by highly leaded gasoline. Can be cleaned.

WORN

- Identified by severely eroded or worn electrodes.
- Caused by normal wear. Should be replaced.

FUSED SPOT DEPOSIT

- Identified by melted or spotty deposits resembling bubbles or blisters.
- Caused by sudden acceleration. Can be cleaned.

OVERHEATING

- Identified by a white or light gray insulator with small black or gray brown spots and with bluish-burnt appearance of electrodes.
- Caused by engine overheating, wrong type of fuel, loose spark plugs, too hot a plug, or incorrect ignition timing. Replace the plug.

PREIGNITION

- Identified by melted electrodes and possibly blistered insulator. Metallic deposits on insulator indicate engine damage.
- Caused by wrong type of fuel, incorrect ignition timing or advance, too hot a plug, burned valves, or engine overheating. Replace the plug.

3

Gapping and Installing the Plugs

New plugs should be carefully gapped to ensure a reliable, consistent spark. You must use a special spark plug gapping tool with a wire gauge.

1. Remove the new plugs from the box. Do *not* use the small threaded pieces that are loose in each box (**Figure 99**). They are not used with the stock plug caps.

2. Insert a wire gauge between the center and the side electrode of each plug (**Figure 100**). The correct gap is found in **Table 14**. If the gap is correct, you will feel a slight drag as you pull the wire through. If there is no drag, or the gauge won't pass through, bend the side electrode *with the gapping tool* (**Figure 101**) to set the proper gap (**Table 14**).

3. Put a small drop of oil or anti-seize compound on the threads of each spark plug.

4. Screw in each spark plug by hand until it seats. Very little effort is required. If force is necessary, you have the plug cross-threaded; unscrew it and check that you haven't damaged the threads in the cylinder head.

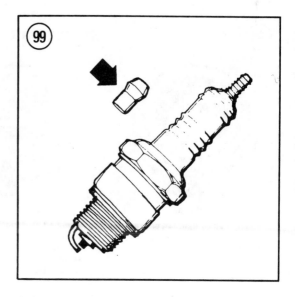

> *NOTE*
> *If a spark plug is difficult to install, the cylinder head threads may be dirty or slightly damaged. To clean the threads, apply grease to the threads of a spark plug tap and screw it carefully into the cylinder head. Turn the tap slowly until it bottoms, then remove it. If the tap cannot be installed, the threads are severely damaged.*

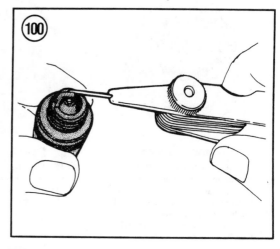

5. Tighten the spark plugs to the torque specification in **Table 2**. If you don't have a torque wrench, an additional 1/4 to 1/2 turn is sufficient after the gasket has made contact with the head. If you are reinstalling old, regapped plugs and are reusing the old gasket, tighten only an additional 1/4 turn.

> *CAUTION*
> *Do not overtighten. Besides making the plug difficult to remove, the excessive torque will deform the gasket and destroy its sealing ability.*

6. Apply dielectric grease to the base of each spark plug cap (**Figure 102**).

> *NOTE*
> *Dielectric grease is a special grease used on electrical systems. It can be found in automotive parts stores.*

7. Install each spark plug cap. Make sure it goes to the correct spark plug.

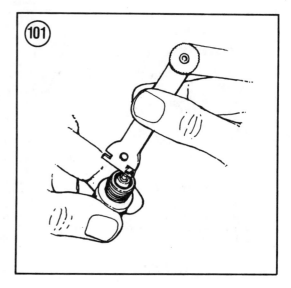

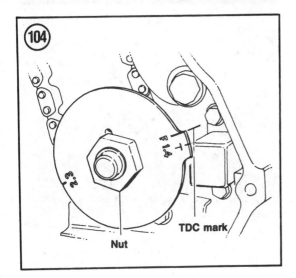

Reading Spark Plugs

Much information about engine and spark plug performance can be determined by careful examination of the spark plugs. This information is more valid after performing the following steps.

1. Ride bike a short distance at full throttle in any gear.
2. Turn off kill switch before closing throttle, and simultaneously, pull in clutch and coast to a stop. *Do not* downshift transmission in stopping.
3. Remove spark plugs and examine them. Compare them to **Figure 98**.

If the insulator tip is white or burned, the plug is too hot and should be replaced with a colder one.

A too-cold plug will have sooty deposits ranging in color from dark brown to black. Replace with a hotter plug and check for too-rich carburetion or evidence of oil blow-by at the piston rings.

If any one plug is found unsatisfactory, replace all 4.

IGNITION TIMING

The models covered in this manual are equipped with a capacitor discharge ignition (CDI) system. This system uses no breaker points and is non-adjustable. The timing should be checked to make sure all ignition components are operating correctly. Incorrect ignition timing can cause a drastic loss of engine performance and efficiency. It may also cause overheating.

Before starting on this procedure, check all electrical connections related to the ignition system. Make sure all connections are tight and free of corrosion and that all ground connections are tight. Refer to *Ignition System* in Chapter Eight.

1. Start the engine and let it reach normal operating temperature. Shut the engine off.
2. Remove the timing hole cap (**Figure 103**) from the pickup coil cover.
3. Connect a portable tachometer following the manufacturer's instructions. Set the tachometer on the 0-2,000 rpm range. The bike's tachometer is not accurate enough in the low rpm range for this adjustment.
4. Connect a timing light to the No. 1 spark plug following the manufacturer's instructions.
5. Start the engine and let it idle at the idle speed listed in **Table 14**.
6. Aim the timing light at the timing hole in the left-hand crankcase and pull the trigger. If the "F" mark aligns with the index mark on the crankcase (**Figure 104**), the timing is correct.

7. Turn the engine off and connect the timing light to the No. 2 spark plug and repeat Step 6.

NOTE
This system uses two ignition coils. One coil fires cylinders No. 1 and No. 4 and the other coil fires cylinders No. 2 and No. 3. This is why timing must be checked at cylinders No. 1 and No. 2.

8. If the timing is incorrect, refer to *Ignition System Troubleshooting* in Chapter Two. There is no method of adjusting ignition timing with stock components.

9. Shut off the engine and disconnect the timing light and portable tachometer. Install the timing hole cap with its O-ring.

CARBURETOR

Idle Speed

Proper idle speed setting is necessary to prevent stalling and to provide adequate engine compression braking, but you can't set it perfectly with the bike's tachometer—it's not accurate at the low rpm range. A portable tachometer is required for this procedure.

1. Place the bike on its center stand.
2. Attach a portable tachometer, following the manufacturer's instructions. Set the tachometer on the 0-2,000 rpm range.
3. Start the engine and warm it to normal operating temperature.
4. Sit on the seat while the engine is idling and adjust your weight to raise the front wheel off the ground. Turn the front wheel from side to side without touching the throttle grip. If the engine speed increases when the wheel is turned, the throttle cable(s) may be damaged, incorrectly routed or misadjusted. Perform the *Throttle Cable Adjustment* as described in this chapter.
5. Turn the throttle stop screw to set the idle speed as specified in **Table 14**. See **Figure 105** (ZX900) or **Figure 106** (ZX1000).
6. Rev the engine a couple of times to see if it returns to the idle speed. Readjust, if necessary.

Carburetor Synchronization

Synchronizing the carburetors makes sure that one cylinder doesn't try to run faster than the other, cutting power and gas mileage. The only accurate way to synchronize the carburetors is to use a set of vacuum gauges that measure the intake vacuum of all four cylinders at the same time.

1. Start the engine and warm it up fully.
2. Adjust the idle speed, as described in this chapter, then turn off the engine.

3. Remove the fuel tank as described in Chapter Seven. Plug the vacuum line to the fuel valve.

WARNING
*The engine and exhaust pipes are **hot**. Do not spill gasoline when disconnecting the fuel hose and removing the fuel tank.*

4. Install an auxiliary fuel tank onto the motorcycle and attach its fuel hose to the carburetor.

NOTE
Carburetor synchronization cannot be performed with the stock fuel tank in place because of the lack of room required to install the gauges and make adjustments. An auxiliary fuel tank is required to supply fuel to the carburetors during this procedure.

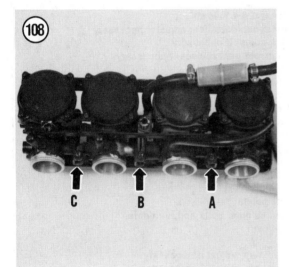

NOTE
Fuel tanks from small displacement motorcycles and ATV's make excellent auxiliary fuel tanks. Make sure the tank is mounted securely and positioned so that connecting fuel hose is not kinked or obstructed.

WARNING
When supplying fuel by temporary means, make sure the fuel tank is secure and that all fuel lines are tight—no leaks.

5. Remove the vacuum port plugs. Install the port adapters, one for each cylinder, and connect to the vacuum gauges. **Figure 107** shows the vacuum ports with the carburetors removed for clarity.
6. Start the engine and check that the difference between the cylinders is less than 2 cmHg. Identical readings are desirable.
7. If the difference is greater, perform the following:
   a. The carburetor adjusting screws are identified in **Figure 108**.
   b. With the engine at idle, synchronize No. 1 to No. 2 carburetor by turning the left-hand adjusting screw (A, **Figure 108**).
   c. Then synchronize No. 3 to No. 4 carburetor by turning the right-hand adjusting screw (C, **Figure 108**).
   d. Finally synchronize the sets to each other; No. 1 and No. 2 carburetors to No. 3 and No. 4 carburetors by turning the middle adjusting screw (B, **Figure 108**).
8. Reset the idle speed and stop the engine. Remove all of the hardware for the synchronization gauges and install the vacuum plugs.
9. Install the fuel tank.

Tables are on the following pages.

Table 1 MAINTENANCE SCHEDULE

Weekly/gas stop
- Check tire pressure cold; adjust to suit load and speed
- Check brakes for a solid feel
- Check brake pedal play; adjust if necessary
- Check throttle grip for smooth opening and return
- Check for smooth but not loose steering
- Check axles, suspension, controls and linkage nuts, bolts and fasteners; tighten if necessary
- Check engine oil level; add oil if necessary
- Check lights and horn operation, especially brake light
- Check for any abnormal engine noise and leaks
- Check coolant level
- Check kill switch operation
- Lubricate drive chain

Monthly/500 miles (800 km)
- Check battery electrolyte level (more frequently in hot weather); add distilled water if necessary
- Check disc brake fluid level; add if necessary
- Check drive chain tension; adjust if necessary

6 months/3,000 miles (5,000 km)
- All above checks and the following
- Check carburetor synchronization; adjust if necessary
- Check idle speed; adjust if necessary
- Check spark plugs, set gap; replace if necessary
- Check air suction valve
- Check evaporative emission control system*
- Check brake pad wear
- Check brake light switch operation; adjust if necessary
- Check rear brake pedal free play; adjust if necessary
- Adjust clutch
- Check steering play; adjust if necessary
- Check drive chain wear
- Change engine oil and filter
- Check tire wear
- Lubricate all pivot points
- Check and tighten all nuts, bolts and fasteners
- Clean air filter element

Yearly/6,000 miles (10,000 km)
- Check throttle free play; adjust if necessary
- Check valve clearance; adjust if necessary
- Lubricate swing arm pivot shaft
- Lubricate Uni-Trak linkage
- Check radiator hoses
- Check fuel system hoses, clamps and all fittings

2 years/12,000 miles (20,000 km)
- Change front fork oil
- Change brake fluid (brakes and clutch)
- Change coolant
- Lubricate steering stem bearings
- Replace master cylinder cups and seals
- Replace caliper piston seal and dust seal
- Replace anti-dive brake plunger parts
- Lubricate wheel bearings
- Lubricate speedometer gear

Every 4 years
- Replace fuel hoses

* California models.

Table 2 MAINTENANCE TORQUE SPECIFICATIONS

Item	N•m	ft.-lb.
Oil drain plugs	20	14.5
Oil filter bolt	20	14.5
Spark plug	14	10
Valve tappet lock nut	25	18
Upper fork tube pinch bolts	21	15
Fork cap		
ZX900		
1984	23	16.5
1985-1986	25	18
ZX1000	23	16.5
Rear axle nut	88	65
Chain adjuster pinch bolts		
ZX900	32	24
ZX1000	39	29
Steering stem nut	39	29
Torque link nuts (ZX1000)	29	22
Handlebar bolts	19	13.5

Table 3 TIRES AND TIRE PRESSURE (ZX900)*

Model/tire size	Pressure	Tire wear limit
Front-110/90 V 16	32 psi (2.25 kg/cm²)	1 mm (1/32 in.)
Rear-130/90 V 16	36 psi (2.50 kg/cm²)	3 mm (1/8 in.)

* Check tire pressure when cold.

Table 4 TIRES AND TIRE PRESSURE (ZX1000)*

Model/tire size	Pressure	Tire wear limit
U.S and Canadian		
Front-128/80 V 16	36 psi (2.50 kg/cm²)	1 mm (1/32 in.)
Rear-150/80 V 16	41 psi (2.90 kg/cm²)	2 mm (3/32 in.)
Other than U.S and Canadian models		
Front-128/80 V 16	36 psi (2.50 kg/cm²)	1 mm (1/32 in.)
Rear-150/80 V 16	36 psi (2.50 kg/cm²)**	2 mm (3/32 in.)

* Check tire pressure when cold.
** Kawasaki recommends to set rear tire pressure @ 41 psi (2.90 kg/cm²) when vehicle speeds exceed 130 mph (210 km/h). When using your vehicle for racing purposes, consult tire manufacturers for additional tire information.

Table 5 BATTERY STATE OF CHARGE

Specific gravity	State of charge
1.110-1.130	Discharged
1.140-1.160	Almost discharged
1.170-1.190	One-quarter charged
1.200-1.220	One-half charged
1.230-1.250	Three-quarters charged
1.260-1.280	Fully charged

3

Table 6 RECOMMENDED LUBRICANTS AND FUEL

Engine oil	SAE 10W40, 10W50, 20W40, 20W50 rated SE, SF or SG
Front fork oil	SAE 10W20
Brake fluid	DOT 4
Clutch hydraulic fluid	DOT 4
Fuel	87 pump octale (RON + MON)/2
	91 Research octane (RON)
Battery	Distilled water
Cooling system	Permanent type antifreeze compounded
	for aluminum engines and radiators

Table 7 ENGINE OIL CAPACITY

	Liter	U.S. qt.
Without filter change		
ZX900	2.6	2.7
ZX1000, ZX1100	3.5	3.7
With filter change		
ZX900	3.0	3.2
ZX1000, ZX1100	4.0	4.2

FRONT FORK OIL CAPACITY AND OIL LEVEL

Model	Change cc (oz.)	Rebuild cc (oz.)	Oil level mm (in.)
ZX900	273	317-325	332-336
	(9.23)	(10.72-11.00)	13.071-13.228)
ZX1000	295	344-352	377-381
	(9.97)	(11.63-11.90)	(14.84-15.00)

COOLING SYSTEM SPECIFICATIONS

Capacity	
ZX900	2.0 L (2.1 U.S. qt.)
ZX1000	3.1 L (3.3 U.S. qt.)
Coolant ratio	50% soft water:50% coolant
Radiator cap	0.95-1.25 kg/cm^2 (14-18 psi)
Thermostat	
Opening temperature	80-84° C (176-183° F)
Valve operating lift	Not less than 8 mm (5/16 in.) @ 95° C (203° F)

FRONT FORK AIR PRESSURE (1984-1987)*

	kg/cm^2	psi
Standard		
ZX900	0.6	8.5
ZX1000	0.5	7.1
Usable range		
ZX900	0.5-0.7	7.1-10.0
ZX1000	0.4-0.6	5.7-85
Maximum	2.50	36

*The 1988-on models are not equipped with air pressurized front forks.

Table 11 REAR SHOCK ABSORBER AIR PRESSURE (ZX900)

Road/load conditions	kg/cm²	psi
Good/light	0	0
Bad/heavy	3.5	35

Table 12 REAR SHOCK ABSORBER AIR PRESSURE (ZX1000)

	kc/cm²	psi
Recommended	0.5	7.1
Maximum	1.5	21

Table 13 DAMPING ADJUSTMENT

Adjuster position	Load	Road	Speed
1	Light	Good	Slow
2			
3			
4	Heavy	Rough	High

Table 14 TUNE-UP SPECIFICATIONS

Spark plug gap	0.6-0.7 mm (0.024-0.028 in.)
Valve clearance (cold)	
Intake	0.13-0.18 mm (0.005-0.007 in.)
Exhaust	0.18-0.23 mm (0.007-0.009 in.)
Idle speed	
ZX900	1,000 $\pm$50 rpm
ZX1000	
U.S. 49-state	1,000 $\pm$50 rpm
California	1,200 $\pm$50 rpm
Canada and Europe	1,000 $\pm$50 rpm
Compression*	
ZX900	9.9 $\pm$2.1 kg/cm² (140 $\pm$31 psi)
ZX1000	10.7 $\pm$2.3 kg/cm² (152 $\pm$33 psi)

*Compression readings listed are for stock engines. If your engine is equipped with non-stock camshafts or pistons, these compression figures cannot be used as reference; ask the camshaft or piston manufacturer for new compression numbers.

Table 15 SPARK PLUGS

	Standard riding	High speed riding	Low speed riding
U.S.	NGK D9EA	NGK D9EA	NGKD8EA
	ND X27ES-U	ND X27ES-U	ND X24EX-U
Canada	NGK DR8ES	NGK DR8ES	NGKDR8ES-L
	ND X27ESR-U	ND X27ESR-U	ND X24ESR-U
Italy	NGK D9EA	NGK D9EA	NGK D8EA
	ND X27ES-U	ND X27ES-U	ND X24ES-U
All Europe	NGK DR8ES	NGK DR8ES	NGK DR8ES-L
except Italy	ND X27ES-U	ND X27ES-U	ND X24ES-U

NOTE: If you own a 1988 or later model, first check the Supplement at the back of this book for any new service information.

CHAPTER FOUR

ENGINE

The engine is a liquid-cooled, inline four. It has two chain-driven overhead cams which operate four valves per cylinder.

This chapter provides complete service and overhaul procedures, including information for disassembly, removal, inspection, service and reassembly of the engine.

Before starting any work, read the service hints in Chapter One. You will do a better job with this information fresh in your mind.

Table 1 lists general engine information. Table 2 lists engine service specifications. Tables 1-5 are at the end of the chapter.

SERVICING ENGINE IN FRAME

Many components can be serviced while the engine is mounted in the frame:
  a. Cylinder head.
  b. Cylinders and pistons.
  c. Gearshift mechanism.
  d. Clutch.
  e. Carburetors.
  f. Starter motor.
  g. Alternator and electrical systems.

ENGINE PRINCIPLES

Figure 1 explains how the engine works. This will be helpful when troubleshooting or repairing your engine.

ENGINE

Removal/Installation

1. Place the motorcycle on its center stand.
2. Remove the fairing assembly. See Chapter Thirteen.
3. Remove the fuel tank (Chapter Seven) and seat.
4. Disconnect the negative battery terminal (Figure 2).
5. Drain the engine oil as described under *Engine Oil and Filter Change* in Chapter Three.
6. Drain the cooling system as described *Coolant Change* in Chapter Three.
7. Disconnect the spark plug wires.
8. *ZX900:* Disconnect the ignition coil electrical connectors and remove the coils (Figure 3).
9. *U.S. models:* Remove the air suction valve as described under *Suction Valve Removal/Installation* in Chapter Seven.
10. Remove the oil cooler as described in this chapter.

4-STROKE OPERATING PRINCIPLES

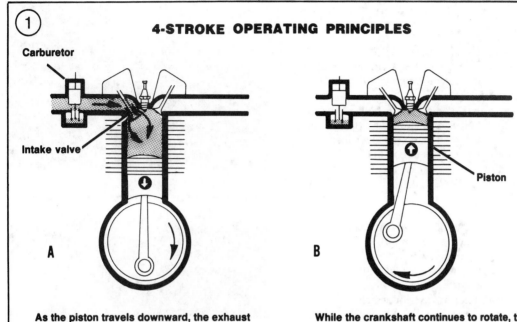

Carburetor

Intake valve

Piston

A

B

As the piston travels downward, the exhaust valve is closed and the intake valve opens, allowing the new air-fuel mixture from the carburetor to be drawn into the cylinder. When the piston reaches the bottom of its travel (BDC), the intake valve closes and remains closed for the next 1 1/2 revolutions of the crankshaft.

While the crankshaft continues to rotate, the piston moves upward, compressing the air-fuel mixture.

Spark plug

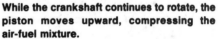

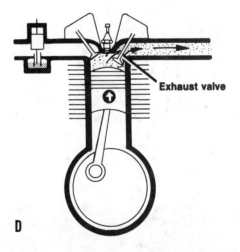

Exhaust valve

C

D

As the piston almost reaches the top of its travel, the spark plug fires, igniting the compressed air-fuel mixture. The piston continues to top dead center (TDC) and is pushed downward by the expanding gases.

When the piston almost reaches BDC, the exhaust valve opens and remains open until the piston is near TDC. The upward travel of the piston forces the exhaust gases out of the cylinder. After the piston has reached TDC, the exhaust valve closes and the cycle starts all over again.

11. Remove the following as described in Chapter Nine:

   a. Radiator.

   b. Thermostat housing.

12. Remove the exhaust system as described under *Exhaust System Removal/Installation* in Chapter Seven.

13. Remove the 2 coolant drain bolts at the front of the cylinder block and drain the cylinder block.

14. Remove the carburetors as described under *Carburetor Removal/Installation* in Chapter Seven.

15. Disconnect the crankcase breather hose.

16. Remove the engine sprocket as described under *Engine Sprocket Removal/Installation* in Chapter Six.

17. Disconnect the following wiring connectors:

   a. Neutral switch (A, **Figure 4**).

   b. Starter motor connector.

   c. Oil pressure switch (B, **Figure 4**).

   d. Oil temperature switch.

   e. *ZX1000:* Rear brake light switch.

18. *Engine disassembly:* If the engine requires disassembly, it will be easier to remove many of the large sub-assemblies while the engine is mounted in the frame. It will also make it easier to lift the engine out of the frame. Remove the following as described in this chapter unless otherwise noted:

   a. Cylinder head.

   b. Cylinders.

   c. Pistons.

   d. Alternator and pickup coil (Chapter Eight).

   e. Starter (Chapter Eight).

   f. Clutch (Chapter Five).

   g. External shift mechanism (Chapter Six).

19. Place a hydraulic jack with wooden blocks under the crankcase to support the engine before the mounting bolts are removed. See **Figure 5**.

20A. *ZX900:* Perform the following.

   a. Remove the upper engine mounting bolts (**Figure 6**).

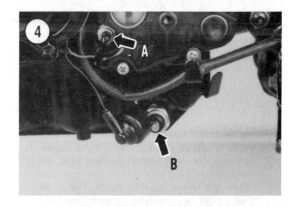

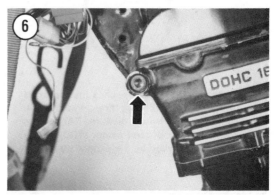

NOTE
*Some models have a shim installed at the point shown in **Figure 7**. If necessary, remove the shim and note its location.*

b. Remove the lower engine mounting bolts and nuts (**Figure 8**). Remove the bracket (**Figure 9**) from the right-hand side.

WARNING
One or more assistants will be required to remove the engine from the frame. Do not attempt engine removal by yourself.

c. Lower the engine and remove it from the frame.

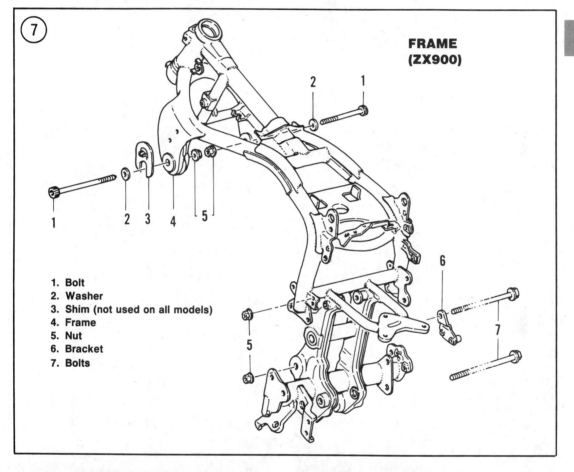

FRAME (ZX900)

4

1. Bolt
2. Washer
3. Shim (not used on all models)
4. Frame
5. Nut
6. Bracket
7. Bolts

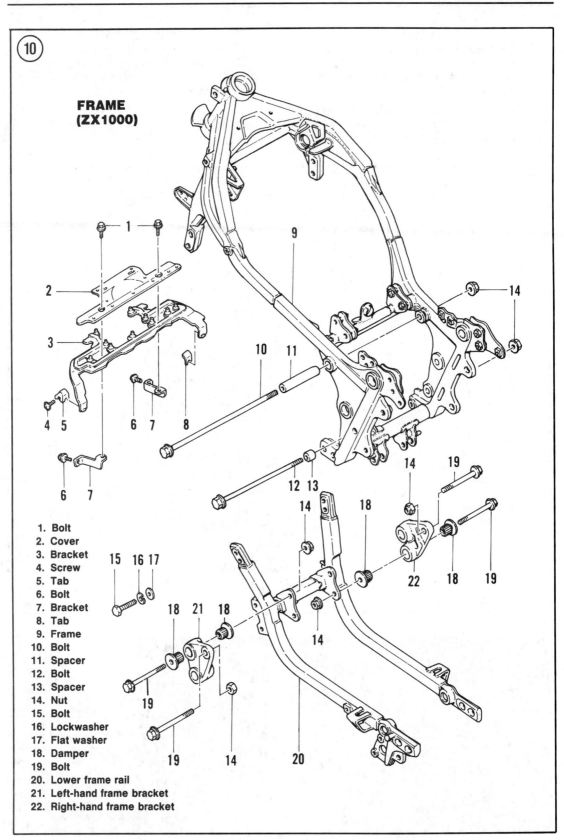

⑩

FRAME
(ZX1000)

1. Bolt
2. Cover
3. Bracket
4. Screw
5. Tab
6. Bolt
7. Bracket
8. Tab
9. Frame
10. Bolt
11. Spacer
12. Bolt
13. Spacer
14. Nut
15. Bolt
16. Lockwasher
17. Flat washer
18. Damper
19. Bolt
20. Lower frame rail
21. Left-hand frame bracket
22. Right-hand frame bracket

20B. *ZX1000:* Referring to **Figure 10**, perform the following:

  a. Remove the front engine mounting bolts.

  b. Remove the down tube mounting bolts and remove the down tubes.

  c. Remove the rear engine mounting bolts and spacers.

> *WARNING*
> *One or more assistants will be required to remove the engine from the frame. Do not attempt engine removal by yourself.*

  d. Lower the engine and remove it from the frame.

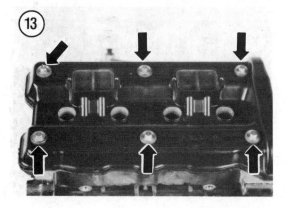

21. While the engine is removed for service, check all of the frame engine mounts for cracks or other damage. If any cracks are detected, take the chassis assembly to a Kawasaki dealer for further examination.

22. Install by reversing the removal steps. Note the following.

23A. *ZX900:* Tighten the engine mount nuts and bolts to 59 N•m (43 ft.-lb.).

23B. *ZX1000:* Tighten the front engine bracket bolts (**Figure 11**) to 44 N•m (33 ft.-lb.). Tighten the remaining engine mount bolts to 52 N•m (38 ft.-lb.).

24. Fill the crankcase with the recommended type and quantity of engine oil. Refer to *Engine Oil and Filter Change* in Chapter Three.

25. Refill the cooling system. See *Coolant Change* in Chapter Three.

26. Adjust the following as described in Chapter Three:

  a. Drive chain.

  b. Rear brake.

  c. Throttle cable(s).

  d. Choke cable.

27. Start the engine and check for leaks.

28. Install the fairing assembly. See Chapter Thirteen.

CYLINDER HEAD COVER

Removal/Installation
(ZX900)

1. Park the bike on the center stand.

2. Remove the upper and lower fairings. See Chapter Thirteen.

3. Remove the fuel tank. See Chapter Seven.

4. Remove the ignition coils (**Figure 3**) and brackets.

5. Remove the air suction valves. See *Suction Valve Removal/Installation* in Chapter Seven.

> *CAUTION*
> *Four dowel pins are used to align the cylinder head cover on the cylinder head. When removing the cylinder head cover, one or more dowel pins may drop into the engine. If a dowel pin does fall, do not turn the engine over until the dowel pin is located and removed.*

6. Remove the cylinder head cover bolts and remove the cover (**Figure 12**).

> *NOTE*
> *Figure 13 shows the cylinder head cover mounting bolts with the engine removed for clarity. It is not necessary to remove the engine for this procedure.*

7. Installation is the reverse of these steps, noting the following.

8. Replace the cylinder head cover gasket (**Figure 14**), if necessary. Note the following:

   a. Remove all residue from the head cover and cylinder head mating surfaces.

   b. Apply a non-hardening gasket sealer (such as RTV) to the 4 cutouts on the cylinder head (**Figure 15**).

   c. Apply a coat of liquid gasket to the cylinder head cover and install the new gasket onto the cover.

   d. Apply a small amount of liquid gasket onto the 4 dowel pins and install them into the cylinder head cover.

9. Install the cylinder head cover and tighten the bolts to the specifications in **Table 3**.

Removal/Installation (ZX1000)

1. Park the bike on the center stand.

2. Remove the upper and lower fairings. See Chapter Thirteen.

3. Remove the fuel tank. See Chapter Seven.

4. Remove the air suction valves. See *Suction Valve Removal/Installation* in Chapter Seven.

5. Remove the carburetors as described under *Carburetor Removal/Installation* in Chapter Seven.

6. Drain the engine coolant as described under *Coolant Change* in Chapter Three.

7. Remove the rear water pipe from the cylinder head.

> *CAUTION*
> *Four dowel pins are used to align the cylinder head cover on the cylinder head. When removing the cylinder head cover, one or more dowel pins may drop into the engine. If a dowel pin does fall, do not turn the engine over until the dowel pin is located and removed.*

8. Remove the cylinder head cover bolts and remove the cover.

> *NOTE*
> *Figure 13 shows the cylinder head cover mounting bolts with the engine removed for clarity. It is not necessary to remove the engine for this procedure.*

9. Installation is the reverse of these steps, noting the following.

10. Replace the cylinder head cover gasket (**Figure 14**), if necessary. Note the following:

   a. Remove all residue from the head cover and cylinder head mating surfaces.

   b. Apply a non-hardening gasket sealer (such as RTV) to the 4 cutouts in the cylinder head (**Figure 15**).

   c. Apply a coat of liquid gasket sealer to the cylinder head cover and install the new gasket onto the cover.

   d. Apply a light coat of gasket sealer to the 4 dowel pins and install them into the cylinder head cover.

12. Replace damaged water pipe O-rings, as required.

13. Install the cylinder head cover and tighten the bolts to the specifications in **Table 3**.

14. Refill the engine coolant as described under *Coolant Change* in Chapter Three.

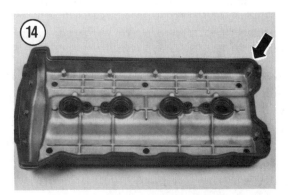

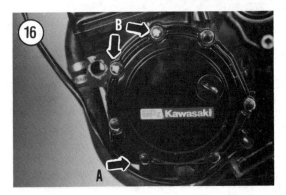

CAMSHAFTS

There are two camshafts mounted in the top of the cylinder head. EX (exhaust) and IN (intake) are cast into each camshaft for easy identification. Each camshaft has a sprocket installed on its

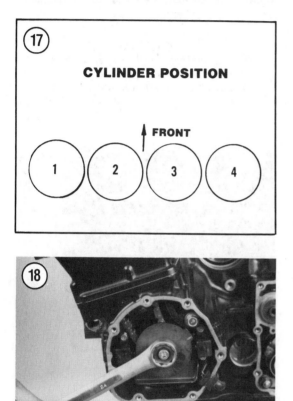

left-hand side. The drive sprocket is mounted on the left-hand side of the crankshaft behind the pulser coils. A chain placed over the sprockets drives the camshafts.

The camshaft sprockets are marked so that valve timing can be checked and reset when the camshafts are removed. Valve timing in degrees is listed in **Table 1**.

Because cam lobe wear, runout and journal wear will change valve timing, camshaft wear should be checked whenever the camshafts are removed or when valve timing troubles are experienced.

Removal

NOTE
The camshafts can be removed with the engine mounted in the frame. The following photographs show camshaft removal with the engine removed for clarity.

1. Remove the cylinder head cover as described in this chapter.
2. Disconnect the battery negative cable (**Figure 2**).
3. Remove the spark plugs. This will make it easier to turn the engine by hand.
4. Remove the pickup coil cover (A, **Figure 16**).

NOTE
Figure 17 identifies cylinder numbering.

5. Use a wrench on the crankshaft nut (**Figure 18**) and rotate the engine counterclockwise until the "T" rotor mark for the No. 1 and No. 4 cylinders aligns with the fixed pointer on the crankcase (**Figure 19**). No. 1 and 4 cylinders are now at top dead center (TDC).

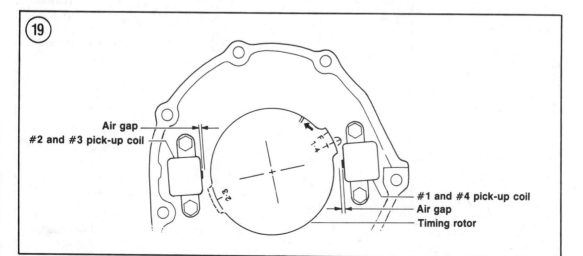

6. Remove the camshaft chain tensioner as described in this chapter.

7. Remove the cam chain guide (**Figure 20**).

8. Loosen the valve adjuster locknuts and loosen the adjusters (**Figure 21**).

NOTE
*Each camshaft cap is marked with an arrow (pointing forward) and with a letter representing position. See **Figure 22**. If the camshaft cap markings on your bike differ from those in **Figure 22** or if there are no marks, label them for direction and position before performing Step 9.*

9. Remove the camshaft cap bolts and remove the caps (**Figure 23**) and dowel pins (**Figure 24**).

10. Secure the camshaft chain with wire to keep it from falling into the engine. Then, remove both camshafts with their sprockets (**Figure 25**). Remove the camshafts slowly to prevent damaging any cam lobe or bearing surface.

CAUTION
The crankshaft can be turned with the camshafts removed. However, pull the camshaft chain tight to prevent it from jamming against the crankshaft sprocket.

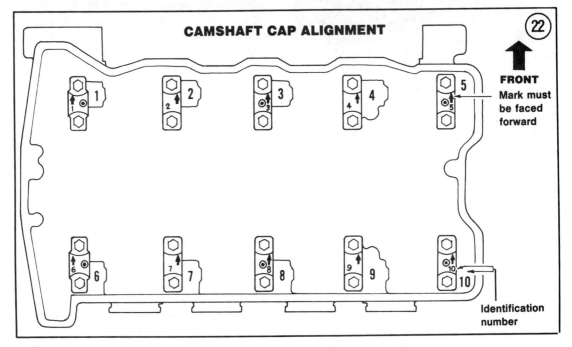

CAMSHAFT CAP ALIGNMENT

FRONT
Mark must be faced forward

Identification number

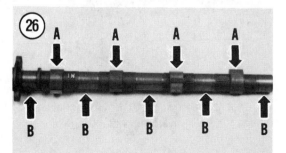

Inspection

1. Check cam lobes (A, **Figure 26**) for wear. The lobes should not be scored and the edges should be square.

2. Even though the cam lobe surface appears to be satisfactory, with no visible signs of wear, they must be measured with a micrometer as shown in **Figure 27**. Replace the shaft(s) if worn beyond the service limits (measurements less than those given in **Table 2**).

3. Check the camshaft bearing journals (B, **Figure 26**) for wear and scoring.

4. Even though the camshaft bearing journal surface appears satisfactory, with no visible signs of wear, the camshaft bearing journals must be measured with a micrometer (**Figure 28**). Replace the shaft(s) if worn beyond the service limits (measurements less than those given in **Table 2**).

5. Place the camshaft on a set of V-blocks and check its runout with a dial indicator. Replace the camshaft if runout exceeds specifications in **Table 2**. Repeat for the opposite camshaft.

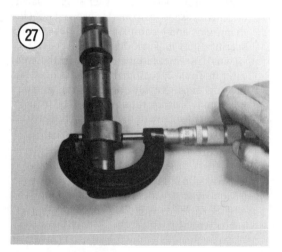

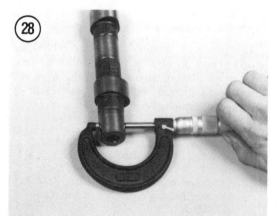

6. Inspect the camshaft sprockets (**Figure 29**) for wear. Replace if necessary.

> *NOTE*
> *If the camshaft sprockets are worn, also check the camshaft chain, chain guides and chain tensioner as described in this chapter.*

7. Check the camshaft bearing journals in the cylinder head (**Figure 30**) and camshaft caps (**Figure 31**) for wear and scoring. They should not be scored or excessively worn. If the camshaft caps appear okay, check them as follows:

a. Check that the camshaft cap dowel pins are in place and loosely install the camshaft caps in their original positions. The arrow on each cap must face to the front of the bike and the location numbering on the cap must correspond to the numbering cast into the cylinder head. Do not install the camshafts.

b. Install the camshaft cap bolts and tighten to the torque specification in **Table 3**.

c. Measure the vertical inside diameter of each bearing with a bore gauge or telescoping gauge.

d. Record each camshaft bearing inside diameter and compare to the service specifications in **Table 2**.

e. If any one measurement exceeds the wear limit in **Table 2**, replace the cylinder head and bearing caps. Replacement of the cylinder head and bearing caps as a set is required because the camshaft caps and cylinder head are align-bored (machined as a set).

> *NOTE*
> *If you don't have access to a bore or telescoping gauge, you can achieve the same results by using Plastigage as detailed in the following procedure.*

**Camshaft Bearing
Clearance Measurement**

This procedure requires the use of a Plastigage set. The camshaft must be installed into the head. Prior to installation, wipe all oil residue from each cam bearing journal and bearing surface in the head and all camshaft caps.

> *NOTE*
> *Plastigage can be purchased from most auto supply stores and is available in several sizes. Make sure you purchase Plastigage small enough to measure the camshaft bearing clearance as specified in **Table 2**.*

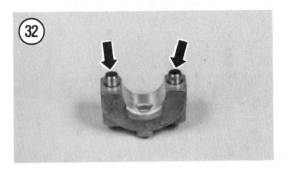

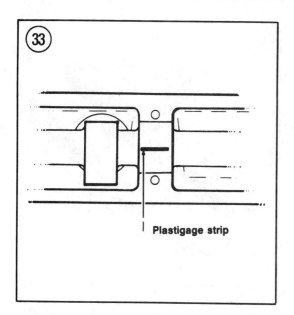

Plastigage strip

1. Install the camshafts into the cylinder head.
2. Install all locating dowels into their camshaft caps (**Figure 32**).
3. Wipe all oil from the cam bearing journals prior to using the Plastigage material.
4. Place a strip of Plastigage material on top of each cam bearing journal (**Figure 33**), parallel to the cam.
5. Place the camshaft cap into position.
6. Install all camshaft cap bolts. Install finger-tight at first, then tighten in a crisscross pattern (**Figure 34**) to the final torque specification listed in **Table 3**.

CAUTION
Do not rotate the camshaft with the Plastigage material in place.

7. Gradually remove the camshaft cap bolts in a crisscross pattern. Remove the camshaft caps carefully.

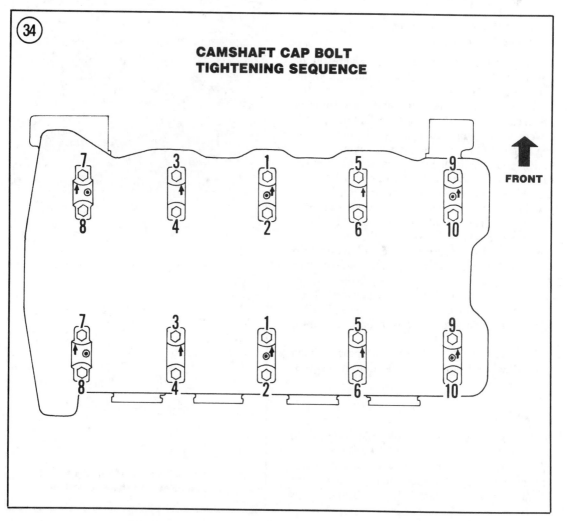

CAMSHAFT CAP BOLT TIGHTENING SEQUENCE

FRONT

8. Measure the width of the flattened Plastigage according to manufacturer's instructions (**Figure 35**).

9. If the clearance exceeds the wear limits in **Table 2**, measure the camshaft bearing journals (**Figure 28**) with a micrometer and compare to the limits in **Table 2**. If the camshaft bearing journal is less than dimension specified, replace the cam. If the cam is within specifications, the cylinder head and camshaft caps (**Figure 36**) must be replaced as a matched set.

> *CAUTION*
> *Remove all particles of Plastigage from all camshaft bearing journals and the camshaft holder. Be sure to clean the camshaft holder groove. This material must not be left in the engine as it can plug up an oil control orifice and cause severe engine damage.*

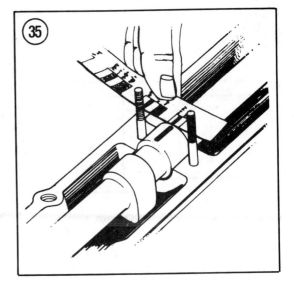

Camshaft Chain and Sprockets
Inspection/Replacement

1. Examine the camshaft sprockets (**Figure 29**) for any signs of wear, cracks or tooth damage. If the camshaft sprockets are worn, also check the camshaft chain and the crankshaft drive sprocket for wear. See *Crankshaft Inspection* in this chapter. Severe wear of one component will require the replacement of both sprockets and chain.

2. *ZX1000:* The intake and exhaust sprockets are identical. If the sprockets were removed from the camshafts, note the following before installation:
   a. Install the sprockets onto each camshaft so that the sprocket sides marked "IN" and "EX" face to the left-hand side (**Figure 37**).
   b. There are 4 holes drilled into each sprocket. Two sprocket holes are marked "IN" and the other two holes are marked "EX." Align the sprocket holes marked "IN" with the intake camshaft bolt holes. Align the sprocket holes marked "EX" with the exhaust camshaft bolt holes. See **Figure 37.**

3. Apply Loctite 242 (blue) to the sprocket bolts and tighten to the torque specifications in **Table 3**.

Installation

1. Replace the upper cam chain guide (**Figure 38**) if necessary.

2. If camshaft bearing clearance was checked, make sure all Plastigage material has been removed from the camshaft and bearing caps surfaces.

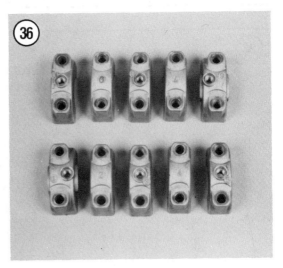

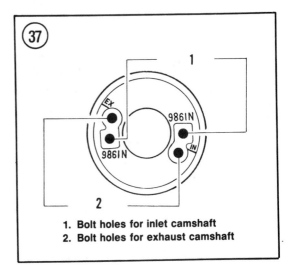

1. **Bolt holes for inlet camshaft**
2. **Bolt holes for exhaust camshaft**

CAUTION
When rotating the crankshaft in Step 3, lift the cam chain tightly on the exhaust side (front) to prevent it from binding on the crankshaft sprocket.

3. Use a wrench on the large crankshaft nut and rotate the engine clockwise until the "T" rotor mark for the No. 1 and 4 cylinders aligns with the fixed pointer on the crankcase (**Figure 39**). No. 1 and 4 cylinders are now at top dead center (TDC).

4. Coat all camshaft lobes and bearing journals with molybdenum disulfide grease or assembly oil.

5. Also coat the bearing surfaces in the cylinder head and camshaft bearing caps.

NOTE
Identification marks are cast into each camshaft. The exhaust camshaft is marked with EX and the intake camshaft with IN. See Figure 40.

6. Lift the cam chain and slide the exhaust camshaft through and set it in the front bearing blocks. Install the intake camshaft through the cam chain and set it in the rear bearing blocks. See **Figure 25**.

7. Without turning the crankshaft, align the "EX" line on the exhaust cam sprocket and the "IN" on the intake cam sprocket with the upper cylinder head surface as viewed from the left-hand side of

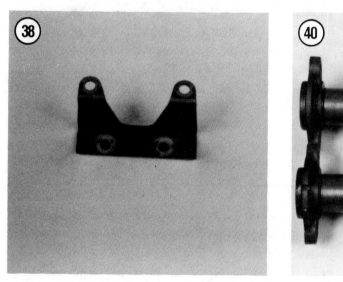

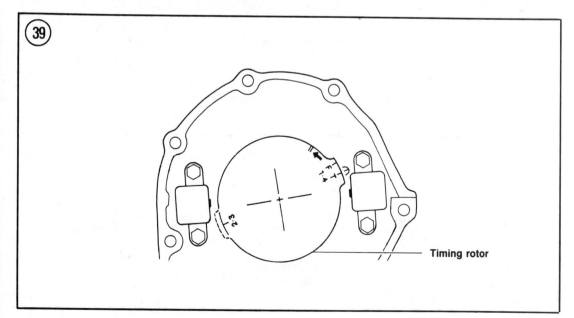

Timing rotor

the engine (**Figure 41**). It will be necessary to lift the cam chain off the sprockets to reposition the camshafts.

8. Refer to **Figure 42** (ZX900) or **Figure 43** (ZX1000). Locate the first cam chain link pin that aligns with the exhaust sprocket "EX" mark. Beginning with this mark, count off 35 cam chain link pins toward the intake sprocket. The 35th pin must align with the intake camshaft "IN" mark. If the pin count is incorrect, recount and reposition the intake or exhaust camshaft as required.

9. Check that the cam chain is properly seated in the front and rear cam chain guides.

10. Check that the camshaft cap dowel pins are in place and loosely install the camshaft caps (**Figure 23**) in their original positions. The arrow on each cap (**Figure 44**) must face to the front of the bike and the location numbering on the cap must correspond to the numbering (**Figure 44**) cast into the cylinder head.

> *CAUTION*
> *The camshaft caps were align-bored with the cylinder head at the time of manufacture. If the caps are not installed in their original position, camshaft seizure may result.*

11. Tighten the camshaft cap bolts marked No. 1 and 6 (**Figure 44**) for the exhaust and intake cams. This will seat the camshafts in position. Then tighten all bolts in a crisscross pattern (**Figure 44**) to the torque specification in **Table 3**.

12. Slowly turn the crankshaft counterclockwise 2 full turns, using the large crankshaft bolt (**Figure**

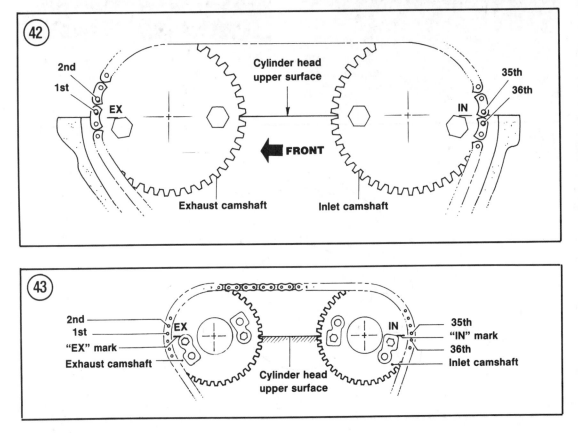

45). Check that all timing marks again align as shown in **Figure 46** when the No. 1 and 4 cylinder "T" mark on the rotor aligns with the crankcase timing mark (**Figure 46**). If all marks align as indicated, cam timing is correct.

> *CAUTION*
> *If there is any binding while turning the crankshaft, **stop**. Recheck the camshaft timing marks. Improper timing can cause valve and piston damage.*

13. If the cam timing is incorrect, remove the camshaft caps and reposition the camshafts as described in Steps 6-12.

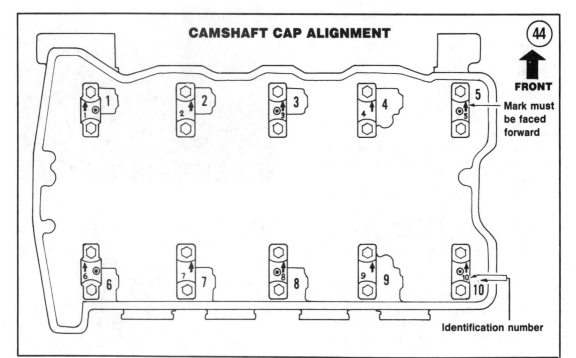

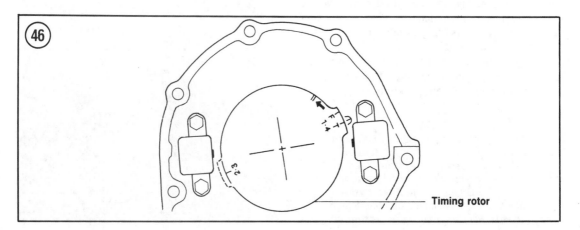

14. Install the upper cam chain guide (**Figure 47**).
15. Install the cam chain tensioner as described in this chapter.
16. Adjust the valves as described under *Valve Adjustment* in Chapter Three.
17. Install the pickup coil cover. Apply Loctite 242 (blue) onto the 2 bolts indicated in B, **Figure 16**.
18. Install the cylinder head cover as described in this chapter.

CAM CHAIN TENSIONER

The automatic tensioner is continually self-adjusting. The tensioner pushrod is free to move inward, but can't move out. Whenever the cam chain tensioner bolts are loosened, the tensioner assembly must be completely removed and reset as described in this section.

Removal/Installation

1. Loosen the cap bolt (A, **Figure 48**).
2. Remove the 2 tensioner mounting bolts and pull the tensioner housing (B, **Figure 48**) away from the engine.
3. Check the tensioner housing (**Figure 49**) for cracks or other damage. If necessary, replace the tensioner as an assembly.
4. When installing the cam chain tensioner, perform the following:

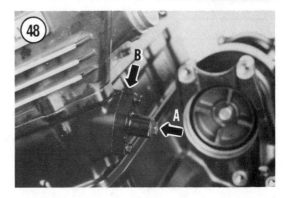

   a. Remove the cap bolt and O-ring.
   b. Insert a screwdriver into the tensioner (**Figure 50**) and compress the pushrod while turning the screwdriver.
   c. Turn the screwdriver clockwise until the pushrod extends about 10 mm from the tensioner housing as shown in **Figure 49**. Do not remove the screwdriver at this time.
   d. Install the tensioner housing into the cylinder, while holding the screwdriver. Press the tensioner against the cylinder, remove the screwdriver, then install tensioner housing mounting bolts finger-tight to hold the tensioner in place.
   f. Tighten the tensioner housing mounting bolts to the torque specification in **Table 3**.
   g. Install the O-ring and cap bolt.

> *NOTE*
> *When purchasing a new cam chain tensioner from Kawasaki, the tensioner will be equipped with a pushrod holder plate. When installing a new tensioner, it is not necessary to hold the pushrod with a screwdriver as long as the holder plate is not removed. After installing*

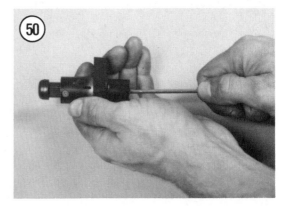

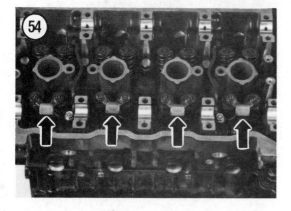

the tensioner mounting bolts, remove the holder plate and install the O-ring and cap bolt.

CAUTION
When working with a replacement cam chain tensioner, do not pull on the pushrod as this would cause the pushrod to disconnect from the assembly. Once it is disconnected, the tensioner is ruined and can't be repaired.

ROCKER ARM ASSEMBLIES

There are 2 rocker arm shafts installed in the cylinder head. Each shaft has 4 rocker arms and springs. The rocker arms are made of a special steel alloy for durability. The rocker arm surface that contacts the cam and the end of the valve adjusters which contact the valve stems have been heat-treated for surface hardness.

The intake and exhaust rocker arms are identical (same Kawasaki part No.) but they will develop different wear patterns during use. All parts should be marked during removal so that they can be assembled in their original positions.

Excessive rocker arm-to-shaft clearance results in excessive engine noise. Whenever the rocker arms and shafts are removed, the clearance should be checked.

The rocker arms and shafts can be removed with the engine installed in the frame.

Removal

1. Remove the camshafts as described in this chapter.
2. Remove the 4 banjo bolts and remove the 2 oil pipes (**Figure 51**).
3. Remove the rocker arm shafts as follows:
   a. Remove the rocker arm shaft plugs with an Allen wrench (**Figure 52**).
   b. Thread a M8×1.25 bolt (approximately 30 mm long) into the end of the intake rocker arm shaft and pull the rocker arm shaft out of the cylinder head (**Figure 53**).
4. Lift the rocker arms and springs (**Figure 54**) out of the cylinder head. See **Figure 55**. Keep the rocker arms in order so that they may be reinstalled in their original positions.
5. Repeat Steps 3 and 4 for the exhaust rocker arm shaft, remaining rocker arms and springs.

Inspection

1. Wash all parts (**Figure 56**) in cleaning solvent and thoroughly dry.

2. Check each rocker arm spring for fatigue, cracks or other damage. Replace if necessary.

3. Inspect the rocker arm pad (A, **Figure 57**) where it rides on the cam lobe and where the adjusters (**Figure 58**) ride on the valve stems. If the pad is scratched or unevenly worn, inspect the cam lobe for scoring, chipping or flat spots. Replace the rocker arm if defective.

NOTE
If the rocker arm pad (A, Figure 57) is worn, also check the mating cam lobe for wear or damage.

4. Measure the inside diameter of the rocker arm bore (B, **Figure 57**) and check against dimension in **Table 2**. Replace if worn to the service limit or greater.

NOTE
The rocker arm bore I.D. can be measured with a small hole gauge. Figure 59 shows a micrometer measuring the gauge diameter after it has been fit into the bore.

5. Inspect the rocker arm shaft (**Figure 60**) for wear or scoring. Measure the outside diameter (**Figure 61**) with a micrometer and check against dimension in **Table 2**. Replace if worn to the service limit or greater.

Oil Pipes
Cleaning/Inspection

1. Examine the oil pipes (**Figure 62**) for damage. Check the brazed joints (**Figure 63**) for cracking or other abnormal conditions.

2. Flush the oil pipes and banjo bolts with solvent and allow to dry before installation.

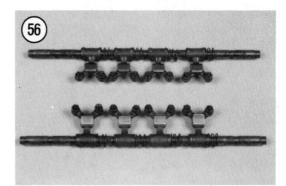

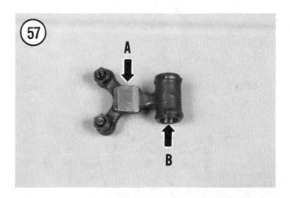

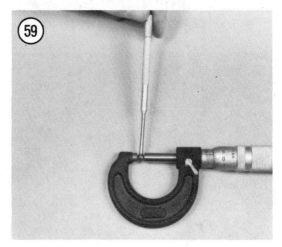

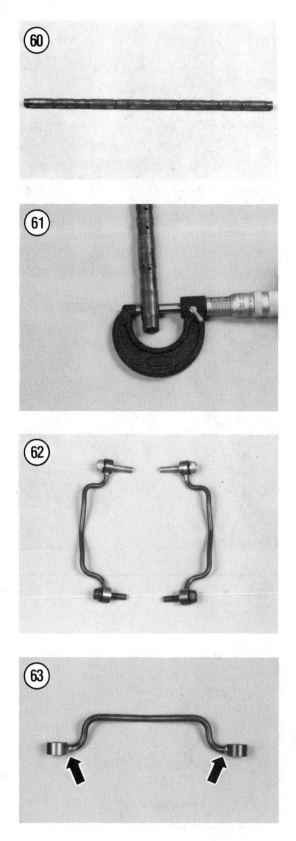

Installation

1. Coat the rocker arm shaft and rocker arm bore with assembly oil.

2. Assemble the spring (**Figure 55**) onto the right-hand side of each rocker arm as the rocker arm faces to the center of the engine. See **Figure 56** for installation reference only. Do not assemble the rocker arms and springs onto the rocker arm shafts.

3. Place the rocker arms and springs into the cylinder head (**Figure 64**). Remember to install the rocker arms in their original positions. The valve adjusters will rest on the valves when the rocker arms are installed correctly.

> *CAUTION*
> *If the rocker arm shafts are installed backwards in Step 4, they will be difficult to remove.*

4. Thread the bolt onto the rocker arm shaft as used during rocker arm shaft removal. Then insert the rocker arm shaft through the cylinder head, rocker arms and springs. See **Figure 53**.

5. Remove the bolt from rocker arm shaft.

6. Install the rocker arm shaft plugs (**Figure 52**) and tighten securely. Make sure an O-ring is installed on each plug.

7. Install the 2 oil pipes (**Figure 51**). Install the 4 oil pipe banjo bolts. The banjo bolt heads are color coded. The bolts facing the exhaust side are white. The bolts installed on the intake side are black. Observe the head color designations when tightening the banjo bolts (see **Table 3**).

8. Install the camshafts as described in this chapter.

CYLINDER HEAD

The cylinder head can be removed with the engine installed in the frame. The following photographs show the engine removed for clarity.

Removal

1. If the engine is installed in the frame, remove the following components:
   a. Remove the oil cooler as described in this chapter.
   b. Drain the cooling system as described under *Coolant Change* in Chapter Three.
   c. Remove the radiator as described under *Radiator Removal/Installation* in Chapter Nine.
   d. Remove the exhaust system as described under *Exhaust System Removal/Installation* in Chapter Seven.
   e. Remove the carburetors as described under *Carburetor Removal/Installation* in Chapter Seven.
2. Remove the cylinder head cover as described under *Cylinder Head Cover Removal/Installation* in this chapter.
3. Remove the camshafts as described in this chapter.
4. Remove the rocker arms as described in this chapter.
5. Remove the main oil pipe assembly at the front of the cylinder head (**Figure 65**).
6. Remove the pickup coil cover (A, **Figure 66**).
7. *ZX900:* Remove the frame-to-cylinder head mounting bolts (**Figure 67**).
8. *ZX1000:* Remove the baffle plate at the cylinder head.
9. Remove the cylinder head 6 mm bolt (**Figure 68**).
10. Remove the 2 cylinder-to-cylinder head 6 mm bolts (**Figure 69**).

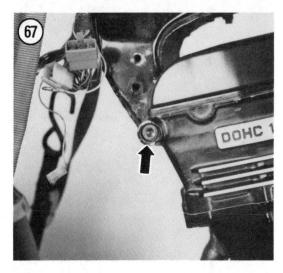

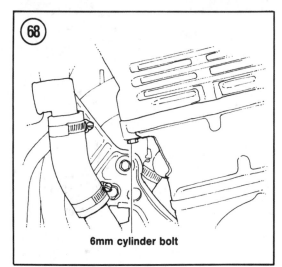

6mm cylinder bolt

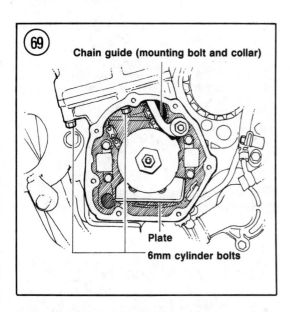

Chain guide (mounting bolt and collar)

Plate

6mm cylinder bolts

11. Loosen the cylinder head bolts in a crisscross pattern (**Figure 70**) and remove the bolts and washers.

> *NOTE*
> *It may not be possible to remove some of the head bolts from the head with the engine in the frame. In this case, lift the bolts up enough to provide removal clearance and take the head off.*

12. Loosen the cylinder head by tapping around the perimeter with a rubber or plastic mallet.
13. Remove the cylinder head (**Figure 71**) by pulling straight up and off the cylinder. Place a clean shop rag into the cam chain tunnel in the cylinder to prevent the entry of foreign matter.

> *NOTE*
> *After removing the cylinder head, check the top and bottom mating surfaces for any indications of leakage. Also check the head gasket for signs of leakage. A blown gasket could indicate possible cylinder head warpage or other damage.*

14. Remove the 2 dowel pins (A, **Figure 72**) and the cylinder head gasket (B, **Figure 72**).

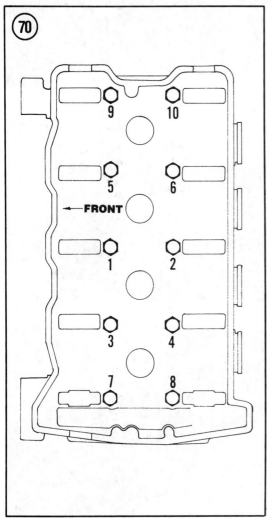

9　10

5　6

←FRONT

1　2

3　4

7　8

Cylinder Head Inspection

1. Remove all traces of gasket residue from the head and cylinder mating surfaces. Do not scratch the gasket surface.

2. Without removing valves, remove all carbon deposits from the combustion chambers with a wire brush or wooden scraper. Take care not to damage the head, valves or spark plug threads.

CAUTION
Do not clean the combustion chambers when the valves are removed. A damaged or even slightly scratched valve seat will cause poor valve seating.

3. Examine the spark plug threads in the cylinder head for damage. If damage is minor or if the threads are dirty or clogged with carbon, use a spark plug thread tap (**Figure 73**) to clean the threads following the manufacturer's instructions. If thread damage is severe, refer further service to a Kawasaki dealer or machine shop.

4. After all carbon is removed from combustion chambers and valve ports and the spark plug thread holes are repaired, clean the entire head in solvent.

5. Check for cracks in the combustion chambers and exhaust ports (A, **Figure 74**). A cracked head must be replaced.

6. After the head has been thoroughly cleaned, place a straightedge across the gasket surface at several points (**Figure 75**). Measure warp by inserting a feeler gauge between the straightedge and cylinder head at each location. Maximum allowable warpage is listed in **Table 2**. Warpage or nicks in the cylinder head surface could cause an air or coolant leak and result in overheating. If warpage exceeds this limit, the cylinder head must be replaced.

7. Check the intake manifold boots for cracks and damage that would allow unfiltered air to enter the engine. Also check the hose clamps for breakage or fatigue. Replace parts as necessary.

8. Check the exhaust pipe studs (B, **Figure 74**) for looseness or thread damage. Slight thread damage can be repaired with a thread file or die. If thread damage is severe, replace the damaged stud(s) as follows:

  a. Screw two 6 mm nuts onto the end of a stud as shown in **Figure 76**.

  b. With 2 wrenches, tighten the nuts against each other (**Figure 77**).

  c. Unscrew the stud with a wrench on the lower nut (**Figure 78**).

  d. Clean the tapped hole with solvent and check for thread damage or carbon build-up. If

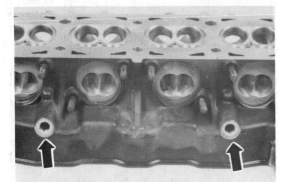

necessary, clean the threads with a 6×1.00 tap.

e. Remove the nuts from the old stud and install them on the end of a new stud.

f. Tighten the nuts against each other.

g. Apply Loctite 242 (blue) to the threads of the new stud.

h. Screw the stud into the cylinder head with a wrench on the upper nut. Tighten the stud securely.

i. Remove the nuts from the new stud.

9. Check the valves and valve guides as described under *Valves and Valve Components* in this chapter.

Installation

1. Clean the cylinder head and cylinder mating surfaces of all gasket residue.

2. Blow out the cylinder head oil passages before installing the head. See **Figure 79**.

3. See **Figure 72**. Install a new head gasket (A) and the 2 dowel pins (B).

NOTE
On 1985 ZX900-A2 models, there was a production change starting with engine No. ZX900AE030894. Starting with this engine number, six of the cylinder head bolt diameters were changed from 10 mm to 11 mm diameter. Starting with the listed engine No., all ZX900 models (including all 1986 models) have the new bolts. Starting with Step 4, ZX900 models will be referred to as early and late models. Early models include all 1984 models and 1985 models with the following engine No.: ZX900AE019001 to ZX900AE030893. Late models will include all 1985 ZX900 models starting with the engine No. ZX900AE030894 and all 1986 models. All ZX1000 models are equipped with the new bolts. The new bolts are not interchangeable on early model ZX900 models. While both bolts use a 1.5 mm thread pitch, a 11 mm bolt installed in a 10 mm bolt hole will strip out the crankcase threads. In addition, to use the larger diameter bolts, the following parts have been changed: Cylinder head and gasket, cylinder block and base gasket, crankcase set, cylinder head bolt washers and the cylinder head dowel pins.

4. *Late model ZX900, all ZX1000:* Apply molybdenum disulfide grease onto both sides of each cylinder head bolt washer (**Figure 80**).

5. *Late model ZX900 and ZX1000:* See **Figure 81**. Two different diameter cylinder head bolts are used. The 11 mm diameter bolts should be installed in the No. 1-6 cylinder head bolt holes. The 10 mm diameter bolts should be installed in the No. 7-10 cylinder head bolt holes.

NOTE
If the cylinder head is being installed with the engine installed on the bike, insert the No. 3, 4, 5 and 6 cylinder head bolts and washers through the cylinder head bolt holes before installing the cylinder head onto the bike. See ***Figure 70*** *and* ***Figure 81***.

6. Install the cylinder head (**Figure 71**).

7A. *Early model ZX900:* Install the cylinder head bolts and washers. Tighten the 10 mm and 11 mm bolts in 2-3 stages in a crisscross pattern (**Figure 70**) to the torque specifications listed in **Table 3**.

7B. *Late model ZX900, all ZX1000:* Kawasaki specifies different cylinder head bolt tightening torques for new and used 10 mm and 11 mm bolts. The bolts installed in your bike now should be considered used. New bolts are those purchased through a dealer and being installed for the *first* time. Perform the following to install and tighten the bolts:

   a. Install the 10 mm and 11 mm bolts in the order shown in **Figure 81**.

   b. *Tightening used bolts:* Tighten used 10 mm bolts to 36 N•m (27 ft.-lb.). Tighten used 11 mm bolts to 48 N•m (35 ft.-lb.).

   c. *Tightening new bolts:* Tighten new 10 mm bolts to 39 N•m (29 ft.-lb.). Tighten new 11 mm bolts to 51 N•m (38 ft.-lb.).

   d. Tighten the bolts in a crisscross pattern in 2 steps in a crisscross pattern (**Figure 81**).

8. Tighten the 6 mm bolts to the torque specifications listed in **Table 3**. See **Figure 68** and **Figure 69**.

9. Tighten the front and rear (**Figure 68** and **Figure 69**) cylinder head bolts and nut to the torque specifications listed in **Table 2**.

10. Reverse Steps 1-8 under *Cylinder Head Removal* to complete assembly. Reinstall the pickup coil cover. Apply Loctite 242 (blue) onto the bolts indicated in B, **Figure 66**.

VALVES AND VALVE COMPONENTS

Correct valve service requires a number of special tools. The following procedures describe how to check for valve component wear and to determine what type of service is required. In most cases, valve troubles are caused by poor valve seating, worn valve guides or burned valves. After removing the cylinder head and performing the following checks and procedures, have the valve

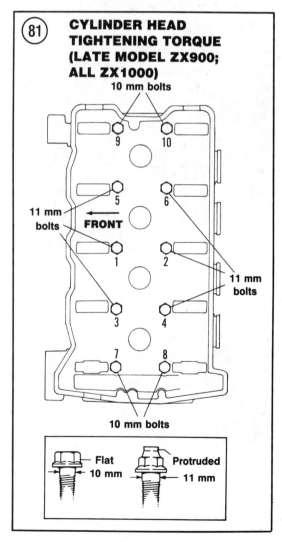

CYLINDER HEAD TIGHTENING TORQUE (LATE MODEL ZX900; ALL ZX1000)

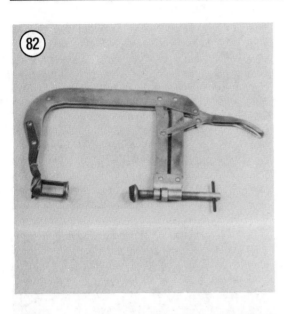

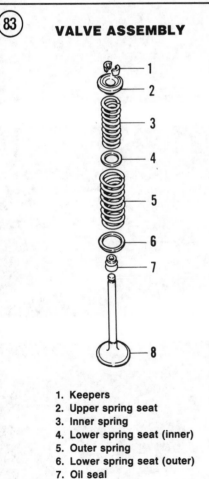

VALVE ASSEMBLY

1. Keepers
2. Upper spring seat
3. Inner spring
4. Lower spring seat (inner)
5. Outer spring
6. Lower spring seat (outer)
7. Oil seal
8. Valve

guides, valves and guides serviced by a Kawasaki dealer. A valve spring compressor (**Figure 82**) will be required to remove and install the valves.

Refer to **Figure 83** for this procedure.

CAUTION
On all 1984 ZX900 and on 1985 ZX900 models with engine No. ZX900AE019001-ZX900AE030462, a small number of vehicles experienced broken valve spring retainers during high rpm use. This resulted in severe engine damage. Starting on 1985 models with engine No. ZX900AE030462, new valve spring retainers made of a new alloy have been installed during engine assembly. If you have an early model, you should discard the old retainers and install new retainers available through your Kawasaki dealer. New valve spring retainers are especially important if the engine has been modified or if it is used under racing or other high speed conditions.

When replacing the valve spring retainers, do not allow the old and new retainers to become mixed together as they appear identical.

If a Kawasaki dealer replaced the valve spring retainers, 2 punch marks will appear on the rear of the cylinder head on the upper left-hand side.

1. Remove the cylinder head as described in this chapter.
2. Install a valve spring compressor squarely over the valve retainer with other end of tool placed against valve head. See **Figure 84**.

3. Tighten valve spring compressor until the valve keepers separate (**Figure 85**). Lift out the valve keepers with needlenose pliers or a magnet.

4. Gradually loosen the valve spring compressor and remove it from the cylinder head. Remove the valve spring retainer (**Figure 86**).

5. Remove the inner and outer valve springs (**Figure 87**).

6. Remove the inner valve spring seat (**Figure 88**).

7. Remove the outer valve spring seat (**Figure 89**).

> *CAUTION*
> *Remove any burrs from the valve stem grooves before removing the valve (**Figure 90**). Otherwise the valve guides will be damaged.*

8. Remove the valve from the combustion chamber side (**Figure 91**).

9. Pull the oil seal (**Figure 92**) off of the valve guide.

> *CAUTION*
> *All component parts of each valve assembly (**Figure 93**) must be kept together. Do not mix with like components from other valves or excessive wear may result.*

10. Repeat Steps 2-9 and remove remaining valve(s).

Inspection

1. Clean valves in solvent. Do not gouge or damage the valve seating surface.

2. Inspect the contact surface of each valve for burning (**Figure 94**). Minor roughness and pitting can be removed by lapping the valve as described in this chapter. Excessive unevenness to the contact surface is an indication that the valve is not serviceable. The contact surface of the valve may be ground on a valve grinding machine, but it is

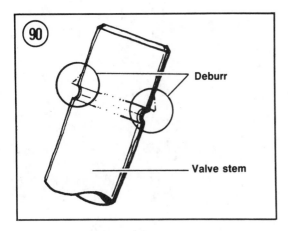

Deburr

Valve stem

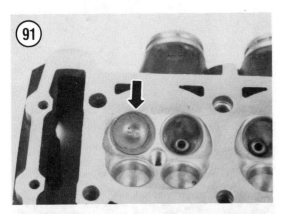

best to replace a burned or damaged valve with a new one.

3. Inspect the valve stems for wear and roughness and measure the vertical runout of the valve stem as shown in **Figure 95**. The runout should not exceed specifications (**Table 2**).

4. Measure valve stems for wear using a micrometer (**Figure 96**). Compare with specifications in **Table 2**.

4

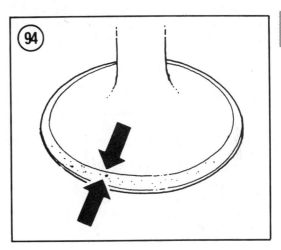

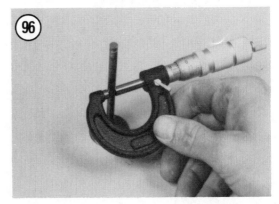

5. Remove all carbon and varnish from the valve guides with a stiff spiral wire brush before checking wear.

NOTE
Step 6 and Step 7 require special measuring equipment. If you do not have the required measuring devices, proceed to Step 8.

6. Measure each valve guide at top, center and bottom with a small hole gauge (**Figure 97**). Measure the small hole gauge with a micrometer (**Figure 98**) and compare measurements with specifications in **Table 2**.

7. Replace any guide or valve that is not within tolerance. Valve guide replacement is described later in this chapter.

8. If a small bore gauge is not available, measure the valve guide clearance as follows. A new intake and exhaust valve and dial indicator will be required.

   a. Clean the valve guides as described in Step 5.

   b. Insert a *new* valve into one guide and set the plunger of a dial indicator so that it rests against the upper valve stem as shown in **Figure 99**.

   c. Move the valve back and forth and then from side to side. Record movement in both directions.

   d. Repeat for each valve guide.

   e. If the valve movement in either direction exceeds the valve guide clearance (wobble method) in **Table 2**, replace the valve guides as described in this chapter.

9. Measure the valve spring length with a vernier caliper (**Figure 100**). All should be of length

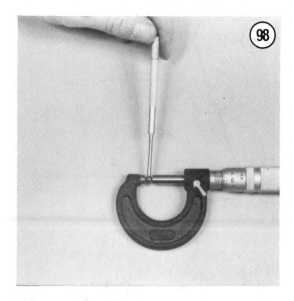

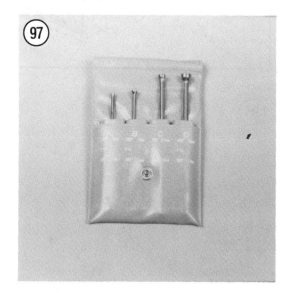

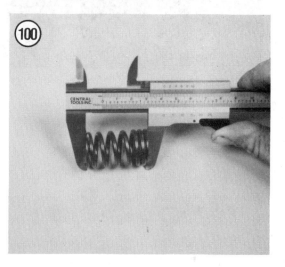

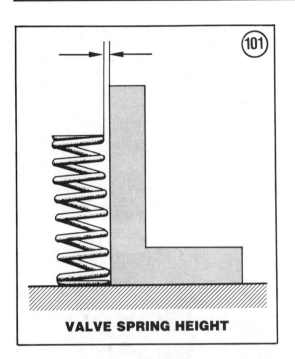

VALVE SPRING HEIGHT

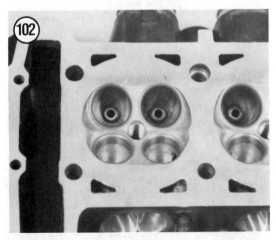

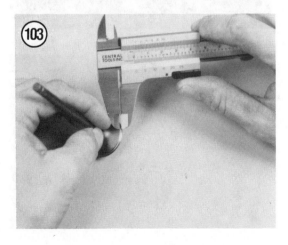

specified in **Table 2** with no bends or other distortion. Replace defective springs.

10. Measure the tilt of all valve springs as shown in **Figure 101**. Replace if tilt exceeds limit in **Table 2**.

11. Check the valve spring retainer and valve keepers. If they are in good condition, they may be reused.

12. Inspect valve seats (**Figure 102**). If worn or burned, they may be reconditioned. Seats and valves in near-perfect condition can be reconditioned by lapping with fine carborundum paste. Lapping, however, is always inferior to precision grinding. Check as follows:

   a. Clean the valve seat and valve mating areas with contact cleaner.

   b. Coat the valve seat with machinist's blue.

   c. Install the valve into its guide and rotate it against its seat with a valve lapping tool. See *Valve Lapping* in this chapter.

   d. Lift the valve out of the guide and measure the seat width with vernier calipers (**Figure 103**).

   e. The seat width for intake and exhaust valves should measure within the specifications listed in **Table 2**.

   f. If the seat width is too narrow or wide or is uneven, regrind the seats as described in this chapter.

   g. Remove all machinist's blue residue from the seats and valves.

Installation

Refer to **Figure 83** for this procedure.

1. Carefully slide a new oil seal over the end of the valve guide (**Figure 104**).

NOTE
Oil seals should be replaced whenever a
valve is removed or replaced.

2. Coat a valve stem with molybdenum disulfide paste and install into its correct guide (**Figure 91**).
3. Install the outer valve spring seat (**Figure 89**).
4. Install the inner valve spring seat (**Figure 88**).
5. Install outer valve spring with the narrow pitch end (end with coils closest together) facing the cylinder head (**Figure 105**). See **Figure 106**.
6. Install the valve spring retainer (**Figure 86**).

CAUTION
On all 1984 ZX900 and on 1985 ZX900 models with engine No. ZX900AE019001-ZX900AE030462, a small number of vehicles experienced broken valve spring retainers during high rpm use. This resulted in severe engine damage. Starting on 1985 models with engine No. ZX900AE030462, new valve spring retainers made of a new alloy have been installed during engine assembly. If you have an early model, you should discard the old retainers and install new retainers available through your Kawasaki dealer. New valve spring retainers are especially important if the engine has been modified or if it is used under racing or other high speed conditions.

7. Push down on the upper valve seat with the valve spring compressor (**Figure 85**) and install the valve keepers. After releasing tension from compressor, examine valve keepers and make sure they are seated correctly (**Figure 107**).
8. Repeat Steps 1-7 for remaining valve(s).

Valve Guide Replacement

The valve guides must be removed and installed with special tools that are available from a Kawasaki dealer. The special tools required for ZX900 and ZX100 models are as follows:
   a. Valve guide driver, Kawasaki part No. 57001-1021.
   b. Valve guide reamer, Kawasaki part No. 57001-1079.
1. The valve guides are installed with a slight interference fit. The cylinder head must be heated to a temperature of approximately 212-300° F (100-150° C) in an oven or on a hot plate.

NOTE
You can check cylinder head temperature by using special wax sticks

(TempSticks) which melt at a certain temperature. These wax sticks are available at welding supply stores and come in different temperature ranges.

CAUTION
Do not heat the cylinder head with a torch (propane or acetylene)—never bring a flame into contact with the cylinder head. The direct heat will cause warpage of the cylinder head.

WARNING
Heavy gloves must be worn when performing this procedure—the cylinder head is very hot.

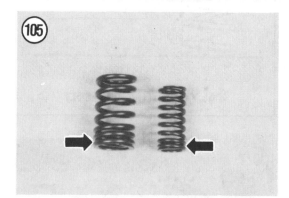

2. Remove the cylinder head from the oven or hot plate and place onto wood blocks with the combustion chamber facing *up*.

3. Drive the old valve guide out from the combustion chamber side of the cylinder head (**Figure 108**) with the valve guide driver.

4. Reheat the cylinder head to approximately 212-300° F (100-150° C).

5. Remove the cylinder head from the oven or hot plate and place it on wood blocks with the combustion chamber facing *down*.

6. Using the valve guide driver, install the new valve guide until it is fully seated.

7. Repeat for each valve guide.

8. After the cylinder head has cooled to room temperature, ream the new valve guides as follows:

   a. Coat the valve guide and valve guide reamer with cutting oil.

   b. See **Figure 109**. Ream the valve guide by rotating the reamer *clockwise* only. Do not turn the reamer counterclockwise.

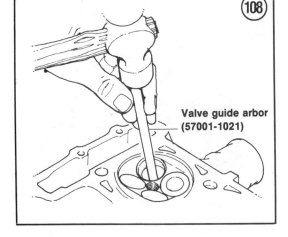

Valve guide arbor (57001-1021)

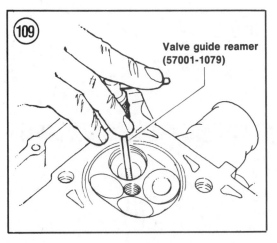

Valve guide reamer (57001-1079)

   c. Measure the valve guide inside diameter with a snap gauge. The valve guide should be within the service specifications listed in **Table 2**.

9. The valve seats must be refaced with a 45° cutter after replacing valve guides. Reface the valve seats as described under *Valve Seat Reconditioning* in this chapter.

10. Clean the cylinder head thoroughly in solvent. Lightly oil the valve guides to prevent rust.

Valve Seat Reconditioning

The valve seats must be cut with special tools that are available from a Kawasaki dealer or a motorcycle accessory dealer. The following tools will be required:

   a. Valve seat cutters (see Kawasaki dealer for part numbers).

   b. Vernier caliper.

   c. Machinist's blue.

   d. Valve lapping stick.

NOTE
Follow the manufacturer's instructions with using valve facing equipment.

1. Inspect valve seats (**Figure 102**). If worn or burned, they may be reconditioned. Seats and valves in near-perfect condition can be reconditioned by lapping with fine carborundum paste. Lapping, however, is always inferior to precision grinding. Check as follows:

   a. Clean the valve seat and valve mating areas with contact cleaner.

   b. Coat the valve seat with machinist's blue.

   c. Install the valve into its guide and rotate it against its seat with a valve lapping tool. See *Valve Lapping* in this chapter.

   d. Lift the valve out of the guide and measure the seat width with vernier calipers.

   e. The seat width for intake and exhaust valves should measure within the specifications listed in **Table 2** all the way around the seat. If the seat width exceeds the service limit (**Table 2**), regrind the seats as follows.

CAUTION
*When grinding valve seats, work **slowly** to prevent grinding the seats too much. Overgrinding the valve seats will sink the valves too far into the cylinder head. Sinking the valves too far may reduce valve clearance and make it impossible to adjust valve clearance. In this condition, the cylinder head would have to be replaced.*

2. Install a 45° cutter onto the valve tool and lightly cut the seat to remove roughness (**Figure 110**). See **Figure 111**.

3. Measure the valve seat with a vernier caliper. Record the measurement to refer to when performing the following.

4. Install a 32° cutter onto the valve tool and lightly cut the seat to remove 1/4 of the existing valve seat.

> *CAUTION*
> *The 60° cutter removes material quickly. Work carefully and check your progress often.*

5. Install a 60° cutter onto the valve tool and lightly cut the seat to remove the lower 1/4 of the existing valve seat.

> *NOTE*
> *The 32° and 60° cutters are used to make the 45° seat a consistent width around its entire surface. Differences in seat width create uneven cooling of the valves and can lead to valve warpage. The 32° and 60° cutters are also used to shift the 45° seat up or down, depending on readings taken with machinist's blue.*

6. Measure the valve seat with a vernier caliper. If necessary, fit a 45° cutter onto the valve tool and cut the valve seat to the specified seat width listed in **Table 2**. See **Figure 110**.

7. When the valve seat width is correct, check valve seating as follows.

8. Clean the valve seat and valve mating areas with contact cleaner.

9. Coat the valve seat with machinist's blue.

10. Insert the valve into the guide and seat it against the valve seat.

11. Remove the valve and check the contact area on the valve. Interpret results as follows:

    a. The valve contact area should be approximately in the center of the valve seat area.

    b. If the contact area is too high on the valve, lower the seat with a 32° flat cutter.

    c. If the contact area is too low on the valve, raise the seat with a 60° interior cutter.

    d. Refinish the seat using a 45° cutter.

12. When the contact area and seat width are correct, lap the valve as described in this chapter.

Valve Lapping

Valve lapping is a simple operation which can restore the valve seal without machining if the amount of wear or distortion is not too great.

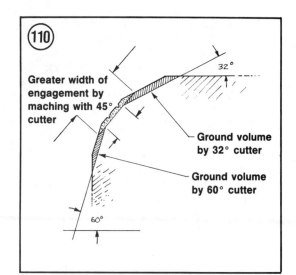

Greater width of engagement by maching with 45° cutter

32°

Ground volume by 32° cutter

Ground volume by 60° cutter

60°

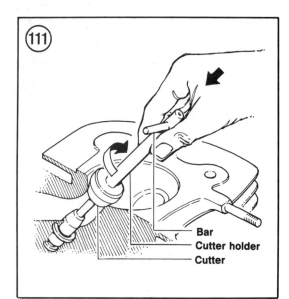

Bar
Cutter holder
Cutter

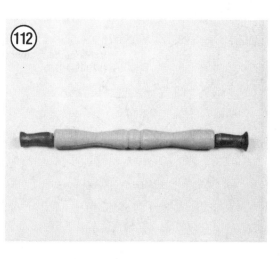

This procedure should only be performed after determining that valve seat width and outside diameter are within specifications. A valve lapping stick (**Figure 112**) will be required.

1. Smear a light coating of fine grade valve lapping compound on the seating surface of the valve.

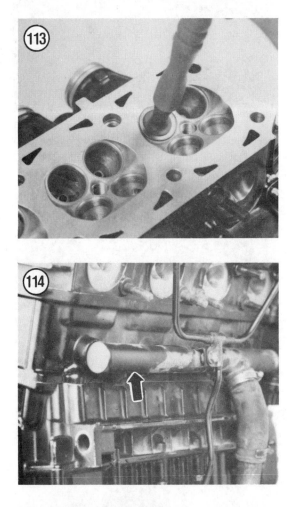

2. Insert the valve into the head.

3. Wet the suction cup of the lapping stick and stick it onto the head of the valve (**Figure 113**). Lap the valve to the seat by spinning the lapping stick in both directions, while pressing it against the valve seat. Every 5 to 10 seconds, rotate the valve 180° in the valve seat. Continue this action until the mating surfaces on the valve and seat are smooth and equal in size.

4. Closely examine valve seat in cylinder head (**Figure 102**). It should be smooth and even with a smooth, polished seating "ring."

5. Thoroughly clean the valves and cylinder head in solvent to remove all grinding compound.

CAUTION
Any compound left on the valves or the cylinder head will end up in the engine and cause excessive wear and damage.

6. After the lapping has been completed and the valve assemblies have been reinstalled into the head the valve seal should be tested. Check the seal of each valve by pouring solvent into each of the intake and exhaust ports. There should be no leakage past the seat. If leakage occurs, combustion chamber will appear wet. If fluid leaks past any of the seats, disassemble that valve assembly and repeat the lapping procedure until there is no leakage.

NOTE
This solvent test does not ensure long-term durability or maximum power. It merely ensures maximum compression will be available on initial start-up after reassembly.

CYLINDER BLOCK, CAM CHAIN AND CHAIN GUIDES

The alloy cylinder block has pressed-in cylinder sleeves, which can be bored to 0.5 mm (0.020 in.) oversize.

Removal

1. Remove the cylinder head as described in this chapter.

2. Remove the screws securing the water pipe to the cylinder block. Then pull the water pipe (**Figure 114**) out of the cylinder block water port holes.

3. Remove the cylinder head gasket.

4. Remove the 2 dowel pins (**Figure 115**).

5. Remove the pickup coil rotor as described in Chapter Eight.

6. If necessary, remove the cam chain plate bolts and remove the plate (**Figure 116**).

7. Remove the rear cam chain guide bolt (**Figure 117**) and pivot spacer (**Figure 118**). Pull the chain guide out through the cylinder tunnel (**Figure 119**).

8. Remove the cam chain (**Figure 120**).

9. Lift the front cam chain guide out through the cylinder tunnel (**Figure 121**).

10. Remove the 6 mm crankcase-to-cylinder block bolts.

11. Loosen the cylinder by tapping around the perimeter with a rubber or plastic mallet.

12. Pull the cylinder block (**Figure 122**) straight up and off the pistons and cylinder studs.

13. Stuff clean shop rags into the crankcase opening to prevent objects from falling into the crankcase.

14. Remove the 2 dowel pins (**Figure 123**) and base gasket. Discard the base gasket.

Inspection

1. Wash the cylinder block in solvent to remove any oil and carbon particles. The cylinder bores must be cleaned thoroughly before attempting any measurement as incorrect readings may be obtained.

2. Remove all gasket residue from the top (**Figure 123**) and bottom (A, **Figure 124**) gasket surfaces.

3. Clean the cylinder block water ports (B, **Figure 124**) of all coolant sludge build-up.

4. Measure the cylinder bores with a cylinder gauge or inside micrometer at the points shown in **Figure 125**. Measure in 2 axes—in line with the

4

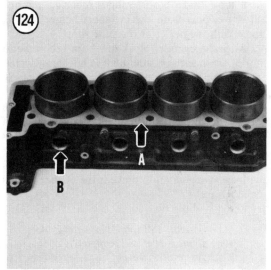

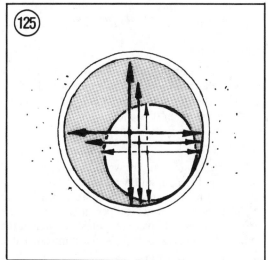

piston pin and at 90° to the pin. If the diameter is greater than specifications (**Table 2**), the cylinders must be rebored to the next oversize and new pistons and rings installed. Rebore all 4 cylinders even though only one may be worn.

NOTE
*The new pistons should be obtained first before the cylinders are bored so that the pistons can be measured. Each cylinder must be bored to match one piston only (**Figure 126**). Piston-to-cylinder clearance is specified in **Table 2**.*

5. If the cylinder bores are not worn past the service limits, check the bore carefully for scratches or gouges. The bore still may require boring and reconditioning.

6. If the cylinder block requires reboring, remove all dowel pins from the cylinders before leaving them with the dealer or machine shop.

7. After the cylinder block has been rebored and honed, wash each cylinder bore in hot soapy water. This is the only way to clean the cylinders of the fine grit material left from the bore or honing job. After washing the cylinder walls, run a clean white cloth through each wall. It should show no traces of grit or other debris. If the rag is dirty, the wall is not thoroughly clean and must be rewashed. After the cylinder is cleaned, lubricate the cylinder walls with clean engine oil to prevent the cylinder liners from rusting.

CAUTION
A combination of soap and water is the only solution that will completely clean cylinder walls. Solvent and kerosene cannot wash fine grit out of cylinder crevices. Grit left in the cylinder will act as a grinding compound and cause premature wear to the new rings.

Chain Guides

Inspect the chain guides (**Figure 127**). Replace them if the chain run is visibly damaged. If the chain guides are worn, also check the cam chain and the cam chain tensioner.

Cam Chain

Check the cam chain for worn, loose or damaged links. Lay the chain on a workbench and stretch a 20-pin segment as shown in **Figure 128**. Measure 20 pins with a vernier caliper at several points around the chain. Replace the camshaft chain if the length of 20 pins exceeds the service limit in **Table 2**.

Installation

1. Check that the top and bottom cylinder surfaces are clean of all gasket residue.

2. Install the 2 dowel pins onto the crankcase (**Figure 123**).

3. Install a new cylinder base gasket. Make sure all holes line up properly.

NOTE
*Because there are no studs to help guide the cylinder block during installation, it will be necessary to support the pistons during cylinder block installation. **Figure 129** shows the No. 2 and No. 3 pistons held with a piece of 1/4 in. plywood. Support the pistons in the front and back with small plywood blocks. The cylinder block will be easier to install with an assistant. It is important to work carefully so as not to break a piston ring.*

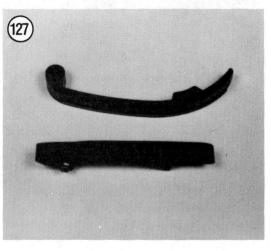

4. Support the No. 2 and No. 3 pistons as described in the previous NOTE. Turn the crankshaft and lower pistons No. 2 and No. 3 so that they put pressure on the wood blocks.

5. Lubricate the cylinder bores and pistons liberally with engine oil prior to installation.

6. Carefully align the cylinder block with the pistons (**Figure 129**) and lower it over pistons No. 2 and No. 3 until the piston rings enter the cylinder.

NOTE
Compress each ring as it enters the cylinder with your fingers or by using aircraft type hose clamps of appropriate diameter.

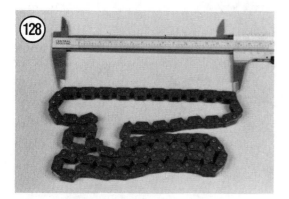

CAUTION
Don't tighten the clamp any more than necessary to compress the rings. If the rings can't slip through easily, the clamp may gouge the rings. Don't use excessive force to install the cylinder. If excessive force is required, one (or more) of the piston rings are caught on the bottom of the cylinder(s).

7. Install the No. 2 and No. 3 pistons first. Then turn the crankshaft to raise pistons No. 1 and No. 4. Move the wood blocks to support these pistons. Turn the crankshaft backwards so the pistons put slight pressure on the wood blocks. Install the cylinder block over the No. 1 and No. 4 pistons. Carefully push the cylinder down until it seats on the base gasket.

8. Compress each ring as it enters the cylinder with your fingers or by using aircraft type hose clamps of appropriate diameter.

CAUTION
Don't tighten the clamp any more than necessary to compress the rings. If the rings can't slip through easily, the clamp may gouge the rings.

9. Install the water pipes (**Figure 114**).

10. Install the front cam chain guide (**Figure 121**) into the chain tunnel. Engage the tabs on the end of the chain guide with the slots in the cylinder block.

11. Install the cam chain through the chain tunnel (**Figure 120**). Engage the chain with the crankshaft sprocket.

12. Insert the rear cam chain guide into the chain tunnel (**Figure 119**). Then install the pivot spacer (**Figure 118**) and the cam chain guide bolt (**Figure 117**). Tighten the bolt securely.

13. Install the cam chain plate and bolts (**Figure 116**). Tighten the bolts securely.

14. Install the pickup coil rotor as described in Chapter Eight.

15. Install the cylinder head as described in this chapter.

16. Install the cylinder head cover as described in this chapter.

PISTONS AND PISTON RINGS

Piston
Removal/Installation

A typical piston assembly is shown in **Figure 130**.

1. Remove the cylinder block as described in this chapter.

2. Stuff the crankcase with clean shop rags to prevent objects from falling into the crankcase.

3. Lightly mark each piston crown with an identification number (1-4), starting with the No. 1 piston (left-hand side).

4. Remove the piston rings as described in this chapter.

5. Before removing the piston, hold the rod tightly and rock the piston. Any rocking motion (do not confuse with the normal sliding motion) indicates wear on the piston pin, rod small end, pin bore, or more likely, a combination of all three. Mark the piston and pin so that they will be reassembled into the same set.

6. Remove the circlips from the piston pin bores (**Figure 131**).

NOTE
Discard the piston circlips. Never reuse old clips. New circlips must be installed during reassembly.

7. Push the piston pin (A, **Figure 132**) out of the piston by hand. If the pin is tight, use a homemade tool (**Figure 133**) to remove it. Do not drive the piston pin out as this action may damage the piston pin or connecting rod.

8. Lift the piston (B, **Figure 132**) off the connecting rod.

9. Repeat Steps 4-8 for the other pistons.

10. Inspect the piston as described in this chapter.

NOTE
New piston circlips must be installed during assembly.

11. Install one circlip in each piston on the side that faces toward the center of the engine.

12. Coat the connecting rod small end, piston pin and piston with assembly oil.

13. Insert the piston pin into the piston (**Figure 134**).

14. Place the piston (B, **Figure 132**) over the connecting rod. If you are installing old parts, make sure the piston is installed on the correct rod as marked during removal. If the cylinders were bored, install the new pistons as marked by the machinist (**Figure 126**). The arrow on each piston crown (**Figure 135**) must face to the front of the engine. Install the pistons in the following order:

  a. No. 2.

  b. No. 1.

  c. No. 3.

  d. No. 4.

15. Insert the piston pin through one side of the piston until it starts to enter the connecting rod. Then it may be necessary to move the piston

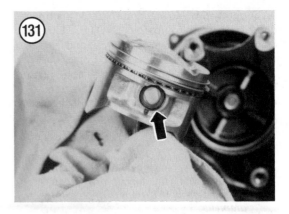

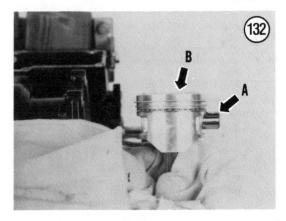

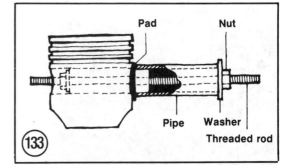

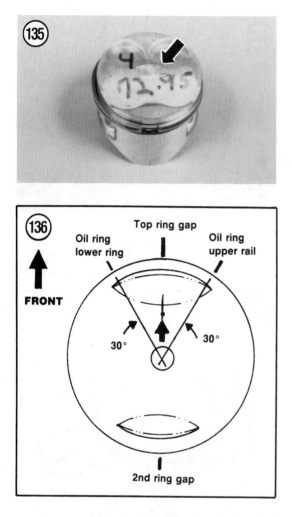

Top ring gap

Oil ring
lower ring

Oil ring
upper rail

FRONT

30° 30°

2nd ring gap

around until the pin enters the connecting rod. Do not force installation or damage may occur. If the pin does not slide easily, something is wrong. One of the mating parts is damaged or dirty. Inspect the parts and correct as necessary. Push the pin in until it is centered in the piston.

16. Install the second circlip in the circlip groove.

17. Make sure the rings are seated completely in their grooves all the way around the piston and that the end gaps are distributed around the piston as shown in **Figure 136**. It is important that the ring gaps are not aligned with each other when installed to prevent compression pressures from escaping past them.

18. Repeat Steps 13-17 for the opposite pistons.

Piston Inspection

1. Carefully clean the carbon from the piston crown (**Figure 135**) with a soft scraper. Large carbon accumulations reduce piston cooling and results in detonation and piston damage. Do not remove or damage the carbon ridge around the circumference of the piston above the top ring. If the pistons, rings and cylinders are found to be dimensionally correct and can be reused, removal of the carbon ring from the top of the piston or the carbon ridges from the cylinders will promote excessive oil consumption.

> *CAUTION*
> *Do not wire brush piston skirts or ring lands. The wire brush removes aluminum and increases piston clearance. It also rounds the corners of the ring lands which results in decreased support for the piston rings.*

2. Examine each ring groove (A, **Figure 137**) for burrs, dented edges and wide wear. Pay particular attention to the top compression ring groove, as it usually wears more than the others.

3. Check the oil control holes in the piston (**Figure 138**) for carbon or oil sludge buildup. Clean the holes with a small diameter drill bit.

4. Check the piston skirts (B, **Figure 137**) for cracks or other damage. If a piston(s) show signs of partial seizure (bits of aluminum build-up on the piston skirts), the pistons should be replaced and the cylinders bored (if necessary) to reduce the possibility of engine noise and further piston seizure.

> *NOTE*
> *Machine shops can remove aluminum from the cylinders without reboring. But, if the surface of the cylinder liner has been scarred by the seizure, it will require reboring.*

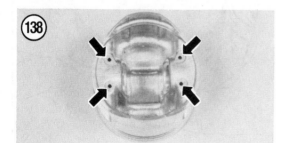

5. Measure piston-to-cylinder clearance as described under *Piston Clearance* in this chapter.
6. Inspect the piston pin for chrome flaking or cracks. Replace if necessary.

Piston Clearance

1. Make sure the piston and cylinder walls are clean and dry.
2. Measure the inside diameter of the cylinder at a point 13 mm (1/2 in.) from the upper edge with a bore gauge.
3. Measure the outside diameter of the piston at a point 5 mm 3/16 in.) from the lower edge of the piston 90° to piston pin axis (**Figure 139**).
4. Subtract the piston diameter from the bore diameter. The difference is piston-to-cylinder clearance. Compare to specification in **Table 2**. If clearance is excessive, the pistons should be replaced and perhaps the cylinders rebored.

> *NOTE*
> *If the cylinder diameters are still within specification, it is possible to merely buy new pistons without reboring. New pistons will take up the piston-to-cylinder clearance. Check carefully before deciding to rebore or just use new pistons.*

5. Purchase the new pistons first. Then, measure its diameter and add the specified clearance to determine the proper cylinder bore diameters.

> *NOTE*
> *If one cylinder requires boring, the other cylinders must also be rebored.*

Piston Ring
Removal/Installation

> *WARNING*
> *The edges of all piston rings are very sharp. Be careful when handling them to avoid cut fingers.*

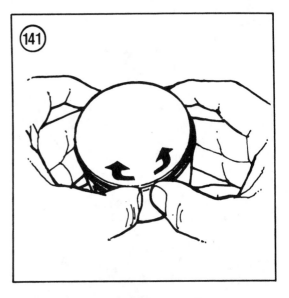

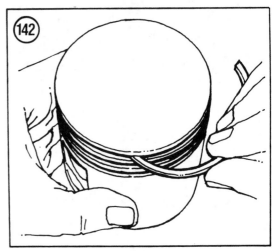

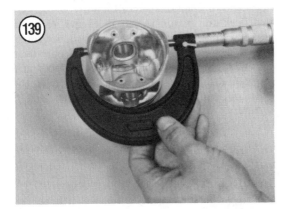

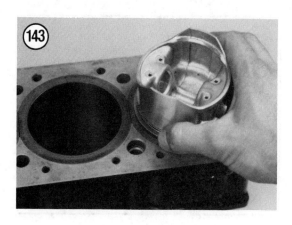

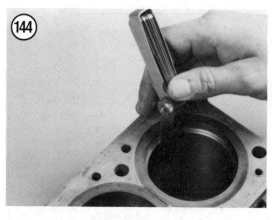

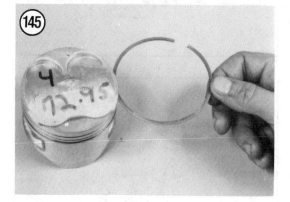

1. Measure the side clearance of each ring in its groove with a flat feeler gauge (**Figure 140**) and compare with the specifications in **Table 2**. If the clearance is greater than specified, the rings must be replaced. If the clearance is still excessive with the new rings, the piston must be replaced.

2. Remove the old rings with a ring expander tool or by spreading the ring ends with your thumbs and lifting the rings up evenly (**Figure 141**).

3. Using a broken piston ring, remove all carbon from the piston ring grooves (**Figure 142**).

4. Inspect grooves carefully for burrs, nicks or broken or cracked lands (A, **Figure 137**). Replace piston if necessary.

5. Check end gap of each ring. To check ring, insert the ring into the bottom of the cylinder bore and square it with the cylinder wall by tapping it with the piston (**Figure 143**). The ring should be pushed in about 15 mm (5/8 in.). Insert a feeler gauge as shown in **Figure 144**. Compare gap with **Table 2**. Replace ring if gap is too large.

> *NOTE*
> *If the gap on the new ring is smaller or larger than specified, check that you have the correct rings. If you have the correct rings and the gap is too big, the cylinder must be rebored.*

6. Roll each ring around its piston groove as shown in **Figure 145** to check for binding. Minor binding may be cleaned up with a fine-cut file.

> *NOTE*
> ***Figure 146*** *shows a piston with the piston rings removed. Each piston ring is different and must be installed as described in Step 7.*

7. Install the piston rings—first the bottom, then the middle, then the top ring—by carefully spreading the ends with your thumbs and slipping the rings over the top of the piston. Remember that piston rings must be installed with the marks on them facing up toward the top of the piston or there is the possibility of oil pumping past the rings.

   a. Install the oil ring assembly into the bottom ring groove. The assembly is comprised of 2 steel rails and 1 expander. The expander is installed in the middle of the steel rails. Install the expander ring first, so that the ends of the ring butt together. They must not overlap. Install the bottom steel rail, then the top steel rail.

   b. *ZX900:* The top piston ring is symmetrical and can be installed either way. The second ring is not symmetrical and must be installed as shown in **Figure 147** with the 2N mark facing up.

   c. *ZX1000:* The top and second piston rings are not symmetrical and must be installed as shown in **Figure 148A**.

8. Make sure the rings are seated completely in their grooves all the way around the piston and that the end gaps are distributed around the piston as shown in **Figure 148B**. It is important that the ring gaps are not aligned with each other when installed to prevent compression pressures from escaping past them.

9. If installing oversize compression rings, check the number to make sure the correct rings are being installed. The ring numbers should be the same as the piston oversize number.

10. If new rings are installed, the cylinders must be lightly deglazed or honed. This will help to seat the new rings. Refer honing service to a Kawasaki dealer. After honing, measure the end clearance of each ring (**Figure 144**) and compare to dimensions in **Table 2**.

> *CAUTION*
> *If the cylinders were deglazed or honed, clean the cylinders with soap and water as described under **Cylinder Block Inspection**, Step 8, in this chapter. An improperly cleaned cylinder block will cause rapid wear to the cylinder bore, piston and ring.*

OIL PUMP

The oil pan and oil pump can be removed with the engine mounted in the frame. The following procedures is shown with the engine removed for clarity.

Service Notes

Because the lubrication system is a vital key to engine reliability, note the following during service and inspection:

   a. Was the engine oil level correct?

   b. Was the engine oil contaminated with sludge or coolant?

   c. Was the oil pump properly mounted?

   d. Were external oil lines damaged or their fittings loose?

   e. Were banjo bolts loose or clogged?

   f. Was the oil filter element clogged?

   g. Was the oil pump screen clogged?

   h. Was the relief valve working properly, clogged or damaged?

   i. Were all O-rings properly installed or were they damaged?

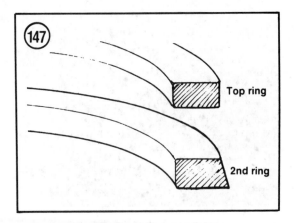

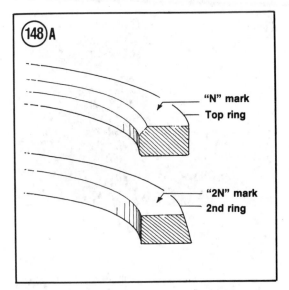

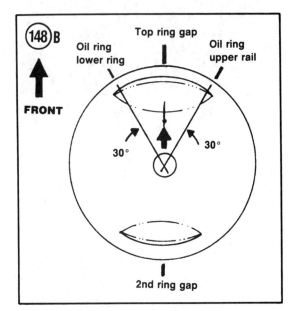

j. Was the oil cooler damaged or improperly installed?

k. Were the oil passages partially restricted or clogged?

Oil Pan
Removal/Installation

1. Remove the mufflers as described under *Exhaust System Removal/Installation* in Chapter Seven.

> *NOTE*
> *If the engine is being checked for a possible oil system malfunction, drain the engine oil in a clean container so that it can be checked for contamination.*

2. Drain the engine oil and remove the oil filter as described under *Engine Oil and Filter Change* in Chapter Three.

3. Remove the bolt and washer and disconnect the electrical connector at the oil pressure switch (**Figure 149**).

4. Disconnect the connector at the oil temperature switch (**Figure 150**).

5. Remove the oil cooler hoses' banjo bolts at the oil pan.

6. Remove the lower crankcase-to-oil pan banjo bolts and external oil line (**Figure 151**).

7. Disconnect the cylinder head-to-oil pan oil line (**Figure 152**).

8. Keep the oil drain pan underneath the engine. Then loosen the oil pan mounting bolts all the way around the pan and allow more oil to drain into the pan.

9. Completely remove the oil pan mounting bolts and lower the pan (**Figure 153**) away from the crankcase and remove it.

10. Remove the oil pan gasket.

11. Remove the large O-ring (**Figure 154**) from the oil pan.

12. Before cleaning the oil pan, check inside the pan for signs of excessive metal or fiber debris that may indicate engine, clutch or transmission problems.

13. Service the oil pan screen as follows:

 a. Remove the 3 Phillips screws and remove the oil screen plate (**Figure 155**).

 b. Lift the oil screen (**Figure 156**) out of the oil pan.

 c. Clean the oil pan screen area (**Figure 157**) of all sludge buildup.

 d. Check the oil screen (**Figure 158**) for tears or other damage. Replace the screen if necessary.

 e. Reverse to install the screen. Apply Loctite 242 (blue) onto each Phillips screw. Tighten the screws securely.

14. Check the 5 exposed O-rings (**Figure 159**) for wear or damage. Replace the O-rings if necessary.

15. Installation is the reverse of these steps, noting the following:

 a. The O-ring installed between the oil pump bracket and oil pan must be installed so that its flat side faces the bracket.

 b. Apply clean engine oil to all O-rings.

 c. Install the large O-ring (**Figure 154**) on the oil pan.

 d. Remove all gasket residue from the oil pan and crankcase. Then install a new gasket. Make sure the bolt holes align properly.

 e. Install the relief valve and/or oil pressure switch if removed.

NOTE
If the engine oil was contaminated with metal debris or clutch particles,

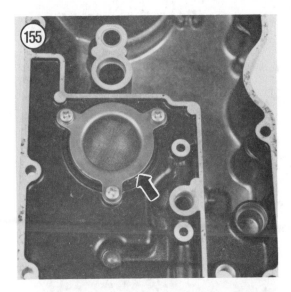

(158)

thoroughly clean the relief valve to ensure it will function properly.

g. Four of the oil pan mounting bolt holes are identified with a triangle mark adjacent to the hole **(Figure 160).** Apply Locite 242 (blue) onto these 4 oil pan mounting bolts before installation.

h. Tighten the oil pan mounting bolts securely.

i. Install a new oil filter and refill the engine oil as described in Chapter Three.

Oil Pump Removal

The oil pump can be removed with the engine installed in the frame.

1. Remove the oil pan as described in this chapter.
2. Remove nozzle **(Figure 161A)**.
3. Pull the oil pump screen **(Figure 161B)** up and remove it.

(161)A

(159)

(160)

(161)B

4. Pull the large oil pipe (**Figure 162**) out of the crankcase.

5. Pull the small oil pipe (**Figure 163**) out of the crankcase.

6. Remove the 2 oil pump O-rings (**Figure 164**).

7. Remove the oil pump (**Figure 165**) as follows:

   a. Remove the oil pump mounting bolts.

   b. The oil pump drive gear shaft engages with the oil pump drive shaft. If the water pump and the oil pump drive gear are installed on the engine, remove the pickup coil cover. Then rotate the crankshaft clockwise so that the oil pump shaft (**Figure 166**) and the oil pump gear shaft (**Figure 167**) slots face up. If the slots are not facing up, it will be difficult to remove the oil pump.

   c. Lift the oil pump assembly up and remove it.

   d. Remove the dowel pin (**Figure 168**).

> *NOTE*
> *The dowel pin shown in **Figure 168** sometimes stays in the oil pump when it is removed.*

8. Remove and discard all external O-rings.

Preliminary Inspection/Installation

1. Check the oil pump screen (**Figure 169**) for debris buildup or damage. Clean the screen thoroughly in solvent and allow to dry. Replace the screen assembly if necessary.

> *NOTE*
> *If the screen was contaminated with metal or clutch particles, clean as much*

of this contamination from the underside of the engine as possible. Also, clean all oil lines.

2. Replace the oil pump screen O-ring (**Figure 170**).

3. Check the large oil pipe soldered joints (**Figure 171**) for cracks or other damage. Replace the 4 oil pipe O-rings (**Figure 172**).

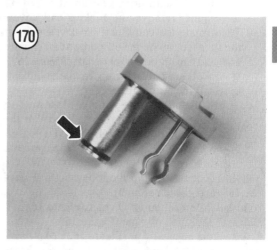

4. Replace the O-ring (**Figure 173**) and install the dowel pin (**Figure 174**).

5. Replace the 3 oil pipe O-rings. **Figure 163** shows the oil pipe.

6. Install the oil pump as follows:

    a. Pour new engine oil into the oil pump.

    b. The oil pump drive gear shaft engages with the oil pump drive shaft. If the water pump and the oil pump drive gear are installed on the engine, remove the pickup coil cover. Then rotate the crankshaft clockwise so that the slots face up on the oil pump shaft (**Figure 166**) and the oil pump gear shaft (**Figure 167**). If the slots are not facing up, it will be difficult to install the oil pump.

    c. Install the oil pump assembly. Make sure to engage the shafts in sub-step "a" and that the dowel pin and O-ring installed on the bottom of the pump housing (**Figure 174**) engage the crankcase correctly.

    d. Install the oil pump mounting bolts (**Figure 165**) and tighten securely.

7. Install 2 new oil pump O-rings (**Figure 164**).

8. Install the small oil pipe (**Figure 163**).

9. Install the large oil pipe (**Figure 162**). Make sure both ends of the pipe seat into the crankcase completely.

10. Install the oil screen (**Figure 175**). Engage the screen hook with the large oil pipe (**Figure 176**).

11. Install the oil pan as described in this chapter.

Disassembly/Inspection/Assembly

Refer to **Figure 177** for this procedure.

1. Remove the oil pump as described in this chapter.

2. Remove the dowel pin and O-ring (**Figure 174**).

3. Remove the oil pump mounting bolts (**Figure 178**) and remove the oil pump (**Figure 179**) off of the mounting base.

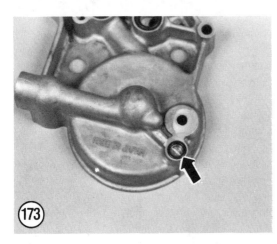

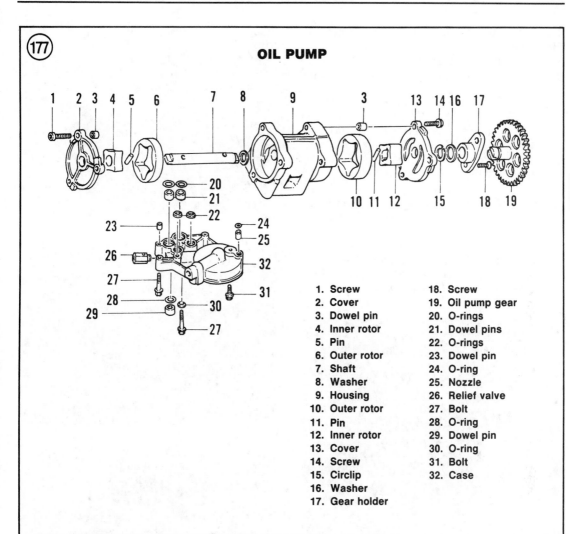

OIL PUMP

1. Screw
2. Cover
3. Dowel pin
4. Inner rotor
5. Pin
6. Outer rotor
7. Shaft
8. Washer
9. Housing
10. Outer rotor
11. Pin
12. Inner rotor
13. Cover
14. Screw
15. Circlip
16. Washer
17. Gear holder
18. Screw
19. Oil pump gear
20. O-rings
21. Dowel pins
22. O-rings
23. Dowel pin
24. O-ring
25. Nozzle
26. Relief valve
27. Bolt
28. O-ring
29. Dowel pin
30. O-ring
31. Bolt
32. Case

4

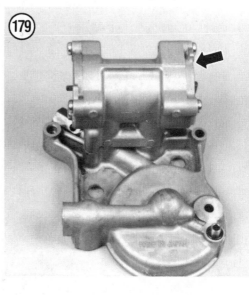

4. Remove the 2 dowel pins and O-rings (A, **Figure 180**).

5. Remove the 2 O-rings (B, **Figure 180**).

6. If necessary, unscrew the relief valve (**Figure 181**).

NOTE
*The oil pump covers are marked with an "A" and a "B." See A, **Figure 182**. The side marked "A" will be disassembled first, then side "B".*

7. Disassemble the "A" pump side as follows:
   a. Remove the 3 Phillips screws (B, **Figure 182**) and remove the "A" cover (**Figure 183**).
   b. Remove the dowel pin (**Figure 184**).
   c. Remove the inner rotor (**Figure 185**).
   d. Remove the outer rotor (**Figure 186**).
   e. Remove the pin (**Figure 187**).

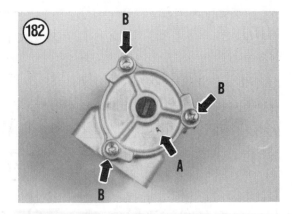

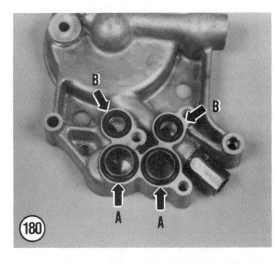

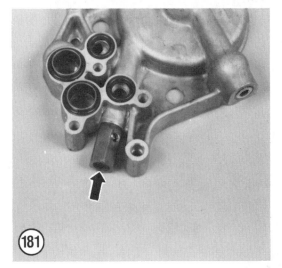

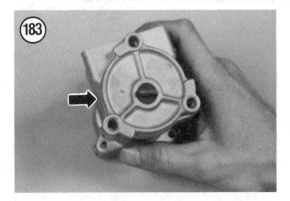

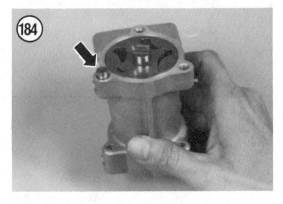

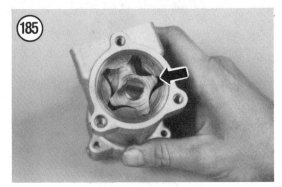

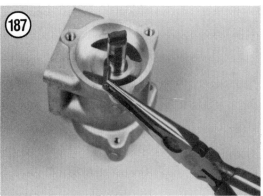

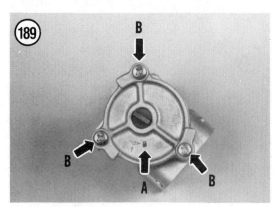

f. Remove the washer (**Figure 188**).

NOTE
Keep the parts for sides A and B
separated to avoid mixups.

8. Disassemble the "B" pump side (A, **Figure 189**)
as follows:

   a. Remove the 3 Phillips screws (B, **Figure 189**)
      and remove the "A" cover (**Figure 190**).
   b. Remove the dowel pin (**Figure 191**).
   c. Remove the outer rotor (**Figure 192**).

4

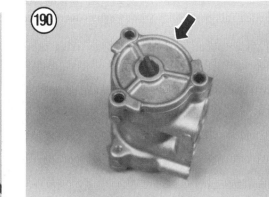

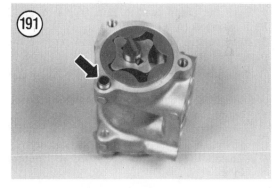

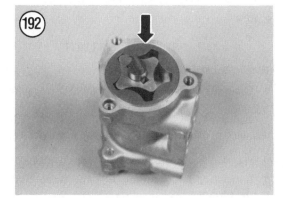

d. Remove the inner rotor (**Figure 193**).

e. Remove the pin (**Figure 194**).

9. Remove the oil pump shaft (**Figure 195**).

10. Inspect the oil pump housing (**Figure 196**) for cracks or bore damage.

11. Check the pump shaft for scoring, pin hole damage or seizure.

12. Check the rotors for scoring or damage.

NOTE
Proceed with Step 13 only when the above inspection and measurement steps have been completed and all parts are known to be good.

13. Coat all parts with fresh engine oil prior to assembly.

14. Assemble the oil pump by reversing these steps. Note the following:

a. Assemble the "A" pump side first.

b. Lubricate all parts with clean engine oil.

c. When installing the oil pressure relief valve, apply Loctite 242 (blue) onto the valve threads and install it.

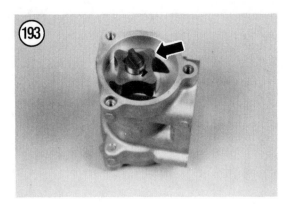

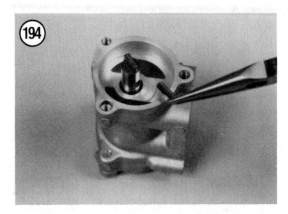

Oil Pump Gear
Removal/Installation

1. Remove the clutch as described in Chapter Five.

2. Turn the pump gear to gain access to the 2 Phillips screws (A, **Figure 197**).

3. Remove the Phillips screws and remove the pump gear assembly (B, **Figure 197**).

4. Install by reversing these steps. Note the following:

a. Align the notch in the gear shaft with the oil pump shaft and install the gear assembly.

b. Apply Loctite 242 (blue) onto the 2 Phillips screws (A, **Figure 197**) and tighten securely.

c. Install the clutch as described in Chapter Five.

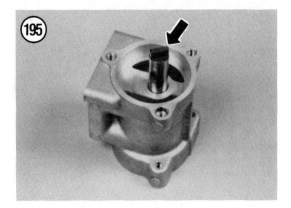

OIL PRESSURE SWITCH

Removal/Installation

1. Drain the engine oil as described under *Engine Oil and Filter Change* in Chapter Three.

2. Remove the bolt and lockwasher and disconnect the electrical connector from the oil pressure switch.

3. Unscrew the oil pressure switch (**Figure 198**).

4. Installation is the reverse of these steps. Note the following.

a. Make sure the area around the switch mounting position is clean of all dirt and debris.

b. Refill the engine oil as described in Chapter Three.

OIL TEMPERATURE SWITCH

Removal/Installation

1. Drain the engine oil as described under *Engine Oil and Filter Change* in Chapter Three.

2. Disconnect the electrical connector at the oil temperature switch (**Figure 199**).

3. Unscrew the oil temperature switch (**Figure 199**).

4. Installation is the reverse of these steps. Note the following.

a. Make sure the area around the switch mounting position is clean of all dirt and debris.

b. Refill the engine oil as described in Chapter Three.

OIL COOLER

Removal/Installation

Refer to **Figure 200** (ZX900) or **Figure 201** (ZX1000).

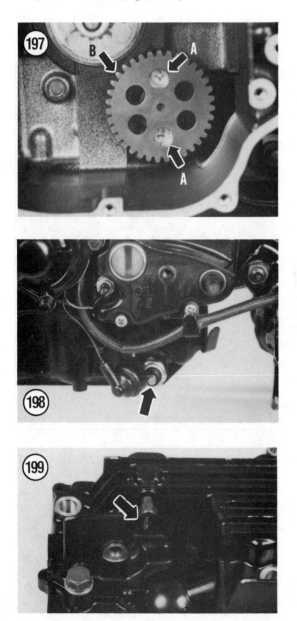

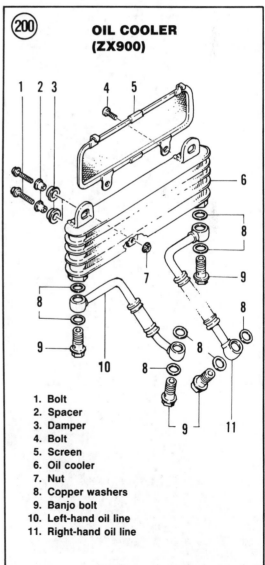

OIL COOLER (ZX900)

1. Bolt
2. Spacer
3. Damper
4. Bolt
5. Screen
6. Oil cooler
7. Nut
8. Copper washers
9. Banjo bolt
10. Left-hand oil line
11. Right-hand oil line

1. Remove the lower fairing assembly. See Chapter Thirteen.

2. Put the bike up on its center stand and put an oil pan under the engine.

3. Drain the engine oil as described under *Engine Oil and Filter Change* in Chapter Three.

4. Remove the oil cooler banjo bolts and washers.

5. Remove the oil cooler mounting screws and remove the oil cooler assembly.

6. To install the cooler, reverse the removal steps. Note the following:

   a. Clean the banjo bolts in solvent and allow to thoroughly dry.

   b. Check all cooler hoses and fittings for leakage or damage.

   c. Tighten the mounting bolts securely.

   d. Make sure to install a washer on both sides of the oil hose banjo bolts.

   e. Refill engine oil as described in Chapter Three.

   f. Recheck the oil level and after the engine has run a short time and add oil if necessary. See *Engine Oil Level Check* in Chapter Three.

ALTERNATOR SHAFT AND STARTER MOTOR CLUTCH

Chain Tensioner
Removal/Installation

Refer to **Figure 202** (ZX900) or **Figure 203** (ZX1000).

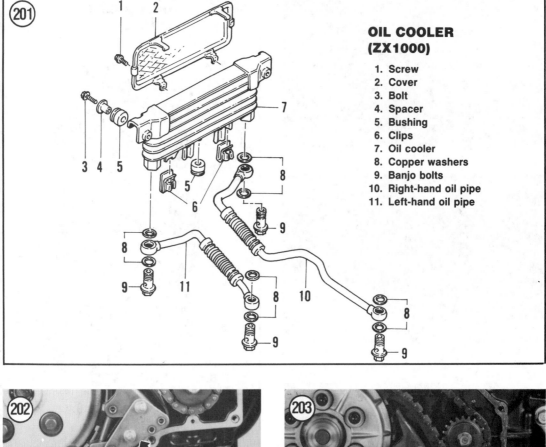

201

OIL COOLER (ZX1000)

1. Screw
2. Cover
3. Bolt
4. Spacer
5. Bushing
6. Clips
7. Oil cooler
8. Copper washers
9. Banjo bolts
10. Right-hand oil pipe
11. Left-hand oil pipe

202

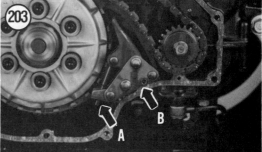

203

1. Remove the clutch cover as described under *Clutch Cover Removal/Installation* in Chapter Five.

2. Push the tensioner guide (A) and the rod stop lever to lock the rod in position.

3. Remove the tensioner mounting bolts and remove the tensioner assembly (B).

4. Installation is the reverse of these steps. Note the following:

   a. Install the tensioner in its locked position.

   b. Apply Loctite 242 (blue) onto the tensioner bolts and install the bolts. Tighten the bolts securely.

   c. After installing the tensioner and tightening its mounting bolts, release the tensioner guide (A) and the rod stop lever.

Chain and Sprocket Removal/Installation

1. Remove the chain tensioner as described in this chapter.

2. Remove the chain guide bolts and remove the guide (**Figure 204**).

3. Using the Kawasaki coupling holder (57001-1189) (**Figure 205**), remove the alternator shaft nut (A, **Figure 206**) and the crankshaft end bolt (B, **Figure 206**).

4. Remove the washer (**Figure 207**).

5. Remove the coupling (**Figure 208**).

6. Remove the 8 rubber dampers (**Figure 209**).

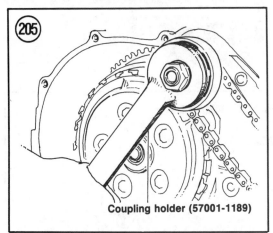

Coupling holder (57001-1189)

7. Remove the chain and sprockets (**Figure 210A**).
8. Check the rubber dampers for wear or damage. Replace the dampers as a set, if necessary.
9. Installation is the reverse of these steps. Tighten the right-hand alternator shaft end nut to the torque specification in **Table 3**. Tighten the crankshaft right-hand end bolt securely.

Alternator Shaft and Starter Clutch
Removal/Inspection/Installation

Refer to the illustration for your model when performing this procedure:

a. **Figure 210B**: This assembly is used on all ZX900 models and on all 1986 ZX1000 models up to engine No. 015992.
b. **Figure 210C**: This assembly is used on all 1986 and later ZX1000 models starting with engine No. 015993.

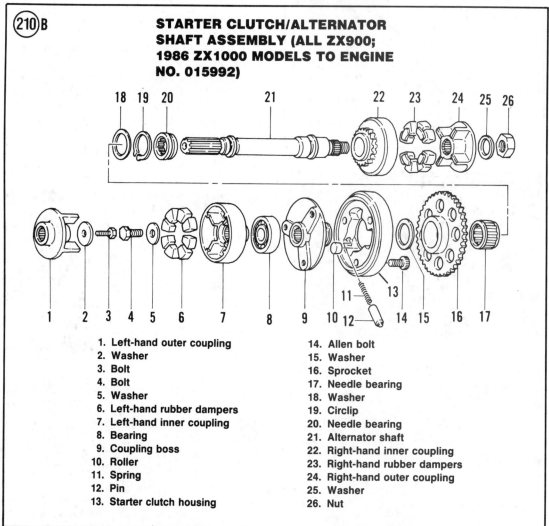

STARTER CLUTCH/ALTERNATOR SHAFT ASSEMBLY (ALL ZX900; 1986 ZX1000 MODELS TO ENGINE NO. 015992)

1. Left-hand outer coupling
2. Washer
3. Bolt
4. Bolt
5. Washer
6. Left-hand rubber dampers
7. Left-hand inner coupling
8. Bearing
9. Coupling boss
10. Roller
11. Spring
12. Pin
13. Starter clutch housing
14. Allen bolt
15. Washer
16. Sprocket
17. Needle bearing
18. Washer
19. Circlip
20. Needle bearing
21. Alternator shaft
22. Right-hand inner coupling
23. Right-hand rubber dampers
24. Right-hand outer coupling
25. Washer
26. Nut

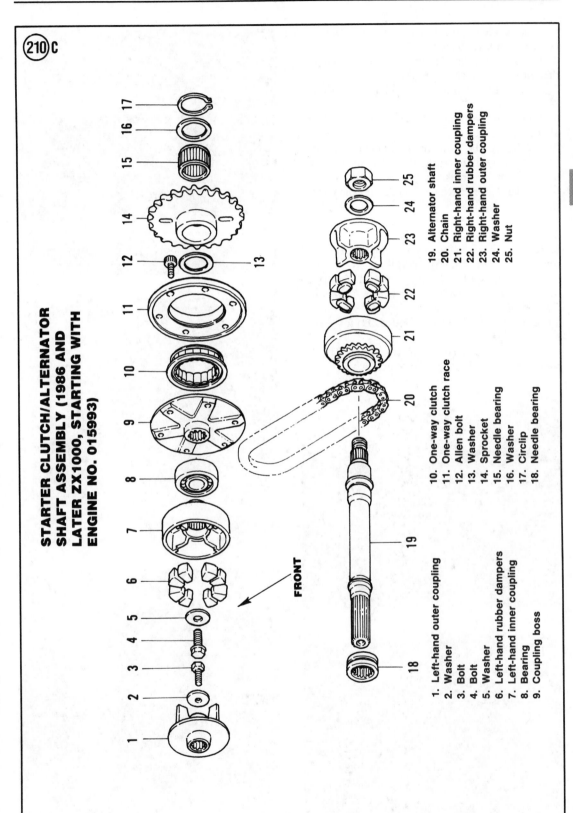

210 C

STARTER CLUTCH/ALTERNATOR SHAFT ASSEMBLY (1986 AND LATER ZX1000, STARTING WITH ENGINE NO. 015993)

1. Left-hand outer coupling
2. Washer
3. Bolt
4. Bolt
5. Washer
6. Left-hand rubber dampers
7. Left-hand inner coupling
8. Bearing
9. Coupling boss
10. One-way clutch
11. One-way clutch race
12. Allen bolt
13. Washer
14. Sprocket
15. Needle bearing
16. Washer
17. Circlip
18. Needle bearing
19. Alternator shaft
20. Chain
21. Right-hand inner coupling
22. Right-hand rubber dampers
23. Right-hand outer coupling
24. Washer
25. Nut

FRONT

4

1. Remove the engine and split the crankcase as described in this chapter.

2. Remove the rubber dampers from the coupling on the left-hand side **(Figure 211)**.

3. Remove the coupling bolt and washer **(Figure 212)**.

4. Slide the coupling **(Figure 213)** off of the alternator shaft.

5. See **Figure 214.** Hold the starter clutch assembly (A) and remove the alternator shaft (B) from the right-hand side of the crankcase.

6. Lift the starter clutch up **(Figure 215)** and remove it.

7. Remove the idler gear bolt and washer **(Figure 216)**.

8. Remove the idler gear shaft **(Figure 217)** and remove the idler gear **(Figure 218)**.

9. Inspect the starter clutch assembly as described under *Starter Clutch Disassembly/Inspection/Reassembly* in this chapter.

10. Check the idler gear (A, **Figure 219**) for gear or tooth damage.

11. Check the idler gear shaft (B, **Figure 219**) for wear, scoring or heat discoloration.

12. Check the alternator shaft **(Figure 220)**. Check the splines for severe wear or cracks. Check the bearing surfaces for deep scoring, excessive wear or heat discoloration.

13. Replace worn or damaged parts as required.

14. Check the alternator shaft crankcase bearings as described under *Crankcase Bearings Inspection/Replacement* in this chapter.

15. Install the alternator shaft and starter clutch assemblies as follows.

16. Apply engine oil onto all bearing surfaces.

17. Install the idler gear into the upper crankcase as shown in **Figure 218.** Apply clean engine oil onto the idler gear shaft and install it through the crankcase and into the idler gear **(Figure 217).**

18. Apply Loctite 242 (blue) onto the idler gear bolt. Install the bolt and washer. Tighten the bolt securely.

NOTE
The washer used with the idler gear bolt holds the idler gear shaft in place. If it is necessary to replace the bolt and washer, make sure to use identical replacement parts from Kawasaki.

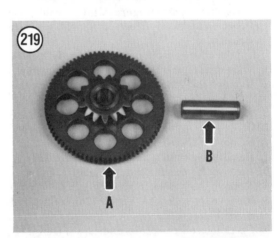

19. Place the starter clutch into the upper crankcase as shown in **Figure 215.**

20. Lift up the starter clutch (A, **Figure 214**) to engage the alternator shaft splines, then install the alternator shaft (B, **Figure 214**).

21. Align the coupling splines with the alternator shaft and install the coupling **(Figure 213).**

22. Install the coupling washer and bolt. Tighten the bolt to the torque specification in **Table 3.**

23. Install the rubber dampers **(Figure 211)** into the coupling.

24. Reassemble and install the engine as described in this chapter.

Starter Clutch (Early Models)
Disassembly/Inspection/Reassembly

Refer to **Figure 210B** for this procedure.

1. To check the starter clutch operation, perform the following:

   a. Remove the starter motor as described in Chapter Eight.

   b. Turn the idler gear by hand **(Figure 218).**

   c. When the starter clutch is operating correctly, the idler gear **(Figure 218)** should turn counterclockwise freely; it should not turn clockwise.

   d. If the idler gear did not turn correctly, remove and disassemble the starter clutch assembly.

2. Remove the starter clutch as described in this chapter.

3. Remove the starter clutch gear circlip **(Figure 221).**

4. Remove the washer **(Figure 222).**

5. Remove the starter clutch gear **(Figure 223).**

6. Remove the needle bearing **(Figure 224).**

7. Remove the washer **(Figure 225).**

8. Remove the rollers (A, **Figure 226**), springs and caps. See **Figure 227.**

9. Check the rollers, springs and caps **(Figure 227)** in the starter clutch for uneven or excessive wear. Replace as a set if any are bad.

10. Check the starter clutch Allen bolts (B, **Figure 226**) for tightness. If the bolts are loose, remove them and apply Loctite 242 (blue) to the threads. Then install the bolts and tighten to 34 N•m (25 ft.-lb.).

11. Installation is the reverse of these steps. Note the following.

12. After installing a spring and plunger **(Figure 227)** it may be difficult to install the plungers. If a plunger is difficult to install, use a piece of wire through one of the holes in the starter clutch housing to compress the spring and plunger for roller installation. See **Figure 228.**

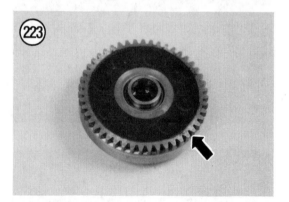

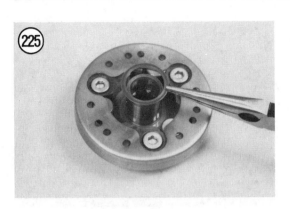

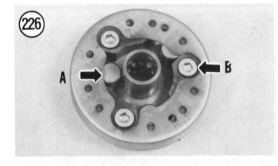

Starter Clutch (Late Models)
Disassembly/Inspection/Reassembly

Refer to **Figure 210C**.

1. Remove the 6 Allen bolts securing the one-way clutch race to the coupling boss.

2. Remove the one-way clutch race and remove the one-way clutch.

3. Check the one-way clutch rollers for pitting, roughness or other damage.

4. Check the coupling boss splines for damage.

5. Replace worn or damaged parts as required.

6. Assemble the starter clutch assembly by reversing Steps 1 and 2. Apply Loctite 242 (blue) to the 6 Allen bolt threads before installation. Tighten the bolts securely.

CRANKCASE

Service to the lower end requires that the crankcase assembly be removed from the motorcycle frame and disassembled (split).

Disassembly

1. Remove the engine as described in this chapter. Remove all exterior assemblies from the crankcase as described in this chapter and other related chapters.

2. Loosen the upper crankcase bolts (**Figure 229**) in the following order:

    a. 6 mm bolts.

    b. 8 mm bolts.

    c. Remove the bolts.

3. Turn the engine so that the bottom end faces up.

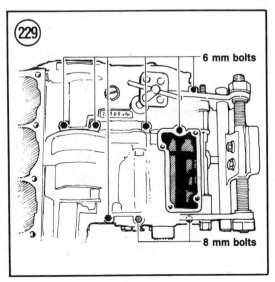

4. Remove the oil pump as described in this chapter.

5. Loosen the lower crankcase bolts (**Figure 230**) in the following order:

    a. 6 mm bolts.

    b. 8 mm bolts.

    c. Remove the bolts.

> *NOTE*
> *It is not necessary to remove the crankshaft main bearing cap and bolts (**Figure 231**) when splitting the crankcase assembly.*

6. Using the 4 pry points cast into the crankcase assembly, pry the lower crankcase (**Figure 232**) and lift it up.

> *CAUTION*
> *Do not pry the crankcase between any gasket surface. The crankcases are machined as a set; damage to one will require replacement of both.*

7. After separating the crankcase halves, the transmission and crankshaft will stay in the upper crankcase half.

8. Remove the transmission, shift forks and shift drum assemblies as described in Chapter Six.

9. Remove the crankshaft and the crankshaft bearing inserts as described in this chapter.

10. Remove the balancer shaft as described in this chapter.

11. Remove the alternator shaft and starter clutch assembly as described in this chapter.

12. Remove the 2 dowel pins from the upper crankcase (**Figure 233**).

Inspection

1. Thoroughly clean the inside and outside of both crankcase halves with cleaning solvent. Dry with

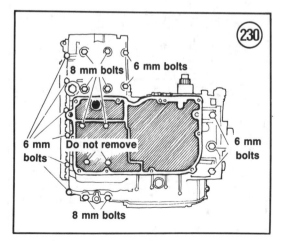

compressed air. Make sure there is no solvent residue left in the cases as it will contaminate the engine oil.

2. Make sure all oil passages are clean. Blow them out with compressed air.

3. Check the crankcases for cracks or other damage. Inspect the mating surfaces of both halves. They must be free of gouges, burrs or any damage that could cause an oil leak.

4. Inspect the crankshaft bearing inserts as described in this chapter.

5. Check the cylinder head bolt stud holes in the upper crankcase (**Figure 234**). If necessary, clean the threads with the appropriate tap. Apply kerosene to the tap before use.

6. Check the shift mechanism studs (**Figure 235**) in the lower crankcase for looseness or thread damage. Slight thread damage can be repaired with a thread file or die. If thread damage is severe, replace the damaged stud(s) as follows:

    a. Screw two 6 mm nuts onto the end of a stud as shown in **Figure 236**.

    b. With 2 wrenches, tighten the nuts against each other (**Figure 237**).

    c. Unscrew the stud with a wrench on the lower nut (**Figure 238**).

    d. Clean the tapped hole with solvent and check for thread damage. If necessary, clean the threads with a 6×1.00 tap.

    e. Remove the nuts from the old stud and install them on the end of a new stud.

    f. Tighten the nuts against each other.

    g. Apply Loctite 242 (blue) to the threads of the new stud.

    h. Screw the stud into the cylinder head with a wrench on the upper nut. Tighten the stud securely.

    i. Remove the nuts from the new stud.

4

7. Remove the gallery plugs (**Figure 239**) and flush with solvent. Allow the galley to thoroughly dry before reinstalling the plug. Install new O-rings onto the plugs. Tighten the plugs securely.

Crankcase Bearings
Inspection/Replacement

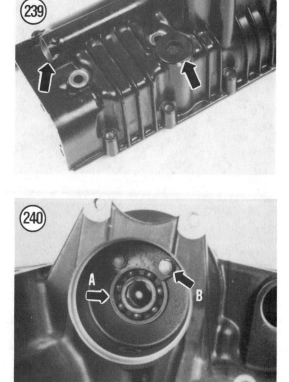

1. Turn the alternator shaft ball bearing (A, **Figure 240**). The bearing should turn smoothly and without any roughness or excessive noise.
2. Check the alternator shaft needle bearing in the crankcase for cracks, scoring, heat discoloration or loose needles.
3. If the bearings are okay, oil the races and rollers with clean engine oil. If necessary, replace the bearings as follows.
4. If the ball bearing (A, **Figure 240**) requires replacement, first remove the bearing stop plate (B, **Figure 240**).

> *NOTE*
> *If bearing replacement is required, purchase the new bearing(s) and place them in a freezer for approximately 2 hours before installation. Chilling the bearings will reduce their overall diameter while the hot crankcase is slightly larger due to heat expansion. This will make installation much easier.*

> *WARNING*
> *When heating the crankcase as described in Step 5, first wash the crankcase thoroughly in soap and water and rinse thoroughly. Make sure there are no gasoline or solvent fumes present.*

5. The bearings are installed with a slight interference fit. The crankcase must be heated to a temperature of about 212° F (100° C) in a shop oven.

> *CAUTION*
> *Do not heat the case with a torch (propane or acetylene)—never bring a flame into contact with the bearing or case. The direct heat will warp the case.*

> *WARNING*
> *Wear insulated gloves when handling heated parts.*

6. Remove the case from the oven and place onto wooden blocks.
7. Tap the bearings out of the crankcase with a block of wood or a large socket and extension.
8. Reheat the crankcase in the oven.
9. Remove the crankcase and place it on wood blocks as before.

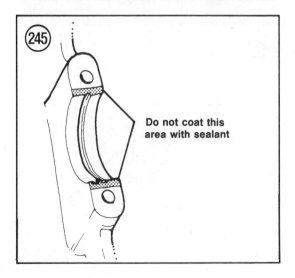

Do not coat this
area with sealant

10. Press the new bearing(s) into place in the crankcase by hand until it seats completely. Do not hammer it in. If the bearing will not seat, remove it and freeze it again. Reheat the crankcase and install the bearing again.

> *CAUTION*
> *The needle bearing should not be driven into the crankcase assembly.*

11. Install the ball bearing stop plate (B, **Figure 240**). Apply Loctite 242 (blue) onto the plate bolts before installation. Tighten the bolts securely.

Assembly

1. Prior to assembly, coat all parts with assembly oil or engine oil.
2. Install the following assemblies before assembling the crankcase assembly:
   a. Crankshaft.
   b. Balancer shaft.
   c. Transmission shafts (Chapter Six).

> *CAUTION*
> *After installing the transmission shafts, double check to make sure the transmission shaft bearings are flush with the crankcase. See **Figure 241** and **Figure 242**. If there is a gap between the bearing and crankcase, the set rings and 1/2 circlips do not engage the bearings correctly. Refer to **Transmission Installation** in Chapter Six.*

   d. Shift drum and forks (Chapter Six).
   e. Alternator shaft and starter clutch assembly.
3. Shift the transmission into NEUTRAL. The shift drum is in NEUTRAL when the neutral positioning lever (**Figure 243**) engages the detent on the shift drum bearing holder.
4. Turn the crankcase over so that the bottom end faces up. Align the dot on the balancer shaft (A, **Figure 244**) with the center of the oil passage hole (B, **Figure 244**). This alignment must be maintained when assembling the crankcase halves.
5. Make sure the case half sealing surfaces are perfectly clean and dry.
6. Install the 2 locating dowel pins. See **Figure 233**.

> *CAUTION*
> *When applying gasket sealer in Step 7, do not apply sealer around the main bearing inserts (**Figure 245**).*

7. Apply a light coat of gasket sealer to the lower crankcase half sealing surface. Cover only flat surfaces, not curved bearing surfaces. Make the

coating as thin as possible. Do not apply sealant close the edge of the bearing inserts as it would restrict oil flow and cause damage.

NOTE
Use Gasgacinch Gasket Sealer, Three Bond No. 4 or equivalent. A black colored silicone sealant (RTV) works well and blends with the black crankcases.

8. In the upper crankcase, position the shift drum into NEUTRAL. See Step 3. Position the shift forks (**Figure 246**) so that they can engage with the slots in the transmission gears (**Figure 247**) when the crankcase halves are assembled together.

CAUTION
Make sure the balancer shaft is aligned properly. See Step 4.

9. Position the lower crankcase onto the upper crankcase. Set the front portion down first and lower the rear while making sure the shift forks engage properly into the transmission assemblies.
10. Lower the crankcase completely.

CAUTION
Do not install any crankcase bolts until the sealing surface around the entire crankcase perimeter has seated completely.

11. Prior to installing the bolts, slowly spin the transmission shafts and shift the transmission through all 6 gears. This is done to check that the shift forks are properly engaged.

NOTE
*The 8 mm bolts indicated in **Figure 248** are installed with flat washers.*

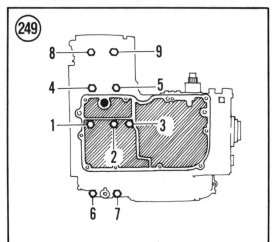

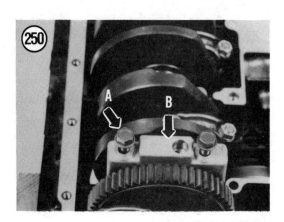

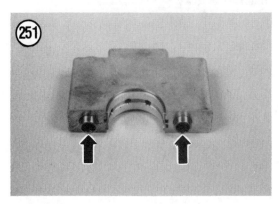

12. Apply oil to the threads of all lower crankcase bolts and install them finger-tight (**Figure 230**).

13. Tighten the 8 mm bolts in three stages by following the torque sequence shown in **Figure 249**. Tighten to the following specifications:

    a. Stage 1: Tighten all bolts finger-tight.

    b. Stage 2: Tighten all bolts to 14 N•m (10 ft.-lb.).

    c. Stage 3: Tighten all bolts to 27 N•m (20 ft.-lb.).

14. Tighten the 6 mm bolts (**Figure 230**) securely.

15. After tightening the crankcase bolts, check that the transmission shafts turn freely.

16. Turn the crankcase assembly over and install all upper crankcase bolts only finger-tight (**Figure 229**). Tighten the 8 mm bolts and then the 6 mm bolts to the torque specifications in **Table 3**.

17. Reverse Step 1 and install all engine assemblies that were removed.

18. Install the engine as described in this chapter.

CRANKSHAFT

Removal/Installation

1. Split the crankcase as described under *Crankcase Disassembly* in this chapter.

2. See **Figure 250**. Remove the crankshaft main bearing cap bolts (A) and washers and remove the cap (B).

3. Remove the 2 dowel pins (**Figure 251**) from the cap.

4. Turn the crankshaft so that the connecting rods are at top dead center and bottom dead center, then lift the crankshaft out of the crankcase (**Figure 252**).

5. Remove the crankcase main bearing inserts from the upper (**Figure 253**) and lower (**Figure 254**) crankcase halves. Mark the backsides of the inserts

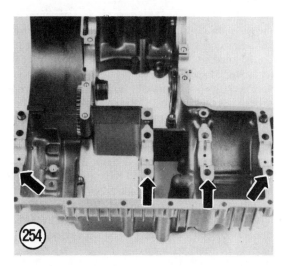

with a 1, 2, 3, 4 or 5 and U (upper) or L (lower) starting from the left-hand side, so they can be reinstalled into the same positions.

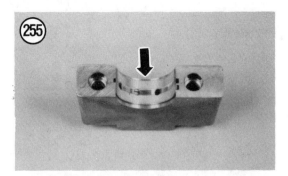

NOTE
*Don't forget to mark the bearing insert in the main bearing cap (**Figure 255**).*

6. Installation is the reverse of these steps. Note the following.
7. If new bearing inserts were installed, check the bearing clearance as described under *Crankshaft Main Bearing Clearance Measurement.*
8. Install the main bearing cap assembly (**Figure 256**) as follows:

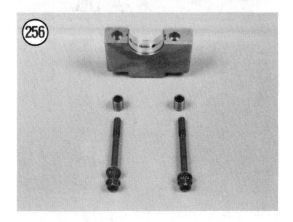

   a. Insert the bearing insert into the cap (**Figure 255**). Make sure the tab on the insert engages the notch in the bearing cap.
   b. Install the 2 dowel pins into the cap.
   c. Install the bearing cap so that the arrow on the cap faces to the front of the engine.
   d. Install the bearing cap bolts with flat washers (**Figure 256**).
   e. Lightly oil the bearing cap bolt threads.
   f. Tighten the bearing cap bolts (A, **Figure 250**) to the torque specification in **Table 3**.

Crankshaft Inspection

1. Clean crankshaft thoroughly with solvent. Clean oil holes with rifle cleaning brushes or pipe cleaners. Flush thoroughly and dry with compressed air. Lightly oil all journal and other machined surfaces immediately to prevent rust.
2. Inspect each journal (**Figure 257**) for scratches, ridges, scoring, nicks, etc.

3. If the surface on all journals is satisfactory, measure the journals with a micrometer (**Figure 258**) and check out-of-roundness, taper and wear on the journals. Check against measurements given in **Table 2**.
4. Check the drive sprocket (**Figure 259**) for worn, broken or cracked teeth. If the gear is damaged, the crankshaft will have to be replaced. If the gear is worn, also check the cam chain.
5. Check the gears on both ends of the crankshaft for worn, broken or cracked teeth. If any gear is damaged, the crankshaft will have to be replaced.
6. Place the crankshaft (**Figure 260**) on V-blocks or between centers in a lathe and check runout with a dial indicator (**Figure 260**). If the runout exceeds the service limit in **Table 2**, the crankshaft will have to be replaced.

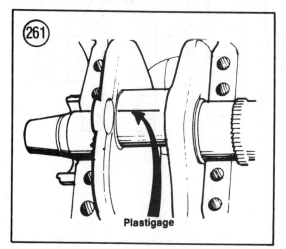

Plastigage

NOTE
If you lack the tools for this check, take the crankshaft to your Kawasaki dealer or to a machine shop.

7. Install the upper crankcase bearing inserts and the crankshaft. Measure the crankshaft side clearance by inserting a feeler gauge between the No. 2 crankcase main journal and the crankshaft machined web. Replace the crankcase assembly if the clearance exceeds the service limit in **Table 2**.

Crankshaft Main Bearing Clearance Measurement

This procedure requires the use of a Plastigage set. The crankshaft must be installed in the crankcases and the crankcases assembled. Before installation, wipe all oil residue from each bearing journal and bearing surface.

NOTE
*Plastigage can be purchased from most auto supply stores and is available in several sizes. Make sure you purchase Plastigage small enough to measure the crankshaft journal clearance as specified in **Table 2**.*

1. Check the inside and outside surfaces of the bearing inserts for wear, bluish tint (burned), flaking abrasion and scoring. If the bearings are good, they may be reused. If any insert is questionable, replace the entire set.
2. Clean the bearing surfaces of the crankshaft and the main bearing inserts.
3. Measure the main bearing clearance by performing the following steps.
4. Set the upper crankcase upside down on the workbench on wood blocks.
5. Install the existing main bearing inserts into the upper (**Figure 253**) and lower (**Figure 254**) crankcase into their original positions.
6. Install the crankshaft (**Figure 252**) into the upper crankcase.
7. Place a piece of Plastigage over each main bearing journal parallel to the crankshaft (**Figure 261**).

CAUTION
Do not rotate crankshaft while Plastigage is in place and do not place the plastigage directly over an oil hole.

8. Install the main bearing cap as described under *Crankshaft Removal/Installation* in this chapter.
9. Install the lower crankcase over the upper crankcase. Install and tighten the lower crankcase 8 mm bolts as described under *Crankcase Assembly* in this chapter.

10. Remove the 8 mm bolts in the reverse order of installation.

11. Carefully remove the lower crankcase and measure the width of the flattened Plastigage according to the manufacturer's instructions (**Figure 262**). Measure at both ends of the strip. A difference of 0.025 mm (0.001 in.) or more indicates a tapered crankpin. Confirm with a micrometer. Remove the Plastigage strips from all bearing journals.

12. New bearing clearance should be 0.020-0.044 mm (0.0007-0.0017 in.) with a service limit of 0.08 mm (0.003 in.). Remove the Plastigage strips from all bearing journals.

13. If the bearing clearance is greater than specified, use the following steps for new bearing selection.

14. If the bearing clearance is between 0.044 mm (0.0017 in.) and 0.08 mm (0.003 in.), replace the bearing inserts with factory inserts painted blue

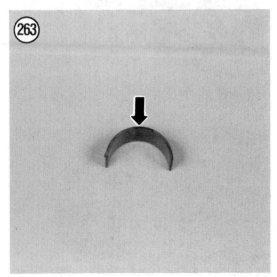

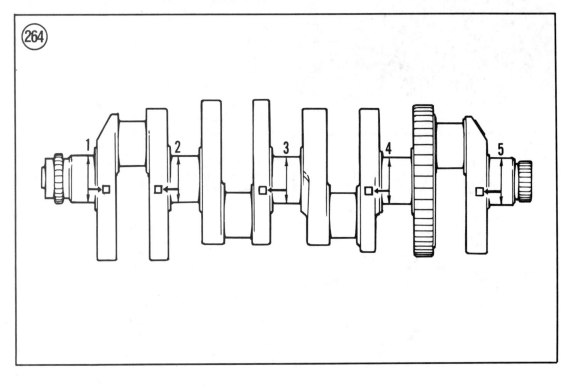

and recheck the bearing clearance. Always replace all 10 inserts at the same time. The clearance may exceed 0.044 mm (0.0017 in.) slightly but it must not be less than the minimum clearance of 0.020 mm (0.0007 in.) or bearing seizure will occur.

NOTE
Bearing inserts are color-coded at the point shown in **Figure 263**.

15. If the bearing clearance exceeds the service limit, measure the crankshaft journal OD with a micrometer (**Figure 258**). See **Table 2** for specifications. If any journal exceeds the wear limit, replace the crankshaft.

16. If the crankshaft has been replaced, determine new bearing inserts as follows:

a. Purchase a new crankshaft. Then cross-reference the main journal crankshaft diameter markings (**Figure 264**) with the upper crankcase half marks (**Figure 265**). Record

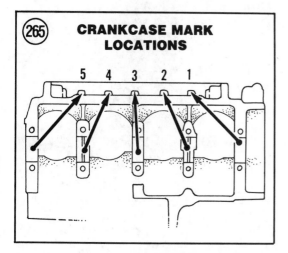

CRANKCASE MARK LOCATIONS

5 4 3 2 1

these marks and cross-reference them with **Table 4** for new crankshaft main bearing insert selection.

b. Recheck the clearance with the new inserts and crankshaft. The clearance should be less than the service limit and as close to the standard as possible, but not less than the standard.

NOTE
If the main bearing clearance is incorrect after performing Step 16, remove all bearing inserts from the crankcases and the main bearing cap. Then assemble the bearing cap and crankcases. Install all case bolts and tighten to the torque specifications in **Table 3**. *With a bore gauge, measure each bearing bore diameter and compare to the crankcase main bearing bore diameter marks in* **Figure 265**. *If a bearing bore is marked with a "0", the diameter should be 39.000-39.008 mm (1.5354-1.5357 in.); if a bearing bore does not have a "0" mark the bore diameter should be 39.009-39.016 mm (1.5358-1.5360 in.). If the bore diameters on your crankcases differ from these specifications, it will be necessary to substitute bearing inserts until the correct clearance is obtained.*

17. Clean and oil the main bearing journals and insert faces.

CONNECTING RODS

Removal/Installation

CAUTION
The connecting rod bolts on ZX1000 models are designed to stretch when tightened. These bolts must be replaced whenever the connecting rods are removed from the crankshaft. Do not install used bolts.

1. Remove the engine as described in this chapter.
2. Split the crankcase and remove the crankshaft as described in this chapter.
3. Measure the connecting rod big end side clearance. Insert a feeler gauge between a connecting rod big end and either crankshaft machined web (**Figure 266**). Record the clearance for each connecting rod and compare to the specifications in **Table 2**. If the clearance is excessive, replace the connecting rod(s) and recheck clearance. If clearance is still excessive, replace the crankshaft.

NOTE
*Before disassembly, mark the rods and caps with a "1", "2", "3" and "4" starting from the left-hand side (**Figure 267**).*

4. Remove the connecting rod cap nuts (**Figure 268**) and separate the rods from the crankshaft (**Figure 269**). Keep each cap with its original rod, with the weight mark on the end of the cap matching the mark on the rod (**Figure 270**).

NOTE
*Some rods do not have a diameter mark at the point indicated in **Figure 270**. If there is no mark, draw a line across the big end cap and connecting rod with an indelible pen to indicate alignment.*

NOTE
*Keep each bearing insert (**Figure 271**) in its original place in the crankcase, rod or rod cap. If you are going to assemble the engine with the original inserts, they must be installed exactly as removed in order to prevent rapid wear.*

5. Install by reversing these removal steps. Note the following procedures.

6. *ZX1000:* Perform the following to install new connecting rod bolts (**Figure 272**):

  a. The new connecting rod bolts and nuts are coated with an anti-rust material. Clean the bolts thoroughly in a strong solvent to remove all anti-rust residue.

  b. Dry the bolts thoroughly after cleaning.

  c. Install the new bolts into the connecting rod (**Figure 272**).

7. Install the bearing inserts into each connecting rod and cap. Make sure the bearing tabs are locked in place correctly. See **Figure 273**.

8. Apply engine oil to the bearing inserts.

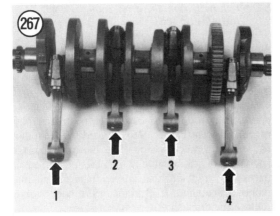

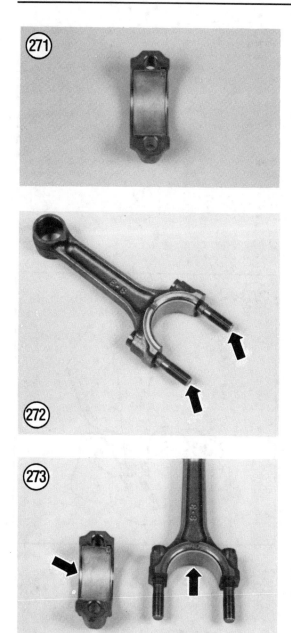

9. If new bearing inserts are going to be installed, check the bearing clearance as described in this chapter.

10. The 2 left- and 2 right-hand rods are matched (same weight) to reduce vibration. If replacing connecting rods, make sure to match weights.

11A. *ZX900:* Tighten the connecting rod nuts (**Figure 268**) to torque specifications in **Table 3**.

11B. *ZX1000:* Perform the following when tightening the connecting rod bolts:

  a. Apply engine oil to the connecting rod bolt threads and to the nut seating surface.

  b. Tighten the connecting rod nuts (**Figure 268**) to the torque specification in **Table 3**.

  c. To complete connecting rod assembly, each bolt must be turned an additional 120°. Referring to **Figure 274**, mark each connecting rod bolt so that it can be turned accurately. Then turn each connecting rod nut 120°. Do not turn the nuts past the 120° mark.

  d. Referring to **Figure 275**, measure the exposed length of each connecting rod bolt. If the length exceeds 0.8 mm (0.031 in.), the bolt has stretched too far. Replace the bolt and nut.

WARNING
A bolt that is excessively stretched may break during engine operation and cause extensive engine damage. This could cause engine lockup and result in loss of control of the motorcycle.

Connecting Rod Inspection

1. Check each rod for obvious damage such as cracks and burns.

2. Check the small end bore for wear or scoring.

3. Take the rods to a machine shop and have them checked for twisting and bending.

4. Examine the bearing inserts (**Figure 273**) for wear, scoring or burning. They are reusable if in

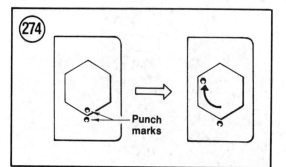

Punch marks

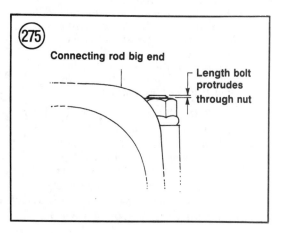

Connecting rod big end

Length bolt protrudes through nut

good condition. Make a note of the bearing color marked on the side of the insert (**Figure 263**).

5. Check the connecting small end (**Figure 276**) for heat discoloration.

6A. *ZX900:* Remove the connecting rod bearing bolts and check them for cracks or twisting. Replace any bolts as required.

6B. *ZX1000:* Discard all connecting rod bearing bolts and nuts. Refer to *Connecting Rod Removal/Installation* for replacement information. New connecting rod bolts must be installed during reassembly.

7. Check bearing clearance as described in this chapter.

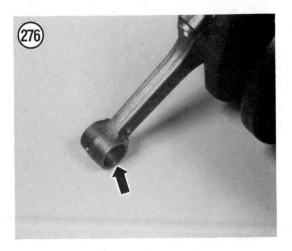

Connecting Rod Bearing and Clearance Measurement

This procedure requires the use of Plastigage. The connecting rods must be installed on the crankshaft. Before installation, wipe all oil residue from each bearing journal and bearing surface.

> *NOTE*
> *Plastigage can be purchased from most auto supply stores and is available in several sizes. Make sure you purchase Plastigage small enough to measure the connecting rod bearing clearance as specified in* **Table 2**.

> *CAUTION*
> *If the old bearings are to be reused, be sure that they are installed in their exact original locations.*

1. Wipe bearing inserts and crankpins clean. Install bearing inserts in rod and cap.

2. Place a piece of Plastigage on one crankpin parallel to the crankshaft. Avoid placing the Plastigage over an oil hole.

> *NOTE*
> *On ZX1000 models, perform this procedure with the old connecting rod bolts. After the bearing clearance has been determined and the new inserts selected, install new connecting rod bolts as described under* **Connecting Rod Removal/Installation**.

3A. *ZX900:* Install the rod and cap. Tighten nuts to the torque specifications in **Table 3**.

3B. *ZX1000:* Perform the following when tightening the connecting rod bolts:

    a. Apply engine oil to the connecting rod bolt threads and to the nut seating surface.

    b. Tighten the connecting rod nuts (**Figure 268**) to the torque specification in **Table 3**.

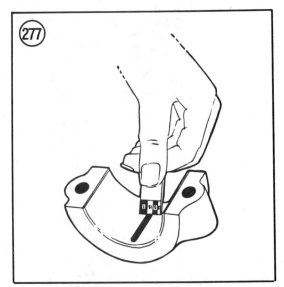

c. Referring to **Figure 274**, mark each connecting rod nut so that it can be turned 120°. Then tighten each connecting rod nut 120°. Do not tighten the nuts past the 120° mark.

> *CAUTION*
> *Do not rotate crankshaft while Plastigage is in place.*

4. Remove the rod cap.

5. Measure width of flattened Plastigage according to the manufacturer's instructions (**Figure 277**). Measure at both ends of the strip. A difference of 0.025 mm (0.001 in.) or more indicates a tapered crankpin. The crankshaft must be replaced. Confirm with a micrometer measurement of the journal OD (**Figure 278**).

6. If the crankpin taper is within tolerance, measure the bearing clearance with the same strip of Plastigage. Correct bearing clearance is specified in **Table 2**. Remove Plastigage strips.

7. If the bearing clearance is greater than specified, use the following steps for new bearing selection.

8. New bearing clearance should be 0.036-0.066 mm (0.0014-0.0026 in.) with a service limit of 0.10 mm (0.0.0039 in.). Remove the Plastigage strips from all bearing journals.

9. If the bearing clearance is greater than specified, use the following steps for new bearing selection.

10. If the bearing clearance is between 0.066 mm (0.0026 in.) and 0.10 mm (0.0039 in.), replace the bearing inserts with factory inserts painted blue and recheck the bearing clearance. Always replace all 8 inserts at the same time. The clearance may exceed 0.066 mm (0.0026 in.) slightly but it must not be less than the minimum clearance of 0.036 mm (0.0014 in.) or bearing seizure will occur.

11. If the bearing clearance exceeds the service limit, measure the crankshaft journal OD with a micrometer (**Figure 278**). See **Table 2** for specifications. If any journal exceeds the wear limit, replace the crankshaft.

12. If the crankshaft has been replaced, determine new bearing inserts as follows:

a. Purchase a new crankshaft. Then cross-reference the crankpin journal diameter markings (**Figure 279**) with the connecting rod mark (**Figure 270**). The connecting rod will either be marked with a "0" around the weight mark or there will be no "0" around the weight mark. Refer to **Table 5** and cross-reference the crankpin diameter markings (**Figure 279**) and the connecting rod marks (**Figure 270**).

b. Recheck the clearance with the new inserts and crankshaft. The clearance should be less than the service limit and as close to the standard as possible, but not less than the standard.

13. Clean and oil the main bearing journals and insert faces.

14. After new bearings have been installed, recheck clearance with Plastigage. If the clearance is still out of specifications, either the connecting rod or the crankshaft is worn beyond the service limit. Refer the engine to a dealer or qualified specialist.

4

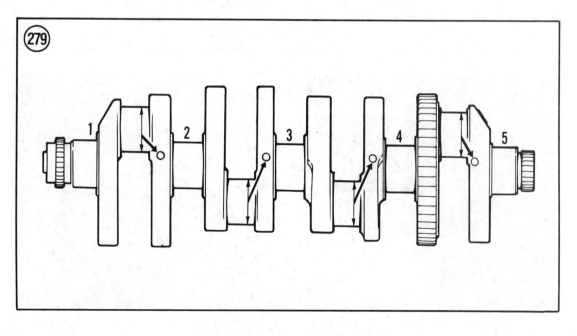

(279)

BALANCER SHAFT

Removal

Refer to **Figure 280** for this procedure.
1. Split the crankcase as described in this chapter.
2. Remove the balancer lever pinch bolt and remove the lever (**Figure 281**).
3. Remove the bolt and remove the balancer shaft guide pin plate (**Figure 282**).
4. Remove the balancer shaft guide pin (**Figure 283**).
5. Pull the balancer shaft (with oil seal attached) out of the crankcase (**Figure 284**).

6. Lift the weight assembly and the 2 washers (**Figure 285**) out of the crankcase. See **Figure 286**.

Disassembly/Inspection/Reassembly

Refer to **Figure 280** for this procedure.
1. Disassemble the balancer shaft assembly in the order shown in **Figure 287**.
2. Clean all parts in solvent and allow to thoroughly dry.
3. Check the balancer shaft (**Figure 288**) for cracks, deep scoring, excessive wear or heat discoloration. Make sure the oil holes in the shaft are clear of all debris.

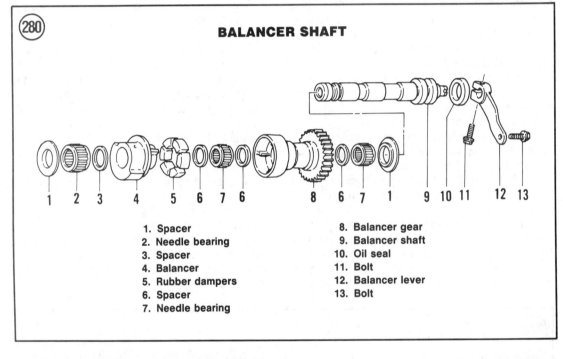

BALANCER SHAFT

1. Spacer
2. Needle bearing
3. Spacer
4. Balancer
5. Rubber dampers
6. Spacer
7. Needle bearing
8. Balancer gear
9. Balancer shaft
10. Oil seal
11. Bolt
12. Balancer lever
13. Bolt

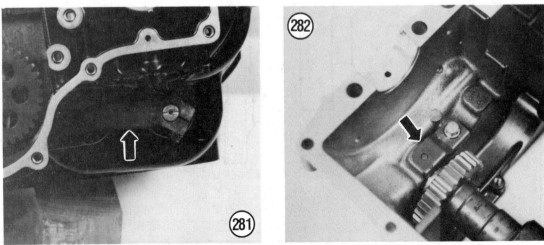

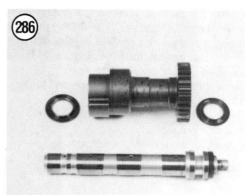

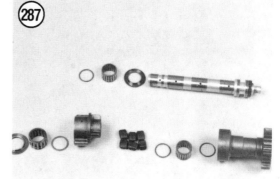

4

4. Replace the balancer shaft oil seal (**Figure 289**).

5. Check the needle bearings (**Figure 290**) for loose or damaged needles or a cracked needle cage.

6. Check the copper washers (**Figure 291**) for cracks, deep scoring or excessive wear.

7. Check the rubber dampers (**Figure 292**) for age deterioration or cracks.

8. Check the balancer gear (**Figure 293**) for cracked or worn teeth.

9. Replace all worn or damaged parts.

10. Assemble the balancer weight assembly as follows.

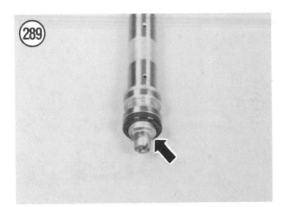

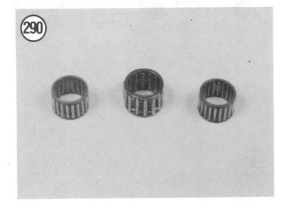

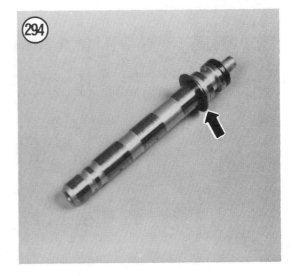

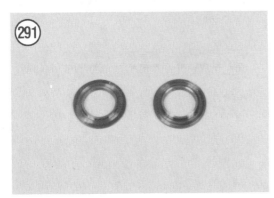

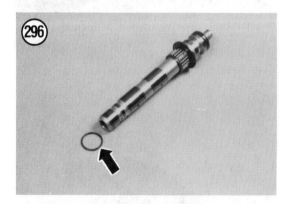

NOTE
It will be easier to assemble the balancer weight assembly if the parts are assembled over the balancer shaft. When the weight assembly is complete, the balancer shaft will be removed.

11. Install the copper washer (**Figure 294**) onto the balancer shaft. The shoulder on the washer must face away from the oil seal.

12. There are 2 different sizes of needle bearings. The largest needle bearing (**Figure 290**) is installed in the middle of the shaft. Install one of the small needle bearings (**Figure 295**) onto the shaft and slide it next to the washer.

13. Install the washer (**Figure 296**).

14. Install the gear assembly (**Figure 297**) onto the balancer shaft.

15. See **Figure 298**. Install the following parts in order:

    a. Washer (A).

    b. Large needle bearing (B).

    c. Washer (C).

16. With the balancer shaft upright, install the 6 rubber dampers (**Figure 299**). Make sure the dampers fit into the housing as shown in **Figure 300**.

17. See **Figure 301**. Align the dot on the weight with the mark on the gear assembly and install the weight. See **Figure 302**.

18. Install the washer (**Figure 303**).

19. Install the remaining small needle bearing (**Figure 304**).

20. Install the copper washer (**Figure 305**). The shoulder on the washer must face toward the needle bearing and fit flush next to the weight assembly (**Figure 306**).

21. See **Figure 307**. Hold onto the washers (A) and withdraw the balancer shaft (B) from the weight assembly.

Installation

1. Set the weight assembly (with the copper washers) (**Figure 308**) into the crankcase. See **Figure 285**.

2. Oil the balancer shaft bearing surfaces.

3. Insert the balancer shaft through the crankcase and into the weight assembly (**Figure 284**). Insert the shaft until it bottoms out.

4. Install the guide pin through the crankcase and into the balancer shaft slot. Install the guide pin so that the end with the point faces up (**Figure 309**).

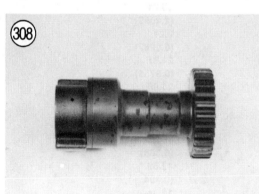

5. Install the guide pin plate. Make sure the hole in the plate engages the point on the pin (**Figure 282**). Apply Loctite 242 (blue) onto the plate mounting bolt and tighten the bolt securely.

6. See **Figure 310**. Turn the balancer shaft (**Figure 284**) so that the mark on the end of the shaft points to the front. Then install the clamp lever so that the mark on the lever aligns with the balancer shaft mark as shown in **Figure 310**.

7. After the engine is assembled, perform the *Balancer Shaft Gear Backlash Check* in this chapter.

Balancer Shaft Gear Backlash Check

Adjust the balancer shaft when the engine is cold. Refer to **Figure 310** and **Figure 311**.

1. Start the engine and allow to idle.

2. Loosen the clamp bolt and turn the balancer shaft counterclockwise until the balancer shaft gear makes a noise.

3. Slowly turn the balancer shaft clockwise until the balancer gear noise stops. Tighten the clamp bolt securely.

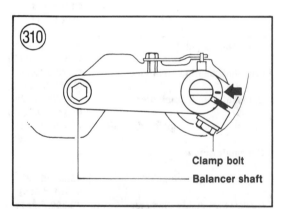

Clamp bolt
Balancer shaft

Table 1 GENERAL ENGINE INFORMATION

Engine type	4-stroke, DOHC, 4-cylinder
Cooling system	Liquid cooled
Bore and stroke	
ZX900	72.5×55 mm (2.85×2.16 in.)
ZX1000	74×58 mm (2.91×2.28 in.)
Compression ratio	
ZX900	11.0
ZX1000	10.2
Cylinder alignment	Left to right, 1-2-3-4
Firing order	1-2-4-3
Valve timing	
ZX900	
Intake opens	45° BTDC
Intake closes	65° ABDC
Exhaust opens	65° BBDC
Exhaust closes	45° ATDC
ZX1000	
Intake opens	40° BTDC
Intake closes	70° ABDC
Exhaust opens	65° BBDC
Exhaust closes	45° ATDC

Table 2 ENGINE SPECIFICATIONS

	Standard mm (in.)	Wear limit mm (in.)
Cam lobe height	35.824-35.940 (1.4104-1.4149)	35.71 (1.4059)
Camshaft bearing clearance	0.078-0.121 (0.003-0.0047)	0.21 (0.0082)
Camshaft journal diameter	24.900-24.922 (0.9803-0.9812)	24.87 (0.9791)
Camshaft bearing inside diameter	25.000-25.021 (0.9843-0.9851)	25.08 (0.9874)
Camshaft runout	—	0.1 (0.0039)
Camshaft chain (20 links)	158.8-159.2 (6.252-6.268)	161.5 (6.358)
Rocker arm inside diameter	12.500-12.518 (0.4921-0.4928)	12.55 (0.4941)
Rocker arm shaft diameter	12.466-12.484 (0.4907-0.4915)	12.44 (0.4897)
Cylinder diameter		
ZX900	72.494-72.506 (2.8540-2.8547)	72.60 (2.8583)
ZX1000	73.994-74.006 (2.9131-2.9136)	74.11 (2.9177)
Piston diameter		
ZX900	72.435-72.450 (2.8518-2.8523)	72.30 (2.8464)
ZX1000	73.935-73.964 (2.9108-2.9119)	73.79 (2.9051)
Piston-to-cylinder clearance	0.044-0.071 (0.0017-0.0028)	

(continued)

Table 2 ENGINE SPECIFICATIONS (continued)

	Standard mm (in.)	Wear limit mm (in.)
Piston ring groove clearance		
Top	0.03-0.07 (0.0012-0.0027)	0.17 (0.007)
Second	0.02-0.06 (0.0007-0.0024)	0.16 (0.006)
Piston ring groove width		
Top	1.02-1.04 (0.040-0.041)	1.12 (0.044)
Second	1.01-1.03 (0.039-0.041)	1.12 (0.044)
Oil	2.51-2.53 (0.098-0.099)	2.6 (0.102)
Piston ring thickness		
Top and second	0.97-0.99 (0.038-0.039)	0.9 (0.035)
Piston ring end gap		
Top and second	0.2-0.35 (0.008-0.014)	0.7 (0.028)
Oil	0.2-0.7 (0.008-0.028)	1.0 (0.394)
Cylinder head warpage		0.05 (0.002)
Valve head margin thickness		
Intake	0.05 (0.0197)	0.25 (0.010)
Exhaust	1.0 (0.0394)	0.7 (0.028)
Valve stem runout		0.05 (0.002)
Valve stem diameter		
Intake	5.475-5.490 (0.2155-0.2161)	5.46 (0.215)
Exhaust	5.455-5.470 (0.2147-0.2154)	5.44 (0.214)
Valve guide inside diameter	5.500-5.512 (0.2165-0.2170)	5.58 (0.2197)
Valve-to-valve guide clearance (wobble method)		
Intake	0.02-0.08 (0.0007-0.0031)	0.22 (0.0087)
Exhaust	0.07-0.14 (0.0027-0.0055)	0.27 (0.0106)
Valve spring free length		
Inner	36.3 (1.429)	35.0 (1.378)
Outer	40.4 (1.591)	39.0 (1.535)
Valve seat surface		
Outside diameter		
Intake	28.3-28.5 (1.114-1.122)	
Exhaust	24.0-24.2 (0.945-0.953)	
Width (intake and exhaust)	0.5-1.0 (0.0196-0.039)	

(continued)

4

Table 2 ENGINE SPECIFICATIONS (continued)

	Standard mm (in.)	Wear limit mm (in.)
Valve spring tilt		1.5 (0.059)
Connecting rod side clearance	0.13-0.33 (0.005-0.013)	0.50 (0.019)
Connecting rod bearing clearance		
ZX900	0.036-0.066 (0.0014-0.0026)	0.10 (0.0039)
ZX1000	0.046-0.076 (0.0018-0.0029)	0.11 (0.0043)
Crankpin diameter		
Identification mark		
0	34.993-35.000 (1.3776-1.3779)	34.97 (1.3767)
No mark	34.984-34.992 (1.3773-1.3776)	34.97 (1.3767)
Crankshaft runout		0.05 (0.0019)
Crankshaft journal clearance	0.020-0.044 (0.0007-0.0017)	0.08 (0.0031)
Crankshaft main journal diameter		
Identification mark		
1	35.993-36.000 (1.4170-1.4173)	35.96 (1.4157)
No mark	35.984-35.992 (1.4167-1.4170)	35.96 (1.4157)
Crankcase main bearing bore diameter		
Identification mark		
0	39.000-39.008 (1.5354-1.5357)	
No mark	39.009-39.016 (1.5358-1.5360)	
Crankshaft side clearance	0.05-0.07 (0.0019-0.0078)	0.40 (0.016)

Table 3 ENGINE TIGHTENING TORQUES

	N·m	ft.-lb.
Cylinder head cover	9.8	7.2
Upper chain guide bolts	9.8	7.2
Rear chain guide bolts *	20	14.5
Chain tensioner bolts	9.8	7.2
Camshaft sprocket bolts*	15	11
Valve adjusting screw locknuts	25	18
Rocker arm shaft Allen bolts	9.8	7.2
Main oil pipe banjo bolts	25	18
Cylinder head oil pipe banjo bolts		
White		
ZX900	9.8	7.2
ZX1000	7.8	5.8
Black	9.8	7.2
Camshaft cap bolts	12	9
Cylinder head bolts	See text	
Cylinder bolts	15	11
Cylinder drain bolts	7.8	5.8

(continued)

Table 3 ENGINE TIGHTENING TORQUES (continued)

	N·m	ft.-lb.
Connecting rod cap nuts		
ZX900	36	27
ZX1000	26	19.5
Rotor bolt	25	18
Alternator shaft		
Left end bolt	25	18
Right end nut	59	43
Alternator coupling blades bolt	9.8	7.2
Alternator one-way clutch bolts*	34	25
Crankshaft main bearing cap bolts	27	20
Crankcase bolts		
6 mm	15	11
8 mm	27	20
Neutral switch	15	11
Engine sprocket nut	98	72
Lower crankcase 25 mm dia. plug	18	13
Crankcase outside oil pipe banjo bolts		
ZX900	25	18
ZX1000	18	13
Oil pump mounting bolts*	12	9
Oil pressure switch	15	11
Oil pan bolts	See text	
Oil cooler pipe banjo bolts		
Oil pan side	34	25
Oil cooler side	25	18
Oil filter bolt	20	14.5
Engine mounting nuts and bolts (ZX900)	59	43
Engine mounting nuts (ZX1000)		
Front	44	33
Rear	52	38
Down tube mounting bolts (ZX1000)	52	38

* Apply Loctite 242 (blue) to bolt threads before installation.

Table 4 CRANKSHAFT MAIN BEARING SELECTION

Crankcase bore mark	Crankshaft main journal Diameter mark	Insert color	Journal number
0	1	Brown	2, 4
0	1	Brown	1, 3, 5
None	None	Blue	2, 4
None	None	Blue	1, 3, 5
0	None	Black	2, 4
None	1	Black	1, 3, 5

Table 5 CONNECTING ROD BEARING SELECTION

Connecting rod mark	Crankpin diameter mark	Insert color
0	0	Black
None	None	Black
0	None	Blue
None	0	Brown

NOTE: If you own a 1988 or later model, first check the Supplement at the back of this book for any new service information.

CLUTCH

This chapter provides complete service procedures for the clutch and the clutch release mechanism.

The clutch is a wet-multi-plate type which operates immersed in engine oil. It is mounted on the right-hand side of the transmission mainshaft. The clutch can be serviced with the engine in the frame.

The clutch hydraulic release mechanism consists of the clutch lever, master cylinder, hydraulic clutch line and slave cylinder. When the clutch lever is pulled, the piston in the master cylinder moves and pressurizes hydraulic fluid in the clutch line. The pressurized fluid moves against the slave cylinder piston to push the clutch pushrod and disengage the clutch.

With a hydraulic clutch assembly, no periodic clutch adjustment is required. Normally, clutch adjustment is required due to clutch cable stretch and friction plate wear. However, no cable is used with a hydraulic system. As the friction plates wear, the slave cylinder piston is extended beyond the elastic limit of its seal. The seal slips slightly which allows the piston to move to a new position. This compensates for the difference in plate wear and the clutch lever stroke remains unchanged.

Table 1 and **Table 2** (end of chapter) lists clutch specifications.

CLUTCH COVER
(ALL MODELS)

Removal/Installation

1. Remove the lower fairing. See Chapter Thirteen.

2. Drain the engine oil as described under *Engine Oil and Filter Change* in Chapter Three.

3. Remove the bolts securing the clutch cover (**Figure 1**) in place and remove it and the gasket.

NOTE
If the clutch cover is tight, tap it lightly with a plastic tipped hammer to break the gasket seal. Do not pry the cover off or the crankcase and cover mating surfaces may be damaged and cause an oil leak.

4. If the gasket tears when removing the cover, use a single-edge razor blade in a holder or a gasket scraper and remove all gasket residue from the crankcase and cover mating surfaces. Make sure the mating surfaces are not cut as this may cause engine oil leakage. If the torn gasket is difficult to remove in some spots, apply a small amount of gasket remover onto a small metal brush and scrub the gasket off. Because gasket remover will also remove engine paint, do not use an excessive amount or spray the remover directly onto the engine or cover. Read the instructions on the gasket remover can before use.

5. See **Figure 2**. Check the oil pipe (A) in the clutch cover for a loose banjo bolt (B) or mounting screw (C). If the engine is being rebuilt or if the engine oil appeared dirty and contaminated, remove the banjo bolt (B) and blow compressed air through the oil pipe. Replace the oil pipe if damaged or severely contaminated. Tighten the banjo bolt securely after service.

6. The metal plate (**Figure 3**) held in the clutch cover by the 5 Phillips screws is a cover for a sound

damper. The metal plate and sound damper are non-wearing items. Whenever the clutch cover is removed, check that the Phillips screws are tight. If the screws are loose, remove each screw and reinstall with a drop of Loctite 242 (blue) applied to each screw thread. Tighten the screws securely.

7. Installation is the reverse of these steps. Note the following.

8. Install a new clutch cover gasket. Because there are no dowel pins used on the clutch cover, insert 2 bolts through the clutch cover and install the gasket on the cover. The bolts will hold the gasket in place when installing the cover.

CAUTION
If the clutch cover gasket is not aligned properly, it may become damaged when installing a bolt and leak.

9. Apply a small amount of RTV sealant onto the clutch cover gasket where it mates against the crankcase split line.

10. Apply Loctite 242 (blue) onto the 4 clutch cover bolts indicated in **Figure 4**.

NOTE
When installing the cover bolts, check that each one sticks up the same amount before you screw them all in. If

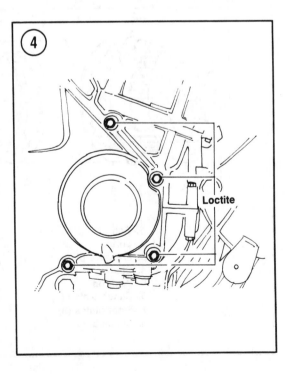

*not, you've got a short bolt in a long
hole or vice versa.*

11. Install the remaining clutch cover bolts and
tighten securely.

12. Refill the engine oil as described under *Engine
Oil and Filter Change* in Chapter Three.

CLUTCH (ZX900)

The clutch is installed behind the clutch cover
on the right-hand side. Refer to **Figure 5** when
performing procedures in this section.

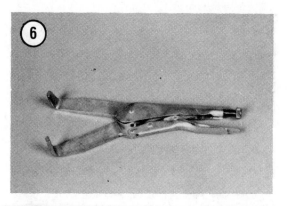

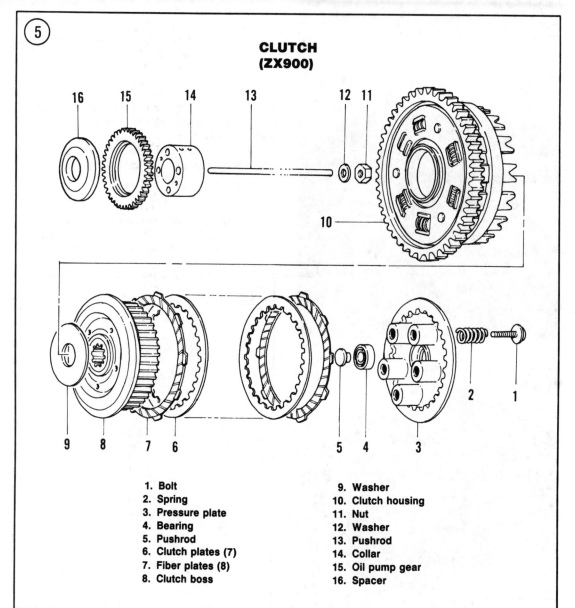

**CLUTCH
(ZX900)**

1. Bolt
2. Spring
3. Pressure plate
4. Bearing
5. Pushrod
6. Clutch plates (7)
7. Fiber plates (8)
8. Clutch boss
9. Washer
10. Clutch housing
11. Nut
12. Washer
13. Pushrod
14. Collar
15. Oil pump gear
16. Spacer

Removal

The following special tool and overhaul part will be required when removing and installing the clutch:

    a. Universal clutch holding tool (**Figure 6**).
    b. Clutch nut.

NOTE
The clutch nut is a self-locking type. Kawasaki recommends replacing the clutch nut whenever it is removed.

1. Remove the clutch cover as described in this chapter.
2. Loosen the 5 pressure plate bolts (**Figure 7**) in a crisscross pattern. Then remove the bolts and washers.
3. Remove the pressure plate springs (**Figure 8**).
4. Remove the pressure plate (**Figure 9**).
5. Remove a friction (fiber) plate (**Figure 10**) and a clutch plate (**Figure 11**). Continue until all plates are removed. Stack plates in order.
6. Install a universal clutch holding tool (A, **Figure 12**) onto the clutch boss to prevent it and the transmission mainshaft from turning when loosening the clutch nut (B, **Figure 12**).

5

7. Loosen the clutch nut by turning it counterclockwise. Remove the clutch nut (**Figure 13**).

8. Remove the washer (**Figure 14**).

9. Slide the clutch boss (**Figure 15**) off of the mainshaft.

10. Remove the large flat washer (**Figure 16**).

11. Install one of the clutch cover bolts into the collar as shown in A, **Figure 17** and pull the collar (B) off of the mainshaft.

NOTE
To prevent installing the clutch collar backwards, leave the bolt installed into the collar until reassembly.

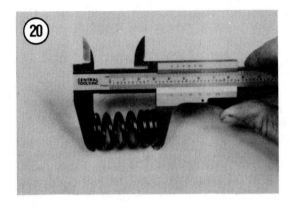

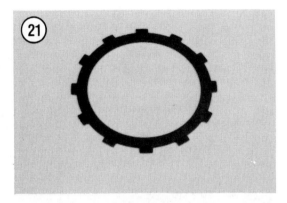

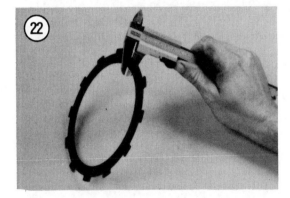

12. Remove the clutch housing (**Figure 18**) and the oil pump drive gear.

13. Remove the tapered washer (A, **Figure 19**).

14. Remove the pushrod (B, **Figure 19**) by pulling it out of the mainshaft.

Inspection

1. Clean all clutch parts in a petroleum-based solvent such as kerosene, and thoroughly dry with compressed air.

2. Measure the free length of each clutch spring as shown in **Figure 20**. Replace any springs that are too short (**Table 1**).

3. The stock ZX900 clutch uses 8 friction plates (**Figure 21**). The friction material is made of cork that is bonded onto an aluminum plate for warp resistance and durability. Measure the thickness of each friction plate at several places around the disc with a vernier caliper (**Figure 22**). See **Table 1** for specifications. Replace all 8 friction plates if any one is found too thin. Do not replace only 1 or 2 plates.

4. The stock ZX900 clutch uses 7 clutch metal plates (**Figure 23**). Place each clutch metal plate on a surface plate or a thick piece of glass and check for warpage with a feeler gauge as shown in **Figure 24**. If any plate is warped more than specified (**Table 1**), replace the entire set of plates. Do not replace only 1 or 2 plates.

> *CAUTION*
> *If the clutch was damaged by excessive abuse (drag racing, excessive slipping or road racing), there is a good chance that clutch particles have been spread throughout the lubrication system. In such cases, the inside of the engine should be cleaned as thoroughly as possible. Especially important are the oil pump pickup, oil pump and all oil lines. Failure to clean these areas after severe clutch damage can lead to engine failure.*

5

5. The clutch metal plate inner teeth (**Figure 23**) mesh with the clutch boss splines (A, **Figure 25**). Check the splines for cracks or galling. They must be smooth for chatter-free clutch operation. If the clutch boss splines are worn, check the clutch metal plate teeth for wear or damage.

6. Inspect the shaft splines (B, **Figure 25**) in the clutch boss assembly. If damage is only a slight amount, remove any small burrs with a fine cut file. If damage is severe, replace the assembly.

7. Inspect the clutch boss bolt studs (C, **Figure 25**) for thread damage or cracks at the base of the studs. Thread damage may be repaired with a M6×1 metric tap. Use kerosene on the tap threads. If a bolt stud is cracked, the clutch boss must be replaced.

8. Push the clutch release bearing and pushrod (**Figure 26**) out of the pressure plate. Rotate the bearing race (**Figure 27**) by hand and check for excessive play or roughness. Replace the bearing if necessary.

9. Inspect the pressure plate (**Figure 28**) for signs of damage or warpage. Check the release bearing bore (A) for cracks or damage. Check the spring towers (B) for cracks or damage. Check the pressure plate teeth (C) where they engage the clutch boss for cracks or damage. Replace the pressure plate if necessary.

10. The friction plates (**Figure 21**) have tabs that slide in the clutch housing grooves (**Figure 29**). Inspect the tabs for cracks or galling in the grooves. They must be smooth for chatter-free clutch operation. Light damage can be repaired with an oilstone. Replace the clutch housing if damage is severe.

11. Check clutch housing bearing bore (**Figure 30**) for cracks, deep scoring, excessive wear or heat

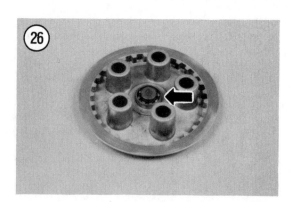

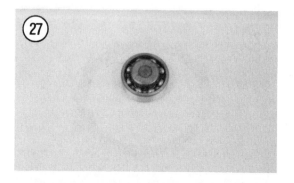

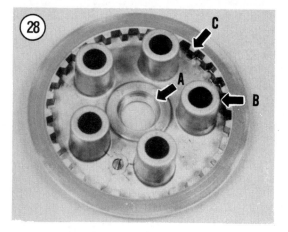

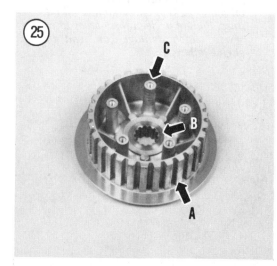

discoloration. If the bearing bore is damaged, also check the clutch collar for damage. Replace worn or damaged parts.

12. Check the clutch housing driven gear (**Figure 31**) for tooth wear, damage or cracks. Replace the clutch housing if necessary.

NOTE
*If the clutch housing driven gear teeth are damaged, the drive gear on the crankshaft (**Figure 32**) may also be damaged. Refer to **Crankshaft** in Chapter Four.*

13. See **Figure 33**. The tabs on the back of the oil pump drive gear (A) mesh with the 2 notches (B) in the clutch housing. See **Figure 34**. Inspect all mating parts for wear or damage. If the oil pump drive gear teeth are damaged, also check the oil pump driven gear teeth (C, **Figure 19**) for wear or damage. Replace worn parts as required.

14. Check the ends of the pushrod for wear or damage. Also roll the pushrod on a surface plate or thick piece of glass and check for bending; a bent pushrod may bind inside the mainshaft when under load. Replace if necessary.

5

Installation

Refer to **Figure 5** for this procedure.

1. Apply clean engine oil to all mating parts (shafts, splines, bearings) during assembly.

2. Oil the pushrod (B, **Figure 19**) and insert it through the mainshaft so that the flat end faces out (right-hand side).

3. The washer (A, **Figure 19**) has one flat and one tapered side. Install the washer so that the tapered side faces in (left-hand side).

4. Mesh the oil pump drive gear tabs (A, **Figure 33**) with the notches in the clutch housing (B, **Figure 33**). See **Figure 34**.

5. Install the clutch housing (**Figure 18**).

NOTE
*When installing the collar (**Figure 17**) in Step 6, make sure the threaded holes face out (right-hand side).*

6. Install the collar so that it fits into the clutch housing (**Figure 17**).

NOTE
*Remove the bolt from the collar (A, **Figure 17**) if installed.*

7. Install the flat washer (**Figure 16**) so that it seats against the clutch housing.

8. Install the clutch boss (**Figure 15**).

9. Install the washer (**Figure 14**).

NOTE
*When tightening the clutch nut in Step 10, use the same tool (**Figure 12**) as during removal to prevent the clutch boss from turning.*

10. Install a new clutch nut (**Figure 13**) by turning it clockwise. Tighten to the torque specification in **Table 2**.

NOTE
If you are installing new friction plates, soak them in engine oil to prevent clutch plate seizure.

NOTE
*Stock Kawasaki friction plates have radial grooves cut into the cork material. Install these discs so that the grooves will run into the center of the clutch housing when it rotates in a counterclockwise direction (viewed from the right-hand side). See **Figure 35**.*

11. Install the clutch plates. The sequence is friction (**Figure 10**) and then metal (**Figure 11**) and ending with a friction plate. Friction plates have tabs that slide in the clutch housing grooves. The clutch metal plates' inner teeth mesh with the clutch boss splines. Take care to align the clutch plates correctly.

12. When installing the last friction plate, align the plate's tabs with the clutch housing outer groove (**Figure 36**).

13. Install the pressure plate (**Figure 9**) with the clutch release bearing and pushrod installed in the plate.

14. Install the 5 clutch springs (**Figure 8**).

15. Install the 5 clutch spring bolts and washers. Tighten the bolts in a crisscross pattern to the torque specifications in **Table 2**.

16. Install the clutch cover as described in this chapter.

CLUTCH
(ZX1000)

The clutch is installed behind the clutch cover on the right-hand side. Refer to **Figure 37** when performing procedures in this section.

Removal

The following special tools and part will be required when removing and installing the clutch:
    a. Universal clutch holding tool (**Figure 6**).

    b. Clutch nut.

    c. Hydraulic press (to disassemble the clutch boss, if necessary).

NOTE
The clutch nut is a self-locking type. Kawasaki recommends replacing the clutch nut whenever it is removed.

1. Remove the clutch cover as described in this chapter.

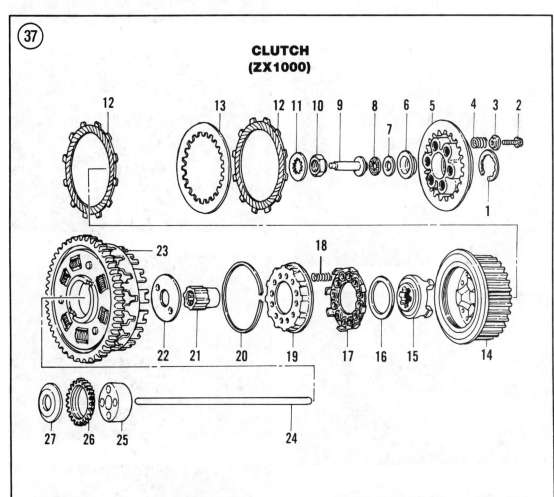

37

CLUTCH (ZX1000)

1. Circlip	10. Nut	19. Left-hand damper spring plate
2. Bolt	11. Lockwasher	20. Snap ring
3. Washer	12. Friction plates (9)	21. Clutch shaft
4. Spring	13. Clutch plates (8)	22. Thrust washer
5. Pressure plate	14. Clutch boss	23. Clutch housing
6. Spacer	15. Damper cap	24. Pushrod
7. Washer	16. Spacer	25. Collar
8. Bearing	17. Right-hand damper spring plate	26. Gear
9. Pushrod	18. Spring	27. Tapered washer

2. Loosen the 6 pressure plate bolts (**Figure 38**) in a crisscross pattern. Then remove the bolts, washers and springs.

3. Remove the pressure plate (**Figure 39**).

4. Remove the clutch release bearing assembly as follows:

    a. Remove the spacer (**Figure 40**) from the pressure plate. It is not necessary to remove the large circlip from the pressure plate.

    b. Remove the flat washer (**Figure 41**).

    c. Remove the bearing (**Figure 42**).

    d. Remove the pushrod (**Figure 43**).

5. Remove a friction plate (**Figure 44**) and a clutch plate (**Figure 45**). Continue until all plates are removed. Stack plates in order.

6. Install a universal clutch holding tool onto the clutch boss (**Figure 46**) to prevent it and the transmission mainshaft from turning when loosening the clutch nut.

7. Loosen the clutch nut (**Figure 47**) by turning it counterclockwise. Remove the clutch nut.

8. Remove the washer (**Figure 48**).

9. Slide the clutch boss (**Figure 49**) off of the mainshaft.

10. Remove the clutch shaft (**Figure 50**) from the damper cam assembly.

5

WARNING
*The damper cam assembly installed in the clutch boss is secured with a large circlip and held under spring pressure. Do not attempt to remove the circlip without the use of a hydraulic press. Refer to **Clutch Boss Disassembly/ Inspection/Reassembly** in this chapter. If the clutch boss assembly is disassembled improperly, personal injury may occur from parts flying out of the clutch boss while under pressure.*

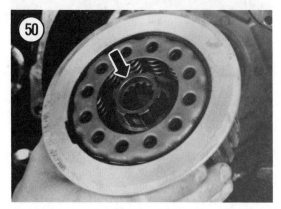

NOTE
Step 11 describes removal of the large thrust washer and collar. These items must be removed before removing the clutch housing so that the clutch housing can be positioned away from the alternator sprocket and the chain tensioner.

11. The thrust washer (**Figure 51**) has 2 holes drilled in it that can be aligned with the threaded holes in the collar. **Figure 52** shows the collar with the thrust washer removed for clarity. Align one of the holes in the flat washer with the threaded hole in the collar. Then install one of the clutch cover bolts through the washer and thread it into the collar (**Figure 53**) and pull the washer and collar off of the mainshaft.

NOTE
To prevent installing the clutch collar backwards, leave the bolt installed into the collar until reassembly.

12. Remove the clutch housing (**Figure 54**) and the oil pump drive gear.
13. Remove the tapered washer (**Figure 55**).

Inspection

CAUTION
If the clutch was damaged by excessive abuse (drag racing, excessive slipping or road racing), there is a good chance that clutch particles have been spread throughout the lubrication system. In such cases, the inside of the engine should be cleaned as thoroughly as possible. Especially important are the oil pump pickup, oil pump and all oil lines. Failure to clean these areas after severe clutch damage can lead to engine failure.

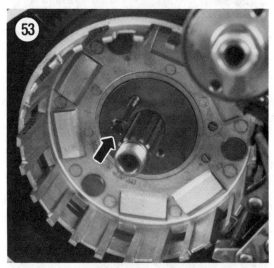

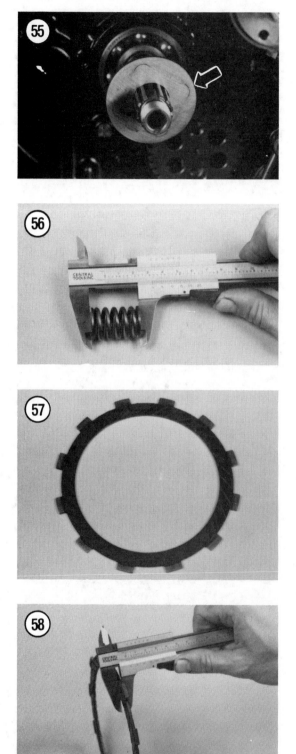

1. Clean all clutch parts in a petroleum-based solvent such as kerosene, and thoroughly dry with compressed air.

2. Measure the free length of each clutch spring as shown in **Figure 56**. Replace any springs that are too short (**Table 1**).

3. The stock ZX1000 clutch uses 9 friction plates (**Figure 57**). The friction material is made of cork that is bonded onto an aluminum plate for warp resistance and durability. Measure the thickness of each friction plate at several places around the disc as shown in **Figure 58** with a vernier caliper. See **Table 1** for specifications. Replace all 9 friction plates if any one is found too thin. Do not replace only 1 or 2 plates.

4. The stock ZX1000 clutch uses 8 clutch metal plates (**Figure 59**). Place each clutch metal plate on a surface plate or a thick piece of glass and check for warpage with a feeler gauge as shown in **Figure 60**. If any plate is warped more than specified (**Table 1**), replace the entire set of plates. Do not replace only 1 or 2 plates.

5

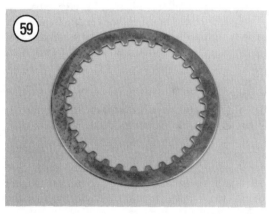

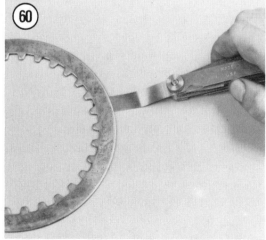

5. The clutch metal plate inner teeth (**Figure 59**) mesh with the clutch boss splines (A, **Figure 61**). Check the splines for cracks or galling. They must be smooth for chatter-free clutch operation. If the clutch boss splines are worn, check the clutch metal plate teeth for wear or damage.

6. Inspect the clutch boss bolt studs (B, **Figure 61**) for thread damage or cracks at the base of the studs. Thread damage may be repaired with a M6×1 metric tap. Use kerosene on the tap threads. If a bolt stud is cracked, the clutch boss must be replaced.

7. Check the clutch release bearing and pushrod assembly (**Figure 62**). Check the needle bearing for wear or damage. Check all bearing surfaces for galling or damage. Replace worn or damaged parts.

8. Inspect the pressure plate (**Figure 63**) for signs of damage or warpage. Check the release bearing spacer bore (A) for cracks or damage. Check the spring towers (B) for cracks or damage. Check the pressure plate teeth (C) where they engage the clutch boss for cracks or damage. Replace the pressure plate if necessary.

9. The friction plates (**Figure 57**) have tabs that slide in the clutch housing grooves (A, **Figure 64**). Inspect the tabs for cracks or galling in the grooves. They must be smooth for chatter-free clutch operation. Light damage can be repaired with an oilstone. Replace the clutch housing if damage is severe.

10. Check the clutch housing bearing bore (B, **Figure 64**) for cracks, deep scoring, excessive wear or heat discoloration. If the bearing bore is damaged, also check the clutch collar (**Figure 65**) for damage. Replace worn or damaged parts.

11. Check the clutch housing driven gear (**Figure 66**) for tooth wear, damage or cracks. Replace the clutch housing if necessary.

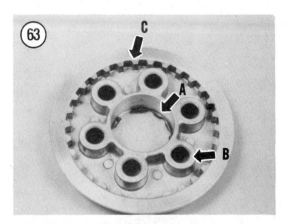

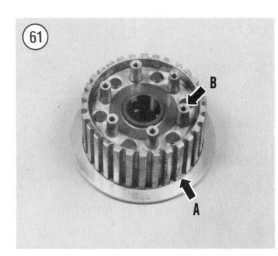

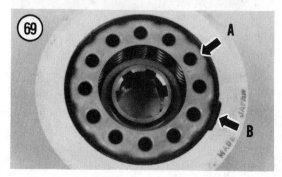

NOTE
*If the clutch housing driven gear teeth are damaged, the drive gear on the crankshaft may also be damaged. Refer to **Crankshaft** in Chapter Four.*

12. See **Figure 67**. The tabs on the back of the oil pump drive gear (A) mesh with the 2 notches (B) in the clutch housing. See **Figure 68**. Inspect all mating parts for wear or damage. If the oil pump drive gear teeth are damaged, also check the oil pump driven gear teeth (C, **Figure 67**) for wear or damage. Replace worn parts as required.

Clutch Boss
Disassembly/Inspection/Reassembly

A hydraulic press is required to service the clutch boss assembly.

WARNING
*The clutch boss damper assembly (A, **Figure 69**) is held under spring pressure. Do not attempt to disassemble the clutch boss without the use of a press.*

1. Remove the clutch boss as described under *Clutch Removal* in this chapter.
2. Remove the clutch shaft (**Figure 50**) from the clutch boss.
3. Place the clutch boss in a press bed so that the snap ring (B, **Figure 69**) faces up.
4. Place bearing driver (Kawasaki part No. 57001-1149) or a similar piece of metal or large diameter pipe on the left-hand damper spring plate as shown in **Figure 70**.
5. Press the damper spring assembly to release all pressure from the snap ring. Then carefully pry the snap ring out of the clutch boss groove. When the snap ring is removed, slowly release pressure on

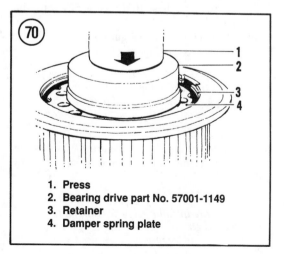

1. **Press**
2. **Bearing drive part No. 57001-1149**
3. **Retainer**
4. **Damper spring plate**

the damper spring plate. Remove the following parts in order:

a. Left-hand damper spring plate.
b. 12 damper springs.
c. Right-hand damper spring plate.
d. Spacer.
e. Damper cam.

6. Wash all parts in solvent and allow to dry.

7. Inspect all parts for wear or damage. Kawasaki does not specify spring free length for the 12 damper springs.

8. Install by reversing these steps. Make sure the snap ring seats in the clutch boss groove completely before releasing damper spring tension.

Installation

Refer to **Figure 37**.

1. Apply clean engine oil to all mating parts (shafts, splines, bearings) during assembly.

2. The washer (**Figure 55**) has one flat and one tapered side. Install the washer so that the tapered side faces in (left-hand side).

3. Mesh the oil pump drive gear tabs (A, **Figure 67**) with the notches in the clutch housing (B, **Figure 67**). See **Figure 68**.

4. Install the clutch housing (**Figure 54**).

> *NOTE*
> *When installing the collar (**Figure 52**) in Step 5, make sure the threaded holes face out (right-hand side).*

5. Install the collar so that it fits into the clutch housing (**Figure 52**).

6. Install the flat washer (**Figure 51**) so that it seats against the clutch housing.

7. Install the clutch shaft (**Figure 50**) into the clutch boss.

8. Install the clutch boss (**Figure 49**).

9. Install the washer (**Figure 48**).

> *NOTE*
> *When tightening the clutch nut in Step 10, use the same tool (**Figure 46**) as during removal to prevent the clutch boss from turning.*

10. Install a new clutch nut (**Figure 47**) by turning it clockwise. Tighten to the torque specification in **Table 2**.

> *NOTE*
> *If you are installing new friction plates, soak them in engine oil to prevent clutch plate seizure.*

NOTE
*Stock Kawasaki friction plates have radial grooves cut into the cork material. Install these discs so that the grooves will run into the center of the clutch housing when it rotates in a counterclockwise direction (viewed from the right-hand side). See **Figure 44**.*

11. Install the clutch plates. The sequence is friction (**Figure 44**) and then metal (**Figure 45**) and ending with a friction plate. Friction plates have tabs that slide in the clutch housing grooves. The clutch metal plates inner teeth mesh with the clutch boss splines. Take care to align the clutch plates correctly. See **Figure 71**.

12. When installing the last friction plate, align the plate's tabs with the clutch housing outer groove (**Figure 72**).

13. Install the clutch release bearing assembly as follows:

    a. Install the pushrod (**Figure 73**).

    b. Install the bearing (**Figure 74**).

    c. Install the flat washer (**Figure 75**).

    d. Insert the spacer into the pressure plate as shown in **Figure 76**. Make sure the circlip is installed in the pressure plate.

14. Install the pressure plate (**Figure 77**).

15. Install the 6 clutch springs.

16. Install the 6 clutch spring bolts (**Figure 78**) and washers. Tighten the bolts in a crisscross pattern to the torque specifications in **Table 2**.

17. Install the clutch cover as described in this chapter.

CLUTCH HYDRAULIC SYSTEM

The clutch is actuated by hydraulic fluid pressure and is controlled by the hand lever on the clutch master cylinder. As clutch components wear, the slave cylinder piston is extended beyond the elastic limit of its seal. The seal slips slightly which allows the piston to move to a new position. This automatically adjusts for wear. There is no routine adjustment necessary or possible.

When working on the clutch hydraulic system, it is necessary that the work area and all tools be absolutely clean. Any tiny particles of foreign matter and grit in the clutch slave cylinder or the clutch master cylinder can damage the components. Also, sharp tools must not be used inside the slave cylinder or on the piston. If there is any doubt about your ability to correctly and safely

carry out major service on the clutch hydraulic system, take the job to a dealer.

CAUTION
*Throughout the text, reference is made to hydraulic fluid. Hydraulic fluid is the same as DOT 4 brake fluid. Use only DOT 4 brake fluid; do **not** use other types of fluids as they are not compatible. Do not intermix silicone base (DOT 5) brake fluid as it can cause clutch component damage leading to clutch system failure.*

CLUTCH MASTER CYLINDER

The clutch master cylinder includes the reservoir, piston, primary and secondary cups, spring and pushrod. See **Figure 79**.

Removal/Installation

CAUTION
Cover the fuel tank and instrument cluster with a heavy cloth or plastic tarp to protect them from accidental hydraulic fluid spills. Wash fluid off any painted or plated surfaces

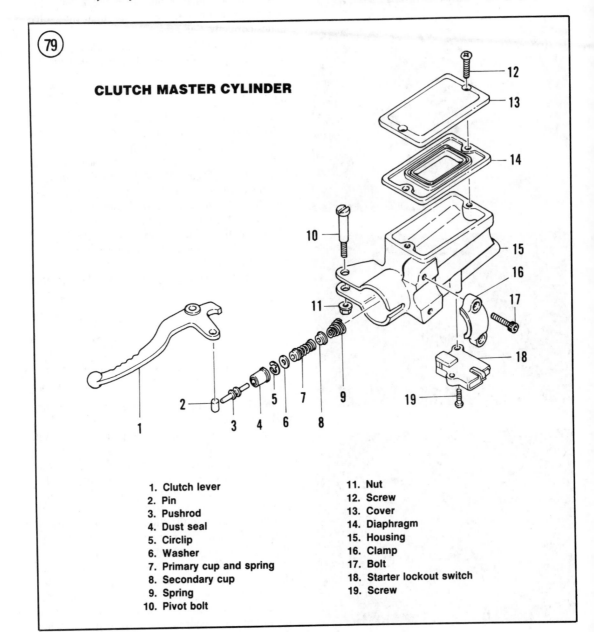

79

CLUTCH MASTER CYLINDER

1. Clutch lever
2. Pin
3. Pushrod
4. Dust seal
5. Circlip
6. Washer
7. Primary cup and spring
8. Secondary cup
9. Spring
10. Pivot bolt
11. Nut
12. Screw
13. Cover
14. Diaphragm
15. Housing
16. Clamp
17. Bolt
18. Starter lockout switch
19. Screw

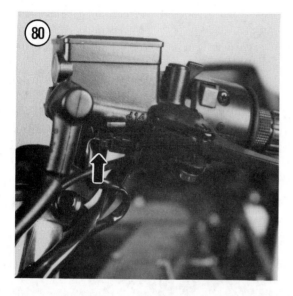

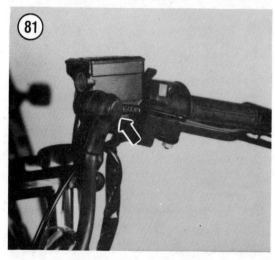

immediately as it will destroy the finish. Use soapy water and rinse completely.

1. Disconnect the electrical connector to the starter lockout switch (**Figure 80**).

2. Pull back the rubber boot (**Figure 81**) and remove the banjo bolt securing the clutch hose to the clutch master cylinder. Remove the clutch hose; tie the hose up and cover the end to prevent entry of foreign matter.

3. Remove the clamping bolts and clamp (A, **Figure 82**) securing the clutch master cylinder to the handlebar and remove the clutch master cylinder assembly (B, **Figure 82**).

4. Install by reversing these removal steps. Note the following:

   a. Install the clamp (A, **Figure 82**) so that the arrow faces up.

   b. Install the clamp screws and tighten securely.

   c. Install the clutch hose (**Figure 81**) onto the clutch master cylinder. Be sure to place a sealing washer on each side of the fitting and install the banjo bolt. Tighten the banjo bolt to the torque specification in **Table 2**.

   d. Attach the electrical connector (**Figure 80**) to the starter lockout switch.

   e. Bleed the clutch as described in this chapter.

Disassembly

> *NOTE*
> *Before disassembly, check for hydraulic fluid around the clutch lever. If hydraulic fluid is noted, the primary and secondary cups are worn and should be replaced.*

Refer to **Figure 79** for this procedure.

1. Remove the clutch master cylinder as described in this chapter.

2. Remove the screw (A, **Figure 83**) securing the starter lockout switch to the bottom of the master cylinder housing and remove the switch (B, **Figure 83**).

3. Loosen and remove the pivot bolt nut (**Figure 84**).

4. Remove the pivot bolt (**Figure 85**) and pull the clutch lever out of the master cylinder (**Figure 86**).

5. Remove the pushrod bushing (**Figure 87**) from the clutch lever.

6. Remove the pushrod (**Figure 88**).

7. Remove the rubber cover (**Figure 89**) from the groove in the master cylinder.

8. Using circlip pliers, remove the circlip and washer (**Figure 90**).

9. Remove the piston (A, **Figure 91**) with the primary cup (B, **Figure 91**) attached.

10. Remove the spring (A, **Figure 92**) with the secondary cup (B, **Figure 92**) attached.

Inspection

1. Clean all parts (**Figure 93**) in denatured alcohol or fresh DOT 4 hydraulic fluid. Inspect the cylinder bore and piston contact surfaces for signs of wear and damage. If either part is less than perfect, replace it.

NOTE
The primary cup, spring and secondary cup are sold as part of the piston assembly. If any one of these parts are worn or damaged, a new piston assembly must be purchased.

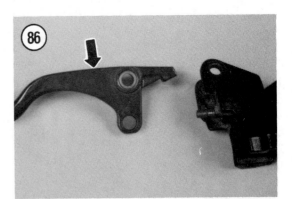

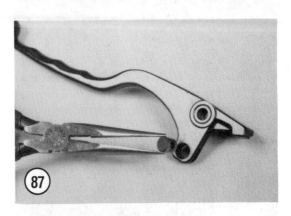

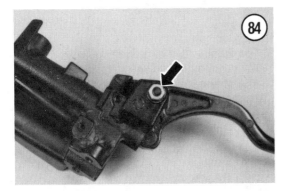

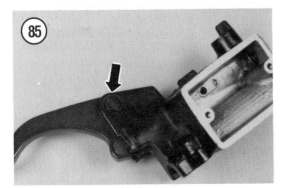

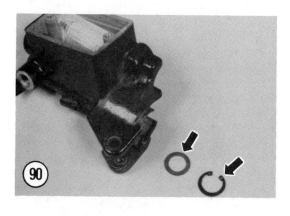

NOTE
The primary and secondary cups prevent hydraulic fluid from leaking around the piston when the piston is moved forward by the clutch lever to pressurize the hydraulic hose.

2. Check the end of the piston (A, **Figure 94**) for wear caused by the pushrod. Check the primary cup (B, **Figure 94**) for tearing, wear, softness or swelling.

3. Check the spring (A, **Figure 95**) for fatigue, cracks or other damage. Check the secondary cup (B, **Figure 95**) for tearing, wear, softness or swelling.

4. There are 2 ports at the bottom of the master cylinder reservoir (**Figure 96**). The large port

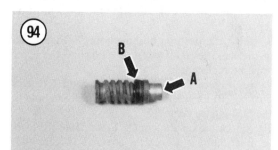

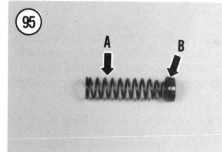

supplies hydraulic fluid to the line and the small port allows fluid to return to the reservoir when the clutch lever is released. Check that both ports are open and clear of all debris. Clean the ports with compressed air from either a compressor or from an air container sold by photography dealers.

NOTE
If the small port is plugged, the clutch will not disengage.

5. Check the hand lever pivot bore (A, **Figure 97**) in the clutch master cylinder. If worn or elongated, the master cylinder must be replaced.

6. Check the threads (B, **Figure 97**) in the master cylinder housing for damage. Repair threads with a tap if necessary.

7. Inspect the pivot bore (A, **Figure 98**) in the hand lever. If worn or elongated the lever must be replaced.

8. Check the pushrod bushing bore (B, **Figure 98**) in the hand lever. If worn or elongated the lever must be replaced.

9. See **Figure 99**. Check the pushrod (A) and bushing (B) for wear or damage. Check the hole in the bushing for wear.

10. Check the diaphragm (A, **Figure 100**) for tears or other damage. Check the cover (B, **Figure 100**) for cracks or damage.

11. Replace worn or damaged parts as required.

Assembly

1. Soak the new cups in fresh DOT 4 hydraulic fluid for at least 15 minutes to make them pliable. Coat the inside of the cylinder with fresh fluid prior to assembly of parts.

CAUTION
When installing the piston assembly, do not allow the cups to turn inside out as they will be damaged and allow hydraulic fluid to leak within the cylinder bore.

2. Install the spring and secondary cup into the piston bore as shown in **Figure 92**.

3. Install the piston and primary cup into the piston bore as show in **Figure 91**.

4. Install the washer and circlip over the end of the piston (**Figure 90**).

5. Compress the piston assembly and install the circlip (**Figure 90**) into the groove in the master cylinder using circlip pliers. Make sure the circlip seats in the groove completely.

NOTE
When installing the circlip in Step 5, it will be easier if the master cylinder is

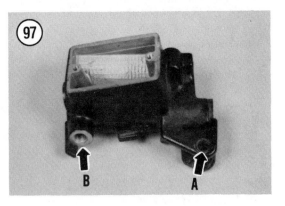

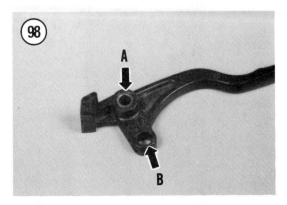

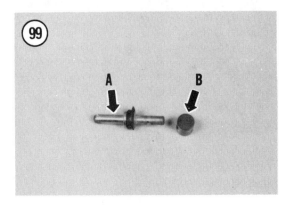

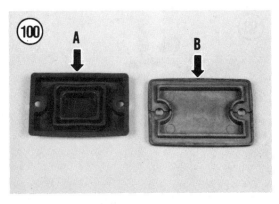

mounted in a vise with soft jaws. Then have an assistant compress the piston assembly with a long wood dowel. This will give you room to install the circlip with the pliers.

6. Insert the rubber cover into the piston bore (**Figure 89**). Make sure the cover seats in the bore completely.

7. Install the pushrod (**Figure 88**) into the master cylinder so that the curved end of the pushrod faces the piston.

8. Install the pushrod bushing into the clutch lever. Turn the bushing so that the hole in the bushing faces the hole in the clutch lever (**Figure 87**).

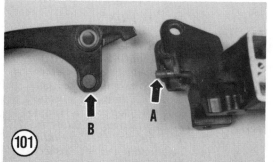

9. Assemble the clutch lever. Align the end of the pushrod (A, **Figure 101**) with the hole in the bushing (B, **Figure 101**) and install the clutch lever. The pushrod must engage with the bushing in the hand lever.

10. Apply a small amount of grease onto the clutch lever pivot bolt. Then install the pivot bolt from the top of the master cylinder and through the hand lever pushrod bushing (**Figure 85**). Install the pivot bolt nut (**Figure 84**) and tighten securely. Operate the clutch lever and make sure it moves smoothly; the lever should not bind or catch.

11. Install the starter lockout switch (B, **Figure 83**) and secure with the Phillips screw (A, **Figure 83**).

12. Install the diaphragm and top cover.

13. Install the clutch master cylinder and bleed the clutch system as described in this chapter.

SLAVE CYLINDER

Removal/Installation

1. Attach a hose to the bleed valve on the clutch slave cylinder (A, **Figure 102**).

2. Place the loose end of the hose into a container and open the bleed valve. Operate the clutch lever until all fluid is pumped out of the system. Close the bleed valve and remove the hose.

> *WARNING*
> *Dispose of this fluid—never reuse hydraulic fluid. Contaminated fluid can cause clutch failure.*

3. Place a container under the clutch hose at the clutch slave cylinder to catch any remaining fluid. Remove the banjo bolt and sealing washers (B, **Figure 102**) securing the clutch hose to the clutch slave cylinder. Remove the clutch hose and let any remaining fluid drain out into the container.

4. Remove the bolts securing the clutch slave cylinder (C, **Figure 102**) to the sprocket cover and withdraw the unit from the cover.

5. Discard the slave cylinder gasket.

6. Installation is the reverse of these steps. Note the following:

   a. Install a new slave cylinder gasket.

   b. Tighten the slave cylinder bolts securely.

   c. Install the banjo bolt and new sealing washers onto the slave cylinder. Tighten the banjo bolt to the torque specification in **Table 2**.

   d. Turn the handlebar to level the clutch master cylinder. Clean the top of the clutch master cylinder of all dirt and foreign matter. Remove the cap (**Figure 103**) and diaphragm. Fill the reservoir almost to the top line; insert the diaphragm and install the cap loosely.

   e. Bleed the clutch as described in this chapter.

Disassembly/Inspection/Assembly

Refer to **Figure 104** for this procedure.

1. To remove the piston, perform the following:
   a. Remove the banjo bolt from the slave cylinder.
   b. Hold the slave cylinder body in your hand with the piston facing away from you. Place a clean shop cloth behind the piston to catch it.

> *WARNING*
> *Do not use your hand to catch the piston as it is removed from the slave cylinder body.*

> *CAUTION*
> *Be sure to catch the piston with a shop cloth when it is pushed out of the body. Failure to do so will result in damage to the piston.*

   c. Apply compressed air in the hole where the banjo bolt was attached. The air pressure will force the piston out of the body.
2. Remove the spring from the piston.
3. Check the spring for damage or sagging. Replace the spring if its condition is doubtful.
4. Remove the piston seal from the cylinder.
5. Check the piston and cylinder body for scratches, severe wear or damage. Replace questionable parts.
6. Apply a light coat of hydraulic fluid to the piston and new piston seal prior to installation.
7. Install a new seal on the piston.

8. Insert the piston into the slave cylinder. With your fingers, push the piston all the way into the cylinder.
9. Install the slave cylinder as described in this chapter.

BLEEDING THE CLUTCH

This procedure is not necessary unless the clutch feels spongy (air in the line), there has been a leak in the system, a component has been replaced or the hydraulic fluid is being replaced. If the clutch operates when the engine is cold or in cool weather but operates erratically (or not at all) after the engine warms up or in hot weather, there is air in the hydraulic line and the clutch must be bled.

> *CAUTION*
> *Throughout the text, reference is made to hydraulic fluid. Hydraulic fluid is the same as DOT 4 brake fluid. Use only DOT 4 brake fluid; do **not** use other types of fluids as they are not compatible. Do not intermix silicone base (DOT 5) brake fluid as it can cause clutch component damage leading to clutch system failure. The hydraulic system uses aluminum crush washers at the hose joints. If the hoses have been disconnected, use new washers during reassembly.*

1. Remove the dust cap from the bleed valve on the clutch slave cylinder (A, **Figure 102**).

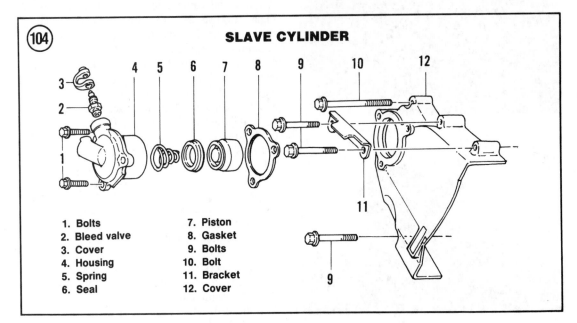

(104)   **SLAVE CYLINDER**

1. Bolts	7. Piston
2. Bleed valve	8. Gasket
3. Cover	9. Bolts
4. Housing	10. Bolt
5. Spring	11. Bracket
6. Seal	12. Cover

2. Connect a length of clear tubing to the bleed valve.

3. Place the other end of the tube into a clean container. Fill the container with enough fresh hydraulic fluid to keep the end submerged.

CAUTION
Cover the clutch slave cylinder and lower frame with a heavy cloth or plastic tarp to protect them from accidental fluid spillings. Wash any fluid off of any painted or plated surface immediately, as it will destroy the finish. Use soapy water and rinse completely.

4. Clean the top of the clutch master cylinder of all dirt and foreign matter. Remove the cap (**Figure 103**) and diaphragm. Fill the reservoir to the upper level mark. Insert the diaphragm and install the cap loosely.

CAUTION
Failure to install the diaphragm on the master cylinder will allow fluid to spurt out when the clutch lever is released.

CAUTION
Use hydraulic fluid clearly marked DOT 4 only. Others may vaporize and cause clutch failure. Always use the same brand name; do not intermix as many brands are not compatible. Do not intermix silicone based (DOT 5) brake fluid as it can cause clutch component damage leading to clutch system failure.

NOTE
If the entire system or master cylinder was drained, you must first bleed the master cylinder and hose joints of air.

5. Disconnect the fluid hose at the master cylinder. Wrap a plastic bag around the hose end and secure

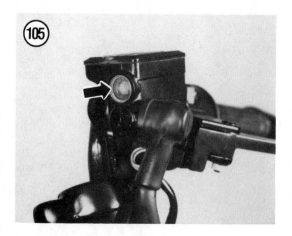

the hose up and out of your way. While holding your thumb securely over the hose opening in the master cylinder, pump the clutch lever three or four times and hold it in. Slightly release thumb pressure from the hole. Some air and brake fluid should seep out. Apply thumb pressure when the lever bottoms on the hand grip. Repeat this procedure until you feel resistance when you pump the lever.

6. Reconnect the fluid hose. Add fluid to the clutch master cylinder as necessary. Pump the lever again and hold it in. Loosen the fluid hose fitting at the master cylinder 1/2 turn. Air and brake fluid should seep out. When the lever bottoms on the hand grip, tighten the hose fitting. Repeat this procedure until no more air bubbles come out of the hose fitting.

7. Pump the lever again and hold it in. Loosen the bleed valve about 1/2 turn at the slave cylinder. Slowly apply the clutch lever several times. Hold the lever in the applied position. Open the bleed valve about one-half turn. Allow the lever to travel to its limit. When the limit is reached, tighten the bleed valve. Occasionally tap or jiggle the clutch flexible hoses to loosen any trapped air bubbles that won't come out the normal way. Turn the handlebars so that the clutch lever end of the master cylinder is the highest point in the hydraulic system. As the fluid enters the system, the level will drop in the reservoir. Maintain the level at the top of the reservoir to prevent air from being drawn into the system.

8. Repeat Step 7 until fluid emerging from the hose is completely free of bubbles.

NOTE
Do not allow the reservoir to empty during the bleeding operation or air will enter the system. If this occurs, the entire procedure must be repeated.

9. Hold the lever in, tighten the bleed valve, remove the bleed tube and install the bleed valve dust cap.

10. If necessary, add fluid to the upper level mark in the reservoir (**Figure 105**).

11. Install the diaphragm and reservoir cap (**Figure 103**).

12. Test the feel of the clutch lever. It should be firm and should offer the same resistance each time it's operated. If it feels spongy, it is likely that there still is air in the system and it must be bled again. When all air has been bled from the system and the fluid level is correct in the reservoir, double-check for leaks and tighten all the fittings and connections.

5

Table 1 CLUTCH SPECIFICATIONS

	Standard mm (in.)	Wear limits mm (in.)
Clutch spring free length		
ZX900	33-34.2 (1.30-1.346)	32.6 (1.283)
ZX1000	33.2 (1.307)	32.1 (1.263)
Friction plate thickness		
ZX900	2.9-3.1 (0.114-0.122)	2.75 (0.108)
ZX1000	2.9-3.1 (0.114-0.122)	2.8 (0.110)
Friction and clutch plate warpage		0.3 (0.011)

Table 2 CLUTCH TIGHTENING TORQUES

	N•m	ft.-lb.
Clutch nut	130	98
Clutch spring bolts	9.8	7.2
Clutch hose banjo bolt	29	22
Clutch master cylinder clamp bolt	11	8

CHAPTER SIX

TRANSMISSION

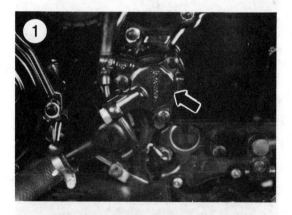

This chapter covers all the parts that transmit power from the clutch to the drive chain: engine sprocket, transmission gears, shift drum and forks and shift linkage. **Table 1** (end of chapter) lists transmission specifications.

SPROCKET COVER

Removal/Installation

> *NOTE*
> *It is not necessary to remove the clutch slave cylinder (**Figure 1**) and its mounting bolts when removing the sprocket cover.*

2. Remove the screws securing the engine sprocket cover and remove the cover. See **Figure 2** (ZX900) or **Figure 3** (ZX1000).
3. Remove the 2 dowel pins (A, **Figure 4**).

> *CAUTION*
> *While the sprocket cover is removed, take care not to damage the clutch pushrod (B, **Figure 4**).*

3. To install the sprocket cover, reverse the removal steps.

NEUTRAL SWITCH

Removal/Installation

The neutral light is activated by a switch mounted in the shift linkage cover (**Figure 5**) under the sprocket cover. The switch is turned on when the shift drum end plate is in its NEUTRAL position.

1. Drain the engine oil as described under *Engine Oil and Filter Change* in Chapter Three.

2. Disconnect the electrical connector at the neutral switch.

3. Using a socket, unscrew the neutral switch and remove it.

4. Reverse to install.

5. Refill the engine oil as described in Chapter Three.

ENGINE SPROCKET

The engine sprocket is on the left-hand end of the transmission countershaft, behind the sprocket cover. See **Figure 6** (ZX900) or **Figure 7** (ZX1000).

Removal

1. Remove the engine sprocket cover as described in this chapter.

2. Pry the lockwasher tab away from the sprocket nut. See **Figure 6** or **Figure 7**.

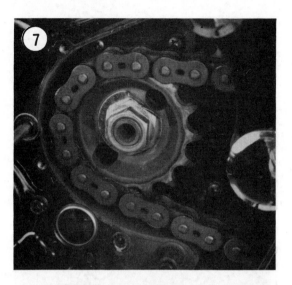

3. Shift the transmission into gear and have an assistant apply the rear brake. Then loosen the sprocket nut with a socket and breaker bar. Remove the sprocket.

4. Remove the lockwasher (**Figure 8**).

> *NOTE*
> *You may have to loosen the drive chain to allow sprocket removal in Step 5. See* **Drive Chain Free Play** *in Chapter Three. If drive chain removal is necessary, see Chapter Eleven.*

5. Slide the sprocket and chain off the countershaft (**Figure 9**).

6. Installation is the reverse of these steps. Note the following:

   a. Before installing the sprocket, check the oil seal (**Figure 10**) in the shift cover. If the seal is leaking, replace it as described under *External Shift Mechanism* in this chapter.

   b. On ZX1000 models, the sprocket recess (**Figure 7**) must face to the outside.

   c. Position the drive chain on the sprocket, then slide the sprocket onto the countershaft (**Figure 9**).

   d. Install a new lockwasher (**Figure 8**).

   e. Tighten the sprocket nut to 98 N•m (72 ft.-lb.).

   f. Bend a new section of the lockwasher tab over the sprocket nut to lock it. See **Figure 6** or **Figure 7**.

   g. Adjust the drive chain. See *Drive Chain Free Play* in Chapter Three.

Inspection

Inspect the engine sprocket for wear. If the teeth are undercut as shown in **Figure 11**, install a new sprocket.

> *NOTE*
> *When replacing the engine sprocket, it is a good idea to replace the drive chain and rear sprocket as well. This will prevent rapid wear to the new part.*

EXTERNAL SHIFT MECHANISM

Refer to **Figure 12**. The external shift mechanism can be serviced with the engine in the frame.

Removal/Installation

1. Remove the engine sprocket as described in this chapter.
2. Drain the engine oil as described under *Engine Oil and Filter Change* in Chapter Three.
3. Drain the cooling system as described under *Coolant Change* in Chapter Three.
4. Remove the water pump as described under *Water Pump Removal/Installation* in Chapter Nine.
5. Disconnect the electrical connector at the neutral switch (**Figure 5**).

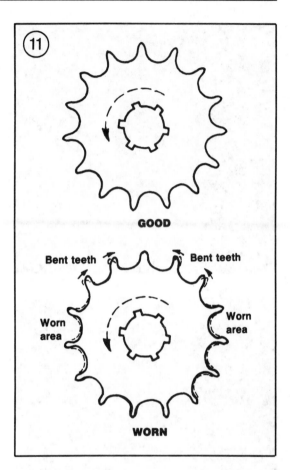

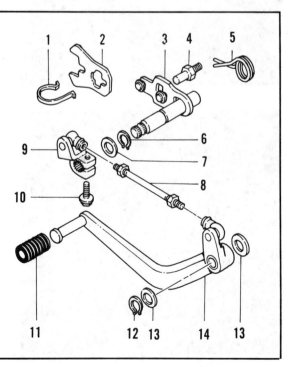

EXTERNAL SHIFT MECHANISM

1. Spring
2. Shift pawl
3. Shift shaft
4. Pin bolt
5. Return spring
6. Circlip
7. Washer
8. Adjust rod
9. Boss
10. Bolt
11. Foot rubber
12. Circlip
13. Washer
14. Shift lever

6. Pull the pushrod (B, **Figure 4**) out of the engine.

7. Remove the gearshift lever.

8. Remove the screws, then remove the shift linkage cover (**Figure 13**) and gasket. Tap the cover loose with a soft mallet, if necessary. Use care when removing the cover; it is positioned with dowel pins.

9. Remove the 2 dowel pins (**Figure 14**).

10. Remove the washer (**Figure 15**) from the shift lever.

11. Move the shift mechanism arm (A, **Figure 16**) away from the shift drum and pull the shift linkage assembly (B, **Figure 16**) out of the engine.

12. See **Figure 17**. Service to the neutral (A) and gear (B) positioning levers are described under *Shift Drum and Forks Removal/Installation* in this chapter.

Inspection

1. Inspect the seals in the shift linkage cover. Replace any damaged seals; heat the cover in a shop oven to about 212° F and tap the old seals out. Install new seals flush with the surface of the cover, with their numbered side out.

2. Check that the circlip (A, **Figure 18**) is installed on the shift shaft.

3. Check the shift shaft for bending and spline damage.

4. Check the arm spring (B, **Figure 18**) for damage.

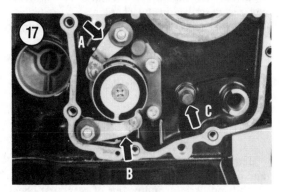

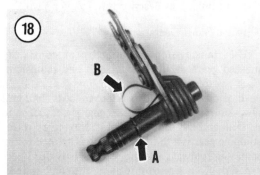

5. Check the shift mechanism arms (**Figure 19**) for wear or damage at the contact areas.

6. Check that the return spring arms fit onto the pin as shown in **Figure 20**. Check that the spring is not damaged.

7. Replace any other broken, bent, binding or worn parts.

Installation

Refer to **Figure 12** for this procedure.

1. Check return spring pin (C, **Figure 17**) for looseness or damage. Replace the pin by unscrewing it from the crankcase. When installing a new or used pin, apply Loctite 242 (blue) onto the pin threads and tighten the pin securely.

2. Install the shift linkage assembly by engaging the shift mechanism arms with the shift drum. See **Figure 16**.

3. Install the washer (**Figure 15**) on the shift shaft.

4. Install the 2 dowel pins (**Figure 14**) and a new cover gasket.

5. Install the shift linkage cover (**Figure 13**).

6. Apply Loctite 242 (blue) onto all of the shift linkage cover screws. Tighten the screws securely.

7. Install the pushrod (B, **Figure 4**) into the engine so that the end of the pushrod with the round end faces out.

8. Reconnect the electrical connector at the neutral switch (**Figure 5**).

9. Install the engine sprocket and the sprocket cover as described in this chapter.

10. Install the water pump as described in Chapter Nine.

11. Refill the cooling system as described in Chapter Three.

12. Refill the engine oil as described in Chapter Three.

TRANSMISSION

Transmission repair requires engine removal and crankcase separation. If the transmission fails to shift properly or jumps out of gear, first check the shift linkage as described in Chapter Two.

Gear and Shaft Operation

The transmission has 6 pairs of constantly meshed gears on the countershaft and mainshaft. Each pair of meshed gears gives one gear ratio. In each pair, one of the gears is locked to its shaft and always turns with it. The other gear is not locked to its shaft and can spin freely on it. Next to each free spinning gear is a third gear which is splined to the same shaft, always turning with it. This third gear can slide from side to side along the shaft splines.

The side of the sliding gear and the free spinning gear have mating "dogs" and slots." When the sliding gear moves up against the free spinning gear, the 2 gears are locked together by the dogs and slots, locking the free spinning gear to its shaft. Since both meshed countershaft and mainshaft gears are now locked to their shafts, power is transmitted from one shaft to the other at that gear ratio.

Neutral Finder Operation

The countershaft fifth gear has 3 holes machined 120° apart that are fitted with 3/32 in. steel balls. These balls keep the transmission from overshooting NEUTRAL when the rider shifts from first gear to NEUTRAL, with the clutch lever pulled in and the bike stopped. When the bike is moving and the countershaft is turning, the balls are forced away from the shaft by centrifugal force. This allows upshifting to second. When the bike is stopped, the ball on the top falls into a groove in the shaft and prevents the gear from sliding into position for higher gears.

Shift Drum and Fork Operation

Each sliding gear has a deep groove machined around its outside. The curved shift fork arm rides in this groove, controlling the side-to-side sliding of the gear and therefore the selection of different gear ratios.

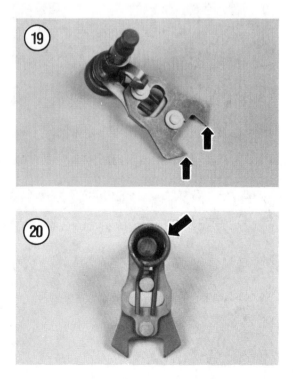

Each shift fork slides back and forth on a guide shaft and has a peg that rides in a groove on the face of the shift drum. When the shift linkage rotates the shift drum, the zigzag grooves move the shift forks and sliding gears back and forth.

TRANSMISSION GEARS

Removal

Refer to **Figure 21** for this procedure.

1. Remove the engine and split the crankcase as described under *Crankcase Disassembly* in Chapter Four.

> *NOTE*
> *It is not necessary to remove crankshaft, primary chain or starter clutch when removing the transmission shafts.*

2. The transmission shafts are identified in **Figure 22**:
   a. Countershaft (A).
   b. Mainshaft (B).

3. Before removing the transmission shafts, check gear backlash as follows:
   a. Mount a dial indicator onto a magnetic stand or some other support and place the plunger against one gear. See **Figure 23**.
   b. Rotate the gear slightly back and forth with the plunger while holding the mating gear and note the dial indicator reading.
   c. The difference between the highest and lowest readings recorded in sub-step "b" is gear backlash. Replace both gears if the backlash exceeds the service limit specified in **Table 1**.
   d. Repeat for each set of mating gears.

6

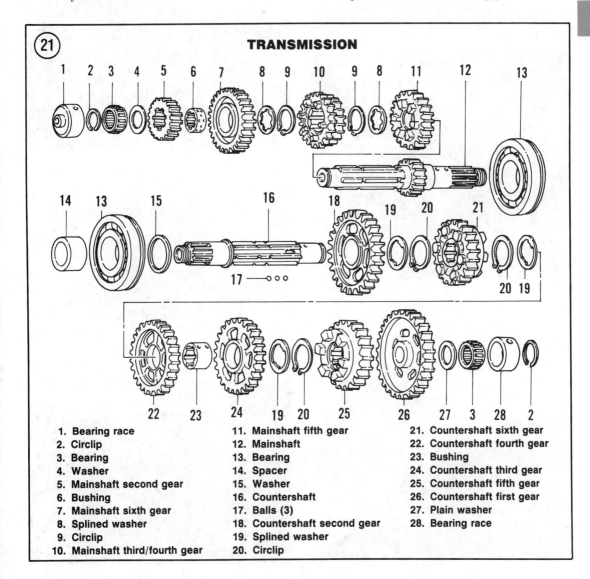

(21) TRANSMISSION

1. Bearing race	11. Mainshaft fifth gear	21. Countershaft sixth gear
2. Circlip	12. Mainshaft	22. Countershaft fourth gear
3. Bearing	13. Bearing	23. Bushing
4. Washer	14. Spacer	24. Countershaft third gear
5. Mainshaft second gear	15. Washer	25. Countershaft fifth gear
6. Bushing	16. Countershaft	26. Countershaft first gear
7. Mainshaft sixth gear	17. Balls (3)	27. Plain washer
8. Splined washer	18. Countershaft second gear	28. Bearing race
9. Circlip	19. Splined washer	
10. Mainshaft third/fourth gear	20. Circlip	

3. See **Figure 22**. Carefully lift the countershaft (A) and then the mainshaft (B) out of the upper crankcase.

4. Remove the dowel pins (A) and 1/2 circlips (B) from the upper crankcase. See **Figure 24** and **Figure 25**.

Inspection

1. Transmission disassembly, reassembly and assembly is described in this chapter.

2. Check the transmission bearing mounting area in both crankcase halves for cracks or other damage.

3. Fit each dowel pin (**Figure 24** and **Figure 25**) into its mounting hole in the upper crankcase. The fit should be snug with no noticeable side play.

4. Check each 1/2 circlip (**Figure 24** or **Figure 25**) for cracks or wear. If replacing a 1/2 circlip, first measure the thickness of the old circlip. Kawasaki

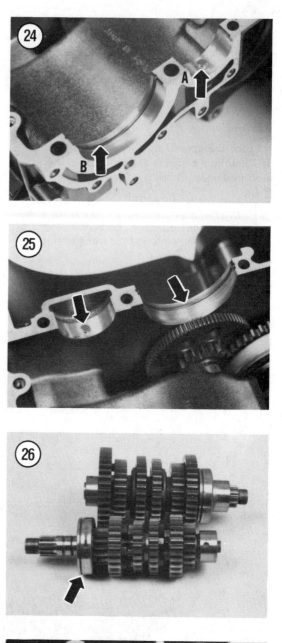

offers 2 different thickness 1/2 circlips to allow for small differences in bearing grooves. The standard 1/2 circlip thickness is 1.98 mm; the other 1/2 circlip thickness is 1.90 mm.

5. Replace worn or damaged parts. Some minor crankcase damage may be repaired by a qualified machinist. If not, the crankcase assembly will have to be replaced as a set. Refer to *Crankcase* in Chapter Four.

Installation

1. Clean the transmission mounting areas in both crankcase halves with a lint-free cloth.
2. Coat all bearing surfaces with assembly oil.
3. Install the dowel pins in the upper crankcase (**Figure 24** and **Figure 25**).

> *NOTE*
> *If the transmission ball bearings were replaced (**Figure 26**), the standard 1/2 circlips may be too wide for the new ball bearing circlip grooves. Before installing the 1/2 circlips and transmission shafts into the crankcase, insert each 1/2 circlip in the transmission ball bearing circlip groove. If the standard 1/2 circlips are too thick, you will need to order the thin 1/2 circlips (Kawasaki part No. 14013-1006).*

> *CAUTION*
> *Installing the incorrect size 1/2 circlip will cause crankcase damage.*

4. Install the 1/2 circlips in the upper crankcase. See **Figure 24** and **Figure 25**.
5. Align the pin hole in the bearing race (A, **Figure 27**) and the circlip groove in the ball bearing (B, **Figure 27**) with the pins and 1/2 circlips (**Figure 24** and **Figure 25**) and install the mainshaft (**Figure 28**). Repeat for the countershaft (**Figure 29**).

> *NOTE*
> *When the transmission shafts are correctly installed, there will be no clearance between the crankcase and the outer bearing races. See **Figure 30** and **Figure 31**.*

6. Assemble the crankcase assembly as described under *Crankcase Assembly* in Chapter Four.

Transmission Engagement Check

If the transmission shaft(s) were disassembled, the transmission gears should be checked for proper engagement at each gear position. It is better to find out that a gear has been installed backwards or a shim misplaced while the engine is disassembled than when the engine is assembled and installed in the frame.

1. A spinning gear is positioned by either a shim and circlip on both sides or a shim and circlip on one side and a shoulder (either from a gear or shaft) on the other side. To work properly a spinning gear must have side play. (Kawasaki does not specify actual side play specifications.) If there is no side play, the gear will bind when under load. If there is too much side play, the gear may move too far when a sliding gear tries to engage it. This will cause the sliding gear dogs to wear rapidly since they do not have maximum engagement. Check side play as follows:

    a. Place the transmission shaft on V-blocks or in the upper crankcase so that the transmission shaft is horizontal with no load placed against any gear.

    b. While holding the transmission shaft in place with one hand, locate each spinning gear and spin it by hand. The gear should spin freely and not bind or turn slowly.

    c. If a spinning gear binds while turning by hand and you disassembled the transmission shaft, check for an incorrectly installed thrust washer or a deformed or damaged circlip.

2. For correct operation, each gear dog must have 50-75% engagement with the corresponding dog or slot. A less than 50% engagement will cause gear dog wear, which will eventually cause the gears to "pop" out of engagement. This will bend the shift fork that moves the sliding gear. Dog engagement cannot be checked accurately because the crankcase halves must be assembled and the transmission operated by turning the shift drum and moving the shift forks. With the crankcase halves assembled together, it is impossible to see how far gears are engaged. Because of this, the gear dogs must be closely examined during disassembly as described in this chapter. When the crankcase halves are assembled, check each gear position as described under *Crankcase Assembly* in Chapter Four.

Transmission Service Notes

1. Circlip pliers will be required to disassemble and reassemble the transmission shafts.

2. A hydraulic or arbor press will be required to replace ball bearings on both transmission shafts. A press, however, is not required for transmission gear disassembly.

3. A long thin metal rod can be used to hold each gear, circlip and washer as they are removed from the transmission shaft to maintain correct alignment and positioning of the parts. See **Figure 32** (countershaft) and **Figure 33** (mainshaft).

4. The circlips must fit tightly on the transmission shafts, but they can wear rapidly since they face spinning parts. Replace all circlips during reassembly.

> *WARNING*
> *After installing a circlip on a shaft, check that the circlip seats completely in the shaft groove. Circlips with rounded edges are directional; they must be installed with the rounded edge facing the spinning part. If a circlip was damaged during removal or if it is weak from having lost its temper and tension*

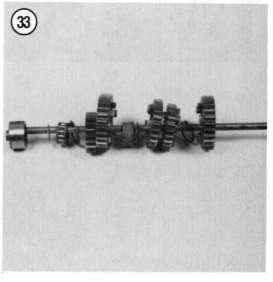

from excessive heat, it could unseat. This would allow the retained gear to slide out and possibly cause the transmission to lock up. This would destroy the transmission and crankcase assembly as well as lock up the rear wheel and cause loss of control.

5. When installing circlips on splined shafts, position them so that their openings fall on top of a spline groove and do not align with a splined washer tooth (**Figure 34**).

6. Circlips will turn and fold over, making removal and installation difficult. To ease replacement, open the circlip with a pair of circlip pliers while at the same time holding the back of the circlip with a pair of pliers and remove it. See **Figure 35**. Repeat for installation.

6

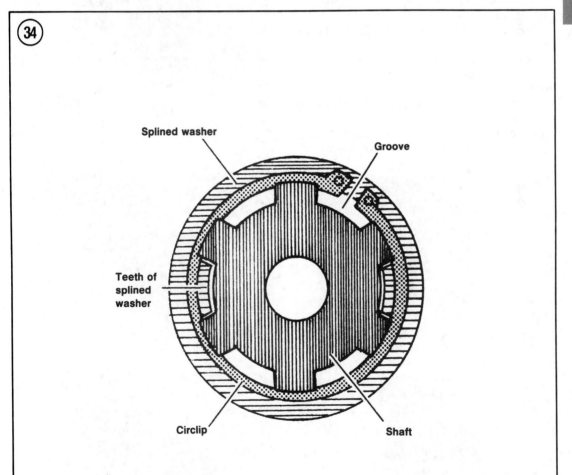

Mainshaft Disassembly

Refer to **Figure 21** for this procedure.

1. Slide the bearing race (**Figure 36**) off of the mainshaft.

2. Pry the clip (**Figure 37**) out of the mainshaft groove.

3. Remove the needle bearing (**Figure 38**).

4. Remove the thrust washer (**Figure 39**).

5. Remove mainshaft second gear (**Figure 40**).

6. Remove mainshaft sixth gear (**Figure 41**) and its bushing (**Figure 42**).

7. Remove the splined thrust washer (A, **Figure 43**).

8. Use circlip pliers and remove the third/fourth gear circlip (B, **Figure 43**) from the mainshaft.

9. Remove the third/fourth combination gear (**Figure 44**) from the mainshaft.

10. Use circlip pliers and remove the fifth gear circlip (A, **Figure 45**).

11. Remove the splined thrust washer (B, **Figure 45**).

12. Remove fifth gear (**Figure 46**).

13. Inspect the mainshaft assembly as described in this chapter.

14. If necessary remove the mainshaft ball bearing (A, **Figure 47**) as follows:

   a. Support the mainshaft ball bearing with a press plate with its circlip groove down.

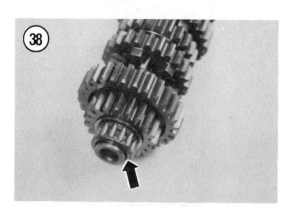

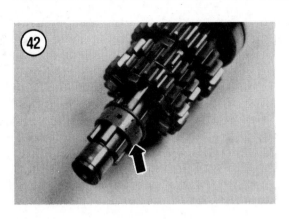

b. Place an aluminum adapter on the end of the mainshaft to protect the mainshaft threads.

c. Apply a thin film of clean engine oil onto the mainshaft between the ball bearing and the end of the shaft.

d. Press on the adapter to push the mainshaft out of the ball bearing.

e. Catch the mainshaft as it falls away from the press plate once the ball bearing is free.

Mainshaft Assembly

1. If the mainshaft ball bearing was removed or replaced, install the new ball bearing as follows:

a. Support the ball bearing inner race on a press plate. Do not support the outer race or the bearing will be damaged during installation.

b. Insert the end of the mainshaft through the ball bearing until it stops.

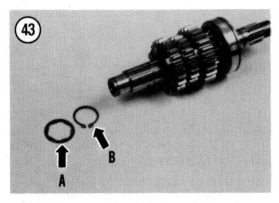

NOTE
*When pressing the ball bearing onto the mainshaft, make sure the circlip groove in the ball bearing faces toward the mainshaft threads as shown in B, **Figure 47**.*

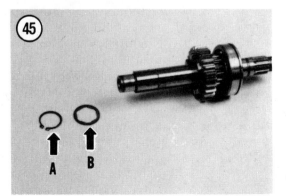

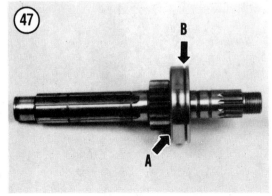

c. Hold the mainshaft upright (vertical) and lower the press ram so that it touches the end of the mainshaft.

d. Press the mainshaft onto the ball bearing inner race until first gear bottoms against the bearing.

2. Install mainshaft fifth gear (**Figure 46**) so that the gear dogs face away from the ball bearing.

3. Slide the splined washer (B, **Figure 45**) onto the mainshaft.

4. Using circlip pliers, install the mainshaft fifth gear circlip (A, **Figure 45**). Make sure the circlip seats completely in the groove (**Figure 48**).

5. See **Figure 49**. Install the mainshaft third/fourth gear combination. Install the combination gear so that the smaller diameter gear (A) faces toward the ball bearing. When installing the combination gear, align the oil hole between the gears (B) with the oil hole in the mainshaft (C).

6. Install the third/fourth gear circlip (B, **Figure 43**) with circlip pliers. Make sure the circlip seats completely in the groove (**Figure 50**).

8. Install the splined washer (A, **Figure 43**).

9. See **Figure 51**. Install the sixth gear bushing (A). Align the oil hole in the bushing (B) with the oil hole in the mainshaft (C).

10. Install sixth gear (**Figure 41**) so that the gear dogs face toward the ball bearing.

11. Install second gear (**Figure 40**).

12. Install the bushing and needle bearing (**Figure 52**) assembly as follows:

a. Install the plain thrust washer (**Figure 39**).

b. Install the needle bearing (**Figure 38**).

c. Install the clip (**Figure 37**) in the mainshaft groove. Make sure the clip seats in the groove completely.

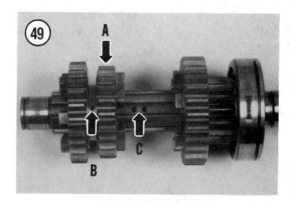

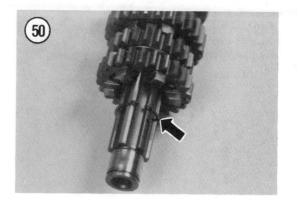

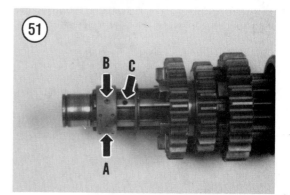

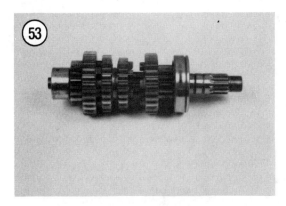

d. Install the bearing race (**Figure 36**) over the bearing.

13. Refer to **Figure 53** for correct placement of the gears. Make sure each gear engages properly to the adjoining gear where applicable.

Countershaft Disassembly

Refer to **Figure 21**.

1. Slide the bearing race (**Figure 54**) off of the countershaft.

2. Pry the clip (**Figure 55**) out of the countershaft groove.

3. Remove the needle bearing (**Figure 56**).

4. Remove the thrust washer (**Figure 57**).

5. Remove countershaft first gear (**Figure 58**).

6

6. Remove countershaft fifth gear (**Figure 59**) as follows. Fifth gear (**Figure 60**) has 3 steel balls located between the gear and the shaft. These are used for neutral location when shifting from first gear. To remove the gear, spin the shaft in a vertical position while holding onto third gear. Pull fifth gear up and off the shaft.

7. Using circlip pliers, remove the third gear circlip (**Figure 61**).

8. Remove the splined washer (**Figure 62**).

9. Remove countershaft third gear (**Figure 63**).

10. See **Figure 64**. Remove countershaft fourth gear (A) and its bushing (B).

11. Remove the splined washer (**Figure 65**).

12. Using circlip pliers, remove the circlip (**Figure 66**).

13. Remove countershaft sixth gear (**Figure 67**).

14. Using circlip pliers, remove the circlip (**Figure 68**).

15. Remove the splined washer (**Figure 69**).

16. Remove countershaft second gear (**Figure 70**).

17. Inspect the countershaft assembly as described in this chapter.

18. If necessary remove the countershaft ball bearing (A, **Figure 71**) as follows:

NOTE
*The collar (B, **Figure 71**) will be removed with the ball bearing. Also there is a washer installed between the ball bearing and the countershaft shoulder (C, **Figure 71**).*

a. Support the countershaft bearing with a press plate.
b. Place an aluminum adapter on the end of the countershaft to protect the countershaft threads.

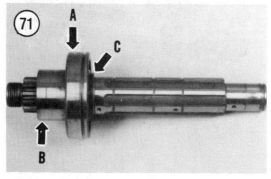

c. Apply a thin film of clean engine oil onto the countershaft between the collar and the end of the shaft.

d. Press on the adapter to push the countershaft out of the collar and ball bearing.

e. Catch the countershaft as it falls away from the press plate once the ball bearing is free.

Countershaft Assembly

1. If the countershaft ball bearing (A, **Figure 71**) was removed, reverse to install the bearing.

> *NOTE*
> *When pressing the ball bearing onto the countershaft, make sure the circlip groove in the ball bearing faces away from the countershaft threads as shown in Figure 72.*

2. Install countershaft second gear **(Figure 70)** so that the side of the gear showing sliding wear between the slots faces away from the bearing.

3. Install the splined washer **(Figure 69)**.

4. Using circlip pliers, install the second gear circlip **(Figure 68)**. Make sure the circlip seats completely in the countershaft groove.

5. Install sixth gear **(Figure 67)**. Align the oil hole in the sixth gear shift fork slot (A, **Figure 73**) with the oil hole in the countershaft (B, **Figure 73**). In addition, install the gear so that the shift fork slot faces away from the bearing (C, **Figure 73**).

6. Using circlip pliers, install the sixth gear circlip **(Figure 66)**. Make sure the circlip seats completely in the countershaft groove.

7. Install the splined washer **(Figure 65)**.

8. See **Figure 74**. Install the fourth gear bushing. Align the oil hole in the bushing (A) with the oil hole in the countershaft (B).

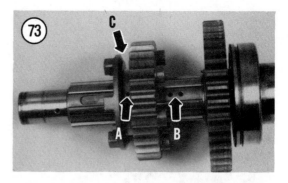

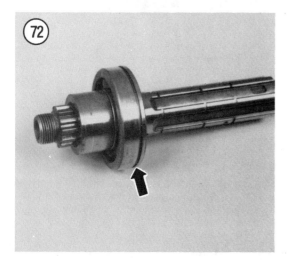

9. Install countershaft fourth gear (A, **Figure 64**).

10. Install countershaft third gear (**Figure 63**).

11. Install the splined washer (**Figure 62**).

12. Using circlip pliers, install the third gear circlip (**Figure 61**). Make sure the circlip seats completely in the countershaft groove.

NOTE
When installing the 3 balls into fifth gear (Figure 60) do not use grease to hold them in place. The balls must be able to move freely during normal transmission operation.

13. Install countershaft fifth gear as follows:
   a. Insert one 5/32 in. ball into each of the fifth gear holes (**Figure 75**).
   b. See **Figure 76**. Align the 3 ball holes in the gear with the 3 countershaft ball slots and install fifth gear.
   c. Make sure that the shift fork groove faces toward the ball bearing when installing fifth gear (**Figure 76**).

14. Install countershaft first gear (**Figure 58**).

15. Install the bushing and needle bearing (**Figure 77**) assembly as follows:
   a. Install the plain thrust washer (**Figure 57**).
   b. Install the needle bearing (**Figure 56**).
   c. Install the clip (**Figure 55**) in the countershaft groove. Make sure the clip seats in the groove completely.
   d. Install the bearing race (**Figure 54**) over the bearing.

16. Refer to **Figure 78** for correct placement of the gears. Make sure each gear engages properly to the adjoining gear where applicable.

Inspection

1. Clean all parts in cleaning solvent and thoroughly dry.

2. Inspect the gears visually for cracks, chips, broken teeth and burnt teeth.

3. Check the gear dogs (A, **Figure 79**) to make sure they are not rounded off. If dogs are rounded off, check the shift forks as described later in this chapter. More than likely, one or more of the shift forks is bent.

4. Inspect the idle gear slots (A, **Figure 80**) for rounding off, cracks or other damage. If the slots are worn or damaged, check the mating gear dogs as described in Step 3.

5. Inspect all free wheeling gear bearing surfaces (B, **Figure 80**) for wear, discoloration and galling. Inspect the mating shaft bearing surface also. If there is any metal flaking or visible damage, replace both parts.

6. Inspect the mainshaft and countershaft splines (A, **Figure 81**) for wear or discoloration. Check the mating gear internal splines also (B, **Figure 79**). If no visible damage is apparent, install each sliding gear on its respective shaft and work the gear back and forth to make sure it slides smoothly.

7. Check each transmission shaft circlip groove for cracks or wear. If in doubt, install a new circlip into the questionable groove. The circlip should be fairly tight with no appreciable side play. Because there are no service specifications for transmission shaft-to-circlip groove fit, wear will have to be determined by sight and feel. If a circlip groove is damaged, the transmission shaft will have to be replaced.

8. Check all washers and circlips. Replace the circlips as they may have been damaged during operation or removal. Check the thrust washers for signs of heat or wear. Thrust washers damaged by heat will appear blue in color. Because thrust washers and circlips determine transmission end play, always replace questionable washers and used circlips.

WARNING
Splined washers are used to retain all idle gears on one or both sides. When replacing a splined washer, make sure to use a splined washer and not a plain washer. Splined washers reduce friction at the circlips because they are made to turn with the shaft and not the gear. If a plain washer is used, it will spin with the gear and cause excessive friction and weakening of the circlip. It could even force the circlip out of its groove. Either condition could cause two gears to engage at one time. Double engagement would cause transmission lockup and loss of control.

6. Inspect the needle bearings and their housings for wear or damage. Replace if necessary.

7. Check the countershaft slot (B, **Figure 81**) where the fifth gear ball bearings engage. If the slot is worn or damaged, the countershaft must be replaced.

NOTE
*Defective gears should be replaced, and it is a good idea to replace the mating gear (**Figure 82**) even though it may not show as much wear or damage. Accelerated wear to new parts is normally caused by contact from worn parts.*

Shift Drum and Forks
Removal

The shift drum and shift forks are installed in the lower crankcase assembly.

Refer to **Figure 83** for this procedure.

1. Separate the crankcase assembly as described in Chapter Four.

NOTE
The gear positioning and neutral positioning levers removed in Steps 2 and 3 are identical. The springs installed behind the levers are different. The neutral positioning lever spring has been painted blue for identification. It is suggested to store both lever assemblies in separate plastic bags.

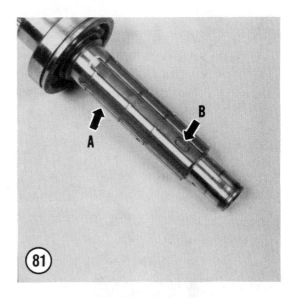
(81)

(82)

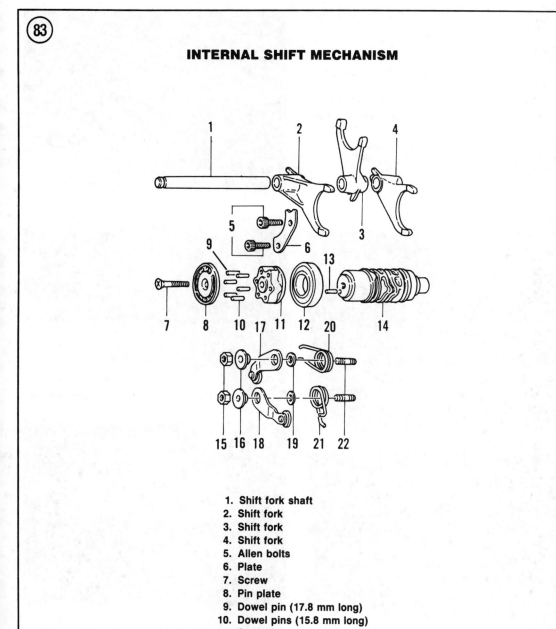

INTERNAL SHIFT MECHANISM

1. Shift fork shaft
2. Shift fork
3. Shift fork
4. Shift fork
5. Allen bolts
6. Plate
7. Screw
8. Pin plate
9. Dowel pin (17.8 mm long)
10. Dowel pins (15.8 mm long)
11. Segment
12. Bearing
13. Dowel pin (8 mm long)
14. Shift drum
15. Nut
16. Washer
17. Neutral positioning lever
18. Gear positioning lever
19. Washer
20. Spring
21. Spring
22. Dowel pin

6

2. Remove the gear positioning lever (A, **Figure 84**) as follows:

  a. Remove the lever nut (**Figure 85**).

  b. Remove the flat washer (**Figure 86**).

  c. Remove the gear positioning lever and spring (**Figure 87**).

  d. Remove the small flat washer (**Figure 88**).

3. Remove the neutral positioning lever (B, **Figure 84**) as follows:

  a. Remove the lever nut (**Figure 89**).

  b. Remove the flat washer (**Figure 90**).

  c. Remove the neutral positioning lever and spring (**Figure 91**).

  d. Remove the small flat washer (**Figure 92**).

4. Remove the shift drum/shift fork shaft bracket Allen bolts (A, **Figure 93**) and remove the bracket (B, **Figure 93**).

NOTE
Label the shift forks so that they can be reinstalled in their original positions.

5. Withdraw the shift fork shaft and remove the shift forks one at a time. See **Figure 94**.

6. Remove the shift drum assembly by pulling it out of the lower crankcase (**Figure 95**). Remove the drum slowly to prevent damaging the crankcase bearing surface.

Inspection

1. Inspect each shift fork (**Figure 96**) for signs of wear, bending or cracking.

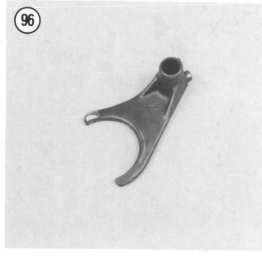

2. Examine the shift forks at the points where they contact the slider gear (**Figure 97**). This surface should be smooth with no signs of wear or damage. Also check each shift fork mating gear groove (**Figure 98**).

3. Make sure the forks slide smoothly on the shaft (**Figure 99**) or shift drum. Make sure the shaft is not bent. This can be checked by removing the shift forks from the shaft and rolling the shaft on a piece of thick glass. Any clicking noise detected indicates a bent shaft.

4. Measure the tips of each shift fork (**Figure 100**) and compare to the specifications in **Table 1**. Replace a shift fork if the tip thickness is too thin.

5. Check grooves in the shift drum (A,**Figure 101**) for wear or roughness. Measure the groove width with a vernier caliper (**Figure 102**). Replace the shift drum if any groove is too wide (**Table 1**).

6. Measure the shift fork guide pin diameter (**Figure 103**). Replace the shift fork(s) if the guide pin diameter is too small (**Table 1**).

7. Inspect the shift drum bearing (B, **Figure 101**) as follows:

   a. Wash the shift drum bearing by rotating it slowly in clean solvent.

   b. Hold the bearing with your hand (so it cannot spin) and dry the bearing with compressed air.

> *WARNING*
> *Do not spin the bearing with compressed air while drying it. The bearing is not lubricated and it can become damaged. In addition, the bearing may fly apart and cause injury.*

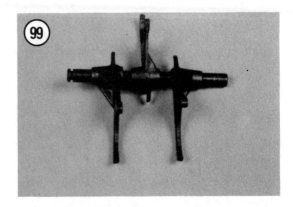

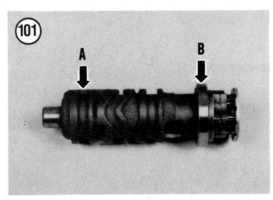

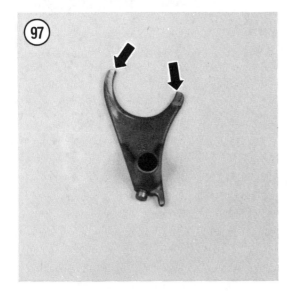

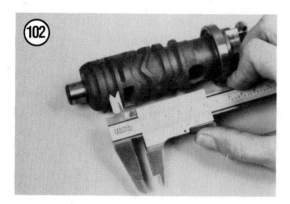

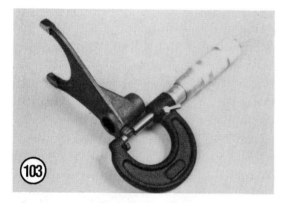

c. When the bearing is dry of all solvent, lubricate it lightly with clean engine oil.

d. Hold the bearing by the inner ring and spin the outer ring. If the outer ring turns roughly or stops, reclean and lubricate the bearing. If the bearing is till rough after 2 or 3 cleanings, replace it as described under *Shift Drum Disassembly/Reassembly*.

Shift Drum Disassembly/Reassembly

The shift drum contains a number of different size pins. Before disassembling the shift drum, have on hand 3 or 4 small containers that can be used to store parts. This will also help to prevent the loss of any component as the pins are very small.

Refer to **Figure 83** when performing this procedure.

NOTE
An impact driver with a Phillips bit (described in Chapter One) or an air gun will be necessary to loosen the screw in Step 1. Attempting to loosen the screw with a Phillips screwdriver may ruin the screw head.

1. Remove the Phillips screw (**Figure 104**) from the end of the shift drum.
2. Remove the plate (**Figure 105**).
3. Lift the segment (**Figure 106**) off of the shift drum.

NOTE
Steel pins are used to locate different shift drum components. Because 3 different pin lengths are used, the pins are identified in the following steps by their length. All of the pins are 4 mm in diameter.

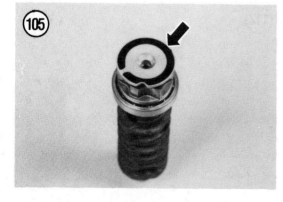

4. Remove the 1 long (17.8 mm) (**Figure 107**) and the 5 short (15.8 mm) (**Figure 108**) pins from the segment.

5. Remove ball bearing (**Figure 109**).

6. Remove the 8 mm pin from the end of the shift drum (**Figure 110**).

7. Wash all of the parts in clean solvent (**Figure 111**).

8. Inspect the shift drum as described in this section.

9. Inspect the pin holes in the shift drum and segment for wear or cracks.

10. Replace the bearing (**Figure 112**), if necessary.

11. Install the 8 mm pin into the end of the shift drum (**Figure 110**).

12. Install the ball bearing onto the shift drum (**Figure 109**).

13. The segment has 6 pin holes. Install the 15.8 mm pins into the 5 segment holes adjacent to the pointed ears (**Figure 108**). Install the 17.8 mm pin in the hole adjacent to the flat ear (**Figure 107**).

14. Align the hole in the back of the segment (A, **Figure 113**) with the pin in the shift drum (B, **Figure 113**) and install the segment. See **Figure 106**.

15. Align the hole in the back of the plate (A, **Figure 114**) with the 17.8 mm pin (B, **Figure 114**) in the segment and install the plate. See **Figure 105** and **Figure 115**.

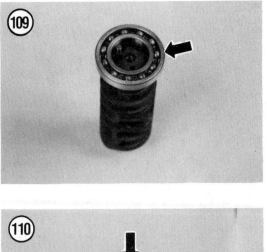

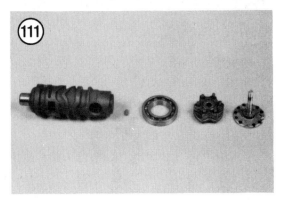

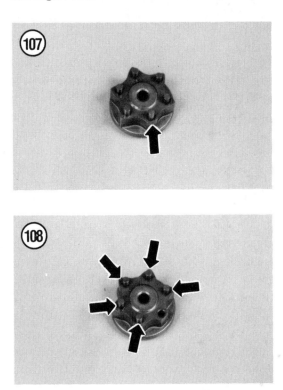

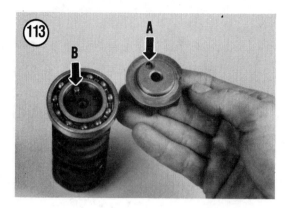

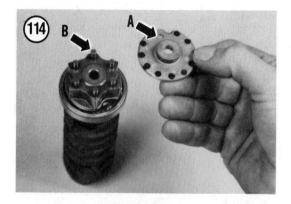

NOTE
The plate must lay perfectly flat across the pins installed in the segment. If the plate is not flat, the 17.8 mm pin is installed in the wrong hole. Refer to Step 13 and reassemble the pins.

16. Apply Loctite 242 (blue) to the screw and install it into the shift drum (**Figure 104**). Tighten the screw securely.

Shift Drum and Forks
Installation

1. Oil both ends of the shift drum bearing surfaces and insert the shift drum into the lower crankcase. See **Figure 116**.

2. Insert the shift fork shaft partway into the lower crankcase (A, **Figure 117**). The end of the shaft with the groove must face out as shown in B, **Figure 117**.

3. The shift forks are identified by shape (**Figure 118**):

    a. Left-hand shift fork (A).
    b. Center shift fork (B).
    c. Right-hand shift fork (C).

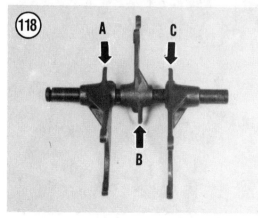

4. Slide the left-hand shift fork onto the shaft (**Figure 119**).

5. Push the shift fork shaft into the case slightly and install the center shift fork (**Figure 120**).

6. Push the shift fork shaft into the case slightly and install the right-hand shift fork (**Figure 121**).

7. Push the shift fork shaft all the way into the crankcase until it bottoms.

8. Secure the shift fork shaft and shift drum as follows:

    a. Install the locating plate (A, **Figure 122**) so that the notch in the end of the plate engages with the shift fork shaft groove.

    b. Apply Loctite 242 (blue) onto the 2 Allen bolts (B, **Figure 122**). Install the bolts and tighten securely.

9. Install the neutral positioning lever as follows:

    a. Install the small flat washer (**Figure 123**).

b. Install the neutral positioning lever and spring (**Figure 124**). Engage the lever roller into the shift drum segment.

NOTE
The neutral positioning lever spring is painted blue.

c. Install the flat washer (**Figure 125**).
d. Apply Loctite 242 (blue) onto the lever nut threads. Install the nut (**Figure 126**) and tighten securely.
10. Install the gear positioning lever as follows:
a. Install the small flat washer (**Figure 127**).
b. Install the gear positioning lever and spring (**Figure 128**). Engage the lever roller into the shift drum segment.
c. Install the flat washer (**Figure 129**).
d. Apply Loctite 242 (blue) onto the lever nut threads. Install the nut (**Figure 130**) and tighten securely.

6

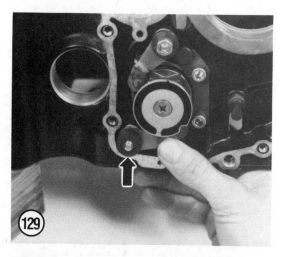

Table 1 TRANSMISSION SPECIFICATIONS

	Standard mm (in.)	Wear limit mm (in.)
Gear backlash	0.06-0.23 (0.002-0.009)	0.3 (0.0012)
Gear shift fork groove width	5.05-5.15 (0.199-0.203)	5.3 (0.209)
Shift fork guide pin diameter	7.9-8.0 (0.311-0.315)	7.8 (0.307)
Shift fork tip thickness	4.9-5.0 (0.193-0.197)	4.8 (0.189)
Shift drum groove width	8.05-8.20 (0.317-0.323)	8.3 (0.327)

NOTE: If you own a 1988 or later model, first check the Supplement at the back of this book for any new service information.

CHAPTER SEVEN

FUEL, EMISSION CONTROL AND EXHAUST SYSTEMS

7

This chapter describes complete procedures for servicing the fuel, emission control and exhaust systems. Carburetor specifications are listed in **Table 1** (ZX900) and **Table 2** (ZX1000). **Table 1** and **Table 2** are found at the end of the chapter.

CARBURETOR

Removal/Installation

Remove all 4 carburetors as an assembled unit.
1. Park the motorcycle on the center stand.
2. Remove the top fairing assembly and the side rails. See Chapter Thirteen.
3. Remove the fuel tank as described in this chapter.
4. Remove the battery as described under *Battery Removal/Installation and Electrolyte Level Check* in Chapter Three.
5. Remove the air cleaner housing mounting bolts and hose clamps and remove the housing assembly. See **Figure 1** (ZX900) or **Figure 2** (ZX1000).

> *NOTE*
> *Label the 2 throttle cables before removal.*

6. Disconnect the throttle cables at the carburetor (**Figure 3**).
7. Loosen the choke cable bracket screw and disconnect the cable at the carburetor (**Figure 4**).

8. Remove the carburetor-to-intake manifold boot clamps (**Figure 5**).
9. Grasp the carburetors on both ends and work them up and down and remove from the intake manifold boots (**Figure 6**).
10. Stuff a clean shop rag into each intake manifold to prevent dirt from entering the engine.
11. Installation is the reverse of these steps. Note the following:
   a. Make sure the carburetors are fully seated forward in the rubber carburetor holders. You should feel a solid "bottoming out" when they're correctly installed. Tighten the boot clamps securely.

> *CAUTION*
> *Make sure the carburetor boots are air tight. Air leaks can cause severe engine damage because of a lean mixture or the intake of dirt.*

   b. Tighten the air cleaner housing mounting screws after the carburetors have been installed.
   c. Check throttle cable routing after installation. The cables must not be twisted, kinked or pinched.
   d. Adjust the throttle cables as described under *Throttle Cable Adjustment* in Chapter Three.

e. Adjust the choke cable as described under *Choke Cable Adjustment* in Chapter Three.

f. Check carburetor adjustment as described under *Carburetor* in Chapter Three. Adjust if necessary.

Disassembly/Reassembly

Figure 7 (ZX900) and **Figure 8** (ZX1000) show external carburetor brackets and hoses. **Figure 9** shows internal carburetor components for all models.

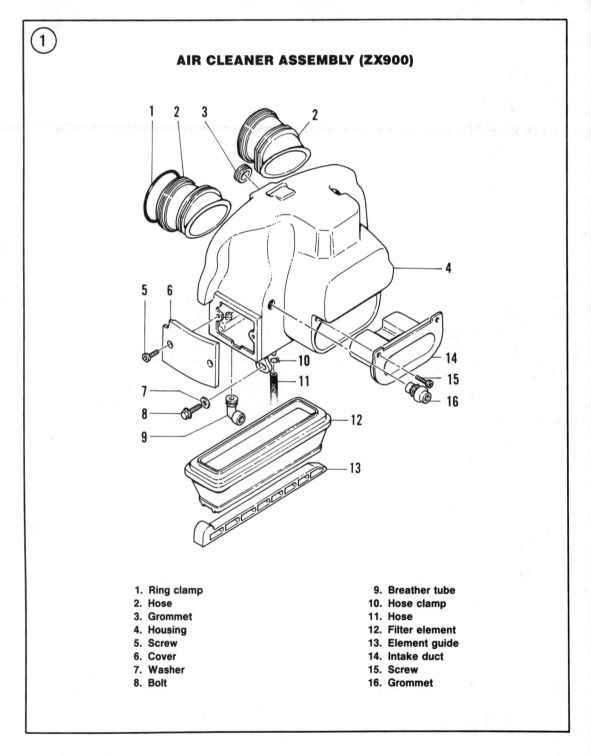

① **AIR CLEANER ASSEMBLY (ZX900)**

1. Ring clamp
2. Hose
3. Grommet
4. Housing
5. Screw
6. Cover
7. Washer
8. Bolt
9. Breather tube
10. Hose clamp
11. Hose
12. Filter element
13. Element guide
14. Intake duct
15. Screw
16. Grommet

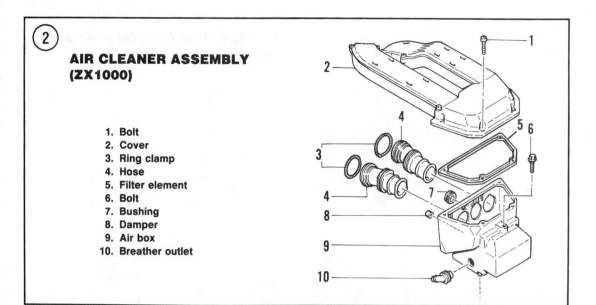

② **AIR CLEANER ASSEMBLY (ZX1000)**

1. Bolt
2. Cover
3. Ring clamp
4. Hose
5. Filter element
6. Bolt
7. Bushing
8. Damper
9. Air box
10. Breather outlet

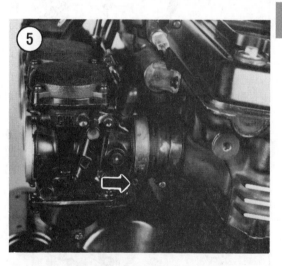

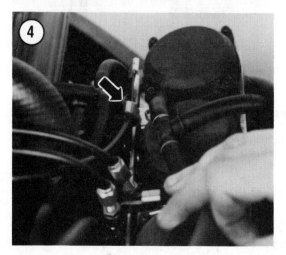

7

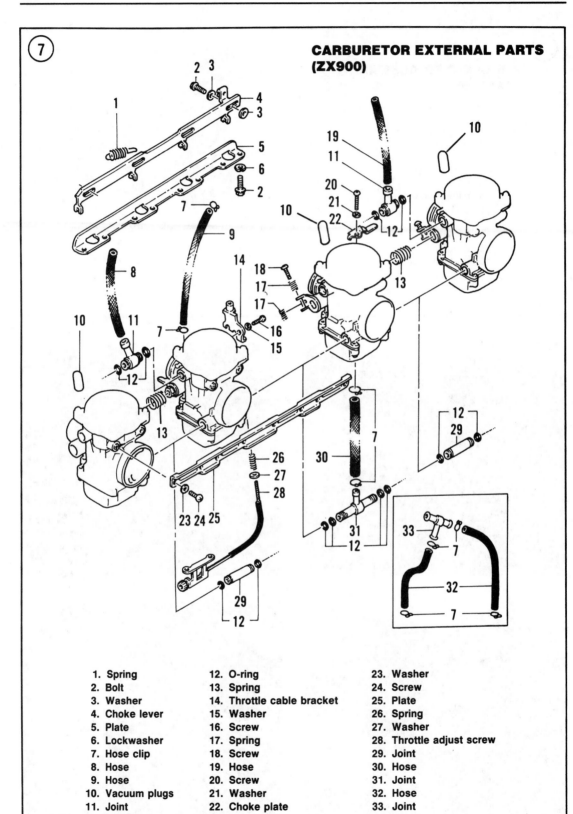

⑦   **CARBURETOR EXTERNAL PARTS (ZX900)**

1. Spring	12. O-ring	23. Washer
2. Bolt	13. Spring	24. Screw
3. Washer	14. Throttle cable bracket	25. Plate
4. Choke lever	15. Washer	26. Spring
5. Plate	16. Screw	27. Washer
6. Lockwasher	17. Spring	28. Throttle adjust screw
7. Hose clip	18. Screw	29. Joint
8. Hose	19. Hose	30. Hose
9. Hose	20. Screw	31. Joint
10. Vacuum plugs	21. Washer	32. Hose
11. Joint	22. Choke plate	33. Joint

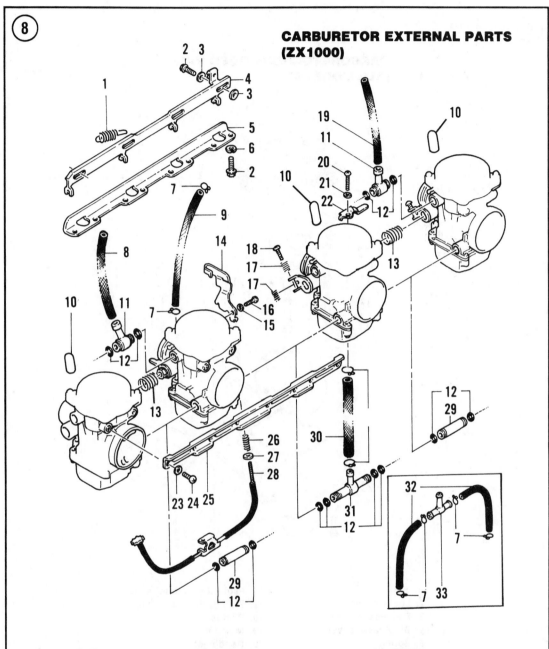

CARBURETOR EXTERNAL PARTS (ZX1000)

1. Spring	12. O-ring	23. Washer
2. Bolt	13. Spring	24. Screw
3. Washer	14. Throttle cable bracket	25. Plate
4. Choke lever	15. Washer	26. Spring
5. Plate	16. Screw	27. Washer
6. Lockwasher	17. Spring	28. Throttle adjust screw
7. Hose clip	18. Screw	29. Joint
8. Hose	19. Hose	30. Hose
9. Hose	20. Screw	31. Joint
10. Vacuum plugs	21. Washer	32. Hose
11. Joint	22. Choke plate	33. Joint

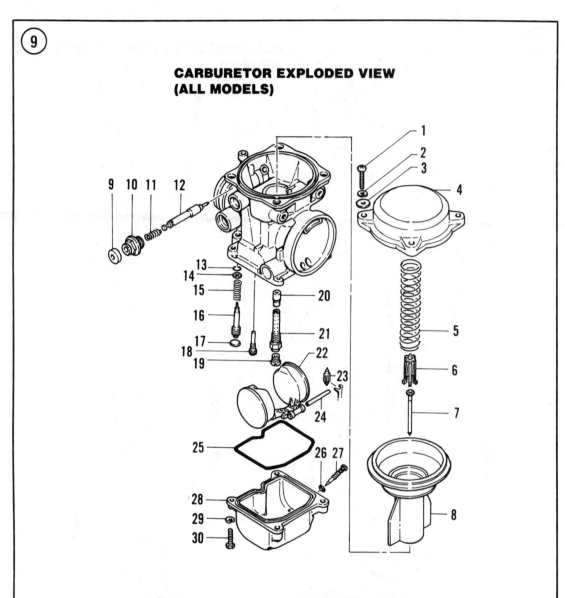

**CARBURETOR EXPLODED VIEW
(ALL MODELS)**

1. Screw
2. Lockwasher
3. Flat washer
4. Diaphragm cover
5. Spring
6. Spring seat
7. Jet needle
8. Vacuum slide
9. Seal
10. Nut
11. Spring
12. Choke shaft
13. O-ring
14. Washer
15. Spring
16. Pilot (idle mixture) screw
17. Plug (U.S. models only)
18. Pilot jet
19. Main jet
20. Needle jet
21. Air bleed pipe
22. Floats
23. Float valve
24. Float pivot pin
25. O-ring
26. O-ring
27. Drain screw
28. Float bowl
29. Lockwasher
30. Bolt

1. Remove the upper cover (**Figure 10**).
2. Remove the spring (**Figure 11**).
3. Lift the diaphragm out of the carburetor (**Figure 12**).
4. Remove the spring seat (**Figure 13**) and remove the jet needle (**Figure 14**).
5. Remove the float bowl (**Figure 15**).

NOTE
When removing the No.1 and No. 2 float bowls, it will be necessary to disconnect the throttle adjust screw holder. **Figure 16** *shows the adjuster on ZX900 models.*

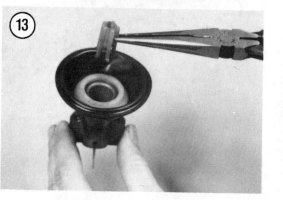

6. See **Figure 17**. Remove the float pin (A) and float (B).

> *NOTE*
> *Be sure to remove the float valve needle and its hanger clip off of the float (**Figure 18**).*

7A. *All models except U.S.:* Carefully screw in the mixture screw until it seats *lightly* while counting and recording the number of turns so it can be installed in the same position during assembly. Then remove the idle mixture screw (**Figure 19**), spring, washer and O-ring. See **Figure 20**.

7B. *U.S. models:* The idle mixture is sealed at the factory. If necessary, remove it as described under *Idle Mixture Screw Removal/Installation (U.S. Models)* in this chapter.

8. Unscrew and remove the main jet (**Figure 21**).

9. Unscrew and remove the needle jet holder (**Figure 22**).

10. Remove the needle jet (**Figure 23**).

11. Unscrew and remove the pilot jet (**Figure 24**).

12. Repeat for the remaining carburetors.

13. Separation of the carburetors is not required for cleaning.

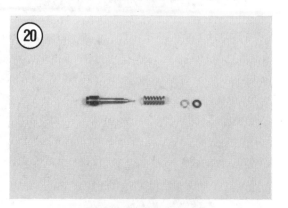

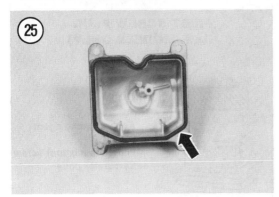

NOTE
With all of the jets removed, you can easily clean most orifices and passages with spray carburetor cleaner. This type of cleaning is effective to clear jets clogged by long-term storage. In rare cases, this type of cleaning won't remove all contamination. If the carburetors are very dirty, separate the carburetors as described in this chapter.

14. Clean and inspect the carburetors as described in this chapter.

15. Installation is the reverse of these steps. Note the following.

16. Replace the float bowl O-ring (**Figure 25**) if deformed, cracked or if the bowl leaked.

17. Install the needle jet as follows:
   a. Install the needle jet (**Figure 23**) so that the small diameter end goes in first.
   b. Carefully screw the jet needle holder (**Figure 22**) into the carburetor. As the jet needle holder is screwed into the carburetor, it will push the end of the needle jet into the carburetor bore.

18. Assemble and install the jet needle and diaphragm assembly (**Figure 14**) as follows:
   a. Install the jet needle (**Figure 26**) through the center hole in the vacuum piston (A, **Figure 27**).
   b. Install the spring seat (**Figure 13**). Turn the spring seat so that it does not block the off-center hole at the bottom of the vacuum piston (B, **Figure 27**).

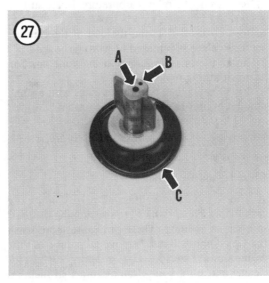

7

c. Install the spring into the diaphragm and install the diaphragm assembly. Push down on the spring to hold the jet needle and spring seat in position (**Figure 28**).

d. When installing the upper cover, insert the spring into the boss inside the cover (**Figure 29**).

> *CAUTION*
> *It is easy to damage the diaphragm while installing the cover. Make sure that the sealing lip around the outer edge of the diaphragm is fully seated into its groove in the carburetor body.*

19. Check the fuel level. See *Fuel Level Inspection/Adjustment* in this chapter.

Idle Mixture Screw Removal/Installation (U.S. Models)

The idle mixture screws are sealed at the factory with a plug bonded to the top of the pilot screw bore (**Figure 30**). When disassembling the carburetors for overhaul, the bonding agent and cover must be removed for access to the screw, O-ring and spring.

1. Carefully scrape out the bonding agent from the recess in the carburetor body.

2. Punch and pry out the plug with a small screwdriver or awl.

3. Carefully screw in the idle mixture screw (**Figure 19**) until it seats *lightly*. Count and record the number of turns so it can be installed in the *same* position during assembly.

4. Remove the mixture screw, O-ring and spring from the carburetor body.

5. Repeat for the other carburetors. Make sure to keep each carburetor's parts separate.

6. Inspect the O-ring and the end of the mixture screw. Replace if damaged or worn (grooved).

7. Install the mixture screws in the same position as noted during removal (Step 3).

8. Install new plugs. Secure the plugs with a small amount of non-hardening bonding agent.

> *CAUTION*
> *Apply only a small amount of bonding agent.*

Cleaning and Inspection

1. Thoroughly clean and dry all parts. Do not use carburetor cleaners which require dipping the parts in a strong solution. These can cause more harm than good and will also remove all paint from the carburetor's exterior. Use a spray carburetor cleaner and limit your cleaning to actual fuel and

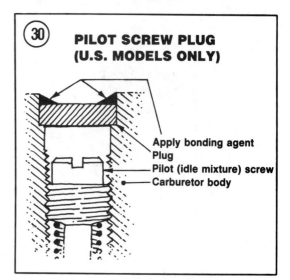

PILOT SCREW PLUG (U.S. MODELS ONLY)

Apply bonding agent
Plug
Pilot (idle mixture) screw
Carburetor body

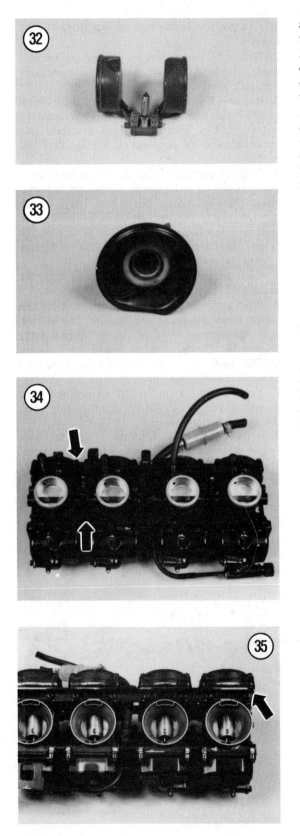

air orifices. Separate the carburetors as described in this chapter.

2. Blow out all the passages and jets with compressed air. Don't use wire to clean any of the orifices. Wire will enlarge or gouge them and alter the air/fuel ratio.

3. Check the cone of the float needle (**Figure 31**) and replace it if it is scored or pitted.

4. Check each float assembly (**Figure 32**) for cracks or leakage. Submerge the float assembly in a cup of water and check for leaks. Replace the float(s) as required.

5. Examine the end of the air mixture screw for grooves or roughness. Replace it if damaged. Replace a worn O-ring.

6. Inspect the throttle slide for scoring and wear. Replace if necessary.

7. Inspect the diaphragm (C, **Figure 27** and **Figure 33**) for tears, cracks or other damage. Replace the throttle slide assembly if the diaphragm is damaged.

Separation

See **Figure 7** (ZX900) or **Figure 8** (ZX1000). The carburetors are joined by upper and lower mounting plates on the front side (**Figure 34**) and an upper plate on the rear side (**Figure 35**). Almost all carburetor parts can be replaced without separating the carburetors. If the carburetors must be cleaned internally or if the pipe fittings (**Figure 36**) must be replaced, the carburetors must be separated.

1. Remove the throttle adjusting screw holder (**Figure 16**).

NOTE
An impact drive with a Phillips bit (described in Chapter One) will be

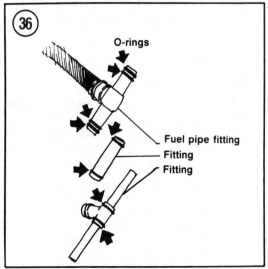

O-rings

Fuel pipe fitting
Fitting
Fitting

necessary to loosen the screws securing the holding plates onto the carburetor housings. Attempting to loosen the screws with a Phillips screwdriver may ruin the screw heads.

2. Remove the carburetor mounting plates. See **Figure 7** or **Figure 8**.

3. Carefully separate the carburetors. Note the position of any springs and cable brackets.

4. Assemble the carburetors by reversing these steps. Note the following:

    a. Replace all fuel pipe O-rings.

    b. Assemble the fuel pipe O-rings as shown in **Figure 36**.

    c. The carburetor bores (**Figure 37**) must be parallel. If not, place the assembly on a flat surface and align the carburetors (**Figure 37**).

    d. Apply Loctite 242 (blue) to all carburetor mounting plate screws before installation. Tighten the screws securely.

FUEL LEVEL

The fuel level in the carburetor float bowls is critical to proper performance. The fuel flow rate from the bowl up to the carburetor bore depends not only on the vacuum in the throttle bore and the size of the jets, but also on the fuel level. Kawasaki gives a specification of actual fuel level, measured from the top edge of the float bowl with the carburetor held level (**Figure 38**).

This measurement is more useful than a simple float height measurement because the actual fuel level can vary from bike to bike, even when their floats are set at the same height. Fuel level inspection requires a special fuel level gauge (Kawasaki Part No. 57001-1017). See **Figure 38**.

The fuel level is adjusted by bending the float arm tang.

Inspection/Adjustment

Carburetors leave the factory with float levels properly adjusted. Rough riding, a worn needle valve or bent float arm can cause the float level to change. To adjust the float level on these carburetors, perform the following.

> *WARNING*
> *Some gasoline will drain from the carburetors during this procedure. Work in a well-ventilated area, at least 50 feet from any open flame, including gas appliance pilot lights. Do not smoke. Wipe up spills immediately.*

1. Remove the carburetors as described in this chapter.

2. Mount the carburetors on a fabricated wooden stand or blocks so that they are in a perfectly vertical position.

3. Remove the fuel tank and place it on wood blocks higher than the carburetors. Then connect a length of fuel hose (6 mm in diameter and approximately 300 mm long) to the fuel tank and carburetors.

4. Connect a length of hose to the float bowl drain outlet as shown in **Figure 38**. Connect a fuel level gauge (Kawasaki part No. 57001-1017) to the opposite end of the hose. Hold the fuel level gauge against the carburetor so that the "0" line on the gauge is several millimeters higher than the bottom edge of the carburetor housing (**Figure 38**).

5. Turn the fuel valve to PRI. Then turn the carburetor drain plug a few turns.

6. Wait until the fuel in the gauge settles. Then slowly lower the gauge until the "0" line is even with the bottom edge of the carburetor body (**Figure 38**). The fuel level should be 0.5 ± 1 mm (ZX900) or 0.2 ± 1 mm (ZX1000) above the edge of the carburetor body.

7. Turn the fuel valve to ON so fuel will stop flowing. Fuel flows in the ON position only when the engine is running.

8. If the fuel level is incorrect, adjust the float height. Remove the float bowl from the carburetor and remove the float. Bend the float tang (**Figure 39**) as required to get the right float level. Increasing float height lowers fuel level. Install the float bowl and recheck the fuel level.

9. Repeat for each carburetor.

10. Install the carburetors as described in this chapter.

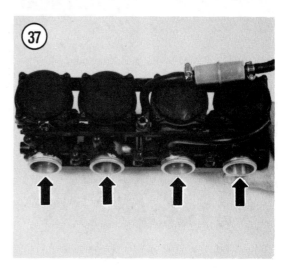

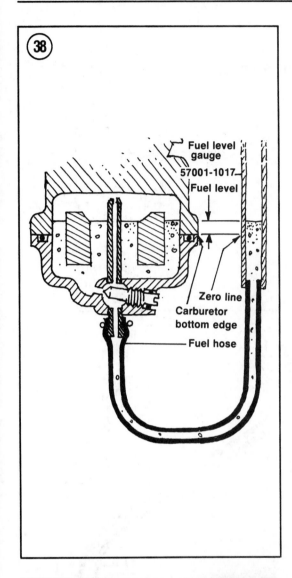

Fuel level gauge

57001-1017

Fuel level

Zero line

Carburetor bottom edge

Fuel hose

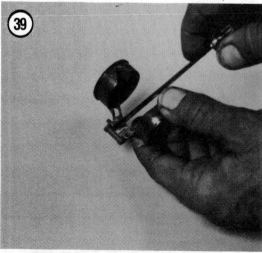

FUEL TANK

WARNING
Some fuel may spill in the following procedure. Work in a well-ventilated area at least 50 feet from any sparks or flames, including gas appliance pilot lights. Do not smoke in the area. Keep a BC rated fire extinguisher handy.

Removal/Installation

Refer to **Figure 40** (ZX900) or **Figure 41** (ZX1000) for this procedure.
1. Check that the ignition switch is OFF.
2. Place the bike on its center stand.
3. Remove the seat and both side covers.
4. Remove the battery cover and disconnect the negative battery terminal.
5. Disconnect the fuel level sensor connector.
6. Turn the fuel tap to ON and disconnect the fuel and vacuum lines at the fuel tap (**Figure 42**).

CAUTION
When servicing the fuel tank, make sure to label all hoses before removal. Improper fuel system hose routing will cause erratic engine operation.

7. Label and disconnect the hose(s) at the rear of the fuel tank (**Figure 43**).

NOTE
Plug the hoses disconnected in Step 7.

8. Remove the bolts from the rear of the fuel tank.
9. Pull the tank up and to the rear and remove it.
10. Pour the fuel in a container approved for gasoline storage.
11. Inspect the fuel tank dampers for damage and replace if necessary. Check the damper mount for looseness. Tighten the mounting bolts if necessary.
12. To install the fuel tank, reverse the removal steps. Note the following:
    a. Don't pinch any wires or control cables during installation.
    b. Reconnect all hoses and connectors.

FUEL VALVE

The vacuum-operated fuel valve (**Figure 42**) has no OFF position. The valve should pass no fuel in ON or RES until a running engine provides the vacuum required to operate the diaphragm valve. In PRI (prime) the valve will pass fuel whether the engine is running or not.

7

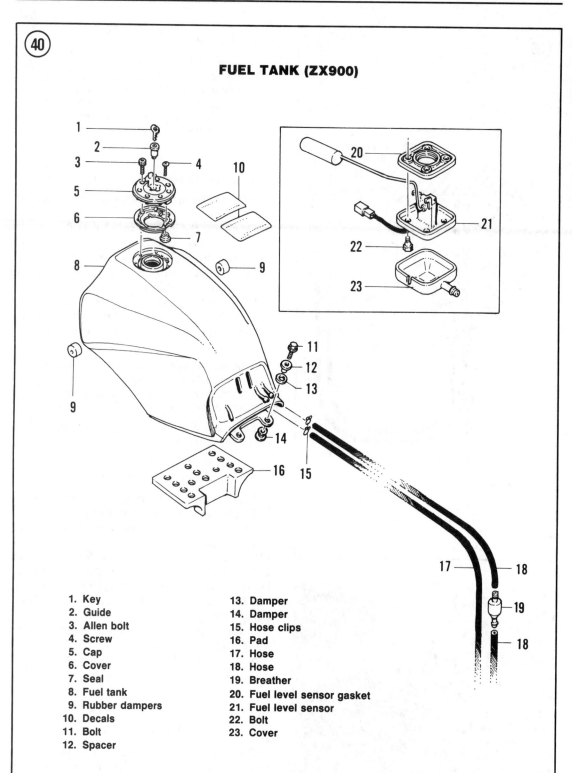

FUEL TANK (ZX900)

1. Key
2. Guide
3. Allen bolt
4. Screw
5. Cap
6. Cover
7. Seal
8. Fuel tank
9. Rubber dampers
10. Decals
11. Bolt
12. Spacer
13. Damper
14. Damper
15. Hose clips
16. Pad
17. Hose
18. Hose
19. Breather
20. Fuel level sensor gasket
21. Fuel level sensor
22. Bolt
23. Cover

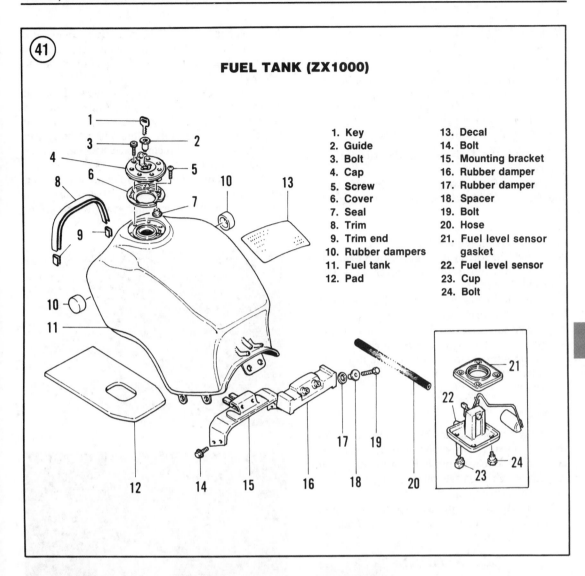

FUEL TANK (ZX1000)

1. Key
2. Guide
3. Bolt
4. Cap
5. Screw
6. Cover
7. Seal
8. Trim
9. Trim end
10. Rubber dampers
11. Fuel tank
12. Pad
13. Decal
14. Bolt
15. Mounting bracket
16. Rubber damper
17. Rubber damper
18. Spacer
19. Bolt
20. Hose
21. Fuel level sensor gasket
22. Fuel level sensor
23. Cup
24. Bolt

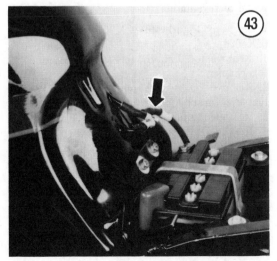

Removal/Installation

> *WARNING*
> *Some fuel may spill in the following*
> *procedure. Work in a well-ventilated*
> *area at least 50 feet from any sparks or*
> *flames, including gas appliance pilot*
> *lights. Do not smoke in the area. Keep*
> *a BC rated fire extinguisher handy.*

1. Remove the fuel tank as described in this chapter.
2. Turn the fuel valve to PRI (prime) and drain the fuel into a container approved for gasoline storage.
3. Remove the 2 fuel valve mounting bolts, the valve and O-ring (**Figure 44**).
4. Inspect the fuel valve mounting O-ring and clean the feed tube screen whenever the valve is removed (**Figure 45**).
5. Install the fuel valve by reversing these steps. Note the following:
   a. Make sure that fuel does not flow in the ON position when the engine is *not* running.
   b. Pour a small amount of gasoline in the tank after installing the fuel valve and check for leaks.

Inspection

See **Figure 45**. Disassemble the valve and check that the O-ring and diaphragm are clean and undamaged. Look for pin holes in the diaphragm. Any bit of debris on the valve O-ring will prevent the valve from closing.

Make sure the diaphragm spring is in place. Install the diaphragm cover as shown in **Figure 45**.

FUEL LEVEL SENSOR

Removal/Installation

Refer to **Figure 40** (ZX900) or **Figure 41** (ZX1000).
1. Remove and drain the fuel tank as described in this chapter.
2. Remove the cover (**Figure 46**) and remove the fuel level sensor mounting bolts.
3. Remove the fuel level sensor.
4. Install by reversing these steps. When installing the sensor, make sure the gasket is in good condition.

AIR SUCTION SYSTEM
(U.S. MODELS)

The air suction system consists of a vacuum switch, 2 air suction valves (reed valves) and air

and vacuum hoses. This system does not pressurize air, but uses the momentary pressure differentials generated by the exhaust gas pulses to introduce fresh air into the exhaust ports.

The vacuum switch normally allows fresh air pulses into the exhaust ports but shuts off air flow during engine braking. This helps prevent backfiring in the exhaust system due to the greater amount of unburned fuel in the exhaust gas during deceleration.

The air suction valves, on top of the valve cover, are one-way valves. They allow the fresh air to enter the exhaust port but prevent any air or exhaust from reversing back into the system.

Suction Valve
Removal/Installation

If the engine idle is not smooth, if engine power decreases seriously or if there are any abnormal engine noises, remove the air suction valves and inspect them.

> *WARNING*
> *Some fuel may spill in the following procedure. Work in a well-ventilated area at least 50 feet from any sparks or flames, including gas appliance pilot lights. Do not smoke in the area. Keep a BC rated fire extinguisher handy.*

1. Check that the ignition switch is OFF.
2. Remove the fuel tank as described in this chapter.
3. *ZX900:* Remove the ignition coils as described in Chapter Eight.
4. Slide up the lower hose clamps and pull the hose (**Figure 47**) off the air suction valve cover.

> *NOTE*
> *The air suction valves (**Figure 47**) can be removed with the cylinder head cover installed on the engine. The following steps show the cylinder head cover removed for clarity.*

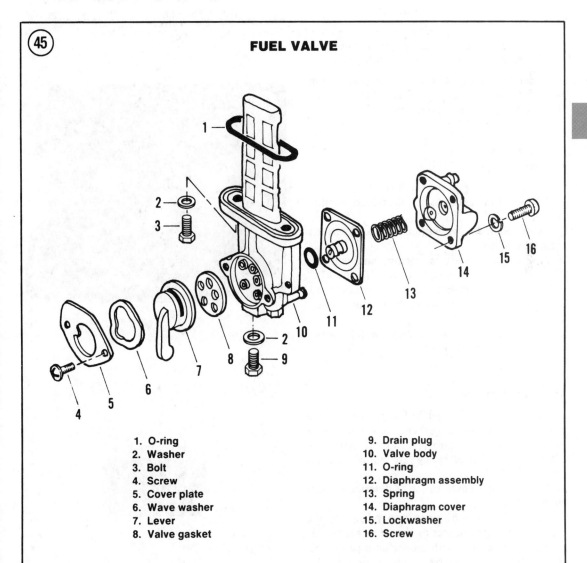

FUEL VALVE

1. O-ring
2. Washer
3. Bolt
4. Screw
5. Cover plate
6. Wave washer
7. Lever
8. Valve gasket
9. Drain plug
10. Valve body
11. O-ring
12. Diaphragm assembly
13. Spring
14. Diaphragm cover
15. Lockwasher
16. Screw

7

5. Remove the bolts securing the air suction valve cover and remove the cover (**Figure 48**) and gasket.
6. Pull the air suction valve (**Figure 49**) out of the cylinder head cover.
7. Check the suction valves for cracks, folds, warpage or any other damage (**Figure 50**).
8. Check the sealing lip around the perimeter of the suction valve. It must be free of grooves, scratches or signs of damage.

NOTE
The valve assembly cannot be repaired. If damaged, it must be replaced.

9. Wash off any carbon deposits between the reed and the reed contact area with solvent.

CAUTION
Do not scrape deposits off the suction valve or the assembly will be damaged.

10. Carefully remove any carbon deposits from the cylinder head cover port (**Figure 51**).
11. Install by reversing these steps.

Vacuum Switch
Removal/Installation

1. Check that the ignition switch is OFF.
2. Remove the fuel tank as described in this chapter.
3. *ZX900:* Remove the ignition coils as described in Chapter Eight.
4. Slide up the lower hose clamps and pull the hoses off the air suction valve covers (**Figure 47**).
5. Label and disconnect the vacuum lines and hoses at the switch and remove the vacuum switch (**Figure 52**).
6. Check all hoses for cuts, damage or soft spots.
7. Install by reversing these steps.

Vacuum Switch Test

Inspect the vacuum switch if there is backfiring during deceleration or other abnormal engine noise. A vacuum gauge (Kawasaki part No. 57001-1152) and small syringe are required for this test.
1. Remove the vacuum switch as described in this chapter.
2. Attach the vacuum gauge and syringe to the battery and vacuum hoses as shown in **Figure 53**.
3. Raise the vacuum with the vacuum gauge and check valve operation by pumping air into the vacuum hose. When the vacuum is low, the vacuum switch should allow air to flow. When the vacuum rises to 54-68 kPa (410-510 mm HG), the

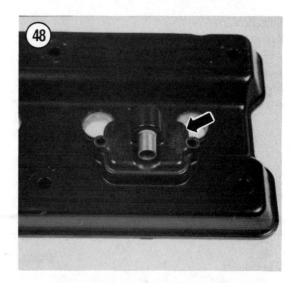

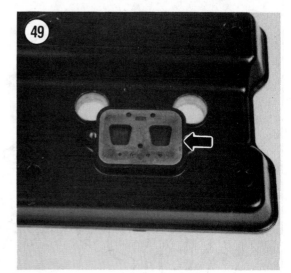

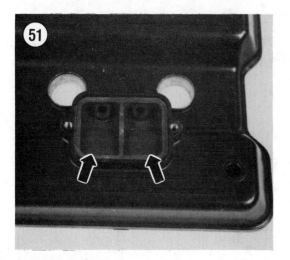

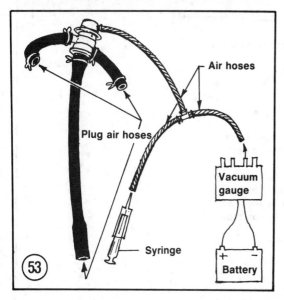

vacuum switch should stop the flow of air from the syringe.

4. If the vacuum switch failed to operate as described in Step 3, replace it.

EMISSION CONTROL

All 1984-on models sold in California are equipped with an evaporative emission control system to meet the CARB regulations in effect at the time of the model's manufacture. When the engine is running, fuel vapors are routed into the engine for burning. When the engine is stopped, fuel vapors are routed into a charcoal canister.

Inspection/Replacement

Maintenance to the evaporative emission control system consists of periodic inspection of the hoses for proper routing and a check of the canister mounting brackets.

When removal or replacement of an emission part is required, refer to **Figure 54** (1984-1985) or **Figure 55** (1986-1987).

> *WARNING*
> *Because the evaporative emission control system stores fuel vapors, make sure the work area is free of all flame or sparks before working on the emission system.*

1. Whenever servicing the evaporative system, make sure the ignition switch is turned OFF.
2. Make sure all hoses are attached as indicated in **Figure 54** or **Figure 55** and that they are not damaged or pinched.
3. When removing the separator, it is important not to turn the separator upside down or sideways. Doing so will allow gasoline to flow into the canister.
4. Replace any worn or damaged parts immediately.
5. The canister is capable of working through the motorcycle's life without maintenance, provided that it is not damaged or contaminated.

EXHAUST SYSTEM

Removal/Installation

Refer to **Figure 56** (ZX900) or **Figure 57** (ZX1000) for this procedure.
1. Remove the lower fairing and its mounting brackets as described in Chapter Thirteen.
2. Remove the radiator as described in Chapter Nine.

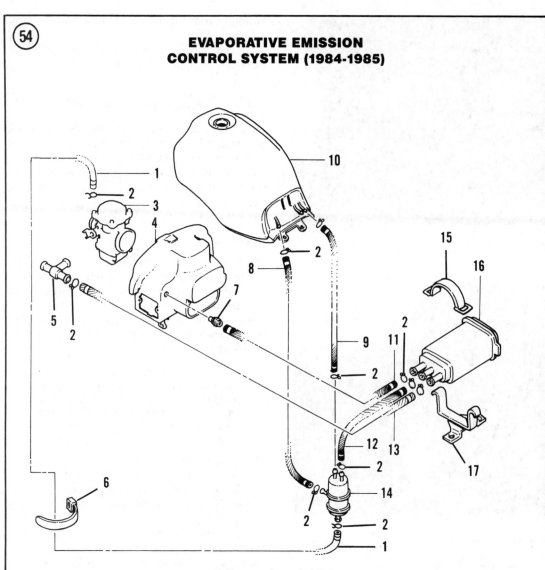

54

**EVAPORATIVE EMISSION
CONTROL SYSTEM (1984-1985)**

1. Vacuum hose (white)
2. Hose clamp
3. Carburetor
4. Air box
5. T-connector
6. Clamp
7. Hose fitting
8. Fuel return hose (red)
9. Breather hose (blue)
10. Fuel tank
11. Purge hose (green)
12. Breather hose (blue)
13. Breather hose (yellow)
14. Liquid/vapor separator
15. Clamp
16. Canister
17. Clamp

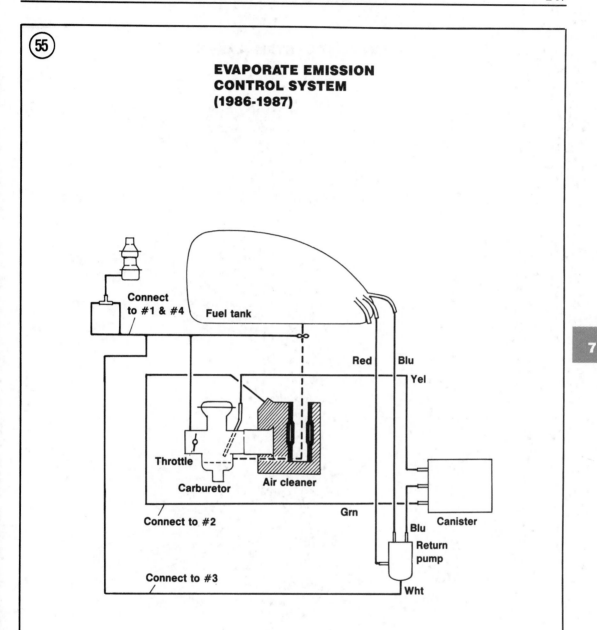

EVAPORATE EMISSION CONTROL SYSTEM (1986-1987)

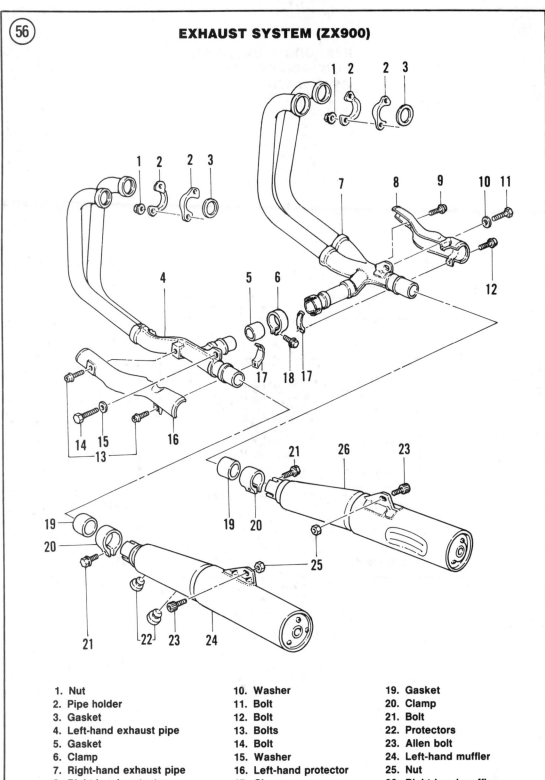

EXHAUST SYSTEM (ZX900)

1. Nut
2. Pipe holder
3. Gasket
4. Left-hand exhaust pipe
5. Gasket
6. Clamp
7. Right-hand exhaust pipe
8. Right-hand protector
9. Bolt
10. Washer
11. Bolt
12. Bolt
13. Bolts
14. Bolt
15. Washer
16. Left-hand protector
17. Clamp
18. Bolt
19. Gasket
20. Clamp
21. Bolt
22. Protectors
23. Allen bolt
24. Left-hand muffler
25. Nut
26. Right-hand muffler

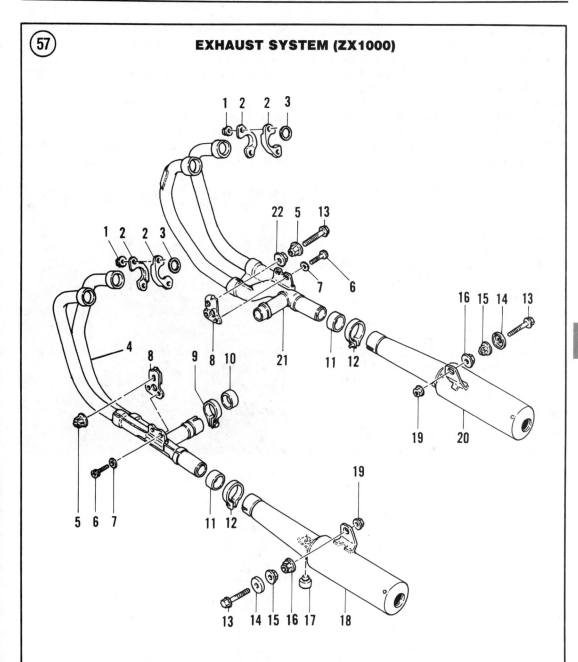

EXHAUST SYSTEM (ZX1000)

1. Nut
2. Pipe holder
3. Gasket
4. Left-hand exhaust pipe
5. Nut
6. Allen bolt
7. Washer
8. Nut plate
9. Clamp
10. Gasket
11. Gasket
12. Clamp
13. Bolt
14. Cover
15. Nut
16. Nut
17. Damper
18. Left-hand muffler
19. Nut
20. Right-hand muffler
21. Right-hand exhaust pipe
22. Nut

3. Remove the oil cooler as described under *Oil Cooler Removal/Installation* in Chapter Four.

4. Remove the exhaust pipe holder nuts and work the holders free from the studs (**Figure 58**).

5. Remove the rear exhaust pipe mounting nuts and bolts.

6. Pull the exhaust pipe and muffler assemblies out of the cylinder head and remove the split collars.

7. Remove the exhaust pipe assembly.

8. To install, reverse the removal steps. Note the following:
   a. Use new gaskets in the cylinder head exhaust ports.
   b. Tighten the exhaust pipe holder nuts at the cylinder head first, gradually and evenly. Then tighten the rear bolts and nuts.
   c. Start the engine and check for leakage. Tighten the clamps again after the engine has cooled down.

NOTE
It may be necessary to loosen the cross-over pipe clamps and the muffler clamps to ease alignment of bolt holes. If these were loosened, tighten them after all bolts are loosely installed.

Maintenance

The exhaust system is a vital key to the motorcycle's operation and performance. You should periodically inspect, clean and polish (if required) the exhaust system. Special chemical cleaners and preservatives compounded for exhaust systems are available at most motorcycle shops.

Severe dents which cause flow restrictions require replacement of the damaged part. When washing your motorcycle, avoid spraying water directly at the exhaust outlet since this will allow excessive moisture to enter the mufflers.

Table 1 CARBURETOR SPECIFICATIONS (ZX900)

	1984-1985 49-state	1984-1985 Calif.	1984-1985 European
Make	Keihin	Keihin	Keihin
Type	CVK34	CVK34	CVK34
Main jet	135	138	132
Main air jet	100	100	100
Jet needle	N27A	N27A	N27B
Pilot jet	35	35	35
Pilot air jet	160	160	160
Pilot screw	—	—	2 1/2 turns out
Starter jet	42	38	42
Fuel level	-0.5 mm (0.19 in.)	-0.5 mm (0.19 in.)	-0.5 mm (0.19 in.)
Float height	17.0 mm (0.669 in.)	17.0 mm (0.669 in.)	17.0 mm (0.669 in.)

Type	1986 All U.S.	1986 European
Make	Keihin	Keihin
Type	CVK34	CVK34
Main jet	135	132
Main air jet	100	100
Jet needle	N27A	N27B
Pilot jet	35	35
Pilot air jet	160	160
Pilot screw	—	2 1/2 turns out
Starter jet	42	42
Fuel level	-0.5 (0.19 in.)	-0.5 (0.19 in.)
Float height	17.0 mm (0.669 in.)	17.0 mm (0.669 in.)

7

Table 2 CARBURETOR SPECIFICATIONS (ZX1000)

	1986-1987 49-state And European	1986-1987 Calif.	1986-1987 High altitude
Make	Keihin	Keihin	Keihin
Type	CVK36	CVK36	CVK36
Main jet	132	138	135
Main air jet	100	100	100
Jet needle	N36D	N36D	N36D
Pilot jet	35	35	32
Pilot air jet	140	140	140
Pilot screw	1 3/4 turns out*	—	—
Starter jet	50	45	50
Fuel level	-0.2 mm (0.078 in.)	-0.2 mm (0.078 in.)	-0.2 mm (0.078 in.)
Float height	17.0 mm (0.669 in.)	17.0 mm (0.669 in.)	17.0 mm (0.669 in.)

* Pilot screw adjustment is for European models only. See text for U.S. pilot screw information.

NOTE: If you own a 1988 or later model, first check the back of Supplement at the back of this book for any new service information.

CHAPTER EIGHT

ELECTRICAL SYSTEM

This chapter describes service procedures for the electrical system. **Tables 1-3** are at the end of the chapter.

ALTERNATOR

Refer to **Figure 1** (ZX900) or **Figure 2** (ZX1000) when performing procedures in this section.

Troubleshooting

Refer to *Charging System* in Chapter Two.

Removal/Installation

1. Park the bike on its center stand.
2. Remove the lower fairing assembly. See Chapter Thirteen.
3. Disconnect the alternator electrical connector.
4. Remove the alternator mounting bolts. Then pull the alternator away from the engine (**Figure 3**).
5. If necessary, remove the rubber dampers (**Figure 4**) from the coupling.
6. Check the alternator O-ring (**Figure 5**) for flat spots or wear. Replace if necessary.
7. The mounting bolt lugs on the crankcase (**Figure 4**) and the alternator (A, **Figure 6**) ground the alternator. Clean both areas with contact cleaner before installing the alternator.

8. Clean the alternator connector with contact cleaner.
9. Check the coupling blades (B, **Figure 6**) on the back of the alternator for looseness, cracks or other damage. Replace the coupling blades as described under *Alternator Disassembly/Reassembly* in this chapter.
10. Install the alternator as follows:
   a. Apply a light coat of engine oil to the O-ring (**Figure 5**) and the rubber dampers (**Figure 4**).
   b. If removed, install the rubber dampers (**Figure 4**). Position the rubber dampers so that there is a gap between each set of dampers. See **Figure 4**.
   c. Align the alternator coupling blades (B, **Figure 6**) with the slots between the rubber dampers (**Figure 4**) and install the alternator. If the alternator is hard to install, one of the rubber dampers has moved and closed its gap. Remove the alternator and reposition the rubber damper(s).
   d. Apply a few drops of Loctite 242 (blue) onto each of the alternator mounting bolts and install the bolts. Tighten the bolts in a crisscross pattern to pull the alternator coupling into the rubber dampers evenly. When the alternator is completely flush with the crankcase, tighten the mounting bolts to 25 N•m (18 ft.-lb.).

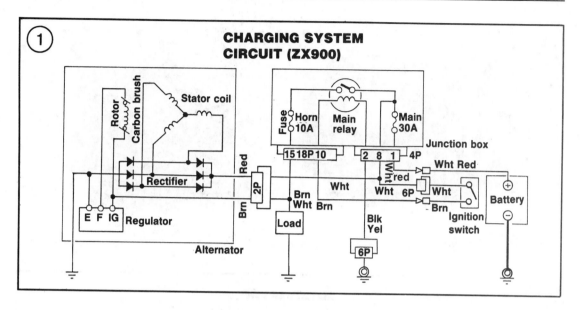

CHARGING SYSTEM CIRCUIT (ZX900)

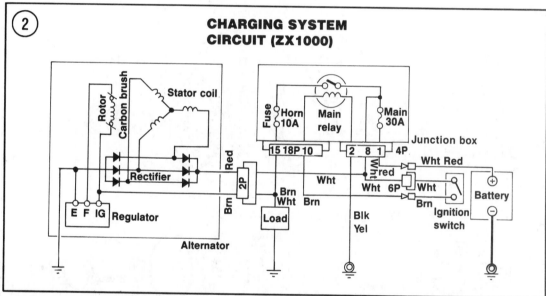

CHARGING SYSTEM CIRCUIT (ZX1000)

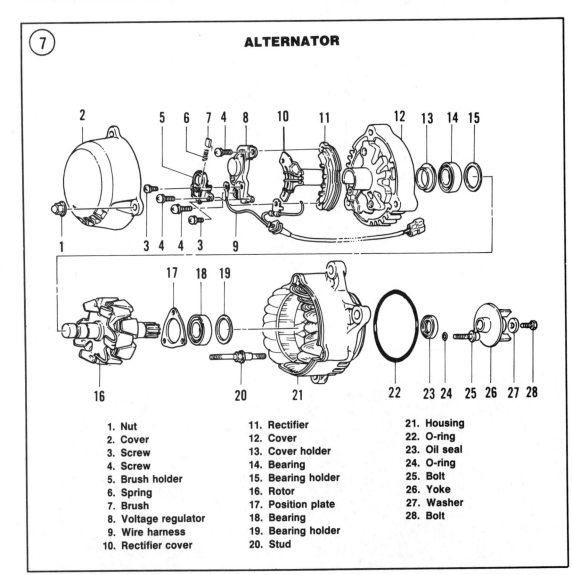

ALTERNATOR

1. Nut
2. Cover
3. Screw
4. Screw
5. Brush holder
6. Spring
7. Brush
8. Voltage regulator
9. Wire harness
10. Rectifier cover
11. Rectifier
12. Cover
13. Cover holder
14. Bearing
15. Bearing holder
16. Rotor
17. Position plate
18. Bearing
19. Bearing holder
20. Stud
21. Housing
22. O-ring
23. Oil seal
24. O-ring
25. Bolt
26. Yoke
27. Washer
28. Bolt

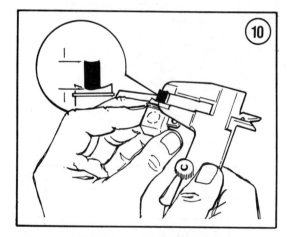

Carbon Brush
Removal/Inspection/Installation

The carbon brush assembly can be serviced with the alternator installed on the motorcycle. Refer to **Figure 7** when performing this procedure.

1. Remove the alternator cover.

2. Remove the screws securing the brush holder (**Figure 8**) and remove the brushes and springs. See **Figure 9**.

3. Measure the brushes (**Figure 10**) with a vernier caliper at the projected portion. Replace the brush holder assembly if the brush length is too short. See **Table 1**.

4. Install by reversing these steps.

Regulator
Removal/Installation

The regulator can be replaced with the alternator installed on the motorcycle.

1. Remove the alternator cover.

2. Remove the screws securing the brush holder (**Figure 8**) and remove the brushes and springs.

3. Remove the screw securing the wire to the regulator (A, **Figure 11**).

4. Remove the regulator mounting screws (A, **Figure 12**) and remove the regulator (B, **Figure 12**).

5. Install by reversing these steps.

Rectifier
Removal/Installation

The rectifier can be replaced with the alternator installed on the motorcycle.

Special tools required for rectifier replacement:

  a. Soldering iron or gun.

  b. Rosin core solder.

1. Remove the alternator cover.

2. Remove the screws securing the brush holder (**Figure 8**) and remove the brushes and springs.

3. Remove the 2 screws. See A and B, **Figure 11**.

8

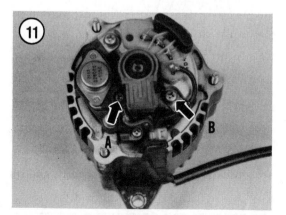

4. Unsolder the alternator wire at the rectifier (A, **Figure 13**) and remove the rectifier (B, **Figure 13**).
5. Install by reversing these steps. Note the following.
6. When resoldering the alternator wires to the rectifier, only rosin core solder should be used. Do not use acid core solder on electrical wires and components.

Disassembly

Special tools required for alternator disassembly, inspection and reassembly:
　a. Hydraulic mechanical press.
　b. Universal bearing puller.
　c. Vernier caliper.
　d. Ohmmeter.
Refer to **Figure 7** for this procedure.
1. Remove the alternator from the motorcycle as described in this chapter.
2. Remove the following alternator components as described in this chapter:
　a. Carbon brushes.
　b. Regulator.
　c. Rectifier.
3. Secure the alternator coupling (B, **Figure 6**) and remove the coupling bolt (C, **Figure 6**).
4. Wrap the splined portion of the alternator shaft with Teflon tape. The tape will prevent the shaft splines from damaging the oil seal during disassembly.

> *NOTE*
> *Teflon tape is available at plumbing supply stores.*

5. Remove the screws securing the left- and right-hand housings together. Then, pull the right-hand housing off of the rotor assembly.
6. Support the left-hand housing in a press as shown in **Figure 14**. Then press the rotor and bearing (**Figure 14**) out of the left-hand housing. Catch the rotor as it is pressed out of the housing or it will fall to floor.

> *NOTE*
> *Label the left- and right-hand bearings so that they can be installed in their original positions.*

7. Remove the left- and right-hand bearings off of the rotor shafts with universal bearing puller. See **Figure 15**.

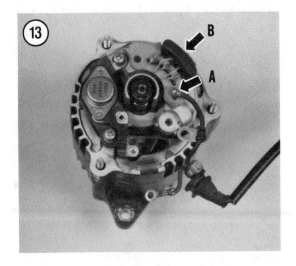

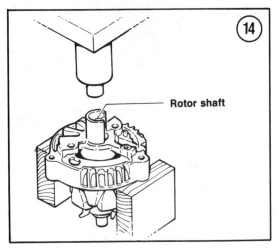

Rotor shaft

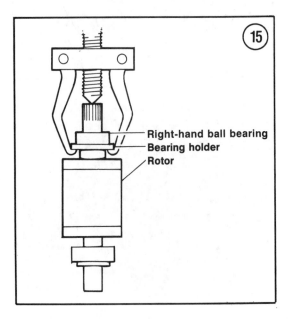

Right-hand ball bearing
Bearing holder
Rotor

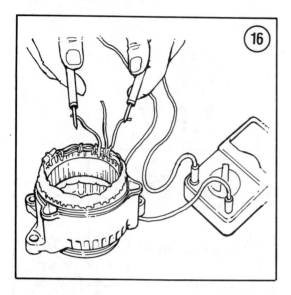

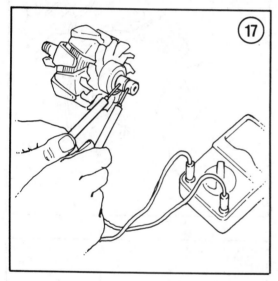

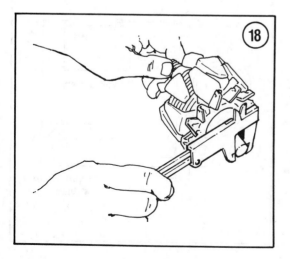

Inspection/Testing

1. Inspect each of the bearings for roughness or excessive noise by turning the inner race by hand. Also check the bearing seal for tears or other damage. Replace the bearings if necessary.

2A. *Stator coil resistance check:* Perform the following:
   a. Set an ohmmeter on the R×1 scale.
   b. Check resistance between each of the 3 stator coil wires (**Figure 16**). The resistance between each set of wires should be less than 1.0 ohm.
   c. Replace the stator coil if the resistance is 1.0 ohm or higher.

2B. *Stator coil continuity check:* Perform the following:
   a. Set an ohmmeter on the R×100 scale.
   b. Check continuity between the stator coil core and each of the coil windings. There should be no continuity (ohmmeter reads infinity).
   c. If continuity was recorded in sub-step "b", the stator coil winding has a short; replace the stator coil.

3A. *Rotor coil resistance check:* Perform the following:
   a. Set an ohmmeter on the R×1 scale.
   b. Check resistance between slip rings (**Figure 17**). The resistance should be approximately 4 ohms.
   c. Replace the rotor if the ohm reading varied considerably from that specified in sub-step "b".

3B. *Rotor coil continuity check:* Perform the following:
   a. Set an ohmmeter on the R×100 scale.
   b. Check continuity between rotor shaft and each of the slip rings. There should be no continuity (ohmmeter reads infinity).
   c. If there was continuity was recorded in sub-step "b", the rotor coil has a short; replace the rotor coil.

4. Inspect the slip rings as follows:
   a. Inspect the slip rings for pitting, corrosion buildup or other abnormal wear patterns.
   b. If necessary, dress the slip rings with No. 300 to No. 500 emery cloth.
   c. Measure the slip ring diameter with a vernier caliper or micrometer (**Figure 18**) and compare to the service specifications in **Table 1**. Replace the rotor if the slip ring outside diameter is less than the limit specified in **Table 1**.

8

5. Check the rectifier (B, **Figure 13**) as follows:
   a. Set an ohmmeter on the R x 1000 scale.
   b. Set one of the ohmmeter leads onto the recti-
      fier chassis (E, **Figure 19**). Then use the other
      ohmmeter lead and check the resistance be-
      tween the B, P1, P2, and P3 terminals.
   c. Reverse the ohmmeter leads and repeat
      sub-step "b".
   d. The resistance should be low in one direction
      and more than 10 times higher when the ohm-
      meter leads were reversed.

If any one reading was low or high in both directions, a diode is defective. Replace the rectifier assembly.

6. Check the regulator (B, **Figure 12**) as follows:
   a. The following tools and equipment will be re-
      quired: test light (12-volt, 3.4 watt bulb), two
      12-volt batteries and 3 auxiliary test wires
      with alligator clips.

   > *CAUTION*
   > *Do not use an ammeter in place of the
   > test light or the regulator may be dam-
   > aged.*

   > *CAUTION*
   > *When attaching the batteries to the
   > regulator in the following steps, do
   > not allow the wires from the batteries
   > to contact the regulator metal hous-
   > ing.*

   b. Connect the test light and one 12-volt battery
      to the regulator as shown in **Figure 20A**. The
      test light should go on.
   c. Connect the test light and two 12-volt batter-
      ies to the regulator as shown in **Figure 20B**.
      The test light should not go on.
   d. If the test light failed to operate as described
      in sub-step b or c, the regulator is damaged
      and must be replaced.
   e. With an ohmmeter, check the regulator inter-
      nal resistance by referring to the regulator ter-
      minal test points in **Figure 21** and matching
      them to the test specifications and ohmmeter
      connection points in **Table 2**.

The meter readings in **Table 2** are approximates.
If the resistance is infinite, the regulator is damaged
and requires replacement. Make sure that all other
possibilities of malfunction are eliminated before
purchasing a non-returnable electrical component.

Assembly

Refer to **Figure 7** for this procedure.

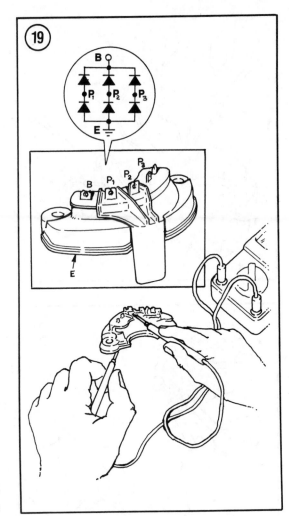

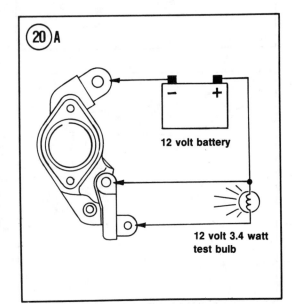

12 volt battery

12 volt 3.4 watt
test bulb

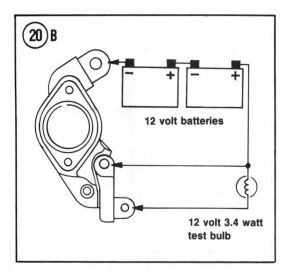

20 B

12 volt batteries

12 volt 3.4 watt
test bulb

1. Place the right-hand housing in a press as shown in **Figure 22**.

2. Press the right-hand bearing into the right-hand housing.

3. Install the right-hand bearing holder and its mounting screws.

4. Position the right-hand bearing so that the bearing's inner race is supported as shown in **Figure 23**.

CAUTION
Do not support the right-hand housing or the outer bearing race when performing Step 5 or Step 6.

5. Align the rotor shaft with the right-hand bearing inner race. Then press the rotor shaft into the right-hand bearing.

6. With the bearing supported as described in Step 4, press the left-hand bearing and bearing covers onto the rotor shaft (**Figure 24**).

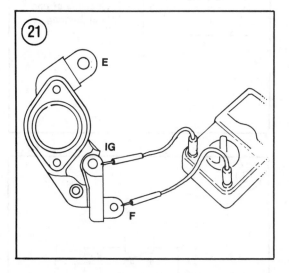

21

E

IG

F

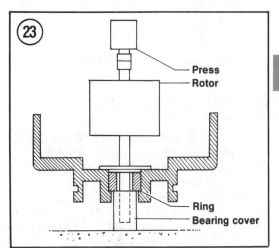

23

Press
Rotor

Ring
Bearing cover

8

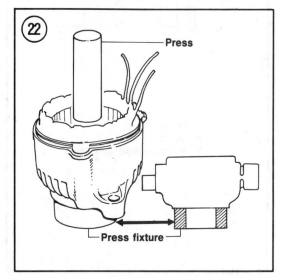

22

Press

Press fixture

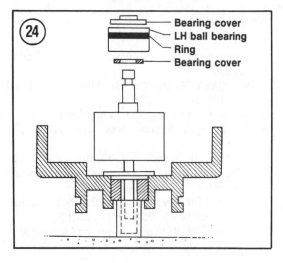

24

Bearing cover
LH ball bearing
Ring
Bearing cover

7. Align the left-hand bearing ring so that the tabs align with the ring positioning groove (**Figure 25**). Then install the left-hand housing.

8. If the oil seal in the right-hand cover was removed, install a new seal as follows:

   a. Align the new oil seal with the left-hand housing so that the spring band side of the seal faces out.

   b. Tap or press the new seal into the left-hand housing (**Figure 26**).

9. Apply Teflon tape to the rotor shaft splines. Then install the left-hand housing.

10. Install the housing screws and tighten securely.

11. Install the regulator, rectifier and brush holder as described in this chapter.

TRANSISTORIZED IGNITION

The ignition system wiring diagram is shown in **Figure 27** (ZX900) and **Figure 28** (ZX1000).

Troubleshooting

Refer to *Ignition System* in Chapter Two.

Left-hand Side Cover
Removal/Installation

1. *ZX1000:* Remove the lower fairing and the left-hand side fairing. See Chapter Thirteen.

2. Remove the left-hand side cover bolts and remove the side cover (A, **Figure 29**).

3. Remove the side cover gasket.

4. Install the side cover and gasket. Install a new gasket if necessary. Apply Loctite 242 (blue) onto the threads of the 2 bolts indicated in B, **Figure 29**.

Timing Rotor
Removal/Installation

1. Remove the left-hand side cover as described in this chapter.

2. See **Figure 30**. Remove the Allen bolt (A) and remove the large nut (B).

3. Remove the timing rotor (**Figure 31**).

4. Install by reversing these steps. Note the following:

   a. Align the dowel pin on the end of the crankshaft with the slot in the rotor and install the rotor.

   b. Install the large nut and Allen bolt. Tighten the Allen bolt to 25 N•m (18 ft.-lb.).

   c. Install the left-hand side cover as described in this chapter.

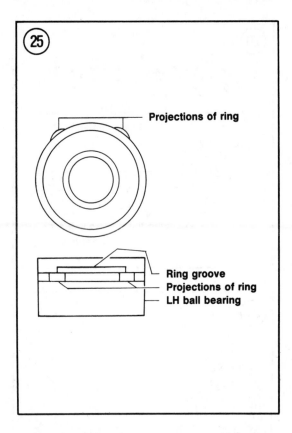

25

Projections of ring

Ring groove
Projections of ring
LH ball bearing

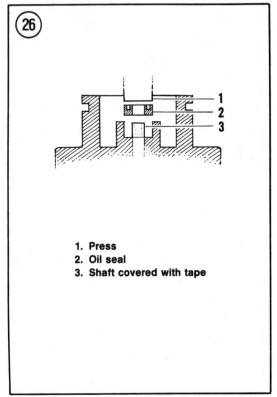

26

1. Press
2. Oil seal
3. Shaft covered with tape

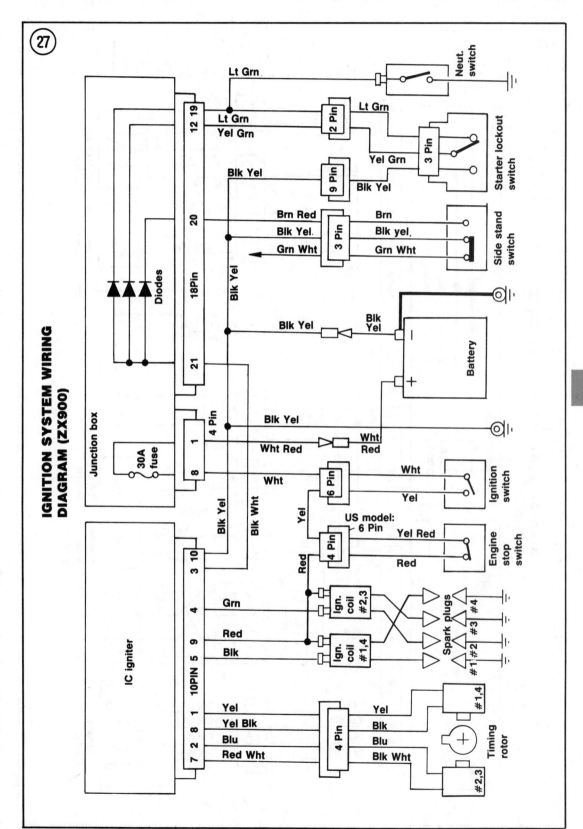

IGNITION SYSTEM WIRING DIAGRAM (ZX900)

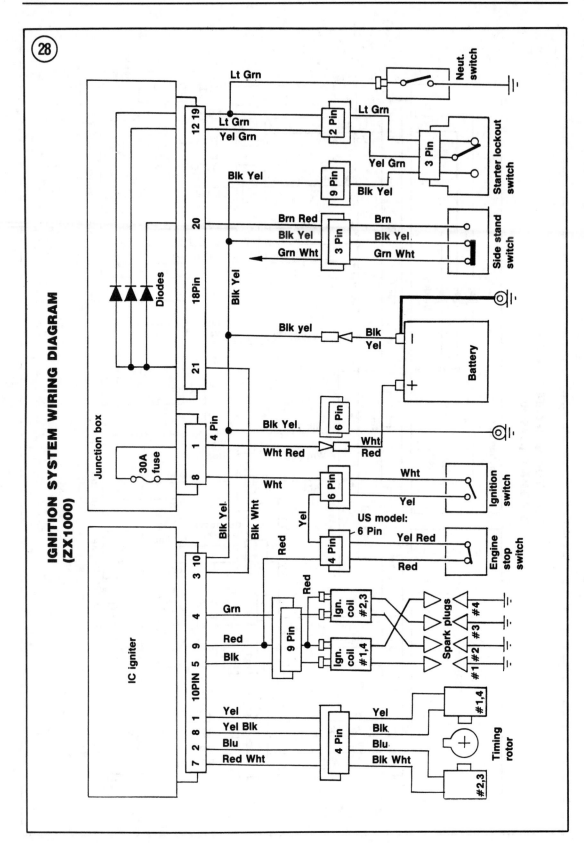

IGNITION SYSTEM WIRING DIAGRAM
(ZX1000)

Pickup Coil
Removal/Installation

1. Remove the left-hand side cover as described in this chapter.
2. Disconnect the pickup coil connector.
3. Pull the wire harness away from the frame and engine. Note the path of the wire harness as it must be routed the same during installation.

29

30

31

4. Pull the wire harness wire plug (A, **Figure 32**) out of the crankcase.
5. Remove the 4 pickup coil screws (B, **Figure 32**) and remove the pickup coil assembly.
6. Installation is the reverse of these steps, noting the following:
   a. Fit the wire harness rubber plug into the crankcase notch (A, **Figure 32**).
   b. The pickup coils must be adjusted so that air gaps (clearance between the timing rotor projection and the pickup coil core) of both coils are equal. Perform the *Pickup Coil Air Gap Inspection/Adjustment* in this chapter.

Pickup Coil Air Gap
Inspection/Adjustment

1. Remove the left-hand side cover as described in this chapter.
2. Rotate the crankshaft with a wrench (**Figure 33**) until the timing rotor projection (**Figure 34**) aligns

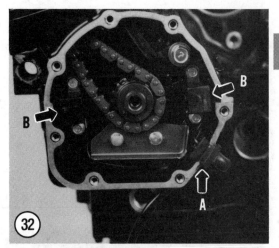

32

8

33

with one of the pickup coils. Measure the air gap with a feeler gauge (**Figure 35**). The correct pickup coil air gap is 0.5-0.9 mm (0.019-0.035 in.).

3. If the pickup coil air gap is incorrect, loosen the 2 pickup coil mounting bolts (**Figure 34**) and reposition the coil. Tighten the bolts and recheck the air gap.

4. Repeat for the opposite pickup coil.

5. Install the left-hand side cover as described in this chapter.

Ignition Coils
Removal/Installation

1A. *ZX900:* Remove the fuel tank as described under *Fuel Tank Removal/Installation* in Chapter Seven.

1B. *ZX1000:* Remove the front fairing as described under *Front Fairing Removal/Installation* in Chapter Thirteen.

NOTE
Label all wires and cables disconnected in Steps 2 and 3.

2. Disconnect the spark plug leads by grasping the connectors and pulling them off the plugs (**Figure 36**).

3. Disconnect the primary leads to the ignition coil.

4. Remove the coil mounting nuts and washers and remove the coil(s). See **Figure 37** (ZX900) or **Figure 38** (ZX1000).

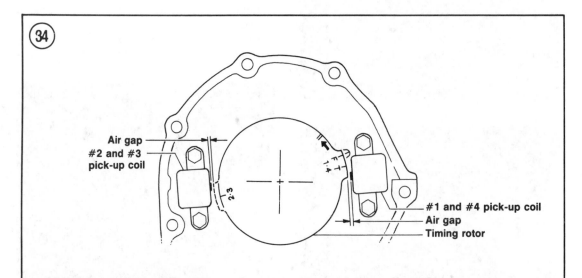

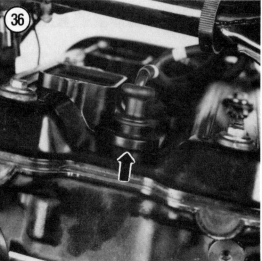

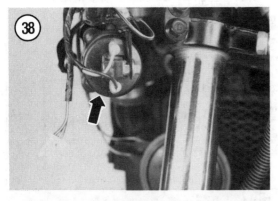

5. Install by reversing these steps. Note the following.

6. Connect the primary wires to the ignition coil primary terminals as follows:

   a. The black and red wires connect to the No. 1 and No. 4 ignition coil. See **Figure 27** or **Figure 28**.

   b. The green and red wires connect to the No. 2 and No.3 ignition coil. See **Figure 27** or **Figure 28**.

   c. When connecting the 2 primary wires to each ignition coil, it doesn't matter what terminal each wire goes to.

8. Apply electrical grease to the base of each ignition coil cap where it seats against the cylinder head cover (**Figure 39**).

IC Igniter
Removal/Installation

1A. *ZX900:* Remove the fuel tank as described under *Fuel Tank Removal/Installation* in Chapter Seven.

1B. *ZX1000:* Remove the seat as described in Chapter Thirteen.

2. Unplug the connector and pull the igniter out of its mounting bracket. See **Figure 40** (ZX900) or **Figure 41** (ZX1000).

3. Installation is the reverse of these steps. Note the following:

   a. Check the rubber igniter mount for cracks or damage. Replace the mount if necessary.

   b. Clean the connector with electrical contact cleaner before assembly.

8

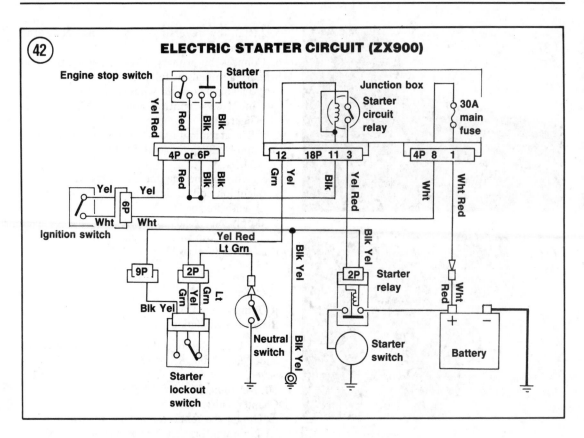

ELECTRIC STARTER CIRCUIT (ZX900)

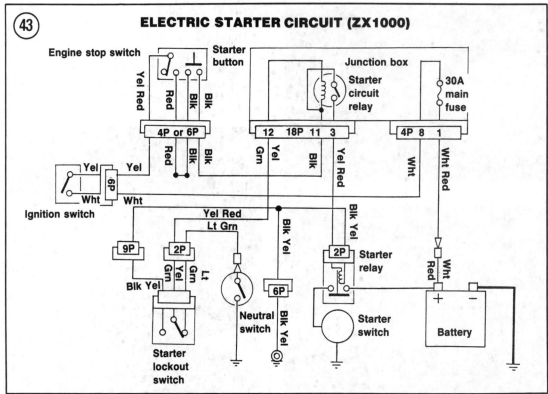

ELECTRIC STARTER CIRCUIT (ZX1000)

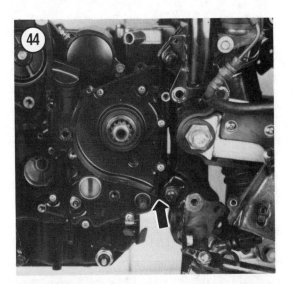

ELECTRIC STARTER

The starter circuit includes the starter button, starter relay, battery and starter motor. The starter circuit is shown in **Figure 42** (ZX900) and **Figure 43** (ZX1000).

Removal/Installation

1. Remove the lower fairing as described in Chapter Thirteen.

2. Drain the engine oil as described under *Engine Oil and Filter Change* in Chapter Three.

3. Drain the cooling system as described under *Coolant Change* in Chapter Three.

3. Remove the water pump as described under *Water Pump Removal/Installation* in Chapter Nine.

4. Remove the engine sprocket as described under *Engine Sprocket Removal/Installation* in Chapter Six.

5. Remove the external shift mechanism cover screws and remove the cover (**Figure 44**). Remove the 2 dowel pins and gasket (**Figure 45**).

6. Disconnect the negative cable at the battery. Then, disconnect the cable at the starter.

7. Remove the starter mounting bolts and pull the starter (**Figure 46**) away from the crankcase.

8. Install by reversing these removal steps. Note the following:

   a. Clean the starter motor lugs at the starter case and crankcase with contact cleaner. The starter is grounded at these points and the surfaces must be clean of all dirt and oil residue.

   b. Apply engine oil to the starter O-ring (**Figure 47**) before assembly.

   c. Refill the cooling system as described in Chapter Three.

   d. Refill the engine oil as described in Chapter Three.

   e. Adjust the drive chain as described under *Drive Chain Adjustment* in Chapter Three.

8

Disassembly
(ZX900)

Refer to **Figure 48** for this procedure.
1. Loosen the 2 case screws (**Figure 49**). Then remove the screws, lockwashers and flat washers.
2. Slide the front cover (A, **Figure 50**) off of the armature shaft.
3. Slide the rear cover (**Figure 51**) off of the bearing and commutator.
4. Slide the case (**Figure 52**) off of the armature.
5. Remove the O-rings from both covers. See A, **Figure 53** (front) and **Figure 54** (rear).
6. Remove the nut and washers (A, **Figure 55**) securing the brush plate to the end cover and remove the brush plate (B, **Figure 55**).

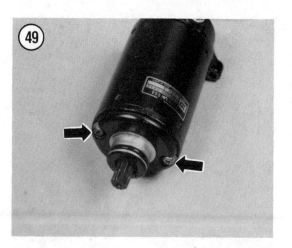

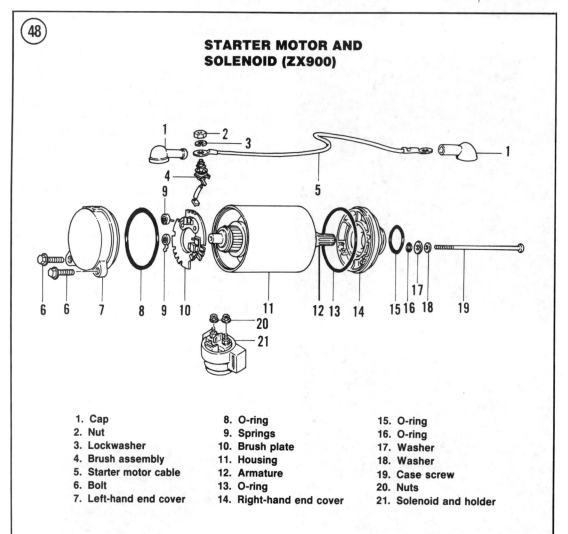

STARTER MOTOR AND
SOLENOID (ZX900)

1. Cap	8. O-ring	15. O-ring
2. Nut	9. Springs	16. O-ring
3. Lockwasher	10. Brush plate	17. Washer
4. Brush assembly	11. Housing	18. Washer
5. Starter motor cable	12. Armature	19. Case screw
6. Bolt	13. O-ring	20. Nuts
7. Left-hand end cover	14. Right-hand end cover	21. Solenoid and holder

7. Clean all grease, dirt and carbon from the armature, case and end covers.

CAUTION
Do not immerse brushes or the wire windings in solvent as the insulation may be damaged. Wipe the windings with a cloth lightly moistened with solvent and dry thoroughly or use electrical contact cleaner.

8. Check the dust seal (B, **Figure 53**) in the front cover for tearing or excessive wear. Replace the seal by prying it out of the front cover with a screwdriver. Work carefully when removing the seal so that you don't damage the front cover. Drive the new seal into the cover with a suitable size socket placed on the outer portion of the seal. Service old and new seals by applying a small amount of grease to the seal lips.
9. Test the starter components as described under *Testing* in this section.

8

Assembly
(ZX900)

Refer to **Figure 48** for this procedure.

1. Install the O-rings onto both cover grooves. See A, **Figure 53** and **Figure 54**.

2. Assemble the brush holder onto the end cover. Install the washers and nut (A, **Figure 55**).

3. Insert the brushes into the holders and secure the brushes with the springs.

4. Align the notch in the end cover (A, **Figure 56**) with the notch in the brush holder plate and install the brush holder.

5. Insert the armature (**Figure 57**) into the end cover. Rotate the armature during installation so that the brushes engage the commutator properly.

6. Align the notch on the end cover/brush holder assembly (**Figure 57**) with the raised tab inside the housing (B, **Figure 56**) then, slide the case over the armature (**Figure 51**).

7. Align the notch in the front cover with the raised tab inside the housing (B, **Figure 50**), then install the front cover (A, **Figure 50**).

8. Install the case screws, flat washers and lockwashers (**Figure 49**). Tighten the bolts securely.

9. Replace the front cover O-ring (**Figure 47**) if deteriorated or damaged. Apply clean engine oil to the O-ring.

10. Clean the end cover mounting lugs of all dirt and other contamination.

Disassembly/Reassembly
(ZX1000)

Refer to **Figure 58** for this procedure.

1. Loosen the 2 through bolts. Then remove the through bolts and lock washers.

2. Remove the 2 end covers.

3. Remove the armature.

4. Slide the case off of the armature.

5. Remove the brush plate (**Figure 59**).

6. Remove the springs from the brush plate.

7. Remove the terminal nut. Then remove the washers in the order shown in **Figure 58**.

8. If necessary, remove the terminal holder.

9. Clean all grease, dirt and carbon from the armature, case and end covers.

> *CAUTION*
> *Do not immerse brushes or the wire windings in solvent as the insulation may be damaged. Wipe the windings with a cloth lightly moistened with solvent and dry thoroughly or use electrical contact cleaner.*

10. Test the starter components as described under *Testing* in this section.

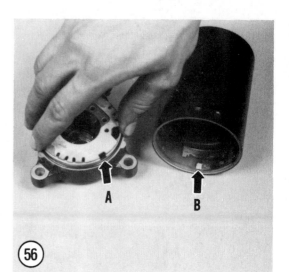

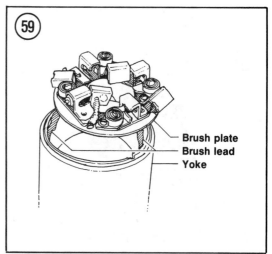

Brush plate
Brush lead
Yoke

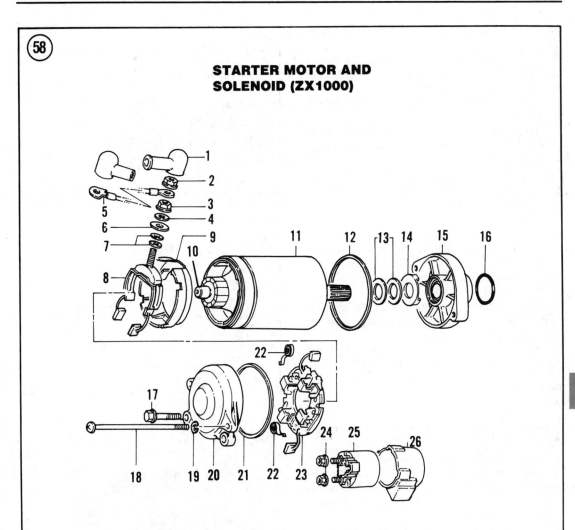

**STARTER MOTOR AND
SOLENOID (ZX1000)**

1. Cover
2. Nut
3. Nut
4. Washer
5. Starter motor cable
6. Large plastic washer
7. Small plastic washers
8. Terminal bolt and holder
9. Plastic holder
10. Armature
11. Housing
12. O-ring
13. Washers

14. Lockplate
15. Right-hand end cover
16. O-ring
17. Bolt
18. Through bolt
19. Lockwasher
20. Left-hand end cover
21. O-ring
22. Springs
23. Brushes and brush plate
24. Nuts
25. Solenoid
26. Holder

8

11. Assembly is the reverse of these steps. Note the following.

12. Install the O-rings onto both cover grooves.

13. Install the terminal bolt. Install the washers in the order shown in **Figure 58**.

14. Install the brush plate and armature as follows (**Figure 60**):

   a. Install the brush leads into the notches in the brush plate and install the brush plate on the housing.

   b. Holding the starter with the brush plate facing up, install the brush springs into the brush post halfway.

   c. Position the post so that so that it is in the D-shaped part of the spring.

   d. Turn the other half of the spring clockwise 1/2 turn and insert it into the brush groove.

   e. Push the spring into the post until it stops at the stepped portion.

15. When installing the end cover on the housing, align the notch in the cover with the tab on the housing (**Figure 61**).

16. When installing the end covers, align the marks on the case as shown in **Figure 62**.

Testing
(All Models)

1. Pull the spring away from each brush (**Figure 63**) and pull the brushes out of their guide.

2. Measure the length of each brush with a vernier caliper (**Figure 64**). If the length is worn to the wear limit specified in **Table 1**, the brush holder assembly must be replaced. The brushes cannot be replaced individually.

3. Use an ohmmeter (R×1) and check for continuity between the brush plate and each brush (**Figure 65**); there should be continuity (low resistance). Also check for continuity between the brush plate and each brush holder (**Figure 66**) with the ohmmeter set on R×100; there should be no

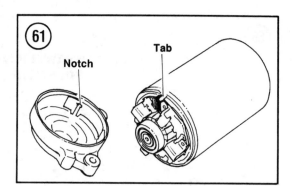

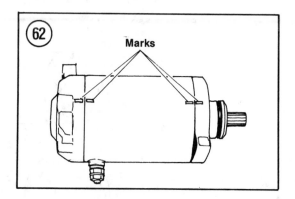

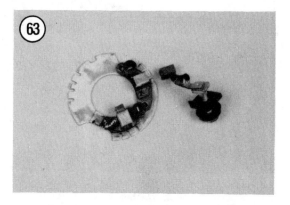

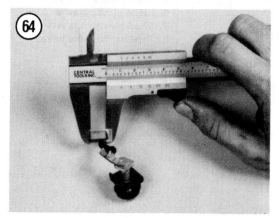

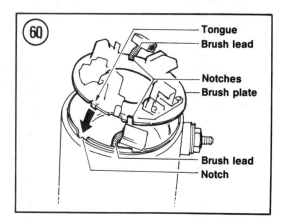

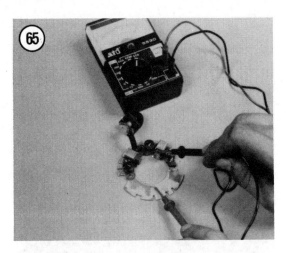

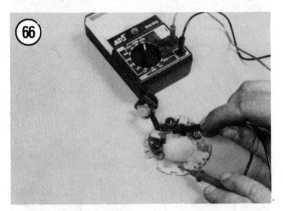

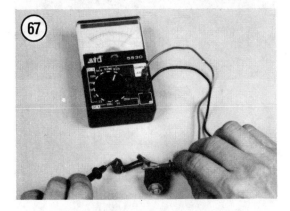

continuity. Replace the brush holder if it tested incorrectly.

4. *ZX900:* Set an ohmmeter on R×1 and check for continuity between the terminal bolt and brush (**Figure 67**); there should be continuity (low resistance). Replace the terminal bolt if it tested with high resistance or infinity.

5. Inspect the commutator (**Figure 68**). The mica in a good commutator is below the surface of the copper bars. On a worn commutator the mica and copper bars may be worn to the same level. See **Figure 69**. If necessary, have the commutator serviced by a dealer or electrical repair shop.

6. Inspect the commutator copper bars (**Figure 68**) for discoloration. If a pair of bars are discolored, grounded armature coils are indicated. Use an ohmmeter (R×1) and check for continuity between the commutator and armature. If there is continuity, the armature is grounded and must be replaced.

7. Measure the commutator diameter with a vernier caliper or micrometer (**Figure 70**). Replace the armature if the commutator diameter is worn to the service limit in **Table 1**.

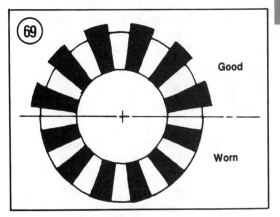

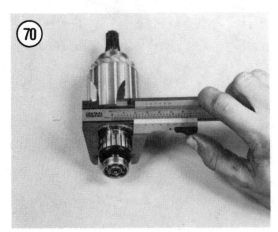

8. Use an ohmmeter (R×1) and check for continuity between the commutator bars (**Figure 71**); there should be continuity between pairs of bars. Also check for continuity between the commutator bars and the shaft (**Figure 72**) with the ohmmeter set on R×100; there should be no continuity. If the unit fails either of these tests the armature is faulty and must be replaced.

9. Replace worn or damaged parts as determined by these tests.

Starter Relay
Removal/Installation

The starter relay is installed on the left-hand side of the bike. See **Figure 73** (ZX900) or **Figure 74** (ZX1000).

> *CAUTION*
> *Because the battery positive lead at the starter relay is connected directly to the battery, even when the ignition switch is OFF, do not allow the end of the lead to touch any part of the bike during the following procedure.*

1. Remove the left-hand side cover.
2. Make sure the ignition switch is turned OFF.
3. Label and disconnect the wires at the starter relay and pull it out of its holder.
4. Install by reversing these steps.

Starter Relay
Testing

1. Remove the left-hand side cover.

> *CAUTION*
> *Because the battery positive lead at the starter relay is connected directly to the*

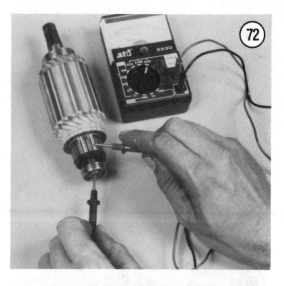

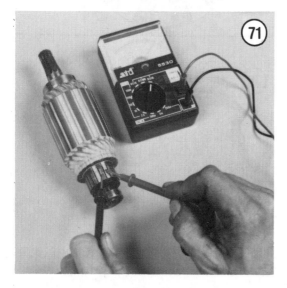

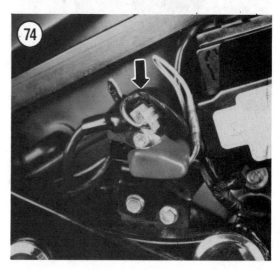

battery, even when the ignition switch is OFF, do not allow the end of the lead to touch any part of the bike during the following procedure.

2. Disconnect the starter motor lead and the battery positive cable from the starter relay terminal. Do not disconnect the 2-pin connector.
3. Connect an ohmmeter across the relay terminals. Switch the ohmmeter to the R×1 scale.
4. Press the starter button. The relay should click and the ohmmeter should indicate zero resistance. If the relay clicks but the meter indicates any value greater than zero, replace the relay.
5. If the relay does not click, replace it.

(75)

LIGHTING SYSTEM

The lighting system consists of the headlight, taillight/brakelight combination, directional signals, warning lights and speedometer and tachometer illumination lights. In the event of trouble with any light, the first thing to check is the affected bulb itself. If the bulb is good, check all wiring and connections with a test light.

Headlight Replacement

CAUTION
*All models are equipped with quartz-halogen bulbs (**Figure 75**). Do not touch the bulb glass with your fingers because traces of natural skin oil on the bulb will create hot spots which drastically reduce the life of the bulb. Clean any traces of oil from the bulb with a cloth moistened in alcohol or lacquer thinner.*

WARNING
If the headlight has just burned out or turned off it will be HOT! Don't touch the bulb until it cools off.

ZX900

Refer to **Figure 76** for this procedure.
1. Disconnect the connector at the bulb.
2. Lift the rubber dust cover away from the bulb.

8

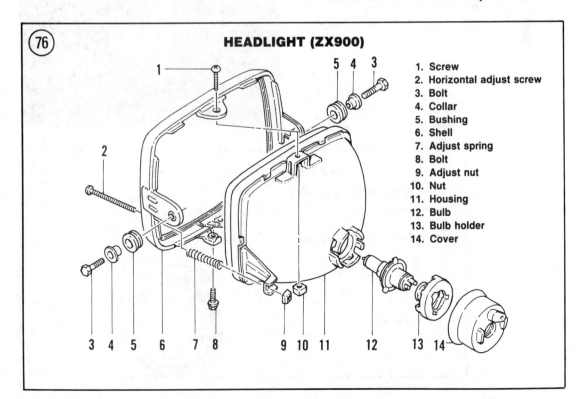

(76) **HEADLIGHT (ZX900)**

1. Screw
2. Horizontal adjust screw
3. Bolt
4. Collar
5. Bushing
6. Shell
7. Adjust spring
8. Bolt
9. Adjust nut
10. Nut
11. Housing
12. Bulb
13. Bulb holder
14. Cover

3. Turn the bulb holder to release it from the headlight housing.

4. Lift the bulb out of the headlight housing.

5. Install by reversing these steps. Note the following:

   a. Align the tabs on the bulb with the notches in the bulb socket when installing the bulb.

   b. Make sure to lock the bulb holder into the headlight housing.

ZX1000

The following procedure is shown with the front fairing assembly removed for clarity. It is not necessary to remove the fairing when replacing the headlight bulb.

1. Disconnect the connector at the bulb.

2. Lift the rubber dust cover away from the fairing mount. Then remove it from around the bulb. See **Figure 77**.

3. Lift the hook spring up and pivot it away from the bulb (**Figure 78**).

4. Lift the bulb (**Figure 79**) out of the headlight assembly.

5. Install by reversing these steps. Note the following:

   a. Align the tabs on the bulb with the notches in the bulb socket when installing the bulb.

   b. Make sure to lock the hook spring into the bulb socket.

   c. Install the dust cover so that the end labeled TOP faces up.

Headlight Adjustment

> *NOTE*
> *When performing this procedure, make*
> *sure the tire pressure is correct and that*

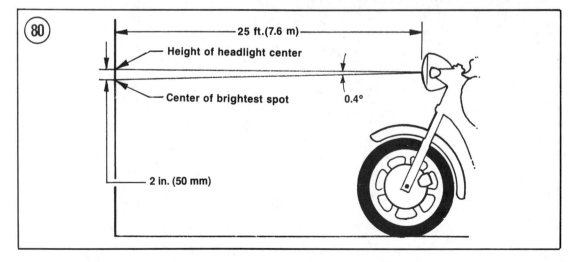

*the fuel tank is approximately 1/2 full.
Check with your state highway police
for headlight beam measurements
which may differ from those listed
below.*

Park the motorcycle on a level surface so that the front of the headlight is 25 feet (7.6 m) away from

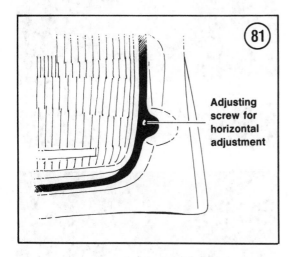

Adjusting
screw for
horizontal
adjustment

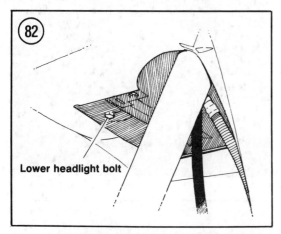

Lower headlight bolt

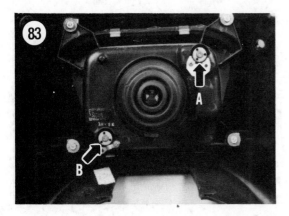

a vertical wall (**Figure 80**). When checking the headlight, the motorcycle must be off of its side or center stand and with a rider seated and wearing normal riding gear. Have an assistant measure the distance from the center of the headlight to the ground. Then make a horizontal mark on the wall the same distance as that from the headlight to ground to represent the headlight height center. Consider the following when adjusting the headlight:

    a. Horizontal adjustment: Turn the headlight on high beam. The beam should be pointing straight ahead.

    b. Vertical adjustment: With the headlight on high beam, the brightest point of the light should be 2 in. (50 mm) below the horizontal mark at a distance of 25 feet (7.6 m).

    c. If necessary, adjust the headlight for your model as described in the following procedures.

ZX900

    There are 2 adjustments: horizontal and vertical. The adjusters are identified in **Figure 81** (horizontal) and **Figure 82** (vertical).

1. Perform the steps described in the introduction to this procedure.

2. *Horizontal adjustment:* Perform the following:

    a. Insert a screwdriver into the horizontal adjuster (**Figure 81**).

    b. Turn the adjuster clockwise or counterclockwise until the headlight beam points straight ahead.

3. *Vertical adjustment:* Perform the following:

    a. Remove the adjustment cover bolts and remove the cover at the bottom of the front fairing.

    b. Insert a screwdriver into the vertical adjuster guide (**Figure 82**).

    c. Turn the adjuster clockwise or counterclockwise to adjust the headlight beam vertically.

    d. Reinstall the adjustment cover.

ZX1000

1. There are 2 adjustments: horizontal and vertical. The adjusters are identified in **Figure 83**; A (horizontal) and B (vertical). To adjust, proceed as follows.

2. *Horizontal adjustment:* Perform the following:

    a. Remove the screws securing the adjustment cover and remove the cover.

8

b. Insert a screwdriver into the horizontal adjuster guide (A, **Figure 83**).

c. Turn the adjuster clockwise or counterclockwise until the headlight beam points straight ahead.

3. *Vertical adjustment:* Perform the following:

a. Insert a screwdriver into the vertical adjuster guide (B, **Figure 83**).

b. Turn the adjuster clockwise or counterclockwise to adjust the headlight beam vertically.

4. Install the adjustment cover.

Taillight Replacement

1. Remove the seat.

2. Pull the socket assembly out of the taillight housing.

3. Replace the bulb.

License Plate Light

1. Remove the Phillips screws and remove the outer cover (**Figure 84**).

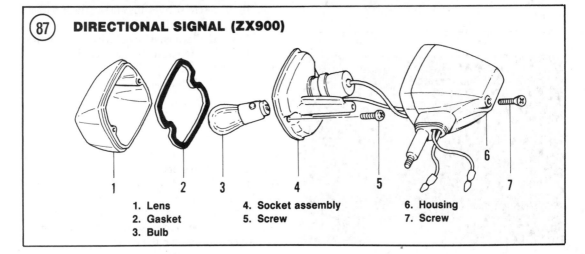

DIRECTIONAL SIGNAL (ZX900)

1. Lens
2. Gasket
3. Bulb
4. Socket assembly
5. Screw
6. Housing
7. Screw

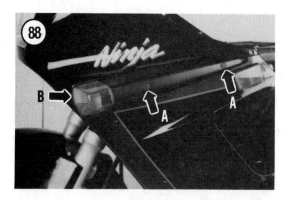

2. Remove the Phillips screws and remove the inner cover (**Figure 85**).

3. Replace the bulb (**Figure 86**). When installing the inner cover (**Figure 85**), make sure the "TOP" mark faces up.

Directional Signal Light Replacement (ZX900)

Remove the two screws securing the lens (**Figure 87**) and remove it. Wash out the inside and outside of the lens with a mild detergent. Replace the bulb. Install the lens; do not overtighten the screws as that will crack the lens.

Directional Signal Light Replacement (ZX1000)

Front

1. Remove the 2 lens mounting screw plugs (A, **Figure 88**).

2. Remove the 2 mounting screws (A, **Figure 88**) and pull the lens (B) housing slightly away from the fairing assembly.

3. Disconnect the electrical connector and remove the lens housing.

4. Replace the bulb (**Figure 89**).

5. Install by reversing these steps.

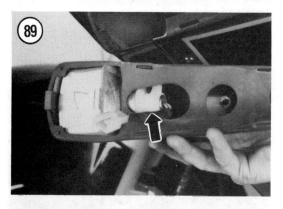

Rear

1. Remove the screw securing the lens assembly (**Figure 90**).

2. Pull the lens housing away from the fender assembly.

3. Remove the socket (**Figure 91**) from the lens assembly.

4. Replace the bulb (**Figure 92**).

5. Install by reversing these steps.

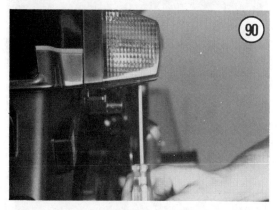

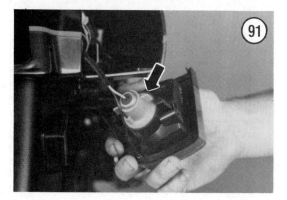

Speedometer and Tachometer
Illumination Bulb Replacement

1. Remove the upper fairing assembly as described in Chapter Thirteen.
2. Remove the socket from the meter assembly and remove the bulb. See **Figure 93**, typical.
3. Install a new bulb and push the socket into the meter.
4. Installation is the reverse of these steps.

SWITCHES

Switches can be tested for continuity with an ohmmeter (see Chapter One) or a test light at the switch connector plug by operating the switch in each of its operating positions and comparing results with the switch operation. For example, **Figure 94** shows a continuity diagram for a typical horn button. It shows which terminals should show continuity when the horn button is in a given position.

When the horn button is pushed, there should be continuity between terminals BK/W and BK/Y. This is indicated by the line on the continuity diagram. An ohmmeter connected between these 2 terminals should indicate little or no resistance and a test lamp should light. When the horn button is free, there should be no continuity between the same terminals.

If the switch or button doesn't perform properly, replace it. Refer to the following figures when testing the switches:

a. **Figure 95**: All models.
b. **Figure 96**: U.S. and Canada models only.
c. **Figure 97**: All models other than U.S and Canada.

When testing switches, note the following:

a. First check the fuses as described under *Fuses* in this chapter.
b. Check the battery as described under *Battery* in Chapter Three. Bring the battery to the correct state of charge, if required.
c. Disconnect the negative cable from the battery if the switch connectors are not disconnected in the circuit.

> *CAUTION*
> *Do not attempt to start the engine with the battery negative cable disconnected or you will damage the wiring.*

d. When separating 2 connectors, pull on the connector housings and not the wires.

e. After locating a defective circuit, check the connectors to make sure they are clean and properly connected. Check all wires going into a connector housing to make sure each wire is properly positioned and that the wire end is not loose.
f. To properly connect connectors, push them together until they click into place.
g. When replacing handlebar switch assemblies, make sure the cables are routed correctly so that they are not crimped when the handlebar is turned from side to side.

Ignition Switch Replacement

1. Remove the upper fairing assembly as described in Chapter Thirteen.
2. Disconnect the ignition switch electrical connector.

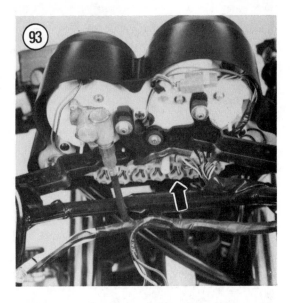

HORN BUTTON

	Blk/Wht	Blk/Yel
Free		
Push on	O————	————O

(95)

SWITCHES (ALL MODELS)

IGNITION SWITCH

	Brn	Wht	Yel	Blu	Red	Wht/Blk	Org/Grn
Off, lock							
On	O——O	——O	O	O——O		O——O	O
P (park)		O——O			O	O——O	O
						US, Canada	

STARTER LOCKOUT SWITCH

	Blk/Yel	Yel/Grn	Lt Grn
Clutch lever is pulled in	O——O		
Clutch lever is released		O——O	

SIDESTAND SWITCH

	Brn	Blk Yel	Grn Wht
Sidestand is up	O——O		
Sidestand is down		O——O	

ENGINE STOP SWITCH

	Red	Yel/Red
Off		
Run	O——O	

STARTER BUTTON

	Blk	Blk
Free		
Push on	O——O	

TURN SIGNAL SWITCH

	Gry	Org	Grn
L		O——O	
N			
R	O——O		

HAZARD SWITCH

	Gry	Org	Grn
On	O——O——O		
Off			

FRONT BRAKE LIGHT SWITCH

	Blu	Brn
Brake lever pulled in	O——O	

REAR BRAKE LIGHT SWITCH

	Blu	Brn
Brake pedal pushed down	O——O	

NEUTRAL SWITCH

	Lt Grn	Ground
Transmission is in neutral	O——O	
Transmission is not in neutral		

OIL PRESSURE SWITCH

	SW Term	Ground
Engine is stopped	O——O	
Engine is running		

8

3. Remove the bolt(s) securing the ignition switch to the steering stem and remove the switch (**Figure 98**).

4. Installation is the reverse of these steps.

Neutral Switch Replacement

Refer to *Neutral Switch Removal/Installation* in Chapter Six.

Oil Pressure Switch Replacement

Refer to *Oil Pressure Switch Removal/Installation* in Chapter Four.

Starter Lockout Switch Replacement

The starter lockout switch is mounted underneath the clutch master cylinder (**Figure 99**). Disconnect the connector and remove the switch screw. Reverse to install.

Front Brake Light Switch Replacement

The front brake switch is mounted underneath the front brake master cylinder (**Figure 100**). Disconnect the connector and remove the switch screw. Reverse to install. Check switch operation. The rear brake light should come on when applying the front brake lever.

Rear Brake Light Switch Replacement

The rear brake switch is mounted behind the right-hand side cover.

1. Remove the right-hand footpeg bracket as described in Chapter Thirteen. See **Figure 101** (ZX900) or **Figure 102** (ZX1000).

2. Disconnect the electrical connector at the switch.

SWITCHES (ALL MODELS EXCEPT U.S. AND CANADA)

HEADLIGHT SWITCH

	Red Wht	Red Blu	Blu	Blu Yel
Off				
On	O——O	O——O	O——O	

DIMMER SWITCH

	Red Blk	Blu Yel	Red Yel
Hi	O——O		
Lo		O——O	

PASSING BUTTON

	Brn	Red/Blk
Free		
Push on	O——O	

DIMMER SWITCH (U.S. AND CANADA ONLY)

	Blu/Yel	Blu/Org	Red/Yel	Red/Blk
Hi	O——————————O			O
		O——————O		
Lo	O——————O			
		O——————O		O

3. Disconnect the spring at the switch.

4. Unscrew the switch and remove it. See **Figure 103** (ZX900) or **Figure 104** (ZX1000).

5. Screw a new switch into the switch mount. Attach the spring and plug-in the connector.

6. Reinstall the right-hand footpeg bracket.

7. Adjust the rear brake switch as described under *Rear Brake Light Switch Adjustment* in Chapter Three.

8

Sidestand Switch
Replacement

1. Place the bike on its center stand.
2. Pull the side stand down to gain access to the switch.
3. Disconnect the connector and remove the switch screws.
4. Remove the side stand switch. See **Figure 105** (ZX900) or **Figure 106** (ZX1000).
5. Install by reversing these steps.

Left Handlebar Switch
Replacement

1A. *U.S. and Canada:* The left handlebar switch housing is equipped with the following switches:
   a. Horn.
   b. Hazard.
   c. Turn signal.
   d. Dimmer.
   e. Starter lockout.
1B. *All models except U.S. and Canada:* The left handlebar switch housing is equipped with the following switches:
   a. Horn.
   b. Turn signal.
   c. Dimmer.
   d. Passing.
   e. Starter lockout.
2. Remove the upper fairing as described in Chapter Thirteen.
3. Disconnect the switch connector(s).
4. Remove the switch housing screws and separate the housings. Pull the throttle grip out of the housings.
5. Remove the switch housing and wiring harness. See **Figure 107**.
6. Installation is the reverse of these steps. Adjust the throttle cable(s) as described under *Throttle Cable Adjustment* in Chapter Three.

Right Handlebar Switch
Replacement

1A. *U.S. and Canada:* The right handlebar switch housing is equipped with the following switches:
   a. Engine stop.
   b. Starter.
1B. *All models except U.S. and Canada:* The right handlebar switch housing is equipped with the following switches:
   a. Engine stop.
   b. Starter.
   c. Headlight.
   d. Front brake light.

2. Remove the upper fairing as described in Chapter Thirteen.
3. Disconnect the switch connector(s).
4. Remove the switch housing screws and separate the housings. Pull the choke cable at the lower housing.
5. Remove the switch housing and wiring harness. See **Figure 108**.
6. Installation is the reverse of these steps. Adjust the choke cable as described under *Choke Cable Adjustment* in Chapter Three.

INSTRUMENT CLUSTER

CAUTION
Whenever the instrument cluster is removed from the bike, it must be placed so that the gauges face up. If the meter is left in any other position it will become damaged.

(105)

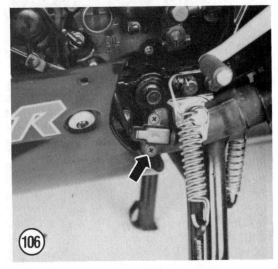
(106)

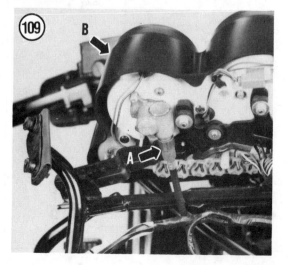

Removal/Installation

1. Remove the upper fairing assembly as described in Chapter Thirteen.
2. Disconnect the speedometer cable (A, **Figure 109**).
3. Disconnect the instrument cluster wiring harness connectors.
4. Remove the screws securing the instrument cluster bracket and remove the instrument cluster (B, **Figure 109**).

> *CAUTION*
> *Do not turn or store the instrument cluster on its side or back as this would damage the instruments.*

5. Install by reversing these steps.

WIRING AND CONNECTORS

Wiring Check

Many electrical troubles can be traced to damaged wiring or to contaminated or loose connectors.

1. Inspect all wiring for fraying, burning, etc.
2. Connectors can be serviced by disconnecting them and cleaning with electrical contact cleaner. Multiple pin connectors should be packed with a dielectric silicone grease.
3. Check wiring continuity as follows:
   a. This test checks the continuity of individual circuits.
   b. Disconnect the negative cable from the battery.

> *NOTE*
> *When making a continuity test, it is best not to disconnect a connector. Instead, insert the test leads into the back of the connectors and check both sides. Because corrosion between the connector contacts may be causing an open circuit, your trouble may be at the connector instead of with the wiring.*

   c. Zero the ohmmeter according to the manufacturer's instructions. Switch the meter to the R×1 scale.
   d. Attach the test leads to the circuit you want to check.
   e. There should be continuity (indicated low resistance). If there is no continuity, there is an open in the circuit.

8

GAUGES

Tachometer/Voltmeter Testing

The tachometer/voltmeter circuit is shown in **Figure 110**.

1. Check that rubber dampers are installed at all mounting brackets. Replace missing dampers or dampers that have become cracked or hardened.

2. Referring to **Figure 110**, perform the *Wiring Check* as described in this chapter. Interpret results as follows:

a. If there is no continuity, there is an open in the circuit.

b. If the tachometer/voltmeter still is not operating correctly after the wiring is repaired, replace the tachometer/voltmeter.

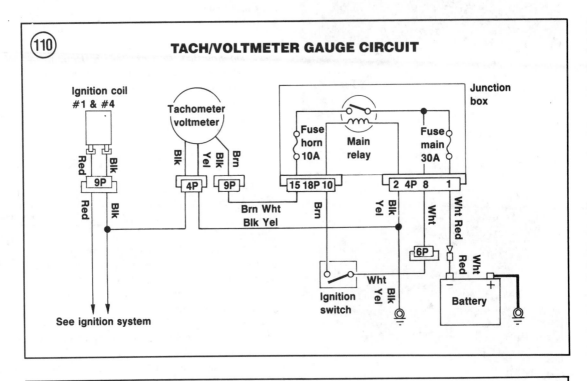

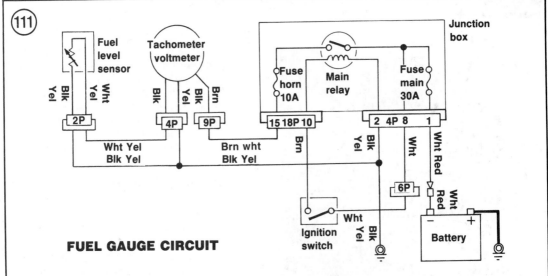

Fuel Gauge Testing

The fuel gauge circuit is shown in **Figure 111**.
1. Perform a fuel gauge operation check as follows:
    a. Disconnect the fuel level sensor 2-prong connector. It has 2 wires; black/yellow and white/yellow. See **Figure 111**.
    b. Turn the ignition switch ON. The fuel gauge should read empty (E).
    c. Use a jumper cable and short out the 2 connector wires. The fuel gauge should read full (F).
    d. Turn the ignition switch OFF.
    e. If the gauge readings are correct, the fuel level sensor is faulty. If the gauge readings were incorrect, the wiring and/or the fuel gauge is faulty.
    f. Perform Step 2 to isolate the damaged component.
2. Perform the *Wiring Check* in this chapter. If the wiring is okay, the fuel gauge is faulty and must be replaced.

Water Temperature Gauge Testing

The water temperature gauge circuit is shown in **Figure 112** (ZX900) or **Figure 113** (ZX1000).

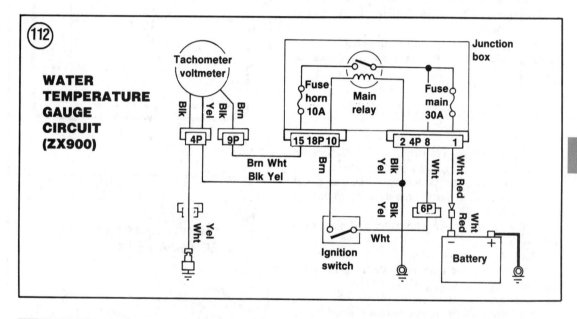

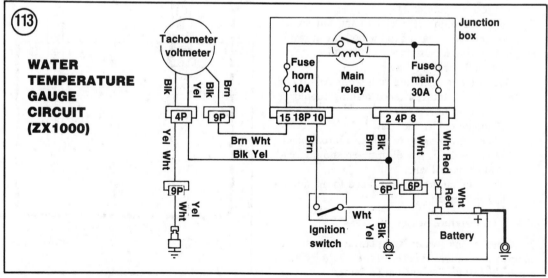

1. Perform a water temperature gauge operation check as follows:
    a. Disconnect the water temperature sensor connector (yellow/white). See **Figure 112** or **Figure 113**.
    b. Turn the ignition switch ON. The water temperature gauge should read cold (C).
    c. Use a jumper wire and ground the water temperature connector. The water temperature gauge should read hot (H).
    d. Turn the ignition switch OFF.
    e. If the test results are correct, the water temperature sensor is faulty.
    f. If the test results are incorrect, the wiring and/or the water temperature gauge is faulty. Perform Step 2 to isolate the damaged component.

2. Perform the *Wiring Check* in this chapter. If the wiring is okay, the fuel gauge is faulty and must be replaced.

THERMOSTATIC FAN SWITCH

Testing

The fan switch controls the radiator fan according to engine coolant temperature.

1. Remove the fan switch as described under *Thermostatic Fan Switch Removal/Installation* in Chapter Nine.

2. Fill a beaker or pan with water and place on a stove.

3. Mount the fan switch so that the temperature sensing tip and the threaded portion of the body are submerged as shown in **Figure 114**.

4. Place a thermometer in the pan of water (use a cooking or candy thermometer that is rated higher than the test temperature).

5. Attach one ohmmeter lead to the fan switch terminal and the other lead to the body as shown in **Figure 114**. Check resistance as follows:
    a. Gradually heat the water.
    b. When the temperature rises from 201-212° F (94-100° C), the resistance reading should be 0.5 ohms or less.
    c. Gradually reduce the heat.
    d. When the temperature falls to approximately 194° F (90° C), the ohmmeter should read 1,000 ohms or higher.

6. Replace the fan switch if it failed to operate as described in Step 5.

Water Temperature Sensor

1. Remove the water temperature sensor as described under *Thermostatic Fan Switch Removal/Installation* in Chapter Nine.

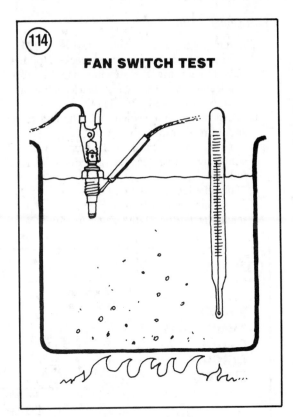

(114)

FAN SWITCH TEST

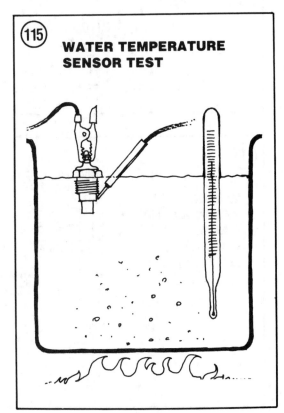

(115)

WATER TEMPERATURE SENSOR TEST

2. Fill a beaker or pan with water and place on a stove.

3. Mount the water temperature sensor so that the temperature sensing tip and the threaded portion of the body are submerged as shown in **Figure 115**.

4. Place a thermometer in the pan of water (use a cooking or candy thermometer that is rated higher than the test temperature).

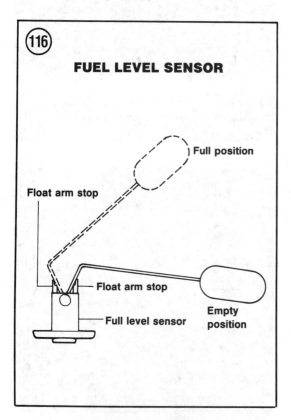

FUEL LEVEL SENSOR

Full position

Float arm stop

Float arm stop

Full level sensor

Empty position

5. Attach one ohmmeter lead to the water temperature terminal and the other lead to the body as shown in **Figure 115**. Check resistance as follows:

   a. Gradually heat the water.

   b. When the temperature reaches 176° F (80° C), the resistance reading should be approximately 52 ohms.

   c. Continue to heat the water. When the temperature reaches 212° F (100° C), the resistance reading should be approximately 27 ohms.

6. Replace the water temperature sensor if it failed to operate as described in Step 5.

FUEL LEVEL SENSOR

Testing

Refer to **Figure 116** for this procedure.

1. Remove the fuel level sensor as described under *Fuel Level Sensor Removal/Installation* in Chapter Seven.

2. Pivot the float arm up and down. The arm should move smoothly without any binding. Raise the float arm all the way up and release it. The arm should drop under its own weight. Replace the fuel level sensor if necessary.

3. Connect an ohmmeter onto the fuel level sensor connectors.

4. Raise the float (full position). The ohmmeter should read within the specifications in **Table 3**.

5. Lower the float (empty position). The ohmmeter should read within the specifications in **Table 3**.

6. Replace the fuel level sensor if the test results in Step 4 or Step 5 were incorrect.

HEADLIGHT RESERVE LIGHTING SYSTEM (U.S. AND CANADA)

Inspection

Models sold in the U.S. and Canada contain a relay in the headlight circuit. The headlight goes on when the starter button is used to start the engine. The headlight will stay on until the ignition switch is turned off. If the engine stalls, the headlight will go off when the starter button is depressed to start the engine and come on when the engine starts. Replace the reserve lighting device if defective. The reserve lighting device is mounted on the upper fairing mount. **Figure 117** shows the reserve lighting device for ZX1000 models. Mounting for the ZX900 model is similar.

8

COOLING FAN RELAY

Removal/Installation (ZX900)

1. Remove the left-hand side cover.
2. Disconnect the cooling fan relay connector and remove the relay (**Figure 118**).
3. Install by reversing these steps.

Removal/Installation (ZX1000)

1. Remove the right-hand side cover.
2. Disconnect the cooling fan relay connector and remove the relay (**Figure 119**).
3. Install by reversing these steps.

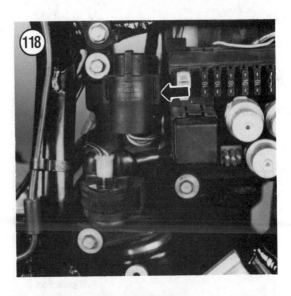

HORN

Removal/Installation (ZX900)

1. Remove the oil cooler as described under *Oil Cooler Removal/Installation* in Chapter Four.
2. Remove the exhaust pipes as described in Chapter Seven.
3. Disconnect the horn electrical connector.
4. Remove the bolts securing the horn bracket and remove the horn assembly.
5. Installation is the reverse of these steps.

Removal/Installation (ZX1000)

1. Disconnect the horn electrical connector.
2. Remove the mounting bolt and remove the horn (**Figure 120**).
3. Install by reversing these steps. Make sure to insert the horn mounting bracket tab into the mounting bracket hole.

Horn Testing

1. Disconnect horn wires from harness.
2. Connect horn wires to 12-volt battery. If it is good, it will sound.

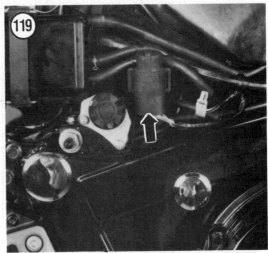

JUNCTION BOX AND FUSES

The junction box is mounted on the left-hand side behind the side cover. The decal placed on the junction box cover (**Figure 121**) identifies component functions. Remove the cover to gain access to the components (**Figure 122**). The junction box circuit is shown in **Figure 123**.

Junction Box
Removal/Installation

To remove the junction box, disconnect the electrical connectors and remove the fastening screws. Reverse to install.

Fuse Replacement

There are 8 fuses located in the junction box. See **Figure 122** and **Figure 123**. If there is an electrical failure, first check for a blown fuse. Remove the seat and remove the junction box cover (**Figure 121**). Remove the fuse by pulling it out of the

junction box with needlenose pliers. Install a new fuse with the same amperage rating.

NOTE
The junction box is equipped with one 10 amp and one 30 amp replacement fuse. Always carry extra fuses.

Whenever a fuse blows, find out the reason for the failure before replacing the fuse. Usually, the trouble is a short circuit in the wiring. Check by testing the circuit that the fuse protects. A blown fuse may be caused by worn-through insulation or a disconnected wire shorting to ground.

CAUTION
Never substitute tinfoil or wire for a fuse. Never use a higher amperage fuse than specified. An overload could cause a fire, resulting in complete loss of the bike.

Diode Circuit Test

1. Remove the diode(s) from the junction box. See A, **Figure 122**.
2. Connect an ohmmeter to each diode lead. Measure the resistance.
3. Reverse the ohmmeter leads made in Step 2. Measure the resistance.
4. The resistance should be low in one direction and more than 10 times higher with the ohmmeter leads reversed. If a diode shows low or high resistance readings in both directions, replace it.

Relay Test

The junction box (**Figure 122**) is equipped with the following relays:
   a. Turn signal relay (B, **Figure 122**).
   b. Headlight relay (C, **Figure 122**).
   c. Main relay (D, **Figure 122**).
   d. Starter circuit relay (E, **Figure 122**).
To test any relay, perform the following.

Main, starter circuit and
headlight relay test

1. Remove the relay from the junction box.
2. Connect an ohmmeter and a 12-volt battery to the relay as shown in **Figure 124**. Set the ohmmeter on the R×1 scale. Interpret results as follows:
   a. Battery connected: Ohmmeter should read 0 ohms.
   b. Battery disconnected: Ohmmeter should read infinity.
3. Replace the relay if it failed the tests in Step 2.

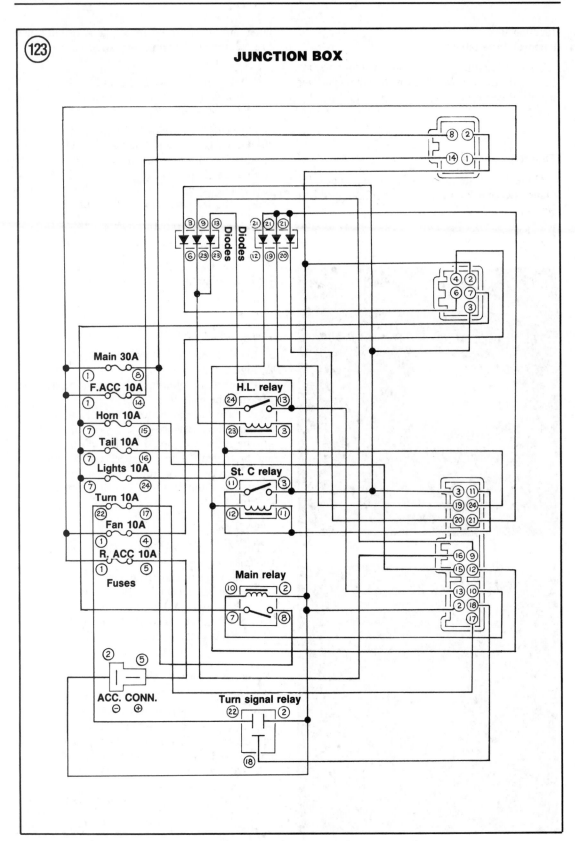

(123)

JUNCTION BOX

Turn signal relay test

1. Remove the relay from the junction box.
2. Using a 12-volt battery and the turn signal relay with accessory wiring, wire the relay to the turn signal lights as shown in **Figure 125**.
3. After the battery is connected, count how many times the turn signal lights flash for 1 minute.

4. If the lights do not flash as specified in **Figure 125**, replace the relay.

WIRING DIAGRAMS

Complete wiring diagrams are located at the end of this book.

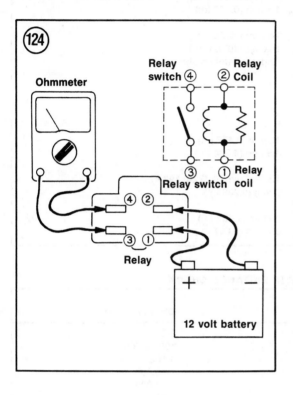

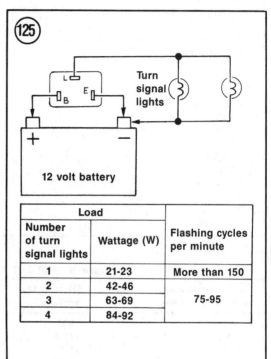

Load			
Number of turn signal lights	Wattage (W)		Flashing cycles per minute
1	21-23		More than 150
2	42-46		
3	63-69		75-95
4	84-92		

Tables 1-3 are on the following page.

Table 1 ELECTRICAL SPECIFICATIONS

Battery	
Type	12 volt; 14 amp hour
Specific gravity	See text
Charge rate	See text
Alternator	
Brush length	
New	10.5 mm (0.413 in.)
Wear limit	4.5 mm (0.177 in.)
Slip ring diameter	
New	14.4 mm (0.566 in.)
Wear limit	14.0 mm (0.551 in.)
Rotor coil resistance	Approximately 4 ohms
Ignition system	
Pickup coil air gap	0.5-0.9 mm (0.019-0.035 in.)
Starter motor	
Brush length	
ZX900	
New	12 mm (0.472 in.)
Wear limit	8.5 mm (0.334 in.)
ZX1000	
New	12-12.5 mm (0.472-0.492 in.)
Wear limit	6 mm (0.236 in.)
Commutator diameter	
New	28 mm (1.102 in.)
Wear limit	0.2 mm (0.007 in.)

Table 2 REGULATOR RESISTANCE CHECK

Test connections (+ lead to − lead)	Ohmmeter setting	Ohm reading
F to E	x100	0-50
E to F	x1000	100-10,000
IG to E	x100	0-100
E to IG	x1000	1-10,000
F to IG	x1000	1-10,000
IG to F	x100	0-50

Table 3 FUEL LEVEL SENSOR TEST SPECIFICATIONS

Fuel level sensor resistance	
ZX900	
Full position	3-12 ohms
Empty position	70-120 ohms
ZX1000	
Full position	4-10 ohms
Empty position	90-100 ohms

NOTE: If you own a 1988 or later model, first check the Supplement at the back of this book for any new service information.

CHAPTER NINE

COOLING SYSTEM

The pressurized cooling system consists of the radiator, water pump, radiator cap, thermostat, electric cooling fan and a coolant reservoir tank.

The coolant temperature gauge on the instrument panel monitors coolant temperature. During engine operation, check the gauge reading often. Normally the needle should operate within the white zone, indicating normal coolant temperature. If the needle should start to climb rapidly or reach the "H" line, turn the engine off and allow the engine to cool down. Then check the coolant level. It is important to keep the coolant level to the FULL mark on the coolant reservoir tank. See **Figure 1** (ZX900) or **Figure 2** (ZX1000). Always add coolant to the reservoir tank, not to the radiator.

> *NOTE*
> *Always make initial checks to the coolant reservoir tank when the engine is cold as the coolant level will rise in the tank when the engine is operating at normal conditions.*

> *CAUTION*
> *Drain and flush the cooling system at least every 2 years. Refill with a mixture of ethylene glycol antifreeze (formulated for aluminum engines) and distilled water. Do not reuse the old coolant as it deteriorates with use. **Do not** operate the cooling system with only distilled water (even in climates where antifreeze protection is not required). This is important because the engine is all aluminum; it will not rust but it will oxidize internally and have to be replaced. Refer to **Coolant Change** in Chapter Three.*

This chapter describes repair and replacement of cooling system components. **Table 1** at the end of the chapter lists cooling system specifications. For routine maintenance of the system, refer to *Cooling System Inspection* in Chapter Three.

> *WARNING*
> *Do not remove the radiator cap when the engine is hot. The coolant is very hot and is under pressure. Severe scalding could result if the coolant comes in contact with your skin.*

> *WARNING*
> *The radiator fan and fan switch are connected to the battery. Whenever the engine is warm or hot, the fan may start even with the ignition switch turned OFF. Never work around the fan or touch the fan until the engine is completely cool.*

The cooling system must be cooled prior to removing any component of the system.

9

COOLING SYSTEM INSPECTION

1. If a substantial coolant loss is noted, the head gasket may be blown. In extreme cases sufficient coolant will leak into a cylinder(s) when the bike is left standing for several hours so the engine cannot be turned over with the starter. White smoke (steam) might also be observed at the muffler(s) when the engine is running. Coolant may also find its way into the oil. To check, observe the oil level window on the shift cover (**Figure 3**). If the oil is foamy or milky-looking, there is coolant in the oil system. If so, correct the problem immediately.

> **CAUTION**
> *After the problem is corrected, drain and thoroughly flush out the engine oil system to eliminate all coolant residue. Refill with fresh engine oil; refer to* **Engine Oil and Filter Change** *in Chapter Three.*

2. Check the radiator for clogged or damaged fins. If more than 15 percent of the radiator fin area is damaged, repair or replace the radiator.
3. Check all coolant hoses for cracks or damage. Replace all questionable parts. Make sure the hose clamps are tight, but not so tight that they cut the hoses. Refer to *Hoses* in this chapter.
4. Pressure test the cooling system as described under *Cooling System Inspection* in Chapter Three.

COOLANT RESERVOIR

On ZX900 models the coolant reservoir tank is mounted on the right-hand side of the motorcycle above the rear wheel (**Figure 1**). On ZX1000 models, the coolant reservoir tank is located inside the lower fairing at the front of the engine (**Figure 4**). To remove the reservoir tank, remove the right-hand side cover (ZX900) or the lower fairing (ZX1000) as described in Chapter Thirteen. Replace the reservoir tank if cracked or otherwise damaged.

RADIATOR AND FAN

> **WARNING**
> *The radiator fan and fan switch are connected to the battery. Whenever the engine is warm or hot, the fan may start with the ignition switch turned OFF. Never work around the fan or touch the fan until the engine is completely cool.*

Removal/Installation (ZX900)

The radiator and fan are removed as an assembly. Refer to **Figure 5**.
1. Place the bike on the center stand.
2. Remove the upper and lower fairings as described in Chapter Thirteen.
3. Drain the cooling system as described under *Coolant Change* in Chapter Three.
4. Disconnect the fan switch lead (**Figure 6**) at the radiator.

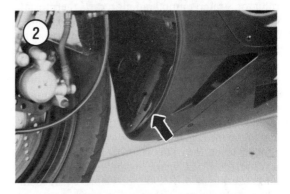

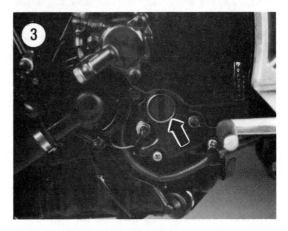

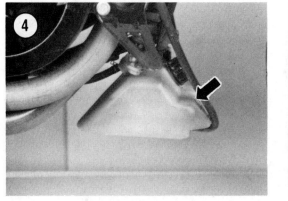

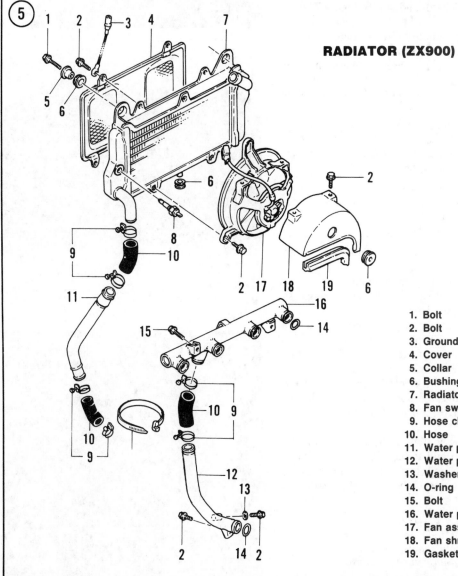

RADIATOR (ZX900)

9

1. Bolt
2. Bolt
3. Ground wire
4. Cover
5. Collar
6. Bushing
7. Radiator
8. Fan switch
9. Hose clamps
10. Hose
11. Water pipe
12. Water pipe
13. Washer
14. O-ring
15. Bolt
16. Water pipe
17. Fan assembly
18. Fan shroud
19. Gasket

5. Disconnect the fan motor connector.

6. Disconnect the radiator ground wire at the front of the radiator.

7. At the radiator, loosen the hose clamps for the upper (A, **Figure 7**) and lower radiator hoses. Move the clamps back onto the hoses. Carefully slip the hose ends off of the necks of the radiator.

> *CAUTION*
> *If a hose is tight on its joint, refer to* **Hoses** *in this chapter. Excessive force applied to a hose during removal could damage the connecting joint.*

8. Remove the radiator mounting bolts (**Figure 5**).

9. Remove the radiator and fan (B, **Figure 7**) as an assembly.

10. Remove the radiator screen (**Figure 8**) and clean it thoroughly in soap and water.

11. Replace the radiator hoses if deterioration or damage is noted.

12. Installation is the reverse of these steps. Note the following:

    a. Make sure the fan switch ground lead is attached as shown in **Figure 6**.

    b. Refill the coolant as described under *Coolant Change* in Chapter Three.

Removal/Installation (ZX1000)

The radiator and fan are removed as an assembly. Refer to **Figure 9**.

1. Place the bike on the center stand.

2. Remove the upper and lower fairings as described in Chapter Thirteen.

3. Drain the cooling system as described under *Coolant Change* in Chapter Three.

4. Disconnect the fan switch lead (A, **Figure 10**).

5. Disconnect the fan motor connector.

6. Disconnect the horn electrical connector at the horn. Then remove the horn mounting bolt and remove the horn (B, **Figure 10**). Repeat for the opposite horn.

7. At the radiator, loosen the hose clamps for the upper (**Figure 11**) and lower (**Figure 12**) radiator hoses. Move the clamps back onto the hoses. Then, carefully slip the hoses off the necks of the radiator.

> *CAUTION*
> *If a hose is tight on its joint, refer to* **Hoses** *in this chapter. Excessive force applied to a hose during removal could damage the connecting joint.*

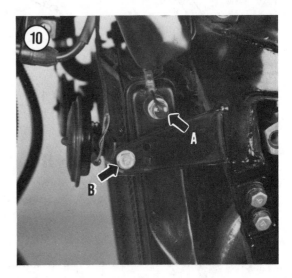

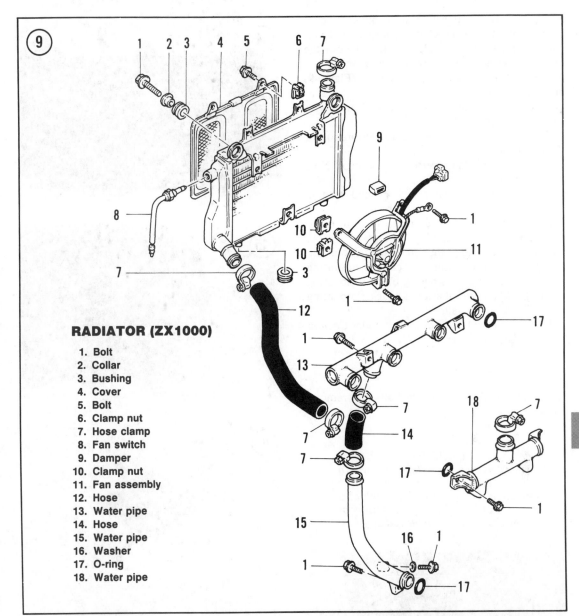

RADIATOR (ZX1000)

1. Bolt
2. Collar
3. Bushing
4. Cover
5. Bolt
6. Clamp nut
7. Hose clamp
8. Fan switch
9. Damper
10. Clamp nut
11. Fan assembly
12. Hose
13. Water pipe
14. Hose
15. Water pipe
16. Washer
17. O-ring
18. Water pipe

8. Remove the oil cooler mounting bolts at the oil cooler bracket (A, **Figure 13**). Then remove the oil cooler bracket bolts (B, **Figure 13**) and push the bracket down and away from the radiator.

9. Remove the radiator mounting bolts (**Figure 9**) and remove the radiator.

10. Remove the radiator screen and clean it with soap and water.

11. Replace the radiator hoses if deterioration or damage is noted.

12. Installation is the reverse of these steps. Note the following:

   a. Make sure the fan switch ground lead is attached as shown in A, **Figure 10**.

   b. Test the horns after installing them to make sure they work properly.

   c. When installing the oil cooler mounting bracket, insert the oil cooler mounting projections into the fairing bracket mounting holes. Make sure that the 3 bracket mounting bushings are installed.

   d. Refill the coolant as described under *Coolant Change* in Chapter Three.

Inspection

1. Remove the radiator screen bolts and remove the screen.

> *CAUTION*
> *When flushing the radiator fins with a hose, always point the hose perpendicular to the radiator and at a distance of 20 in. Never point a water or air hose at an angle to the radiator fins.*

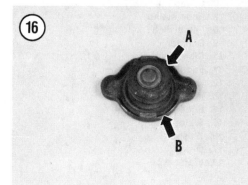

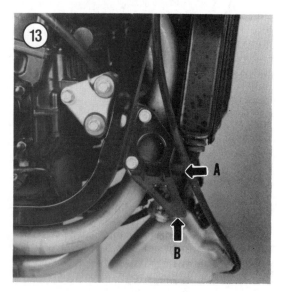

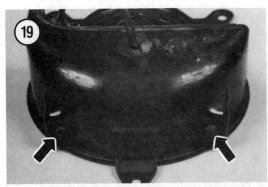

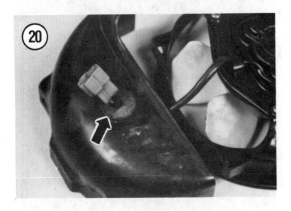

2. Flush off the exterior of the radiator with a garden hose on low pressure. Spray both the front and the back to remove all road dirt and bugs. Carefully use a whisk broom or stiff paint brush to remove any stubborn dirt.

CAUTION
Do not press too hard or the cooling fins and tubes may be damaged causing a leak.

3. Carefully straighten out any bent cooling fins (**Figure 14**) with a broad tipped screwdriver.
4. See **Figure 15**. Check for cracks or leakage (usually a moss-green colored residue) at the filler neck, the inlet and outlet hose fittings and the upper and lower tank seams.
5. Refer to **Figure 16**. Inspect the radiator cap top (A) and bottom (B) seals for deterioration or damage. Check the spring for damage. Pressure test the radiator cap as described under *Cooling System Inspection* in Chapter Three. Replace the radiator cap if necessary.

Cooling Fan
Removal/Installation

ZX900

See **Figure 5** for this procedure.
1. Remove the radiator as described in this chapter.
2. Remove the bolts (**Figure 17**) securing the fan shroud and fan assembly and remove the assembly.
3. Check the fan blades (**Figure 18**) for cracks or other damage. Check the fan blade screws for tightness. If the fan blades are damaged or if the motor does not work properly, the fan assembly will have to be replaced as a unit; individual parts are not available. The fan shroud can be replaced separately from the fan motor assembly.
4. To separate the fan and shroud assembly, perform the following:
   a. Remove the shroud-to-fan bolts (**Figure 19**).
   b. Pull the rubber grommet (**Figure 20**) out of the shroud and slip the connector out of the grommet.
   c. When installing the shroud, align it with the fan assembly as shown in **Figure 21**.
   d. Make sure the fan wires are routed and secured around the fan housing as shown in **Figure 22**.
5. Installation is the reverse of these steps. Apply Loctite 242 (blue) to the fan mounting bolts and tighten securely. Make sure to attach the fan switch ground lead onto the radiator.

9

ZX1000

See **Figure 9** for this procedure.

1. Remove the radiator as described in this chapter.

2. Remove the bolts securing the fan to the radiator and remove the fan.

3. Check the fan blades for cracks or other damage. Check the fan blade screws for tightness. If the fan blades are damaged or if the motor does not work properly, the fan assembly will have to be replaced as a unit; individual parts are not available.

4. Installation is the reverse of these steps. Apply Loctite 242 (blue) to the fan mounting bolts and tighten securely. Make sure to attach the fan switch ground lead onto the radiator.

THERMOSTAT

The thermostat is a temperature controlled valve that regulates coolant flow between the engine and radiator. When the engine is cold, the thermostat is closed, thus blocking the coolant passage. This allows the engine to reach its operating temperature quickly. When the coolant reaches a certain temperature, the thermostat will open and allow coolant circulation. If a thermostat does not open properly, the coolant flow is blocked and the engine overheats. If the thermostat is stuck open, the engine will take much longer to reach its normal operating temperature.

Removal/Installation (ZX900)

Refer to **Figure 23** for this procedure.

1. Remove the seat and both side covers.

2. Remove the upper and lower fairings as described in Chapter Thirteen.

3. Remove the fuel tank as described in Chapter Seven.

4. Drain the cooling system as described under *Coolant Change* in Chapter Three.

5. Remove the ignition coils as described under *Ignition Coil Removal/Installation* in Chapter Eight.

6. *U.S. models:* Remove the air suction valves and hoses. See Chapter Seven.

7. Disconnect the thermostat housing-to-radiator cap water hose at the thermostat housing.

8. Loosen the choke cable locknut (**Figure 24**) on the right-hand side of the carburetor. Then remove the choke cable and the clamp screw at the carburetor.

9. Disconnect the water pipe-to-thermostat mounting bolt at the bottom of the thermostat housing.

10. See **Figure 25**. Disconnect the water temperature sensor (A) and the thermostatic fan switch connectors at the thermostat housing.

11. Remove the thermostat housing. Don't lose the O-ring on the water pipe when removing the thermostat housing.

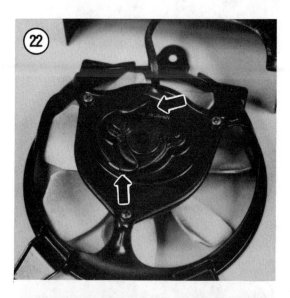

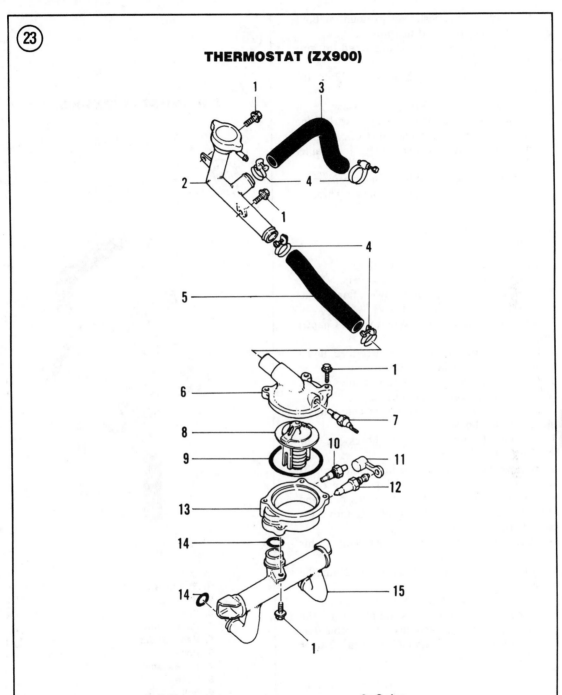

㉓

THERMOSTAT (ZX900)

1. Bolt
2. Radiator cap/thermostat housing
3. Hose
4. Hose clamps
5. Hose
6. Thermostat cover
7. Water temperature sensor
8. Thermostat
9. O-ring
10. Fan switch
11. Cover
12. Bleeder bolt
13. Housing
14. O-ring
15. Water pipe

9

12. Remove the thermostat cover mounting bolts and remove the cover and thermostat.

13. Test the thermostat as described in this chapter.

14. Install by reversing these steps. Note the following:

    a. Replace the cover O-ring, if necessary.

    b. Refill the cooling system with the recommended type and quantity of coolant as described under *Coolant Change* in Chapter Three.

    c. Adjust the choke cable as described under *Choke Cable Adjustment* in Chapter Three.

Removal/Installation (ZX1000)

Refer to **Figure 26** for this procedure.

1. Remove the seat and both side covers.

2. Remove the upper and lower fairings as described in Chapter Thirteen.

3. Remove the fuel tank as described in Chapter Seven.

4. Drain the cooling system as described under *Coolant Change* in Chapter Three.

5. Disconnect the water temperature sensor connector at the thermostat housing.

6. Disconnect the fan switch sensor connector at the thermostat housing.

7. Disconnect both radiator hoses at the thermostat housing.

8. Remove the thermostat housing mounting bolts and remove the thermostat housing (**Figure 27**).

9. Remove the thermostat housing cover bolts and remove the cover and thermostat. Remove the cover O-ring.

10. Test the thermostat as described in this chapter.

11. Install by reversing these steps. Note the following:

    a. Replace the cover O-ring, if necessary.

    b. Refill the cooling system with the recommended type and quantity of coolant as described under *Coolant Change* in Chapter Three.

Inspection

Test the thermostat (**Figure 28**) to ensure proper operation. The thermostat should be replaced if it remains open at normal room temperature or stays closed after the specified temperature has been reached during the test procedure.

Place the thermostat on a small piece of wood in a pan of water (**Figure 29**). Place a thermometer in the pan of water (use a cooking or candy

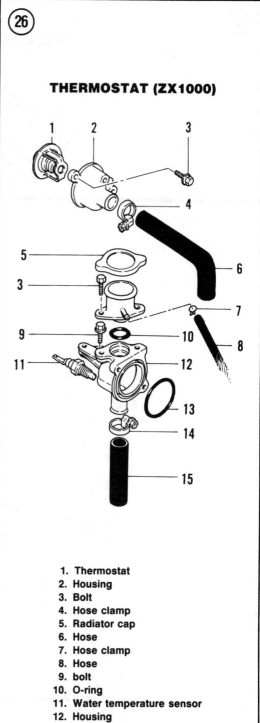

(26)

THERMOSTAT (ZX1000)

1. Thermostat
2. Housing
3. Bolt
4. Hose clamp
5. Radiator cap
6. Hose
7. Hose clamp
8. Hose
9. bolt
10. O-ring
11. Water temperature sensor
12. Housing
13. O-ring
14. Hose clamp
15. Hose

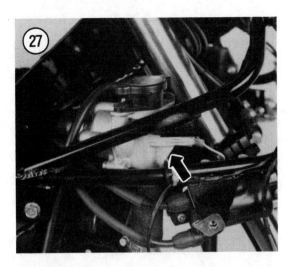

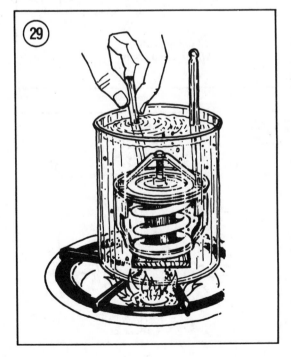

thermometer that is rated higher than the test temperature). Gradually heat the water and continue to gently stir the water until it reaches 176-183° F (80-84° C). At this temperature the thermostat should begin to open.

NOTE
Valve operation is sometimes sluggish; it usually takes 3-5 minutes for the valve to open fully.

If the valve fails to open, the thermostat should be replaced (it cannot be serviced). Be sure to replace it with one of the same temperature rating.

WATER PUMP

Removal/Installation

1. Drain the engine oil as described under *Engine Oil and Filter Change* in Chapter Three.
2. Drain the cooling system as described under *Coolant Change* in Chapter Three.
3. Loosen the hose clamps at the water pump cover radiator hose (**Figure 30**). Then twist the hose and slide if off the cover neck.
4. Remove the sprocket cover as described under *Sprocket Cover Removal/Installation* in Chapter Six.
5. Remove the water pipe mounting bolt and pull the pipe off of the water pump fitting (**Figure 31**).

9

6. Remove the water pump mounting bolts and pull the water pump (**Figure 32**) out of the crankcase.

7. Installation is the reverse of these steps. Note the following:

   a. Replace the water pump O-ring (**Figure 33**) if damaged.

   b. Replace the O-rings on the water pipe that attaches to the water pump.

   c. See **Figure 34**. Align the slot in the water pump shaft with the tab on the oil pump shaft (in the engine), then install the water pump. If the water pump will not seat fully, the shafts are not aligned properly.

   d. Refill the engine oil as described under *Engine Oil and Filter Change* in Chapter Three.

   e. Refill the cooling system with the recommended type and quantity of coolant as described under *Coolant Change* in Chapter Three.

Disassembly/Inspection/Reassembly

> *NOTE*
> *The water pump is sold as a complete unit only. If any component is damaged, the entire water pump must be replaced. The 2 O-rings, however, can be replaced separately.*

1. If the coolant level has been dropping, check the water pump weep hole (**Figure 35**) for leakage. If coolant leaks from the hole, an internal seal is damaged; replace the water pump unit. If there is no indication of coolant leakage from the hole, reinstall the water pump and pressure test the cooling system as described under *Cooling System Inspection* in Chapter Three.

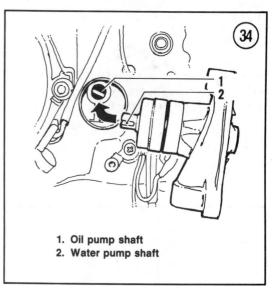

1. Oil pump shaft
2. Water pump shaft

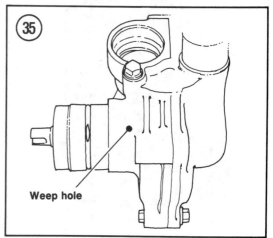

Weep hole

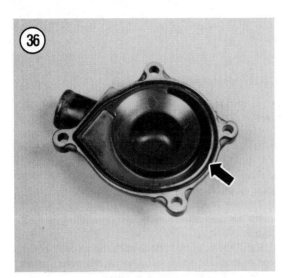

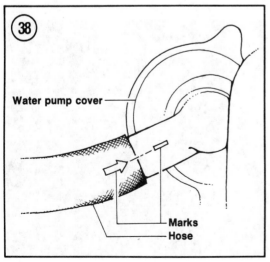

Water pump cover

Marks
Hose

2. Remove the water pump cover bolts and separate the pump assembly.

3. Check the O-rings for flat spots or damage; replace if necessary. See **Figure 33** or **Figure 36**.

4. Check the impeller blades (**Figure 37**) for corrosion or damage. If corrosion is minor, clean the blades. If corrosion is severe or if the blades are cracked or broken, replace the water pump unit.

5. Turn the impeller shaft and check the bearing for excessive noise or roughness. If the bearing operation is rough, replace the water pump unit.

6. Inspect the water pump inlet and outlet passages (**Figure 35**) for corrosion or sludge buildup. If corrosion is minor, clean the passage. If corrosion is severe or if the water passage is pitted, replace the water pump unit.

7. Reverse Step 2 to assemble the water pump assembly. Tighten the bolts securely. On ZX1000 models, align the mark on the pump housing with the arrow mark on the hose (**Figure 38**).

HOSES

Hoses deteriorate with age and should be replaced periodically or whenever they show signs of cracking or leakage. To be safe, replace the hoses every 2 years. The spray of hot coolant from a cracked hose can injure the rider and passenger. Loss of coolant can also cause the engine to overheat, causing damage.

Whenever any component of the cooling system is removed, inspect the hoses(s) and determine if replacement is necessary.

Inspection

1. With the engine cool, check the cooling hoses for brittleness or hardness. A hose in this condition will usually show cracks and must be replaced.

2. With the engine hot, examine the hoses for swelling along the entire hose length. Eventually a hose will rupture at this point.

3. Check area around hose clamps. Signs of rust around clamps indicate possible hose leakage.

Replacement

Hose replacement should be performed when the engine is cool.

1. Drain the cooling system as described under *Coolant Change* in Chapter Three.

2. Loosen the hose clamps from the hose to be replaced. Slide the clamps along the hose and out of the way.

3. Twist the hose end to break the seal and remove from the connecting joint. If the hose has been on

for some time, it may have become fused to the joint. If so, cut the hose parallel to the joint connections with a knife or razor. The hose then can be carefully pried free with a screwdriver.

> *CAUTION*
> *Excessive force applied to the hose during removal could damage the connecting joint.*

4. Examine the connecting joint for cracks or other damage. Repair or replace parts as required. If the joint is okay, clean it of any rust with sandpaper.
5. Inspect hose clamps and replace as necessary.
6. Slide hose clamps over outside of hose and install hose to inlet and outlet connecting joint. Make sure the hose clears all obstructions and is routed properly.

> *NOTE*
> *If it is difficult to install a hose on a joint, soak the end of the hose in hot water for approximately 2 minutes. This will soften the hose and ease installation.*

7. With the hose positioned correctly on joint, position clamps back away from end of hose slightly. Tighten clamps securely, but not so much that hose is damaged.
8. Refill cooling system as described under *Coolant Change* in Chapter Three. Start the engine and check for leaks. Retighten hose clamps as necessary.

THERMOSTATIC FAN SWITCH AND WATER TEMPERATURE SENSOR

Thermostatic Fan Switch
Removal/Installation

On radiator

1. Drain the cooling system as described under *Coolant Change* in Chapter Three.
2. Remove the upper and lower fairings as described in Chapter Thirteen.
3. Disconnect the connector at the switch. See **Figure 39** (ZX900) or **Figure 40** (ZX1000).
4. Unscrew the switch from the radiator and remove it.
5. Apply a liquid gasket sealer to the fan switch threads before installation.

6. Install the switch and tighten to 7.4 N•m (65 in.-lb.).

On thermostat housing

1. Remove the thermostat as described in this chapter.
2. Unscrew the sensor from the thermostat housing. See **Figure 23** (ZX900) or **Figure 26** (ZX1000).
3. Apply a liquid gasket to the sensor threads before installation.
4. Tighten the sensor to 7.8 N•m (69 in.-lb.).
5. Install the thermostat as described in this chapter.
6. Refill the cooling system with the recommended type and quantity of coolant as described under *Coolant Change* in Chapter Three.

Water Temperature Sensor
Removal/Installation

1. Remove the thermostat as described in this chapter.
2. Unscrew the sensor from the thermostat housing. See **Figure 23** (ZX900) or **Figure 26** (ZX1000).
3. Apply a liquid gasket to the sensor threads before installation.
4. Tighten the sensor to 7.8 N•m (69 in.-lb.).

5. Install the thermostat as described in this chapter.
6. Refill the cooling system with the recommended type and quantity of coolant as described under *Coolant Change* in Chapter Three.

Testing

Refer to *Electrical Components* in Chapter Eight.

Table 1 COOLING SYSTEM SPECIFICATIONS

Capacity	
ZX900	2.9 L (3.06 qt.)
ZX1000	3.1 L (3.28 qt.)
Coolant ratio	57% water/43% coolant
Radiator cap	0.75-1.05 kg/cm² (11-15 psi)
Thermostat	
Opening temperature	80-84° C (176-183° F)
Valve opening lift	Not less than 8 mm (5/16 in.) @ 203° F (95° C)

9

NOTE: If you own a 1988 or later model, first check the Supplement at the back of this book for any new service information.

CHAPTER TEN

FRONT SUSPENSION AND STEERING

This chapter discusses service operations on suspension components, steering, wheels and related items. **Table 1** lists service specifications. **Tables 1-4** are at the end of the chapter.

FRONT WHEEL

Removal/Installation

1. Remove the lower fairing as described in Chapter Thirteen.
2. Support the motorcycle with a jack so that the front wheel is clear of the ground.
3. Loosen the speedometer cable nut (**Figure 1**) and pull the cable out of the speedometer drive unit.
4. Remove the left brake caliper's mounting bolts (**Figure 2**) and lift the caliper off of the brake disc. Support the caliper with a Bunjee cord (**Figure 3**) or mechanic's wire to prevent stress buildup on the brake hose.
4. Loosen the right-hand side axle clamp bolt (A, **Figure 4**). Then loosen the axle on the right-hand side (B, **Figure 4**).
5. Remove the axle (B, **Figure 4**) from the right-hand side.
6. Pull the wheel forward to disengage the attached caliper from the brake disc. See **Figure 5**.
7. Remove the speedometer drive gear (**Figure 6**) from the left-hand side.
8. Remove the spacer (**Figure 7**) from the right-hand side.
9. If necessary, loosen the left-hand axle clamp bolt (A, **Figure 8**) and remove the axle nut (B, **Figure 8**).

CAUTION
Do not set the wheel down on the disc surface as it may become scratched or bent. Either lean the wheel against a wall or place it on a couple of wood blocks.

NOTE
Insert a piece of wood in the calipers in place of the disc. That way, if the brake lever is inadvertently squeezed, the piston will not be forced out of the cylinder. If this does happen, the calipers might have to be disassembled to reseat the piston and the system will have to be bled.

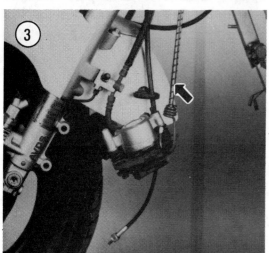

10

10. When servicing the wheel assembly, install the spacer, speedometer drive gear, washer and nut on the axle to prevent their loss. See **Figure 9**.

11. Installation is the reverse of these steps. Note the following:

   a. To prevent axle seizure, coat the axle with an anti-seize compound such as Bostik Never-Seez Lubricating & Anti-Seize Compound (part No. 49501).

   b. See **Figure 10**. Align the 2 tabs in the speedometer gear housing with the 2 speedometer drive slots in the front wheel and install the gear housing. See **Figure 6**.

   c. When installing the front wheel, align the lug on the speedometer gear housing (**Figure 11**) with the slot in the back of the left-hand fork tube (**Figure 12**). This procedure locates the speedometer drive gear housing and prevents it from rotating when the wheel turns.

   d. Make sure that the speedometer gear housing does not move as the axle nut is tightened.

   e. Tighten the axle nut to specifications in **Table 2** or **Table 3**.

   f. Remove the brake caliper from the Bunjee cord and carefully align it with the brake disc and install it. Install the 2 caliper bolts and tighten to the torque specification in **Table 2** or **Table 3**.

   g. Apply the front brake and compress the front forks several times to make sure the axle is installed correctly without binding the forks. Then tighten the axle pinch bolts to the torque specification in **Table 2** or **Table 3**.

Inspection

1. Remove any corrosion on the front axle with a piece of fine emery cloth.

2. Check axle runout. Place the axle on V-blocks that are set 100 mm (4 in.) apart (**Figure 13**). Place

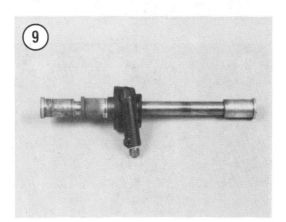

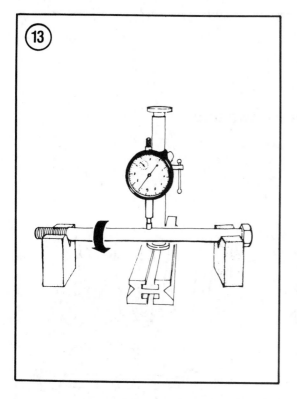

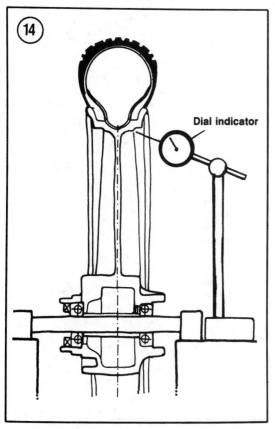

Dial indicator

the tip of a dial indicator in the middle of the axle. Rotate the axle and check runout. If the runout exceeds 0.2 mm (0.008 in.) but does not exceed 0.7 mm (0.027 in.), have it straightened by a dealer or machine shop to read less than 0.2 mm (0.008 in.) runout. If the runout exceeds 0.7 mm (0.027 in.), replace the axle. Do not attempt to straighten it.

3. Check rim runout as follows:

   a. Measure the radial (up and down) runout of the wheel rim with a dial indicator as shown in **Figure 14**. If runout exceeds 0.8 mm (0.03 in.), check the wheel bearings.

   b. Measure the axial (side to side) runout of the wheel rim with a dial indicator as shown in **Figure 14**. If runout exceeds 0.5 mm (0.01 in.), check the wheel bearings.

   c. If the wheel bearings are okay, the wheel cannot be serviced, but must be replaced.

   d. Inspect and replace the front wheel bearings as described under *Front Hub* in this chapter.

4. Inspect the wheel rim for dents, bending or cracks. Check the rim and rim sealing surface for scratches that are deeper than 0.5 mm (0.01 in.). If any of these conditions are present, replace the wheel.

Speedometer Gear Lubrication

The speedometer gear should be lubricated with high-temperature grease.

1. Remove the front wheel from the motorcycle.

2. Clean all old grease from the gear housing (**Figure 15**) and gear. Pack the gear with high-temperature grease.

3. Install the front wheel as described in this chapter.

10

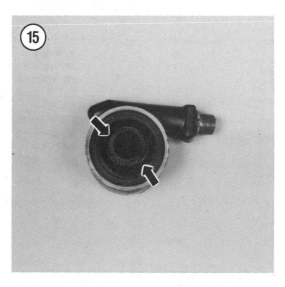

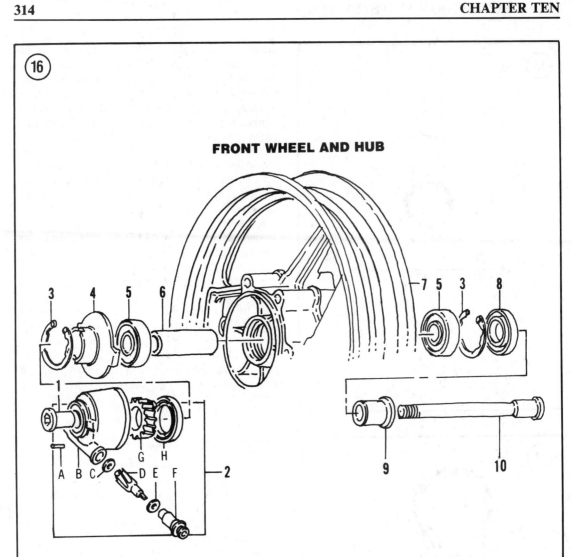

FRONT WHEEL AND HUB

1. Axle nut
2A. Spring pin
2B. Housing
2C. Washer
2D. Gear
2E. Washer
2F. Bushing
2G. Gear
2H. Oil seal

3. Circlip
4. Receiver
5. Bearing
6. Spacer
7. Wheel
8. Oil seal
9. Spacer
10. Axle

FRONT HUB

Disassembly/Inspection/Reassembly

Refer to **Figure 16**.

1. Check the wheel bearings by rotating the inner race. Check for bearing roughness, excessive noise or damage. If necessary, replace the bearings as follows. Always replace bearings in a set.

> *NOTE*
> *When removing wheel bearings from a hub, the first bearing removed is usually damaged. Because wheel bearings must be replaced as a set, do not remove the bearings unless replacement is required. Factory installed bearings are sealed and do not require periodic lubrication.*

2. Remove the circlip (**Figure 17**) and lift the receiver out of the wheel (**Figure 18**).
3. Using a long drift or screwdriver, pry the oil seal from the right-hand side. See **Figure 19**.
4. Remove the circlip from the right-hand side (3, **Figure 16**).
5. Using a long drift and hammer, tilt the center spacer away from one side of the left-hand bearing (**Figure 20**). Then drive the left-hand bearing out of the hub. See **Figure 20**.
6. Remove the center spacer and drive the right-hand bearing out of the hub.
7. Clean the axle spacer and hub thoroughly in solvent.

10

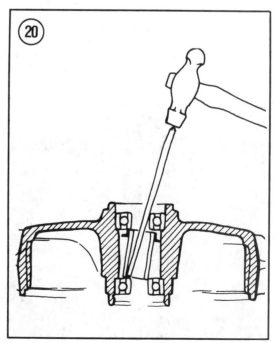

8. Tap the right-hand bearing into place carefully using a suitable size socket placed on the outer bearing race (**Figure 21**).

9. Install the right-hand circlip. Make sure it seats in its groove.

10. Install the center spacer and install the left-hand bearing (**Figure 22**) as described in Step 8.

11. Align the 2 tabs on the receiver with the 2 slots in the hub (**Figure 23**) and install the receiver. See **Figure 18**.

12. Install the receiver circlip (**Figure 17**). Make sure the circlip seats in the hub groove.

13. Install a new right-hand grease seal. Drive the seal in squarely with a large diameter socket on the outer portion of the seal. Drive the seal until it seats against the circlip.

WHEEL BALANCE

An unbalanced wheel results in unsafe riding conditions. Depending on the degree of unbalance and the speed of the motorcycle, the rider may experience anything from a mild vibration to a violent shimmy and loss of control.

Weights are attached to the rim (**Figure 24**) by two different methods. Adhesive-backed weights are available from motorcycle dealers. The weight shown (**Figure 24**) comes in a kit with test weights and strips of adhesive-backed weights that can be cut to the desired length and attached directly to the rim. Kawasaki offers weights that can be crimped on the aluminum rims (**Figure 25**).

NOTE
The Kawasaki balance weights cannot be reused. In addition, replace any Kawasaki balance weight that is loose on the rim.

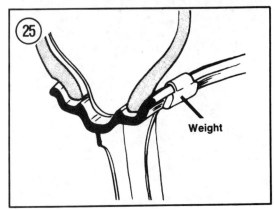

Weight

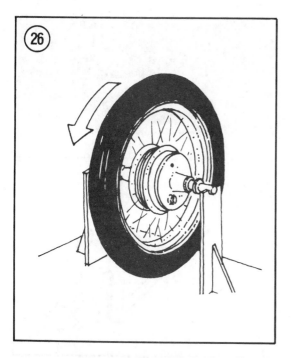

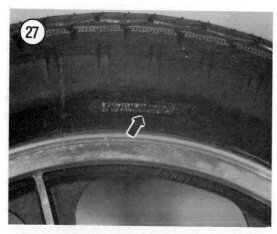

NOTE
Be sure to balance the wheel with the brake disc(s) attached as it also affects the balance.

Before attempting to balance the wheels, check to be sure that the wheel bearings are in good condition and properly lubricated. The wheel must rotate freely.

1. Remove the wheel as described in this chapter or in Chapter Eleven.

2. Mount the wheel on a fixture such as the one in **Figure 26** so it can rotate freely.

3. Give the wheel a spin and let it turn until it stops. Mark the tire at the lowest point (6 o'clock).

4. Spin the wheel several more times. If the wheel keeps coming to rest at the same point, it is out of balance.

5. Tape a test weight to the upper (or light) side of the wheel.

6. Experiment with different weights until the wheel, when spun, comes to rest at a different position each time.

7. Remove the test weight and install the correct size weight.

NOTE
*When installing crimp-type weights onto aluminum rims, it may be necessary to let some air out of the tire. After installing the weight, refill the tire to the correct air pressure. See **Tire Pressure** in Chapter Three.*

TUBELESS TIRES

WARNING
Do not install an inner tube inside a tubeless tire. The tube will cause an abnormal heat buildup in the tire and could result in a blowout.

Tubeless tires have the word TUBELESS molded in the tire sidewall (**Figure 27**) and the rims have TUBELESS cast on them (**Figure 28**).

When a tubeless tire is flat, it best to take it to a motorcycle dealer for repair. Punctured tubeless tires should be removed from the rim to inspect the inside of the tire and to apply a combination plug/patch from the inside. Don't rely on a plug or cord repair applied from outside the tire. They might be okay on a car, but they're too dangerous on a motorcycle.

After repairing a tubeless tire, don't exceed 50 mph (80 kph) for the first 24 hours. After 24 hours, you can ride faster, but never over 80 mph (128 kph). Never race on a repaired tubeless tire. The patch could work loose from tire flexing and heat.

10

Repair

Do not rely on a plug or cord patch applied from outside the tire. Use a combination plug/patch applied from inside the tire (**Figure 29**).

1. Remove the tire from the rim as described in this chapter.

2. Inspect the rim inner flange. Smooth any scratches on the sealing surface with emery cloth. If a scratch is deeper than 0.5 mm (0.020 in.), the wheel should be replaced.

3. Inspect the tire inside and out. Replace a tire if any of the following is found:

    a. A puncture larger than 1/8 in. (3 mm) diameter.

    b. A punctured or damaged sidewall.

    c. More than 2 punctures in the tire.

4. Apply the plug/patch, following the instructions supplied with the patch.

TUBELESS TIRE CHANGING

The wheels can easily be damaged during tire removal. Special care must be taken with tire irons when changing a tire to avoid scratches and gouges to the outer rim surface. Insert scraps of leather between the tire iron and the rim to protect the rim from damage.

The stock cast wheels are designed for use with tubeless tires.

Tire repair is covered under *Tubeless Tires* in this chapter.

When removing a tubeless tire, take care not to damage the tire beads, inner liner of the tire or the wheel rim flange. Use tire levers or flat handled tire irons with rounded ends.

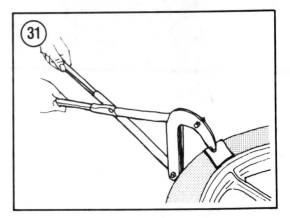

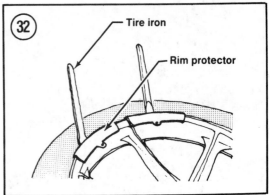

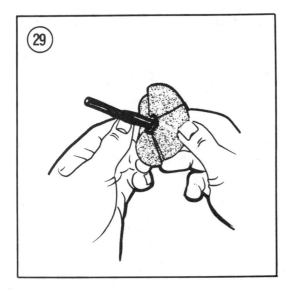

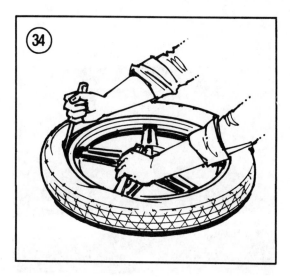

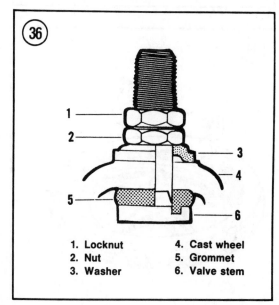

1. Locknut
2. Nut
3. Washer
4. Cast wheel
5. Grommet
6. Valve stem

Removal

> *NOTE*
> *While removing a tire, support the wheel on 2 blocks of wood, so the brake disc doesn't contact the floor.*

1. Mark the valve stem location on the tire, so the tire can be installed in the same position for easier balancing. See **Figure 30**.
2. Remove the valve core to deflate the tire.

> *NOTE*
> *Removal of tubeless tires from their rims can be very difficult because of the exceptionally tight bead/rim seal. Breaking the bead seal may require the use of a special tool (**Figure 31**). If you have trouble breaking the seal, take the tire to a motorcycle dealer.*

> *CAUTION*
> *The inner rim and tire bead area are sealing surfaces on a tubeless tire. Do not scratch the inside of the rim or damage the tire bead.*

3. Press the entire bead on both sides of the tire into the center of the rim.
4. Lubricate the beads with soapy water.

> *NOTE*
> *Use rim protectors (**Figure 32**) or insert scraps of leather between the tire irons and the rim to protect the rim from damage.*

5. Insert the tire iron under the bead next to the valve (**Figure 33**). Force the bead on the opposite side of the tire into the center of the rim and pry the bead over the rim with the tire iron.
6. Insert a second tire iron next to the first to hold the bead over the rim. Then work around the tire with the first tool prying the bead over the rim (**Figure 34**).

> *NOTE*
> *Step 7 is required only if it is necessary to completely remove the tire from the rim.*

7. Turn the wheel over. Insert a tire tool between the second bead and the same side of the rim that the first bead was pried over (**Figure 35**). Force the bead on the opposite side from the tool into the center of the rim. Pry the second bead off the rim, working around the wheel with 2 tire irons as with the first.
8. Inspect the valve stem seal. Because rubber deteriorates with age, it is advisable to replace the valve stem when replacing a tire. See **Figure 36**.

10

Installation

1. Carefully inspect the tire for any damage, especially inside.

2. A new tire may have balancing rubbers inside. These are not patches and should not be disturbed. A colored spot near the bead indicates the lightest point on the tire. This spot should be placed next to the valve stem (**Figure 30**). In addition, most tires have directional arrows labeled on the side of the tire that indicates at which direction the tire should rotate (**Figure 37**). Make sure to install the tire accordingly.

3. Lubricate both beads of the tire with soapy water.

4. Place the backside of the tire into the center of the rim. The lower bead should go into the center of the rim and the upper bead outside. Work around the tire in both directions (**Figure 38**). Use a tire iron for the last few inches of bead (**Figure 39**).

5. Press the upper bead into the rim opposite the valve (**Figure 40**). Pry the bead into the rim on both sides of the initial point with a tire tool, working around the rim to the valve.

6. Check the bead on both sides of the tire for an even fit around the rim.

7. Place an inflatable band around the circumference of the tire. Slowly inflate the band until the tire beads are pressed against the rim. Inflate the tire enough to seat it, deflate the band and remove it.

> *WARNING*
> *Never exceed 56 psi (4.0 k/cm²) inflation pressure as the tire could burst causing severe injury. Never stand directly over the tire while inflating it.*

8. After inflating the tire, check that the beads are fully seated and that the tire rim lines (**Figure 41**) are the same distance from the rim all the way around the tire. If the beads won't seat, deflate the tire, relubricate the rim and beads with soapy water and reinflate the tire.

9. Inflate the tire to the required pressure. See *Tire Pressure* in Chapter Three. Screw on the valve stem cap.

10. Balance the wheel assembly as described in this chapter.

HANDLEBARS

Removal/Installation

The Ninja uses separate handlebar assemblies that slip over the top of the fork tubes and bolt directly to the upper steering stem.

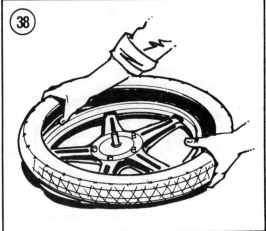

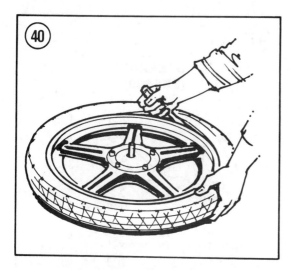

1. Remove the fork tube cap.

2. Remove the steering stem cover (**Figure 42**).

3. Remove the Allen bolts (**Figure 43**) and lift the handlebar off of the upper steering stem. Allow the handlebar(s) to hang by their control cables while performing service procedures.

4. If it is necessary to replace a handlebar, remove the handlebar switches as described under *Switches* in Chapter Eight. Remove the brake master cylinder as described in Chapter Twelve. Remove the clutch master cylinder as described in Chapter Five.

5. Tighten the handlebar Allen bolts to the specifications in **Table 2** or **Table 3**.

Inspection

Check the handlebars at their bolt holes and along the entire mounting area for cracks or damage. Replace a bent or damaged handlebar immediately. If the bike is involved in a crash, examine the handlebars, steering stem and front forks carefully.

STEERING HEAD

Disassembly

Refer to **Figure 44** (ZX900) or **Figure 45** (ZX1000) for this procedure.

1. Support the bike on the center stand.

2. Remove the upper and lower fairings as described in Chapter Thirteen.

3. Remove the front wheel as described in this chapter.

4. Remove the fuel tank as described in Chapter Seven.

10

5. Remove the ignition switch bolts and separate the switch (**Figure 46**) from the upper steering stem.

6. Remove the instrument cluster as described under *Electrical Components* in Chapter Eight.

NOTE
It is not necessary to disconnect the brake lines when performing Step 7.

7. Remove the bolts securing the brake hose joint to the steering stem (**Figure 47**) pull it away from the stem.

8. Remove the front fairing bracket and allow the bracket to hang down .

9. Remove the handlebars as described in this chapter.

10. Remove the front forks as described in this chapter.

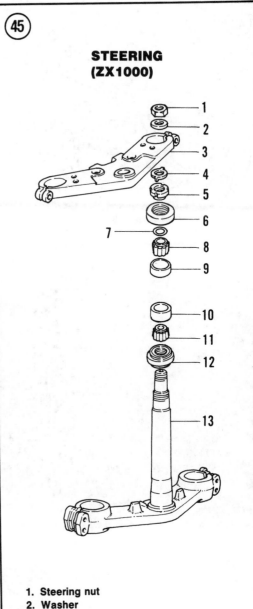

STEERING (ZX1000)

1. Steering nut
2. Washer
3. Upper fork bridge
4. Lockwasher
5. Nut
6. Oil seal
7. O-ring
8. Inner bearing race
9. Outer bearing race
10. Outer bearing race
11. Inner bearing race
12. Oil seal
13. Lower fork bridge and steering stem

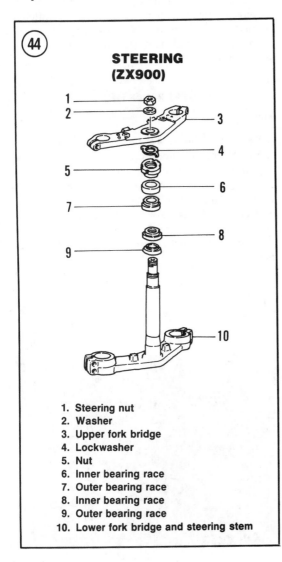

STEERING (ZX900)

1. Steering nut
2. Washer
3. Upper fork bridge
4. Lockwasher
5. Nut
6. Inner bearing race
7. Outer bearing race
8. Inner bearing race
9. Outer bearing race
10. Lower fork bridge and steering stem

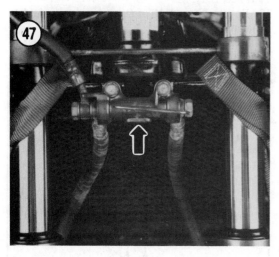

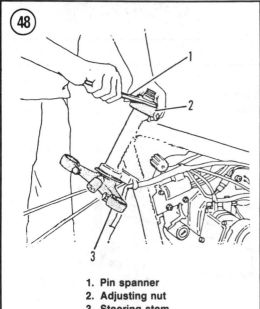

1. Pin spanner
2. Adjusting nut
3. Steering stem

11. Remove the steering nut and flat washer.

12. Lift the upper steering stem head off the steering stem shaft.

13. Remove the lockwasher and remove the steering adjust nut (**Figure 48**) with a spanner wrench.

14. Pull the steering stem out of the frame.

15. Remove the steering stem cap and upper bearing from the frame.

16. Remove the lower bearing (**Figure 49**) as follows:

    a. Install a bearing puller (**Figure 50**) onto the steering stem and bearing.

    b. Pull the bearing off of the steering stem.

    c. Slide the seal (**Figure 49**) off the steering stem.

Assembly

Refer to **Figure 44** (ZX900) or **Figure 45** (ZX1000) for this procedure.

1. If the lower bearing was removed from the steering stem, install a new bearing as follows:

    a. Clean the steering stem thoroughly in solvent.

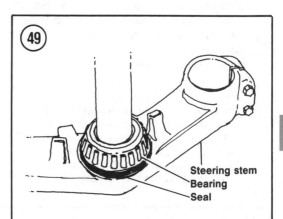

Steering stem
Bearing
Seal

10

b. Slide a new seal (**Figure 49**) onto the steering stem.

c. Slide the new bearing (**Figure 49**) onto the steering stem until it stops.

d. Align the bearing with the machined portion of the shaft and slide a long hollow pipe over the steering stem (**Figure 51**). Drive down the bearing until it rests against the seal.

2. Apply a coat of wheel bearing grease to both bearings.

3. Apply a coat of wheel bearing grease to both bearing races.

4. Carefully slide the steering stem up through the frame neck.

5. Install the upper bearing and the bearing cap.

6. Install the steering stem locknut finger tight.

7. Align the lockwasher arms with the notches in the steering adjust nut and install the locknut.

8. Install the upper steering stem.

9. Install the washer and the steering stem nut. Install the nut loosely.

10. Seat the bearings by performing the following:

a. Using a steering stem nut wrench (**Figure 52**), tighten the steering adjust nut to 39 N•m (29 ft.-lb.). This torque can be obtained by using a nut wrench with the dimensions in **Figure 52** and pulling the wrench until a torque of 22.2 kg (48 ft.-lb.) is reached.

NOTE
If the proper steering stem nut wrench is not available, it will be necessary to tighten the steering adjust nut by feel and with the use of a drift punch and hammer. Tighten the adjust nut until it meets the conditions in sub-step "b".

b. When the steering adjust nut is tightened properly, the steering stem should turn smoothly with no play.

c. Loosen the adjust nut a small amount.

d. Turn the steering stem by hand to make sure it turns freely and does not bind. Repeat if necessary.

11. Tighten the steering stem nut to the torque specification in **Table 2** or **Table 3**.

12. Turn the steering stem again by hand to make sure it turns freely and does not bind. If the steering stem is too tight, the bearings can be damaged. If the steering stem is too loose, the steering will become unstable. Repeat Steps 10 and 11 if necessary.

13. Reverse Steps 1-10 of *Disassembly* to complete installation.

14. Recheck the steering adjustment. Repeat if necessary.

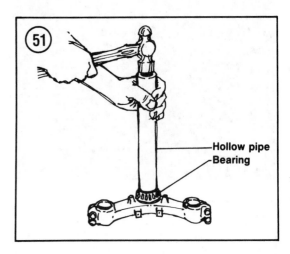

Hollow pipe
Bearing

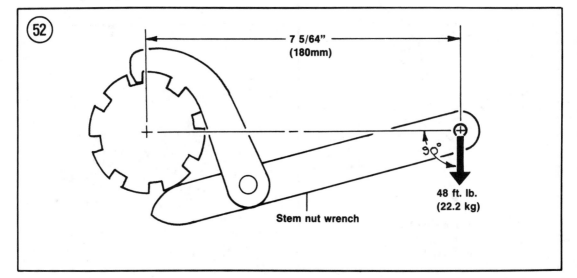

7 5/64"
(180mm)

90°

48 ft. lb.
(22.2 kg)

Stem nut wrench

15. If a brake line was disconnected, bleed the brake system as described under *Bleeding the System* in Chapter Twelve.

Inspection

1. Clean the bearing races in the steering head and both bearings with solvent.
2. Check for broken welds on the frame around the steering stem. If any are found, having the repaired by a competent frame shop or welding service familiar with motorcycle frame repair.

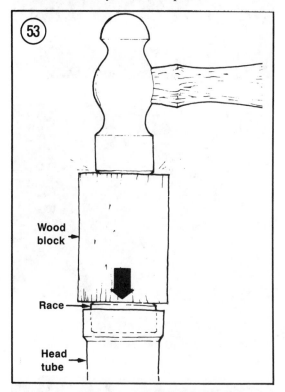

Wood block

Race

Head tube

3. Check the bearings for pitting, scratches, or discoloration indicating wear or corrosion. Replace them in sets if any are bad.
4. Check the upper and lower races in the steering head for pitting, galling and corrosion. If any of these conditions exist, replace them as described under *Bearing Race Replacement* in this chapter.
5. Check steering stem for cracks and check its race for damage or wear. Replace if necessary.

Bearing Race Replacement

The steering stem bearing races are pressed into place. Because they are easily damaged, do not remove them unless they are worn and require replacement.

To remove a bearing race, insert a long drift punch into the head tube and carefully tap the race out from the inside. Tap all around the race so that neither the race nor the head tube are bent. To install a race, fit it into the end of the head tube. Tap it in slowly and squarely using a large socket or tube which contacts the outside edge of the bearing race (**Figure 53**).

FRONT FORK

If the front fork is going to be removed without disassembly, perform the *Removal/Installation* procedures in this chapter. If the front fork is going to be disassembled, refer to *Disassembly* in this chapter.

Removal/Installation

1. Place the motorcycle on the center stand.
2. Remove the front fairing assembly as described in Chapter Thirteen.
3. Remove the brake caliper(s) as described under *Front Caliper Removal/Installation* in Chapter Twelve.

> *NOTE*
> *Insert a piece of wood in the calipers in place of the disc. That way, if the brake lever is inadvertently squeezed, the piston will not be forced out of the calipers. If it does happen, the calipers might have to be disassembled to reseat the piston.*

5. Remove the air valve cap and depress the valve (**Figure 54**) to release fork air pressure from both fork tubes.
6. Remove the handlebars as described in this chapter.

7A. *ZX900:* Remove the front fender bolts (**Figure 55**) and the fender nut (**Figure 56**). Remove the front fender (**Figure 57**).

7B. *ZX1000:* Remove the front fender bolts (**Figure 58**). Then remove the fender brace (A, **Figure 59**) and the front fender (B, **Figure 59**).

NOTE
Do not disconnect any hydraulic line
when performing Step 8 and Step 9.

8. Remove the Allen bolts securing the brake plunger (**Figure 60**) to the anti-dive housing and pull the brake plunger away from the fork tube.

9. Remove the junction block bolts and pull the junction block (**Figure 61**) away from the fork tube. Secure the brake caliper with a Bunjee cord or mechanic's wire to prevent brake line damage.

10. Loosen the air joint hose clamp (A, **Figure 62**) on each fork tube.

11. Loosen the upper and lower fork tube pinch bolts (**Figure 63**).

12. Twist the fork tube and remove it.

13. Repeat for the opposite side.

14. Install by reversing these removal steps. Note the following:

    a. Check the air joint O-rings (**Figure 64**) for wear or damage. Replace all 4 O-rings as a set, if necessary.

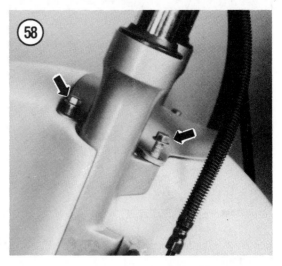

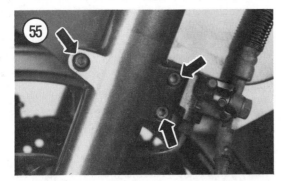

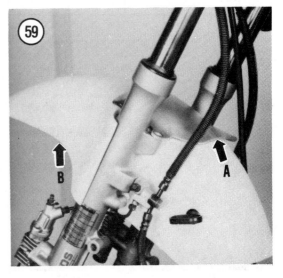

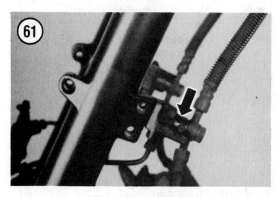

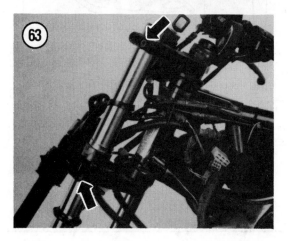

b. When installing the fork tube, make sure to slide the tube through the air joint (B, **Figure 62**) and then the circlip. Make sure the screw head on the clamp faces out (A, **Figure 62**).

c. Tighten the upper and lower fork tube pinch bolts to the specifications in **Table 2** or **Table 3**.

d. Tighten the junction block and brake plunger bolts securely.

e. Apply Loctite 242 (blue) to the front fender bolts and tighten securely.

f. After installing the front wheel, squeeze the front brake lever. If the brake lever feels spongy, bleed the brake(s) as described under *Bleeding the System* in Chapter Twelve.

g. Refill the front fork air pressure as described under *Suspension Adjustment* in Chapter Three.

Disassembly

Refer to **Figure 65** for this procedure.

1. Perform Steps 1-10 described under *Front Fork Removal/Installation*.

2. Depress the air valve(s) to release all fork air pressure, then remove the air valve caps (**Figure 54**).

> *NOTE*
> *The lower fork tube Allen bolt is normally secured with Loctite and can be very difficult to remove because the damper rod may turn inside the lower fork tube. The Allen bolt can be removed easily with an air impact driver. If you do not have access to an air impact driver, it is best to loosen the Allen bolt before removing the fork tube cap and spring. This method allows the fork spring to apply pressure to the damper rod to keep it from turning when the Allen bolt is loosened.*

10

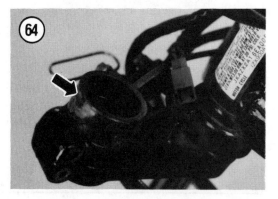

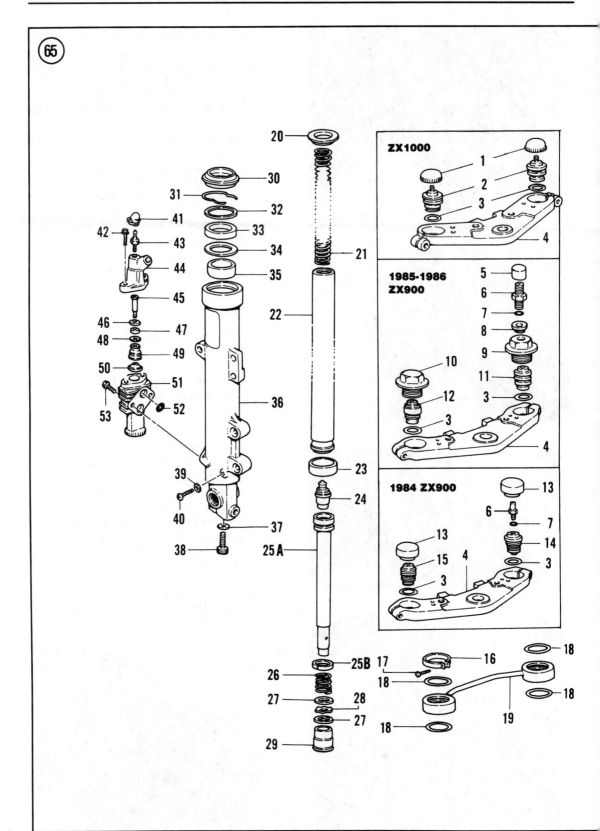

FRONT FORK

1. Air valve cap
2. Fork cap
3. O-rings
4. Upper fork bridge
5. Air valve cap
6. Air valve
7. O-ring
8. Gasket
9. Right-hand fork cap
10. Left-hand fork cap
11. Right-hand spring seat
12. Left-hand spring seat
13. Air valve cap
14. Right-hand fork cap
15. Left-hand fork cap
16. Clamp
17. Screw
18. O-rings
19. Air tube assembly
20. Spring seat (ZX1000)
21. Fork spring
22. Upper fork tube
23. Bushing
24. Travel control valve
25A. Damper rod
25B. Piston ring
26. Spring

27. Spring washers
28. Wave washer
29. Oil lock piece
30. Dust seal
31. Spring clip
32. Washer
33. Oil seal
34. Washer
35. Bushing
36. Lower fork tube
37. Washer
38. Allen bolt
39. Washer
40. Drain screw
41. Cap
42. Bolt
43. Bleed valve
44. Brake plunger
45. Plunger
46. Washer
47. Seal ring
48. Seal ring
49. Plug case
50. Separator
51. Housing
52. O-ring
53. Bolt

10

3. Place a drain pan underneath one of the fork tubes.

4. Remove the fork tube Allen bolt (**Figure 66**).

> *NOTE*
> *With the front fender removed, the lower fork tube will turn when the Allen bolt is turned. Hold the lower fork tube with a large adjustable wrench as shown in **Figure 67**.*

> *WARNING*
> *The fork caps preload the fork springs. Take precautions to prevent the fork caps from flying into your face during removal. If the fork tubes have been bent in a compressed position by an accident, the fork caps will be under considerable pressure. Have them removed by a Kawasaki dealer.*

5. See **Figure 68**. Loosen the upper fork tube pinch bolt (A) then loosen the fork cap (B).

> *NOTE*
> *The pinch bolt actually compresses the fork tube slightly and makes fork cap removal difficult. Always loosen the pinch bolt before unscrewing the fork cap.*

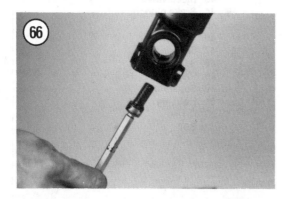

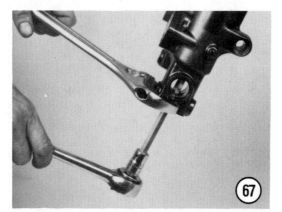

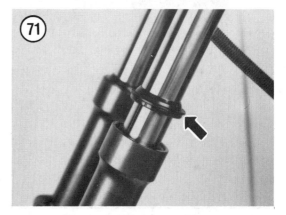

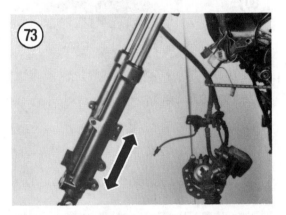

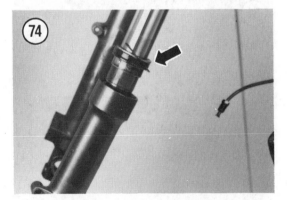

6. Remove the fork cap (**Figure 69**). On ZX1000 models, remove the spring seat (20, **Figure 65**).

7. Remove the fork spring (**Figure 70**). Cover the bottom of the spring with a shop rag as it is removed to prevent oil from dripping down the steering stem and fork tube. Place the fork spring on some clean newspapers to avoid making a mess on your workbench.

8. Carefully pry the dust seal (**Figure 71**) out of the lower fork tube and slide it up the fork tube.

9. Pry the snap ring (**Figure 72**) out of the lower fork tube.

10. Before separating the fork tubes, compress and extend the forks their full travel. If you feel any roughness or harsh spots in the stroke it is an indication of a bent fork tube or a damaged (dented) lower fork tube.

11. The fork tube and lower fork tube are held together by a bushing that is pressed into the top of the lower fork tube. In order to separate the lower fork tube from the fork tube, pull hard on the lower fork tube using quick in-and-out strokes (**Figure 73**). Doing this will withdraw the upper washer, oil seal, lower washer and bushing (**Figure 74**).

12. Loosen the lower fork pinch bolts (**Figure 63**), then remove the fork assembly by turning it as you pull down.

13. Invert the fork so that the travel control valve (**Figure 75**) slides out.

14. See **Figure 76**. Slide the following pars off of the fork tube:

    a. Dust seal (A).
    b. Snap ring (B).
    c. Upper washer (C).
    d. Oil seal (D).
    e. Lower washer (E).
    f. Bushing (F).

10

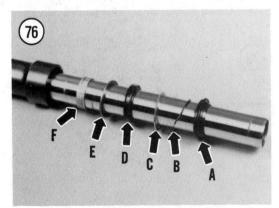

15. Slide the oil lock piece (**Figure 77**) off of the damper rod.

16. See **Figure 78**. Remove the following parts from the damper rod:

a. Spring washer (A).
b. Flat washer (B).
c. Spring washer (C).

16. See **Figure 79**. Slide the damper rod (A) and spring (B) out through the top of the fork tube.

Inspection

1. Thoroughly clean all metal parts in solvent and dry them. Clean the seals with contact cleaner.

2. Check both fork tubes for wear or scratches. Check the upper fork tube for straightness. If bent, refer service to a Kawasaki dealer.

3. Check the upper fork tube for chrome pitting, flaking or creasing; this condition will damage oil seals. Replace the fork tube if necessary.

4. Check the lower fork tube oil seal area (**Figure 80**) for dents or other damage that would allow oil leakage. Replace the fork tube if necessary.

5. Check the damper rod for straightness (**Figure 81**).

6. Check the damper rod piston ring (**Figure 82**) for tearing, cracks or damage.

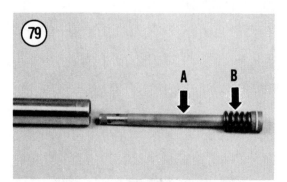

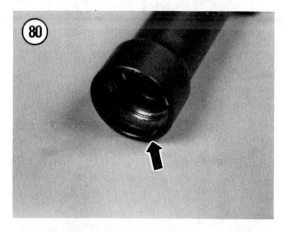

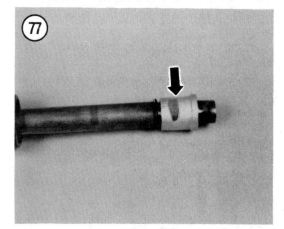

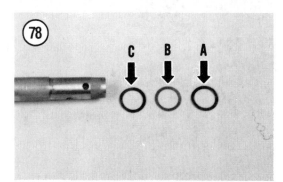

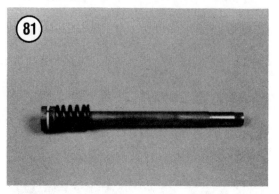

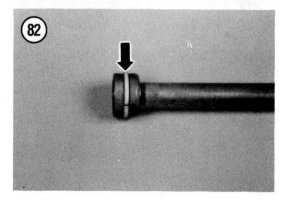

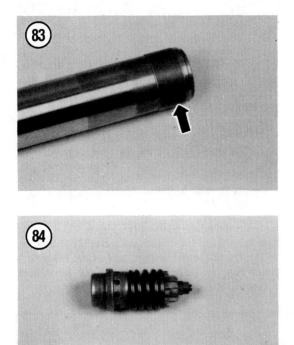

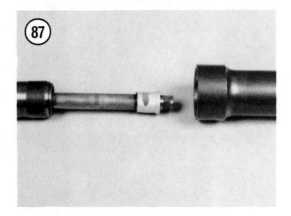

7. Check the outside surface of the guide bushing on the fork tube (**Figure 83**) for scoring, nicks or damage. Replace if necessary by pulling off the fork tube.

8. Check the inside surface of the lower fork tube guide bushing (F, **Figure 76**) for scoring, nicks or damage. Replace if necessary.

NOTE
Do not disassemble the travel control valve in Step 9. If the valve is damaged, it must be replaced.

9. Check the travel control valve (**Figure 84**) for any signs of damage.

10. Measure the uncompressed (free) length of the fork springs (**Figure 85**) with a tape measure and compare to specifications in **Table 1**. Replace both fork springs as a set if one is found too short.

NOTE
It is best to replace both springs to keep the forks balanced for steering stability.

11. Replace the fork cap O-ring (**Figure 86**) if damaged.

12. Check the oil and dust seals for wear or damage. Replace if necessary.

Assembly

Refer to **Figure 65** for this procedure.

1. Slide the spring onto the damper rod and insert the damper rod and spring into the top of the upper fork tube (**Figure 79**).

2. See **Figure 78**. Install the following onto the damper rod:

a. Spring washer (C).
b. Flat washer (B).
c. Spring washer (A).

3. Slide the oil lock piece (**Figure 77**) onto the damper rod.

4. Insert the damper rod/upper fork tube into the lower fork tube (**Figure 87**).

10

NOTE
*When installing and tightening the fork tube Allen bolt in Step 5, it will be necessary to prevent the damper rod from turning. One way is to temporarily install the travel control valve, fork spring and fork cap. Or the damper rod can also be held stationary by installing the Kawasaki adapter 57001-1057 on a long 3/8 in. T-handle extension and inserting the adapter into the end of the damper rod (**Figure 88**).*

5. Apply Loctite 242 (blue) onto the fork tube Allen bolt (**Figure 89**). Install the Allen bolt and tighten to the torque specification in **Table 2** or **Table 3**.

NOTE
If the fork cap, fork spring and travel control valve were used to hold the

damper rod when installing the fork tube Allen bolt, remove them from the fork tube.

NOTE
*The guide bushing can be installed with a piece of galvanized pipe or other piece of tubing that fits snugly over the fork tube. If both ends of the pipe are threaded, wrap one end with duct tape (**Figure 90**) to prevent the threads from damaging the interior of the lower fork tube. The bottom of this homemade driver must be flat so it installs the parts squarely.*

6. Slide the guide bushing (F, **Figure 91**) over the fork tube. Turn the bushing (**Figure 92**) so that the split faces to the left or right side of the lower fork tube. Tap the guide bushing into the lower fork tube until it bottoms.

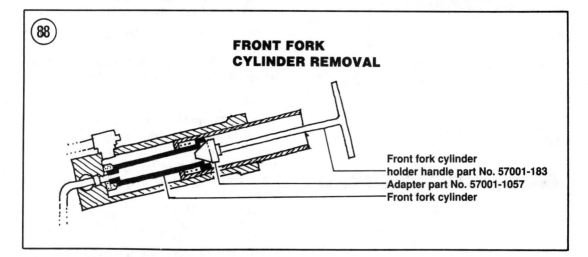

88

FRONT FORK CYLINDER REMOVAL

Front fork cylinder holder handle part No. 57001-183
Adapter part No. 57001-1057
Front fork cylinder

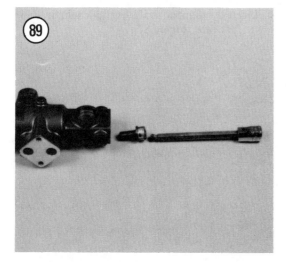

89

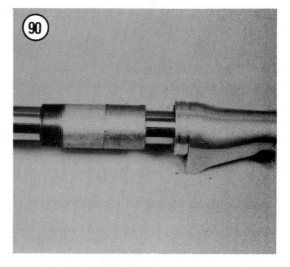

90

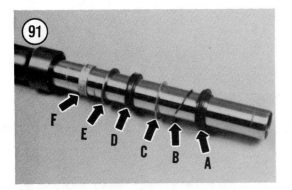

7. Slide the washer (**Figure 93**) down the fork tube until it rests against the bushing.

8. Position the oil seal with its markings facing upward and slide down onto the fork tube (**Figure 94**). Drive the seal into the lower fork tube with the same tool used in Step 6. Drive the oil seal in until it rests against the washer.

9. Slide the washer (C, **Figure 91**) down the inner fork tube until it rests against the oil seal. Make sure the circlip groove in the lower fork tube can be seen above the top surface of the washer. If not, the oil seal will have to driven farther into the lower fork tube. See Step 8.

10. Slide the circlip (B, **Figure 91**) down the upper fork tube and seat it in the lower fork tube groove. Make sure the circlip is completely seated in the groove (**Figure 95**).

11. Slide the dust seal down the inner fork tube and seat it in the lower fork tube (**Figure 96**) using a plastic hammer.

CAUTION
The dust seal has a raised lip which may be damaged by your homemade bushing/seal driver. Use a plastic hammer to tap the dust seal into place.

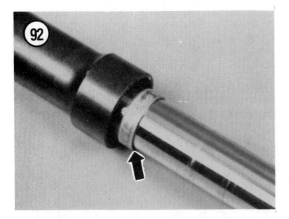

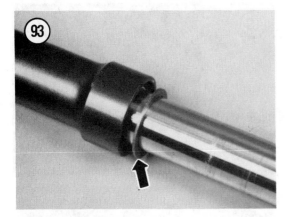

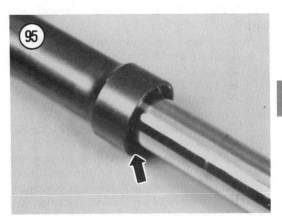

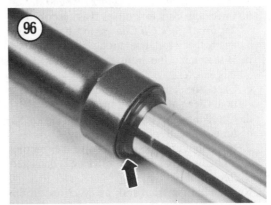

10

12. Fill the fork tube with the correct quantity of 10W fork oil as specified in **Table 4**. Check the oil level as described under *Front Fork Oil Change* in Chapter Three.

13. Install the travel control valve through the upper fork tube so that the nuts face to the top of the fork. See **Figure 97**.

14. Install the fork spring with the closer wound coils toward the top of the fork (**Figure 98**).

15. *ZX1000:* Install the upper spring seat.

16. Extend the upper and lower fork tubes as far apart as possible. Apply a light coat of oil to the fork cap and install it by slightly compressing the fork spring. Once the fork cap is installed, it can be tightened after installing the fork tube onto the motorcycle. See *Front Fork Removal/Installation* in this chapter.

> *NOTE*
> *It may be easier to install the fork caps after the fork is installed in the steering stem on the bike.*

Automatic Variable Damping System Troubleshooting

If the front fork does not operate correctly, perform the following:

1. *No damping during the fork compression stroke:*
   a. Check the front fork oil level as described under *Front Fork Oil Change* in Chapter Three and recheck fork operation.
   b. Disassemble the front fork as described in this chapter.
   c. Check the damper rod piston ring (**Figure 82**) for damage. Replace if necessary.
   d. If the damper rod piston ring is okay, the travel control valve may be damaged. Check the valve (**Figure 84**) for damage. No adjustment is provided for the valve. Replace the valve if necessary.

2. *No damping force during fork rebound stroke:*
   a. Check the front fork oil level as described under *Front Fork Oil Change* in Chapter Three and recheck fork operation.
   b. Disassemble the front fork as described in this chapter.
   c. Check the damper rod orifices for contamination. Clean in solvent if necessary.
   d. Check the damper rod piston ring (**Figure 82**) for damage. Replace if necessary.
   e. If the above checks do not solve the damping problem, the travel control valve is damaged. Replace the valve.

3. Reassemble the front fork as described in this chapter.

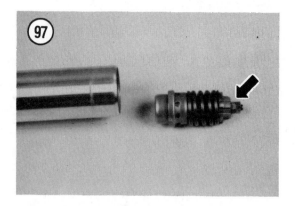

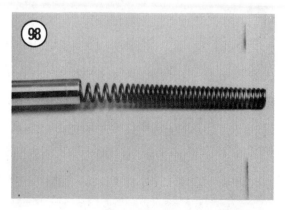

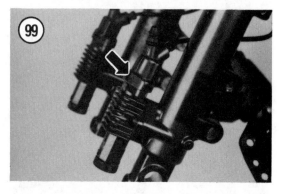

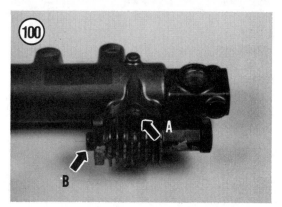

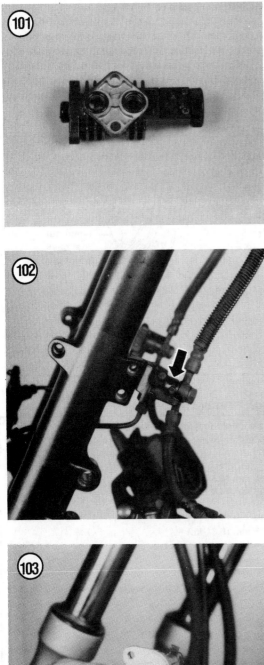

BRAKE PLUNGER
AND ANTI-DIVE

Removal/Installation

The anti-dive assembly can be removed with the front fork installed on the bike.

1. Drain the fork oil as described under *Front Fork Oil Change* in Chapter Three.

2. Remove the Allen bolts securing the brake plunger (**Figure 99**) to the anti-dive housing and pull the brake plunger away from the fork tube. Disconnect the brake line at the brake plunger and remove it.

3. Remove the Allen bolts securing the anti-dive housing (A, **Figure 100**) to the lower fork tube and remove it.

4. Check the anti-dive O-rings (**Figure 101**) for flat spots or damage. Replace if necessary.

5. The anti-dive unit cannot be disassembled. If damaged, replace the unit.

6. Install by reversing these steps.

7. Bleed the front brake as described under *Bleeding the System* in Chapter Twelve.

Brake Plunger Test

1. Remove the brake plunger (**Figure 99**) from the anti-dive unit but do not disconnect the brake line.

2. Remove the junction block screws and pull the junction block away from the fork tube (**Figure 102**). This will prevent oil pipe damage when performing this procedure.

3. Lightly apply the front brake lever and check that the brake plunger (**Figure 103**) extends 2 mm (3/32 in.). Release the brake lever and push the brake plunger back in with your finger. If the plunger did not extend correctly or if it is tight, replace the brake plunger assembly (**Figure 104**).

10

Brake Plunger
Seal Replacement

At the service intervals specified in Chapter Three (**Table 1**), the brake plunger rubber cap, O-ring and seal ring should be replaced.
1. Remove the brake plunger as described in this chapter.
2. Insert a 14 mm nut into the end of the brake plunger and unscrew the seal case (**Figure 105**).
3. Replace the rubber parts.
4. Reverse to install.

Anti-dive Assembly Test

Anti-dive operation can be checked as follows.

> *NOTE*
> *Do not drain the fork oil when performing this procedure. Apply tape over the fork tube equalizing hole to prevent fork oil leakage.*

1. Remove the front wheel, fork cap and spring as described in this chapter.
2. Hold the front fork upright.
3. Compress the upper fork tube a few times. Then compress the upper fork tube while holding the anti-dive rod (B, **Figure 100**) in with your finger.

4. Interpret results as follows:
   a. The fork compression stroke should be light and smooth when the valve is not pushed in.
   b. A noticeable difference in damping should occur when the anti-dive rod is held in.
5. If the anti-dive did not operate as described in Step 4, replace the anti-dive unit as described in this chapter.

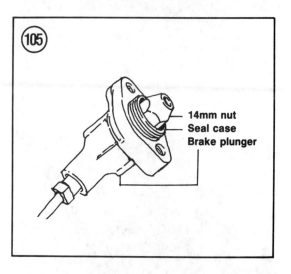

14mm nut
Seal case
Brake plunger

Table 1 FRONT SUSPENSION SPECIFICATIONS

Front fork type	Telescopic fork (pneumatic)
Front fork oil type	10 wt.
Caster	28°
Trail	
ZX900	114 mm (4.5 in.)
ZX1000	108 mm (4.3 in.)
Front wheel travel	
ZX900	140 mm (5.51 in.)
ZX1000	135 mm (5.31 in.)
Front fork spring free length	
ZX900	
New	522 mm (20.55 in.)
Wear limit	511 mm (20.12 in.)
ZX1000	
New	504.5 mm (19.86 in.)
Wear limit	494.0 mm (19.45 in.)
Axle runout	See text
Rim runout	
Axial	0.5 mm (0.020 in.)
Radial	0.8 mm (0.031 in.)

Table 2 FRONT SUSPENSION TIGHTENING TORQUES (ZX900)

	N·m	ft.-lb.
Front axle	88	65
Front axle pinch bolt	20	14.5
Fork cap		
1984	23	16.5
1985-1986	25	18
Fork tube damper rod Allen bolt	29	22
Upper fork tube pinch bolts	21	15
Steering stem pinch bolts	21	15
Steering stem nut	39	29
Handlebar Allen bolts	19	13.5
Front caliper bolts	32	24

Table 3 FRONT SUSPENSION TIGHTENING TORQUES (ZX1000)

	N·m	ft.-lb.
Front axle	64	47
Front axle pinch bolt	20	14.5
Fork cap	23	16.5
Fork tube damper rod Allen bolt	39	29
Upper fork tube pinch bolts	21	15
Steering stem pinch bolts	21	15
Steering stem nut	39	29
Handlebar Allen bolts	19	13.5
Front caliper bolts	32	24

Table 4 FRONT FORK OIL CAPACITY

Model	Change cc (oz.)	Rebuild cc (oz.)	Oil level mm (in.)
ZX900	273	317-325	332-336
	9.23	10.72 (11.00)	(13.071-13.228)
ZX1000	295	344-352	377-381
	(9.97)	(11.63-13.86)	(14.84-15.00)

10

REAR SUSPENSION

This chapter includes repair and replacement procedures for the rear wheel, drive chain and rear suspension components.

Rear suspension specifications are listed in **Table 1**. **Tables 1-3** are found at the end of the chapter.

REAR WHEEL

Removal/Installation

1. Support the bike so that the rear wheel clears the ground.

2A. *ZX900:* See **Figure 1**. Loosen the collar bolt locknut and loosen the collar bolt (A). Then loosen the caliper fixing bolt (B).

2B. *ZX1000:* Loosen the rear torque link nut (**Figure 2**).

3. Remove the rear brake caliper as described in under *Rear Caliper Removal/Installation* in Chapter Twelve.

4. Remove the right-hand retaining ring (**Figure 3**).

5. Loosen the right-hand axle pinch bolt (**Figure 4**).

6. Loosen the axle nut with an Allen wrench (**Figure 5**).

7. Remove the axle nut (**Figure 6**) and washer (**Figure 7**).

8. Remove the left-hand retaining ring (**Figure 8**).

9. Loosen the left-hand axle pinch bolt (A, **Figure 9**).

10. Remove the axle (B, **Figure 9**) from the left-hand side. On ZX900 models, remove the rear caliper bracket (**Figure 10**).

11

11. If necessary, remove the chain adjusters (**Figure 11**).

12. Lift the drive chain off the sprocket and pull the wheel (**Figure 12**) away from the swing arm.

13A. *ZX900:* Remove the right- (**Figure 13**) and left-hand (**Figure 14**) axle spacers.

13B. *ZX1000:* Remove the left- (**Figure 15**) and right-hand (**Figure 16**) axle spacers.

CAUTION
Do not set the wheel down on the disc surface as it may be scratched or bent. Either lean the wheel against a wall or place it on a couple of wood blocks.

NOTE
Insert a piece of wood in the caliper in place of the disc. That way, if the brake lever is inadvertently squeezed, the piston will not be forced out of the cylinder. If this does happen, the caliper might have to be disassembled to reseat the piston and the system will have to be bled.

CAUTION
The rear sprocket is bolted onto a separate coupling assembly. Do not lift the wheel assembly by the sprocket as this will pull the sprocket assembly out of the hub and allow the wheel to fall to the ground.

14. If the wheel is going to be off for any length of time, or if it is to be taken to a shop for repair, install the chain adjusters and axle spacers on the axle along with the axle nut to prevent losing any parts (**Figure 17**).

15. If necessary, service the rear sprocket as described under *Rear Sprocket and Coupling* in this chapter.

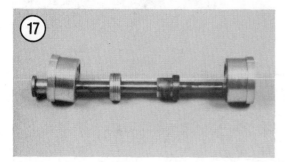

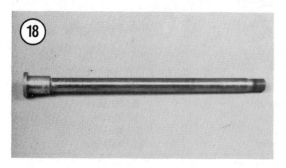

16. Installation is the reverse of these steps. Note the following:

   a. To prevent axle seizure, coat the axle and the axle nut with an anti-seize compound such as Bostick Never-Seez Lubricating & Anti-Seize compound (part No. 49501).

   b. If removed, insert the rear sprocket/coupling assembly into the rear hub as described under *Rear Sprocket and Coupling Removal/ Installation* in this chapter.

   c. Adjust the drive chain and check its alignment as described in Chapter Three.

   d. Tighten the axle nut to the torque specification in **Table 2** or **Table 3**.

   e. Make sure both retaining rings (**Figure 3**) are secured tightly in the chain adjuster grooves.

   f. Adjust the rear brake as described under *Rear Brake Pedal Height Adjustment* and *Rear Brake Light Switch Adjustment* in Chapter Three.

   g. Spin the wheel several times to make sure it rotates freely and that the brake works properly.

Inspection

1. Remove any corrosion on the rear axle (**Figure 18**) and axle nut with a piece of fine emery cloth.

2. Check axle runout. Place the axle on V-blocks that are set 100 mm (4 in.) apart (**Figure 19**). Place the tip of a dial indicator in the middle of the axle. Rotate the axle and check runout. If the runout exceeds 0.2 mm (0.008 in.) but does not exceed 0.7 mm (0.027 in.), have it straightened by a dealer or machine shop to read less than 0.2 mm (0.008 in.) runout. If the runout exceeds 0.7 mm (0.027 in.), replace the axle. Do not attempt to straighten it.

11

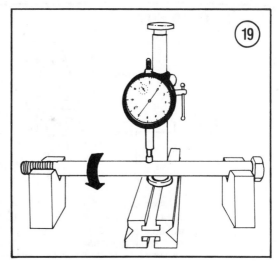

3. Check rim runout as follows:

  a. Measure the radial (up-and-down) runout of
the wheel rim with a dial indicator as shown in
Figure 20. If runout exceeds 0.8 mm (0.03 in.),
check the wheel bearings as described under
Rear Hub in this chapter.

  b. Measure the axial (side-to-side) runout of the
wheel rim with a dial indicator. If runout
exceeds 0.5 mm (0.01 in.), check the wheel
bearings as described under *Rear Hub* in this
chapter.

  c. If the wheel bearings are okay, the wheel
cannot be serviced, but must be replaced.

  d. Replace the rear wheel bearings as described
under *Rear Hub* in this chapter.

4. Inspect the wheel rim for dents, bending or
cracks. Check the rim and rim sealing surface for
scratches that are deeper than 0.5 mm (0.01 in.). If
any of these conditions are present, replace the
wheel.

5. Check the chain adjusters (**Figure 21**) for
corrosion buildup or damage. Replace if necessary.

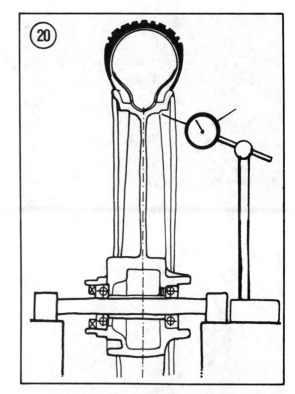

REAR HUB

Disassembly/Inspection/Reassembly

Refer to **Figure 22** for this procedure.

1. Lift the rear sprocket/coupling assembly (**Figure
23**) out of the rear hub.

> *NOTE*
> *When removing wheel bearings from a
> hub, the first bearing removed is usually
> damaged. Because wheel bearings must
> be replaced as a set, do not remove the
> bearings unless replacement is
> required. Factory installed bearings are*

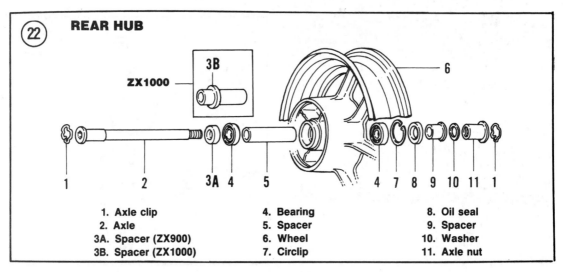

REAR HUB

ZX1000

1. Axle clip
2. Axle
3A. Spacer (ZX900)
3B. Spacer (ZX1000)
4. Bearing
5. Spacer
6. Wheel
7. Circlip
8. Oil seal
9. Spacer
10. Washer
11. Axle nut

sealed and do not require periodic lubrication.

2. Check the wheel bearings by rotating the inner race (**Figure 24**). Check for bearing roughness, excessive noise or damage. If necessary, replace the bearings as follows. Always replace bearings in a set.

3. Using a long drift or screwdriver and pry the oil seal from the right-hand side. See **Figure 25**.

4. Remove the circlip from the right-hand side (**Figure 22**).

5. Using a long drift and hammer, tilt the center spacer away from one side of the left-hand bearing (**Figure 26**). Then drive the left-hand bearing out of the hub. See **Figure 26**.

6. Remove the center spacer and drive the right-hand bearing out of the hub.

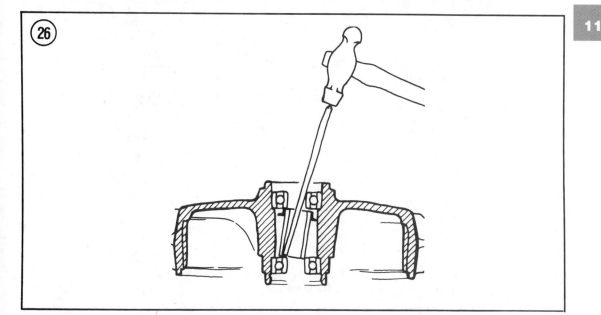

7. Clean the center spacer and hub thoroughly in solvent.

8. Tap the right-hand bearing into place carefully using a suitable size socket placed on the outer bearing race.

9. Install the right-hand circlip. Make sure it seats in its groove.

10. Install the center spacer and install the left-hand bearing as described in Step 8.

11. Install a new right-hand grease seal. Drive the seal in squarely with a large diameter socket on the outer portion of the seal (**Figure 27**). Drive the seal in until it seats against the circlip (**Figure 28**).

REAR SPROCKET AND COUPLING

The rear wheel coupling connects the rear sprocket to the rear wheel. See **Figure 29** (ZX900) or **Figure 30** (ZX1000). The coupling housing is equipped with an oil seal, ball bearing and spacer. Rubber shock dampers installed in the coupling absorb some of the shock that results from torque changes during acceleration or braking.

Removal/Installation

1. Remove the rear wheel as described in this chapter.

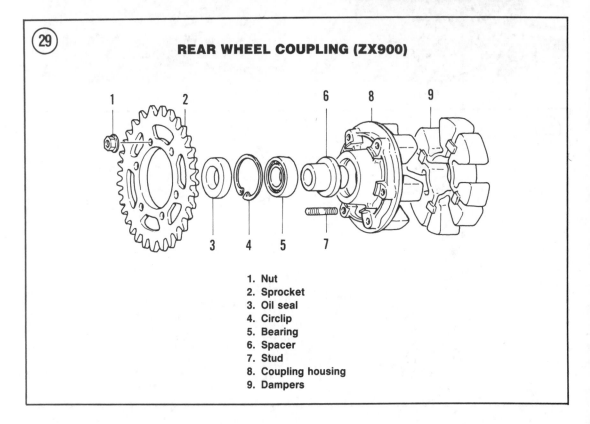

REAR WHEEL COUPLING (ZX900)

1. Nut
2. Sprocket
3. Oil seal
4. Circlip
5. Bearing
6. Spacer
7. Stud
8. Coupling housing
9. Dampers

2. Pull the rear wheel coupling assembly (**Figure 23**) up and out of the wheel hub.

3. Pull the dampers (**Figure 31**) out of the housing.

4. Remove the spacer. See **Figure 32** (ZX900) or **Figure 33** (ZX1000).

5. To remove the sprocket loosen and remove the nuts and lift the sprocket (**Figure 34**) off the housing.

6. Perform *Inspection/Disassembly/Reassembly* as described in this chapter.

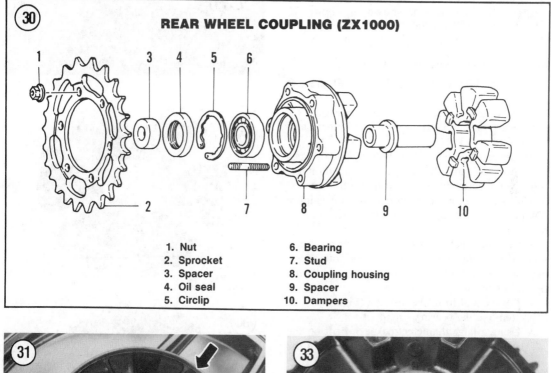

30

REAR WHEEL COUPLING (ZX1000)

1. Nut
2. Sprocket
3. Spacer
4. Oil seal
5. Circlip
6. Bearing
7. Stud
8. Coupling housing
9. Spacer
10. Dampers

31

33

32

34

11

7. Install by reversing these steps. Note the following:

    a. Install the sprocket so that its chamfered inner diameter faces toward the housing.

    b. Apply Loctite 242 (blue) to the sprocket nuts and tighten them to the torque specification in **Table 2** or **Table 3**.

    c. Install the spacer as shown in **Figure 35** (ZX900) or **Figure 36** (ZX1000).

Inspection/Disassembly/Reassembly

Refer to **Figure 29** (ZX900) or **Figure 30** (ZX1000).

1. Visually inspect the rubber dampers (**Figure 37**) for damage or deterioration. Replace, if necessary, as a complete set.

2. Inspect the flange assembly housing and damper separators (**Figure 38**) for cracks or damage. Replace the coupling housing if necessary.

3. Check the damper separators in the hub (**Figure 39**) for cracks or damage. Replace the wheel if necessary.

4. Check the wheel bearing by rotating the inner race (**Figure 40**). Check for bearing roughness, excessive noise or damage. If necessary, replace the bearing as follows:

    a. Pry the seal from the housing (**Figure 41**).

    b. Remove the bearing circlip.

    c. Using a large diameter socket or drift on the bearing, drive it out of the housing (from the inside out).

    d. Discard the bearing.

    e. Clean the housing thoroughly in solvent and check for cracks or damage in the bearing area.

    f. Blow any dirt or foreign matter out of the housing prior to installing the bearings.

    g. Pack non-sealed bearings with grease before installation. Sealed bearings do not require packing.

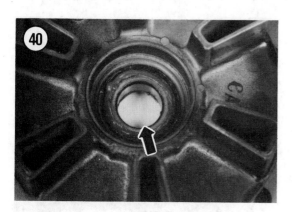

h. Tap the bearing into position with a socket placed on the outer bearing race.

i. Install the circlip. Make sure it seats in the housing groove.

j. Install a new seal by driving it in squarely with a socket and hammer.

Sprocket Inspection

Inspect the teeth of the sprocket. If the teeth are visibly worn, replace both sprockets and the drive chain. Never replace any one sprocket or chain as a separate item; worn parts will cause rapid wear of the new component. If necessary, replace the front sprocket as described in under *Engine Sprocket* in Chapter Six.

Measure the sprocket diameter with a vernier caliper placed across the base of the teeth. Replace the sprocket if it is worn to the service limit specified in **Table 1**.

DRIVE CHAIN

All models are equipped with an endless drive chain. No master link is used. On ZX900 models, the drive chain can be removed without having to remove the swing arm. However, on ZX1000 models, the swing arm must be removed to remove the drive chain.

> *WARNING*
> *Kawasaki uses an endless chain on all ZX900 and ZX1000 models for strength and reliability. Do not cut the chain with a chain cutter or install chain with a master link. The chain may fail and rear wheel lockup and an accident could result.*

Removal/Installation (ZX900)

1. Remove the left-hand footpeg bracket (**Figure 42**).

2. Remove the engine sprocket as described under *Engine Sprocket Removal/Installation* in Chapter Six.

3. Remove the drive chain cover bolts and remove the cover.

4. Remove the rear wheel as described in this chapter.

5. Remove the drive chain (**Figure 43**).

6. Installation is the reverse of these steps. Note the following:

   a. Adjust the drive chain and check its alignment as described in Chapter Three.

   b. Tighten the axle nut to the torque values in **Table 2**.

c. Rotate the wheel several times to make sure it rotates smoothly. Apply the brake several times to make sure it operates correctly.

d. Adjust the rear brake as described under *Rear Brake Pedal Height Adjustment* and *Rear Brake Light Switch Adjustment* in Chapter Three.

Removal/Installation (ZX1000)

1. Remove the left-hand footpeg bracket.

2. Remove the engine sprocket as described under *Engine Sprocket Removal/Installation* in Chapter Six.

3. Remove the drive chain cover bolts and remove the cover.

4. Remove the rear wheel as described in this chapter.

5. Remove the swing arm as described in this chapter.

6. Remove the drive chain.

7. Installation is the reverse of these steps. Note the following:

a. Adjust the drive chain and check its alignment as described in Chapter Three.

b. Tighten the axle nut to the torque values in **Table 3**.

c. Rotate the wheel several times to make sure it rotates smoothly. Apply the brake several times to make sure it operates correctly.

d. Adjust the rear brake as described under *Rear Brake Pedal Height Adjustment* and *Rear Brake Light Switch Adjustment* in Chapter Three.

Cleaning

> *CAUTION*
> *The factory drive chain is equipped with O-rings between the side plates that seal lubricant between the pins and bushings. To prevent damaging these O-rings, use only kerosene or diesel oil for cleaning. Do not use gasoline or other solvents that will cause the O-rings to swell or deteriorate.*

Occasionally, the drive chain should be removed from the bike for a thorough cleaning and soak lubrication. Perform the following:

a. Brush off excess dirt and grit.

b. Remove the drive chain as described in this chapter.

c. Soak the chain in kerosene or diesel oil for about half an hour and clean it thoroughly. Then hang the chain from a piece of wire and allow it to dry. Place a drip pan under the chain to catch the excess oil.

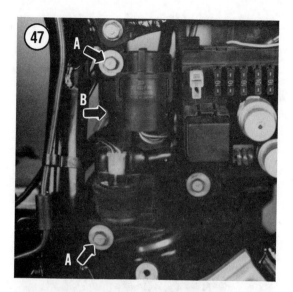

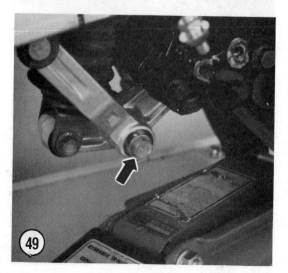

d. Install the chain on the motorcycle as described in this chapter.

Lubrication

For lubrication of the drive chain, refer to *Drive Chain Lubrication* in Chapter Three.

WHEEL BALANCING

For complete information refer to *Wheel Balance* in Chapter Ten.

TIRE CHANGING AND REPAIR

Refer to *Tubeless Tires* and *Tubeless Tire Changing* in Chapter Ten.

REAR SHOCK ABSORBER

Removal/Installation (ZX900)

1. Park the bike on its center stand.
2. Remove the side covers.
3. Remove the coolant reservoir tank (**Figure 44**) mounting bolts. Then disconnect the hoses at the tank and remove it. Plug the tank to prevent coolant leakage.
4. Remove the air valve mounting nut and pull the air valve (**Figure 45**) out of the frame mounting ring.
5. Loosen the adjust rod locknut at the shock absorber (**Figure 46**) and unscrew the rod. Remove the knob and rod assembly (**Figure 45**).
6. See **Figure 47**. Remove the starter relay bracket bolts (A) and remove the bracket (B). Position the bracket to gain access to the upper shock absorber bolt.
7. Loosen but do not remove the upper shock absorber nut (**Figure 48**).
8. Remove the lower tie-rod bolt (**Figure 49**).
9. Remove the lower shock absorber bolt (**Figure 50**).

11

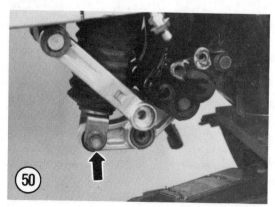

WARNING
When removing the shock absorber in Step 10, do not damage the shock's air hose.

10. Remove the upper shock absorber bolt and nut (**Figure 48**) and remove the shock absorber from underneath the swing arm (**Figure 51**).

WARNING
*The shock absorber contains highly compressed air. Do not tamper with or attempt to open the cylinder or air valve fitting (**Figure 52**). Do not place it near an open flame or other extreme heat. Do not weld on the frame near it. Do not dispose of the shock absorber yourself. Take it to a Kawasaki dealer where it can be deactivated and disposed of properly. Observe the cautions on your shock's decal (**Figure 53**).*

11. Inspect the shock absorber boot (**Figure 54**) for tears, deterioration or damage. Replace the boot if necessary.

12. Install by reversing these steps. Note the following:

   a. Tighten the shock absorber and tie-rod pivot bolts to the specifications in **Table 2**.

   b. Check the shock absorber air and damping adjustment as described under *Suspension Adjustment* in Chapter Three.

   c. Refill the coolant reservoir tank as described in Chapter Three.

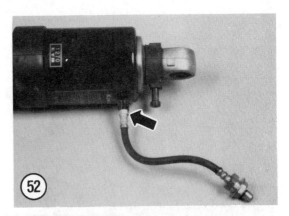

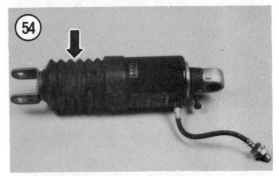

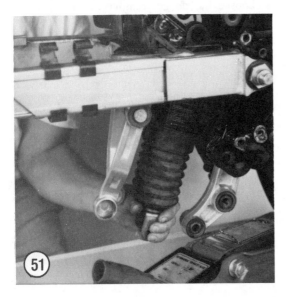

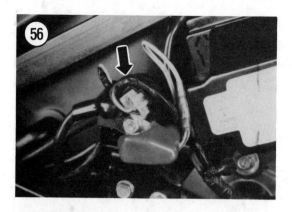

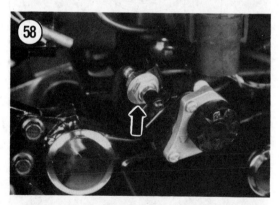

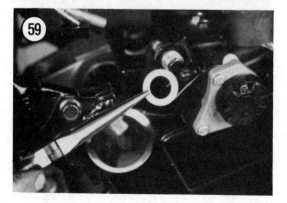

**Removal/Installation
(ZX1000)**

1. Place the bike on the center stand.
2. Remove the side covers.
3. Remove the seat.
4. Remove the fuel tank and its bracket. See Chapter Seven.
5. Remove the battery and battery case.
6. Remove the air cleaner housing.
7. Remove the mufflers.
8. Remove the junction box (**Figure 55**) mounting bolts. Then disconnect the electrical connectors at the junction box and remove it.
9. Remove the starter relay from its mounting bracket (**Figure 56**).
10. *California models:* Label the canister hoses and remove the canister (A, **Figure 57**).
11. Remove the fan relay (B, **Figure 57**) from its mounting bracket.
12. Remove the air valve nut (**Figure 58**) and washer (**Figure 59**). Pull the air valve out of its mounting bracket (**Figure 60**).
13. Remove the damping adjuster mounting bolt and remove the lower battery bracket.
14. Either remove the rear wheel or place a wood block underneath the wheel. If the rear wheel is removed, block the swing arm.
15. Remove the upper shock absorber nut and bolt.
16. See **Figure 61**. From the left-hand side of the shock absorber, loosen the nut and pull the damper adjuster cable out of the shock absorber.

*NOTE
Make sure the damper adjuster pinion gear does not fall out of the top of the shock absorber.*

11

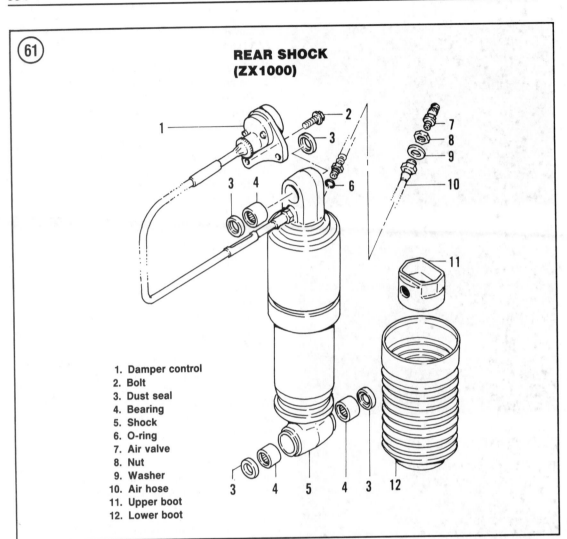

**REAR SHOCK
(ZX1000)**

1. Damper control
2. Bolt
3. Dust seal
4. Bearing
5. Shock
6. O-ring
7. Air valve
8. Nut
9. Washer
10. Air hose
11. Upper boot
12. Lower boot

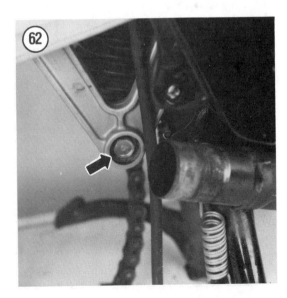

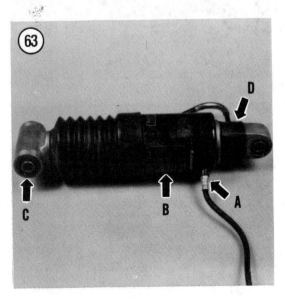

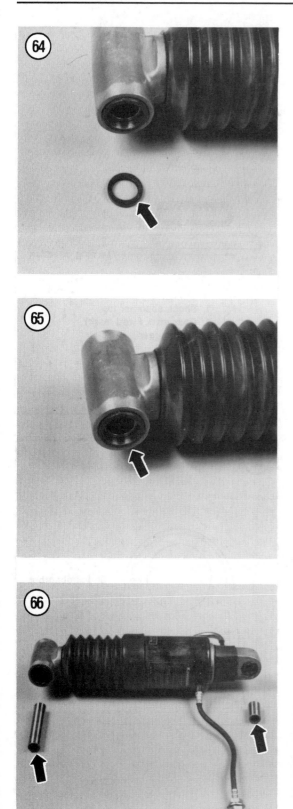

17. Support the shock absorber and remove the lower shock absorber bolt (**Figure 62**).

18. Remove the shock absorber from underneath the bike.

> *WARNING*
> *The shock absorber is a sealed unit and cannot be rebuilt. It contains highly compressed air. Do not tamper with or attempt to open the cylinder or air valve fitting (A, **Figure 63**). Do not place it near an open flame or other extreme heat. Do not weld on the frame near it. Do not dispose of the shock absorber yourself. Take it to a Kawasaki dealer where it can be deactivated and disposed of properly. Observe the cautions on your shock's decal (B, **Figure 63**).*

19. Remove the 2 bearing sleeves (C, **Figure 63**) from the shock absorber.

20. Remove the oil seals (**Figure 64**). Replace the oil seals if torn or damaged.

21. The shock absorber is equipped with 3 needle bearings (**Figure 65**): one on top and two on the bottom. Check each bearing and sleeve for wear and damage. Turn the bearing with your finger and check for roughness or damaged needles. Replace the bearings with the use of a press. If the bearings are replaced, install new oil seals (**Figure 64**).

22. Inspect the shock absorber boot for tears, deterioration or damage. Replace the boot if necessary.

23. Install by reversing these steps. Note the following.

24. Install the bearing sleeves as shown in **Figure 66**.

25. Before installing the shock absorber, check that the damper adjuster dial matches the plastic gear mark in the shock absorber. Perform the following:

   a. Turn the damping adjuster dial so that the No. 1 damping position aligns with the mounting bracket index mark (**Figure 67**).

11

b. Slide the dust cover (D, **Figure 63**) off of the shock absorber.

c. The top of the shock absorber has a window that shows a plastic gear. Check the gear to see if the red mark is in the middle of the window as shown in **Figure 68**. If the gear mark alignment is incorrect, turn the gear *clockwise* until the mark is in the middle of the window (**Figure 68**).

d. After the gear alignment in sub-step "c" is correct, turn the pinion gear so that the square hole is centered as shown in **Figure 69**.

26. Reinstall the shock from underneath the bike. Tighten the shock absorber and tie-rod pivot bolts to the specifications in **Table 3**.

27. After inserting the damping adjuster cable in the shock absorber, tighten the cable nut securely.

28. Check the shock absorber air pressure and damping adjustments as described under *Suspension Adjustment* in Chapter Three.

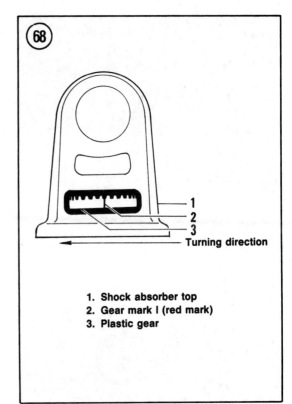

1. **Shock absorber top**
2. **Gear mark I (red mark)**
3. **Plastic gear**

REAR SWING ARM
(ZX900)

The rear suspension system consists of a shock absorber, rocker arm, 2 tie rods and swing arm (**Figure 70**). The rocker arm, tie rods and swing arm are equipped with caged needle bearings. The components are linked together and pivot on machined journals and shafts. Oil seals are installed on the outside of each bearing to prevent contamination. It is critical that the torque specifications in **Table 2** are observed when reinstalling the assembly to prevent binding or bearing damage.

For proper operation, the needle bearings must be lubricated at the intervals specified in Chapter Three. The needle bearings were initially lubricated with molybdenum disulfide grease. When servicing the bearings, this same type of grease should be used.

The following procedure describes service to the swing arm, rocker arm and tie rods.

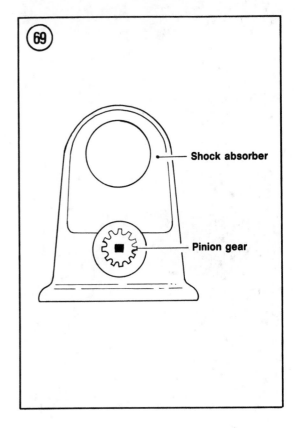

Removal

Refer to **Figure 70** for this procedure.

1. Park the motorcycle on its center stand.
2. Remove the mufflers.
3. Remove the rear wheel as described in this chapter.

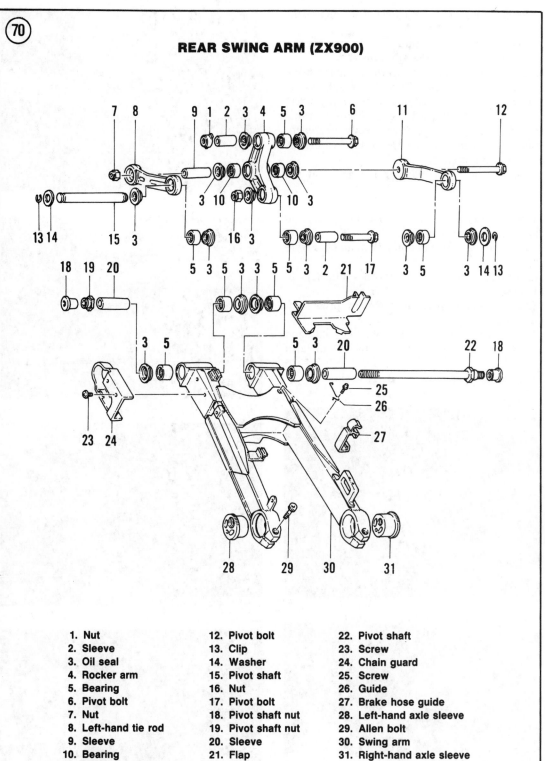

REAR SWING ARM (ZX900)

1. Nut
2. Sleeve
3. Oil seal
4. Rocker arm
5. Bearing
6. Pivot bolt
7. Nut
8. Left-hand tie rod
9. Sleeve
10. Bearing
11. Right-hand tie rod
12. Pivot bolt
13. Clip
14. Washer
15. Pivot shaft
16. Nut
17. Pivot bolt
18. Pivot shaft nut
19. Pivot shaft nut
20. Sleeve
21. Flap
22. Pivot shaft
23. Screw
24. Chain guard
25. Screw
26. Guide
27. Brake hose guide
28. Left-hand axle sleeve
29. Allen bolt
30. Swing arm
31. Right-hand axle sleeve

11

4. Remove rocker arm-to-tie rod nut and remove the pivot shaft **(Figure 71)**.

5. Remove the rocker arm-to-shock absorber nut and remove the pivot shaft **(Figure 72)**.

6. Before removing the swing arm, grasp the swing arm as shown in **Figure 73** and move the swing arm from side to side and up and down. If you feel any more than a very slight movement of the swing arm and the pivot bolt is correctly tightened, remove the swing arm and check the bearings as described in this chapter.

7. Remove the right-hand swing arm nut (A, **Figure 74**).

8. Remove the right-hand footpeg bracket (B, **Figure 74**). Then tie the bracket up to prevent damaging the rear brake line.

9. Remove the left-hand swing arm nut (A, **Figure 75**).

10. Remove the left-hand footpeg bracket (B, **Figure 75**).

11. Loosen and remove the swing arm pivot shaft nut **(Figure 76)**.

12. Remove the pivot shaft from the right-hand side **(Figure 77)** and remove the swing arm assembly.

13. If necessary, remove the drive chain.

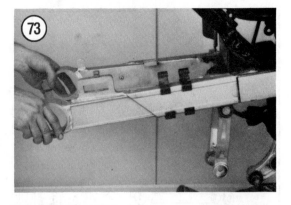

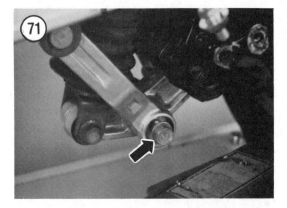

NOTE
If the center stand is being used to support the bike, a jack and wood blocks will be needed to support bike because the center stand must be retracted to remove the rocker arm-to-frame pivot shaft.

14. Remove the rocker arm-to-frame pivot shaft nut. Then remove the pivot shaft (A, **Figure 78**) and rocker arm (B, **Figure 78**).

15. Remove the tie-rods by performing the following:

    a. Remove one of the pivot shaft snap rings (**Figure 79**).

    b. Remove the washer (**Figure 80**).

    c. Remove one of the tie-rods (**Figure 81**).

    d. Remove the remaining tie-rod, washer and the pivot shaft (**Figure 82**).

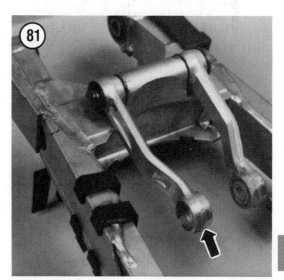

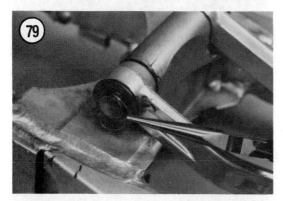

11

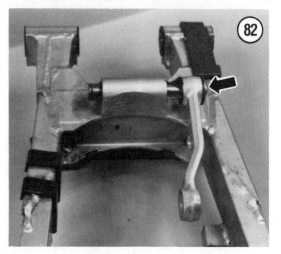

Inspection

Refer to **Figure 70** for this procedure.

1. Check the swing arm (**Figure 83**) for cracks, twisting, weld breakage or other damage. Refer repair to a competent welding shop.

2. Remove the swing arm bearing sleeves (**Figure 84**).

3. Pry the 4 oil seals (**Figure 85**) out of the swing arm.

4. Check the swing arm chain pad (**Figure 86**) for wear or damage. If necessary, remove the 2 Phillips screws and replace the chain pad.

5. Check the flap (**Figure 87**) for tearing, cracks or other damage. Replace the flap if necessary.

NOTE
*When checking the swing arm, tie rod and rocker arm needle bearings (**Figure 88**) in the following steps, wear will be difficult to measure. Instead, check the needle bearings for needle damage or looseness, pitting, cage damage and color change brought on from lack of lubrication (overheating). Turn the bearings by hand. Make sure they rotate smoothly and without any signs of roughness or excessive noise. In*

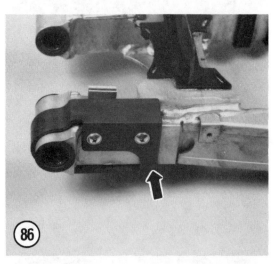

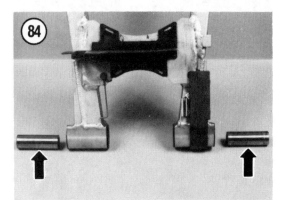

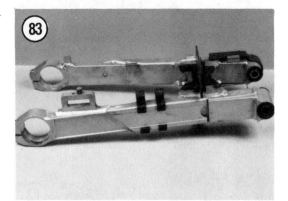

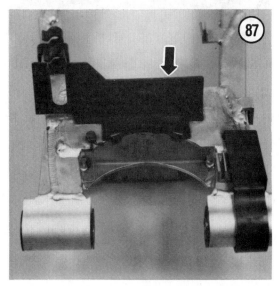

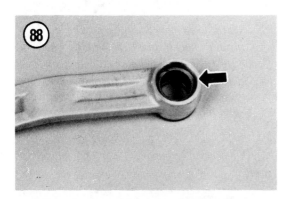

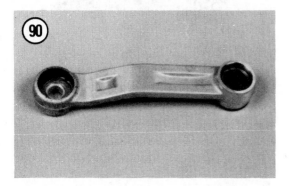

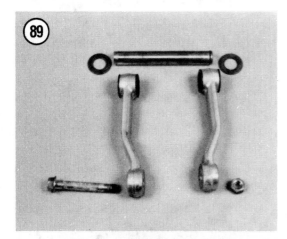

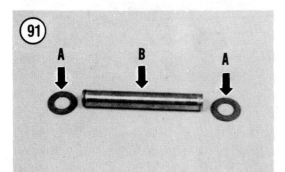

severe instances, the needles will fall out of the bearing cage. If a needle bearing is damaged, both the bearing and bearing sleeve must be replaced as a set.

6. Check the swing arm bearings and journals as follows:

    a. Check the pivot shaft sleeves (**Figure 84**) for galling, surface cracks, deep scoring or excessive wear. If a sleeve is worn, the needle bearing is probably worn.

    b. Check the swing arm needle bearings as described in the previous *Note*.

    c. Replace worn or damaged parts as required. Replace the bearings as described under *Suspension Bearing Replacement*.

7. Check the tie rod assembly (**Figure 89**) as follows:

    a. Pry the oil seals out of the tie rods.

    b. Check each tie rod (**Figure 90**) for cracks, especially at both ends of the rod near the pivots.

    c. Check the tie rod washers (A, **Figure 91**) for abrasion, cracks or other damage.

    d. Check the pivot shaft sleeve (B, **Figure 91**) for galling, surface cracks, deep scoring or excessive wear. If the journal is worn, the needle bearing is probably worn or damaged.

    e. Check the pivot shaft sleeve bore in the swing arm (**Figure 92**). Slide the sleeve through the bore and check for binding or out of round. Also check the bore for cracks.

    f. Check the tie rod needle bearings as described in the previous *Note*.

    g. Replace worn or damaged parts as required. Replace the bearings as described under *Suspension Bearing Replacement*.

11

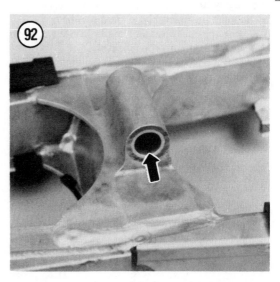

8. Check the rocker arm assembly (**Figure 93**) as follows:

    a. Remove the pivot shaft sleeves (**Figure 94**).

    b. Pry the oil seals (**Figure 95**) out of the connecting rod.

    c. Check the connecting rod for cracks or other damage.

    d. Check the pivot shaft sleeves (**Figure 94**) for galling, surface cracks, deep scoring or excessive wear. If a sleeve is worn, the needle bearing(s) are probably worn or damaged.

    e. Check the rocker arm needle bearings as described in the previous *Note*.

    f. Replace worn or damaged parts as required. Replace bearings as described under *Suspension Bearing Replacement*.

Suspension Bearing Replacement

A press is required to replace the bearings. Attempting to drive the bearings with a drift or similar tool will damage the needle bearings.

1. Remove any bearing sleeves and oil seals as required.

2. Measure the bearing's installed depth (**Figure 96**) in the assembly with a pair of vernier calipers. Record the bearing position so that the new bearing can be installed into the same position.

3. Support the assembly in the press bed.

4. Using a suitable adapter, press the old bearing out. When pressing bearings out of the tie-rods or rocker arm, it will be necessary to support the opposite end of the assembly to prevent it from cocking sideways and binding the bearing.

5. Clean the bearing bore in solvent and allow to thoroughly dry.

6. Support the assembly in the press bed.

7. Using the measurement made in Step 2, press the new bearing into the assembly.

8. Apply a coat of molybdenum disulfide grease to the inner needle bearing surfaces.

Assembly/Installation

1. Apply a coat of molybdenum disulfide grease to each inner needle bearing surface. Lightly grease all pivot shaft journals, sleeves and bolts.

2. Install the tie rods (**Figure 89**) onto the swing arm as follows:

    a. Install a new snap ring on one end of the pivot shaft journal.

    b. Slide on a washer (**Figure 89**) and one of the connecting rods (**Figure 89**).

NOTE
*Make sure a connecting rod is not installed backwards. Refer to **Figure 89** for correct positioning.*

    c. Install the partially assembled tie rod assembly (**Figure 97**) into the swing arm. See **Figure 80**.

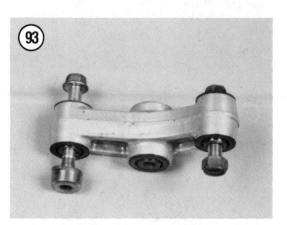

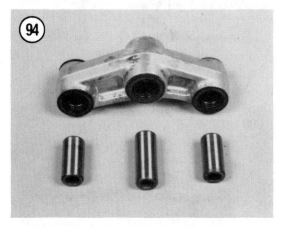

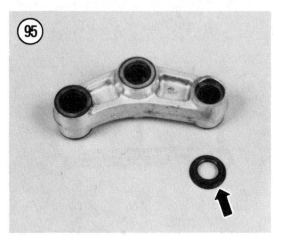

d. Install the opposite tie rod (**Figure 81**).

e. Install the washer (**Figure 80**).

f. Install a new snap ring (**Figure 79**).

g. Make sure both snap rings seat in the pivot shaft journal completely.

3. Install the rocker arm as follows:

a. Install an oil seal next to each bearing (**Figure 95**). Make sure the oil seals press all the way into the rocker arm.

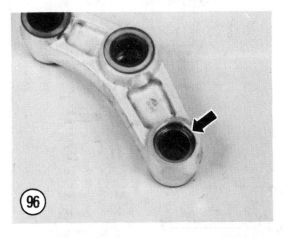

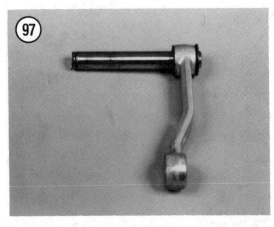

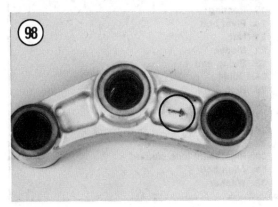

b. Install the pivot shaft sleeves into each of the rocker arm bearings (**Figure 94**). The 50 mm long sleeve fits into the center bearings. The 40 mm long sleeves fit into both end bearings.

c. The rocker arm has an arrow cast into its side for alignment purposes (**Figure 98**). Install the rocker arm so that the arrow is on the left-hand side and facing to the front of the bike.

d. Insert the pivot bolt through the rocker arm from the right-hand side (**Figure 78**).

e. Install the special pivot bolt nut (rocker arm nut) and tighten the bolt to the torque specification in **Table 2**.

4. Install the swing arm as follows:

a. Install an oil seal next to each bearing (**Figure 85**). Make sure the oil seals press all the way into the swing arm.

b. Install the pivot shaft sleeves into each side of the swing arm (**Figure 84**).

c. Lift the swing arm up and align the bearing holes with the frame pivot shaft holes. Install the pivot shaft through the frame and swing arm from the right-hand side (**Figure 77**).

d. Install the swing arm pivot shaft nut (**Figure 76**). Tighten the nut to the torque specification in **Table 2**.

e. Grasp the swing arm as shown in **Figure 73** and check up-and-down and side-to-side play. The swing arm should pivot up-and-down smoothly without any binding. Side-to-side play should be minimal.

5. Install the shock absorber, if removed.

6. Install the shock absorber to rocker arm pivot shaft from the right-hand side (**Figure 72**). Install the nut and tighten to the torque specification in **Table 2**.

7. Install the tie-rod to rocker arm pivot bolt from the right-hand side (**Figure 71**). Install the nut and tighten to the torque specification in **Table 2**.

8. Slip the drive chain over the swing arm.

9. Install the left-hand footpeg bracket (B, **Figure 75**).

10. Install the right-hand footpeg bracket (B, **Figure 74**).

11. Install the left-hand swing arm nut (A, **Figure 75**) and tighten to the torque specification in **Table 2**.

12. Install the right-hand swing arm nut (A, **Figure 74**) and tighten to the torque specification in **Table 2**.

13. Install the rear wheel.

14. Adjust the drive chain as described under *Drive Chain Adjustment* in Chapter Three.

15. Install the mufflers.

11

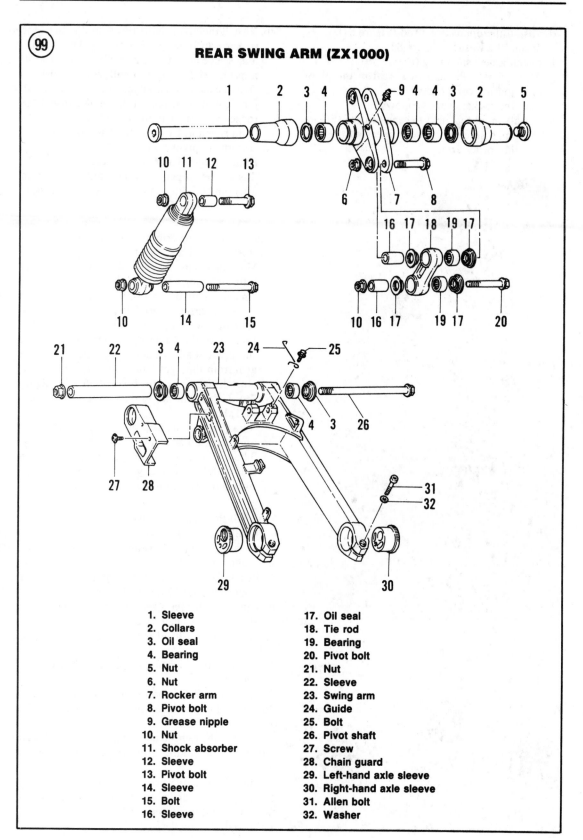

REAR SWING ARM (ZX1000)

1. Sleeve
2. Collars
3. Oil seal
4. Bearing
5. Nut
6. Nut
7. Rocker arm
8. Pivot bolt
9. Grease nipple
10. Nut
11. Shock absorber
12. Sleeve
13. Pivot bolt
14. Sleeve
15. Bolt
16. Sleeve
17. Oil seal
18. Tie rod
19. Bearing
20. Pivot bolt
21. Nut
22. Sleeve
23. Swing arm
24. Guide
25. Bolt
26. Pivot shaft
27. Screw
28. Chain guard
29. Left-hand axle sleeve
30. Right-hand axle sleeve
31. Allen bolt
32. Washer

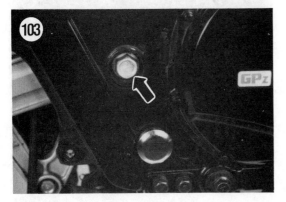

REAR SWING ARM
(ZX1000)

The rear suspension system consists of a shock absorber, rocker arm, tie rod and swing arm (**Figure 99**). The rocker arm, tie rod and swing arm are equipped with caged needle bearings. The components are linked together and pivot on machined sleeves and shafts. Oil seals are installed on the outside of each bearing to contain lubrication and prevent contamination. It is critical that the torque specifications in **Table 3** are observed when reinstalling the assembly to prevent binding or bearing damage.

For proper operation, the needle bearings must be lubricated at the intervals specified in Chapter Three. The needle bearings were initially lubricated with molybdenum disulfide grease. When servicing the bearings, this same type of grease should be used.

The following procedure describes service to the swing arm, rocker arm and tie rod.

Removal

Refer to **Figure 99** for this procedure.

1. Park the motorcycle on its center stand.
2. Remove the mufflers.
3. Remove the rear wheel as described in this chapter.
4. Remove the left-hand footpeg bracket (A, **Figure 100**).
5. Remove the lower shock absorber nut and pivot shaft (**Figure 101**).
6. Remove the upper tie rod nut and pivot shaft (**Figure 102**).
7. Remove the left- and right-hand pivot shaft covers. See B, **Figure 100**.
8. Before removing the swing arm, grasp the swing arm as shown in **Figure 73** and move the swing arm from side to side and up and down. If you feel any more than a very slight movement of the swing arm and the pivot bolt is correctly tightened, remove the swing arm and check the bearings as described in this chapter.
9. Loosen and remove the pivot shaft nut.
10. Remove the pivot shaft from the right-hand side (**Figure 103**) and remove the swing arm assembly. See **Figure 104**.
11. If necessary, remove the drive chain.
12. If necessary, remove the rocker arm assembly (**Figure 105**) as follows:

11

CAUTION
When disconnecting the upper shock absorber bolt in sub-step "a", support the shock with a Bunjee cord or mechanic's wire to prevent damaging the shock's air hose.

a. Remove the upper shock absorber pivot bolt from the rocker arm.
b. Remove the rocker arm sleeve nut from the right-hand side (**Figure 106**).
c. Remove the rocker arm sleeve shaft (C) from the left-hand side.
d. Remove the rocker arm (B) with both collars (A).
13. If necessary, remove the tie rod (A, **Figure 107**) from the swing arm as follows:
a. Loosen and remove the tie rod nut (B).
b. Remove the pivot bolt (C) and the tie rod (A).

Inspection

Refer to **Figure 99** for this procedure.
1. Check the swing arm for cracks, twisting, weld breakage or other damage. Refer repair to a competent welding shop.
2. Check the swing arm chain pad (**Figure 108**) for wear or damage. If necessary, remove the 2 Phillips screws and replace the chain pad.

NOTE
*When checking the swing arm, tie rod and rocker arm needle bearings (**Figure 109**) in the following steps, bearing*

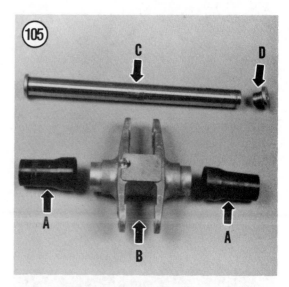

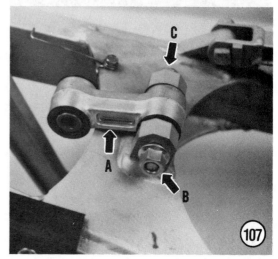

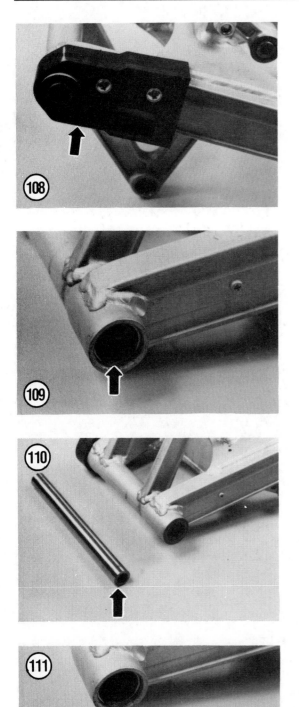

wear will be difficult to measure. Instead, check the needle bearings for needle damage or looseness, pitting, cage damage and color change brought on from lack of lubrication (overheating). Turn the bearings by hand. Make sure they rotate smoothly and without any signs of roughness or excessive noise. In severe instances, the needles will fall out of the bearing cage. If a needle bearing is damaged, both the bearing and bearing sleeve must be replaced as a set.

3. Check the swing arm bearings and sleeves as follows:
   a. Remove the pivot shaft sleeve (**Figure 110**).
   b. Remove the 2 swing arm oil seals (**Figure 111**).
   c. Check the pivot shaft sleeve (**Figure 110**) for galling, surface cracks, deep scoring or excessive wear. If the sleeve is worn, the needle bearings are probably worn also.
   d. Check the swing arm needle bearings as described in the previous *Note*.
   e. Replace worn or damaged parts as required. Replace the bearings as described under *Suspension Bearing Replacement*.
4. Check the tie rod assembly (**Figure 112**) as follows:
   a. Remove the pivot shaft sleeves (**Figure 113**).

11

b. Pry the oil seals (**Figure 114**) out of the tie rod.

c. Check the tie rod for cracks or other damage.

d. Check the pivot shaft sleeves (**Figure 113**) for galling, surface cracks, deep scoring or excessive wear. If the sleeve is worn, the needle bearing is probably worn or damaged.

e. Check the tie rod mounting lugs on the swing arm.

f. Check the tie rod needle bearings as described in the previous *Note*.

g. Replace worn or damaged parts as required. Replace the bearings as described under *Suspension Bearing Replacement*.

5. Check the rocker arm assembly (**Figure 105**) as follows:

a. Pull the collars (**Figure 115**) off of the rocker arm.

b. Pry the oil seals (**Figure 116**) out of the rocker arm.

c. Check the connecting rod for cracks or other damage.

d. Check the pivot shaft journal (**Figure 117**) for galling, surface cracks, deep scoring or excessive wear. If the sleeve is worn, the needle bearings are probably worn or damaged.

e. Check the rocker arm needle bearings as described in the previous *Note*.

f. Replace worn or damaged parts as required. Replace bearings as described under *Suspension Bearing Replacement*.

Suspension Bearing Replacement

A press is required to replace the bearings. Attempting to drive the bearings with a drift or similar tool will damage the needle bearings.

1. Remove any bearing sleeves and oil seals as required.

2. Measure the bearing's installed depth (**Figure 109**) in the assembly with a pair of vernier calipers. Record the bearing position so that the new bearing can be installed into the same position.

3. Support the assembly in the press bed.

4. Using a suitable adapter, press the old bearing out. When pressing bearings out of the tie rods or rocker arm, it will be necessary to support the opposite end of the assembly to prevent it from cocking sideways and binding the bearing.

5. Clean the bearing bore in solvent and allow to thoroughly dry.

6. Support the assembly in the press bed.

7. Using the measurement made in Step 2, press the new bearing into the assembly.

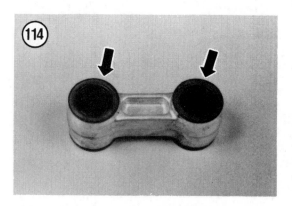

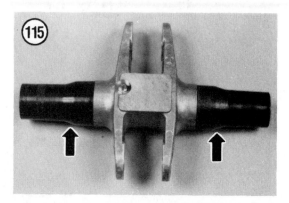

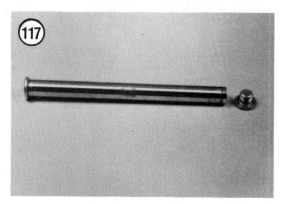

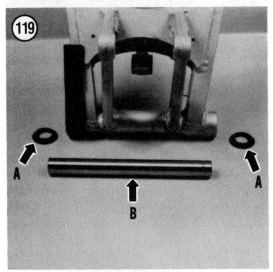

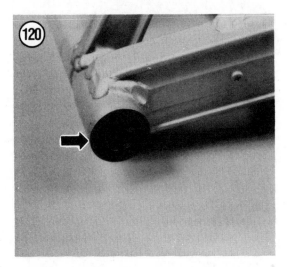

8. Apply a coat of molybdenum disulfide grease to the inner needle bearing surfaces.

Assembly/Installation

1. Apply a coat of molybdenum disulfide grease to each inner needle bearing surface. Lightly grease all pivot shaft sleeves and bolts with the same type grease.

2. Install the rocker arm (**Figure 105**) as follows:
   a. See **Figure 118**. Install the rocker arm so that the arrow mark (A) faces to the front and the grease nipple (B) faces up.
   b. Install the collars onto the rocker arm as shown in **Figure 115**.
   c. Install the 2 oil seals (**Figure 116**) onto the rocker arm.
   d. Install the rocker arm by aligning the sleeves with the frame holes.
   e. Install the rocker arm sleeve shaft (C, **Figure 105**) through the rocker arm from the left-hand side.
   f. Install the sleeve shaft nut (**Figure 106**) and tighten to the torque specification in **Table 3**.
   g. Pivot the rocker arm back and forth to make sure it turns smoothly and doesn't bind.
   h. Install the upper shock absorber bolt and nut. Install the bolt through the rocker arm from the right-hand side. Tighten the shock absorber bolt to the torque specification in **Table 3**.

3. Install the tie rod (**Figure 112**) as follows:
   a. Install the 4 oil seals (**Figure 114**) onto the tie rod.
   b. Install the pivot shaft sleeves into the tie rod (**Figure 113**).
   c. Install the tie rod onto the swing arm. Install the pivot bolt through the tie rod as shown in **Figure 107**.
   d. Install the tie rod nut and tighten it to the torque specification in **Table 3**.
   e. Rotate the tie rod back and forth to make sure it turns smoothly and does not bind.

4. Install the swing arm as follows:
   a. Install an oil seal next to each bearing (A, **Figure 119**). Make sure the oil seals press all the way into the swing arm. See **Figure 120**.
   b. Install the pivot shaft sleeve (B, **Figure 119**) into the swing arm.

> *NOTE*
> *If the pivot shaft sleeve knocks one of the oil seals out as the journal is slid through the seal, install journal through the end of the swing arm so*

11

*that it sticks out as shown in A, **Figure 121**. Then slide the oil seal over the end of the journal and seat it into the swing arm (B, **Figure 121**). When the oil seals are properly seated, insert the journal into the swing arm.*

c. Install the drive chain over the swing arm.

d. Lift the swing arm up and align the bearing holes with the frame pivot shaft holes. Install the pivot shaft through the frame and swing arm from the right-hand side (**Figure 103**).

e. Install the pivot shaft nut. Tighten the nut to the torque specification in **Table 3**.

f. Grasp the swing arm as shown in **Figure 73** and check up-and-down and side-to-side play. The swing arm should pivot up-and-down smoothly without any binding. Side-to-side play should be minimal.

g. Install the left- and right-hand side pivot shaft covers. See B, **Figure 100**.

5. Install the upper tie rod pivot shaft from the right-hand side (**Figure 102**). Install the nut and tighten to the torque specification in **Table 3**.

6. Install the lower shock absorber pivot shaft from the right hand side (**Figure 101**). Install the nut and tighten to the torque specification in **Table 3**.

7. Install the left-hand footpeg bracket (A, **Figure 100**).

8. Install the rear wheel as described in this chapter.

9. Adjust the drive chain as described under *Drive Chain Adjustment* in Chapter Three.

10. Install the mufflers.

Table 1 REAR SUSPENSION SPECIFICATIONS

Rear wheel travel	
ZX900	115 mm (4.52 in.)
ZX1000	130 mm (5.12 in.)
Axle runout	See text
Rim runout	
Axial	0.5 mm (0.020 in.)
Radial	0.8 mm (0.031 in.)
Drive chain 20-link check	
ZX900	
Standard	317.5-318.4 mm (12.50-12.54 in.)
Wear limit	323 mm (12.72 in.)
ZX1000	
Standard	381.0-381.8 mm (15.00-15.03 in.)
Wear limit	389 mm (15.31 in.)
Front sprocket diameter	
ZX900	
Standard	75.67-75.87 mm (2.979-2.987 in.)
Wear limit	75.0 mm (2.952 in.)
ZX1000	
Standard	79.19-79.21 mm (3.117-3.118 in.)
Wear limit	389 mm (15.31 in.)

(continued)

Table 1 REAR SUSPENSION SPECIFICATIONS (continued)

Rear sprocket diameter (ZX900)	
48 tooth	
Standard	233.07-233.12 (9.175-9.177 in.)
Wear limit	232.8 mm (9.165 in.)
49 tooth	
Standard	237.54-238.04 mm (9.351-9.371 in.)
Wear limit	237.2 mm (9.338 in.)
50 tooth	
Standard	242.72-243.22 mm (9.555-9.575 in.)
Wear limit	242.4 mm (9.543 in.)
Rear sprocket diameter (ZX1000)	
40 tooth	
Standard	229.60-230.10 mm (9.039-9.059 in.)
Wear limit	229.3 mm (9.027 in.)
41 tooth	
Standard	235.48-235.98 mm (9.270-9.290 in.)
Wear limit	235.2 mm (9.260 in.)
Rear sprocket warpage	
Standard	Less than 0.4 mm (0.015 in.)
Wear limit	0.5 mm (0.019 in.)

Table 2 REAR SUSPENSION TIGHTENING TORQUES (ZX900)

	N•m	ft.-lb.
Rear axle nut	88	65
Front sprocket nut	125	92
Rear sprocket nuts		
Through frame number ZX900A-016130	69	51
From frame number ZX900A-016131	86	64
Swing arm pivot shaft nut	88	65
Upper shock absorber nut		
1984	24	17.5
1985-1986	29	22
Lower shock absorber nut	59	43
Rocker arm nuts	59	43
Tie rod nuts	59	43
Chain adjuster clamp bolts	39	29

Table 3 REAR SUSPENSION TIGHTENING TORQUE (ZX1000)

	N•m	ft.-lb.
Rear axle nut	88	65
Front sprocket nut	98	72
Rear sprocket nuts	110	80
Shock absorber nuts	59	43
Rocker arm sleeve shaft	88	65
Tie rod nuts	59	43
Swing arm pivot shaft nut	88	65
Torque link nuts	29	22
Chain adjuster clamp bolts	39	29

11

BRAKES

All models are equipped with front and rear disc brakes. This chapter describes repair and replacement procedures for all brake components.

Refer to **Table 1** for brake specifications. **Tables 1** and **2** are found at the end of the chapter.

DISC BRAKES

The disc brake units are actuated by brake fluid controlled by the hand lever (front brake) or brake pedal (rear brake). As the brake pads wear, they move out slightly to automatically adjust for wear. This drops the fluid level in the reservoir by a small amount.

When working on a hydraulic brake system, it is necessary that the work area and all tools be absolutely clean. Any tiny particles of foreign matter or grit in the caliper assembly or the master cylinder can damage the components. Also, sharp tools must not be used inside the caliper or on a caliper piston. If there is any doubt about your ability to correctly and safely carry out major service on the brake components, take the job to a Kawasaki dealer or independent motorcycle repair shop.

When adding brake fluid use only a type clearly marked DOT 4 and use it from a sealed container. Brake fluid will over a long period draw moisture from the air, which greatly reduces its ability to perform correctly, so it is a good idea to purchase brake fluid in small containers.

Whenever *any* component has been removed from the brake system the system is considered "opened" and must be bled to remove air bubbles. Also, if the brake feels "spongy," this usually means there are air bubbles in the system and it must be bled. For safe brake operation, refer to *Bleeding the System* in this chapter for complete details.

> **CAUTION**
> *Disc brake components rarely require disassembly, so do not disassemble unless necessary. Do not use solvents of any kind on the brake systems internal components. Solvents will cause the seals to swell and distort. When disassembling and cleaning brake components (except brake pads) use new brake fluid.*

BRAKE PAD REPLACEMENT

There is no recommended mileage interval for changing the friction pads on the disc brakes. Pad wear depends greatly on riding habits and conditions. The pads should be checked for wear at specified intervals. See Chapter Three (**Table 1**).

Service Notes

Observe the following service notes before replacing brake pads.

1. Brake pads should be replaced only as a set.
2. Disconnecting the brake hose is not required for brake pad replacement. Disconnect the hose only if caliper disassembly is required.

WARNING
Use brake fluid clearly marked DOT 4 from a sealed container. Other types may vaporize and cause brake failure. Always use the same brand name; do not intermix brake fluids, many brands are not compatible. Do not intermix silicone based (DOT 5) brake fluid as it can cause brake component damage leading to brake system failure.

WARNING
Do not ride the motorcycle until you are sure the brake is operating correctly. If necessary, bleed the brake as described under **Bleeding the System** *in this chapter.*

Front Pad Replacement

CAUTION
When working on the brake system avoid touching the friction surfaces of the disc or brake pads with your hands. Natural skin oils or other contamination can affect braking efficiency. If you must touch the disc, wash it with brake cleaner after it is reassembled.

Refer to **Figure 1** for this procedure.

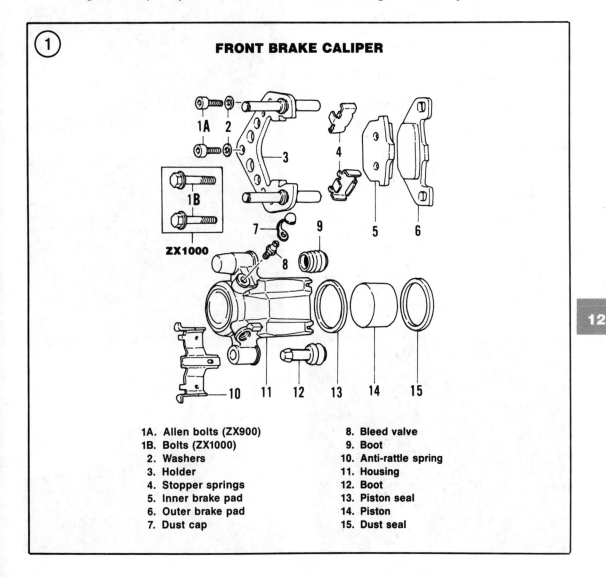

① **FRONT BRAKE CALIPER**

1A. Allen bolts (ZX900)
1B. Bolts (ZX1000)
 2. Washers
 3. Holder
 4. Stopper springs
 5. Inner brake pad
 6. Outer brake pad
 7. Dust cap
 8. Bleed valve
 9. Boot
10. Anti-rattle spring
11. Housing
12. Boot
13. Piston seal
14. Piston
15. Dust seal

12

1. Remove the 2 caliper bolts (**Figure 2**) and lift the caliper off the brake disc (**Figure 3**).

2. Lift the brake pad next to the piston (A, **Figure 4**) out of the caliper.

3. Push the caliper holder (B, **Figure 4**) toward the piston.

4. Remove the outer brake pad (C, **Figure 4**).

5. Remove the anti-rattle spring (A, **Figure 5**).

6. Check that the 2 clips (B, **Figure 5**) are installed on the caliper holder.

7. Remove the cap and diaphragm from the master cylinder (**Figure 6**). To gain clearance for the new brake pads, you'll need to force the caliper piston back into the caliper. Slowly push the piston (C, **Figure 5**) into the caliper while checking the reservoir to make sure it doesn't overflow. The piston should move freely. You may need to use a C-clamp to push the piston back into the caliper. If the piston sticks, remove the caliper and rebuild it as described in this chapter.

8. If necessary, install a new anti-rattle spring into the caliper (A, **Figure 5**).

9. Drop the inner brake pad (A, **Figure 7**) into the caliper.

10. Push the caliper holder (B, **Figure 7**) toward the piston. Then align the holes in the outer brake pad plate and install it onto the caliper holder (C, **Figure 4**).

NOTE
*The friction material on both brake pads (**Figure 8**) must face inward.*

11. Carefully slip the brake pads over the brake disc as you install the caliper (**Figure 3**). Install the caliper bolts (**Figure 2**) and tighten to the torque specification in **Table 2**.

12. Support the motorcycle with the front wheel off the ground. Spin the wheel and pump the brake until the pads are seated against the disc.

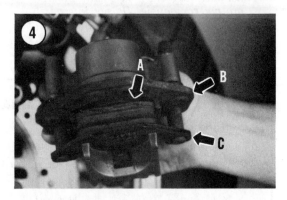

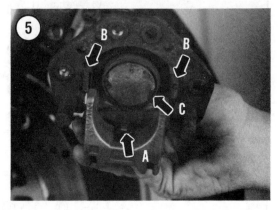

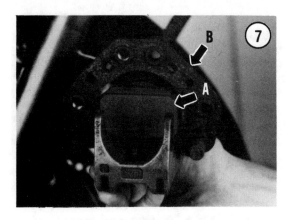

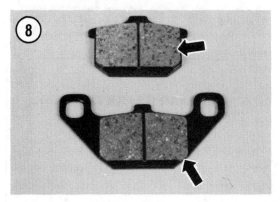

13. If necessary, correct the fluid level in the master cylinder reservoir. Install the diaphragm and top cap.

WARNING
Use brake fluid clearly marked DOT 4 from a sealed container. Other types may vaporize and cause brake failure. Always use the same brand name. Do not intermix silicone based (DOT 5) brake fluid as it can cause brake component damage leading to brake system failure.

WARNING
Do not ride the motorcycle until you are sure the brakes are working correctly.

Rear Pad Replacement

CAUTION
When working on the brake system avoid touching the friction surfaces of the disc or brake pads with your hands. Natural skin oils or other contamination can affect braking efficiency. If you must touch the disc, wash it with brake cleaner after it is reassembled.

Refer to **Figure 9** (ZX900) or **Figure 10** (ZX1000) for this procedure.

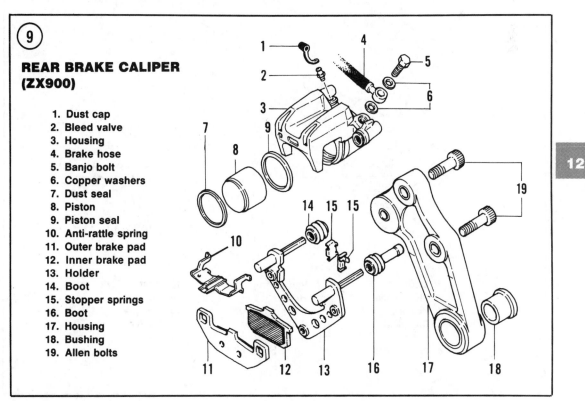

REAR BRAKE CALIPER (ZX900)

1. Dust cap
2. Bleed valve
3. Housing
4. Brake hose
5. Banjo bolt
6. Copper washers
7. Dust seal
8. Piston
9. Piston seal
10. Anti-rattle spring
11. Outer brake pad
12. Inner brake pad
13. Holder
14. Boot
15. Stopper springs
16. Boot
17. Housing
18. Bushing
19. Allen bolts

12

1. Remove the right-hand side muffler.

2. Remove the 2 caliper bolts and lift the caliper off the brake disc. See **Figure 11** (ZX900) or A, **Figure 12** (ZX1000).

3. Push the caliper holder (A, **Figure 13**) toward the piston.

4. Remove the outer (B, **Figure 13**) and inner (**Figure 14**) brake pads.

5. Remove the anti-rattle spring (A, **Figure 15**).

6. Check that the 2 clips (B, **Figure 15**) are installed on the caliper holder.

7. Remove the cap and diaphragm from the master cylinder (**Figure 16**). Slowly push the piston (C, **Figure 15**) into the caliper while checking the reservoir to make sure it doesn't overflow. The piston should move freely. You may need to use a C-clamp to push the piston back into the caliper. If

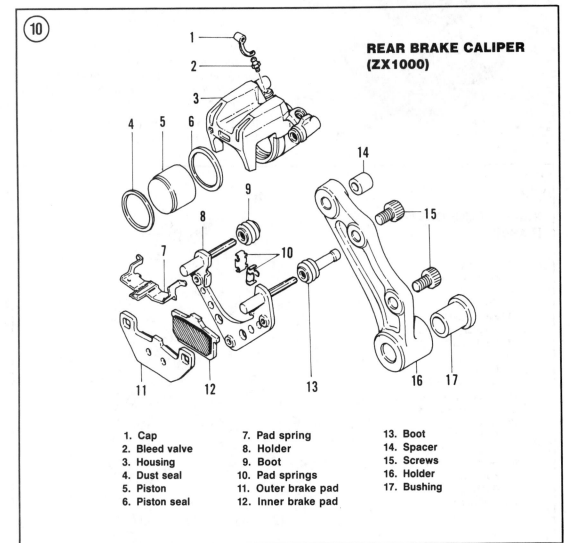

REAR BRAKE CALIPER (ZX1000)

1. Cap	7. Pad spring	13. Boot
2. Bleed valve	8. Holder	14. Spacer
3. Housing	9. Boot	15. Screws
4. Dust seal	10. Pad springs	16. Holder
5. Piston	11. Outer brake pad	17. Bushing
6. Piston seal	12. Inner brake pad	

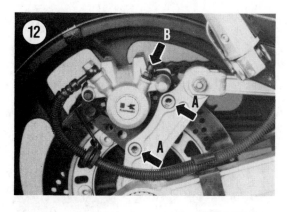

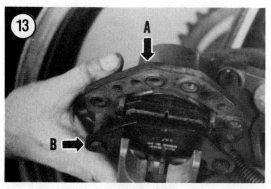

the piston sticks, remove the caliper and rebuild it as described in this chapter.

8. If necessary, install a new anti-rattle spring into the caliper (A, **Figure 15**).

9. Set the inner brake pad (**Figure 14**) into the caliper.

10. Push the caliper holder (A, **Figure 13**) toward the piston. Then align the holes in the outer brake pad plate (B, **Figure 13**) and install it onto the caliper holder.

NOTE
*The friction material on both brake pads (**Figure 8**) must face inward.*

11. Carefully slip the brake pads over the brake disc while installing the caliper. Install the caliper bolts and tighten to the torque specification in **Table 2**. See **Figure 11** (ZX900) or A, **Figure 12** (ZX1000).

12. Support the motorcycle with rear wheel off the ground. Spin the wheel and pump the brake until the pads are seated against the disc.

13. If necessary, correct the fluid level in the master cylinder reservoir. Install the diaphragm and top cap.

WARNING
Use brake fluid clearly marked DOT 4 from a sealed container. Other types may vaporize and cause brake failure. Always use the same brand name. Do not intermix silicone based (DOT 5) brake fluid as it can cause brake component damage leading to brake system failure.

WARNING
Do not ride the motorcycle until you are sure the brakes are working correctly.

14. Install the right-hand muffler.

12

BRAKE CALIPERS

Front Caliper
Removal/Installation

Refer to **Figure 1**.

> *CAUTION*
> *Some brake fluid will come out when the brake hose is disconnected at the caliper. Put some plastic bags over the surrounding parts and have some shop towels ready to clean up spilled fluid.*

1. Remove the bolt and washers attaching the brake hose to the caliper (**Figure 17**). To prevent the loss of brake fluid, cap the end of the brake hose and tie it up to the fender. Be sure to cap or tape the ends to prevent the entry of moisture and dirt.
2. Remove the brake caliper as described under *Brake Pad Replacement* in this chapter.
3. Installation is the reverse of these steps. Note the following:
   a. Tighten the caliper attaching bolts to the torque specification in **Table 2**.
   b. Install the brake hose using new washers.
   c. Tighten the brake hose banjo bolt to the torque specification in **Table 2**.
   d. Bleed the brakes as described under *Bleeding the System* in this chapter.

> *WARNING*
> *Do not ride the motorcycle until you are sure that the brakes are operating properly.*

Rear Caliper
Removal/Installation

Refer to **Figure 9** (ZX900) or **Figure 10** (ZX1000).

> *CAUTION*
> *Some brake fluid will come out when the brake hose is disconnected at the caliper. Put some plastic bags over the surrounding parts and have some shop towels ready to clean up spilled fluid.*

1. Remove the bolt and washers attaching the brake hose to the caliper. To prevent the loss of brake fluid, cap the end of the brake hose and tie it up to the fender. Be sure to cap or tape the ends to prevent the entry of moisture and dirt.
2. Remove the brake caliper as described under *Brake Pad Replacement* in this chapter.

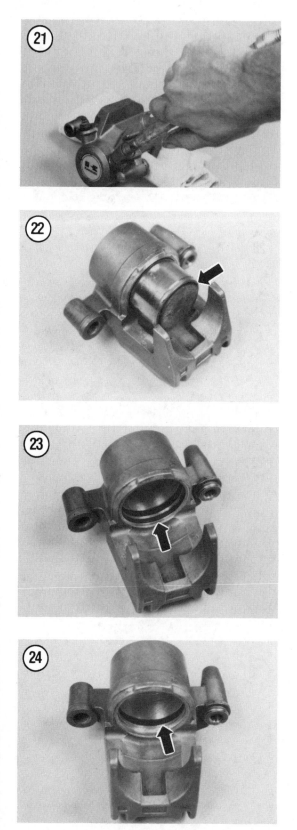

3. Installation is the reverse of these steps. Note the following:
   a. Tighten the caliper attaching bolts to the torque specification in **Table 2**.
   b. Install the brake hose using new washers.
   c. Tighten the brake hose banjo bolt to the torque specification in **Table 2**.
   d. Bleed the brakes as described under *Bleeding the System* in this chapter.

> *WARNING*
> *Do not ride the motorcycle until you are sure that the brakes are operating properly.*

Caliper Rebuilding

Procedures used to rebuild the front and rear brake calipers are the same.

Refer to **Figure 1**, **Figure 9** or **Figure 10** for this procedure.

> *NOTE*
> *Compressed air will be required to completely disassemble the caliper assembly.*

1. Remove the brake caliper as described in this chapter.
2. Remove the anti-rattle spring and the 2 clips from the caliper holder.
3. Pull the caliper holder (**Figure 18**) out of the housing.
4. Pull the rubber boots (**Figure 19**) off of the housing.

> *NOTE*
> *Compressed air will be required to remove the piston (**Figure 20**).*

> *WARNING*
> *Keep your fingers and hand out of the caliper bore area when removing the piston in Step 5. The piston may fly out of the bore with considerable force and could crush your fingers or hand.*

5. Pad the piston with shop rags or wood blocks as shown in **Figure 21**. Then apply compressed air through one of the caliper ports and blow the piston out of the caliper (**Figure 22**).
6. Remove the dust (**Figure 23**) and piston (**Figure 24**) seals from the caliper bore.
7. Clean all caliper parts (except brake pads) in new DOT 4 brake fluid. Place the cleaned parts on a lint-free cloth while performing the following inspection procedures.

12

8. Check the caliper bore (**Figure 25**) for cracks, deep scoring or excessive wear.

9. Check the caliper piston (**Figure 26**) for deep scoring, excessive wear or rust.

10. Replace the caliper housing or piston if necessary.

11. See **Figure 27**. The piston seal (A) maintains correct brake pad-to-disc clearance. If the seal is worn or damaged, the brake pads will drag and cause excessive pad wear and brake fluid temperatures. Replace the piston (A) and dust (B) seals if the following conditions exist:

    a. Brake fluid leaks around the inner brake pad.

    b. The piston seal (A) is stuck in the caliper groove.

    c. There is a large difference in inner and outer brake pad wear (**Figure 28**).

12. Measure the brake pad friction material with a ruler or caliper and compare to wear limits in **Table 1**. Replace both brake pads if any one pad is too thin.

13. Check the caliper holder (**Figure 29**) for cracks or other damage. Replace the support if necessary.

14. Check the rubber boots (**Figure 30**) for tearing or weather damage. Replace if necessary.

15. See **Figure 31**. Check the anti-rattle spring (A) and the 2 clips (B) for cracks or damage. Replace if necessary.

16. After all worn or damaged parts have been replaced, assemble the caliper assembly as follows.

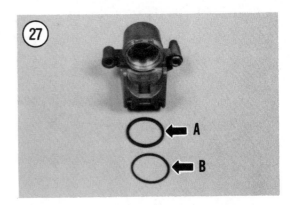

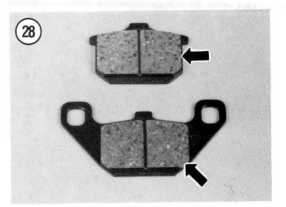

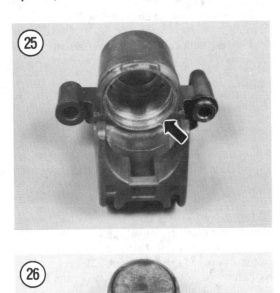

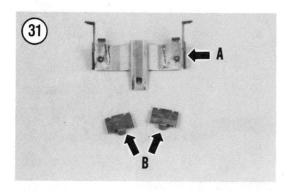

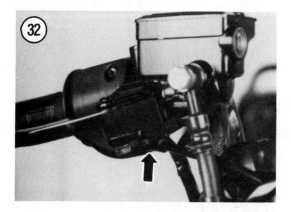

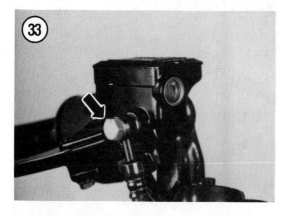

17. See **Figure 27**. Soak the piston seal (A) and dust (B) seal in new DOT 4 brake fluid.

18. Coat the caliper bore with new DOT 4 brake fluid.

19. Install the piston seal (**Figure 24**) into the rear caliper seal groove.

20. Install the dust seal (**Figure 23**) into the front caliper seal groove.

21. Coat the piston O.D. with new DOT 4 brake fluid.

22. Align the piston with the caliper bore as shown in **Figure 22** and install the piston. Push the piston all the way into the caliper bore (**Figure 20**).

23. Install the rubber boots (**Figure 19**) onto the caliper housing.

24. Align the caliper holder with the caliper housing and install the holder. See **Figure 18.**

25. Install the anti-rattle spring and the 2 clips.

26. Install the brake pads and caliper as described in this chapter.

FRONT MASTER CYLINDER

Removal/Installation

> *CAUTION*
> *Cover the fuel tank, front fender and instrument cluster with a heavy cloth or plastic tarp to protect them from accidental spilling of brake fluid. Wash any spilled brake fluid off any painted or plated surfaces immediately, as it will destroy the finish. Use soapy water and rinse completely.*

1. Drain the master cylinder as follows:
   a. Attach a hose to the brake caliper bleed screw.
   b. Place the end of the hose in a clean container.
   c. Open the bleed screw and operate the brake lever to drain all brake fluid from the master cylinder reservoir.
   d. Close the bleed screw and disconnect the hose.
   e. Discard the brake fluid.

2. Disconnect the brake switch connector (**Figure 32**) at the master cylinder.

3. Remove the banjo bolt securing the brake hose to the master cylinder (**Figure 33**). Remove the brake hose and both washers. Cover the end of the hose to prevent the entry of foreign matter and moisture. Tie the hose end up to the handlebar to prevent the loss of brake fluid.

4. Remove the 2 clamping bolts (A, **Figure 34**) and clamp securing the master cylinder to the handlebar and remove the master cylinder (B, **Figure 34**).

12

5. Install by reversing these removal steps. Note the following:

a. Install the master cylinder clamp with the arrow facing upward.

b. Tighten the upper clamp bolt first, then the lower bolt to the torque specification in **Table 2**.

c. Install the brake hose onto the master cylinder. Be sure to place a washer on each side of the hose fitting and install the banjo bolt. Tighten the banjo bolt to the torque specification in **Table 2**.

d. Bleed the brake system as described under *Bleeding the System* in this chapter.

> *WARNING*
> *Do not ride the motorcycle until the front brake is operating correctly.*

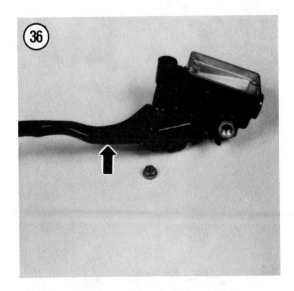

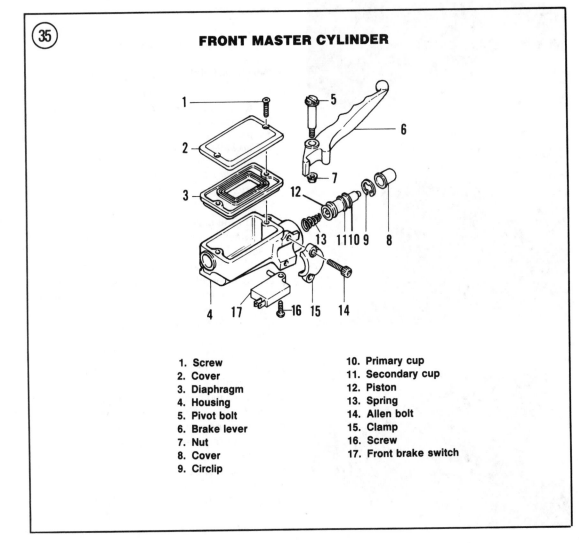

FRONT MASTER CYLINDER

1. Screw
2. Cover
3. Diaphragm
4. Housing
5. Pivot bolt
6. Brake lever
7. Nut
8. Cover
9. Circlip
10. Primary cup
11. Secondary cup
12. Piston
13. Spring
14. Allen bolt
15. Clamp
16. Screw
17. Front brake switch

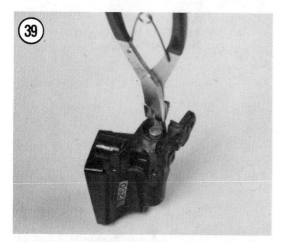

Disassembly/Reassembly

Refer to **Figure 35** for this procedure.
1. Remove the brake master cylinder as described in this chapter.
2. Remove the pivot bolt nut and pivot bolt. Then pull the brake lever out of the master cylinder (**Figure 36**).

> *NOTE*
> *Before cleaning parts, check for brake fluid around the brake lever. If brake fluid is noted, the primary and secondary cups are worn and should be replaced.*

3. Remove the screw (A, **Figure 37**) securing the brake light switch to the bottom of the master cylinder housing and remove the switch (B, **Figure 37**).
4. Remove the rubber cover (**Figure 38**) from the groove in the master cylinder.
5. Using circlip pliers, remove the circlip and washer (**Figure 39**).
6. Remove the piston (A, **Figure 40**) with the secondary cup (B, **Figure 40**) attached.
10. Remove the spring (A, **Figure 41**) with the primary cup (B, **Figure 41**) attached.

Inspection

1. Clean all parts (**Figure 42**) in denatured alcohol or fresh DOT 4 brake fluid. Inspect the cylinder

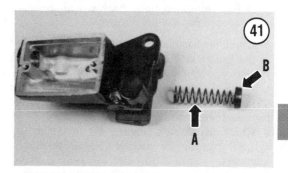

bore and piston contact surfaces for signs of wear and damage. If either part is less than perfect, replace it.

> *NOTE*
> *The primary cup, spring and secondary cup are sold as part of the piston assembly. If any one of these parts are worn or damaged, a new piston assembly must be purchased.*

> *NOTE*
> *The primary and secondary cups prevent brake fluid from leaking around the piston when the piston is moved forward by the brake lever to pressurize the brake hose.*

2. Check the end of the piston (A, **Figure 43**) for wear caused by the lug on the brake lever. Check the secondary cup (B, **Figure 43**) for tearing, wear, softness or swelling.

3. Check the spring (A, **Figure 44**) for fatigue, cracks or other damage. Check the primary cup (B, **Figure 44**) for tearing, wear, softness or swelling.

4. There are 2 ports at the bottom of the master cylinder reservoir (**Figure 45**). The large port supplies brake fluid to the line and the small port releases excess brake fluid from the line. Check that both ports are open and clear of all debris. Clean the ports with compressed air.

> *NOTE*
> *If the small port becomes plugged by contamination, the brakes can be applied but will not release.*

5. Check the hand lever pivot bore (A, **Figure 46**) in the master cylinder. If worn or elongated, the master cylinder must be replaced.

6. Check the hand lever pivot bolt hole (B, **Figure 46**) for wear or damage. If worn or elongated, the hand lever must be replaced.

7. Check the threads (**Figure 47**) in the master cylinder housing for damage. Repair threads if necessary.

8. Check the diaphragm (A, **Figure 48**) for tears or other damage. Check the cover (B, **Figure 48**) for cracks or damage.

9. Replace worn or damaged parts as required.

Assembly

Refer to **Figure 35** for this procedure.

1. Soak the new cups in fresh DOT 4 brake fluid for at least 15 minutes to make them pliable. Coat the inside of the cylinder with fresh brake fluid prior to assembly of parts.

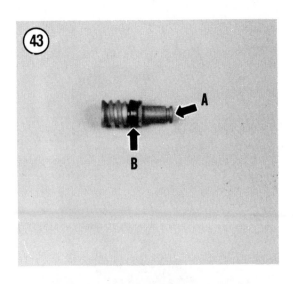

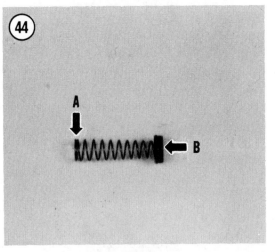

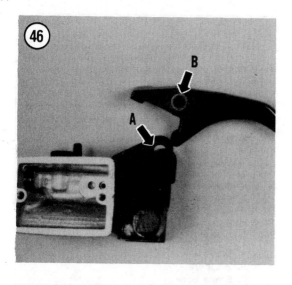

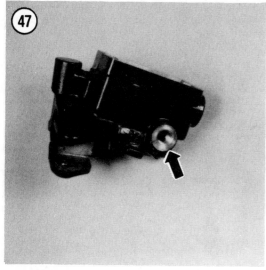

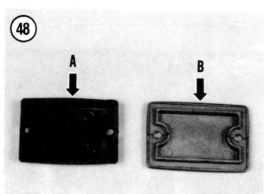

2. Install the spring and primary cup into the piston bore as shown in **Figure 41**.

3. Install the piston and secondary cup into the piston bore as show in **Figure 40**.

4. Slip the circlip over the end of the piston.

5. Compress the piston assembly and install the circlip (**Figure 39**) into the groove in the master cylinder using circlip pliers. Make sure the circlip seats in the groove completely.

NOTE
When compressing the piston assembly
in Step 5, it will be easier if the master
cylinder is mounted in a vise with soft
jaws. Then have an assistant compress
the piston assembly with a long wood
dowel. This will give you room to install
the circlip with the pliers.

6. Insert the rubber cover into the piston bore (**Figure 38**).

7. Install the brake light switch (B, **Figure 37**) and secure with the Phillips screw (A, **Figure 37**).

8. Assemble the brake lever (**Figure 36**). Lightly grease the pivot bolt. Then install the pivot bolt from the top of the master cylinder and through the hand lever pushrod bushing. Install the pivot bolt nut and tighten securely. Operate the brake pedal and make sure it moves smoothly. The lever should not bind or catch.

9. Install the diaphragm and top cover.

10. Install the brake master cylinder and bleed the front brake as described under *Bleeding The System* in this chapter.

12

REAR MASTER CYLINDER (ZX900)

Removal/Installation

Refer to **Figure 49** for this procedure.

CAUTION
Cover the swing arm with a heavy cloth
or plastic tarp to protect it from
accidental spilling of brake fluid. Wash
any spilled brake fluid off any painted
or plated surfaces immediately, as it
will destroy the finish. Use soapy water
and rinse completely.

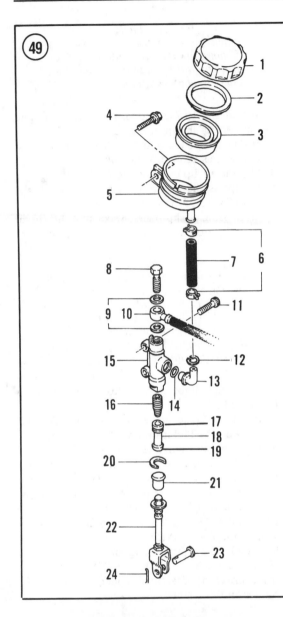

49

REAR MASTER CYLINDER (ZX900)

1. Cap
2. Diaphragm plate
3. Diaphragm
4. Bolt
5. Reservoir
6. Hose clamps
7. Brake hose
8. Banjo bolt
9. Washers
10. Brake hose
11. Bolt
12. Circlip
13. Joint
14. O-ring
15. Housing
16. Spring
17. Primary cup
18. Piston
19. Secondary cup
20. Retainer
21. Cover
22. Pushrod
23. Pin
24. Circlip

50

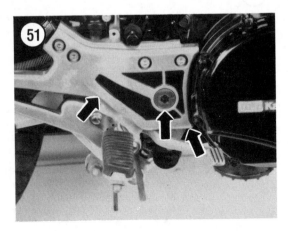

51

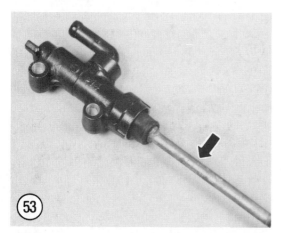

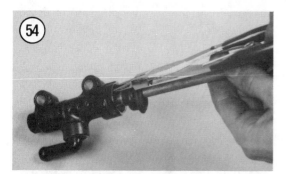

1. Remove the right-hand side cover.
2. Drain the master cylinder as follows:
   a. Attach a hose to the brake caliper bleed screw.
   b. Place the end of the hose in a clean container.
   c. Open the bleed screw and operate the brake lever to drain all brake fluid from the master cylinder reservoir.
   d. Close the bleed screw and disconnect the hose.
   e. Discard the brake fluid.
3. Remove the reservoir mounting bolt (A, **Figure 50**).
4. Remove the master cylinder banjo bolt (B, **Figure 50**). Plug the hose to prevent brake fluid from draining out and onto other components.
5. Remove the master cylinder mounting bolts (C, **Figure 50**).
6. Remove the right-hand footpeg bracket assembly (**Figure 51**) with the master cylinder attached. See Chapter Thirteen.
7. Disconnect the brake rod (A, **Figure 52**) from the footpeg assembly.
8. Install by reversing these removal steps. Note the following:
   a. Install the brake hose into the U-shaped notch in the master cylinder. Be sure to place a copper sealing washer on each side of the hose fitting and install the banjo bolt. Tighten the banjo bolt to the torque specification in **Table 2**.
   b. Insert the reservoir hose into the master cylinder and secure it.
   c. Bleed the brake system as described under *Bleeding the System* in this chapter.
   d. Adjust the rear brake pedal as described in Chapter Three. Refer to *Rear Brake Pedal Height Adjustment* and *Rear Brake Light Switch Adjustment*.

> *WARNING*
> *Do not ride the motorcycle until the rear brake is operating correctly.*

Disassembly

Refer to **Figure 49** for this procedure.
1. Remove the master cylinder as described in this chapter.
2. Remove the pushrod assembly (**Figure 53**) as follows:
   a. Pull the rubber boot out of the way, then remove the circlip (**Figure 54**).
   b. Pull the pushrod assembly (**Figure 55**) out of the master cylinder.

12

3. Remove the piston (A, **Figure 56**) with the secondary cup (B, **Figure 56**) attached.

4. Remove the spring (A, **Figure 57**) with the primary cup (B, **Figure 57**) attached.

5. If necessary, remove the circlip and remove the elbow (**Figure 58**) from the master cylinder housing.

Inspection

1. Clean all parts (**Figure 59**) in denatured alcohol or fresh DOT 4 brake fluid. Inspect the cylinder bore and piston contact surfaces for signs of wear and damage. If either part is less than perfect, replace it.

> *NOTE*
> *The primary cup, spring and secondary cup are sold as part of the piston assembly. If any one of these parts are worn or damaged, a new piston assembly must be purchased.*

> *NOTE*
> *The primary and secondary cups prevent brake fluid from leaking around the piston when the piston is moved forward by the brake lever to pressurize the brake hose.*

2. Check the end of the piston (A, **Figure 60**) for wear caused by the pushrod. Check the secondary cup (B, **Figure 60**) for tearing, wear, softness or swelling.

3. Check the spring (A, **Figure 61**) for fatigue, cracks or other damage. Check the primary cup (B, **Figure 61**) for tearing, wear, softness or swelling.

4. There are 2 ports in the side of the master cylinder (**Figure 62**). The large port supplies brake fluid to the line and the small port releases excess brake fluid from the line. Check that both ports are open and clear of all debris. Clean the ports with compressed air from either a compressor or from an air container sold by photography dealers.

> *NOTE*
> *If the small port becomes plugged by contamination, the brakes can be applied, but will not release.*

5. Check the threads in the master cylinder for damage. Repair threads if necessary.

6. Check the pushrod for damage. Check the boot on the pushrod for deterioration.

7. Check the diaphragm for tears or other damage. Check the cover for cracks or damage.

8. Replace worn or damaged parts as required.

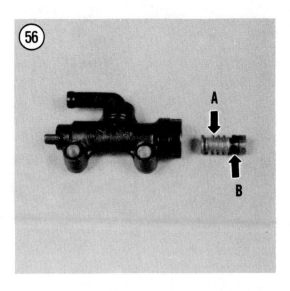

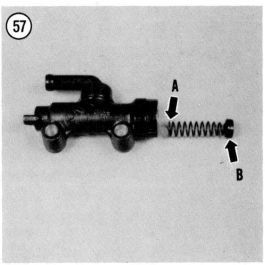

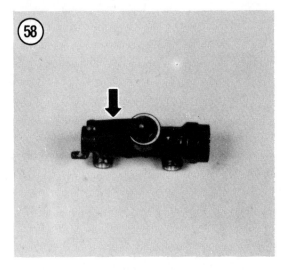

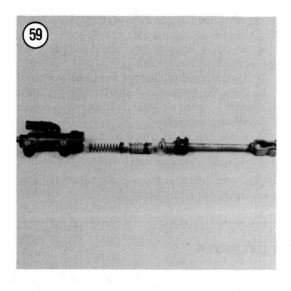

(59)

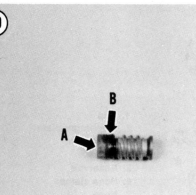

(60)

B

A

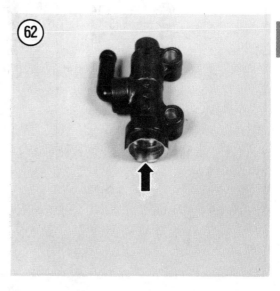

(61)

A

B

Assembly

Refer to **Figure 49** for this procedure.

1. Soak the new cups in fresh DOT 4 brake fluid for at least 15 minutes to make them pliable. Coat the inside of the cylinder with fresh brake fluid prior to assembly of parts.

> *CAUTION*
> *When installing the piston assembly, do not allow the cups to turn inside out as they will be damaged and allow brake fluid to leak in the cylinder bore.*

2. Install the spring and primary cup into the piston bore as shown in **Figure 57**.

3. Install the piston and secondary cup into the piston bore as shown in **Figure 56**.

4. Insert the pushrod into the master cylinder so that it rests against the piston with the pushrod washer below the circlip groove. See **Figure 55**.

> *NOTE*
> *When compressing the piston assembly in Step 5, it will be easier if the master cylinder is mounted in a vise with soft jaws.*

5. Slide the circlip down the pushrod and install it in the circlip groove (**Figure 54**). Make sure the circlip seats in the groove completely. Install the rubber boot.

6. Install the elbow, if removed.

7. Install the brake master cylinder and bleed the rear brake as described under *Bleeding the System* in this chapter.

8. Torque the footpeg bracket bolts in the sequence shown under *Footpeg Brackets,* Chapter Thirteen.

(62)

12

REAR MASTER CYLINDER
(ZX1000)

Removal/Installation

Refer to **Figure 63** for this procedure.

> *CAUTION*
> *Cover the swing arm with a heavy cloth or plastic tarp to protect it from accidental spilling of brake fluid. Wash any spilled brake fluid off any painted or plated surfaces immediately, as it will destroy the finish. Use soapy water and rinse completely.*

1. Remove the right-hand side cover.
2. Drain the master cylinder as follows:
   a. Attach a hose to the brake caliper bleed screw.
   b. Place the end of the hose in a clean container.
   c. Open the bleed screw and operate the brake pedal to drain all brake fluid from the master cylinder reservoir.
   d. Close the bleed screw and disconnect the hose.
   e. Discard the brake fluid.
3. Remove the cotter pin and disconnect the joint pin (**Figure 64**) at the pushrod.

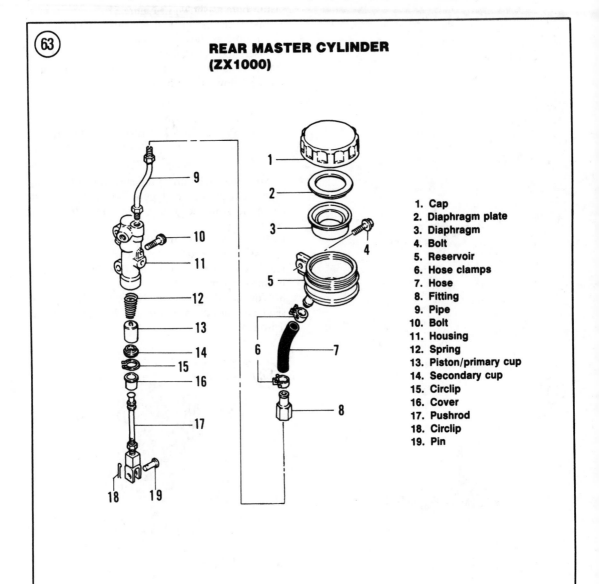

REAR MASTER CYLINDER (ZX1000)

63

1. Cap
2. Diaphragm plate
3. Diaphragm
4. Bolt
5. Reservoir
6. Hose clamps
7. Hose
8. Fitting
9. Pipe
10. Bolt
11. Housing
12. Spring
13. Piston/primary cup
14. Secondary cup
15. Circlip
16. Cover
17. Pushrod
18. Circlip
19. Pin

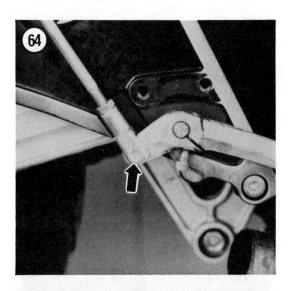

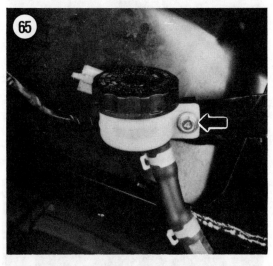

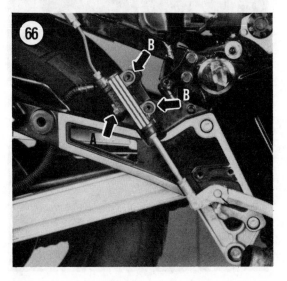

4. Remove the bolt (**Figure 65**) securing the reservoir to the frame.

5. Disconnect the brake line (A, **Figure 66**) at the master cylinder and remove the reservoir assembly.

6. Loosen and remove the banjo bolt at the master cylinder. Plug the hose to prevent brake fluid from leaking on other parts.

7. Remove the bolts securing the master cylinder assembly (B, **Figure 66**) and remove it.

8. Install by reversing these removal steps. Note the following:

    a. Install the brake hose into the U-shaped notch in the master cylinder. Be sure to place a sealing washer on each side of the hose fitting and install the banjo bolt. Tighten the banjo bolt to the torque specification in **Table 2**.

    b. Insert the reservoir hose into the master cylinder and secure it.

    c. Bleed the brake system as described under *Bleeding the System* in this chapter.

    d. Adjust the rear brake pedal as described in Chapter Three. Refer to *Rear Brake Pedal Height Adjustment* and *Rear Brake Light Switch Adjustment*.

> *WARNING*
> *Do not ride the motorcycle until the front brake is operating correctly.*

Disassembly

Refer to **Figure 63** for this procedure.

1. Remove the master cylinder as described in this chapter.

2. Remove the pushrod assembly as follows:

    a. Remove the circlip.

    b. Pull the pushrod assembly out of the master cylinder.

3. Remove the piston/primary cup, secondary cup and spring.

Inspection

1. Clean all parts (**Figure 63**) in denatured alcohol or fresh DOT 4 brake fluid. Inspect the cylinder bore and piston contact surfaces for signs of wear and damage. If either part is less than perfect, replace it.

> *NOTE*
> *The primary cup, spring and secondary cup are sold as part of the piston assembly. If any one of these parts are worn or damaged, a new piston assembly must be purchased.*

12

NOTE
The primary and secondary cups prevent brake fluid from leaking around the piston when the piston is moved forward by the brake lever to pressurize the brake hose.

2. Check the end of the piston for wear caused by the pushrod. Check the secondary cup for tearing, wear, softness or swelling.
3. Check the spring for fatigue, cracks or other damage. Check the primary cup for tearing, wear, softness or swelling.
4. There are 2 ports in the side of the master cylinder. The large port supplies brake fluid to the line and the small port releases excess brake fluid from the line. Check that both ports are open and clear of all debris. Clean the ports with compressed air.

NOTE
If the small port becomes plugged by contamination, the brakes can be applied, but will not release.

5. Check the threads in the master cylinder for damage. Repair threads if necessary.
6. Check the pushrod for damage. Check the boot cover on the pushrod for deterioration.
7. Check the diaphragm for tears or other damage. Check the cover for cracks or damage.
8. Replace worn or damaged parts as required.

Assembly

Refer to **Figure 63** for this procedure.
1. Soak the new cups in fresh DOT 4 brake fluid for at least 15 minutes to make them pliable. Coat the inside of the cylinder with fresh brake fluid prior to assembly of parts.

CAUTION
When installing the piston assembly, do not allow the cups to turn inside out as they will be damaged and allow brake fluid leak in the cylinder bore.

2. Install the spring and primary cup into the piston bore.
3. Install the piston and secondary cup into the piston bore.
4. Slide the circlip down the pushrod and install it in the circlip groove. Make sure the circlip seats in the groove completely.
5. Install the rubber boot into the master cylinder.

BRAKE HOSE REPLACEMENT

A brake hose should replaced whenever it shows cracks, bulges or other damage. The deterioration of rubber by ozone and other atmospheric elements may require hose replacement every 4 years or sooner.

CAUTION
Cover components with a heavy cloth or plastic tarp to protect them from the accidental spilling of brake fluid. Wash any spilled brake fluid off of any painted or plated surface immediately, as it will destroy the finish. Use soapy water and rinse completely.

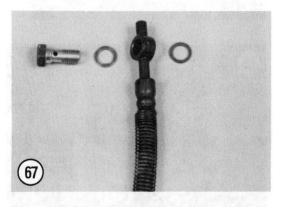

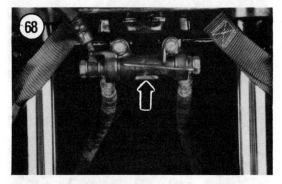

1. Before replacing a brake hose, inspect the routing of the old hose carefully, noting any guides and grommets the hose may go through.

2. Drain the master cylinder as described under *Front Master Cylinder Removal/Installation* or *Rear Master Cylinder Removal/Installation* in this chapter.

3. Disconnect the banjo bolts securing the hose at both ends and remove the hose with the banjo bolts and washers (**Figure 67**).

4. On front brakes, to remove the brake banjo joint, disconnect the hoses at the joint. Then remove the attaching bolts and remove the joint (**Figure 68**).

5. On front brakes, to remove the anti-dive brake pipe (**Figure 69**), loosen the 2 pipe nuts and remove the pipe.

6. Install new brake hoses, sealing washers and bolts in the reverse order of removal. Be sure to install the new sealing washers in their correct positions. Tighten all banjo bolts to the torque specification in **Table 2**.

7. Refill the master cylinder(s) with fresh brake fluid clearly marked DOT 4. Bleed the brake as described under *Bleeding the System* in this chapter.

> *WARNING*
> *Do not ride the motorcycle until you are sure that the brakes are operating properly.*

BRAKE DISC

Inspection

It is not necessary to remove the disc from the wheel to inspect it. Small marks on the disc are not important, but deep radial scratches, deep enough to snag a fingernail, reduce braking effectiveness and increase brake pad wear. If these grooves are found, the disc should be replaced.

1. Measure the thickness around the disc at several locations, 90° apart, with a micrometer (**Figure 70**). The disc must be replaced if the thickness at any point is less than the minimum specified in **Table 1**.

2. Make sure the disc bolts (**Figure 71**) are tight prior to performing this check. Check the disc runout with a dial indicator as shown in **Figure 72**. Slowly rotate the wheel and watch the dial indicator. If the runout is 0.3 mm (0.012 in.) or greater, the disc must be replaced.

3. Clean the disc of any rust or corrosion and wipe clean with lacquer thinner or brake cleaner. Never use an oil based solvent that may leave an oil residue on the disc.

12

Removal/Installation

1. Remove the front or rear wheel as described in Chapter Ten or Chapter Eleven.

> *CAUTION*
> *When working on the brake system avoid touching the friction surfaces of the disc or brake pads with your hands. Natural skin oils or other contamination can affect braking efficiency. If you must touch the disc, wash it with brake cleaner after it is reassembled.*

> *NOTE*
> *Place a piece of wood in the calipers in place of the disc. This way, if the brake lever or pedal is inadvertently squeezed, the piston will not be forced out of the cylinder. If this does happen, the caliper might have to be disassembled to reseat the piston and the system will have to be bled.*

2. Remove the bolts securing the disc to the wheel and remove the disc (**Figure 71**).

3. Install by reversing these removal steps. Note the following:

   a. Apply Loctite 242 (blue) to the bolts before installation.

   b. Tighten the disc bolts to the torque specification in **Table 2**.

BLEEDING THE SYSTEM

This procedure is necessary only when the brakes feel spongy, there is a leak in the hydraulic system, a component has been replaced or the brake fluid has been replaced.

All models are equipped with an anti-dive unit and junction block mounted onto the front forks. It is necessary to bleed the anti-dive mechanism and junction block as well as the brake caliper. When bleeding the front brake calipers, bleed the following components in order:

   a. Caliper air bleed valve (A, **Figure 73**).

   b. Anti-dive bleed valve (B, **Figure 73**).

   c. Junction block bleed valve (C, **Figure 73**).

1. Flip off the dust cap from the brake bleeder valve.

2. Connect a length of clear tubing to the bleeder valve on the caliper. See **Figure 74**. Place the other end of the tube into a clean container. Fill the container with enough fresh DOT 4 brake fluid to

keep the end submerged, which prevents air from being drawn in during the bleeding procedure.

> *CAUTION*
> *Cover parts with a heavy cloth or plastic tarp to protect them from the accidental spilling of brake fluid. Wash any spilled brake fluid off of any painted or plated surface immediately, as it will destroy the finish. Use soapy water and rinse completely.*

3. Disconnect the hose at the master cylinder. Wrap the end of the hose with a shop towel and tie the hose out of the way.

4. Clean the top of the master cylinder of all dirt and foreign matter. Remove the cap and diaphragm. Fill the reservoir to the upper level

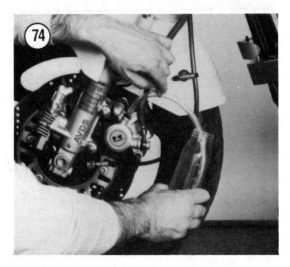

line. Install the diaphragm to prevent the entry of dirt and moisture.

> *WARNING*
> *Use brake fluid clearly marked DOT 4 only. Others may vaporize and cause brake failure. Always use the same brand name; do not intermix the brake fluids, as many brands are not compatible. Do not intermix silicone based (DOT 5) brake fluid as it can cause brake component damage leading to brake system failure.*

5. Hold your thumb securely over the hole in the master cylinder, then pump the lever (front) or pedal (rear) three or four times and hold it depressed. Slightly release your thumb pressure. Some air and fluid with seep out. Press down hard with your thumb and release the lever (front) or pedal (rear). Repeat this several times until you feel resistance when you pump the lever (front) or pedal (rear). Check the reservoir to avoid introducing more air into the master cylinder.

6. Reconnect and tighten the brake hose. Again, pump the lever or pedal and hold it depressed. Loosen the brake hose bolt (at the master cylinder) 1/2 turn. More air and fluid will seep out. Tighten the bolt and release the lever or pedal. Repeat this until only fluid seeps out. Check the master cylinder fluid level often to avoid introducing more air into the system.

7. If you are bleeding the front brake, bleed the brake hose junction block. Use the same technique used in Step 6 and bleed both sides (individually) of the junction.

8. Slowly apply the brake lever (front) or pedal (rear) several times. Hold the lever in the applied position and open the bleeder valve about 1/2 turn. Allow the lever to travel to its limit. When this limit is reached, tighten the bleeder screw. As the brake fluid enters the system, the level will drop in the master cylinder reservoir. Maintain the level at about 10 mm (3/8 in.) from the top of the reservoir to prevent air from being drawn into the system.

9. Continue to pump the lever or pedal and open the bleed valve until the fluid emerging from the hose is completely free of air bubbles.

10. Tighten the bleeder valve. Remove the bleeder tube and install the bleeder valve dust cap.

> *NOTE*
> *If you are bleeding the front brakes, repeat Steps 8-10 for the other side.*

11. If necessary, add fluid to correct the level in the master cylinder reservoir. It must be between the LOWER and UPPER level lines.

12. Install the cap and tighten the screws.

> *NOTE*
> *After bleeding the front brake caliper(s), also bleed the anti-dive bleed valve (B, **Figure 73**) and the junction block (C, **Figure 73**) in order.*

13. Test the feel of the brake lever or pedal. It should feel firm and should offer the same resistance each time it's operated. If it feels spongy, it is likely that air is still in the system and it must be bled again. When all air has been bled from the system, and the brake fluid level is correct in the reservoir, double-check for leaks and tighten all fittings and connections.

> *WARNING*
> *Before riding the motorcycle, make certain that the brakes are operating correctly by operating the lever several times. Then make the test ride a slow one at first to make sure the brake is operating correctly.*

12

Tables are on the following page.

Table 1 BRAKE SPECIFICATIONS

	Standard mm (in.)	Wear limit mm (in.)
Pad lining thickness		
Front and rear	4.85 (0.190)	1.0 (0.039)
Disc thickness		
Front	4.8-5.1	4.5
	(0.189-0.200)	(0.177)
Rear	6.8-7.1	6.0
	(0.267-0.279)	(0.236)
Disc runout	under 0.15	0.3
	(0.006 in.)	(0.012)

Table 2 BRAKE TIGHTENING TORQUES

	N•m	ft.-lb.
Brake lever pivot nut	5.9	4.3
Front master cylinder clamp nuts		
ZX900	8.8	6.5
ZX1000	11	8
Brake hose banjo bolts	29	22
Caliper mounting bolts	32	24
Brake disc mounting bolts	23	16.5
Torque link nuts (ZX1000)	29	22
Rear master cylinder mounting bolts		
ZX900	*	
ZX1000	23	16.5
Brake pushrod clevis locknut		
ZX900	*	
ZX1000	18	13
Rear brake hose clamp bolt		
ZX900	*	
ZX1000	23	16.5

* Torque specifications not specified.

NOTE: If you own a 1988 or later model, first check the Supplement at the back of this book for any new service information.

CHAPTER THIRTEEN

FAIRING

This chapter contains removal and installation procedures for the fairing assembly.

When removing a fairing component, it is best to reinstall all mounting hardware onto the removed part or store them in plastic bags taped to the inside of the fairing. After removal, fairing components should be placed away from area to prevent accidental damage.

> *CAUTION*
> *Painted fairing parts are usually secured with rubber washers and special metal washers, bolts or screws. To avoid permanent damage, always use the correct parts. Use of normal washers or fasteners will result in fairing damage.*

FAIRING
(ZX900)

Lower Fairing
Removal/Installation

Refer to **Figure 1** for this procedure.
1. Remove the lower fairing mounting bolts and screws and lower the fairing away from the bike.
2. Remove the left- and right-hand lower fairing covers.

3. Installation is the reverse of these steps. Note the following:
   a. Install the lower fairing and install the mounting bolts and screws finger tight.
   b. Install the left- and right-hand lower fairing covers to the inside of the lower fairing.
   c. Tighten all bolts and screws securely.

Middle Fairing
Removal/Installation

Refer to **Figure 1** for this procedure.
1. Remove the lower fairing as described in this chapter.
2. Remove the middle fairing mounting bolts and remove the fairing.
3. Remove the middle fairing cover screws and remove the left- and right-hand covers.
4. Installation is the reverse of these steps.

Upper Fairing
Removal/Installation

Refer to **Figure 1** and **Figure 2** for this procedure.
1. Remove the lower and middle fairings as described in this chapter.
2. Remove the ignition switch as described in Chapter Eight.

13

① **LOWER FAIRING ASSEMBLY (ZX900)**

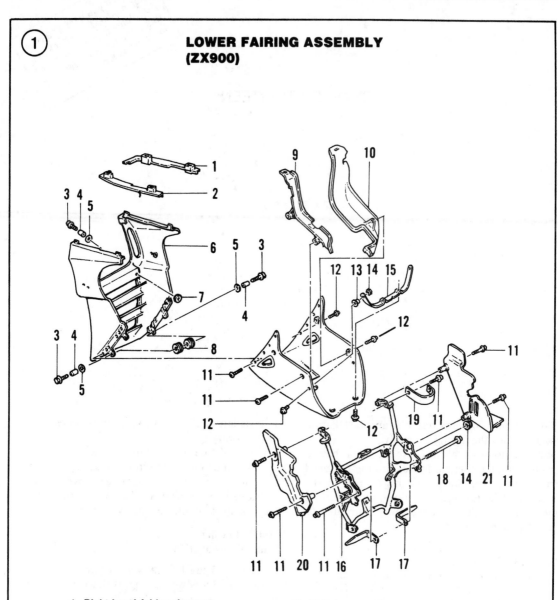

1. Right-hand fairing damper
2. Left-hand fairing damper
3. Bolt
4. Spacer
5. Damper
6. Middle fairing
7. Damper
8. Damper
9. Cover
10. Cover
11. Screw

12. Bolt
13. Spacer
14. Flange locknut
15. Bracket
16. Bracket
17. Nut
18. Bolt
19. Harness clamp
20. Left-hand middle fairing cover
21. Right-hand middle fairing cover

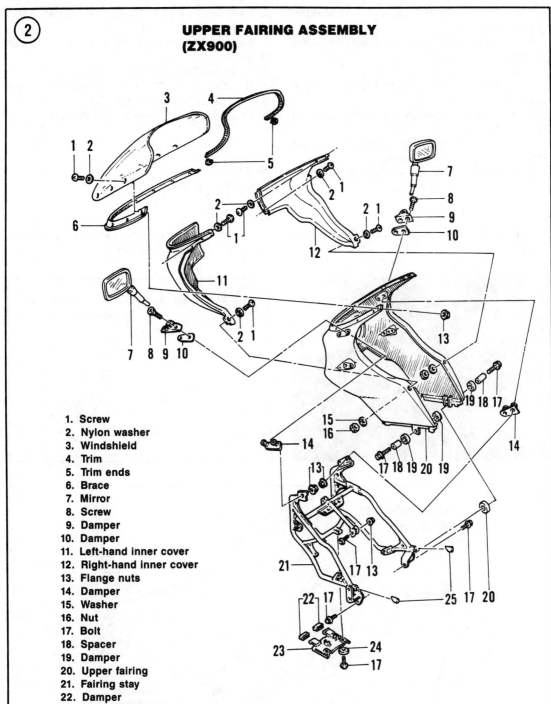

② UPPER FAIRING ASSEMBLY
(ZX900)

1. Screw
2. Nylon washer
3. Windshield
4. Trim
5. Trim ends
6. Brace
7. Mirror
8. Screw
9. Damper
10. Damper
11. Left-hand inner cover
12. Right-hand inner cover
13. Flange nuts
14. Damper
15. Washer
16. Nut
17. Bolt
18. Spacer
19. Damper
20. Upper fairing
21. Fairing stay
22. Damper
23. Headlight cover
24. Washer
25. Cap

13

3. Remove the instrument cluster as described in Chapter Eight.

4. Remove the inner fairing mounting screws and remove the inner fairing.

5. Remove the rear view mirrors.

6. Disconnect the front turn signal electrical connectors.

7. Remove the headlight cover from the bottom of the upper fairing.

8. Remove the upper fairing mounting bolts and remove the upper fairing (**Figure 3**).

9. Installation is the reverse of these steps.

Fairing Stay
Removal/Installation

1. Remove the lower fairing as described in this chapter.

2. Remove the middle fairing as described in this chapter.

3. Remove the upper fairing as described in this chapter.

4. Remove all wiring from the fairing stay.

5. Remove the fairing stay mounting bolt and remove the fairing stay (**Figure 2**).

6. Installation is the reverse of these steps.

Side Cover
Removal/Installation

Remove the mounting screws and washers and remove the side covers (**Figure 4**). Reverse to install. Make sure the rubber dampers are installed on the top of each side cover.

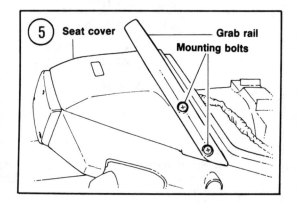

5. Seat cover — Grab rail — Mounting bolts

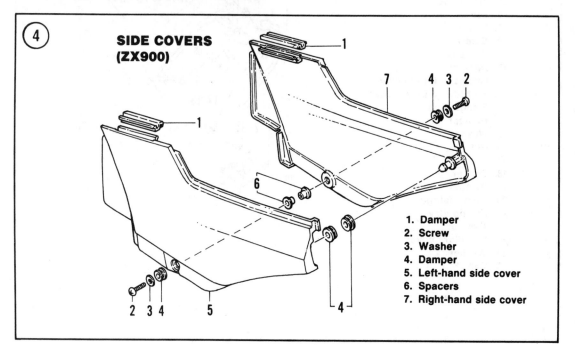

SIDE COVERS (ZX900)

1. Damper
2. Screw
3. Washer
4. Damper
5. Left-hand side cover
6. Spacers
7. Right-hand side cover

Seat Cover
Removal/Installation

1. Remove the seat.
2. Remove the left- and right-hand side covers (**Figure 4**).
3. Disconnect the tail light electrical connector.
4. Remove the grab rail bolts and remove the grab rail (**Figure 5**).
5. Remove the left- and right-hand turn signal bolts and pull the turn signals out of the seat cover. Secure the turn signals with Bunjee cords.

6. Remove the seat cover mounting bolts and remove the seat cover.
7. Installation is the reverse of these steps.

FAIRING
(ZX1000)

Lower Fairing
Removal/Installation

Refer to **Figure 6** for this procedure.

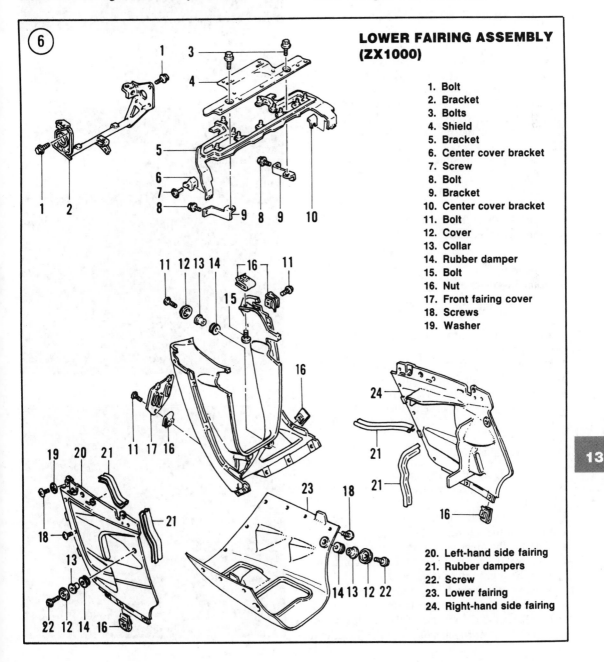

LOWER FAIRING ASSEMBLY (ZX1000)

1. Bolt
2. Bracket
3. Bolts
4. Shield
5. Bracket
6. Center cover bracket
7. Screw
8. Bolt
9. Bracket
10. Center cover bracket
11. Bolt
12. Cover
13. Collar
14. Rubber damper
15. Bolt
16. Nut
17. Front fairing cover
18. Screws
19. Washer
20. Left-hand side fairing
21. Rubber dampers
22. Screw
23. Lower fairing
24. Right-hand side fairing

13

1. Remove the lower fairing mounting bolts and screws and remove the lower fairing (**Figure 7**).

2. Installation is the reverse of these steps. Note the following:

   a. Make sure all rubber dampers are in place (**Figure 6**).

   b. Make sure to insert the lower fairing tabs into the slots in the side fairing during installation.

Side Fairing
Removal/Installation

Refer to **Figure 6** for this procedure.

1. Remove the caps and mounting screws (A, **Figure 8**) and pull the turn signal brackets (B, **Figure 8**) away from the side fairings.

2. Unplug the turn signal electrical connector and remove the turn signal brackets (**Figure 9**).

3. Remove the side cover mounting screws and remove the side cover.

4. Installation is the reverse of these steps. Note the following:

   a. Make sure all rubber dampers are in place (**Figure 6**).

   b. Insert the side fairing tabs into the slots in the front fairings.

   c. Check that the turn signals work after completing installation.

Front Fairing
Removal/Installation

Refer to **Figure 6** and **Figure 10** for this procedure.

1. Remove the front fairing (A, **Figure 11**) mounting screws.

2. Remove the front fairing cover (B, **Figure 11**) mounting screws and remove the cover.

3. Remove the front fairing.

4. Installation is the reverse of these steps.

Upper Fairing
Removal/Installation

Refer to **Figure 10** for this procedure.

1. Disconnect the headlight connector from inside the fairing.

2. Remove the rear view mirror mounting screws and remove the mirrors.

3. Remove the inner fairing mounting screws.

4. Remove the inner cover mounting bolts and remove the inner covers (**Figure 12**).

5. Remove the upper fairing mounting bolts and screws and remove the upper fairing.

6. Installation is the reverse of these steps. Make sure the front turn signals and the headlight

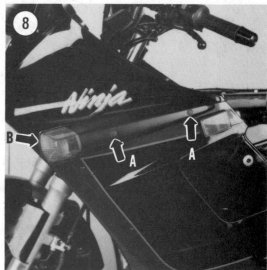

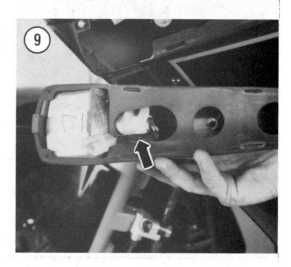

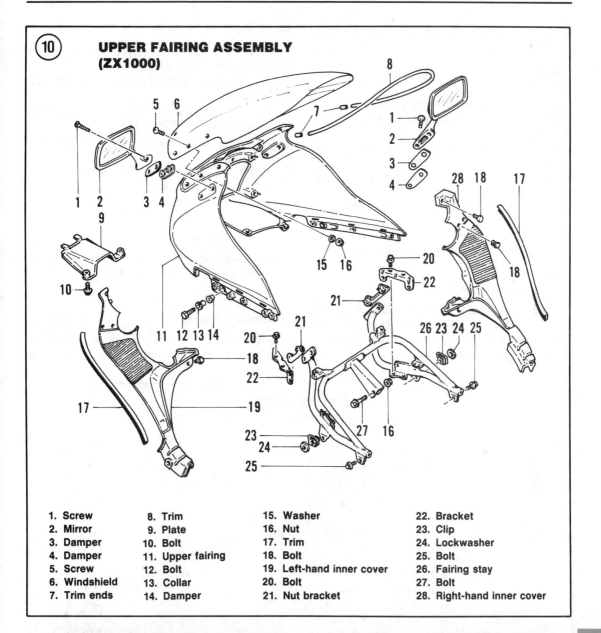

10 **UPPER FAIRING ASSEMBLY (ZX1000)**

1. Screw	8. Trim	15. Washer	22. Bracket
2. Mirror	9. Plate	16. Nut	23. Clip
3. Damper	10. Bolt	17. Trim	24. Lockwasher
4. Damper	11. Upper fairing	18. Bolt	25. Bolt
5. Screw	12. Bolt	19. Left-hand inner cover	26. Fairing stay
6. Windshield	13. Collar	20. Bolt	27. Bolt
7. Trim ends	14. Damper	21. Nut bracket	28. Right-hand inner cover

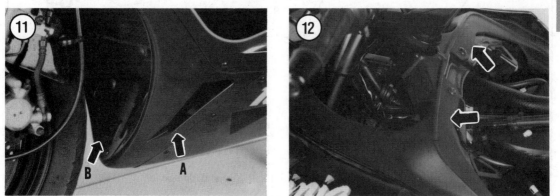

operate properly after installing the upper fairing assembly.

Fairing Stay
Removal/Installation

Refer to **Figure 10** for this procedure.
1. Remove the front fairing as described in this chapter.
2. Remove the upper fairing as described in this chapter.
3. Disconnect all electrical connectors from the fairing stay.
4. Remove all components from the fairing stay.
5. Remove the fairing stay mounting bolts and remove the fairing stay.
6. Installation is the reverse of these steps.

Side Cover
Removal/Installation

Remove the mounting screws and washers and remove the side covers (**Figure 13**). Reverse to install. Make sure the rubber dampers are installed on the top of each side cover.

Seat Cover

1. Remove the side covers (**Figure 13**).
2. Remove the passenger seat.
3. Disconnect the electrical connectors underneath the seat cover.
4. Open the strap hooks (**Figure 14**) and remove the mounting screws (**Figure 15**).
5. Lift the seat cover assembly (**Figure 16**) up and remove it.
6. Installation is the reverse of these steps.

WINDSHIELD

Removal/Installation

The windshield can be removed by removing the mounting screws. Reverse to install.

Windshield Cleaning

Be very careful when cleaning the windshield as it can be easily scratched or damaged. Do not use a

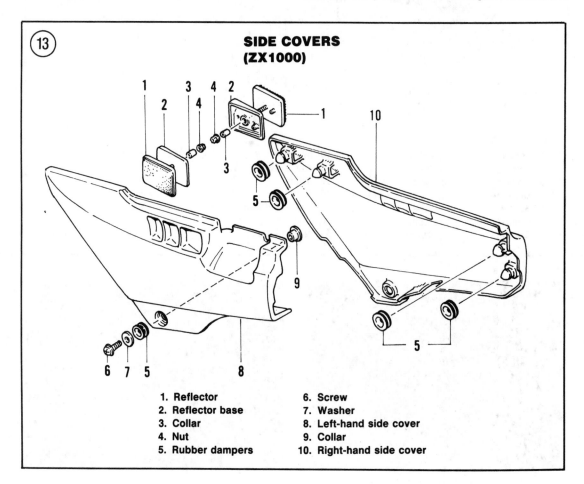

(13)

SIDE COVERS
(ZX1000)

1. Reflector
2. Reflector base
3. Collar
4. Nut
5. Rubber dampers
6. Screw
7. Washer
8. Left-hand side cover
9. Collar
10. Right-hand side cover

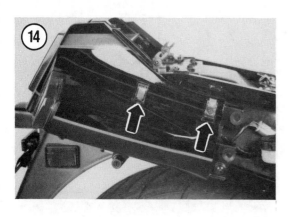

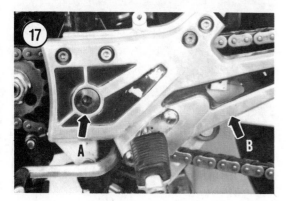

cleaner with an abrasive, a combination cleaner and wax or any solvent that contains ethyl or methyl alcohol. Never use gasoline or cleaning solvent. These products either scratch or destroy the surface of the windshield.

To remove oil, grease or road tar use isopropyl alcohol which is available at any drugstore. Then, wash the windshield with a solution of mild soap and water. Dry gently with a soft cloth or chamois—do not press hard.

CAUTION
When removing road tar, make sure there are no small stones or sand imbedded in it. Carefully remove any abrasive particles prior to performing any rubbing action with a cleaner. This will help minimize scratching.

Many commercial windshield cleaners are available. If using a cleaner, make sure it is safe for use on plastic and test it on a small area first.

FOOTPEG BRACKETS
(ZX900)

**Left-hand Footpeg Bracket
Removal/Installation**

1. Remove the left-hand side cover.
2. Remove the swing arm pivot shaft nut (A, **Figure 17**).
3. Remove the left-hand footpeg bracket mounting bolts and remove the footpeg bracket (B, **Figure 17**) with the shift pedal attached.
4. Remove the circlip and washer (A, **Figure 18**) and remove the shift shaft pedal (B, **Figure 18**) from the footpeg bracket.

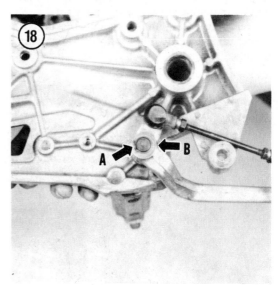

13

5. If necessary, remove the pinch bolt (A, **Figure 19**) and pull the shift pedal boss (B, **Figure 19**) off of the shift shaft.

6. Installation is the reverse of these steps. Note the following.

7. After installing the left-hand footpeg bracket assembly onto the frame, install the swing arm pivot shaft nut (A, **Figure 17**) and tighten it slightly to seat the side cover. Then install the side cover mounting bolts snug but not tight.

8. Referring to **Figure 20**, tighten the bolts in numerical order to the following tightening torques:

    a. Swing arm pivot shaft nut: 88 N•m (65 ft.-lb.).
    b. Mounting bolts: 27 N•m (20 ft.-lb.).

Right-hand Footpeg Bracket
Removal/Installation

1. Remove the right-hand side cover.

2. Disconnect the rear brake light switch electrical connector.

3. Remove the rear brake fluid reservoir mounting bolt (**Figure 21**).

4. Remove the rear swing arm pivot nut (A, **Figure 22**).

5. Remove the right-hand footpeg bracket mounting bolts and remove the footpeg bracket (B, **Figure 22**).

6. If necessary, remove the rear master cylinder (**Figure 23**) as described in Chapter Twelve.

7. Installation is the reverse of these steps. Note the following.

8. After installing the right-hand footpeg bracket assembly onto the frame, install the swing arm pivot shaft nut (A, **Figure 22**) and tighten it slightly to seat the side cover. Then install the footpeg bracket mounting bolts snug but not tight.

9. Referring to **Figure 24**, tighten the bolts in numerical order to the following tightening torques:

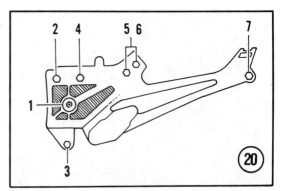

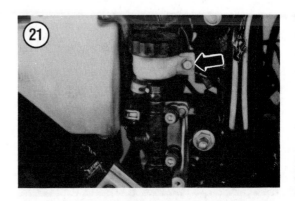

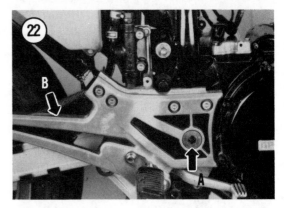

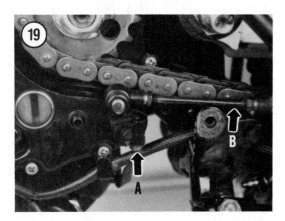

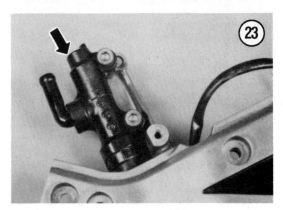

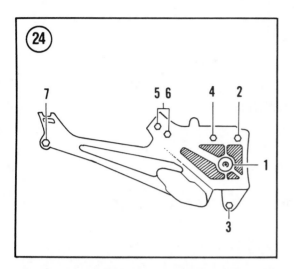

a. Swing arm pivot shaft nut: 88 N•m (65 ft.-lb.).
b. Mounting bolts: 27 N•m (20 ft.-lb.).

10. If the brake hose was disconnected, bleed the rear brake as described under *Bleeding The System* in Chapter Twelve.

11. Make sure the rear brake light works properly. If not, the brake light switch may need adjustment. See Chapter Eight.

FOOTPEG BRACKETS (ZX1000)

Left-hand Footpeg Bracket Removal/Installation

Remove the left-hand footpeg bracket mounting bolts and remove the bracket (**Figure 25**). Installation is the reverse of these steps. Tighten the mounting bolts securely.

Right-hand Footpeg Bracket Removal/Installation

1. Remove the right-hand side cover.
2. Disconnect the rear brake light switch electrical connector.
3. Remove the brake pedal pinch bolt and remove the brake pedal (**Figure 26**).
4. Remove the rear brake master cylinder as described in Chapter Twelve. It is not necessary to disconnect the brake line when removing the master cylinder.
5. Remove the right-hand footpeg bracket mounting bolts and remove the footpeg bracket (**Figure 27**).
6. Installation is the reverse of these steps. Note the following.
7. Tighten all mounting bolts securely.
8. If the brake hose was disconnected, bleed the rear brake as described under *Bleeding the System* in Chapter Twelve.
9. Make sure the rear brake light works properly. If not, the brake light switch may need adjustment. See Chapter Eight.

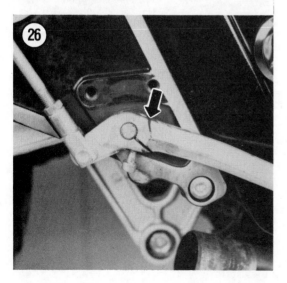

13

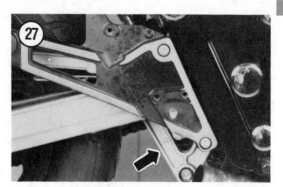

SUPPLEMENT

1988 AND LATER SERVICE INFORMATION

This chapter contains all procedures and specifications unique to the Kawasaki ZX1000 (ZX-10) and ZX1100 (ZX-11) from 1988-on. If a specific procedure is not included in this supplement, unless otherwise specified refer to ZX1000 models in the chapters of the main body.

The headings in this supplement correspond to those in the chapters of this book.

CHAPTER ONE

GENERAL INFORMATION

Table 1 ENGINE SERIAL NUMBERS (U.S. MODELS)

Year and model	Engine serial No. start to end	VIN serial No. start to end
1988 ZX1000-B1	ZXT00AE-028501 to *	JKAZXCB1-JA000001-*
1989 ZX1000-B2	ZXT00AE-040311 to *	JKAZXCB1-KA012001-*
1990 ZX1000-B3	ZXT00AE-028501 to *	JKAZXCB1-LA028001-*
1990 ZX1100-C1	ZXT10CE-000001 to *	JKAZXBC1-NB501700-NB504601
1991 ZX1100-C2	ZXT10CE-013001 to *	JKAZXBC1-MB501701-MB504600
1992 ZX1100-C3	ZXT10CE-024001 to *	JKAZXBC1-NB504601-*
1993 ZX1100-C4	ZXT10CE-*	JKAZXBC1-PB508201-*
1993 ZX1100-D1	ZXT10DE-000001 to *	JKAZXBD1-PB500001-*
1994-on	NA	NA
1994 ZX1100-D2	ZXT10D-020001~	JKAZXBD1-RA020001~
1995 ZX1100-D3	ZXT10D-032001~	JKAZXBD1-SA032001~
1996 ZX1100-D4	ZXT10D-039001~	JKAZXBD1-TA039001~
1997 ZX1100-D5	ZXT10D-045001~	JKAZXBD1-VA045001~
1998 ZX1100-D6	NA	NA
1999 ZX1100-D7	NA	JKAZXBD1-XA058001~
2000 ZX1100-D8	NA	JKAZXBD1-YA069001~
2001 ZX1100-D9	NA	JKAZXBD1-1A075001~
*Not specified.		

CHAPTER TWO

TROUBLESHOOTING

NOTE
This chapter covers all procedures unique to the Kawasaki ZX1000 (ZX-10) and ZX1100 (ZX-11) from 1988-on. If a specific procedure is not included in this chapter, unless otherwise specified refer to ZX1000 models in Chapter Two at the front of this manual for service procedures.

CHARGING SYSTEM TROUBLESHOOTING

The charging system troubleshooting procedure is the same as on previous models with the exception of the circuit layout. Refer to **Figure 1** for this procedure.

Refer to **Table 1** for alternator coil resistance specifications.

IGNITION SYSTEM

The ignition system is the same as on previous models with the exception of the circuit layout. Refer to **Figure 2** for this procedure.

Ignition Coil Testing

The test procedure is the same as on previous models. Refer to **Table 1** for ignition coil primary and secondary resistance specifications.

14

STARTING SYSTEM

The starting system is the same as on previous models with the exception of the circuit layout. Refer to **Figure 3** for this procedure.

FRONT SUSPENSION AND STEERING

The fork assemblies used on these models do not have the anti-dive unit that was equipped on previous models.

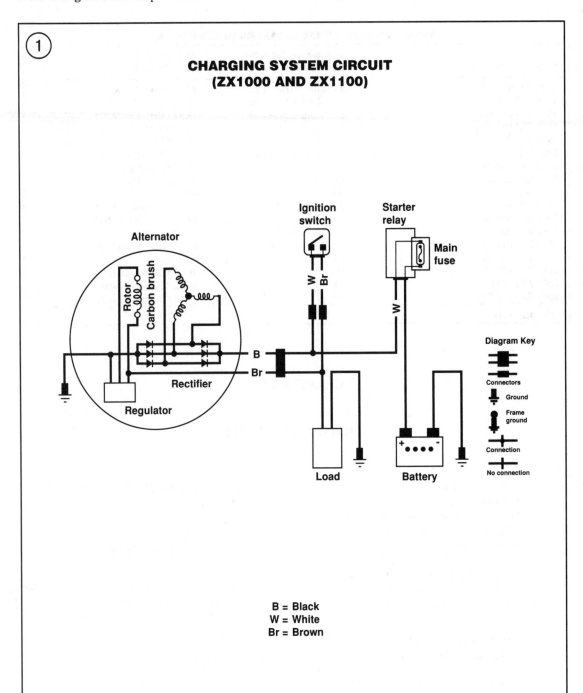

CHARGING SYSTEM CIRCUIT (ZX1000 AND ZX1100)

B = Black
W = White
Br = Brown

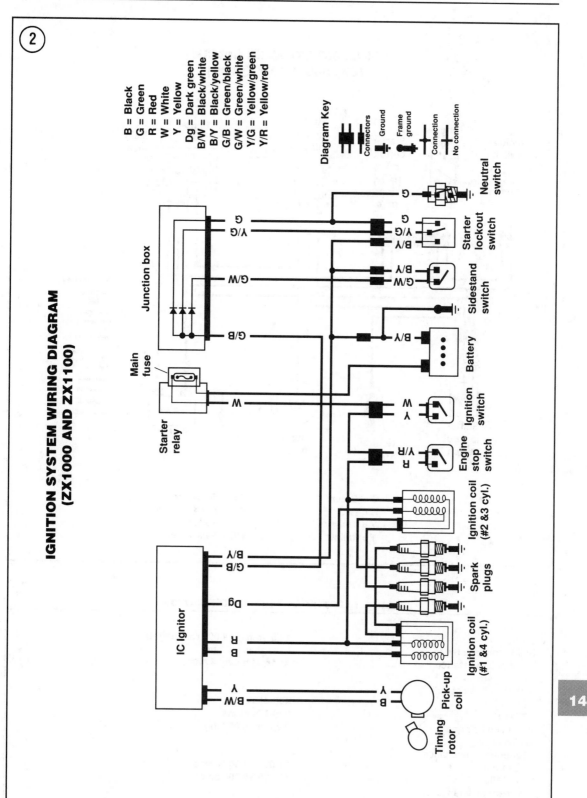

IGNITION SYSTEM WIRING DIAGRAM (ZX1000 AND ZX1100)

B = Black
G = Green
R = Red
W = White
Y = Yellow
Dg = Dark green
B/W = Black/white
B/Y = Black/yellow
G/B = Green/black
G/W = Green/white
Y/G = Yellow/green
Y/R = Yellow/red

Diagram Key

Connectors
Ground
Frame ground
Connection
No connection

Neutral switch
Starter lockout switch
Sidestand switch
Battery
Ignition switch
Engine stop switch
Junction box
Main fuse
Starter relay
Ignition coil (#2 & 3 cyl.)
Spark plugs
Ignition coil (#1 & 4 cyl.)
IC Ignitor
Pick-up coil
Timing rotor

14

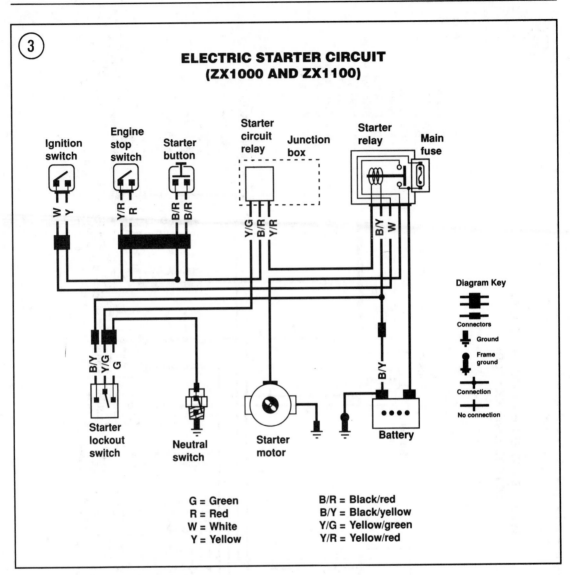

③ ELECTRIC STARTER CIRCUIT
(ZX1000 AND ZX1100)

G = Green   B/R = Black/red
R = Red   B/Y = Black/yellow
W = White   Y/G = Yellow/green
Y = Yellow   Y/R = Yellow/red

Table 1 ELECTRICAL TEST SPECIFICATIONS

Alternator	
Output	14.5 volts @ 4,000 rpm (night)
Stator coil resistance	Less than 1.0 ohm
Rotor coil resistance	Approximately 4 ohms
Ignition system	
Pickup coil resistance	
ZX1000	400-490 ohms
ZX1100	380-570 ohms
Pickup coil air gap	0.7 mm (0.027 in.)
Ignition coil	
Secondary resistance	
ZX1000	13,000-17,000 ohms
ZX1100	12,000-18,000 ohms
Primary resistance	
ZX1000	2.6-3.2 ohms
ZX1100	2.3-3.5 ohms

CHAPTER THREE

PERIODIC LUBRICATION, MAINTENANCE AND TUNE-UP

Your bike can be cared for by two methods: preventive and corrective maintenance. Because a motorcycle is subjected to tremendous heat, stress and vibration—even in normal use—preventive maintenance prevents costly and unexpected corrective maintenance. When neglected, any bike becomes unreliable and actually dangerous to ride. When properly maintained, the Kawasaki ZX-10 and ZX-11 will provide many miles and years of dependable and safe riding. By maintaining a routine service schedule as described in this chapter, costly mechanical problems and unexpected breakdowns can be prevented.

The procedures presented in this chapter can be easily performed by anyone with average mechanical skills. **Table 1** presents a factory recommended maintenance schedule. **Tables 1-5** are at the end of the chapter.

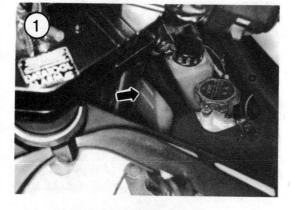

NOTE
This chapter covers all procedures unique to the Kawasaki ZX1000 (ZX-10) and ZX1100 (ZX-11) from 1988-on. If a specific procedure is not included in this chapter, unless otherwise specified refer to ZX1000 models in Chapter Three at the front of this manual for service procedures.

ROUTINE CHECKS

Coolant Level

Check the coolant level when the engine is cool.
1. Park the motorcycle on the centerstand on level ground.
2A. On ZX-10 and ZX-11 C1-4 models, perform the following:
  a. Check the coolant level through the level gauge in the coolant reservoir tank. The reservoir tank is located under the right-hand side of the upper fairing.
  b. The level should be between the "U" (upper) and "L" (lower) level lines on the side of the tank (**Figure 1**).
2B. On ZX-11 D1 models, perform the following:
  a. Remove the seat.
  b. Check the coolant level through the level gauge in the coolant reservoir tank. The reservoir tank is located under the right-hand frame side cover and the level gauge can be seen between the frame rail and the rear fender inner panel.
  c. The level should be between the "U" (upper) and "L" (lower) level lines on the side of the tank.
3. If necessary, add coolant to the reservoir tank (not the radiator) so the level is to the "U" upper level line.
4. On ZX-10 and ZX-11 C1-4 models, remove the screw(s) securing the upper fairing right-hand side cover (**Figure 2**) and remove the cover.
5. Add coolant as follows:

14

WARNING
Do not add coolant to the radiator filler cap (A, Figure 3).

a. On ZX-10 and ZX-11 C1-4 models, remove the reservoir cap (B, **Figure 3**).

b. On ZX-11 D1-9 models, remove the cap reservoir (**Figure 4**).

c. Add coolant to the tank and reinstall the cap securely.

6. Install all parts removed.

Tire Pressure

Tire pressure must be checked with the tires cold. Correct tire pressure depends on the load you are carrying. See **Table 2** for recommended tire pressure.

Battery

The ZX-11 D-1 is equipped with a sealed battery that requires no routing maintenance other than to keep the terminals clean and free of corrosion and keep the terminal screws securing the leads to the battery tight.

The electrolyte level cannot be corrected on a sealed battery as the battery top is not removable.

TIRES

Tire Pressure

Tire pressure should be checked and adjusted to accommodate rider and luggage weight. A simple, accurate gauge can be purchased for a few dollars and should be carried in your motorcycle tool kit. The appropriate tire pressures are shown in **Table 2**.

NOTE
*After checking and adjusting the air pressure, make sure to reinstall the air valve cap (**Figure 5**). The cap prevents small pebbles and/or dirt from collecting in the valve stem that could allow air leakage or result in incorrect tire pressure readings.*

BATTERY (SEALED TYPE)

The ZX-11 D is equipped with a sealed battery that requires no routing maintenance other than to keep the terminals clean and free of corrosion. The electrolyte level cannot be checked nor corrected. Do not remove the sealed cap on top of the battery. This cap was used for the initial filling and charging of the battery and is not to be removed.

Removal/Installation

1. Remove the seat.
2. Remove the fuel tank as described in Chapter Seven in this section of the manual.
3. Remove the rubber strap securing the battery cover and remove the cover.
4. Disconnect the negative (–) battery cable from the battery.
5. Disconnect the positive (+) battery cable.
6. Lift the battery out of the battery box and remove it.
7. Rinse the battery off with clean water and wipe dry.

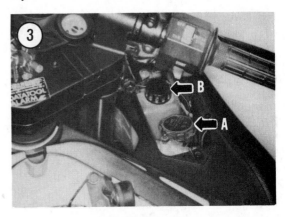

8. Install the battery by reversing these removal steps while noting the following:

   a. Position the battery in the case with the negative (–) terminal on the right-hand side of the bike.

   b. Coat the battery terminals with a thin layer of dielectric grease to retard corrosion and decomposition of the terminals.

   c. Attach the positive (+) cable first then the negative (–) cable.

Inspection

For a preliminary test, connect a digital voltmeter across the battery negative and positive terminals and measure the battery voltage. A fully charged battery should read between 13.0-13.2 volts. If the voltage is 12.3 or less the battery is undercharged.

Clean the battery terminals and surrounding case and reinstall the battery as described in this chapter. Coat the battery terminals with a thin layer of dielectric grease to retard corrosion and decomposition of the terminals.

Charging

The battery is a sealed type and if recharging is required a special type of battery charger must be used. Kawasaki recommends using a constant current type charger used in conjunction with an ammeter that is designed for use with this type of battery. It is recommended that the battery be recharged by a Kawasaki dealer to avoid damage to a good battery that only requires recharging. The following procedure is included if you choose to recharge your battery.

CAUTION
Never connect a battery charger to the battery with the leads still connected. Always disconnect the leads from the battery. During the charging procedure the charger may damage the diodes within the voltage regulator/rectifier if the battery leads were left connected.

1. Remove the battery from the frame.

2. Connect the positive (+) charger lead to the ammeter and then onto to the positive (+) battery terminal and the negative (–) charger lead to the negative (–) battery terminal.

CAUTION
Do not exceed the recommended charging amperage rate or charging time on the battery charging time label attached to the battery.

3. Set the charger to 12 volts. If the output of the charger is variable, it is best to select a low setting. Use the recommended charging amperage rate or charging time on the battery charging time label attached to the battery.

4. Turn the charger ON.

5. After the battery has been charged for the specified amount of time, turn the charger off and disconnect the charger and ammeter leads.

6. Connect a volt meter across the battery negative and positive terminals and measure the battery voltage. A fully charged battery should read 13.0-13.2 volts. If the voltage is 12.3 or less the battery is undercharged.

7. If the battery remains stable for 1 hour at the specified voltage, the battery is considered charged.

8. Clean the battery terminals and surrounding case. Coat the terminals with a thin layer of dielectric grease to retard corrosion and decomposition of the battery.

9. Reinstall the battery as described in this section.

New Battery Installation

When replacing the old battery with a new one, be sure to charge it completely before installing it in the bike. Failure to do so, will permanently damage the battery. When purchasing a new battery, the correct battery capacity for this model is 12 volts/14 amp hours.

14

Always replace the sealed battery with another sealed-type battery. The charging system is designed to have this type of battery in the system.

> *NOTE*
> ***Recycle your old battery****. When you re-place the old battery, be sure to turn in the old battery at that time. The lead plates and the plastic case can be recy-cled. Most motorcycle dealers will ac-cept your old battery in trade when you purchase a new one, but if they will not, many automotive supply store certainly will.* ***Never*** *place an old battery in your household trash since it is illegal, in most states, to place any acid or lead (heavy metal) contents in landfills. There is also the danger of the battery being crushed in the trash truck and spraying acid on the truck operator.*

PERIODIC LUBRICATION

Engine Oil Level Check

Engine oil level is checked through the inspection window (**Figure 6**) in the left-hand side of the crank-case behind the water pump.

1. Start the engine and let it reach normal operating temperature.
2. Stop the engine and allow the oil to settle.
3. Place the bike on level ground and on the center-stand. Make sure the bike is *straight up and level*.

> *CAUTION*
> *If the bike is not parked correctly, an incorrect oil level reading will be ob-served.*

4. The oil level should be between the maximum and minimum window marks. To add oil, remove the oil fill cap and add the recommended oil listed in the *Quick Reference Data* at the front of this book to raise the oil to the proper level. Do not overfill.
5. Reinstall the oil fill cap and tighten securely.

Engine Oil and Filter Change

Engine oil and filter change is the same as on previous models with the exception of the tightening torque on the drain plugs. Refer to **Table 3** for recommended torque specifications.

Front Fork Oil Change

It is a good practice to change the fork oil at the interval listed in **Table 1** or once a year. If it becomes contaminated with dirt or water, change it immedi-ately.

> *NOTE*
> *The ZX-11 models are not equipped with a fork oil drain screw. The fork leg must be removed from the bike in order to change the fork oil.*

NOTE
*If you recycle your old engine oil **never** add used fork oil to the old engine oil. Most oil retailers that accept old oil for recycling may not accept the oil if other fluids (fork oil, brake fluid or any other type of petroleum-based fluids) have been combined with it.*

ZX-10

1. Remove the upper fairing as described in Chapter Thirteen in this section of the manual. This is necessary in order to reach the upper fork bridge bolt.

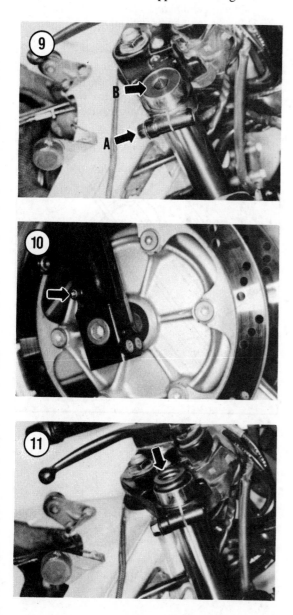

2. Place the bike securely on the centerstand with the front wheel off the ground.

3. Remove the steering stem cover (**Figure 7**).

4. Remove the Allen bolts (**Figure 8**) and lift the handlebar off the upper fork bridge. Move the handlebar assembly out of the way and keep both master cylinders in the upright position to avoid letting air into the brake or clutch hydraulic system while performing service procedures.

5. Loosen the upper fork bridge bolt (A, **Figure 9**).

6. Use a 1/2 in. socket drive extension and loosen the fork cap (B, **Figure 9**).

CAUTION
Cover the brake discs with shop cloths or plastic. Do not allow the fork oil to contact the discs. If any oil comes in contact with them, clean off with lacquer thinner or electrical contact cleaner. Remove all oil residue from the discs or the brake will be useless when applied.

7. Place a drip pan beside one fork tube, then remove the drain screw and sealing washer (**Figure 10**) and allow the fork oil to drain for at least 5 minutes. Never reuse fork oil; discard it but do not mix in with any engine oil that is going to be recycled.

8. Place a shop cloth around the top of the fork tube, the handlebar and the upper fork bridge to catch remaining fork oil while the fork spring is removed. Withdraw the fork spring (**Figure 11**) from the fork tube.

9. Repeat Steps 4-8 for the other fork tube.

10. Take the bike off the centerstand.

11. With both the bike's wheels on the ground, have an assistant steady the bike. Move the front end up and down several times to expel all remaining oil from the fork tubes.

12. Again, place the bike securely on the centerstand.

13. Apply a light coat of liquid gasket to the drain screws prior to installation.

14. Install both drain screws sealing washers and tighten securely.

NOTE
In order to measure the correct amount of fluid, use a baby bottle. These bottles have measurements in cubic centimeters (cc) and fluid ounces (oz.) imprinted on the side.

14

NOTE
The amount of oil poured in is not as accurate a measurement as the actual level of the oil. You may have to add more oil later in this procedure.

15. Fill each fork tube with the specified quantity of SAE 10W-20 oil listed in **Table 4**.

NOTE
Kawasaki recommends that the fork oil level be measured, if possible, to ensure a more accurate filling.

16. Take the bike off the centerstand and slowly compress the forks several times to distribute the oil throughout the lower section of the fork assemblies.
17. Hold the bike vertical and completely compress the fork assemblies.

NOTE
Step 18 is performed with the front fork completely compressed.

18. Measure the distance from the top of the fork tube to the surface of the oil (**Figure 12**) with an accurate ruler or an oil level gauge.
19. Allow the oil to settle completely and recheck the oil level measurement. Adjust the oil level if necessary.
20. Place the bike on the centerstand with the front wheel off the ground.
21. Install the fork spring (**Figure 11**) into the fork tube.
22. Inspect the O-ring seal (**Figure 13**) on the fork cap; replace if necessary.
23. Install the fork cap bolt (**Figure 14**) and start the fork cap bolt slowly while pushing down on the spring. Start the bolt slowly and do not cross-thread it. Tighten it to the torque specification listed in **Table 3**.
24. Tighten the upper fork bridge bolts to the torque specification listed in **Table 3**.
25. Install the handlebar assembly and tighten the bolts to the torque specification listed in **Table 3**.
26. Road test the bike and check for oil and air leaks.

ZX-11

1. Remove the fork assemblies as described in Chapter Ten in this section of the manual.

2. Pull the fork cap straight up and out of the upper fork tube to avoid any damage to the damper adjust rod.
3. Withdraw the fork spring from the fork tube.
4. Turn the fork assembly upside down and drain the fork oil.
5. Move the fork slider in and out several times to expel all remaining oil from the fork tube.

NOTE
In order to measure the correct amount of fluid, use a baby bottle. These bottles have measurements in cubic centimeters (cc) and fluid ounces (oz.) imprinted on the side.

NOTE
The amount of oil poured in is not as accurate a measurement as the actual level of the oil. You may have to add more oil later in this procedure.

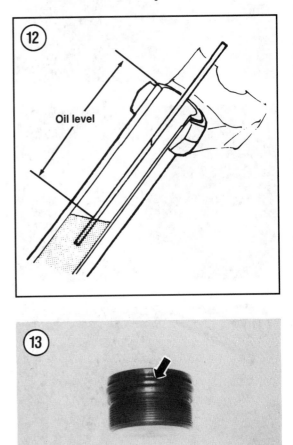

Oil level

6. Fill each fork tube with the specified quantity of SAE 10W-20 oil listed in **Table 4**.

NOTE
Kawasaki recommends that the fork oil level be measured, if possible, to ensure a more accurate filling.

7. Compress the fork assembly several times to distribute the oil throughout the lower section of the fork assembly.

8. Hold the fork assembly vertical and completely compress the assembly.

NOTE
Step 9 is performed with the front forks completely compressed.

9. Measure the distance from the top of the fork tube to the surface of the oil (**Figure 12**) with an accurate ruler or an oil level gauge.

10. Allow the oil to settle completely and recheck the oil level measurement. Adjust the oil level if necessary.

11. Install the fork spring into the fork tube.

12. Inspect the O-ring seal on the fork cap; replace if necessary.

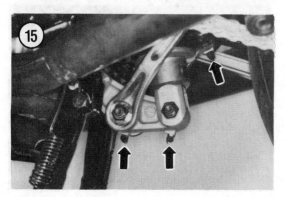

13. Install the fork cap bolt as follows:
   a. Carefully insert the fork cap bolt and adjust rod in the fork spring.
   b. Properly index the flat on the end of the damping adjust rod into the receptacle in the top of the damper rod.
   c. Start the fork cap bolt slowly while pushing down on the spring. Start the bolt slowly and don't cross-thread it. Once the fork cap is installed, it can be tightened after installing the fork tube into the bike.

14. Repeat Steps 2-13 for the other fork assembly.

15. Install the front forks as described in Chapter Ten in this section of the manual.

16. Road test the bike and check for oil and air leaks.

Swing Arm Lubrication

The swing arm needle bearings should be cleaned in solvent and lubricated with molybdenum disulfide grease at the intervals indicated in **Table 1**. The swing arm must be removed to service the needle bearings as described in Chapter Eleven in the front section of the manual.

There is a grease fitting provided to lubricate the pivot collar. Lubricate with molybdenum disulfide grease at the intervals indicated in **Table 1**.

Uni-Trak Lubrication

The Uni-Trak rocker arm and the needle bearings in both tie rods should be cleaned in solvent and lubricated with molybdenum disulfide grease at the intervals indicated in **Table 1**. The Uni-Trak linkage must be removed to service the needle bearings as described in Chapter Eleven in this section of the manual.

There is a grease fitting provided to lubricate the rocker arm and both tie rods (**Figure 15**). Lubricate with molybdenum disulfide grease at the intervals indicated in **Table 1**.

PERIODIC MAINTENANCE

Drive Chain Free Play

The adjustment procedure for drive chain free play is the same as on previous models with the following exceptions.

14

The recommended drive chain free play is as follows:

   a. On ZX-10 and ZX-11 C1-4 models: 30-40 mm (1.2-1.6 in.)

   b. On ZX-11 D1 models: 35-40 mm (1.4-1.6 in.)

The rear brake torque link nut is located below the swing arm instead of above it as on previous models. Refer to **Figure 16** for ZX-10 and ZX-11 C1-4 models or **Figure 17** for ZX-11 D1-9 models.

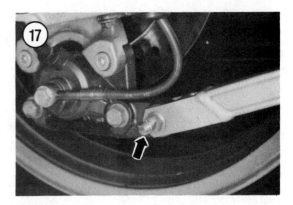

Disc Brake Fluid Level Inspection

1. Place the bike on the centerstand on level ground.
2. Turn the handlebar so the front master cylinder is level.
3. The front master cylinder brake fluid must be between the upper and lower level lines (**Figure 18**).
4. On ZX-11 models, remove the rear seat in order to view the rear master cylinder reservoir.
5. The rear master cylinder brake fluid must be between the upper and lower level lines. Refer to **Figure 19** for ZX-10 models or Figure 20 for ZX-11 models.

Disc Brake Pad Inspection

Inspect the disc brake pad for wear according to the maintenance schedule in this chapter.

The caliper configuration on ZX-11 models makes it impossible to inspect the brake pad thickness with the caliper installed on the disc. On these models, it is necessary to remove the caliper to inspect brake pad thickness. Refer to *Brake Pad Replacement* in Chapter Twelve in this section of the manual.

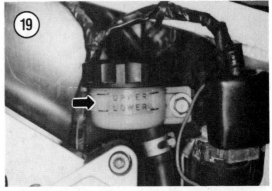

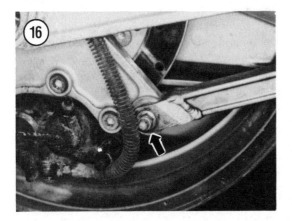

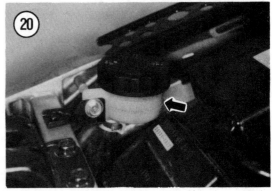

Disc Brake Fluid Change

The procedure for changing brake fluid is the same as on previous models except for the different locations of the bleed valves:

   a. ZX-10 models front caliper bleed valve: **Figure 21**.
   b. ZX-11 models front caliper bleed valve: **Figure 22**.
   c. ZX-10 and ZX-11 C1-4 models rear caliper bleed valves: **Figure 23**.
   d. ZX-11 D1-9 models rear caliper bleed valve: **Figure 24**.

Rear Brake Pedal Height Adjustment

1. Place the bike on the centerstand.

2. Check to be sure the brake pedal is in the at-rest position.

3. The correct height is approximately 45 mm (1 3/4 in.) below the top of the footpeg (**Figure 25**).

4. Loosen the locknut (A, **Figure 26**).

5. Measure the distance between centerlines on the master cylinder lower mounting bolt and the clevis

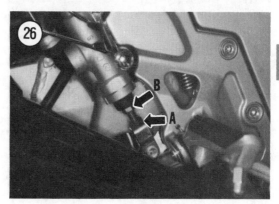

14

pin. Rotate the master cylinder pushrod (B, **Figure 26**) until dimension "A" (**Figure 27**) is achieved as follows:

    a. ZX-10 and ZX-11 C1-4 models: 118-120 mm (4.6-4.72 in.).

    b. ZX-11 D1 models: 79-81 mm (3.1-3.2 in.).

6. Tighten the locknut (A, **Figure 26**) securely.

Air Cleaner

A clogged air cleaner can decrease the efficiency and life of the engine. Never run the bike without the air cleaner installed; even minute particles of dust can cause severe internal engine wear.

The service intervals specified in **Table 1** should be followed with general use. However, the air cleaner should be serviced more often if the bike is ridden in dusty areas.

Refer to the following illustrations for this procedure:

    a. ZX-10 models: **Figure 28**.

    b. ZX-11 C1-4 models: **Figure 29**.

    c. ZX-11 D1 models: **Figure 30**.

1. Place the bike on the centerstand.

2. Remove the seat.

3. Remove the fuel tank as described in Chapter Seven.

4A. On ZX-10 and ZX-11 C1-4 models, perform the following:

    a. Remove the bolts securing the cover to the base and carefully separate the cover from the base. It is not necessary to completely remove the cover.

    b. Remove the element from the base.

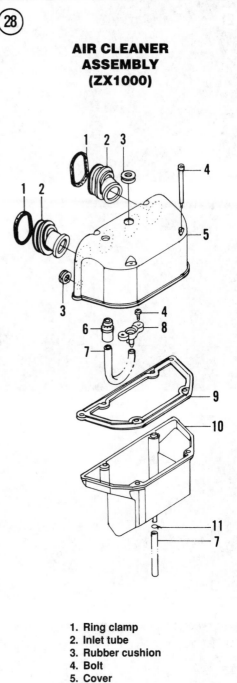

AIR CLEANER ASSEMBLY (ZX1000)

1. Ring clamp
2. Inlet tube
3. Rubber cushion
4. Bolt
5. Cover
6. Grommet
7. Hose
8. Fitting
9. Filter element
10. Base
11. Hose clamp

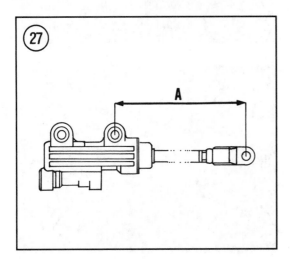

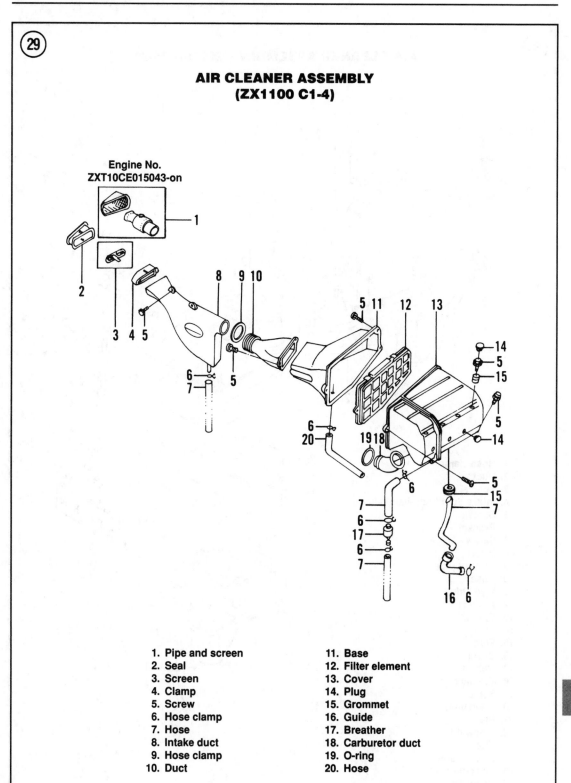

29

AIR CLEANER ASSEMBLY
(ZX1100 C1-4)

Engine No.
ZXT10CE015043-on

1. Pipe and screen
2. Seal
3. Screen
4. Clamp
5. Screw
6. Hose clamp
7. Hose
8. Intake duct
9. Hose clamp
10. Duct
11. Base
12. Filter element
13. Cover
14. Plug
15. Grommet
16. Guide
17. Breather
18. Carburetor duct
19. O-ring
20. Hose

14

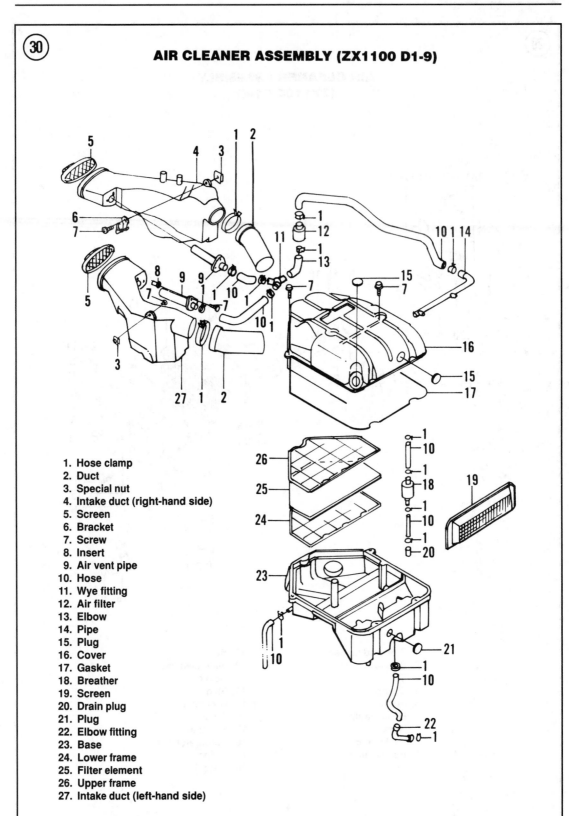

30 **AIR CLEANER ASSEMBLY (ZX1100 D1-9)**

1. Hose clamp
2. Duct
3. Special nut
4. Intake duct (right-hand side)
5. Screen
6. Bracket
7. Screw
8. Insert
9. Air vent pipe
10. Hose
11. Wye fitting
12. Air filter
13. Elbow
14. Pipe
15. Plug
16. Cover
17. Gasket
18. Breather
19. Screen
20. Drain plug
21. Plug
22. Elbow fitting
23. Base
24. Lower frame
25. Filter element
26. Upper frame
27. Intake duct (left-hand side)

4B. On ZX-11 D1-9 models, perform the following:

   a. Remove the bolts securing the cover to the base and remove the cover from the base.

   b. Remove the upper frame, the element and the lower frame.

5. Inspect the element for tears or other damage that would allow unfiltered air to pass into the engine. Replace if necessary.

6. If the element was torn or damaged, clean out the inside of the air box cover and base with a shop rag and cleaning solvent. Remove any foreign matter that may have passed through a broken cleaner element.

7. Clean the air cleaner element as follows:

   a. On ZX-11 D1-9 models, separate the element from the upper and lower frame.

CAUTION
Do not clean the air filter element with gasoline, as it represents an extreme fire hazard.

   b. Fill a clean pan of appropriate size with a non-flammable solvent.

   c. Submerge the air filter element into the cleaning solution and gently work the cleaning solution into the element pores.

   d. Rinse the filter element under warm water and remove all solvent residue.

   e. After cleaning the filter element, inspect it. If torn or broken in any area it should be replaced. Do not run the engine with a damaged filter as it may allow dirt to enter the engine and cause severe engine wear.

   f. Set the filter element aside and allow it to dry thoroughly or apply gentle air pressure to the element.

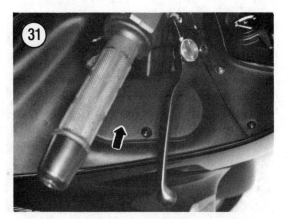

   g. Properly oiling an air filter element is a messy job. You may want to wear a pair of disposable latex gloves when performing the following steps of this procedure.

   h. Purchase a box of gallon size clear reclosable storage bags. These bags can be used when cleaning the filter as well as for storing engine and carburetor parts during disassembly.

   i. Place the cleaned filter element into a plastic storage bag.

   j. Pour SAE 30 motor oil onto the filter to soak it.

   k. Place the filter element and plastic bag on a flat surface and work the oil into the element's pours. Continue until all of the filter's pores are discolored evenly with the oil.

   l. Remove the filter element from the bag and check the pores for uneven oiling. This is indicated by light or dark areas. If necessary re-soak the filter element.

   m. When the filter oiling is even, place the filter element on a shop cloth on a flat surface. Place another cloth on top of the element and press out the residual oil from the filter. Continue until the element is as dry as possible.

8A. On ZX-10 and ZX-11 C1-4 models, perform the following:

   a. Install the element into the base.

   b. Move the cover into place on the base and install the bolts.

   c. Remove the bolts securing the cover to the base and tighten securely.

8B. On ZX-11 D1-9 models, perform the following:

   a. Install the lower frame, the element and the upper frame into the base.

   b. Install the cover and bolts. Tighten the bolts securely.

9. Install the fuel tank as described in Chapter Seven.

10. Install the seat.

Coolant Change

   The coolant change procedure is the same as on previous models with the exception of the radiator cap location.

   Remove the screw(s) securing the upper fairing right-hand side cover (**Figure 31**) and remove the cover.

   Remove the radiator cap (**Figure 32**) as described in Chapter Three in the main body of this manual.

14

SUSPENSION ADJUSTMENT

NOTE
The front fork on ZX-10 models is non-adjustable.

Front Fork
(ZX-11)

The standard setting for an average rider weighing 150 lbs. (68 kg) with no passenger and no accessories is as follows:
  a. Rebound damping force setting: 2nd click.
  b. Spring preload setting: 6th mark from the top.

Rebound damping force adjustment

The rebound damping force can be adjusted to suit various road and riding conditions. The adjuster has 4 different settings with the softest setting, No. 1, all the way *counterclockwise* and the stiffest setting, No. 4, all the way *clockwise*.

WARNING
Set both rebound damper adjusters to the exact same setting. Failure to do so may result in an unsafe riding condition that could lead to the loss of control of the bike leading to an accident.

Use a flat-bladed screwdriver and rotate the rebound damping force adjuster (A, **Figure 33**) in either direction to the desired setting. There is an audible click at each setting. Set both forks to the same *exact* setting.

Spring preload adjustment

The spring preload can be adjusted to suit various road and riding conditions. The preload adjuster has 8 different settings with the softest preload setting, No. 1 is with the adjuster all the way up and the stiffest setting, No. 8 is with the adjuster all the way down.

WARNING
Set both spring preload adjusters to the exact same setting. Failure to do so may result in an unsafe riding condition that could lead to the loss of control of the bike leading to an accident.

Use the open-end wrench provided in the owner's tool kit and rotate the spring preload adjuster (B, **Figure 33**) in either direction to the desired setting. Set both forks to the same *exact* setting.

Rear Shock Absorber Adjustment
(ZX-10)

The standard setting for an average rider weighing 150 lbs. (68 kg) with no passenger and no accessories is as follows:
  a. Air pressure: 0 psi (0 kPa).
  b. Damping force: 2nd position.

Air pressure adjustment

1. Place the bike on the centerstand with the rear wheel off the ground.
2. Remove the special bolt (A, **Figure 34**), then remove the right-hand frame side cover (B, **Figure 34**).
3. Remove the cap from the air valve (**Figure 35**).

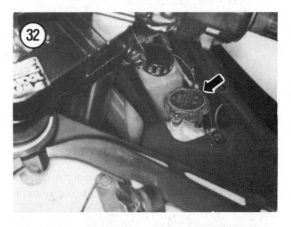

4. Check the air pressure with air pressure gauge provided in the owner's tool kit. Do not use a standard tire pressure gauge due to air leakage when taking the reading.

5. To lower air pressure, depress the valve stem and release the air to the desired pressure level.

CAUTION
Do not pressurize the rear shock to greater than 500 kPa (71 psi) as the

shock's internal oil seals will be damaged.

6. To increase air pressure, connect a small hand-held tire pump to the air valve. Increase air pressure to the desired pressure level.

Damping force adjustment

The damping force adjustment can be adjusted to suit various road and riding conditions. The damping force adjuster has 4 different settings with the softest preload setting No. 1 and the stiffest setting No. 4.

Rotate the damping force adjustment knob (**Figure 36**) and align the triangle mark on the knob with the desired number on the outer ring of the adjuster.

Rear Shock Absorber Adjustment (ZX-11)

The standard setting for an average rider weighing 150 lbs. (68 kg) with no passenger and no accessories is as follows:

    a. Spring preload: 18 mm (0.708 in.).
    b. Damping force: II position.

Spring preload

The spring preload can be adjusted by loosening the locknut and rotating the adjust nut at the top of the shock absorber assembly. Two special tools are required for this adjustment and this should be entrusted to a Kawasaki dealer.

Rebound damper adjustment

The rebound damping force adjustment can be adjusted to suit various road and riding conditions. The rebound damping force adjuster has 4 different settings with the softest preload setting No. 1 and the stiffest setting No. 4.

1. On models so equipped, remove the plastic protective cover at the base of the shock absorber.

2. Rotate the adjustment knob (**Figure 37**) and align the mark on the knob with the alignment mark on the shock absorber.

3. On models so equipped, reinstall the plastic cover. Be sure to reinstall this cover to prevent the knob from getting contaminated with road dirt.

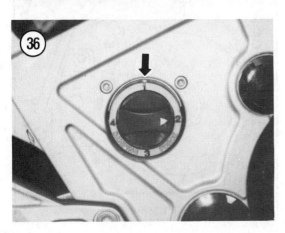

14

TUNE-UP

Valve Clearance Measurement

Valve clearance measurement and adjustment must be performed with the engine cool, at room temperature (below 35° C [95° F]). The correct valve clearance for all models is listed in **Table 5**. The exhaust valves are located at the front of the engine and the intake valves are located at the rear of the engine. There are 2 intake valves and 2 exhaust valves per cylinder.

1. Remove the cylinder head cover as described under *Cylinder Head Cover Removal/Installation* in Chapter Four in this section of the manual.

2. Remove all spark plugs. This will make it easier to rotate the engine.

3. Remove the bolts securing the pickup coil cover (A, **Figure 38**) and remove the cover and gasket.

> *NOTE*
> *The cylinders are numbered 1, 2, 3 and 4 from left to right. The left-hand side refers to a rider sitting on the seat looking forward.*

4. Use a 24 mm wrench on the signal generator rotor (**Figure 39**). Rotate the engine *counterclockwise*, as viewed from the left-hand side of the bike, until the pickup coil rotor "T 1.4" mark (A, **Figure 40**) aligns with the center of the pickup coil (B, **Figure 40**). Also, the lobes on the intake and exhaust camshafts for the No. 4 cylinder must point *away* from the engine (**Figure 41**). If the camshafts are not in this position, rotate the engine 360° (one full turn) until the camshaft lobes are pointing *away* from the engine. Also make sure the "T 1.4" mark is still aligned correctly.

5. With the engine in this position, check the clearance of the intake and exhaust valves as shown in **Figure 42**. The valves to be checked are as follows:

   a. Cylinder No. 4: intake and exhaust valves.

   b. Cylinder No. 3: exhaust valves.

   c. Cylinder No. 2: intake valves.

6. Check the clearance by inserting a flat feeler gauge between the shim and the rocker arm (**Figure**

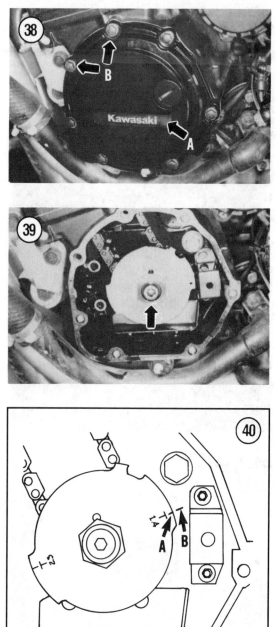

43). When the clearance is correct, there will be a slight drag on the feeler gauge when it is inserted and withdrawn. Write the clearance on a piece of paper and identify it as to cylinder number and intake or exhaust valves. This clearance dimension will be used during the adjustment procedure, if adjustment is necessary.

7. To correct the valve clearance, the small diameter shim on top of the spring retainer must be replaced with a shim of a different thickness. The shims are available from a Kawasaki dealer in 0.05 mm increments that range from 2.00 to 3.00 mm in thickness.

8. If any of the valves in this group require adjustment, do so at this time with the engine in this position. Refer to *Valve Clearance Adjustment* in the following procedure.

9. Use a 24 mm wrench on the signal generator rotor (**Figure 39**). From the position in Step 4, rotate the engine 360° (one full turn) *clockwise* until the pickup coil rotor "T 2.3" mark (A, **Figure 44**) aligns with the center of the pickup coil (B, **Figure 44**). Also, the lobes on the intake and exhaust camshafts for the No. 1 cylinder must point *away* from the engine. If the camshafts are not in this position, rotate the engine 360° (one full turn) until the camshaft lobes are pointing *away* from the engine. Also make sure the "T 2.3" mark is still aligned correctly.

10. With the engine in this position, check the clearance of the intake and exhaust valves as shown in **Figure 45**. The valves to be checked are as follows:

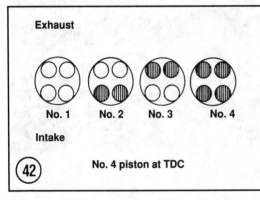

Exhaust

No. 1   No. 2   No. 3   No. 4

Intake

No. 4 piston at TDC

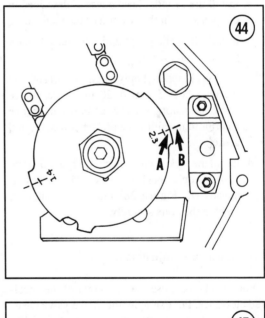

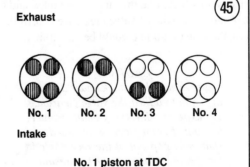

Exhaust

No. 1   No. 2   No. 3   No. 4

Intake

No. 1 piston at TDC

a. Cylinder No. 3: intake valves.

b. Cylinder No. 2: exhaust valves.

c. Cylinder No. 1: intake and exhaust valves.

11. Check the clearance by inserting a flat feeler gauge between the shim and the rocker arm. When the clearance is correct, there will be a slight drag on the feeler gauge when it is inserted and withdrawn. Write the clearance on a piece of paper and identify it as to cylinder number and intake or exhaust valves. This clearance dimension will be used during the adjustment procedure, if adjustment is necessary.

12A. If any of the valves in this group require adjustment, do so at this time with the engine in this position. Refer to *Valve Clearance Adjustment* in the following procedure.

12B. If all valves are within specifications, perform the following:

  a. Install the cylinder head cover as described in Chapter Four in this section of the manual.

  b. Install all spark plugs and connect all spark plug caps and wires.

  c. On ZX-11 models, apply a light coat of silicone sealant, about 5 mm (0.20 in.) wide, to the crankcase mating surfaces as shown in **Figure 46** prior to installing the pickup coil cover and gasket.

  d. Install the pickup coil cover (A, **Figure 38**) and gasket. Apply blue Loctite (No. 242) to the bolt threads (B, **Figure 38**) prior to installation. Tighten the bolts securely.

Valve Clearance Adjustment

For calculations, use the mid-point of the specified clearance. For example, the intake valve clearance is 0.13-0.19 mm, then the mid-point would be 0.16 mm. The exhaust valve clearance is 0.18-0.24 mm, then the mid-point would be 0.21 mm.

> *CAUTION*
> *Never install shim stock under an existing shim to adjust the valve clearance. The existing shim is very small in diameter and if shim stock is installed, the shim may pop out of the receptacle in the spring retainer at high rpm resulting in extensive engine damage.*

> *CAUTION*
> *Do **not** grind a shim to adjust valve clearance. The shim may fracture resulting in extensive engine damage.*

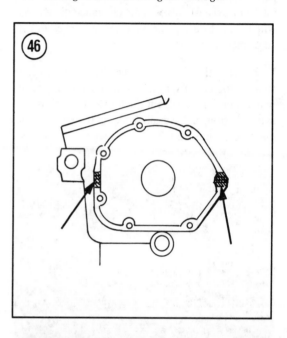

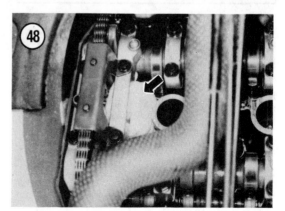

NOTE
If working on a well run-in engine (high milage), measure the thickness of the old shim with a micrometer to make sure of the exact thickness of the shim. If the

shim is worn to less than the indicated thickness marked on it, it will throw off calculations for a new shim. Also measure the new shim to make sure it is marked with the correct thickness.

1. Use a suitable tool and carefully slide the rocker arm off the small shim and rest it on the spring retainer (**Figure 47**).

2. Place a clean shop cloth (**Figure 48**) into the opening in the cylinder head directly under the cam chain guide. This will prevent any small parts from accidentally falling into the crankcase.

3. Use a magnetic tool and remove the shim from the spring retainer (**Figure 49**).

4. Check the number printed on the shim (**Figure 50**). If the number is no longer legible, measure it with a micrometer.

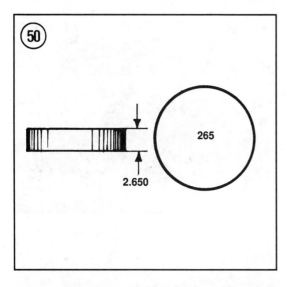

NOTE
*The following numbers are for **example only**. Use the numbers written down during the **Valve Clearance Measurement** procedure.*

Examples:	Intake	Exhaust
Actual measured clearance	0.47 mm	0.41 mm
Subtract specified clearance	–0.16 mm	–0.21 mm
Equals excess clearance	0.31 mm	0.20 mm
Existing shim number	220	245
Add excess clearance	+31	+20
Equals new shim number	251	265
(round off to the nearest shim number)	250	265

5. Apply clean engine oil to both sides of the new shim and to the receptacle in the spring retainer (**Figure 51**). Install the shim with the printed number facing down toward the spring retainer. Make sure the shim is correctly positioned within the spring retainer—it cannot be cocked or the spring retainer will be damaged. After the shim is installed, rotate it (**Figure 52**) to make sure it is correctly seated.

14

6. Hold the shim in place and using a suitable tool (**Figure 53**) slide the rocker arm back onto the small shim.

7. Repeat this procedure for all valve assemblies that are out of specifications.

8. After all valve clearances have been adjusted, use a 24 mm wrench on the pickup coil rotor (**Figure 39**) and rotate the engine *counterclockwise* several complete revolutions to seat the shims and to squeeze out any excess oil between the shim and the spring retainer.

9. Reinspect all valve clearances as described in the preceding procedure. If any of the clearances are still not within specification, repeat this procedure until all clearances are correct.

10. Install the cylinder head cover as described in Chapter Four in this section of the manual.

11. Install all spark plugs and connect all spark plug caps and wires.

12. Install the pickup coil cover (A, **Figure 38**) and gasket. Apply blue Loctite (No. 242) to the bolt threads (B, **Figure 38**) prior to installation. Tighten the bolts securely.

Spark Plug Heat Range

The spark plug heat range for the models covered in this section of the manual differs from previous models. Refer to **Table 5** for factory recommended heat range.

Spark Plug Removal/Cleaning (ZX-11)

Spark plug removal, cleaning and installation is the same as on previous models except that the air cleaner housing is located above the cylinder head and must be removed to gain access to the spark plug leads and spark plugs. Remove the air cleaner housing as described in this chapter.

CARBURETOR

Idle Speed

Idle speed adjustment is the same as on previous models with the exception of the location of the throttle stop screw. Refer to **Figure 54** and adjust idle speed as listed in **Table 5**.

Table 1 MAINTENANCE SCHEDULE*

Weekly/gas stop	Check tire pressure cold; adjust to suit load and speed
	Check brakes for solid feel
	Check brake pedal play; adjust if necessary
	Check throttle grip for smooth opening and return
	Check for smooth but not loose steering
	Check axles, suspension, controls and linkage bolts, nuts and fasteners; tighten if necessary
	Check engine oil level; add oil if necessary
	Check lights and horn operation, especially brake light
	Check for abnormal engine noises and fluid leaks
	Check coolant level
	Check kill switch operation
	Lubricate drive chain
Monthly	Check battery electrolyte level (non-sealed type) (more frequently in hot weather); add distilled water if necessary
	Check disc brake fluid level; add if necessary
	Check clutch fluid level; add if necessary
	Check drive chain tension; adjust if necessary
6 months/3,000 miles (5,000 km)	All above checks and the following
	Check carburetor synchronization; adjust if necessary
	Check idle speed; adjust if necessary
	Check spark plugs, set gap; replace if necessary
	Check air suction valve
	Check evaporative emission control system**
	Check brake pad wear
	Check brake switch operation; adjust if necessary
	Check rear brake pedal free play; adjust if necessary
	Check steering free play; adjust if necessary
	Check drive chain wear
	Check tire wear
	Lubricate all pivot points
	Check and tighten all bolts, nuts and fasteners
	Clean air filter element
	Replace fuel filter
Yearly/6,000 miles (10,000 km)	Check throttle free play; adjust if necessary
	Check valve clearance; adjust if necessary
	Change engine oil and filter
	Check the fuel system hoses, clamps and all fittings
	Lubricate swing arm pivot shaft
	Lubricate Uni-Trak linkage
	Check radiator hoses
2 years/9,000 miles (15,000 km)	Change fork oil
	Change brake fluid
12,000 miles (20,000 km)	Replace air filter element (or every 5 cleanings)
Every 2 years	Change clutch fluid
	Change coolant
	Lubricate steering stem bearings
	Replace master cylinder cups and seals (brake and clutch)
	Replace caliper piston seals and dust seals
	Lubricate wheel bearings
	Lubricate speedometer gear
Every 4 years	Replace all fuel hoses
	Replace all brake fluid hoses

*This Kawasaki Factory maintenance schedule should be considered as a guide to general maintenance and lubrication intervals. Harder than normal use (racing) and exposure to mud, water, sand, high humidity, etc. will naturally dictate more frequent attention to most maintenance items.
**California models.

14

Table 2   TIRE INFLATION PRESSURE*

Tire size	Pressure	Tire wear limit
Front		
ZX1000		
120/70 VR17-V280	36 psi (2.5 kg/cm²)	1 mm (1/32 in.)
ZX1100		
120/70 ZR17	41 psi (2.9 kg/cm2)	1 mm (1/32 in.)
Rear		
ZX1000		
160/60 VR18-V280		
Under 80 mph (130 km/h)	41 psi (2.9 kg/cm²)	2 mm (3/32 in)
Over 80 mph (130 km/h)	41 psi (2.9 kg/cm²)	3 mm (1/8 in)
ZX1100		
180/55 ZR17		
Under 80 mph (130 km/h)	41 psi (2.9 kg/cm²)	2 mm (3/32 in)
Over 80 mph (130 km/h)	41 psi (2.9 kg/cm²)	3 mm (1/8 in)

*Check tire pressure when cold.

Table 3   MAINTENANCE TORQUE SPECIFICATIONS

Item	N•m	ft.-lb.
Oil drain plugs	29	22
Oil filter bolt	20	14.5
Fork cap bolt (ZX1000)	23	16.5
Upper fork bridge bolt (ZX1000)	28	21
Handlebar Allen bolts	20	14.5

Table 4   FRONT FORK OIL CAPACITY AND OIL LEVEL

Model	Change cc (oz.)	Rebuild cc (oz.)	Oil level* mm (in.)
ZX1000	360 (12.17)	415-423 (14.03-14.30)	128-132 mm (5.0-5.19)
ZX1100 C1-4	390 (13.18)	454-462 (15.35-15.62)	147-151 mm (5.78-5.94)
ZX1100 D1-9	410 (13.86)	461-469 (15.59-15.86)	131-135 mm (5.15-5.31)

*Fork assembly fully compressed.

Table 5   TUNE-UP SPECIFICATIONS

Spark plug gap	0.7-0.8 mm (0.028-0.031 in.)
Valve clearance (cold)	
Intake	0.13-0.19 mm (0.005-0.007 in.)
Exhaust	0.18-0.24 mm (0.007-0.009 in.)
Spark plug	
Type	
U.S.	NGK C9E, ND U27ES-N
All other	NGK CR9E, ND U27ESR-N
Idle speed	950-1,050 rpm

CHAPTER FOUR

ENGINE

The engine is a liquid-cooled, inline four. It has two chain-driven overhead camshafts which operate four valves per cylinder.

Table 1 lists general engine information unique to the models covered in this chapter. **Tables 1-3** are at the end of this chapter.

> *NOTE*
> *This chapter covers all procedures unique to the Kawasaki ZX1000 (ZX-10) and ZX1100 (ZX-11) from 1988-on. If a specific procedure is not included in this chapter, unless otherwise specified refer to ZX1000 models in Chapter Four at the front of this manual for service procedures.*

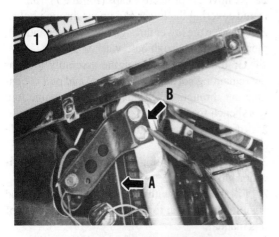

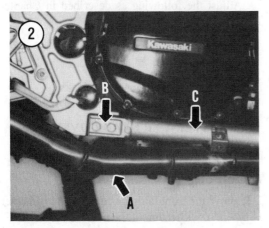

ENGINE

Removal/Installation

1. Remove the seat.

2. Remove the front fairing as described in Chapter Thirteen in this section of the manual.

3. Remove the fuel tank as described in Chapter Seven in this section of the manual.

4. Drain the engine oil as described in Chapter Three in this section of the manual and Chapter Three at the front of this manual.

5. Drain the coolant and remove the radiator (A, **Figure 1**) as described in Chapter Nine at the front of this manual.

6. Remove the oil cooler as described in this chapter (ZX-11) in this section of the manual and Chapter Four (ZX-10) at the front of this manual.

7. Remove the exhaust system (A, **Figure 2**) as described in Chapter Seven in this section of the manual.

8. Disconnect the spark plug leads and tie them up out of the way.

9. Remove the carburetor assembly as described in Chapter Seven in this section of the manual.

10. Remove the fuel pump and filter as described in Chapter Seven in this section of the manual.

11. Remove the clutch slave cylinder as described in Chapter Five at the front of this manual.

12. Remove the engine sprocket as described in Chapter Four at the front of this manual.

13. On U.S. models, remove the air suction valve assembly as described in Chapter Seven at the front of this manual.

14. Disconnect the following electrical connectors:

    a. Alternator.

    b. Neutral indicator.

    c. Pickup coil.

    d. Battery negative lead.

    e. Oil pressure indicator switch.

    f. Starter motor.

    g. Sidestand indicator.

14

NOTE
If you are just removing the engine and are not planning to disassemble it, do not perform Step 15.

15. If the engine is going to be disassembled, remove the following parts while the engine is still in the frame. Refer to this chapter unless otherwise noted:
    a. Alternator and starter (Chapter Seven at the front of this manual).
    b. Camshafts and cylinder head (Chapter Four in this section of this manual).
    c. Cylinder block (Chapter Four at the front of this manual).
    d. Pistons (Chapter Four at the front of this manual).
    e. Signal generator.
    f. Clutch assembly (in Chapter Five [ZX-10] in this section of the manual or in Chapter Five [ZX-11] at the front of this manual).
    g. External shift mechanism (Chapter Six at the front of this manual).
16. Take a final look all over the engine to make sure everything has been disconnected.
17. Place a suitable size jack, with a piece of wood to protect the crankcase, under the engine. Apply a small amount of jack pressure up on the engine.

NOTE
There are many different bolt sizes and lengths, different combinations of washers, conical washers, lock-washers and different spacer lengths. It is suggested that when each set of bolts, nuts, washers, spacers and holding plates are removed that you place them in a separate plastic bag or box to keep them separated. This will save a lot of time when installing the engine.

CAUTION
Continually adjust jack pressure during engine removal and installation to prevent damage to the hardware and the threads on the mounting bolts.

18. Refer to the following illustrations for engine mounting hardware for the various models covered in this chapter:
    a. ZX-10: **Figure 3**.
    b. ZX-11 C1-4: **Figure 4**.
    c. ZX-11 D1-9: **Figure 5**.

NOTE
Refer to the previous illustrations and note the locations of all washers and spacers. They must be reinstalled in the same location.

19. Remove the bolts, washers and nuts securing the front holding plates (**Figure 6**).
20. On ZX-11 D1-9 models, loosen the Allen bolts on the support collars on the upper and lower through bolts.
21. Remove the front bolts (B, **Figure 1**) and rear bolts (B, **Figure 2**) securing the sub-frame (C, **Figure 2**) to the main frame and remove the sub-frame.

CAUTION
The following steps require the aid of a helper to safely remove the engine assembly from the frame. Due to the weight of the engine, it is suggested that at least one helper, preferably 2, assist you in the removal of the engine.

22. Remove the protective caps (**Figure 7**) from the frame covering the lower and upper through bolts.
23. Remove the lower through bolt, washer and nut, then the upper through bolt, washer and nut.
24. Gradually lower the engine assembly to clear the remaining portions of the frame and pull the engine out through either side. Take the engine to a workbench for further disassembly.
25. Install by reversing these removal steps, while noting the following.
26. Tighten the mounting bolts to the torque specifications in **Table 3**.
27. Fill the engine with the recommended type and quantity of oil; refer to Chapter Three at the front of this manual.
28. Adjust the following as described in Chapter Three at the front of this manual.
    a. Drive chain.
    b. Throttle cables.
    c. Choke.
29. Start the engine and check for leaks.

CYLINDER HEAD COVER

Removal/Installation

1. Remove the seat.
2. Remove the front fairing as described in Chapter Thirteen in this section of the manual.

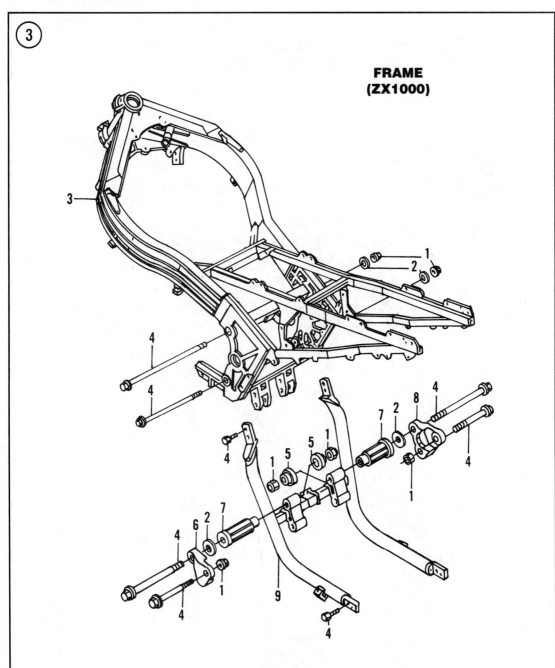

**FRAME
(ZX1000)**

1. Nut
2. Washer
3. Frame
4. Bolt
5. Side damper
6. Hanger plate (left-hand side)
7. Damper
8. Hanger plate (right-hand side)
9. Sub-frame

14

④

FRAME
(ZX1100 C1-4)

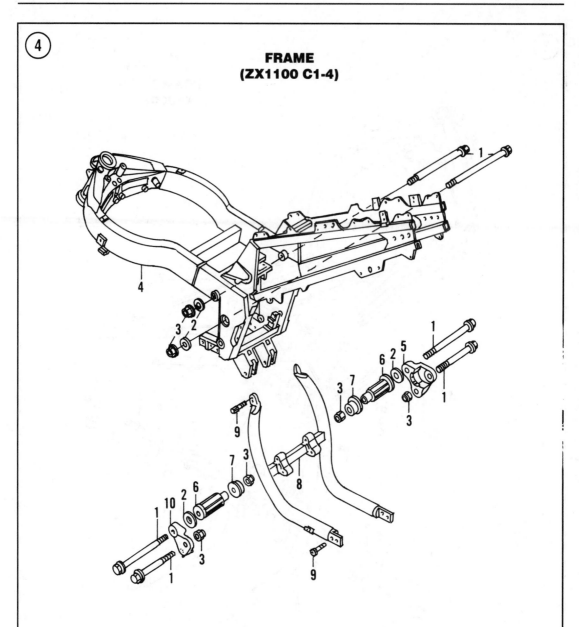

1. Bolt
2. Washer
3. Nut
4. Frame
5. Hanger plate (right-hand side)
6. Damper
7. Side damper
8. Sub-frame
9. Allen bolt
10. Hanger plate (left-hand side)

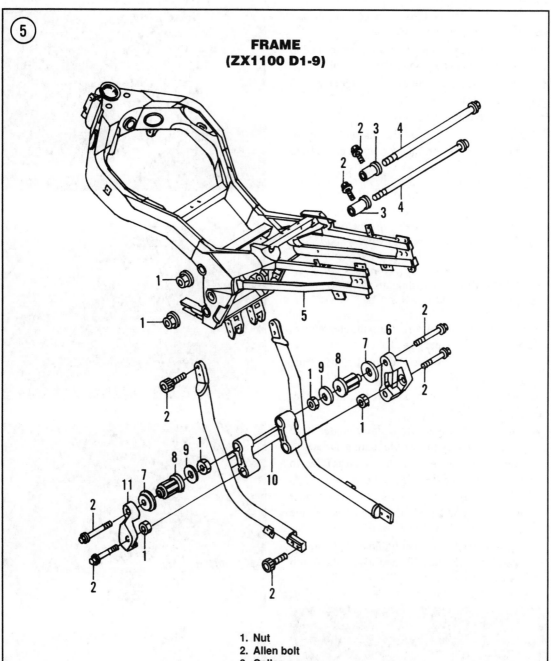

⑤

**FRAME
(ZX1100 D1-9)**

1. Nut
2. Allen bolt
3. Collar
4. Bolt
5. Frame
6. Hanger plate (right-hand side)
7. Side damper
8. Damper
9. Side damper
10. Sub-frame
11. Hanger plate (left-hand side)

14

3. Remove the fuel tank as described in Chapter Seven in this section of the manual.

4. Remove the carburetor assembly as described in Chapter Seven in this section of the manual.

5. Disconnect the spark plug leads (**Figure 8**) and tie them up out of the way.

6. Remove the baffle plate.

7. On U.S. models, remove the air suction valve assembly as described in Chapter Seven at the front of this manual.

> *CAUTION*
> *Four dowel pins are used to align the cylinder head cover to the cylinder head. When removing the cylinder head cover, one or more dowel pins may drop into the engine. If a dowel pin does fall, do not start the engine until the dowel pin is located and removed.*

8. Remove the cylinder head cover bolts and remove the cover (**Figure 9**) and gasket.

9. Install by reversing these removal steps, while noting the following.

10. Replace the cylinder head cover gasket, if necessary. Note the following:

    a. Remove all residue from the cylinder head cover and the cylinder head mating surfaces.

    b. Apply a non-hardening sealer (such as RTV) to the 4 cutouts on the cylinder head.

    c. Apply a coat of liquid gasket to the cylinder head cover and install the new gasket onto the cover.

    d. Apply a small amount of liquid gasket onto the dowel pins (**Figure 10**) and install them into the cylinder head.

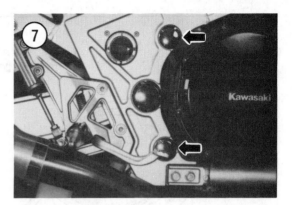

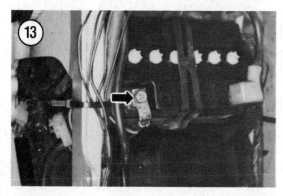

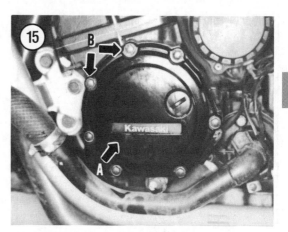

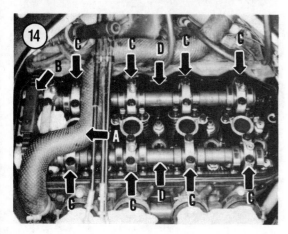

11. Install the small gaskets (**Figure 11**) onto each spark plug receptacle in the cylinder head.

12. Install the cylinder head cover.

13. Make sure the gasket (**Figure 12**) is in place in each bolt hole in the cover, then install and tighten the bolts to the torque specification listed in **Table 3**.

CAMSHAFTS

There are two camshafts mounted in the top of the cylinder head. EX (exhaust) and IN (intake) are cast into each camshaft for easy identification. Each camshaft has a sprocket installed on its left-hand side. The drive sprocket is mounted on the left-hand side of the crankshaft behind the ignition pickup coil assembly. A chain placed over the sprockets drive the camshafts.

Removal

1. Remove the cylinder head cover as described in this chapter.

2. Disconnect the battery negative cable (**Figure 13**).

3. Drain the engine coolant as described in Chapter Nine at the front of this manual.

4. Remove the clamps on the upper coolant hose (A, **Figure 14**) and remove the hose.

5. Remove the spark plugs. This will make it easier to turn the engine by hand.

6. Remove the bolts securing the pickup coil cover (A, **Figure 15**) and remove the cover and gasket.

14

NOTE
*The cylinders are numbered 1, 2, 3 and 4 from left to right (**Figure 16**). The left-hand side refers to a rider sitting on the seat looking forward.*

7. Use a 24 mm wrench on the signal generator rotor (**Figure 17**). Rotate the engine *counterclockwise*, as viewed from the left-hand side of the bike, until the pickup coil rotor "T 1.4" mark (A, **Figure 18**) aligns with the center of the pickup coil (B, **Figure 18**). Also, the lobes on the intake and exhaust camshafts for the No. 4 cylinder must point *away* from the engine (**Figure 19**). If the camshafts are not in this position, rotate the engine 360° (one full turn) until the camshaft lobes are pointing *away* from the engine. Also make sure the "T 1.4" mark is still aligned correctly.

8. Remove the camshaft chain tensioner (**Figure 20**) as described in Chapter Four in the front of this manual.

9. Place a clean shop cloth (**Figure 21**) into the opening in the cylinder head directly under the cam chain guide. This will prevent small parts from accidentally falling into the crankcase.

10. Remove the cam chain guide (B, **Figure 14**).

NOTE
*Each camshaft cap is marked with an arrow (pointing forward) and with a letter representing position. See **Figure 22**. If the camshaft cap markings on your bike differ from those in **Figure 22** or if there are no marks, label them for direction and position before performing Step 11.*

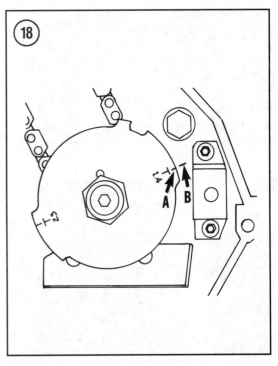

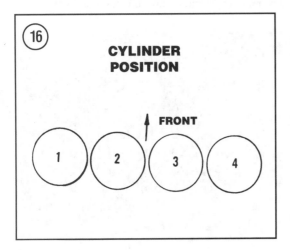

CYLINDER POSITION

11. Remove the camshaft cap bolts and remove the caps (C, **Figure 14**) and dowel pins.

12. Secure the camshaft chain with a piece of wire to keep it from falling into the engine. Then, remove both camshafts (D, **Figure 14**) and sprockets. Remove the camshafts slowly to prevent damaging any cam lobe or bearing surface.

CAUTION
The crankshaft can be rotated with the camshafts removed. However, pull the

chain tight to prevent it from jamming against the crankcase sprocket.

Inspection

The camshaft inspection procedure is identical to previous models. Refer to **Table 1** for specifications.

Installation

1. Replace the cam chain guide (**Figure 23**) if necessary.

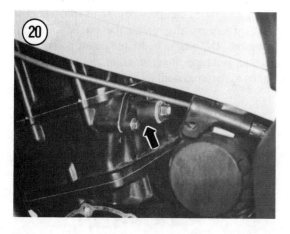

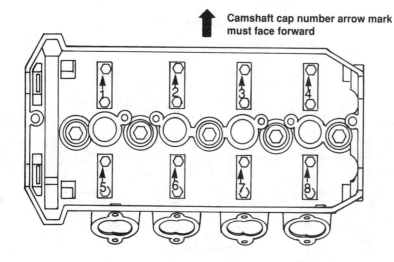

CAMSHAFT CAP ALIGNMENT

Camshaft cap number arrow mark must face forward

14

2. If the camshaft bearing clearance was checked, make sure all Plastigage material has been removed from the camshaft and bearing cap surfaces.

CAUTION
When rotating the crankshaft in Step 3, lift the cam chain tightly on the exhaust side (Front) to prevent it from binding on the crankshaft sprocket.

3. Use a 24 mm wrench on the signal generator rotor (**Figure 17**). Rotate the engine *counterclockwise*, as viewed from the left-hand side of the bike, until the pickup coil rotor "T 1.4" mark (A, **Figure 18**) aligns with the center of the pickup coil (B, **Figure 18**). The No. 1 and No. 4 cylinders are not at top dead center (TDC).

4. Coat all camshaft lobes and bearing journals with molybdenum disulfide grease or assembly oil.

5. Also coat the bearing surfaces in the cylinder head and camshaft bearing caps.

NOTE
Identification marks are cast into each camshaft. The exhaust camshaft is marked with EX and the intake camshaft is marked with IN.

6. Lift the cam chain and slide the exhaust camshaft through and set it in the front bearing blocks. Install the intake camshaft through the cam chain and set it in the rear bearing blocks.

7. Without turning the crankshaft, align the "EX" line on the exhaust camshaft sprocket and the "IN" line on the intake cam sprocket with the cylinder head upper surface as viewed from the left-hand side of the engine (**Figure 24**). It will be necessary to lift the cam chain off the sprockets to reposition the camshafts.

8. Check that the cam chain is properly seated in the front and rear chain guides.

9. Refer to **Figure 24**. Locate the first cam chain link pin that aligns with the exhaust sprocket "EX" mark. Beginning with this mark, count off 30 cam chain link pins toward the intake camshaft sprocket. The 30th pin must align with the intake camshaft sprocket "IN" mark. If the pin count is incorrect, recount and reposition the intake and exhaust camshafts as required until this pin count is correct.

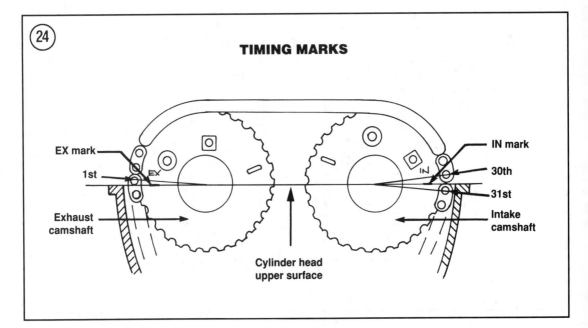

TIMING MARKS

EX mark
1st
Exhaust camshaft

IN mark
30th
31st
Intake camshaft

Cylinder head upper surface

10. Check that the camshaft cap dowel pins are in place and loosely install the camshaft caps in their original position. The arrow on each cap (**Figure 22**) must face to the front of the bike and the location numbering on the cap must correspond to the numbering cast into the cylinder head (**Figure 22**).

> *CAUTION*
> *The camshaft caps were align-bored with the cylinder head at the time of manufacture. If the caps are not installed in their original position, camshaft seizure may result.*

11. Tighten the camshaft cap bolts in the torque sequence shown in **Figure 25**. Tighten the bolts to the torque specification listed in **Table 3**.

> *CAUTION*
> *If there is any binding while turning the crankshaft, **stop**. Recheck the camshaft timing marks. Improper timing can cause valve and piston damage.*

12. Using a 24 mm wrench on the signal generator rotor (**Figure 17**), slowly rotate the engine *counterclockwise*, as viewed from the left-hand side of the bike, 2 full turns. Check that the timing marks on the pickup coil rotor "T 1.4" aligns with the center of the pickup coil (**Figure 18**). If all timing marks align as indicated, cam timing is correct.

13. If cam timing is incorrect, remove the camshaft caps and reposition the camshafts as described in Steps 3-12.

14. Install the cam chain guide and tighten the bolts securely.

> *NOTE*
> *Kawasaki has made an improvement on the cam chain tensioner assembly and it is suggested that this new assembly be installed at this time. The part number for the new assembly is No. 12048-1113.*

15. Install the cam chain tensioner as described in Chapter Four in the front of this manual.

16. Install the pickup coil cover (A, **Figure 15**) and gasket. Apply blue Loctite (No. 242) to the bolt threads (B, **Figure 15**) prior to installation. Tighten the bolts securely.

17. Install all spark plugs and connect all spark plug caps and wires.

18. Install the upper coolant hose and hose clamps. Tighten the hose clamps securely.

19. Install the cylinder head cover as described in this chapter.

20. Refill the engine coolant as described in Chapter Nine at the front of this manual.

21. Connect the battery negative cable.

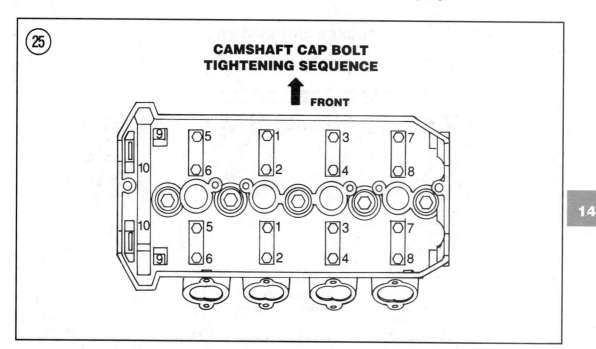

CAMSHAFT CAP BOLT TIGHTENING SEQUENCE
FRONT

14

ROCKER ARM ASSEMBLIES

There are 2 rocker arm shafts installed in the cylinder head. Each shaft has 8 rocker arms and 5 springs.

The intake and exhaust rocker arms are identical (same Kawasaki part No.) but they will develop different wear patterns during use. All parts should be marked during removal so they can be assembled in their original positions.

Only the *exhaust* rocker arm shaft can be removed with the cylinder head installed on the engine in the frame. Due to the frame configuration, the cylinder head must be removed from the engine in order to remove the intake rocker arm shaft.

Refer to **Figure 26** for this procedure.

Removal

1. Remove the camshafts as described in this chapter.
2. If both rocker arm shafts are going to be removed, remove the cylinder head as described in Chapter Four at the front of this manual.

NOTE
Remove one complete rocker arm shaft, rocker arms and springs. Mark all parts and keep them separate from the other set to avoid the intermixing of parts.

3. Remove the special Allen head bolt (**Figure 27**) and spring from the right-hand side of the engine.
4. Thread a M8 × 1.25 bolt (approximately 30 mm [1 1/4 in.] long) into the right-hand end of the rocker arm shaft.
5. Slowly withdraw the rocker arm shaft and remove each spring and rocker arm as they are freed by the shaft. Remove each part and keep them in the order and mark them so that they may be reinstalled in their original positions.
6. Repeat Steps 3-5 for the other rocker arm shaft assembly.
7. Wash all parts in solvent and thoroughly dry with compressed air.

Inspection

1. Inspect the rocker arm pad where it rides on the cam lobe and where it rides on the shim. If the pad is scratched or unevenly worn, inspect the cam lobe for scoring, chipping or flat spots. Replace the rocker arm if defective.
2. Measure the inside diameter of the rocker arm bore with an inside micrometer and check against

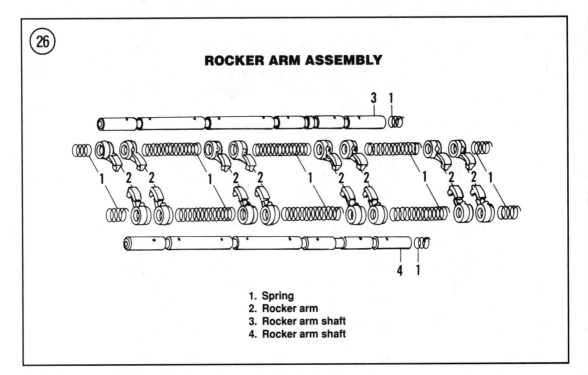

ROCKER ARM ASSEMBLY

1. Spring
2. Rocker arm
3. Rocker arm shaft
4. Rocker arm shaft

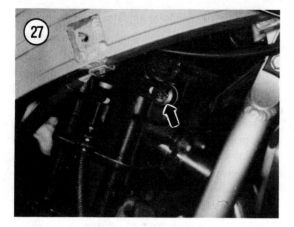

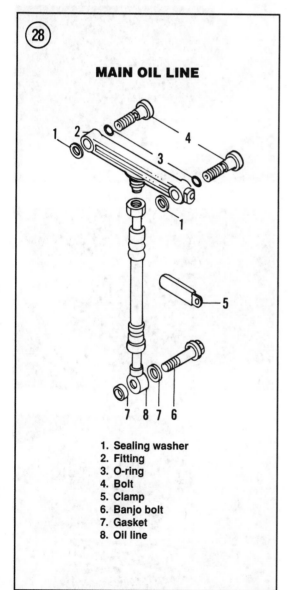

MAIN OIL LINE

1. Sealing washer
2. Fitting
3. O-ring
4. Bolt
5. Clamp
6. Banjo bolt
7. Gasket
8. Oil line

the dimensions in **Table 2**. Replace if worn to the service limit or greater.

3. Inspect the rocker arm shaft for signs of wear or scoring. Measure the outside diameter with a micrometer and check against the dimensions in **Table 2**. Replace if worn to the service limit or less.

4. Make sure the oil holes in the rocker arm shaft are clean and clear. If necessary, clean out with a piece of wire and thoroughly clean with solvent. Dry with compressed air.

5. Check the springs for breakage or distortion; replace if necessary.

Installation

1. Coat the rocker arm shaft, rocker arm bore and the shaft receptacles in the cylinder head with assembly oil or clean engine oil.

2. Refer to marks made in Step 5, *Removal*, and be sure to install the rocker arms and shafts back into their original locations.

3. Install the rocker arms and springs in their original positions in the cylinder head.

4. Position the rocker arm shaft with the bolt hole end going in last.

5. Partially install the rocker arm shaft into the cylinder head and through the first short spring and rocker arm. Continue to install the rocker arm shaft through the cylinder head boss, rocker arm, long spring, rocker arm and cylinder head boss. Continue across the cylinder head though all springs and rocker arms. Don't forget the last short spring on the left-hand end. Push the shaft in until it bottoms out.

6. Install the special Allen head bolt securing the rocker arm shaft and tighten to the torque specification listed in **Table 3**.

CYLINDER HEAD

Removal/Installation

The cylinder head removal and installation is the same as on previous models with the following exceptions.

Main oil line assembly

The main oil pipe assembly (**Figure 28**) is now located on the right-hand side of the cylinder head and is connected to the crankcase. Leave the oil line

14

attached to the cylinder head since the upper rear bolt (**Figure 29**) cannot be easily removed with the cylinder head installed in the frame.

1. Remove the banjo bolt (A, **Figure 30**) and sealing washers securing flexible oil hose to the crankcase.

2. Remove the bolt and clamp (B, **Figure 30**) securing the oil hose to the crankcase.

3. After the cylinder head has been removed, remove the upper fitting and flexible hose from the cylinder head. Don't lose the O-ring seals and gaskets on each of the 2 upper bolts.

4. Install by reversing these removal steps, while noting the following.

5. Be sure to install all O-rings and gasket in the correct location to avoid an oil leak.

6. Tighten the bolts to the torque specification listed in **Table 3**.

Left-hand camshaft bearing cap

If the cylinder head was removed with the engine in the frame and if the left-hand camshaft bearing cap (**Figure 31**) was removed during service to the cylinder head, the bearing cap must be reinstalled and the bolts tightened prior to installing the cylinder head. With the engine in the frame, there is insufficient clearance between the frame and cylinder head to tighten these bolts after the cylinder head is installed.

VALVE AND VALVE COMPONENTS

Service procedures for the valves and valve components are the same as on previous models with the exception of some valve specifications. Refer to **Table 2** for all applicable service specifications.

OIL COOLER (ZX-11)

Removal/Installation

Refer to **Figure 32** for this procedure.

1. Remove the upper and lower fairings as described in Chapter Thirteen in this section of the manual.

2. Drain the engine oil as described in Chapter Three in this section of the manual and Chapter Three at the front of this manual.

3. Loosen the oil cooler banjo bolts.

4. Remove the oil cooler mounting bolts.

5. Remove the lower bolt securing the cover to the bracket.

6. Move the oil cooler down and away from the radiator and remove the banjo bolts and sealing washers. Discard the sealing washers.

7. To remove the oil pipes, remove the exhaust system as described in Chapter Seven in this section of the manual.

8. Remove the banjo bolts and sealing washers securing the oil lines to the engine. Discard the sealing washers.

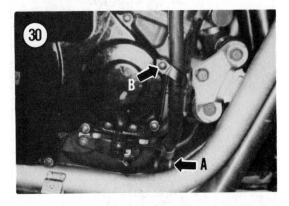

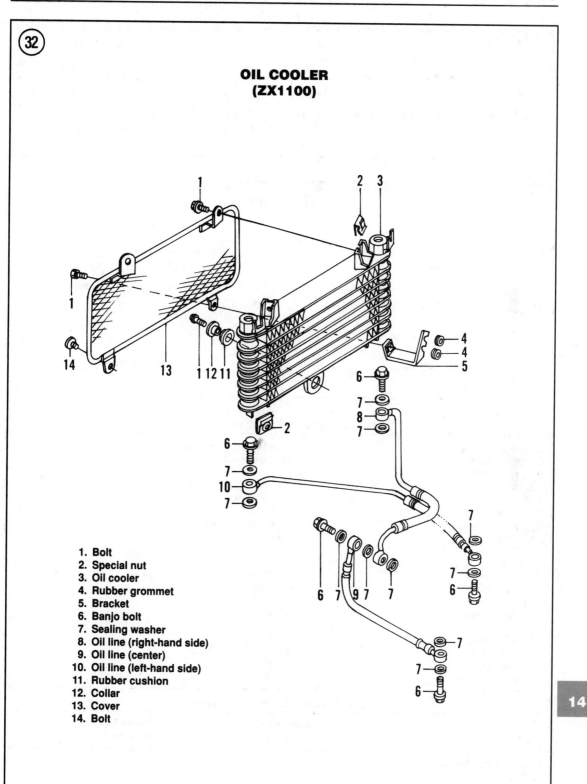

**OIL COOLER
(ZX1100)**

1. Bolt
2. Special nut
3. Oil cooler
4. Rubber grommet
5. Bracket
6. Banjo bolt
7. Sealing washer
8. Oil line (right-hand side)
9. Oil line (center)
10. Oil line (left-hand side)
11. Rubber cushion
12. Collar
13. Cover
14. Bolt

14

9. Install by reversing these removal steps, while noting the following:

a. Clean the banjo bolts in solvent and allow to dry.

b. Check all oil lines and fittings for leakage or damage.

c. Install new sealing washers and install one on each side of all oil line banjo bolts.

d. Position the oil lines onto the oil cooler and crankcase as shown in **Figure 33**.

e. Tighten the banjo bolts to the torque specification listed in **Table 3**.

f. Tighten the mounting bolts securely.

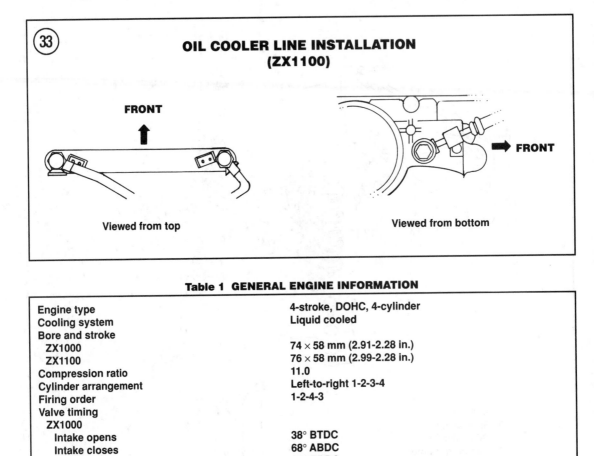

(33) OIL COOLER LINE INSTALLATION (ZX1100)

FRONT

Viewed from top   Viewed from bottom

Table 1 GENERAL ENGINE INFORMATION

Engine type	4-stroke, DOHC, 4-cylinder
Cooling system	Liquid cooled
Bore and stroke	
ZX1000	74 × 58 mm (2.91-2.28 in.)
ZX1100	76 × 58 mm (2.99-2.28 in.)
Compression ratio	11.0
Cylinder arrangement	Left-to-right 1-2-3-4
Firing order	1-2-4-3
Valve timing	
ZX1000	
Intake opens	38° BTDC
Intake closes	68° ABDC
Exhaust opens	60° BBDC
Exhaust closes	40° ATDC
ZX1100	
Intake opens	40° BTDC
Intake closes	70° ABDC
Exhaust opens	63° BBDC
Exhaust closes	43° ATDC

Table 2 ENGINE SPECIFICATIONS

Item	Specifications mm (in.)	Wear limit mm (in.)
Camshaft lobe height		
ZX1000		
Intake and exhaust	36.667-36.807 (1.443-1.449)	36.57 (1.439)
	(continued)	

Table 2 ENGINE SPECIFICATIONS (continued)

Item	Specifications mm (in.)	Wear limit mm (in.)
Camshaft lobe height (continued)		
ZX1100		
Intake	36.872-36.972	36.77
	(1.452-1.455)	(1.447)
Exhaust	36.687-36.787	36.59
	(1.444-1.448)	(1.440)
Camshaft bearing clearance	0.078-0.121	0.21
	(0.003-0.0047)	(0.0082)
Camshaft journal diameter	24.900-24.922	24.87
	(0.9803-0.9812)	(0.9791)
Camshaft bearing inside diameter	25.000-25.021	25.08
	(0.9843-0.9851)	(0.9874)
Camshaft runout	—	0.1 (0.0039)
Camshaft chain (20 links)	158.8-159.2	161.5
	(6.252-6.268)	(6.358)
Rocker arm inside diameter	12.000-12.018	12.05
	(0.4724-0.4737)	(0.4744)
Rocker arm shaft diameter	11.976-11.994	11.44
	(0.4714-0.4722)	(0.4503)
Cylinder inner diameter		
ZX1000	73.994-74.006	74.11
	(2.9131-2.9136)	(2.9177)
ZX1100	75.994-76.006	76.10
	(2.9918-2.9923)	(2.9960)
Piston outer diameter		
ZX1000	73.935-73.950	73.79
	(2.9108-2.9114)	(2.9051)
ZX1100	75.918-75.938	75.77
	(2.9888-2.9896)	(2.9831)
Piston/cylinder clearance	0.044-0.071	—
	(0.0013-0.0027)	
Piston ring groove clearance		
ZX1000 and ZX1100 C1-4		
Top	0.03-0.07	0.17
	(0.0012-0.0027)	(0.0066)
Second	0.02-0.06	0.16
	(0.0007-0.0023)	(0.0063)
ZX1100 D1-9		
Top and second	0.03-0.07	0.17
	(0.0012-0.0027)	(0.0066)
Piston ring groove width		
ZX1000		
Top	0.82-0.84	0.92
	(0.0323-0.0330)	(0.0362)
Second	1.01-1.03	1.12
	(0.0397-0.0405)	(0.0441)
Oil	2.51-2.53	2.6
	(0.0988-0.0996)	(0.1023)
ZX1100 C1-4		
Top	0.84-0.86	0.94
	(0.0331-0.0338)	(0.0370)
Second	1.02-1.04	1.12
	(0.0401-0.0409)	(0.0441)
Oil	2.51-2.53	2.6
	(0.0988-0.0996)	(0.1023)
	(continued)	

14

Table 2 ENGINE SPECIFICATIONS (continued)

Item	Specifications mm (in.)	Wear limit mm (in.)
Piston ring groove width (continued)		
ZX1100 D1-9		
Top	0.84-0.86 (0.0331-0.0338)	0.94 (0.0370)
Second	0.82-0.84 (0.0323-0.0331)	0.92 (0.0362)
Oil	2.51-2.53 (0.0988-0.0996)	2.6 (0.1023)
Piston ring thickness		
ZX1000 and ZX1100 D1-9		
Top and second	0.77-0.79 (0.030-0.031)	0.7 (0.028)
ZX1100 C1-4		
Top	0.77-0.79 (0.030-0.031)	0.7 (0.028)
Second	0.97-0.99 (0.038-0.039)	0.9 (0.035)
Piston ring end gap		
ZX1000		
Top and second	0.2-0.35 (0.008-0.014)	0.7 (0.028)
ZX1100		
Top	0.2-0.32 (0.008-0.0125)	0.7 (0.028)
Second	0.2-0.35 (0.008-0.014)	0.7 (0.028)
Cylinder head warpage	—	0.05 (0.002)
Valve head marginal thickness		
I ntake	0.5 (0.0197)	0.25 (0.010)
Exhaust	0.8 (0.0315)	0.5 (0.0197)
Valve stem runout	—	0.05 (0.002)
Valve stem diameter		
Intake	4.975-4.990 (0.196-0.1964)	4.96 (0.1952)
Exhaust	4.955-4.970 (0.195-0.1956)	4.94 (0.1945)
Valve guide inside diameter		
Intake and exhaust	5.000-5.012 (0.1968-0.1973)	5.08 (2.000)
Valve-to-guide clearance (wobble method)		
Intake	0.02-0.07 (0.0007-0.0031)	0.18 (0.0070)
Exhaust	0.06-0.11 (0.0023-0.0043)	0.21 (0.0083)
Valve spring free length		
Inner	35.5 (0.1397)	33.6 (0.1323)
Outer	40.5 (0.1594)	38.6 (0.1519)
Valve seat surface		
Outer diameter (ZX1000)		
Intake	30.8-31.0 (1.2126-1.2204)	—

(continued)

Table 2 ENGINE SPECIFICATIONS (continued)

Item	Specifications mm (in.)	Wear limit mm (in.)
Exhaust	26.3-26.5 (1.0354-1.0433)	—
Width (intake and exhaust)	0.5-1.0 (0.0196-0.039)	—
Valve spring tilt	—	1.5 (0.059)
Connecting rod side clearance		
ZX1000	0.13-0.33 (0.0052-0.0129)	0.50 (0.0197)
ZX1100	0.13-0.38 (0.0052-0.0149)	0.60 (0.0236)
Connecting rod bearing clearance		
ZX1000	0.036-0.066 (0.0014-0.0026)	0.100 (0.0039)
ZX1100	0.037-0.065 (0.0014-0.0025)	0.100 (0.0039)
Crankpin diameter		
Identification mark (ZX1000)		
0	34.993-35.000 (1.3776-1.3779)	—
No mark	34.984-34.992 (1.3773-1.3776)	—
I dentification mark (ZX1100)		
0	35.993-36.000 (1.4170-1.4173)	—
No mark	35.984-35.992 (1.4166-1.4170)	—
Crankshaft runout	—	0.05 (0.0019)
Crankshaft main journal diameter		
I dentification mark		
1	35.993-36.000 (1.4170-1.4173)	—
No mark	35.984-35.992 (1.4166-1.4170)	—
Crankcase main bearing bore diameter		
Identification mark		
0	39.000-39.008 (1.5354-1.5357)	—
No mark	39.009-39.016 (1.5358-1.5360)	—
Crankshaft side clearance	0.05-0.20 (0.0019-0.0078)	0.40 (0.0157)

Table 3 ENGINE TIGHTENING TORQUES

Item	N•m	ft.-lb.
Engine mounting hardware		
ZX1000, ZX1100 C1-4 all bolts and nuts	44	33
ZX1100 D1-9		
Support collar Allen bolts	20	14.5
All other bolts and nuts	44	33
Cylinder head cover bolt	9.8	87 in.-lb.
Camshaft bearing cap bolts	12	104 in.-lb.

(continued)

14

Table 3 ENGINE TIGHTENING TORQUES (continued)

Item	N·m	ft.-lb.
Rocker arm shaft special Allen bolts	25	18
Main oil pipe assembly bolts	25	18
Oil cooler banjo bolts (ZX1100)		
Oil line-to-oil cooler	25	18
Front oil line and right-hand oil line-to-engine	34	25
Left-hand oil line-to-engine	15	11

CHAPTER FIVE

CLUTCH

The clutch is installed behind the clutch cover on the right-hand side. Refer to **Figure 1** when performing procedures in this section.

NOTE
This chapter covers all procedures unique to the Kawasaki ZX1000 (ZX-10) and ZX1100 (ZX-11) from 1988-on. If a specific procedure is not included in this chapter, unless otherwise specified refer to ZX1000 models in Chapter Five at the front of this manual for service procedures.

Removal

The following special tools and an overhaul part will be required when removing and installing the clutch:

    a. Universal clutch holding tool (**Figure 2**).

    b. New clutch nut.

1. Remove the lower fairing as described in Chapter Thirteen in this section of the manual.

2. Remove the clutch cover (**Figure 3**) as described in Chapter Five in the front section of this manual.

3. Loosen the 6 pressure plate bolts (**Figure 4**) in a crisscross pattern. Then remove the bolts and spring holders.

4. Remove the pressure plate springs.

5. Remove the pressure plate (**Figure 5**).

6. Remove the friction (fiber) plates and clutch plates. Stack the plates in order of removal.

7. Remove the short pushrod, washer and bearing from the end of the transmission shaft.

8. Install a universal clutch holding tool (A, **Figure 6**) onto the clutch boss to prevent it from turning while loosening the clutch nut (B, **Figure 6**).

9. Loosen the clutch nut by turning it counterclockwise, then remove it (**Figure 7**). Discard the clutch nut as a new one must be used during installation.

10. Remove the splined washer (**Figure 8**).

11. Slide the clutch boss (**Figure 9**) off the mainshaft.

12. Remove the large thrust washer (**Figure 10**).

13. Install one or two 6 mm bolts (clutch cover bolts will work) into the collar (**Figure 11**). Pull the collar off of the mainshaft.

NOTE
To prevent installing the collar backwards, leave the bolt(s) in the collar until reinstallation.

CAUTION
Do not damage the bushing surface of the clutch housing on the transmission shaft during removal.

14. Remove the clutch housing as follows:

    a. Pull the clutch housing part way out (**Figure 12**) of the crankcase.

    b. Lift up on the bottom to clear the crankcase lower bolt hole boss (**Figure 13**).

    c. After clearing the bolt hole boss, move the rear portion of the clutch housing out of the crankcase (**Figure 14**) and remove the housing.

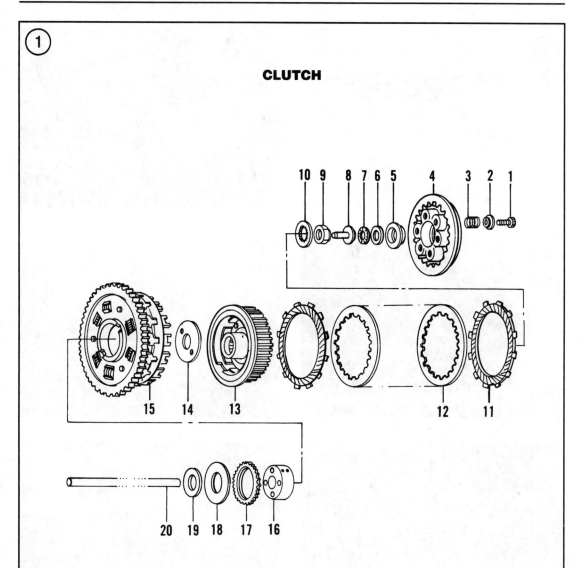

CLUTCH

1. Bolt
2. Spring holder
3. Spring
4. Pressure plate
5. Spacer
6. Washer
7. Bearing
8. Short pushrod
9. Nut
10. Splined washer
11. Fiber plate (9)
12. Clutch plate (8)
13. Clutch boss
14. Thrust washer
15. Clutch housing
16. Collar
17. Oil pump gear
18. Spacer
19. Spacer
20. Long pushrod

14

15. Remove the oil pump drive gear (A, **Figure 15**).

16. Remove the 2 spacer washers (**Figure 16**) from the mainshaft.

17. If necessary, remove the long pushrod by pulling it out of the mainshaft.

Inspection

1. Clean all clutch parts in a petroleum-based solvent such as kerosene and thoroughly dry with compressed air.

14

2. Measure the free length of each clutch spring as shown in **Figure 17**. Replace any springs that are too short (**Table 1**).

3. Measure the thickness of each friction disc (**Figure 18**) at several places around the disc. See **Table 1** for specifications. Replace all friction discs if any one is found too thin. Do not replace only 1 or 2 discs.

4. Inspect the friction disc tabs (A, **Figure 19**) for wear or damage, replace as necessary.

5. Check the clutch metal plates for warpage as shown in **Figure 20**. If any plate is warped more than specified (**Table 1**), replace the entire set of plates. Do not replace only 1 or 2 plates.

6. Check the driven gear teeth on the clutch housing (**Figure 21**). Replace if necessary.

7. Inspect the pressure plate (**Figure 22**) for signs of wear or damage; replace if necessary.

8. Inspect the fingers on the clutch housing (**Figure 23**) and grooves in the clutch boss (**Figure 24**) for cracks or galling where the clutch friction disc tabs and metal plates slide. They must be smooth for chatter-free clutch operation.

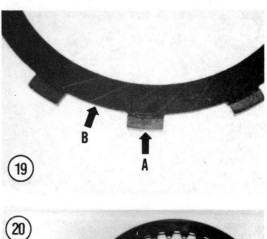

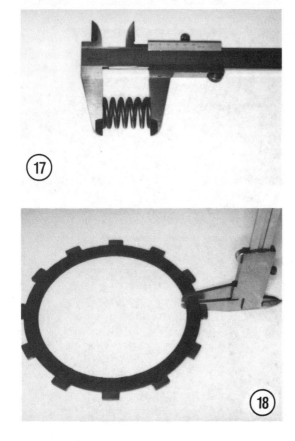

9. Inspect the inner splines (**Figure 25**) in the clutch boss assembly. If damage is only a slight amount, remove any small burrs with a fine cut file; if damage is severe, replace the clutch boss.

10. Make sure the circlip (**Figure 26**) is secure in the pressure place. Replace the circlip if necessary.

11. Inspect the long push rod by rolling it on a flat surface, such as a piece of glass. Any clicking noise detected indicates that the rod is bent and should be replaced.

12. Rotate the short pushrod bearing (**Figure 27**) by hand and check for excessive play or roughness. Replace the bearing if necessary.

13. Inspect the short pushrod bearing surface (**Figure 28**) and shaft (**Figure 29**) for wear or damage, replace if necessary.

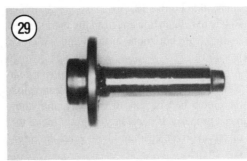

14

14. Check the clutch housing bushing bore (**Figure 30**) for cracks, deep scoring, excessive wear or heat discoloration. If the bearing bore is damaged, also check the clutch collar (**Figure 31**) for wear or damage. Replace worn or damaged parts.

15. See **Figure 32**. The tabs on the back of the oil pump drive gear (A) mesh with the 2 notches (B) in the clutch housing. Inspect all mating parts for wear or damage. If the oil pump drive gear teeth are damaged, also check the oil pump driven gear (B, **Figure 15**) for wear or damage. Replace worn parts as required.

Installation

1. Apply clean engine oil to all mating parts (shafts, splines, bearings) during assembly.

2. If removed, apply clean engine oil to the long pushrod and install it in the mainshaft.

3. Install the smaller diameter washer first and then the larger diameter washer (**Figure 16**) onto the mainshaft. Push them all the way on.

4. Install the oil pump drive gear (A, **Figure 15**) and mesh with oil pump driven gear (B, **Figure 15**) and push it on all the way. Rotate the drive gear so the raised tabs are horizontal at the 3 and 9 o'clock positions.

5. Mark the location of the oil pump drive gear notches on the front of the clutch housing. This will help with the alignment of the clutch housing to the oil pump drive gear.

6. Install the clutch housing onto the mainshaft as follows:

   a. Carefully install the clutch housing behind the alternator drive chain and partially onto the transmission shaft (**Figure 14**)

   b. Carefully guide the bottom portion over the crankcase lower bolt hole boss (**Figure 13**).

   c. After clearing the bolt hole boss, move the rear portion of the clutch housing up and into the crankcase (**Figure 12**).

   d. Rotate the clutch housing until the marks made in Step 5 are horizontal at the 3 and 9 o'clock positions.

   e. Align the raised tabs of the oil pump drive gear with the notches in the clutch housing and push the clutch housing on all the way until they mesh properly. If necessary, slightly move the oil pump driven gear until both gears are properly aligned.

NOTE
Position the collar with the threaded holes facing out.

7. With the clutch housing centered on the main shaft (**Figure 33**), and properly meshed with the oil pump driven gear, insert the collar (**Figure 34**).

8. Install the thrust washer (**Figure 10**) onto the mainshaft.

9. Install the clutch boss (**Figure 9**).

10. Slide on the splined washer (**Figure 8**).

11. Install the *new* clutch nut (**Figure 7**). Tighten to specifications (**Table 2**) using a torque wrench and holding tool to keep the clutch hub from turning (**Figure 6**).

NOTE
If you are installing new clutch friction plates, soak them in clean engine oil prior to installation to prevent clutch plate seizure during initial start-up.

NOTE
Stock factory Kawasaki friction plates have radial grooves cut in to the cork material. Install these discs so that the grooves will run into the center of the clutch housing when it rotates in a counterclockwise direction (as viewed from the right-hand side of the engine). See B, Figure 19.

12. First install a friction plate (**Figure 35**) and then a metal clutch plate (**Figure 36**). Continue to install the friction plate and clutch metal plates until all are installed. Friction plates have tabs that slide in the clutch housing grooves. The clutch metal plates' inner teeth mesh with clutch boss splines. Take care to align the clutch plates correctly.

13. The last item installed is a friction plate (**Figure 37**). Align this friction plate tabs with the special grooves (**Figure 38**) in the clutch housing. These clutch housing grooves are different from the grooves that all other friction plates were installed into.

14. Slowly apply the clutch lever and tie it to the handgrip in this position.

15. Apply molybdenum disulfide grease to the end of the short pushrod and install the bearing (**Figure 39**) onto it.

16. Install the washer (**Figure 40**) onto the bearing.

14

17. Slowly push the short pushrod, bearing and washer into the end of the mainshaft until it stops (**Figure 41**).

18. Make sure the spacer (**Figure 42**) is installed in the pressure plate and is correctly seated.

19. Install the pressure plate (**Figure 5**), springs, spring holders and spring bolts (**Figure 4**). Tighten the bolts in a crisscross pattern to the torque specification listed in **Table 2**.

20. Install the clutch cover as described in Chapter Five in the front section of this manual.

21. Install the lower fairing as described in Chapter Thirteen in this section of the manual.

Table 1 CLUTCH SPECIFICATIONS (ZX1000)

Item	Standard mm (in.)	Minimum mm (in.)
Clutch spring free length	46.3 (1.823)	42.7 (1.681)
Friction plate thickness	2.7-3.0 (0.106-0.118)	2.5 (0.098)
Friction and clutch plate warpage	—	0.3 (0.011)

Table 2 CLUTCH TIGHTENING TORQUES		
Item	N•m	ft.-lb.
Clutch nut	130	98
Clutch spring bolts	9.8	87 in.-lb.

CHAPTER SEVEN

FUEL, EMISSION CONTROL AND EXHAUST SYSTEMS

This chapter describes complete procedures for servicing the fuel, emission control and exhaust systems. Carburetor specifications are listed in **Table 1** and **Table 2**. **Table 1** and **Table 2** are at the end of the chapter.

NOTE
This chapter covers all procedures unique to the Kawasaki ZX1000 (ZX-10) and ZX1100 (ZX-11) from 1988-on. If a specific procedure is not included in this chapter, unless otherwise specified refer to ZX1000 models in Chapter Seven at the front of this manual for service procedures.

CARBURETOR

Removal/Installation

Remove all 4 carburetors as an assembled unit.
1. Park the motorcycle on the centerstand.
2. Remove the seat.
3. Remove the fuel tank as described in this chapter.

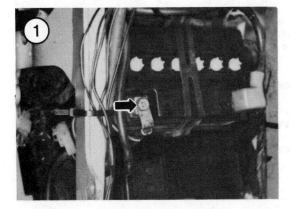

4. Disconnect the battery negative lead (**Figure 1**).
5. Remove the upper faring as described in Chapter Thirteen in this section of the manual.
6. Remove the air cleaner housing mounting bolts and hose clamps and remove the housing assembly. Refer to the following illustrations:
    a. ZX-10 models: **Figure 2**.
    b. ZX-11 C1-4 models: **Figure 3**.
    c. ZX-11 D1-9 models: **Figure 4**.
7. Loosen the clamp screw (A, **Figure 5**) and disconnect the choke cable (B, **Figure 5**) at the carburetor assembly.
8. Remove the carburetor-to-intake manifold boot clamps (**Figure 6**).
9. Disconnect the idle adjust screw from the rubber mount on the frame (**Figure 7**).
10. Grasp the carburetor assembly and work the assembly up and down and remove from the intake manifold boots.

NOTE
Label the 2 throttle cables before removal.

11. Disconnect the throttle cables at the carburetor (**Figure 8**).
12. Stuff a clean shop rag (**Figure 9**) into each intake manifold to prevent dirt from entering the engine.
13. Install by reversing these removal steps. Note the following:
    a. Make sure the carburetors are fully seated forward in the rubber intake manifold boots. You should feel a solid "bottoming out" when they're correctly installed. Tighten the boot clamps securely.

14

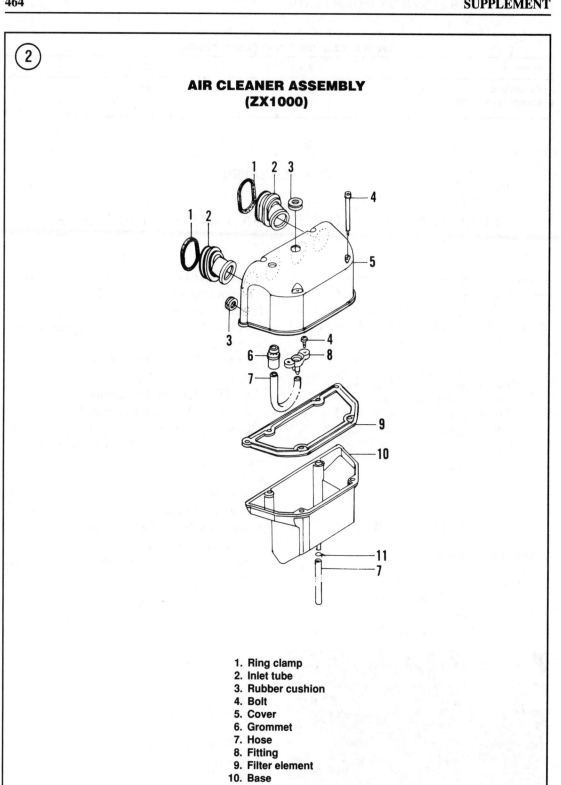

②

AIR CLEANER ASSEMBLY
(ZX1000)

1. Ring clamp
2. Inlet tube
3. Rubber cushion
4. Bolt
5. Cover
6. Grommet
7. Hose
8. Fitting
9. Filter element
10. Base
11. Hose clamp

③

AIR CLEANER ASSEMBLY
(ZX1100 C1-4)

Engine No.
ZXT10CE015043-on

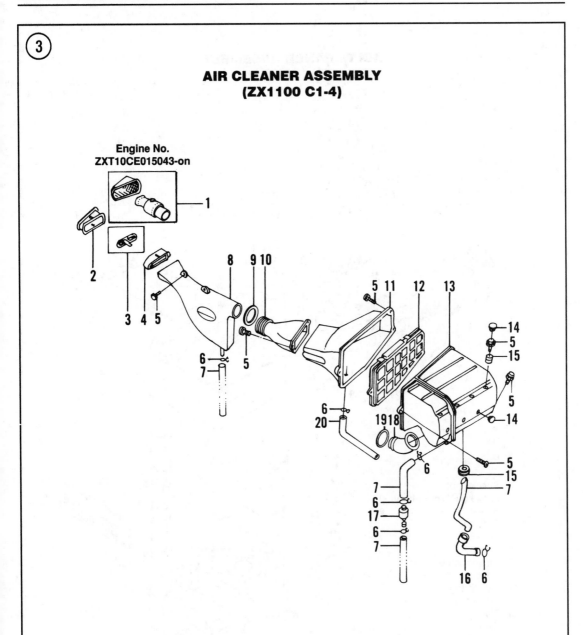

1. Pipe and screen
2. Seal
3. Screen
4. Clamp
5. Screw
6. Hose clamp
7. Hose
8. Intake duct
9. Hose clamp
10. Duct

11. Base
12. Filter element
13. Cover
14. Plug
15. Grommet
16. Guide
17. Breather
18. Carburetor duct
19. O-ring
20. Hose

14

④

AIR CLEANER ASSEMBLY
(ZX1100 D1-9)

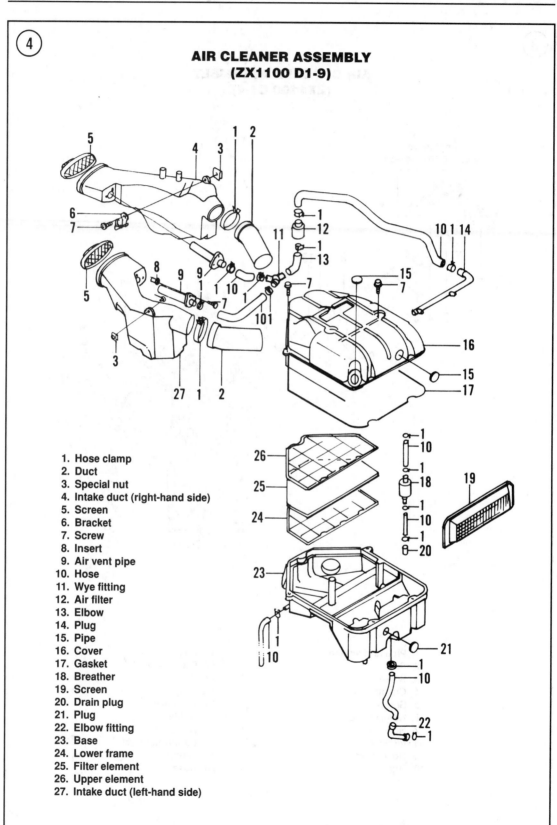

1. Hose clamp
2. Duct
3. Special nut
4. Intake duct (right-hand side)
5. Screen
6. Bracket
7. Screw
8. Insert
9. Air vent pipe
10. Hose
11. Wye fitting
12. Air filter
13. Elbow
14. Plug
15. Pipe
16. Cover
17. Gasket
18. Breather
19. Screen
20. Drain plug
21. Plug
22. Elbow fitting
23. Base
24. Lower frame
25. Filter element
26. Upper element
27. Intake duct (left-hand side)

CAUTION
Make sure the carburetor boots are air-tight. Air leaks can cause severe engine damage because of a lean mixture or the intake of dirt.

b. Tighten the air cleaner housing mounting bolts after the carburetors have been installed.

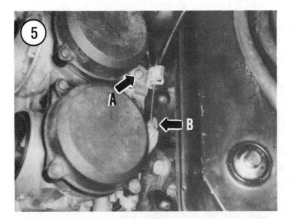

c. Check throttle cable routing after installation. The cables must not be twisted, kinked or pinched.
d. Adjust the throttle cable as described in Chapter Three in the front section of this manual.
e. Adjust the choke cable as described in Chapter Three in the front section of this manual.
f. Check carburetor adjustments as described in Chapter Three in the front section of this manual.

Disassembly/Reassembly

Figure 10 shows internal carburetor components. It is recommended to disassemble only one carburetor at a time to prevent accidental interchange of parts.

1. Remove the air flow inlet guide (**Figure 11**) from the carburetor.

2. Remove the screws and the diaphragm cover (**Figure 12**) and remove the cover.

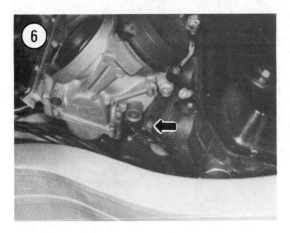

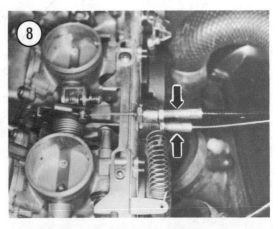

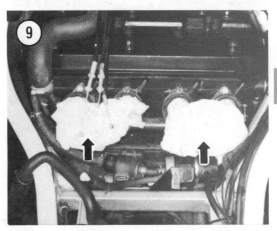

14

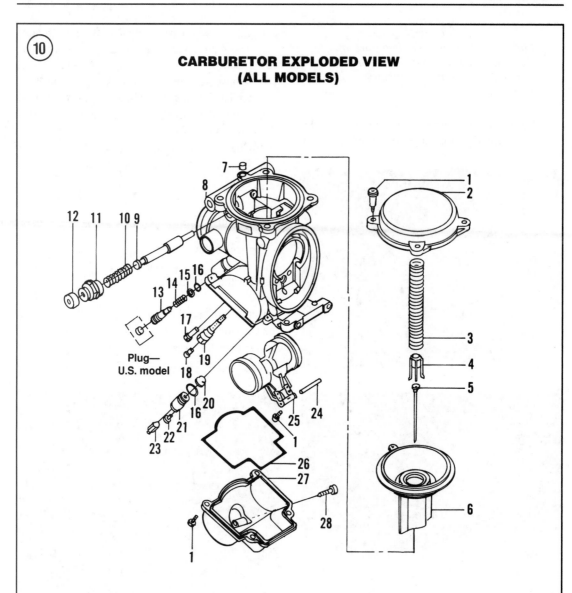

CARBURETOR EXPLODED VIEW
(ALL MODELS)

Plug—
U.S. model

1. Screw
2. Diaphragm cover
3. Spring
4. Spring seat
5. Jet needle
6. Vacuum slide
7. Air leak jet
8. Carburetor body
9. Choke shaft
10. Spring
11. Nut
12. Seal
13. Pilot (idle mixture screw)
14. Spring

15. Washer
16. O-ring
17. Pilot jet
18. Main jet
19. Needle jet holder
20. Screen
21. Float valve seat
22. Screw
23. Float valve
24. Float pin
25. Float
26. O-ring
27. Float bowl
28. Drain screw

3. Remove the spring (**Figure 13**).

4. Lift the diaphragm (A, **Figure 14**) out of the carburetor.

5. Remove the spring seat and remove the jet needle.

6. Remove the float bowl (**Figure 15**).

7. Unscrew and remove the main jet (**Figure 16**).

8. Unscrew and remove the needle jet holder (**Figure 17**).

14

9. Unscrew and remove the pilot jet (**Figure 18**).

10. Remove the screw (**Figure 19**) securing the float pin.

11. Remove the float pin (A, **Figure 20**) and the float (B, **Figure 20**).

> *NOTE*
> *Be sure to remove the float valve needle and its hanger clip off of the float (**Figure 21**).*

12. Remove the screw (A, **Figure 22**) securing the float valve seat and remove the seat assembly (B, **Figure 22**). Don't lose the O-ring seal (**Figure 23**).

13A. *All models except U.S.:* Carefully screw in the idle mixture screw until it seats *lightly* while counting and recording the number of turns so it can be installed in the same position during assembly. Then remove the idle mixture screw, spring, washer and O-ring.

13B. *U.S. models:* The idle mixture screw is sealed with a plug (**Figure 24**) at the factory. If necessary, remove it as described in Chapter Seven in the front section of this manual.

14. Repeat for the remaining carburetors.

15. Separation of the carburetors is not required for cleaning.

> *NOTE*
> *With all of the jets removed, you can clean most orifices and passages with spray carburetor cleaner. This type of cleaning is effective to clear jets clogged by long-term storage. In rare cases, this type of cleaning won't remove all contamination. If the carburetors are very dirty, separate the carburetors as described in this chapter.*

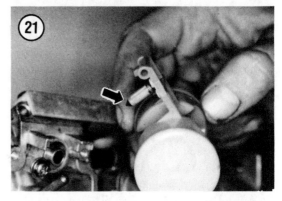

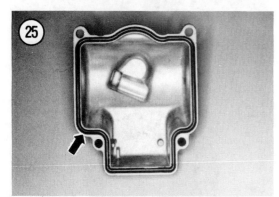

16. Clean and inspect that carburetor as described in this chapter.

17. Installation is the reverse of these steps. Note the following.

18. Replace the float bowl O-ring (**Figure 25**) if deformed or starting to deteriorate or if the bowl has leaked.

19. Assemble and install the jet needle and diaphragm assembly as follows:

a. Install the diaphragm and align the tab (B, **Figure 14**) with the recess in the carburetor body.

b. Install the jet needle so that the small diameter end goes in first.

c. Install the spring seat (**Figure 26**) with the legs going in first. Push the seat all the way down until it captures the jet needle.

d. Carefully push the end of the needle jet in to the carburetor bore (**Figure 27**).

e. Install the spring (**Figure 13**) into the diaphragm and install the diaphragm assembly. Push down on the spring to hold the jet needle and spring seat in position.

f. When positioning the diaphragm cover, insert the spring into the boss inside the cover (**Figure 28**).

CAUTION
It is easy to damage the diaphragm when installing the cover. Make sure that the sealing lip around the outer edge of the diaphragm is fully seated into its groove in the carburetor body.

20. Check the fuel level as described in this chapter.

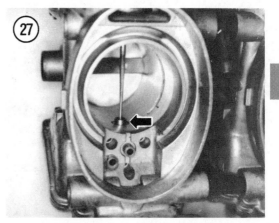

14

Cleaning and Inspection

1. Thoroughly clean and dry all parts. Do not use a caustic carburetor cleaner which requires dipping the parts in a strong solution. These can cause more harm than good and will remove all paint from carburetor's exterior. Use a spray carburetor cleaner and limit your cleaning to actual fuel and air orifices.

2. Allow the carburetor to dry thoroughly before assembly and blow dry with compressed air. Blow out the jets and needle jet holder with compressed air. Do *not* use a piece of wire to clean them as minor gouges in the jet can alter flow rate and upset the fuel/air mixture.

3. Inspect the end of the float valve needle (**Figure 29**) for wear or damage. Replace if it is scored or pitted.

4. Check the float assembly (**Figure 30**) for cracks or leakage. Submerge the float assembly in a cup of water and check for leaks. Replace the float(s) as required.

5. If removed, examine the end of the pilot screw for grooves or roughness. Replace if it is damaged. Replace a worn O-ring.

6. Inspect the vacuum slide (**Figure 31**) for scoring and wear. Replace if necessary.

7. Inspect the diaphragm (**Figure 32**) for tears, cracks or other damage. Replace the throttle slide assembly if the diaphragm is damaged.

8. Make sure the holes in the needle jet holder, main jet and pilot jet are clear (**Figure 33**). Clean out if they are plugged in any way. Replace the main jet nozzle if you cannot unplug the holes.

9. Inspect the filter screen (**Figure 34**) and the O-ring seal (**Figure 35**) on the float valve seat for wear or damage. Replace the O-ring if necessary or

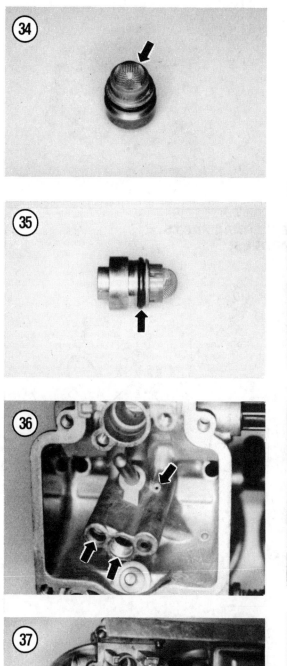

replace the float valve seat if the screen is damaged in any way.

10. Make sure all openings in the carburetor body are clear. Refer to **Figures 36-39**.

11. Inspect the vacuum slide area in the carburetor body. Refer to **Figure 40** and **Figure 41**. Make sure it is clean and free of any burrs or obstructions that may cause the diaphragm assembly to hang up during normal operation.

14

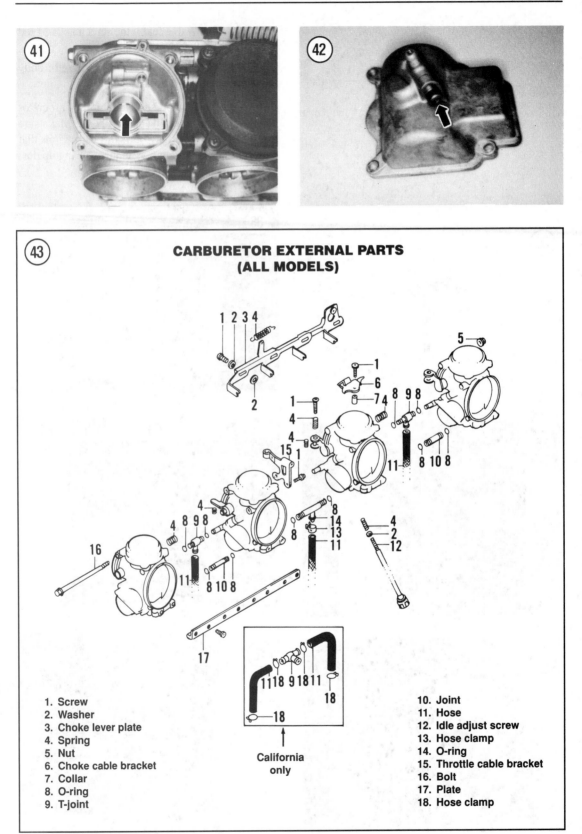

**CARBURETOR EXTERNAL PARTS
(ALL MODELS)**

California
only

1. Screw
2. Washer
3. Choke lever plate
4. Spring
5. Nut
6. Choke cable bracket
7. Collar
8. O-ring
9. T-joint
10. Joint
11. Hose
12. Idle adjust screw
13. Hose clamp
14. O-ring
15. Throttle cable bracket
16. Bolt
17. Plate
18. Hose clamp

12. Remove the drain screw (**Figure 42**) from the float bowl and make sure the opening is free.

Separation/Assembly

Refer to **Figure 43** for this procedure. The carburetors are joined by a rear mounting plate (**Figure 44**) and the front choke lever plate (**Figure 45**). Almost all carburetor parts can be replaced without separating the carburetors. If the carburetors must be cleaned internally or the pipe fittings (**Figure 46**) must be replaced, the carburetors must be separated.

1. Remove the throttle adjust screw holder (**Figure 47**).

2. Disconnect the choke return spring (**Figure 48**).

3. Remove the long bolt and nut (**Figure 49**) holding the carburetor assembly together.

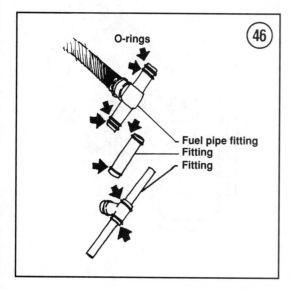

O-rings

Fuel pipe fitting
Fitting
Fitting

14

NOTE
An impact driver and a Phillips bit (de-scribed in Chapter One in the front of this manual) will be necessary to loosen the screws securing the mounting plates onto the carburetor housings. Attempt-ing to loosen the screws with a Phillips screwdriver may ruin the screw heads.

4. Remove the carburetor mounting plates. See **Fig-ure 44** and **Figure 45**.

5. Carefully separate the carburetors. Note the posi-tion of all springs and cable brackets.

6. Assemble the carburetors by reversing these steps. Note the following:

    a. Replace all fuel pipe O-rings.

    b. Assemble the fuel pipe O-rings as shown in **Figure 46**.

    c. The carburetor bores (**Figure 50**) must be par-allel. If not, place the assembly on a flat surface and align the carburetors.

    d. Apply Loctite 242 (blue) to all carburetor mounting plate screws before installation. Tighten the screws securely.

FUEL LEVEL

1. Place the bike on the centerstand on level ground.

2. Remove the fuel tank as described in this chapter.

3. Remove the air cleaner housing as described in Chapter Three in this section of the manual.

4. Use a small auxiliary fuel tank (like one from a lawn mower or small motorcycle) that is equipped with a shutoff valve. Using the correct size fuel hose, connect this fuel tank to the carburetor fuel inlet hose fitting.

5. Connect a length of fuel hose (6 mm diameter and approximately 300 mm long) to the float bowl drain outlet. Connect the fuel level gauge (Kawasaki part No. 57001-1017) into the other end of the fuel hose. Hold the fuel level gauge against the carburetor so that the "0" line (A, **Figure 51**) is even with the mark (B, **Figure 51**) of the carburetor body right-hand side.

6. Open the fuel tank shutoff valve, then turn the carburetor drain screw a few turns.

NOTE
Do not lower the fuel gauge "0" line below the bottom edge of the carburetor body. If the gauge is lowered then raised

again, the fuel level measurement will show a somewhat higher level in the gauge than the actual fuel level in the carburetor.

7. Wait until the fuel level in the gauge settles and note the fuel level. The fuel level (A, **Figure 51**) should be 5.0 mm (0.196 in.) below the float bowl mark line (B, **Figure 51**) on the right-hand side. Note the reading for that carburetor, then turn the drain plug off.

8. Repeat Steps 4-7 for the remaining carburetors.

9. Turn the fuel tank shutoff valve to the OFF posi-tion.

10. If the fuel level is incorrect, adjust the float height. Remove the carburetor assembly as de-scribed in this chapter and remove the float bowl(s).

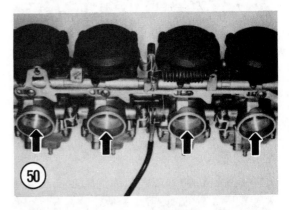

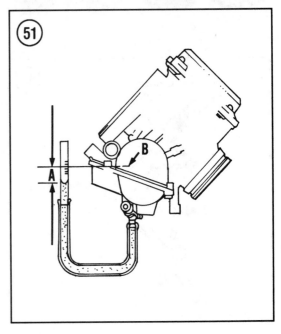

Bend the float tang (**Figure 52**) as required to get the correct fuel level. Increasing float height lowers fuel level and vise-versa. Install the float bowl(s) and reinstall the carburetor assembly and recheck the fuel level.

11. Install the air cleaner housing and the fuel tank.

FUEL TANK

WARNING
Some fuel may spill in the following procedures. Work in a well-ventilated area at least 50 feet from any sparks or flames, including gas appliance pilot lights. Do not allow anyone to smoke in the area. Keep a B:C rated fire extinguisher handy.

Removal/Installation

Refer to the following illustrations for this procedure:
   a. ZX-10: **Figure 53**.
   b. ZX-11 C1-4: **Figure 54**.
   c. ZX-11 D1-9: **Figure 55**.
1. Check that the ignition switch is OFF.
2. Place the bike securely on the sidestand.
3. Remove the seat.
4A. ZX-10: Perform the following:
   a. Remove the seat and both side covers.
   b. Turn the fuel valve to the OFF position.
   c. Remove the bolts (**Figure 56**) on each side at the rear securing the mounting bracket to the frame.
   d. Partially lift up the rear of the fuel tank and disconnect the fuel lines, vacuum lines (**Figure 57**) (models so equipped) and electrical connector (**Figure 58**).

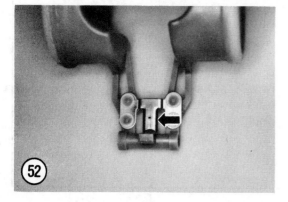

(52)

   e. Disconnect the fuel line (**Figure 59**) from the fuel valve.
   f. Pull the tank to the rear and remove it.
4B. *ZX-11 C1-4:* Perform the following:
   a. Remove both side covers.
   b. Turn the fuel valve to the OFF position.
   c. Remove the fairing inner panels (**Figure 60**).
   d. Disconnect the fuel lines from the fuel tap.
   e. Remove the bolts under the inner panels securing the front of the fuel tank to the frame. Don't lose the metal collar in the rubber cushions.
   f. Remove the bolt on each side securing the rear of the fuel tank to the frame (**Figure 61**).
   g. Partially lift up the rear of the fuel tank and disconnect any vacuum lines (models so equipped) and the electrical connectors.
   h. Pull the tank to the rear and remove it.
4C. *ZX-11 D1-9:* Perform the following:

   a. Turn the fuel valve to the ON or RES position (A, **Figure 62**).
   b. Remove the bolts (**Figure 63**) securing the front of the fuel tank to the frame. Don't lose the metal collar in the rubber cushions.
   c. Remove the bolts (**Figure 64**) securing the rear of the fuel tank to the frame.
   d. Disconnect the fuel line (B, **Figure 62**) from the fuel tap.
   e. Partially lift up the rear of the fuel tank and disconnect any vacuum lines (models so equipped) and the electrical connectors.
   f. Pull the tank to the rear and remove it.
5. Pour the fuel out of the fuel tank into a container approved for gasoline storage.
6. Check the rubber dampers (**Figure 65**) for wear and damage; replace if necessary. Check the damper mount for looseness. Tighten all mounting bolts if necessary.
7. To install the fuel tank, reverse the removal steps. Note the following:
   a. Don't pinch any wires or control cables during installation.
   b. Reconnect all hoses and electrical connectors.

14

FUEL VALVE

The vacuum-operated fuel valve should pass no fuel in the ON or RES position until a running engine provides the vacuum required to operate the diaphragm valve.

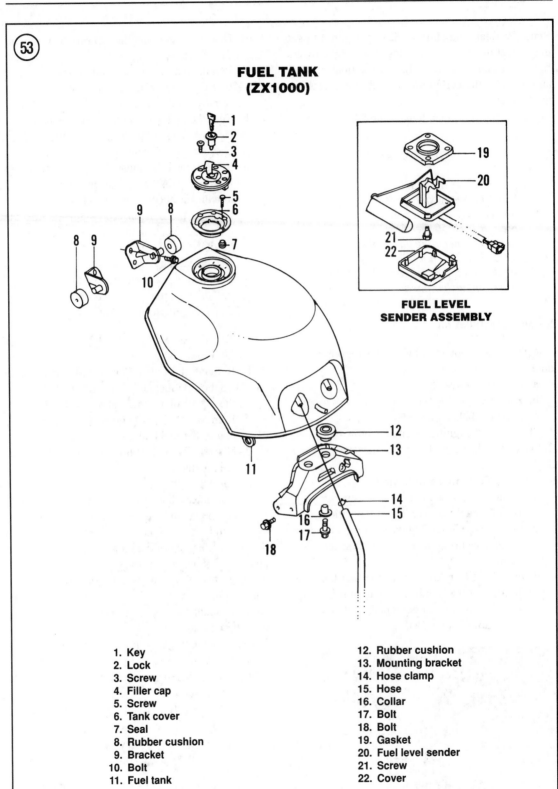

**FUEL TANK
(ZX1000)**

**FUEL LEVEL
SENDER ASSEMBLY**

1. Key
2. Lock
3. Screw
4. Filler cap
5. Screw
6. Tank cover
7. Seal
8. Rubber cushion
9. Bracket
10. Bolt
11. Fuel tank
12. Rubber cushion
13. Mounting bracket
14. Hose clamp
15. Hose
16. Collar
17. Bolt
18. Bolt
19. Gasket
20. Fuel level sender
21. Screw
22. Cover

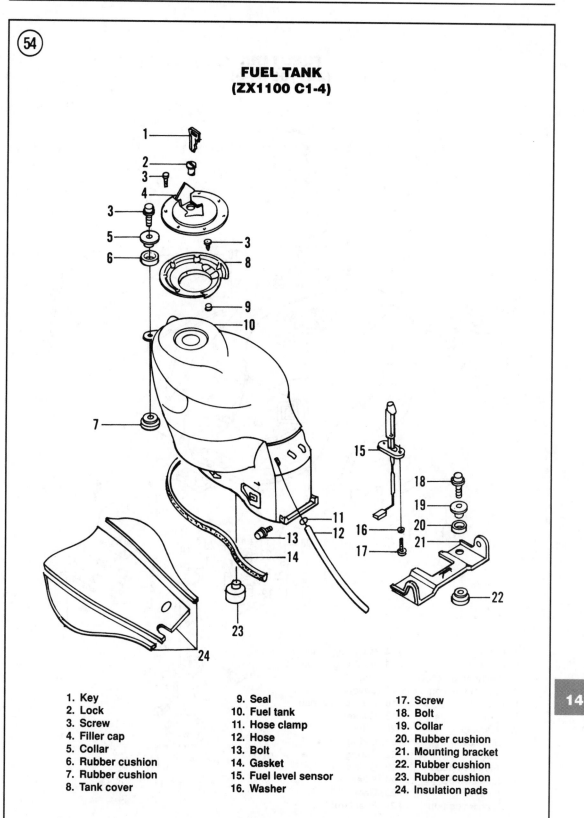

**FUEL TANK
(ZX1100 C1-4)**

1. Key
2. Lock
3. Screw
4. Filler cap
5. Collar
6. Rubber cushion
7. Rubber cushion
8. Tank cover
9. Seal
10. Fuel tank
11. Hose clamp
12. Hose
13. Bolt
14. Gasket
15. Fuel level sensor
16. Washer
17. Screw
18. Bolt
19. Collar
20. Rubber cushion
21. Mounting bracket
22. Rubber cushion
23. Rubber cushion
24. Insulation pads

14

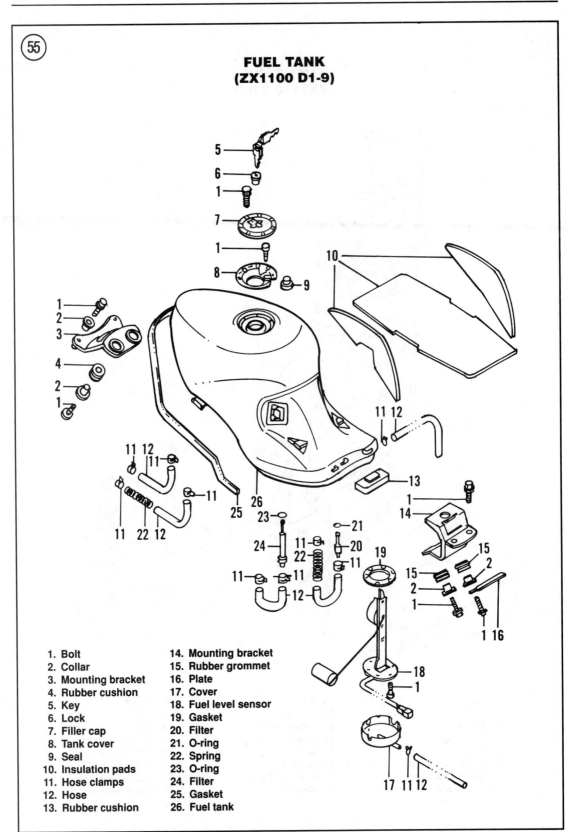

**FUEL TANK
(ZX1100 D1-9)**

1. Bolt
2. Collar
3. Mounting bracket
4. Rubber cushion
5. Key
6. Lock
7. Filler cap
8. Tank cover
9. Seal
10. Insulation pads
11. Hose clamps
12. Hose
13. Rubber cushion
14. Mounting bracket
15. Rubber grommet
16. Plate
17. Cover
18. Fuel level sensor
19. Gasket
20. Filter
21. O-ring
22. Spring
23. O-ring
24. Filter
25. Gasket
26. Fuel tank

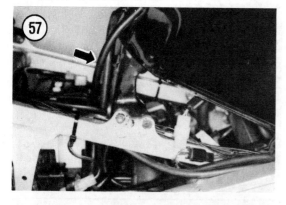

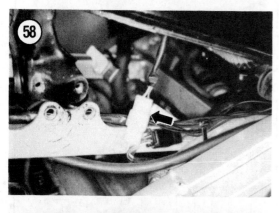

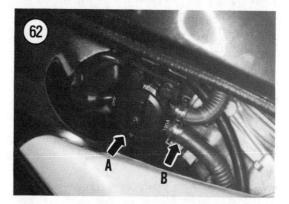

14

Removal/Installation

Refer to the following illustrations for this procedure:

    a. ZX-10: **Figure 66**.

    b. ZX-11 C1-4: **Figure 67**.

    c. ZX-11 D1-9: **Figure 68**.

> *WARNING*
> *Some fuel may spill in the following procedure. Work in a well-ventilated area at least 50 feet from any sparks or flames, including gas appliance pilot lights. Do not allow anyone to smoke in the area. Keep a B:C rated fire extinguisher handy.*

> *NOTE*
> *This sequence is shown on a ZX-10 and illustrates a typical fuel shutoff valve replacement procedure.*

1. Remove the fuel tank as described in this chapter.

2. If still attached, disconnect the fuel line and vacuum line from shutoff valve.

3. Remove the bolts and washers (A, **Figure 69**) securing the shutoff valve to the fuel tank and remove the valve (B, **Figure 69**).

4. Inspect the shutoff valve mounting O-ring and clean the feed tube screen whenever the valve is removed. Replace the O-ring if necessary.

5. Install by reversing these removal steps. Pour a small amount of gasoline in the tank after installing the valve and check for leaks. If a leak is present, solve the problem prior to installing the fuel tank.

FUEL LEVEL SENSOR

Removal/Installation

Refer to the following illustrations for this procedure:

    a. ZX-10: **Figure 53**.

    b. ZX-11 C1-4: **Figure 54**.

    c. ZX-11 D1-9: **Figure 55**.

1. Remove and drain the fuel tank as described in this chapter.

2. Remove the cover (**Figure 70**) and remove the fuel level sensor mounting bolts.

3. Remove the fuel level sensor and gasket.

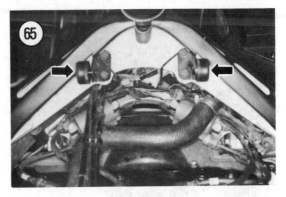

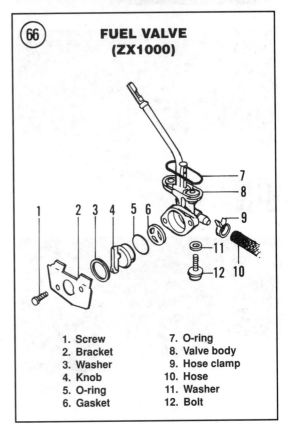

FUEL VALVE (ZX1000)

1. Screw	7. O-ring
2. Bracket	8. Valve body
3. Washer	9. Hose clamp
4. Knob	10. Hose
5. O-ring	11. Washer
6. Gasket	12. Bolt

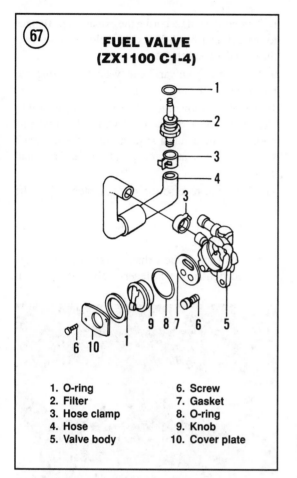

(67)

**FUEL VALVE
(ZX1100 C1-4)**

1. O-ring
2. Filter
3. Hose clamp
4. Hose
5. Valve body
6. Screw
7. Gasket
8. O-ring
9. Knob
10. Cover plate

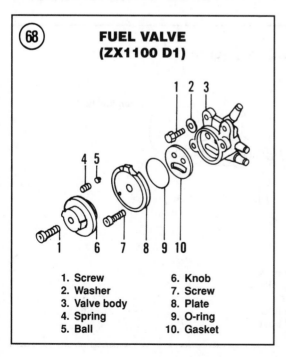

(68)

**FUEL VALVE
(ZX1100 D1)**

1. Screw
2. Washer
3. Valve body
4. Spring
5. Ball
6. Knob
7. Screw
8. Plate
9. O-ring
10. Gasket

4. Install by reversing these removal steps. When installing sensor, make sure the gasket is in good condition.

FUEL PUMP AND FILTER

Removal/Installation

Refer to **Figure 71** for this procedure.
1. Remove the fuel tank as described in this chapter.
2. Remove the carburetors as described in this chapter.
3. Disconnect the fuel pump electrical connector.
4. Carefully remove the fuel pump and filter (**Figure 72**) from the rubber mounts on the frame mounting bracket and remove the assembly from the frame.
5. Install by reversing these removal steps while noting the following.

   a. Check the fuel line clamps for damage; replace if necessary.

   b. Position the fuel filter with the arrow pointing toward the fuel pump.

   c. After installation is complete, thoroughly check for fuel leaks.

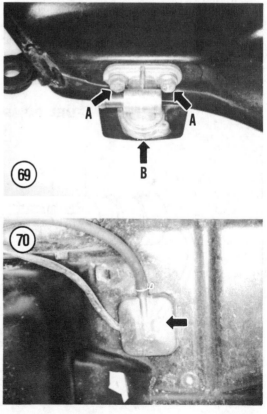

(69)

(70)

14

EMISSION CONTROLS

The emission control system components are basically the same as on previous models with the exception of some of the vacuum hose routing.

Refer to **Figure 73** for ZX-10 models or **Figure 74** for ZX-11 models for component layout and hose routing.

EXHAUST SYSTEM
(ZX-11)

Removal/Installation

Refer to **Figure 75** for this procedure.

1. Place the bike on the centerstand.
2. Remove the fairings as described in Chapter Thirteen in this section of the manual.
3. Remove the radiator as described in Chapter Nine in this section of the manual.
4. Loosen the clamp bolt securing the right-hand muffler to the exhaust pipe/left-hand muffler crossover pipe.
5. Remove the bolt and collar (**Figure 76**) securing the right-hand muffler at the rear.
6. Separate the right-hand muffler from the crossover pipe and remove the muffler.
7. Loosen the nut securing the left-hand muffler at the rear.

8. Remove the nuts securing the exhaust pipe flanges to the cylinder head. Work the holders loose from the cylinder head studs.
9. Remove the nut and cup washer securing the left-hand muffler at the rear.
10. Carefully move the exhaust system forward to clear the threaded studs on the cylinder head exhaust ports. Pull the exhaust system out of the left-hand side of the frame and remove it from the frame and engine.
11. To install, reverse the removal steps. Note the following:

    a. Install new gaskets in the cylinder head exhaust ports.

    b. Install all of the exhaust system components and tighten the fasteners only finger-tight at

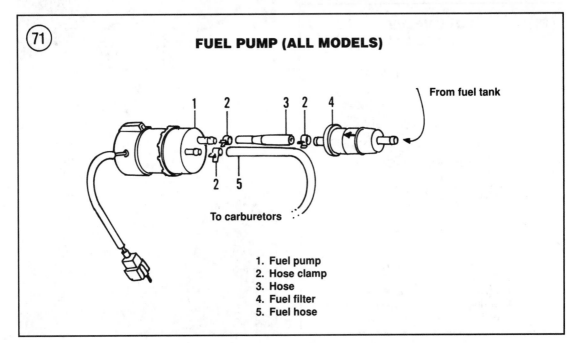

FUEL PUMP (ALL MODELS)

From fuel tank

To carburetors

1. Fuel pump
2. Hose clamp
3. Hose
4. Fuel filter
5. Fuel hose

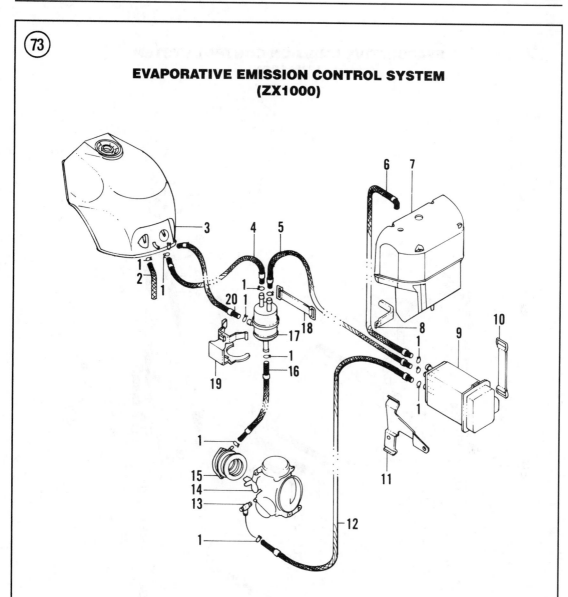

**EVAPORATIVE EMISSION CONTROL SYSTEM
(ZX1000)**

1. Hose clamp
2. Hose
3. Fuel tank
4. Breather hose (blue)
5. Breather hose (blue)
6. Purge hose (green)
7. Air cleaner assembly
8. Bracket
9. Canister
10. Strap
11. Mounting bracket
12. Breather hose (yellow)
13. Fitting
14. Carburetor
15. Intake tube
16. Vacuum hose (white)
17. Liquid/vapor separator
18. Strap
19. Mounting bracket
20. Fuel return hose (red)

14

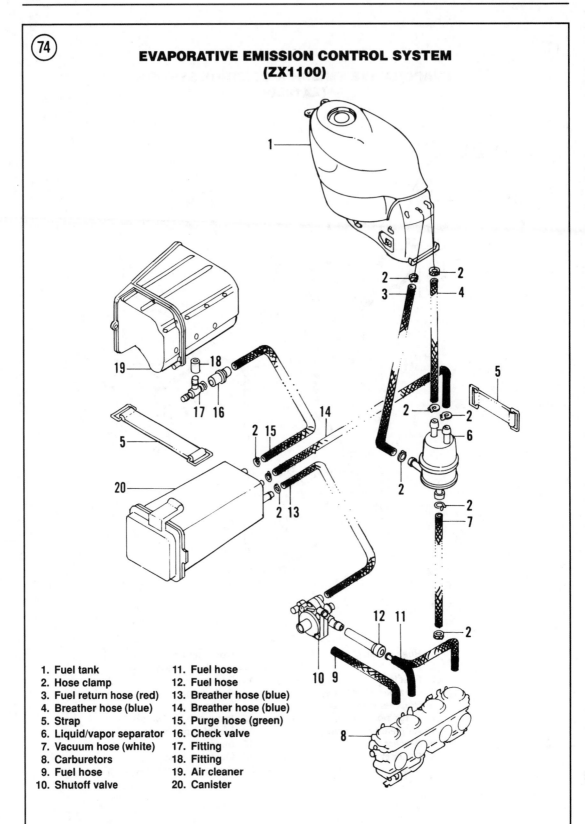

EVAPORATIVE EMISSION CONTROL SYSTEM (ZX1100)

1. Fuel tank
2. Hose clamp
3. Fuel return hose (red)
4. Breather hose (blue)
5. Strap
6. Liquid/vapor separator
7. Vacuum hose (white)
8. Carburetors
9. Fuel hose
10. Shutoff valve
11. Fuel hose
12. Fuel hose
13. Breather hose (blue)
14. Breather hose (blue)
15. Purge hose (green)
16. Check valve
17. Fitting
18. Fitting
19. Air cleaner
20. Canister

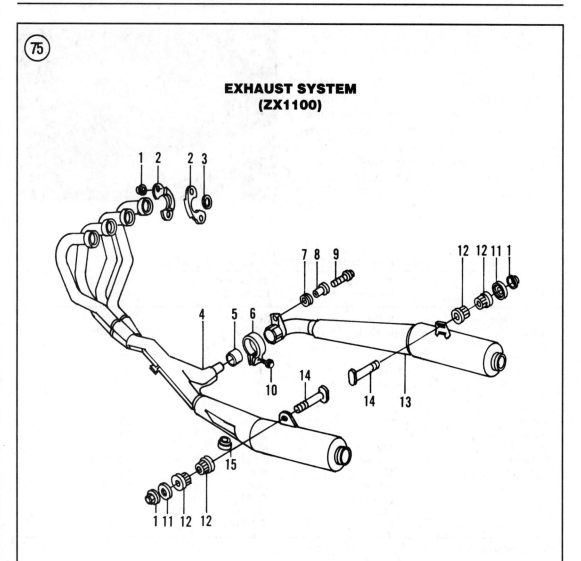

(75)

EXHAUST SYSTEM
(ZX1100)

1. Nut
2. Exhaust pipe flange
3. Gasket
4. Exhaust pipe/left-hand muffler
5. Gasket
6. Clamp
7. Rubber bushing
8. Collar
9. Bolt
10. Bolt
11. Cup washer
12. Rubber bushing
13. Right-hand muffler
14. Bolt
15. Rubber stopper

14

this time. Make sure the exhaust pipe inlets are correctly seated in the cylinder head exhaust ports.

c. Securely tighten the nuts securing the exhaust pipe flange to the cylinder head, then tighten the nuts securing the mufflers to the frame. This will minimize exhaust leakage at the cylinder head.

d. After installation is complete, start the engine and make sure there are no exhaust leaks. Correct any leak prior to riding the bike.

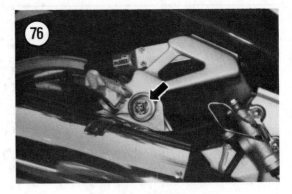

Table 1 CARBURETOR SPECIFICATIONS (ZX1000)

Item	1988, 1989 49-state	1988-1989 California	1988-1989 European
Manufacturer	Keihin	Keihin	Keihin
Model	CVKD36	CVKD36	CVKD36
Main jet			
U.S. (49-state)	130	135	130
High-altitude	128	132	—
Main air jet	100	100	100
Jet needle	N14C	N14C	N54D
Pilot jet			
Standard	38	38	38
High-altitude	35	35	35
Pilot air jet	130	130	140*
Pilot screw	Pre-set	Pre-set	2 turns out
Starter jet	55	45	55
Fuel level	5.0 mm (0.196 in.)	5.0 mm (0.196 in.)	5.0 mm (0.196 in.)
Float height	13.0 mm (0.512 in.)	13.0 mm (0.512 in.)	13.0 mm (0.512 in.)

*Swiss model only.

Table 2 CARBURETOR SPECIFICATIONS (ZX1100)

	ZX1100 C1-4	
Item	1990-1993 U.S.	1990-1993 European
Manufacturer	Keihin	Keihin
Model	CVKD40	CVKD40
Main jet		
1990		
Standard	155	155
High-altitude	152	152
1991-1993		
Standard	140	140
High-altitude	138	138
Main air jet	70	70
Jet needle	N60U	N60U

(continued)

Table 2 CARBURETOR SPECIFICATIONS (continued)

Pilot jet		
Standard	38	38
High-altitude	35	35
Pilot air jet	130	130
Pilot screw	Pre-set	Pre-set
Starter jet	55	55
Fuel level	3.5-5.5 mm	3.5-5.5 mm
	(0.137-0.216 in.)	(0.137-0.216 in.)
Float height	11-15 mm	11-15 mm
	(0.43-0.59 in.)	(0.43-0.59 in.)

	ZX1100 D1-9	
	1993-on	**1993-on**
Item	**U.S.**	**European**
Manufacturer	Keihin	Keihin
Model	CVKD40	CVKD40
Main jet		
Carb. No. 1, No. 4		
Standard	160	160
High-altitude	158	158
Carb. No. 2, No. 3		
Standard	158	158
High-altitude	155	155
Main air jet	70	70
Jet needle	N60U	N96X*
Pilot jet		
Standard	38	38
High-altitude	35	35
Pilot air jet	120	130
Pilot screw	1 5/8-2 turns out	1 3/4-2 turns out
Starter jet	58	58
Fuel level	3.5-5.5 mm	3.5-5.5 mm
	(0.137-0.216 in.)	(0.137-0.216 in.)
Float height	11-15 mm	11-15 mm
	(0.43-0.59 in.)	(0.43-0.59 in.)

*European models except Austria, Sweden and Switzerland.

CHAPTER EIGHT

ELECTRICAL SYSTEM

This chapter describes service procedures for the electrical systems. **Table 1** is located at the end of this chapter.

NOTE
This chapter covers all procedures unique to the Kawasaki ZX1000 (ZX-10) and ZX1100 (ZX-11) from 1988-on. If a specific procedure is not included in this chapter, unless other-wise specified refer to ZX1000 models in Chapter Eight at the front of this manual for service procedures.

ALTERNATOR

The alternator and charging system are the same as on previous years with the exception of the layout of the CHARGING SYSTEM CIRCUIT shown in **Figure 1**.

14

TRANSISTORIZED IGNITION

The ignition system wiring diagram is shown in **Figure 2**.

Left-hand Side Cover
Removal/Installation

1. Remove the left-hand lower fairing panels as described in Chapter Thirteen in this section of the manual.

2. Remove the bolts securing the pickup coil cover (A, **Figure 3**) and remove the cover and gasket.

3. Install the pickup coil cover (A, **Figure 3**) and gasket. Install a new gasket if necessary. Apply blue Loctite (No. 242) to the threads of the 2 bolts indicated in B, **Figure 3**, prior to installation. Tighten the bolts securely.

Pickup Coil
Removal/Installation

1. Remove the left-hand side cover as described in this chapter.

2. Disconnect the electrical connector.

3. Pull the harness away from the frame and engine. Note the path of the harness as it must be routed the same during installation.

4. Remove the bolts (A, **Figure 4**) securing the pickup coil and cover. Remove the cover and rubber

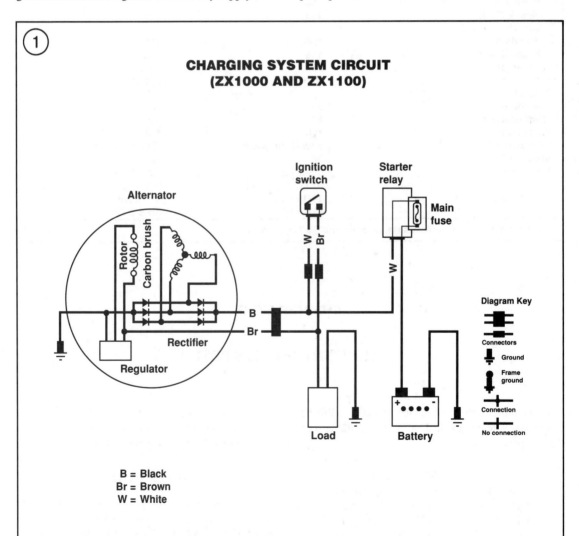

① CHARGING SYSTEM CIRCUIT
(ZX1000 AND ZX1100)

B = Black
Br = Brown
W = White

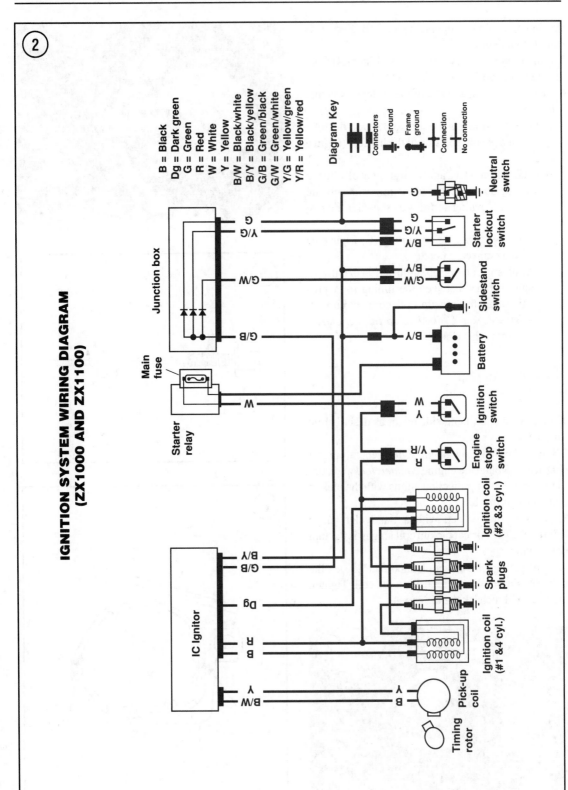

IGNITION SYSTEM WIRING DIAGRAM (ZX1000 AND ZX1100)

B = Black
Dg = Dark green
G = Green
R = Red
W = White
Y = Yellow
B/W = Black/white
B/Y = Black/yellow
G/B = Green/black
G/W = Green/white
Y/G = Yellow/green
Y/R = Yellow/red

Diagram Key

Connectors
Ground
Frame ground
Connection
No connection

14

cushion, then remove the pickup coil (B, **Figure 4**) from the crankcase.

5. Pull the wire harness wire plug (C, **Figure 4**) from the crankcase and remove the assembly.

6. Installation is the reverse of these steps. Note the following:

    a. On ZX-11 models, be sure to position the tube onto the pickup coil side of the harness (**Figure 5**).

    b. On ZX-11 models, apply a light coat of silicone sealant, about 5 mm (0.20 in.) wide, to the crankcase mating surfaces as shown in **Figure 6**.

    c. Fit the wire harness wire plug (C, **Figure 4**) into the crankcase notch.

    d. The pickup coil must be adjusted so that the air gap (clearance between the timing rotor projection and the pickup coil core) is correct. Perform *Pickup Coil Air Gap Inspection/Adjustment* in this chapter.

Pickup Coil Air Gap Inspection/Adjustment

1. Remove the left-hand side cover as described in this chapter.

2. Use a 24 mm wrench on the signal generator rotor (**Figure 7**). Rotate the engine *counterclockwise*, until the timing rotor projection aligns with the pickup coil core (**Figure 8**).

3. Measure the air gap with a flat feeler gauge (**Figure 9**). The correct pickup coil air gap is 0.7 mm (0.027 in.).

4. If the pickup coil air gap is incorrect, loosen the bolts (A, **Figure 4**) and reposition the coil. Tighten the bolts and recheck the air gap.

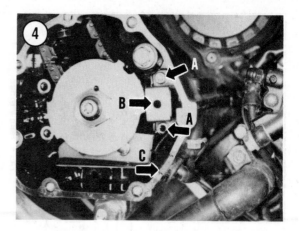

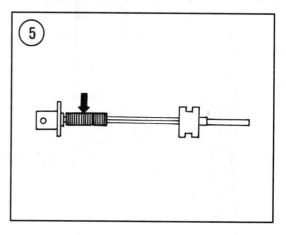

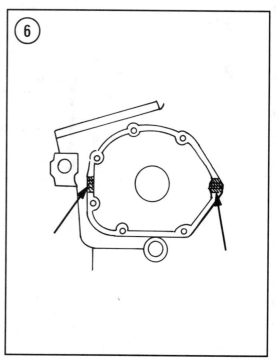

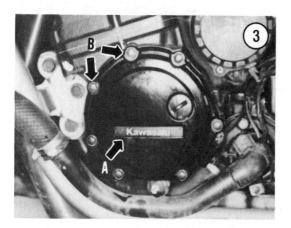

5. Install the left-hand side cover as described in this chapter.

Ignition Coils
Removal/Installation

The ignition coil for the No. 1 and No. 4 cylinder is mounted on the left-hand side and the No. 2 and No. 3 cylinder is mounted on the right-hand side.

Removal/Installation

1. Remove the fuel tank as described in Chapter Seven in this section of the manual.

2. On ZX-11 models, remove the air cleaner air box as described in Chapter Seven.

3. Disconnect the spark plug leads by grasping the connectors and pull them off the spark plugs (**Figure 10**).

NOTE
Label all wires disconnected in Step 4.

4. Disconnect the primary leads (A, **Figure 11**) from the ignition coils.

5. Remove the bolts (B, **Figure 11**) securing the ignition coils and remove them.

6. Installation is the reverse of these steps. Note the following.

7. Attach the primary wires to the ignition coil primary terminals as follows:

    a. The black and red wires connected to the No. 1 and No. 4 ignition coil.

    b. The green and red wires connected to the No. 2 and No. 3 ignition coil.

14

c. When connecting the 2 primary wires to each ignition coil, it doesn't matter what terminal each wire goes to.

8. Apply electrical grease to the base of each ignition coil cap where it seats against the cylinder head cover (**Figure 12**).

IC Igniter
Removal/Installation

1. Remove the seat.

2A. *ZX-10*, remove the frame left-hand side cover.

2B. *ZX-11 C1-4*, remove the frame right-hand side cover.

NOTE
Figure 13 is shown on a ZX-10, others are typical.

3. On models so equipped, remove the mounting screw(s) (A, **Figure 13**).

4. Unplug the connectors (B, **Figure 13**) and remove the igniter (C, **Figure 13**) from the frame.

5. Installation is the reverse of these steps. Note the following.

   a. Check the igniter rubber mount for cracks or damage. Replace the mount if necessary.

   b. Clean the connectors with electrical contact cleaner before assembly.

ELECTRIC STARTER

The starter system is the same as on previous years with the exception of the layout of the ELECTRIC STARTER CIRCUIT shown in **Figure 14**.

LIGHTING SYSTEM

Headlight Replacement

CAUTION
All models are equipped with quartz-halogen bulbs. Do not touch the bulb glass with your fingers because traces of oil on the bulb will drastically reduce the life of the bulb. Clean any traces of oil from the bulb with a cloth moistened in alcohol or lacquer thinner.

WARNING
If the headlight bulb has just burned out or turned off it will be Hot! Don't touch the bulb until it cools off.

1. Remove the inner covers of the upper fairing to gain access to the backside of the headlight assembly. Refer to Chapter Thirteen in this section of the manual.

2. Disconnect the electrical connector from the bulb.

3. Lift the rubber dust cover away from the bulb.

4A. *ZX-10*, lift the spring hook up and pivot it away from the bulb.

4B. *ZX-11*, the bulb is held in place by the rubber dust cover and will be loose after the dust cover is removed.

5. Lift the bulb out of the headlight assembly.

6. Install by reversing these steps. Note the following:

   a. Align the tabs on the bulb with the notches in the bulb socket or headlight assembly when installing the bulb.

   b. On ZX-10 models, make sure to lock the hook spring into the bulb socket.

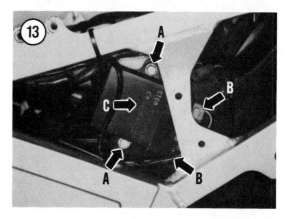

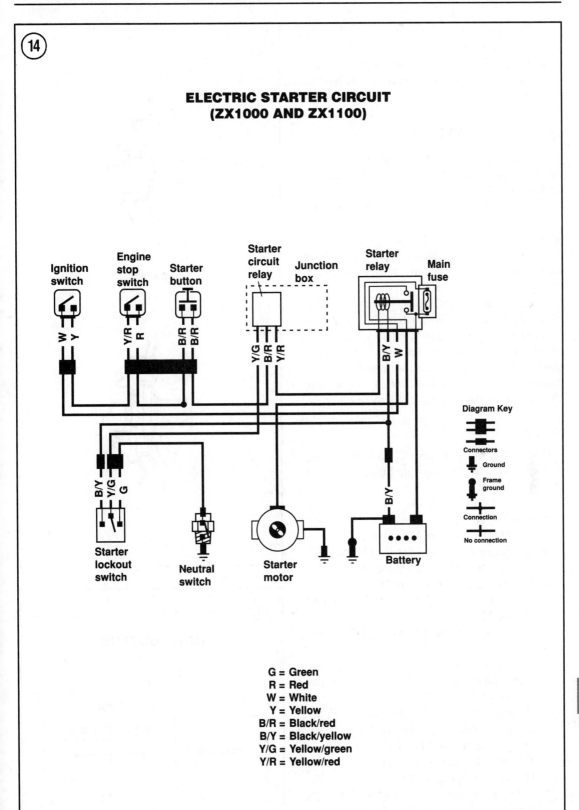

**ELECTRIC STARTER CIRCUIT
(ZX1000 AND ZX1100)**

G = Green
R = Red
W = White
Y = Yellow
B/R = Black/red
B/Y = Black/yellow
Y/G = Yellow/green
Y/R = Yellow/red

c. Install the dust cover so that the end labeled TOP faces up.

d. On ZX-11 models, be sure to push the dust cover all the way on (**Figure 15**) to hold the bulb in place correctly.

SWITCHES

Switches can be tested for continuity with an ohmmeter (see Chapter One at the front of this manual) or a test light at the switch connector plug by operating the switch in each of its operating positions and comparing results with the switch operation. For example, **Figure 16** shows a continuity diagram for a typical horn button. It shows which terminals should show continuity when the horn button is in a given position.

When the horn button is pushed, there should be continuity between terminals BK/Y and BK/W. This is indicated by the line on the continuity diagram. An ohmmeter connected between these 2 terminals should indicate little or no resistance and a test lamp should light. When the horn button is free, there should be no continuity between the same terminals.

Testing

If the switch or button doesn't perform properly, replace it. Refer to the following figures when testing the switches:

a. Horn switch: **Figure 16**.

b. Ignition switch (U.S. and Canada ZX-10, ZX-11 C1-4): **Figure 17**.

c. Ignition switch (ZX-11 D1-9): **Figure 18**.

d. Ignition switch (U.K.): **Figure 19**.

e. Engine stop switch: **Figure 20**.

f. Starter lockout switch (ZX-10, ZX-11 C1-4): **Figure 21**.

g. Starter lockout switch (ZX-11 D1-9): **Figure 22**.

h. Start button: **Figure 23**.

i. Headlight dimmer switch (U.S. and Canada): **Figure 24**.

j. Headlight switch (U.K.): **Figure 25**.

k. Passing switch (U.K.): **Figure 26**.

l. Front brake switch: **Figure 27**.

m. Turn signal switch: **Figure 28**.

n. Hazard switch: **Figure 29**.

When testing switches, note the following:

a. First check the fuses as described under Fuses in this chapter.

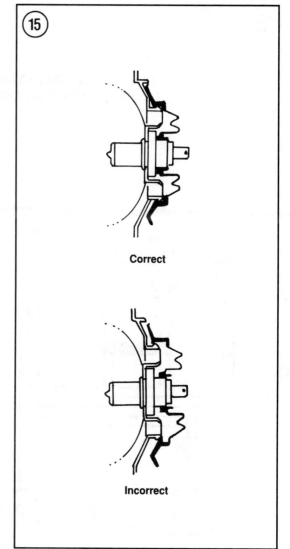

Correct

Incorrect

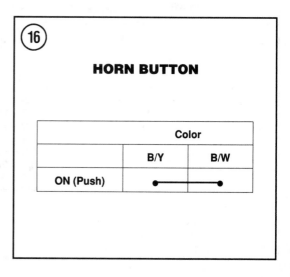

HORN BUTTON

	Color	
	B/Y	B/W
ON (Push)	•——————•	

(17)

IGNITION SWITCH
(U.S. AND CANADA ZX1000 AND ZX1100 C1-4)

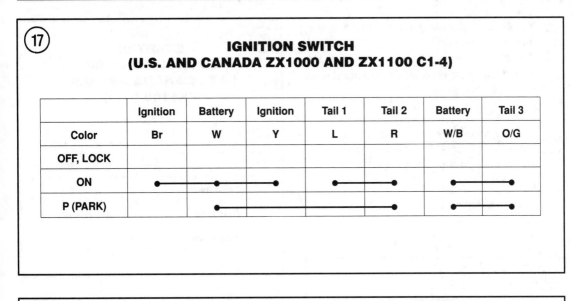

	Ignition	Battery	Ignition	Tail 1	Tail 2	Battery	Tail 3
Color	Br	W	Y	L	R	W/B	O/G
OFF, LOCK							
ON	●————	●————	●	●————	●	●————	●
P (PARK)		●————————————————	●		●	●————	●

(18)

IGNITION SWITCH
(U.S., CANADA AND U.K. ZX1100 D1-9)

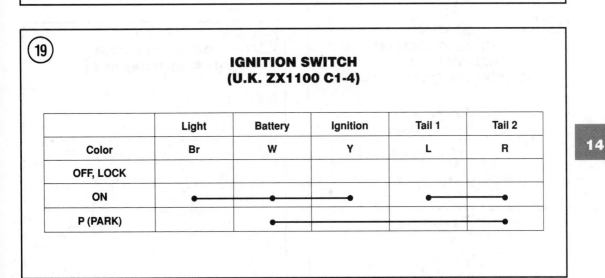

	Ignition	Battery	Ignition	Tail 1	Tail 2	Battery	Tail 3
Color	Br	W	Gy	L	R	W/B	W/G
OFF, LOCK							
ON	●————	●————	●	●————	●	●————	●
P (PARK)		●————————————————	●		●	●————	●

(19)

IGNITION SWITCH
(U.K. ZX1100 C1-4)

	Light	Battery	Ignition	Tail 1	Tail 2
Color	Br	W	Y	L	R
OFF, LOCK					
ON	●————	●————	●	●————	●
P (PARK)		●————————————————	●		●

14

b. Check the battery as described under *Battery* in Chapter Three.

c. Disconnect the negative cable from the battery if the switch connectors are not disconnected in the circuit.

CAUTION
Do not attempt to start the engine with the battery negative cable disconnected or you will damage the wiring harness.

d. When separating 2 connectors, depress the retaining clip and pull on the connector housings and not the wires.

⑳

ENGINE STOP SWITCH

	Color	
	Y/R	R
OFF		
RUN	•———•	

㉒

STARTER LOCKOUT SWITCH (U.S., CANADA AND U.K. ZX1100 D1-9)

	Color		
	B/Y	B	B/R
Clutch lever			
Released		•———•
Pulled in	•———•	

㉓

STARTER BUTTON

	Color	
	B/R	B/R
PUSH	•———•	

㉑

STARTER LOCKOUT SWITCH (U.S. AND CANADA ZX1000 AND ZX1100 C1-4)

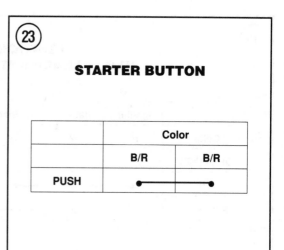

	Color		
	B/Y	Y/G	LG
Released		•———•	
Pulled in	•———•		

㉔

DIMMER SWITCH (U.S. AND CANADA)

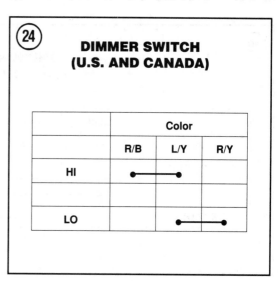

	Color		
	R/B	L/Y	R/Y
HI	•———•		
LO		•———•

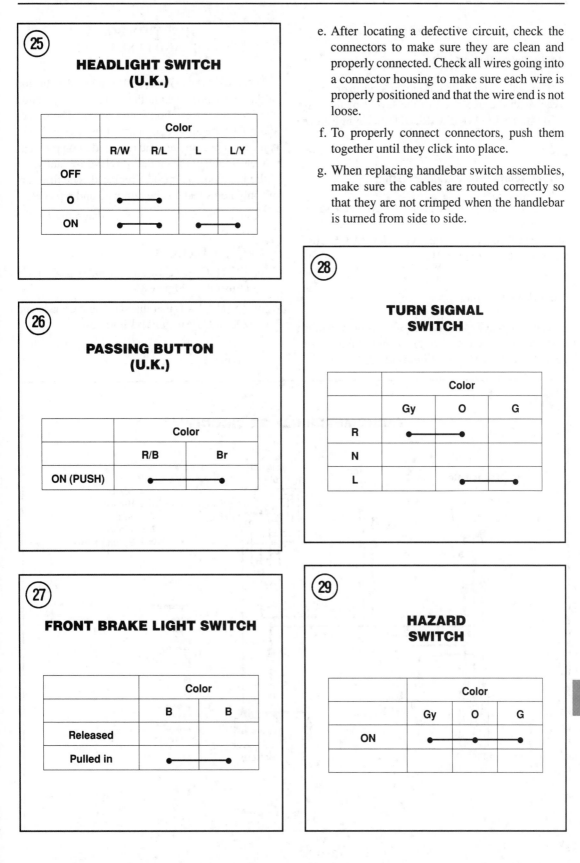

HEADLIGHT SWITCH (U.K.)

	Color			
	R/W	R/L	L	L/Y
OFF				
O	●——●			
ON	●——●		●——●	

PASSING BUTTON (U.K.)

	Color	
	R/B	Br
ON (PUSH)	●——●	

FRONT BRAKE LIGHT SWITCH

	Color	
	B	B
Released		
Pulled in	●——●	

e. After locating a defective circuit, check the connectors to make sure they are clean and properly connected. Check all wires going into a connector housing to make sure each wire is properly positioned and that the wire end is not loose.

f. To properly connect connectors, push them together until they click into place.

g. When replacing handlebar switch assemblies, make sure the cables are routed correctly so that they are not crimped when the handlebar is turned from side to side.

TURN SIGNAL SWITCH

	Color		
	Gy	O	G
R	●——●		
N			
L		●——●	

HAZARD SWITCH

	Color		
	Gy	O	G
ON	●——●——●		

14

GAUGES

Tachometer Testing

The tachometer system is the same as on previous years with the exception of the layout of the TACHOMETER GAUGE CIRCUIT shown in **Figure 30**.

Water Temperature Gauge Testing

The water temperature gauge system is the same as on previous years with the exception of the layout of the WATER TEMPERATURE GAUGE CIRCUIT shown in **Figure 31**.

Fuel Gauge Testing

The fuel gauge system is the same as on previous years with the exception of the layout of the FUEL GAUGE CIRCUIT shown in **Figure 32**.

JUNCTION BOX AND FUSES

The junction box (**Figure 33**) is located on the top of the rear fender behind the battery. The junction box includes fuses, diodes and relays. The diodes and relays are an integral part of the circuit board and cannot be removed and replaced as on previous models. If any of the diodes or relays are faulty, the entire junction box must be replaced. The fuses are the only items that can be removed and replaced.

Refer to the following wiring diagrams for the various models:

a. ZX-10: **Figure 34**.

b. ZX-11 C1-4 (U.S. and Canada), ZX-11 C3 (Australia): **Figure 35**.

c. ZX-11 C1-4 (other than U.S. and Canada and ZX-11 C3 Australia): **Figure 36**.

d. ZX-11 D1-9 (U.S., Canada and Australia): **Figure 37**.

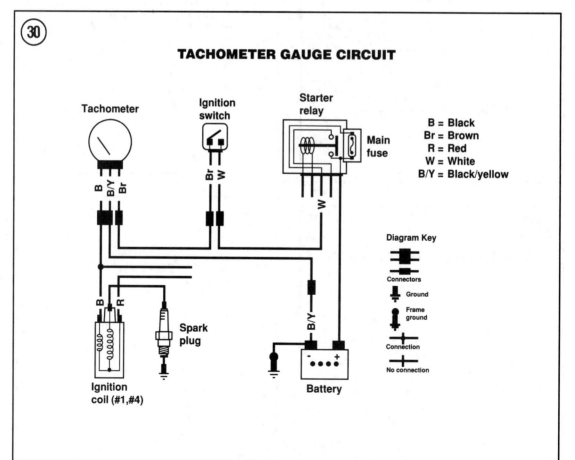

TACHOMETER GAUGE CIRCUIT

B = Black
Br = Brown
R = Red
W = White
B/Y = Black/yellow

Diagram Key

Connectors
Ground
Frame ground
Connection
No connection

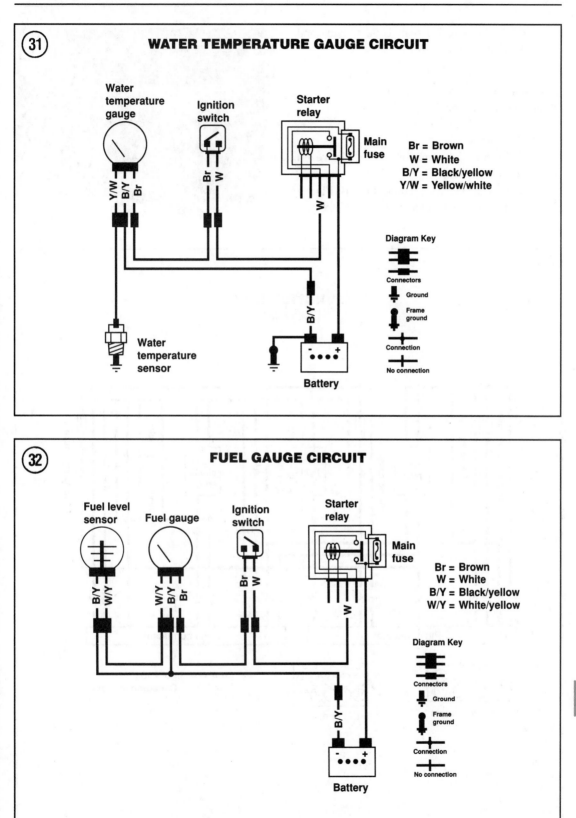

WATER TEMPERATURE GAUGE CIRCUIT

Water temperature gauge

Ignition switch

Starter relay

Main fuse

Br = Brown
W = White
B/Y = Black/yellow
Y/W = Yellow/white

Y/W B/Y Br

Br W

W

B/Y

Diagram Key

Connectors

Ground

Frame ground

Connection

No connection

Water temperature sensor

Battery

FUEL GAUGE CIRCUIT

Fuel level sensor

Fuel gauge

Ignition switch

Starter relay

Main fuse

Br = Brown
W = White
B/Y = Black/yellow
W/Y = White/yellow

B/Y W/Y

W/Y B/Y Br

Br W

W

B/Y

Diagram Key

Connectors

Ground

Frame ground

Connection

No connection

Battery

14

e. ZX-11 D1-9 (other than U.S., Canada and Australia): **Figure 38**.

Junction Box
Removal/Installation

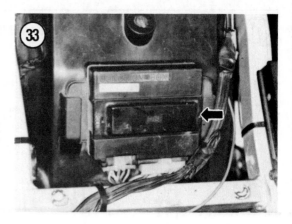

1. Remove the seat.

2. Carefully remove the junction box (A, **Figure 39**) from the rubber mount.

3. Disconnect the electrical connectors (B, **Figure 39**) from the junction box and remove the box.

4. Install by reversing these steps.

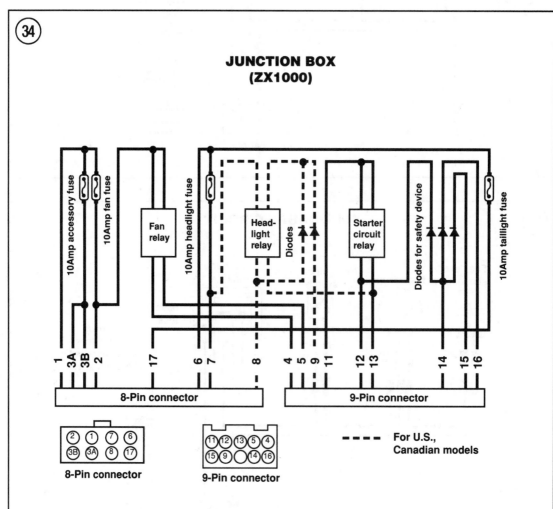

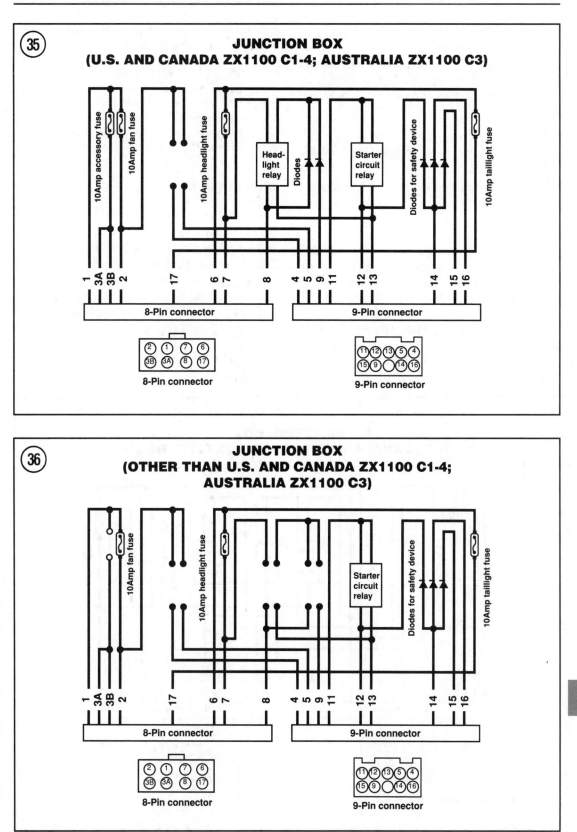

Fuse Replacement

There are 3 or 4 fuses (depending on year and model) located in the junction box. If there is an electrical system failure, first check for a blown fuse.

1. Remove the seat.

2. Remove the fuse cover (**Figure 33**) from the junction box.

3. Use needlenose pliers and pull the fuse straight up and out of the fuse panel.

4. Install a new fuse with the same amperage rating.

NOTE
The junction box is equipped with several replacement fuses. Always carry spare fuses.

Whenever a fuse blows find out the reason for the failure before replacing the fuse. Usually, the trouble is a short circuit in the wiring. Check by testing the circuit that the fuse protects. A blown fuse may be caused by a worn-through insulation or a disconnected wire shorting to ground.

CAUTION
Never substitute aluminum foil or wire for a fuse. Never use a higher amperage fuse than specified. An overload could cause a fire, resulting in complete loss of the bike.

Diode Circuit Test

The ohmmeter test leads are to be placed on the indicated terminal numbers on the junction box.

1. Remove the junction box from the rear fender.

2. Connect the ohmmeter test leads to each of the following junction box terminals:

    a. No. 13 and 8 (U.S. and Canada only).

    b. No. 13 and 9 (U.S. and Canada only).

    c. No. 12 and 14.

    d. No. 15 and 14.

    e. No. 16 and 14.

Measure the resistance and record it.

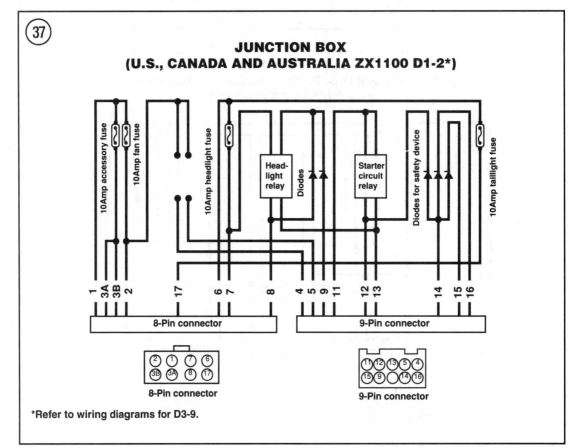

**JUNCTION BOX
(U.S., CANADA AND AUSTRALIA ZX1100 D1-2*)**

*Refer to wiring diagrams for D3-9.

3. Reverse the ohmmeter test leads to the terminals made in Step 2. Measure the resistance and record it.

4. The resistance should be low in one direction and more than 10 times higher with the ohmmeter test leads reversed. If the diode(s) shows low or high resistance readings in both directions, it is faulty and the junction box must be replaced.

5. Replace the junction box if the diodes fail any of the previous tests.

Relay Test

The junction box is equipped with the following relays:

    a. Fan relay (ZX-10 only) (Kawasaki does not provide any test procedures for this relay).

    b. Headlight relay (U.S. and Canada only).

    c. Starter circuit relay.

The 12 volt battery connections and the ohmmeter test leads are to be placed on the indicated terminal numbers on the junction box.

Battery disconnected

1. Remove the junction box from the rear fender.

2. Connect an ohmmeter to the following terminals:

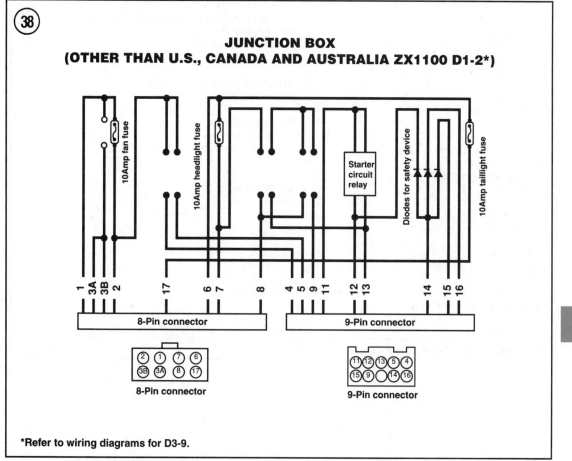

*Refer to wiring diagrams for D3-9.

14

a. Headlight relay (U.S. and Canada): No. 7 and 8, then No. 7 and 13.

b. Starter relay: No. 11 and 13, then No. 12 and 13.

The ohmmeter should read infinity.

3. Replace the junction box if either relay fails any of the previous tests.

Battery connected

1. Remove the junction box from the rear fender.

2. To test the headlight relay (U.S. and Canada), perform the following:

a. Connect a 12-volt battery to terminals No. 9 and 13.

b. Connect an ohmmeter to terminals No. 7 and 8.

The ohmmeter should read 0 ohms.

3. To test the starter relay, perform the following:

a. Connect a 12-volt battery to terminals No. 11 and 12.

b. Connect an ohmmeter to terminals No. 11 and 13.

The ohmmeter should read 0 ohms.

4. Replace the junction box if either relay fails any of the previous tests.

Table 1 ELECTRICAL SPECIFICATIONS

Battery	
ZX1000, ZX1100 C1-4	12 volt; 14 amp hour
ZX1100 D1-9	12 volt; 12 amp hour (sealed type)
Specific gravity	See text, Chapter Three*
Charge rate	See text, Chapter Three*
Alternator	
Brush length	
New	10.5 mm (0.413 in.)
Wear limit	4.5 mm (0.177 in.)
Slip ring diameter	
New	14.4 mm (0.566 in.)
Wear limit	14.0 mm (0.551 in.)
Rotor coil resistance	Approximately 4 ohms
Ignition system	
Pickup coil resistance	
ZX1000	400-490 ohms
ZX1100	380-570 ohms
Starter motor	
Brush length	
New	12 mm (0.472 in.)
Wear limit	8.5 mm (0.334 in.)
Commutator diameter	
New	28 mm (1.102 in.)
Wear limit	27 mm (1.062 in.)
Commutator groove depth	
New	0.7 mm (0.027 in.)
Wear limit	0.2 mm (0.007 in.)
*See Chapter Three in the front section of this manual.	

CHAPTER NINE

COOLING SYSTEM

This chapter describes service procedures for the cooling system. **Table 1** at the end of this chapter lists cooling system specifications.

> *NOTE*
> *This chapter covers all procedures unique to the Kawasaki ZX1000 (ZX-10) and ZX1100 (ZX-11) from 1988-on. If a specific procedure is not included in this chapter, unless otherwise specified refer to ZX1000 models in Chapter Nine at the front of this manual for service procedures.*

COOLANT RESERVOIR

On ZX-10 and ZX-11 C1-4 models, the reservoir tank (**Figure 1**) is located under the right-hand side of the upper fairing. On ZX-11 D1-9 models, the reservoir tank is located under the right-hand frame side cover.

To remove the reservoir tank on ZX-10 and ZX-11 C1-4 models, remove the upper fairing as described in Chapter Thirteen in this section of the manual.

To remove the reservoir tank on ZX-11 D1 models, remove the right-hand side cover as described in Chapter Thirteen in this section of the manual.

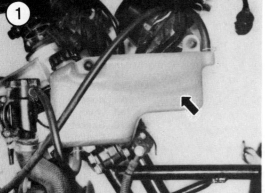

RADIATOR AND FAN

Removal/Installation

The radiator and fan are removed as an assembly. Refer to the following illustrations when working on the cooling system:

   a. ZX-10: **Figure 2**.
   b. ZX-11: **Figure 3**.

1. Place the bike on the centerstand.
2. Remove the upper and lower fairings as described in Chapter Thirteen in this section of the manual.
3. Drain the cooling system as described in Chapter Three in the front section of this manual.
4. Disconnect the fan switch lead (**Figure 4**).
5. Disconnect the fan motor electrical connector.
6. Disconnect the electrical connectors (A, **Figure 5**) from each horn. Then remove the horn bracket mounting bolt (B, **Figure 5**) and remove each horn.
7. At the radiator, loosen the hose clamps for the upper (A, **Figure 6**) and lower (**Figure 7**) radiator hoses. Move the clamps back onto the hoses. Then carefully slip the hoses off the necks on the radiator.

> *CAUTION*
> *If the hoses are tight on the radiator necks, refer to **Hoses** in Chapter Nine in the front section of this manual. Excessive force applied to the hose during removal could damage the radiator neck.*

8. Remove the bolts securing the screen (C, **Figure 5**) and remove the screen.
9. Remove the radiator upper (B, **Figure 6**) and lower mounting bolts and remove the radiator.
10. Replace the radiator hoses if deterioration or damage is noted.
11. Inspect the radiator as described under Radiator Inspection in Chapter Nine in the front section of this manual.
12. Installation is the reverse of these steps. Note the following:
   a. Make sure the fan switch ground lead is attached correctly.
   b. Test the horns to make sure they work properly.

14

② RADIATOR (ZX1000)

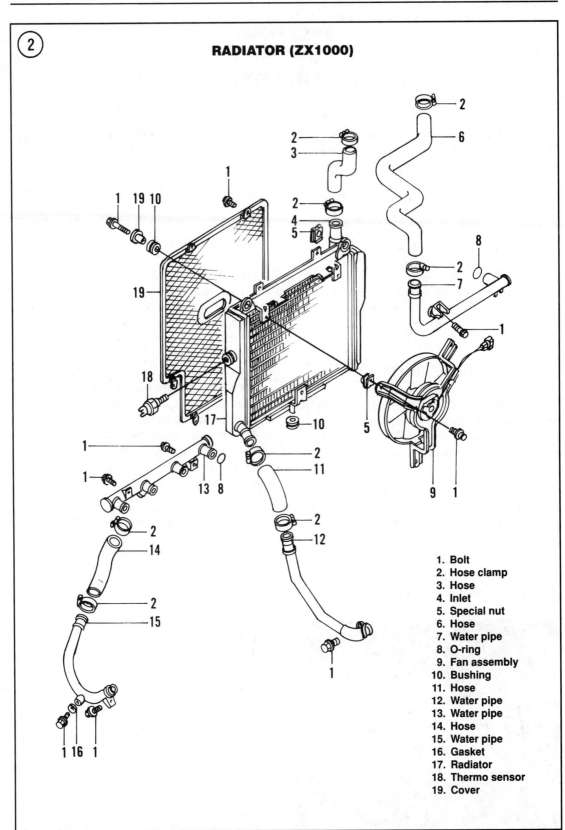

1. Bolt
2. Hose clamp
3. Hose
4. Inlet
5. Special nut
6. Hose
7. Water pipe
8. O-ring
9. Fan assembly
10. Bushing
11. Hose
12. Water pipe
13. Water pipe
14. Hose
15. Water pipe
16. Gasket
17. Radiator
18. Thermo sensor
19. Cover

③

**RADIATOR
(ZX1100)**

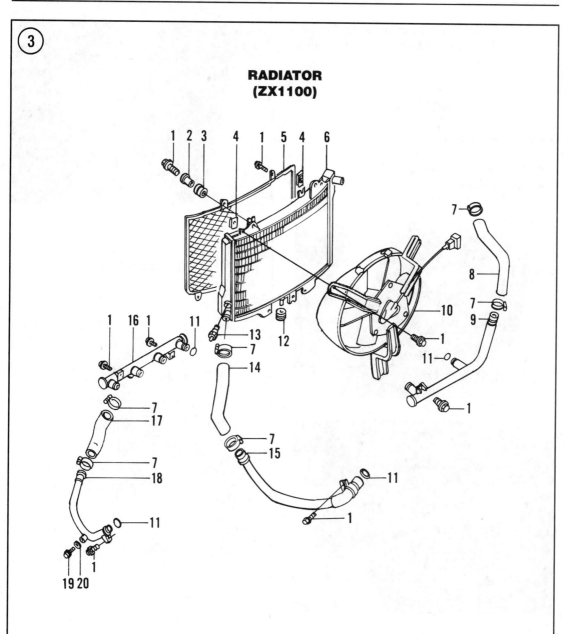

1. Bolt
2. Collar
3. Bushing
4. Special nut
5. Cover
6. Radiator
7. Hose clamp
8. Hose
9. Water pipe
10. Fan assembly

11. O-ring
12. Bushing
13. Thermo sensor
14. Hose
15. Water pipe
16. Water pipe
17. Hose
18. Water pipe
19. Drain bolt
20. Gasket

14

c. Refill the coolant as described under *Coolant Change* in Chapter Three in the front section of the manual.

THERMOSTAT

Removal/Installation

Refer to **Figure 8** for this procedure.

1. Remove the seat.

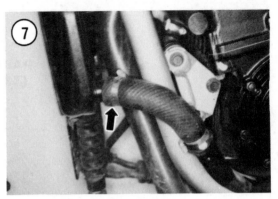

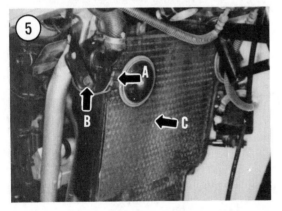

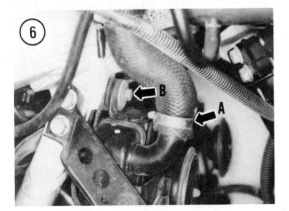

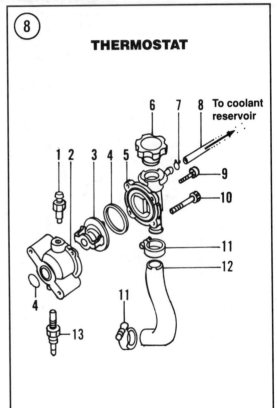

THERMOSTAT

To coolant reservoir

1. Bleeder bolt
2. Thermostat cover
3. Thermostat
4. O-ring
5. Housing
6. Cap
7. Hose clamp
8. Hose
9. Screw
10. Screw
11. Hose clamp
12. Hose
13. Water temperature sensor

2. Remove the fuel tank as described in Chapter Seven in this section of the manual.

3. Remove the front fairing as described in Chapter Thirteen in this section of the manual.

4. Drain the cooling system as described in Chapter Three in the front section of this manual.

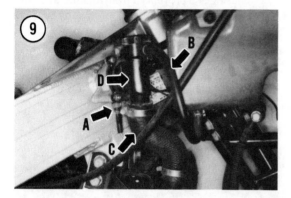

5. Disconnect the water temperature sensor electrical connector (A, **Figure 9**).

6. Disconnect the reservoir tank hose (B, **Figure 9**).

7. Remove the radiator hose (C, **Figure 9**) from the thermostat housing.

8. Remove the 2 long Allen bolts securing the thermostat housing (D, **Figure 9**) to the frame and remove the assembly

9. Remove the 2 short Phillips screws and separate the body from the thermostat housing. Separate the body and O-ring from the housing and remove the thermostat.

10. Test the thermostat as described in Chapter Nine in the front section of this manual.

11. Install by reversing these removal steps while noting the following:

    a. Replace the O-ring if necessary.

    b. Refill the cooling system as described in Chapter Three in the front section of this manual.

Table 1 COOLING SYSTEM SPECIFICATIONS

Capacity	
ZX1000	3.1 L (3.3 U.S. qt.)
ZX1100	2.5 L (2.6 U.S. qt.)
Coolant ratio	50% soft water:50% coolant
Radiator cap	0.95-1.25 kg/cm^2 (14-18 psi)
Thermostat	
Opening temperature	80-84° C (176-183° F)
Valve opening lift	Not less than 8 mm (5/16 in.) @ 95° C (203° F)

CHAPTER TEN

FRONT SUSPENSION AND STEERING

This chapter describes service procedures on front fork and front wheel and hub. **Table 1** at the end of this chapter lists service specifications. **Table 1** and **Table 2** are located at the end of this chapter.

NOTE
This chapter covers all procedures unique to the Kawasaki ZX1000 (ZX-10) and ZX1100 (ZX-11) from 1988-on. If a specific procedure is not included in this chapter, unless otherwise specified refer to ZX1000 models in Chapter Ten

at the front of this manual for service procedures.

FRONT WHEEL

14

Removal/Installation

1. Remove the lower fairing as described in Chapter Thirteen in this section of the manual.

2. Remove the brake caliper mounting bolts (A, **Figure 1**) on each side and remove both calipers.

NOTE
Insert a piece of wood in each caliper in place of the discs. That way, if the brake lever is inadvertently squeezed, the pistons will not be forced out of the cylinder. If this does happen, the caliper(s) might have to be disassembled to reseat the pistons and the system will have to be bled. By using the wood, bleeding the brake is not necessary when installing the wheel.

3. Disconnect the speedometer cable (B, **Figure 1**) at the front wheel.

NOTE
It is not necessary to completely remove the axle pinch bolts.

4. On the right-hand side, loosen both axle pinch bolts (A, **Figure 2**).

5. Loosen the front axle (B, **Figure 2**).

6. On the left-hand side, loosen both axle nut pinch bolts (A, **Figure 3**).

7. Support the bike with a jack so that the front wheel is clear of the ground.

8. Unscrew the axle (B, **Figure 2**) from the nut (B, **Figure 3**) in the left-hand fork leg and remove the axle and the nut.

9. Pull the wheel forward and remove it. Don't lose the spacer (**Figure 4**) on the right-hand side or the speedometer drive gear (**Figure 5**) on the left-hand side.

CAUTION
Do not set the wheel down on the disc surface as it may be scratched or warped. Either lean the wheel against a wall or place it on a couple of wood blocks.

10. When servicing the wheel assembly, install the spacer and the speedometer drive gear and nut onto the axle to prevent their loss (**Figure 6**).

11. Installation is the reverse of these steps. Note the following:

    a. To prevent axle seizure, coat the axle with an anti-seize compound such as Bostik Never-Seez Lubricating & Anti-Seize Compound (part No. 49501).

    b. See **Figure 7**. Align the 2 tabs in the speedometer gear housing with the 2 speedometer drive

slots in the front hub and install the gear housing. See **Figure 5**.

    c. When installing the front wheel, align the lug on the speedometer gear housing with the slot in the back of the left-hand fork slider. This procedure locates the speedometer drive gear housing and prevents it from rotating when the wheel turns.

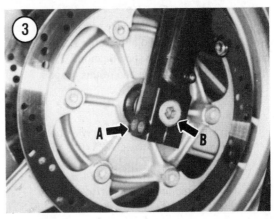

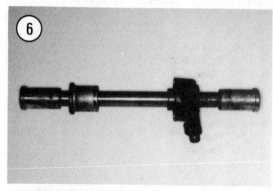

d. Make sure the speedometer gear housing does not move as the axle is tightened.

e. Tighten the axle and nut to the specification listed in **Table 2**.

f. Tighten the caliper mounting bolts to the specification listed in **Table 2**.

g. Apply the front brake and compress the front forks several times to make sure the axle is installed correctly without binding the forks. Then tighten the axle pinch bolts on each side to specifications in **Table 2**.

FRONT HUB
(ZX-11)

The disassembly, inspection and reassembly are the same as on ZX-1000 models with the exception of minor modifications to some of the components. Refer to **Figure 8** for this procedure.

FRONT FORKS

If the front forks are going to be removed without disassembly, perform the *Removal/Installation* procedures in this chapter. If the front forks are going to be disassembled, refer to *Disassembly* in this chapter.

Removal/Installation

1. Place the motorcycle on the centerstand.

2. Remove the front fairing as described in Chapter Thirteen in this section of the manual.

3. Remove both front caliper assembles as described in Chapter Twelve in this section of the manual.

4. Disconnect the speedometer cable (**Figure 9**) at the front wheel.

5. Remove the speedometer cable from the upper (B, **Figure 10**) and lower (A, **Figure 10**) guides on the front fender.

6. Remove the front wheel as described in this chapter.

7. Remove the bolts securing the front fork brace (**Figure 11**) and remove the brace.

8. Remove the bolts (**Figure 12**) securing the front fender and remove the fender assembly.

9. Remove the handlebar assembly as described in this chapter.

14

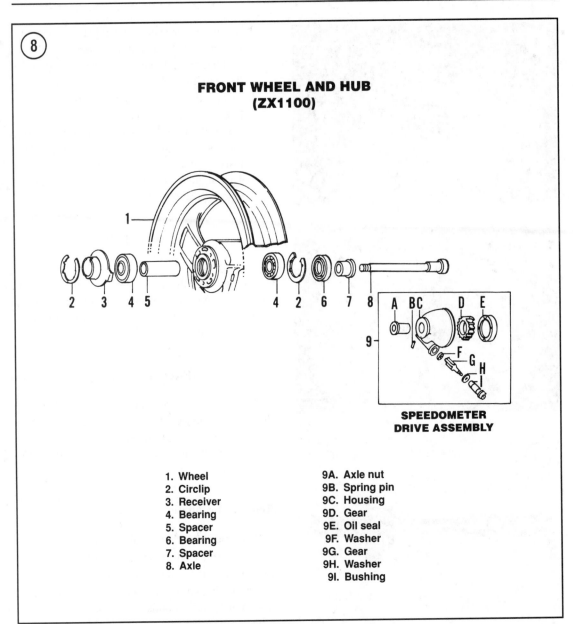

⑧

FRONT WHEEL AND HUB
(ZX1100)

**SPEEDOMETER
DRIVE ASSEMBLY**

1. Wheel
2. Circlip
3. Receiver
4. Bearing
5. Spacer
6. Bearing
7. Spacer
8. Axle

9A. Axle nut
9B. Spring pin
9C. Housing
9D. Gear
9E. Oil seal
9F. Washer
9G. Gear
9H. Washer
9I. Bushing

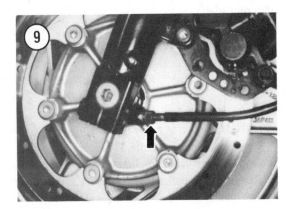

⑨

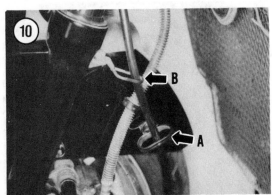

⑩

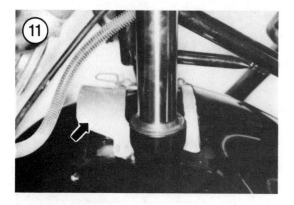

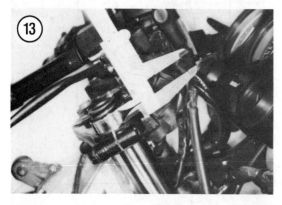

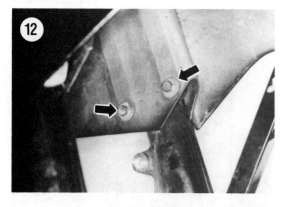

10. Measure the distance from the top surface of the fork tube to the top surface of the upper fork bridge (**Figure 13**). Write down this dimension for installation reference. The specified dimension is 15 mm for the stock fork assembly.

> *NOTE*
> *If the fork assemblies are going to be disassembled for service, refer to the **Disassembly** in this chapter before proceeding.*

11. Loosen the upper (A, **Figure 14**) and lower (**Figure 15**) fork bridge bolts.
12. Twist the fork tube and remove it.
13. Repeat for the opposite side.
14. Install by reversing these removal steps. Note the following:
   a. Push the fork tube up until the top surface is the same distance (**Figure 13**) noted during removal.
   b. Tighten the upper and lower fork bridge bolts to specifications in **Table 2**.
   c. After installing the front wheel, squeeze the front brake lever. If the brake lever feels spongy, bleed the brake as described in Chapter Twelve in the front section of this manual.

Disassembly

Refer to **Figure 16** for this procedure.
1. Perform Steps 1-10 described under *Front Forks Removal/Installation* in this chapter.

> *NOTE*
> *The lower fork tube Allen bolt is normally secured with a locking agent and is often very difficult to remove because*

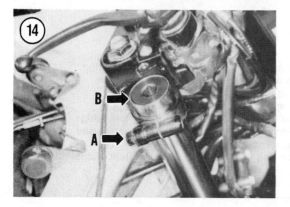

14

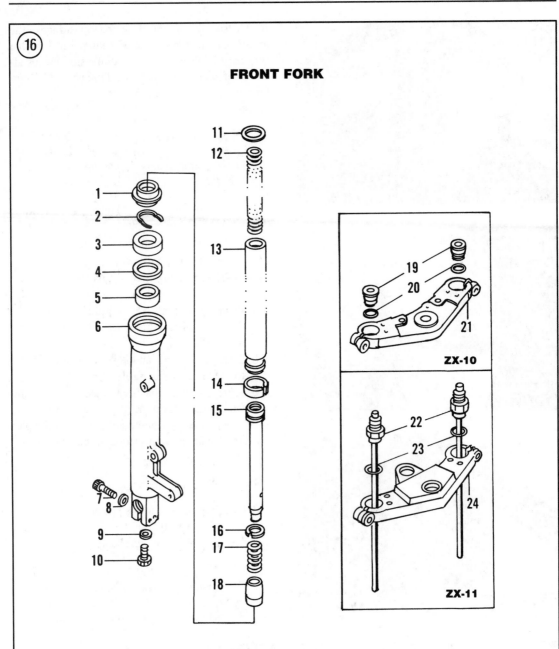

FRONT FORK

ZX-10

ZX-11

1. Dust seal	9. Washer	17. Rebound spring
2. Spring clip	10. Allen bolt	18. Oil lock piece
3. Oil seal	11. Spring seat	19. Fork cap
4. Washer	12. Fork spring	20. O-ring
5. Bushing	13. Upper fork tube	21. Upper fork bridge
6. Lower fork tube	14. Bushing	22. Fork cap/adjuster
7. Drain screw	15. Damper rod	23. O-ring
8. Sealing washer	16. Piston ring	24. Upper fork bridge

the damper rod will turn inside the lower fork tube. The Allen bolt can be removed easily with an air impact driver. If you do not have access to an air impact driver, it is best to loosen the Allen bolt before removing the fork tube cap and spring. This method allows the fork spring to apply pressure to the damper rod to keep it from turning when the Allen bolt is loosened.

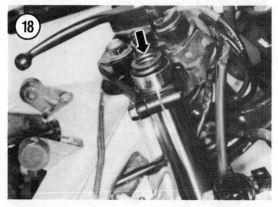

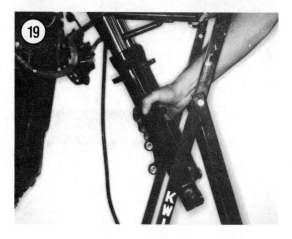

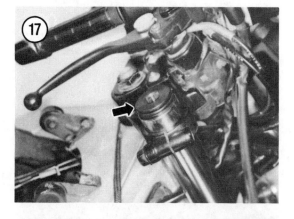

2. Place a drain pan under the fork slider.

NOTE
With the front fender removed, the lower fork tube will turn when the Allen bolt is turned. Install an adjustable wrench on the lower end of the fork tube.

3. Loosen, then remove the Allen bolt and washer and drain the fork oil. After the fork oil has completely drained, reinstall the Allen bolt and washer to avoid misplacing them.

4. Loosen the upper fork bridge pinch bolt (A, **Figure 14**).

5. Use a 1/2 in. socket drive extension and loosen the fork cap (B, **Figure 14**).

NOTE
On ZX-11 models, there is a long adjust rod attached to the fork cap. Pull the fork cap straight up and out of the upper fork tube to avoid any damage to the rod.

6. Remove the fork cap (**Figure 17**) and spring seat.

7. Remove the fork spring (**Figure 18**). Cover the end of the fork spring with a shop rag as it is removed to prevent oil from dripping down the steering stem and fork tube. Place the fork spring on some clean newspapers to avoid making a mess on your workbench.

8. Carefully pry the dust seal out of the lower fork tube and slide it up the fork tube.

9. Pry the spring clip out of the lower fork tube and remove it.

10. Before separating the fork tubes, compress and extend the forks their full travel. If you feel any roughness or harsh spots in the stroke it is an indication of a bent upper fork tube or a damaged (dented) lower fork tube.

11. The upper fork tube and the lower fork tube are held together by a bushing that is pressed into the top of the lower fork tube. In order to separate the lower fork tube from the upper fork tube, pull hard on the lower fork tube using quick up-and-down strokes (**Figure 19**). Doing so will withdraw the oil seal, washer and bushing from the lower fork tube.

12. Remove the lower fork tube (**Figure 20**) from the upper fork tube.

13. Loosen the lower fork bridge pinch bolts (**Figure 15**).

14

14. Slide the upper fork tube from the upper and lower fork bridges. It may be necessary to slightly rotate the fork tube while pulling it down and out. Remove all parts from the upper fork slider.

15. Remove the oil lock piece from the end of the damper rod. In some cases, the oil lock piece will fall off into the lower fork tube, if so remove it from there.

16. Turn the upper fork tube upside down and remove the damper rod and rebound spring.

17. Repeat for the opposite side.

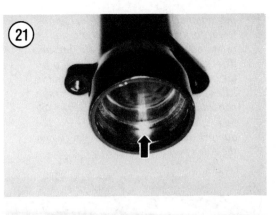

Inspection

1. Thoroughly clean all parts in solvent and dry them.

2. Check both fork tubes for wear or scratches. Check the upper fork tube for straightness. If bent, refer service to a Kawasaki dealer.

3. Check upper fork tube for chrome pitting, flaking or creasing; this condition will damage the oil seals. Replace the upper fork tube if necessary.

4. Check the lower fork tube oil seal area (**Figure 21**) for dents or other damage that would allow oil leakage. Replace the fork tube if necessary.

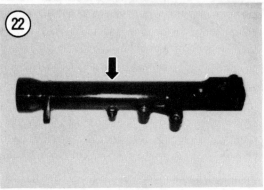

5. Check the lower fork tube (**Figure 22**) for dents or other damage that would allow the upper fork tube to hang up during normal operation. Also check the brake caliper mounts (**Figure 23**) for cracks or damage. Replace the fork tube if necessary.

6. Check the damper rod for straightness.

7. Check the damper rod piston ring (**Figure 24**) for tearing, cracks or damage. Replace if necessary.

8. Make sure the oil hole (**Figure 25**) in the damper rod is clear. Clean out if necessary.

9. Check the outside surface of the guide bushing on the upper fork tube (**Figure 26**) for scoring, nicks or

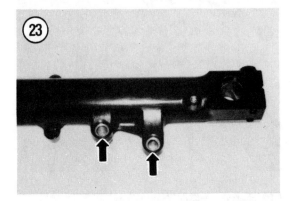

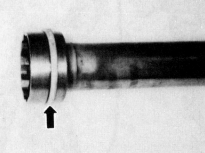

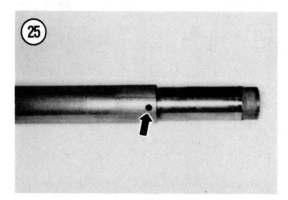

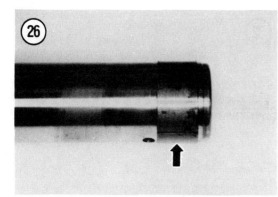

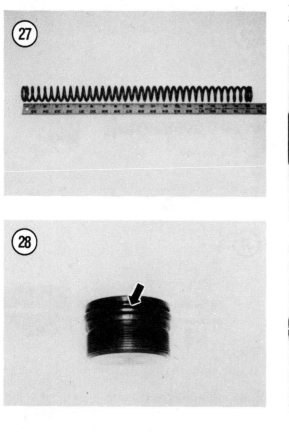

damage. Replace if necessary by pulling it off the upper fork tube.

10. Check the inside surface of the guide bushing on the lower fork tube for scoring, nicks or damage. Replace if necessary.

11. Measure the uncompressed length of the fork spring with a long ruler (**Figure 27**) and compare to specification in **Table 1**. Replace both fork springs as a set if one is found too short.

NOTE
It is best to replace both springs to keep the forks balanced for steering stability.

12. Replace the fork cap O-ring (**Figure 28**) if damaged.

13. Check the oil and dust seals for wear or damage. Replace if necessary.

Assembly

Refer to **Figure 16** for this procedure.

1. If removed, install the drain screw and washer (**Figure 29**). Tighten the screw securely.

2. Apply fork oil to all parts prior to assembly.

3. Slide the spring onto the damper rod (**Figure 30**) and insert the damper rod and spring into the top of

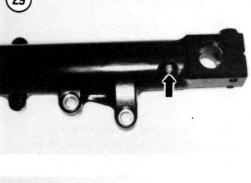

14

the upper fork tube (**Figure 31**). Slide the damper rod all the way down until it exits the bottom of the fork tube.

4. To hold the damper rod in place during the following steps, temporarily install the fork spring (**Figure 32**), the spring seat and the fork cap (**Figure 33**). Tighten the fork cap securely.

5. Position the oil lock piece with the larger end going on last and slide the oil lock piece (**Figure 34**) onto the damper rod.

6. Insert the damper rod/upper fork tube into the lower fork tube (**Figure 35**).

7. Make sure the sealing washer (**Figure 36**) is in place on the Allen bolt.

> *NOTE*
> *When installing and tightening the fork tube Allen bolt in Step 7, it will be necessary to prevent the damper rod from turning. One way is to temporarily install the fork spring and fork cap. Or the damper rod can also be held stationary by installing the Kawasaki adapter (part No. 57001-1057) on a long 3/8 in. T-handle extension and inserting the adapter into the end of the damper rod (**Figure 37**).*

8. Apply Loctite 242 (blue) onto the fork tube Allen bolt and install (**Figure 38**) and tighten it. Tighten to the specification listed in **Table 2**.

> *NOTE*
> *If the fork cap and fork spring were used to hold the damper rod when installing the fork tube Allen bolt, remove them from the upper fork tube.*

> *NOTE*
> *The bushing can be installed with a piece of galvanized pipe (**Figure 39**) or other piece of tubing that fits snugly over the upper fork tube. If both ends of the pipe are threaded, wrap one end with duct tape to prevent the threads from damaging the interior of the lower fork tube. The bottom of this homemade driver must be flat so it installs the parts squarely.*

9. Slide the bushing (A, **Figure 40**) over the fork tube. Turn the bushing so that the split faces to the left or right side of the lower fork tube. Tap the bushing into the lower fork tube until it bottoms out.

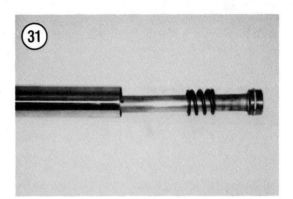

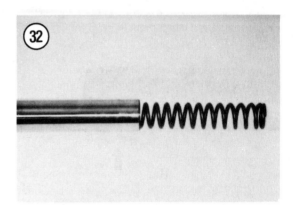

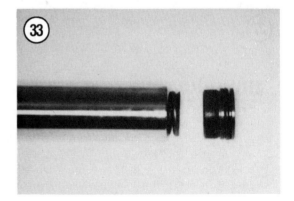

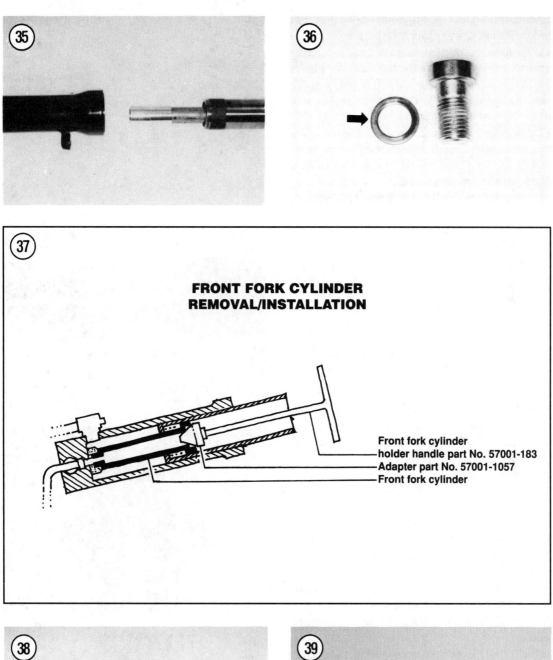

**FRONT FORK CYLINDER
REMOVAL/INSTALLATION**

Front fork cylinder
holder handle part No. 57001-183
Adapter part No. 57001-1057
Front fork cylinder

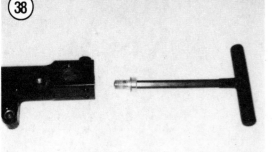

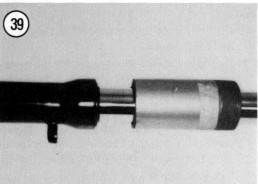

14

10. Slide the washer (B, **Figure 40**) down the upper fork tube until it rests against the bushing.

11. Position the oil seal with its markings facing upward and slide it down the fork tube (C, **Figure 40**). Drive the seal into the lower fork tube with the same tool used in Step 9. Drive the oil seal in until it rests against the washer.

12. Make sure the spring clip groove in the lower fork tube can be seen above the top surface of the oil seal. If not, the oil seal will have to be driven farther down into the lower fork tube.

13. Slide the spring clip (A, **Figure 41**) down the upper fork tube and seat it in the lower fork tube groove. Make sure the clip is correctly seated in the groove (**Figure 42**).

14. Slide the dust seal (B, **Figure 41**) down the upper fork tube and seat it in the lower fork tube (**Figure 43**) using a plastic hammer.

CAUTION
The dust seal has a raised lip which may be damaged by using a homemade bushing/seal driver. Use a plastic hammer to tap the dust seal into place.

15. Fill fork tube with the correct quantity of SAE 10W-20 fork oil as specified in **Table 1**. Check the oil level as described in Chapter Three in this section of the manual.

16. Extend the forks as far apart as possible.

17. Install the fork spring (**Figure 32**) and the spring seat.

18A. On ZX-10 models, apply a light coat of oil to the fork cap O-ring (**Figure 28**) and install it (**Figure 33**) by slightly compressing the fork spring. Once the fork cap is installed, it can be tightened after installing the fork tube into the bike. See *Front Fork Removal/Installation* in this chapter.

18B. On ZX-11 models, install the fork cap bolt as follows:

   a. Carefully insert the fork cap bolt and adjust rod in the fork spring.

   b. Properly index the flat on the end of the damping adjust rod into the receptacle in the top of the damper rod.

   c. Start the fork cap bolt slowly while pushing down on the spring. Start the bolt slowly and don't cross-thread it. Once the fork cap is installed, it can be tightened after installing the fork tube into the bike. See *Front Fork Removal/Installation* in this chapter.

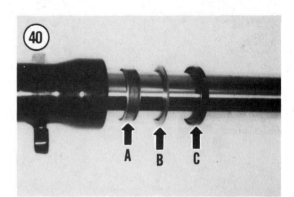
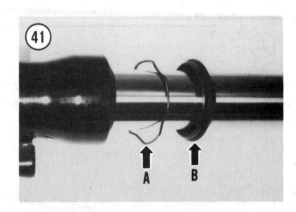
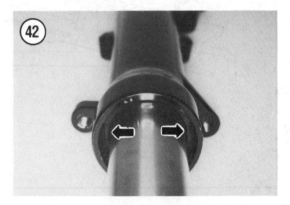
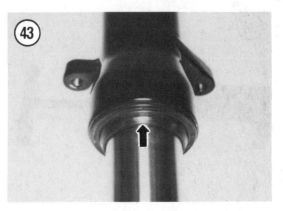

HANDLEBARS

Removal/Installation

The ZX-10 and ZX-11 use handlebar assemblies that slip over the top of the upper fork tubes and bolt directly to the upper fork bridge.

1. Remove the steering stem cover (**Figure 44**).

2. Remove the Allen bolts (**Figure 45**) and lift the handlebar off the upper fork bridge. Move the handlebar assembly out of the way and keep both master cylinders in the upright position to avoid letting air into the brake or clutch hydraulic system while performing service procedures.

3. If it is necessary to replace the handlebar, remove the handlebar switches as described under *Switches* in Chapter Eight in the front section of this manual. Remove the brake master cylinder as described in Chapter Twelve in the front section of this manual. Remove the clutch master cylinder as described in Chapter Five in the front section of this manual.

4. Tighten the Allen bolts to specifications in **Table 2**.

Table 1 FRONT SUSPENSION AND STEERING SPECIFICATIONS

Front fork type	Telescopic fork
Front fork oil type	SAE 10W-20
Front fork oil capacity	
ZX1000	
Change	360 cc (12.17 oz.)
Rebuild	415-423 cc (14.03-14.30 oz.)
ZX1100 C1-4	
Change	390 cc (13.18 oz.)
Rebuild	454-462 cc (15.35-15.62 oz.)
ZX1100 D1	
Change	410 cc (13.86 oz.)
Rebuild D1-2	461-469 cc (15.59-15.86 oz.)
Rebuild D3-9	463-471 mL (15.65-15.93 oz.)
Front fork oil level (fully compressed)	
ZX1000	128-132 mm (5.0-5.19 in.)
ZX1100 C1-4	147-151 mm (5.78-5.94 in.)
ZX1100 D1-2	131-135 mm (5.15-5.31 in.)
ZX1100 D3-9	129-133 mm (5.08-5.24 in.)
Front fork spring free length	
ZX1000	
New	488 mm (19.21 in.)
Wear limit	478 mm (18.82 in.)
ZX1100 C1-4	
New	438 mm (17.24 in.)
Wear limit	429 mm (16.89 in.)
	(continued)

14

Table 1 FRONT SUSPENSION AND STEERING SPECIFICATIONS (continued)

ZX1100 D1-9	
New	295 mm (11.66 in.)
Wear limit	289 mm (11.38 in.)
Caster	
ZX1000	26.5°
ZX1100	26°
Trail	
ZX1000	101 mm (3.97 in.)
ZX1100 C1-4	103 mm (4.05 in.)
ZX1100 D1-9	107 mm (4.21 in.)
Front wheel travel	
ZX1000	135 mm (5.31 in.)
ZX1100 C1-4	125 mm (4.92 in.)
ZX1100 D1-9	120 mm (4.72 in.)
Axle runout	See text
Rim runout (wear limit)	
Axial	0.5 mm (0.019 in.)
Radial	0.8 mm (0.031 in.)

Table 2 FRONT SUSPENSION TIGHTENING TORQUES

Item	N•m	ft.-lb.
Front axle nut	88	65
Front axle pinch bolts	21	15
Upper bridge bolt	28	21
Lower bridge bolt	28	21
Handlebar Allen bolts	20	14.5
Front caliper mounting bolts	34	25

CHAPTER ELEVEN

REAR SUSPENSION

This chapter describes service procedures on rear wheel and suspension components. **Table 1** at the end of this chapter lists service specifications. **Table 1** and **Table 2** are located at the end of this chapter.

> *NOTE*
> *This chapter covers all procedures unique to the Kawasaki ZX1000 (ZX-10) and ZX1100 (ZX-11) from 1988-on. If a specific procedure is not included in this chapter, unless otherwise specified refer to ZX1000 models in Chapter Eleven at the front of this manual for service procedures.*

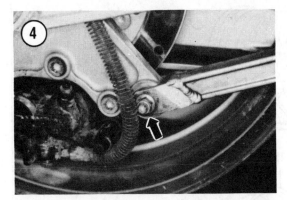

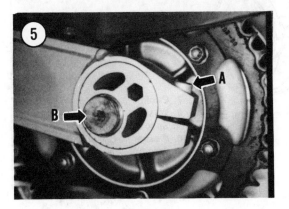

REAR WHEEL

Removal/Installation

1. Support the bike so the rear wheel clears the ground.

2. Remove the right-hand retaining ring (**Figure 1**).

3. Loosen the right-hand axle pinch bolt (**Figure 2**).

4. Loosen the axle nut with an Allen wrench (**Figure 3**).

5. Loosen the brake caliper torque link rear bolt and nut (**Figure 4**).

6. Remove the left-hand retaining ring.

7. Loosen the left-hand axle pinch bolt (A, **Figure 5**).

8. Remove the axle nut (**Figure 6**) from the right-hand side.

9. Remove the axle (B, **Figure 5**) from the left-hand side.

10. Remove the brake caliper torque link rear bolt and nut and lower the torque link (A, **Figure 7**).

11. Lower the caliper and holder assembly (B, **Figure 7**).

14

NOTE
Insert a piece of wood in the caliper in place of the disc. That way, if the brake pedal is inadvertently applied, the pistons will not be forced out of the cylinders. If this does happen, the caliper might have to be disassembled to reseat the pistons and the system will have to be bled. By using the wood, bleeding the brake is not necessary when installing the wheel.

CAUTION
The rear sprocket is bolted onto a separate coupling assembly. Do not lift the wheel assembly by the sprocket as this will pull the sprocket assembly out of the hub and allow the wheel to fall to the ground.

12. Lift the chain off the sprocket and pull the wheel (C, **Figure 7**) away from the swing arm and remove it.

13. If necessary, remove the chain adjusters (D, **Figure 7**).

14. Remove the right- and left-hand axle spacers.

CAUTION
Do not set the wheel down on the disc surface as it may be scratched or warped. Either lean the wheel against a wall or place it on a couple of wood blocks.

15. If the wheel is going to be off for any length of time, or if it is to be taken to a shop for repair, install the chain adjusters and axle spacers on the axle

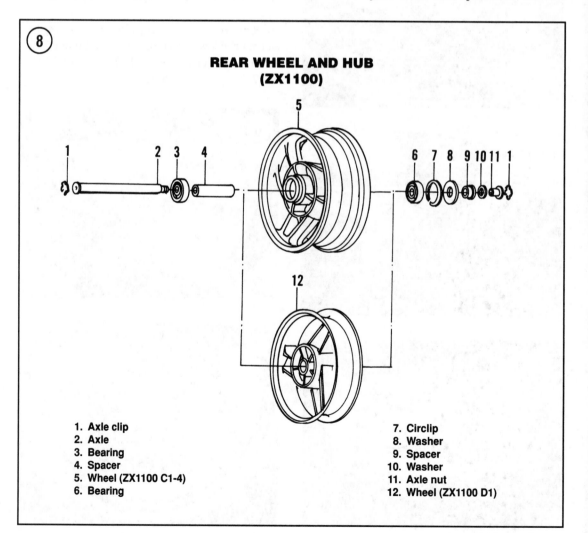

⑧

**REAR WHEEL AND HUB
(ZX1100)**

1. Axle clip
2. Axle
3. Bearing
4. Spacer
5. Wheel (ZX1100 C1-4)
6. Bearing
7. Circlip
8. Washer
9. Spacer
10. Washer
11. Axle nut
12. Wheel (ZX1100 D1)

along with the axle nut to prevent misplacing any parts.

16. If necessary, service the rear sprocket as described in this chapter as well as Chapter Eleven in the front section of this manual.

17. Installation is the reverse of these steps. Note the following:

    a. To prevent axle seizure, coat the axle with an anti-seize compound such as Bostik Never-Seez Lubricating & Anti-Seize Compound (part No. 49501).

    b. If removed, insert the rear sprocket/coupling assembly into the rear hub as described in this chapter as well as Chapter Eleven in the front section of this manual.

    c. Adjust the drive chain as described in Chapter Three.

    d. Tighten the axle nut and pinch bolts to the torque specifications listed in **Table 2**.

    e. Make sure both retaining rings (**Figure 1**) are tightly in the chain adjuster grooves.

    f. Spin the wheel several times to make sure it rotates freely and that the rear brake works properly.

REAR HUB
(ZX-11)

The disassembly, inspection and reassembly are the same as on ZX-1000 models with the exception of minor modifications to some of the components. Refer to **Figure 8** for this procedure.

REAR SPROCKET
AND COUPLING
(ZX-11 D1-9)

The disassembly, inspection and reassembly are the same as on ZX-1000 models with the exception of minor modifications to some of the components. Refer to **Figure 9** for this procedure.

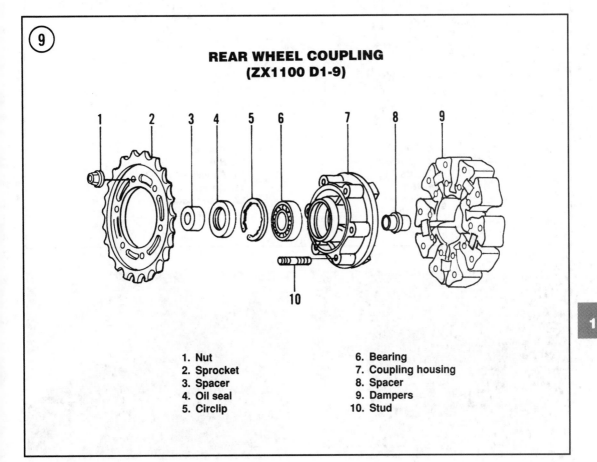

**REAR WHEEL COUPLING
(ZX1100 D1-9)**

1. Nut
2. Sprocket
3. Spacer
4. Oil seal
5. Circlip
6. Bearing
7. Coupling housing
8. Spacer
9. Dampers
10. Stud

14

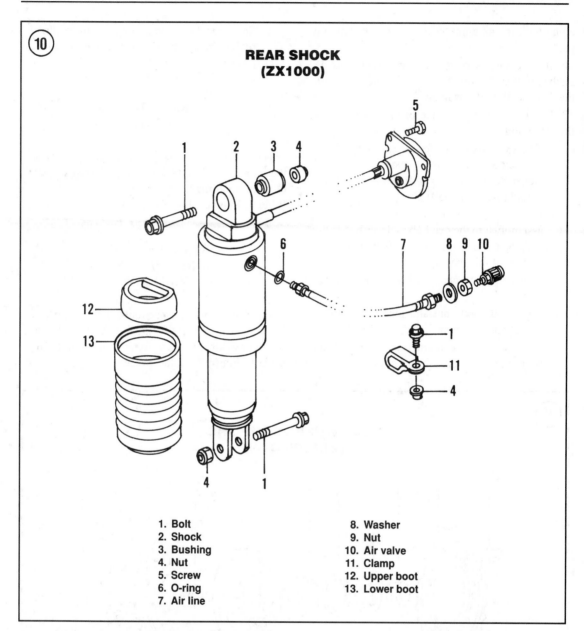

**REAR SHOCK
(ZX1000)**

1. Bolt
2. Shock
3. Bushing
4. Nut
5. Screw
6. O-ring
7. Air line
8. Washer
9. Nut
10. Air valve
11. Clamp
12. Upper boot
13. Lower boot

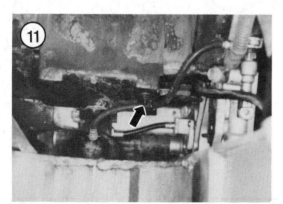

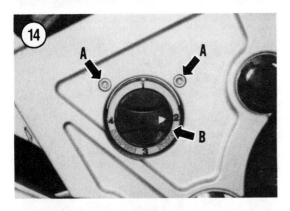

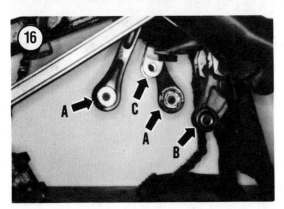

SHOCK ABSORBER

Removal/Installation
(ZX-10)

Refer to **Figure 10** for this procedure.

1. Remove the rear wheel as described in this chapter.

2. Remove the seat.

3. Remove both side covers.

4. Remove the battery and the battery tray.

5. Working in the area where the battery tray was located, remove the bolt (from above) and the nut and bracket (from below) (**Figure 11**) securing the air hose to the rear fender.

6. Remove the air valve cap (**Figure 12**).

7. Then remove the air valve mounting nut and washer (**Figure 13**) and push the air hose back out of the frame hole. Reinstall the nut and washer on the air hose to avoid misplacing them.

8. Remove the screws (A, **Figure 14**) securing the damping adjuster control knob (B, **Figure 14**).

9. Remove the bolt and nut (**Figure 15**) securing the lower portion of the shock absorber to the rocker arm.

10. Remove the lower bolt and nut securing the tie rods to the rocker arm. Move the tie rods (A, **Figure 16**) out of the way.

11. Move the rocker arm (B, **Figure 16**) forward and out of the way.

12. Support the shock absorber.

13. Insert a long socket extension through the damping adjust control knob hole (**Figure 17**) and remove the bolt and nut (**Figure 18**) securing the upper portion of the shock absorber to the frame.

14. Partially lower the shock absorber.

14

15. As viewed from the top, rotate the shock absorber counterclockwise about 50° until the air hose is aligned with the largest part of the cutout in the top surface of the swing arm (**Figure 19**). This is necessary so the air hose will not be damaged during removal.

16. Slowly lower the shock absorber (C, **Figure 16**), air hose and control cable (**Figure 20**) out through the opening in the swing arm and remove the assembly.

NOTE
Move the tie rods back into position onto the rocker arm and install the bolt and nut through them to prevent losing the oil seals and collar.

WARNING
The shock absorber is a sealed unit and cannot be rebuilt. It contains highly compressed nitrogen gas. Do not tamper with or attempt to open the cylinder. Do not place it near an open flame or other extreme heat. Do not weld on the frame near it. Do not dispose of the

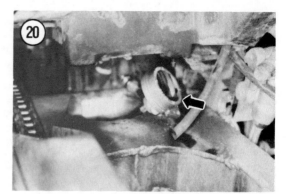

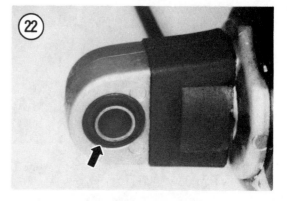

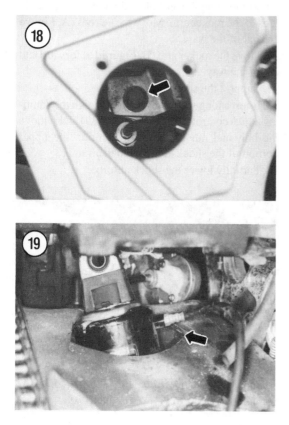

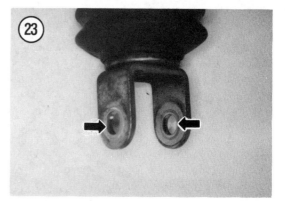

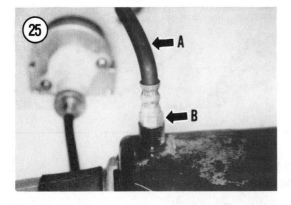

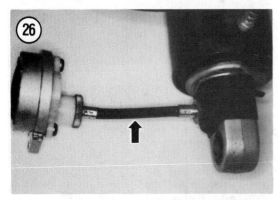

*shock absorber yourself. Take it to a Kawasaki dealer where it can be deactivated and disposed of properly. Observe the cautions on the shock's decal (**Figure 21**).*

17. Inspect the upper rubber damper (**Figure 22**) for galling, cracks or other damage; replace if necessary.

18. Inspect the shock absorber lower mount holes (**Figure 23**) for elongation, cracks or other damage. If damaged, replace the shock absorber assembly.

19. Inspect the rubber boot (**Figure 24**) for tears, deterioration or damage. Replace as necessary.

20. Inspect the air line (A, **Figure 25**) for wear or damage. Replace as necessary. Also make sure the fitting (B, **Figure 25**) is tight on the shock body.

21. Inspect the damping adjuster control cable (**Figure 26**) for wear or damage. Replace if necessary.

22. Pull the rubber boot (A, **Figure 27**) off the damping adjuster control gear. Rotate the control knob and make sure the gear (B, **Figure 27**) operates smoothly.

23. Make sure the screws and cable nut (**Figure 28**) on the damping adjuster control are tight. Tighten if necessary.

24. Install by reversing these steps. Note the following:

    a. Apply molybdenum grease to the bolts and dust seals.

    b. Tighten the shock absorber upper and lower bolts and nuts to the specifications in **Table 2**.

    c. Tighten the tie rod-to-rocker arm bolt and nut to the torque specification listed in **Table 2**.

25. Set the damping adjuster knob as follows:

    a. Set the damping adjuster knob to the No. 1 position (**Figure 29**).

14

b. Slide the upper dust cover off the top of the shock.

c. Check that the gear mark I (red paint mark) is at the middle of the window (**Figure 27**).

d. If the gear mark I is not at the middle of the window, turn the plastic gear clockwise until the mark I is in the middle of the window.

e. Connect the cable to the damping adjuster.

Removal/Installation (ZX-11 C1-4)

Refer to **Figure 30** for this procedure.

1. Place the bike securely on the centerstand with the rear wheel clear of the ground.

2. Remove the seat.

3. Remove both side covers and the tail piece as described in Chapter Thirteen in this section of the manual.

4. Remove the rear fender as described in Chapter Thirteen in this section of the manual.

5. Remove the fuel tank as described in Chapter Seven in this section of the manual.

6. Remove the fuel tank rear mounting bracket.

7. Remove the rear fender front mounting bracket.

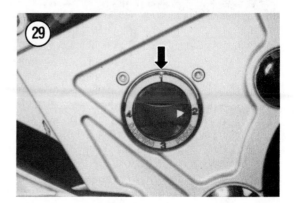

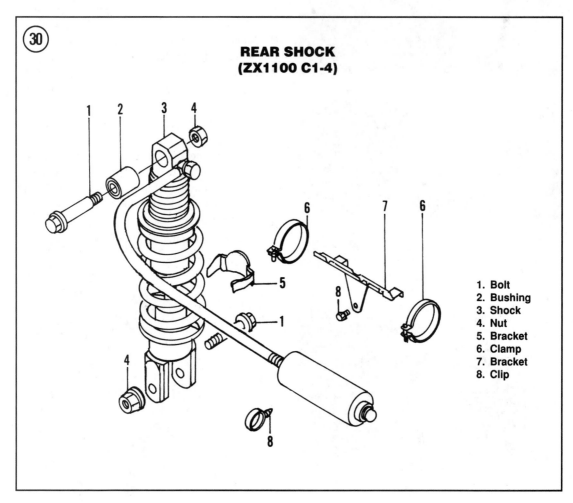

REAR SHOCK (ZX1100 C1-4)

1. Bolt
2. Bushing
3. Shock
4. Nut
5. Bracket
6. Clamp
7. Bracket
8. Clip

8. Loosen the clamp screws and remove the oil reservoir tank from the frame mounting bracket.

CAUTION
When removing the shock absorber mounting bolts, lift up on the swing arm slightly to avoid damaging the bolt threads, sleeve and bearing during bolt removal.

9. Remove the bolt and nut (**Figure 31**) securing the lower portion of the shock absorber to the rocker arm.

10. Support the shock absorber and remove the bolt and nut securing the upper portion of the shock absorber to the frame.

11. Lower the shock absorber out through the swing arm and remove it. Carefully guide the oil reservoir tank and hose out through the frame. Do not kink the hose.

WARNING
*The shock absorber is a sealed unit and cannot be rebuilt. It contains highly compressed nitrogen gas. Do not tamper with or attempt to open the cylinder. Do not place it near an open flame or other extreme heat. Do not weld on the frame near it. Do not dispose of the shock absorber yourself. Take it to a Kawasaki dealer where it can be deactivated and disposed of properly. Observe the cautions on the shock's decal (**Figure 21**).*

12. Inspect the upper rubber damper for galling, cracks or other damage; replace if necessary.

13. Inspect the shock absorber lower mount holes for elongation, cracks or other damage. If damaged, replace the shock absorber assembly.

14. Inspect the reservoir oil line for wear or damage. The hose cannot be replace separately; if damaged, replace the shock absorber assembly.

15. Install by reversing these steps. Note the following:

   a. Apply molybdenum grease to the bolts and dust seals.

   b. Position the shock absorber in the frame with the oil line facing toward the rear.

   c. Tighten the shock absorber upper and lower bolts and nuts to the specifications in **Table 2**.

Removal/Installation (ZX-11 D1-9)

Refer to **Figure 32** for this procedure.

1. Place the bike securely on the centerstand with the rear wheel clear of the ground.

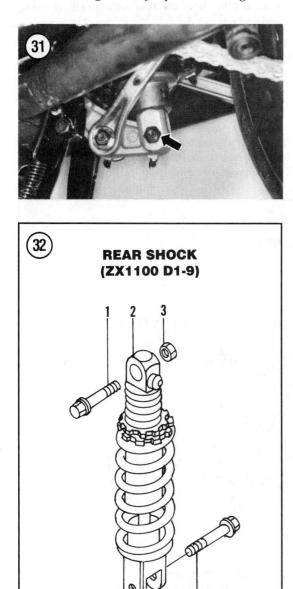

REAR SHOCK (ZX1100 D1-9)

1. Bolt
2. Shock
3. Nut

2. Remove the seat.

3. Remove both side covers and the tail piece as described in Chapter Thirteen in this section of the manual.

4. Remove the rear fender as described in Chapter Thirteen in this section of the manual.

5. Remove the fuel tank as described in Chapter Seven in this section of the manual.

6. Remove the rear wheel as described in this chapter.

CAUTION
When removing the shock absorber mounting bolts, lift up on the swing arm slightly to avoid damaging the bolt threads, sleeve and bearing during bolt removal.

7. Remove the bolt and nut securing the lower portion of the shock absorber to the rocker arm.

8. Support the shock absorber and remove the bolt and nut securing the upper portion of the shock absorber to the frame.

9. Lower the shock absorber out through the swing arm and remove it.

WARNING
The shock absorber is a sealed unit and cannot be rebuilt. It contains highly compressed nitrogen gas. Do not tamper with or attempt to open the cylinder. Do not place it near an open flame or other extreme heat. Do not weld on the frame near it. Do not dispose of the shock absorber yourself. Take it to a

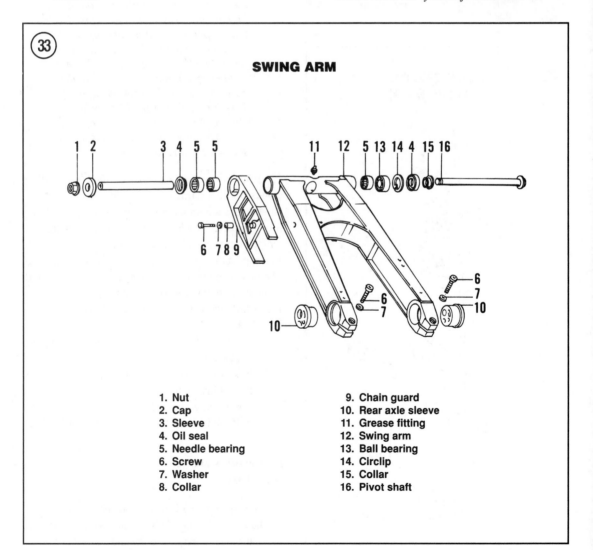

SWING ARM

1. Nut	9. Chain guard
2. Cap	10. Rear axle sleeve
3. Sleeve	11. Grease fitting
4. Oil seal	12. Swing arm
5. Needle bearing	13. Ball bearing
6. Screw	14. Circlip
7. Washer	15. Collar
8. Collar	16. Pivot shaft

*Kawasaki dealer where it can be deactivated and disposed of properly. Observe the cautions on the shock's decal (**Figure 21**).*

10. Inspect the upper rubber damper for galling, cracks or other damage; replace if necessary.

11. Inspect the shock absorber lower mount holes for elongation, cracks or other damage. If damaged, replace the shock absorber assembly.

12. Install by reversing these steps. Note the following:

   a. Apply molybdenum grease to the bolts and dust seals.

   b. Tighten the shock absorber upper and lower bolts and nuts to the specifications in **Table 2**.

REAR SWING ARM

The rear suspension system consists of a shock absorber, rocker arm, tie-rods and a swing arm. The rocker arm, tie-rods and swing arm are equipped with caged needle bearings. The components are linked together and pivot on machined sleeves and shafts. Oil seals are installed on the outside of each bearing to retain lubrication and prevent contamination. It is critical that the torque specifications in **Table 2** are observed when reinstalling the assembly to prevent binding or bearing damage.

For proper operation, the needle bearings must be lubricated at the intervals specified in Chapter Three in this section of the manual. The needle bearings were initially lubricated with molybdenum disulfide grease. When servicing the bearings, this same type of grease should be used.

The following procedure describes service to the swing arm, rocker arm and tie-rods. Refer to the following illustrations for the following procedures:

   a. Swing arm: **Figure 33**.

   b. Rocker arm and tie-rods (ZX-10, ZX11 C1-4): **Figure 34**.

   c. Rocker arm and tie-rods (ZX-11 D1): **Figure 35**.

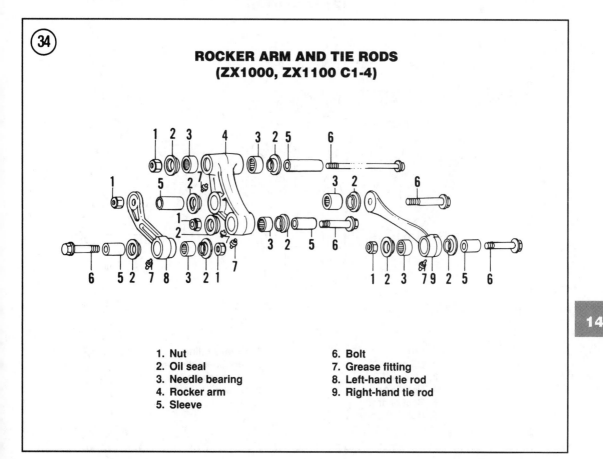

34

ROCKER ARM AND TIE RODS
(ZX1000, ZX1100 C1-4)

1. Nut
2. Oil seal
3. Needle bearing
4. Rocker arm
5. Sleeve
6. Bolt
7. Grease fitting
8. Left-hand tie rod
9. Right-hand tie rod

14

Removal

1. Remove the exhaust system (A, **Figure 36**) as described in Chapter Seven in this section of the manual.

2. Remove the rear wheel (A, **Figure 37**) as described in this chapter.

3. Remove the drive chain guard (B, **Figure 37**).

4. Remove the brake hose guide.

5. Remove the right-hand footpeg bracket as described in Chapter Thirteen in this section of the manual.

6. Remove the bolt and nut (A, **Figure 38**) on each side securing the upper end of each tie rod to the swing arm.

7. Remove the bolt and nut (B, **Figure 38**) securing the lower end of the tie rods to the rocker arm and remove both tie rods (C, **Figure 38**).

CAUTION
When removing the tie rod-to-rocker arm bolt, lift up on the swing arm slightly to avoid damaging the bolt threads, sleeve and bearing during bolt removal.

8. Remove the left-hand trim cap (C, **Figure 37**) covering the pivot shaft nut and the right-hand trim cap (B, **Figure 36**) covering the pivot shaft

9. Before removing the swing arm pivot shaft nut, check swing arm side play. Grasp the swing arm at the rear and hold it in a horizontal position. Check swing arm side play by moving the swing arm from side to side. There should be no noticeable side play. Check swing arm movement by moving it up and down. The swing arm should move smoothly with no tightness or binding. If the swing arm moved

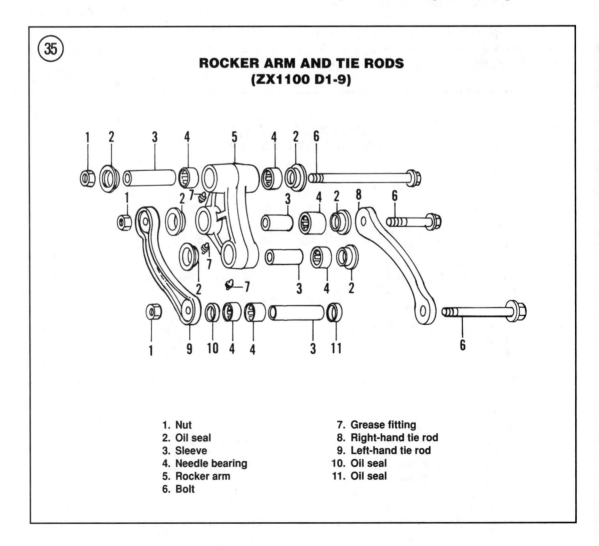

**ROCKER ARM AND TIE RODS
(ZX1100 D1-9)**

1. Nut
2. Oil seal
3. Sleeve
4. Needle bearing
5. Rocker arm
6. Bolt
7. Grease fitting
8. Right-hand tie rod
9. Left-hand tie rod
10. Oil seal
11. Oil seal

abnormally during this test, replace the swing arm bearings as described in this chapter.

10. Remove the pivot shaft nut and cap.

11. Have an assistant hold onto the swing arm or place a box under it to support it after the pivot shaft is removed.

12. Push the pivot shaft out and withdraw it from the right-hand side. If the pivot shaft is tight, use an aluminum or brass drift and tap the pivot shaft out.

13. Carefully pull the swing arm toward the rear and remove it.

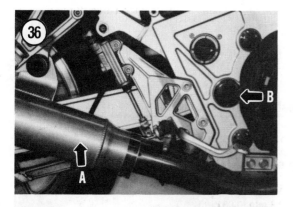

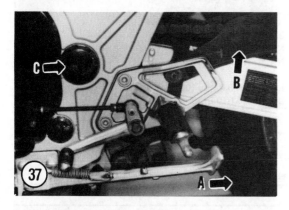

14. If necessary, remove the rocker arm as follows:

   a. Remove the bolt and nut (D, **Figure 38**) securing the shock absorber to the rocker arm.

   b. Remove the bolt and nut securing the rocker arm to the frame pivot point and remove the rocker arm.

Inspection

The inspection procedures are the same as on ZX-1000 models with the exception of minor modifications to some of the components.

Refer to the following illustrations for the following procedures:

   a. Swing arm: **Figure 33**.

   b. Rocker arm and tie-rods (ZX-10, ZX-11 C1-4): **Figure 34**.

   c. Rocker arm and tie-rods (ZX-11 D1-9): **Figure 35**.

Installation

1. Apply molybdenum disulfide grease to each inner needle bearing surface. Lightly grease all pivot shaft sleeves and bolts with the same type grease.

2. Install the rocker arm assembly as follows:

   a. Install the 3 sleeves into the rocker arm

   b. Install the 6 oil seals onto the rocker arm.

   c. Position the rocker arm with the large end going onto the frame and install the bolt and nut securing the rocker arm to the frame pivot point.

   d. Move the shock absorber into position on the rocker arm and install the bolt and nut.

   e. Tighten the bolts and nuts to the torque specification listed in **Table 2**.

3. Install the swing arm as follows:

   a. Install the sleeve into the swing arm, then install an oil seal on each end of the pivot area.

   b. Install the drive chain over the left-hand side of the swing arm.

   c. Lift the swing arm up and align the bearing holes with the frame pivot shaft holes. Install the pivot shaft through the frame and the swing arm from the right-hand side.

   d. Install the cap and nut onto the pivot shaft. Tighten the bolt and nut to the torque specification listed in **Table 2**.

   e. Tighten the bolts and nuts to the torque specification listed in **Table 2**.

14

f. Install the trim cap onto the frame on each side.

4A. On ZX-10 and ZX-11 C1-4 models, install the tie-rods onto the swing arm as follows:

   a. Install the sleeve into each tie-rod.

   b. Install the 2 oil seals onto each tie-rod.

   c. Position the tie-rods with the grease fitting facing toward the rear. Position them onto the swing arm and install the bolts and nuts securing each tie-rod to the swing arm.

   d. Tighten the bolts and nuts to the torque specification listed in **Table 2**.

4B. On ZX-11 D1-9, install the tie-rods onto the swing arm as follows:

   a. Position the tie-rods onto the swing arm and install the bolts and nuts securing the tie-rods to the swing arm.

   b. Tighten the bolts and nuts to the torque specification listed in **Table 2**.

5. Install the brake torque link bolt and nut and tighten securely.

6. Install the right-hand footpeg bracket as described in Chapter Thirteen in this section of the manual.

7. Install the brake hose guide.

8. Install the drive chain guard.

9. Install the rear wheel as described in this chapter.

10. Install the exhaust system as described in Chapter Seven in this section of the manual.

11. Adjust the drive chain as described under *Drive Chain Adjustment* in Chapter Three in the front of this manual.

Table 1 REAR SUSPENSION SPECIFICATIONS

Rear wheel travel	
ZX1000 and ZX1100 C1-4	120 mm (4.72 in.)
ZX1100 D1-9	112 mm (4.41 in.)
Axle runout	See text
Rim runout (wear limit)	
Axial	0.5 mm (0.019 in.)
Radial	0.8 mm (0.031 in.)
Drive chain 20 link check	
Standard	317.5-318.4 mm (12.50-12.54 in.)
Wear limit	323 mm (12.72 in.)
Front sprocket diameter	NA
Rear sprocket diameter	NA
Rear sprocket warpage	
Standard	Less than 0.4 mm (0.015 in.)
Wear limit	0.5 mm (0.019 in.)
NA–Information not available from Kawasaki.	

Table 2 REAR SUSPENSION TIGHTENING TORQUES

Item	N•m	ft.-lb.
Rear axle nut	108	80
Rear axle pinch bolt	39	29
Shock absorber		
ZX1000		
Upper and lower bolts and nuts	59	43
Tie rod-to-rocker arm bolts and nuts	59	43
ZX1100		
Upper and lower bolts and nuts	59	43
Rocker arm bolts and nuts	59	43
Tie rod bolts and nuts	59	43
Swing arm pivot shaft nut	88	65

CHAPTER TWELVE

BRAKES

All models are equipped with front and rear disc brakes. This chapter describes repair and replacement procedures for the brake system. **Table 1** at the end of this chapter lists service specifications. **Table 1** and **Table 2** are located at the end of this chapter.

NOTE
This chapter covers all procedures unique to the Kawasaki ZX1000 (ZX-10) and ZX1100 (ZX-11) from 1988-on. If a specific procedure is not included in this chapter, unless otherwise specified refer to ZX1000 models in Chapter Twelve at the front of this manual for service procedures.

BRAKE PAD REPLACEMENT

There is no recommended mileage interval for changing the friction pads on the disc brakes. Pad wear depends greatly on riding habits and conditions. The pads should be checked for wear at the intervals specified in Chapter Three in this section of the manual and replaced when worn to the minimum thickness listed in **Table 1**. Always replace both pads at the same time.

Front Pad Replacement (ZX-10)

It is not necessary to disassemble the caliper or open the hydraulic brake fluid lines to replace the brake pads.

Refer to **Figure 1** for this procedure:

CAUTION
When working on the brake system avoid touching the friction surface of the disc or brake pads with you hands. Natural skin oils or other contamination can affect braking efficiency. If you must touch the disc, wash it with brake cleaner after it is reassembled.

1. Remove the caliper mounting bolts (A, **Figure 2**) and lift the caliper (B, **Figure 2**) off the brake disc.

2. Remove the outer brake pad next to the pistons (**Figure 3**).
3. Push the caliper holder toward the pistons, then remove the inner pad (**Figure 4**).
4. If necessary, remove the anti-rattle spring (**Figure 5**).
5. Check that the 2 clips are installed on the caliper holder.
6. Remove the screws, cover and diaphragm (**Figure 6**). To gain clearance for the new brake pads, you'll need to force the caliper pistons back into the caliper. Slowly push the pistons into the caliper while checking the reservoir to make sure it doesn't overflow. Remove fluid, if necessary, prior to it overflowing. The pistons should move freely. You may need to use a C-clamp to push the pistons back into the caliper. If the pistons stick, remove and service the caliper as described in this chapter.
7. If removed, install the anti-rattle spring (**Figure 5**).

NOTE
*The friction material on both brake pads (**Figure 7**) must face inward toward the brake disc.*

8. Push the caliper holder toward the pistons. Then align the holes in the outer brake pad plate with the holder pins and install the inner pad (**Figure 4**).
9. Install the outer brake pad next to the pistons (**Figure 3**).
10. Carefully slip the brake pads over the brake disc as you install the caliper (B, **Figure 2**). Install the caliper mounting bolts (A, **Figure 2**) and tighten to the specification in **Table 2**.
11. Support the bike with the front wheel off the ground. Spin the front wheel and pump the brake until the pads are seated against the disc.
12. If necessary, correct the fluid level in the master cylinder reservoir. Install the diaphragm and top cover and tighten the screws securely.

WARNING
Use brake fluid clearly marked DOT 4 from a sealed container. Other types may vaporize and cause brake failure.

14

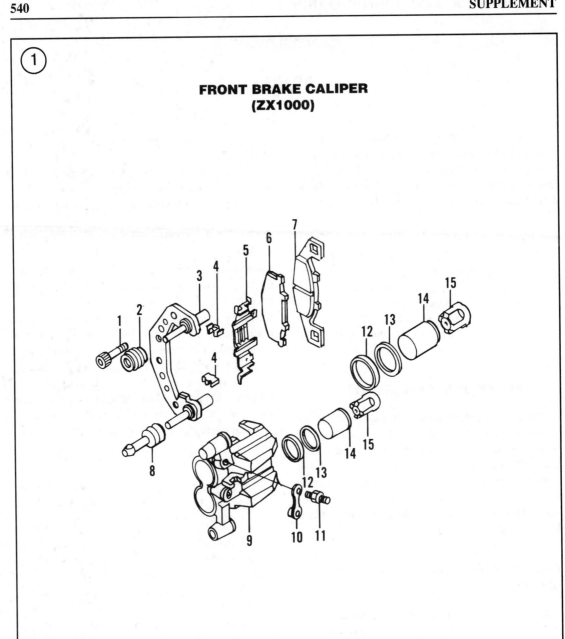

**FRONT BRAKE CALIPER
(ZX1000)**

1. Bolt
2. Boot
3. Holder
4. Stopper spring
5. Anti-rattle spring
6. Outer brake pad
7. Inner brake pad
8. Boot
9. Housing
10. Bleed valve cap
11. Bleed valve
12. Piston seal
13. Dust seal
14. Piston
15. Insulator

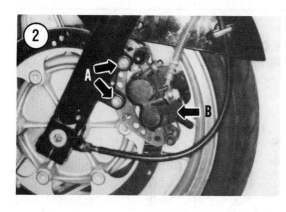

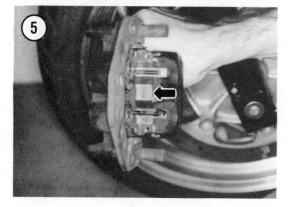

Always use the same brand name; do not intermix brake fluids, many brands are not compatible.

WARNING
Do not ride the motorcycle until you are sure the brake is working correctly.

Front Pad Replacement (ZX-11)

It is not necessary to disassemble the caliper or open the hydraulic brake fluid lines to replace the brake pads.

Refer to the **Figure 8** for this procedure:

CAUTION
When working on the brake system avoid touching the friction surface of the disc or brake pads with you hands. Natural skin oils or other contamination can affect braking efficiency. If you must touch the disc, wash it with brake cleaner after it is reassembled.

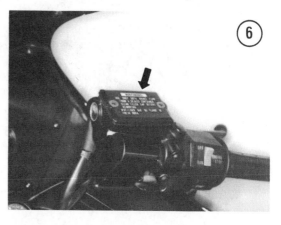

14

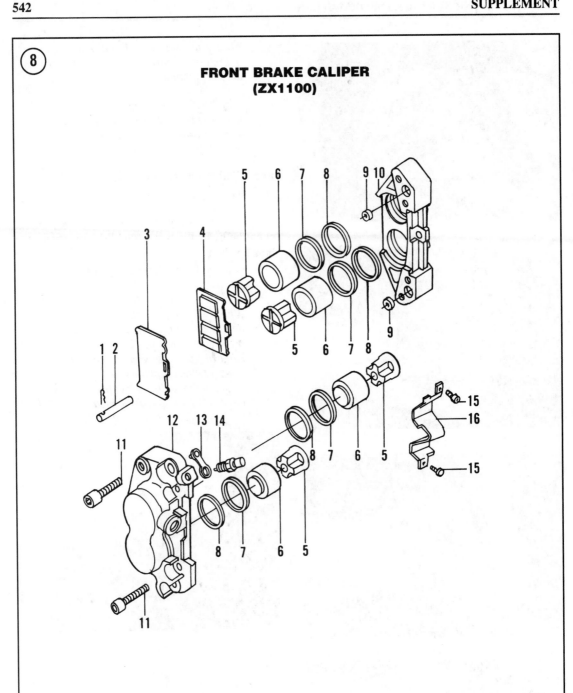

**FRONT BRAKE CALIPER
(ZX1100)**

1. Clip
2. Pin
3. Outer brake pad
4. Inner brake pad
5. Insulator
6. Piston
7. Dust seal
8. Piston seal
9. O-ring
10. Inner housing
11. Bolt
12. Outer housing
13. Bleed valve cap
14. Bleed valve
15. Screw
16. Anti-rattle spring

1. Remove the caliper mounting bolts (A, **Figure 9**) and lift the caliper (B, **Figure 9**) off the brake disc.

2. Remove the screws (A, **Figure 10**) and remove the pad spring (B, **Figure 10**).

3. Remove the clip (A, **Figure 11**) and remove the pad pin (B, **Figure 11**).

4. Slide both brake pads out of the caliper.

5. Remove the screws, cover and diaphragm (**Figure 12**). To gain clearance for the new brake pads, you'll need to force the caliper pistons back into the caliper. Slowly push the pistons, on each side, back into the caliper while checking the reservoir to make sure it doesn't overflow. Remove fluid, if necessary, prior to it overflowing. The pistons should move freely. If the pistons stick, remove and service the caliper as described in this chapter.

NOTE
The friction material on both brake pads must face inward toward the brake disc.

6. Install both brake pads into the caliper.

7. Insert the pad pin and install the clip. The pin must be outside the pads.

8. Carefully slip the brake pads over the brake disc as you install the caliper (B, **Figure 9**). Install the caliper mounting bolts (A, **Figure 9**) and tighten to the specification in **Table 2**.

9. Support the bike with the front wheel off the ground. Spin the front wheel and pump the brake until the pads are seated against the disc.

10. If necessary, correct the fluid level in the master cylinder reservoir. Install the diaphragm and top cover and tighten the screws securely.

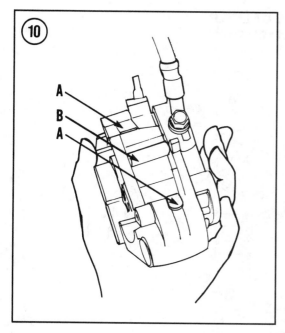

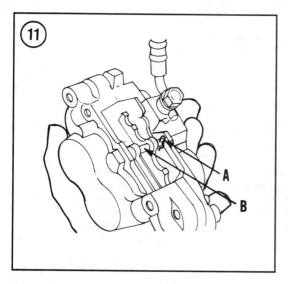

14

**Rear Pad Replacement
(ZX-10 and ZX-11 C1-4)**

It is not necessary to disassemble the caliper or
open the hydraulic brake fluid lines to replace the
brake pads.

Refer to **Figure 13** for this procedure:

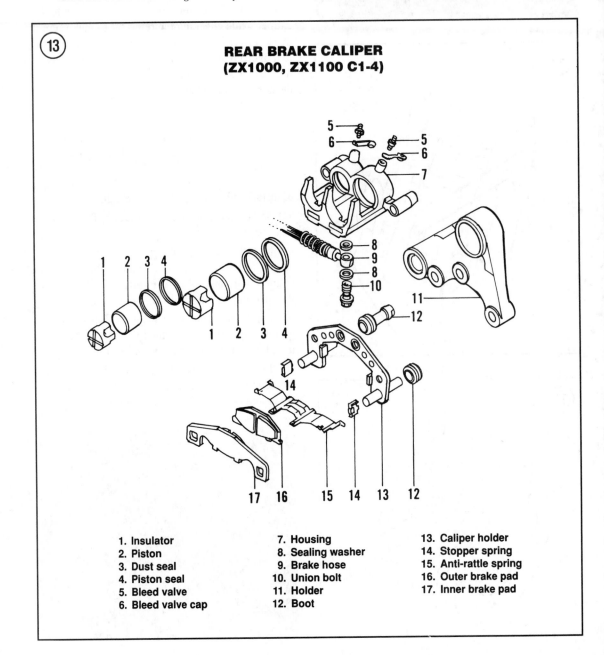

**REAR BRAKE CALIPER
(ZX1000, ZX1100 C1-4)**

1. Insulator
2. Piston
3. Dust seal
4. Piston seal
5. Bleed valve
6. Bleed valve cap
7. Housing
8. Sealing washer
9. Brake hose
10. Union bolt
11. Holder
12. Boot
13. Caliper holder
14. Stopper spring
15. Anti-rattle spring
16. Outer brake pad
17. Inner brake pad

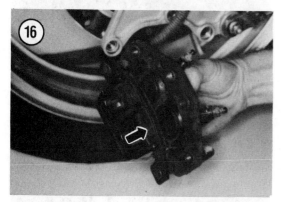

the disc or brake pads with you hands. Natural skin oils or other contamination can affect braking efficiency. If you must touch the disc, wash it with brake cleaner after it is reassembled.

1. Remove the caliper mounting bolts (A, **Figure 14**) and lift the caliper (B, **Figure 14**) off the brake disc.

2. Remove the outer brake pad next to the pistons (**Figure 15**).

3. Push the caliper holder toward the pistons, then remove the inner pad (**Figure 16**).

4. If necessary, remove the anti-rattle spring.

5. Check that the 2 clips are installed on the caliper holder.

6A. On ZX-10 models, remove the right-hand side cover to gain access to the master cylinder reservoir.

6B. On ZX-11 models, remove the seat to gain access to the master cylinder reservoir.

7. Unscrew cover (**Figure 17**) and remove the diaphragm. To gain clearance for the new brake pads, you'll need to force the caliper pistons back into the caliper. Slowly push the pistons into the caliper while checking the reservoir to make sure it doesn't overflow. Remove fluid, if necessary, prior to it overflowing. The pistons should move freely. You may need to use a C-clamp to push the pistons back into the caliper. If the pistons stick, remove and service the caliper as described in this chapter.

8. If removed, install the anti-rattle spring.

9. Make sure the insulators (**Figure 18**) are still in place in the pistons.

10. Push the caliper holder toward the pistons. Then align the holes in the outer brake pad plate with the holder pins and install the inner pad (**Figure 16**).

14

NOTE
The friction material on both brake pads (Figure 7) face inward toward the brake disc.

11. Install the outer brake pad next to the pistons (**Figure 15**).

12. Carefully slip the brake pads over the brake disc as you install the caliper (B, **Figure 14**). Install the caliper mounting bolts (A, **Figure 14**) and tighten to the specification in **Table 2**.

13. Support the bike with the rear wheel off the ground. Spin the rear wheel and pump the brake until the pads are seated against the disc.

14. If necessary, correct the fluid level in the master cylinder reservoir. Install the diaphragm and screw the cover on securely.

WARNING
Use brake fluid clearly marked DOT 4 from a sealed container. Other types may vaporize and cause brake failure. Always use the same brand name; do not intermix brake fluids, many brands are not compatible.

WARNING
Do not ride the motorcycle until you are sure the brake is working correctly.

15A. On ZX-10 models, install the right-hand side cover.

15B. On ZX-11 models, install the seat.

Rear Pad Replacement (ZX-11 D1)

The rear brake pad replacement procedure on these models is the same as on ZX-1000 models as described in Chapter Twelve in the front section of this manual.

BRAKE CALIPERS

Front Caliper
Removal/Installation

Refer to the following illustrations for this procedure:

a. ZX-10: **Figure 1**.
b. ZX-11: **Figure 8**.

CAUTION
Some brake fluid will come out when the brake hose is disconnected at the caliper. Put some plastic bags over the surrounding parts and have some shop towels ready to clean up spilled fluid.

1. Remove the banjo bolt and washers securing the brake hose to the caliper. Refer to **Figure 19** for

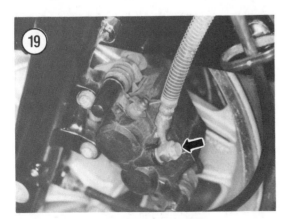

ZX-10 models or **Figure 20** for ZX-11 models. To prevent the loss of brake fluid, cap the end of the brake hose and tie it up to the fender. Be sure to cap or tape the end to prevent the entry of moisture and dirt.

2. Remove the brake caliper as described under *Brake Pad Replacement* in this chapter.

3. Installation is the reverse of these steps. Note the following:

    a. Tighten the caliper mounting bolts to the torque specification listed in **Table 2**.

    b. Install the brake hose using new washers.

    c. Install and tighten the banjo bolt to the torque specification listed in **Table 2**.

    d. Bleed the brakes as described under *Bleeding the System* in this chapter and Chapter Twelve in the front section of this manual.

> *WARNING*
> *Do not ride the motorcycle until you are sure that the brakes are operating properly.*

Rear Caliper
Removal/Installation
(ZX-10 and ZX-11 C1-4)

Refer to **Figure 13** for this procedure.

> *CAUTION*
> *Some brake fluid will come out when the brake hose is disconnected at the caliper. Put some plastic bags over the surrounding parts and have some shop towels ready to clean up spilled fluid.*

㉒

1. Remove the banjo bolt and washers (**Figure 21**) securing the brake hose to the caliper. To prevent the loss of brake fluid, cap the end of the brake hose and tie it up to the fender. Be sure to cap or tape the end to prevent the entry of moisture and dirt.

2. Remove the brake caliper as described under *Brake Pad Replacement* in this chapter.

3. Installation is the reverse of these steps. Note the following:

    a. Tighten the caliper mounting bolts to the torque specification listed in **Table 2**.

    b. Install the brake hose using new washers.

    c. Install and tighten the banjo bolt to the torque specification listed in **Table 2**.

    d. Bleed the brakes as described under *Bleeding the System* in this chapter and Chapter Twelve in the front section of this manual.

> *WARNING*
> *Do not ride the motorcycle until you are sure that the brakes are operating properly.*

Caliper Rebuilding
(Front Caliper ZX-10
and Rear Caliper ZX-10, ZX-11 C1-4)

This same procedure is used for both the front and rear caliper on these models. The calipers are the same.

Refer to the following illustrations for this procedure:

    a. ZX-10 front caliper: **Figure 1**.

    b. ZX-10, ZX-11 C1-4 rear caliper: **Figure 13**.

> *NOTE*
> *Compressed air will be required to completely disassemble the caliper assembly.*

1. Remove the brake caliper as described in this chapter.

2. Remove the brake pads, the anti-rattle spring and 2 stopper springs from the caliper holder and caliper.

3. Disconnect the caliper holder rubber boots from the caliper holder.

4. Pull the caliper holder (**Figure 22**) off of the housing.

5. Remove the insulator (**Figure 23**) from each piston.

 14

NOTE
Compressed air will be required to re-move the pistons.

WARNING
Keep your fingers and hand out of the caliper bore area when removing the pistons in Step 6. The pistons may fly out of the bores with considerable force and could crush your fingers or hand.

6. Pad the pistons with shop rags or wood blocks as shown in A, **Figure 24**. Apply compressed air through one of the caliper ports (B, **Figure 24**) and blow the pistons out of the caliper.

7. Unscrew the bleed screws (**Figure 25**).

8. Remove the dust seals and the piston seals from the caliper bores.

9. Clean all parts (except brake pads) with rubbing alcohol and rinse with clean DOT 4 brake fluid. Place the cleaned parts on a lint-free cloth while performing the following inspection procedures.

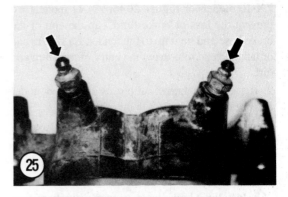

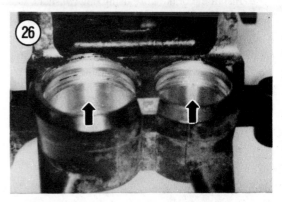

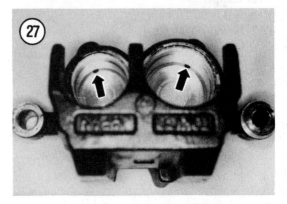

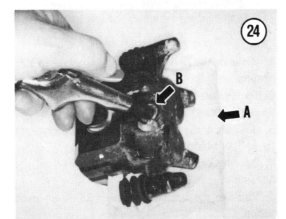

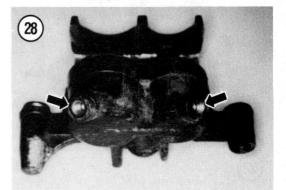

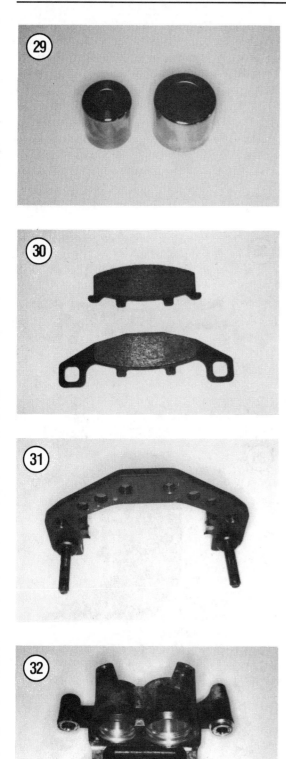

10. Check the caliper bores and seal grooves (**Figure 26**) for cracks, deep scoring or excessive wear.

11. Make sure the fluid opening (**Figure 27**) in the base of each bore is clear. Clean out if necessary.

12. Make sure the bleed screw openings (**Figure 28**) in the housing are clear. Clean out if necessary.

13. Check the caliper pistons (**Figure 29**) for deep scoring, excessive wear or rust.

14. Replace the caliper housing and pistons if necessary.

15. The piston seal maintains correct brake pad-to-disc clearance. If the seal is worn or damaged, the brake pads will drag and cause excessive pad wear and brake fluid temperatures. Replace the piston and dust seals if the following conditions exist:

    a. Brake fluid leaks around the inner brake pad.

    b. The piston seal is stuck in the caliper groove.

    c. There is a large difference in inner and outer brake pad wear (**Figure 30**).

16. Measure the brake pad friction material with a ruler or caliper and compare to the wear limit in **Table 1**. Replace both pads if any one pad is worn too thin.

17. Check the caliper holder (**Figure 31**) for cracks or other damage. Replace the holder if necessary.

18. Check the caliper housing (**Figure 32**) for cracks or other damage. Replace the housing if necessary.

19. Check the piston insulators (**Figure 33**) for heat distortion, cracks or other damage. Replace both as a set if necessary.

20. Check the rubber boots (**Figure 34**) for tearing or weather damage. Replace both as a set if necessary.

14

21. Check the anti-rattle spring (**Figure 35**) and stopper springs (**Figure 36**) for cracks or damage. Replace if necessary.

22. After all worn or damaged parts have been replaced, assemble the caliper assembly as follows.

23. Install the rubber boots (**Figure 37**) onto the caliper housing.

24. Soak the piston and dust seals in new DOT 4 brake fluid.

25. Coat the caliper bores in new DOT 4 brake fluid.

26. Install the piston seal (**Figure 38**) into each lower seal groove.

27. Install the dust seal (**Figure 39**) into each upper seal groove.

28. Coat the pistons O.D. with new DOT 4 brake fluid.

29. Align the pistons with the caliper bores as shown in **Figure 40** and install the pistons. Push both pistons all the way into the caliper bores (**Figure 41**).

30. Install the insulators (**Figure 23**) into the pistons. Push them in until they stop.

31. Install the bleed valves (**Figure 25**) and tighten securely.

32. Align the caliper holder with the caliper housing and install the holder (**Figure 22**).

33. After the holder is installed, hook the rubber boots onto the caliper holder posts (**Figure 42**).

34. Install the brake pads, the anti-rattle spring and 2 stopper springs onto the caliper holder and caliper.

35. Install the brake pads and caliper as described in this chapter.

Caliper Rebuilding
(Front Caliper ZX-11)

Refer to **Figure 43** for this procedure.

> *NOTE*
> *Compressed air will be required to completely disassemble the caliper assembly.*

> *NOTE*
> *In Step 1, just break the 4 Allen bolts loose. If they are loosened too much brake fluid will leak out.*

1. With the caliper still mounted on the front fork leg, *loosen*, but do not remove, all 4 Allen bolts (**Figure 44**) securing the inner and outer caliper housings together.

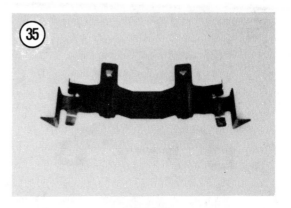

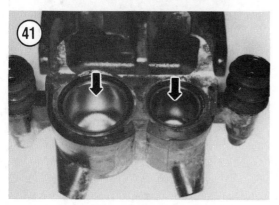

2. Remove the brake caliper as described in this chapter.

3. Remove the screws (A, **Figure 45**) and remove the pad spring (B, **Figure 45**).

4. Remove the clip (A, **Figure 46**) and remove the pad pin (B, **Figure 46**).

5. Slide both brake pads out of the caliper.

6. Remove the 4 Allen bolts loosened in Step 1.

7. Separate the caliper housings.

8. Remove the 2 O-ring seals and discard them. They must be replaced every time the caliper is disassembled.

9. On models so equipped, remove the plastic insulators from each piston.

> *NOTE*
> *Compressed air will be required to remove the pistons.*

> *WARNING*
> *Keep your fingers and hand out of the caliper bore area when removing the pistons in Step 10. The pistons may fly out of the bores with considerable force and could crush your fingers or hand.*

10. Turn the caliper housing, with the piston side facing down, on shop rags or wood blocks. Apply compressed air through one of the caliper ports and blow the pistons out of the caliper.

11. Remove the dust seals and the piston seals from the caliper bores.

12. Repeat Steps 10 and 11 for the other caliper housing half.

13. Clean all parts (except brake pads) with rubbing alcohol and rinse with clean DOT 4 brake fluid. Place the cleaned parts on a lint-free cloth while performing the following inspection procedures.

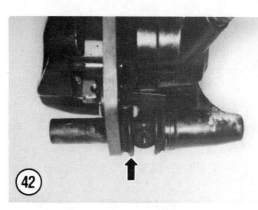

14

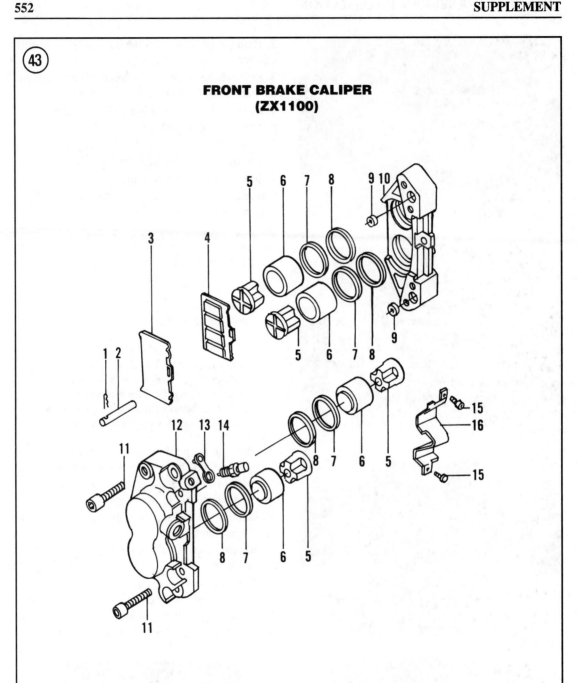

FRONT BRAKE CALIPER
(ZX1100)

1. Clip
2. Pin
3. Outer brake pad
4. Inner brake pad
5. Insulator
6. Piston
7. Dust seal
8. Piston seal
9. O-ring
10. Inner housing
11. Bolt
12. Outer housing
13. Bleed valve cap
14. Bleed valve
15. Screw
16. Anti-rattle spring

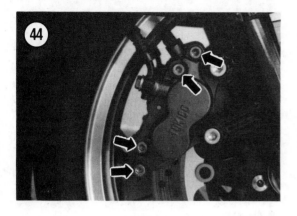

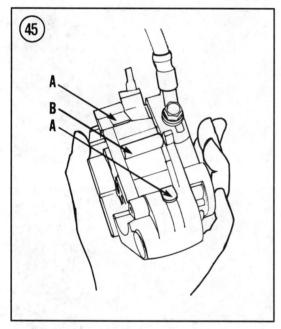

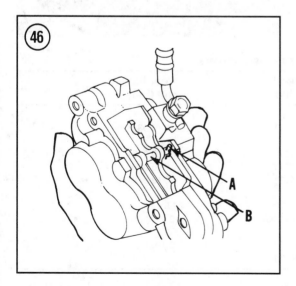

14. Check the caliper bores for cracks, deep scoring or excessive wear.

15. Check the caliper pistons for deep scoring, excessive wear or rust.

16. Replace both caliper housings and pistons as a complete assembly if necessary.

17. The piston seal maintains correct brake pad-to-disc clearance. If the seal is worn or damaged, the brake pads will drag and cause excessive pad wear and brake fluid temperatures. Replace the piston and dust seals if the following conditions exist:

    a. Brake fluid leaks around the inner brake pad.

    b. The piston seal is stuck in the caliper groove.

    c. There is a large difference in inner and outer brake pad wear.

18. Measure the brake pad friction material with a ruler or caliper and compare to the wear limit in **Table 1**. Replace both pads if any one pad is worn too thin.

19. Check the pad spring for cracks or damage. Replace if necessary.

20. After all worn or damaged parts have been replaced, assemble the caliper assembly as follows:

21. Soak the piston and dust seals in new DOT 4 brake fluid.

22. Coat the caliper bores with new DOT 4 brake fluid.

23. Install the piston seal into the rear caliper seal groove.

24. Install the dust seal into the front caliper seal groove.

25. Coat the pistons O.D. with new DOT 4 brake fluid.

26. Align the pistons with the caliper bores and install the pistons. Push both pistons all the way into the caliper bores.

27. Install the rubber boots onto the caliper housing.

28. On models so equipped, install the plastic insert into each piston.

29. Install 2 new O-rings into the receptacle in the caliper housing. Apply new DOT 4 brake fluid to the O-rings.

30. Assemble the caliper housings together and make sure they are correctly aligned and that the bolt holes line up.

31. Install the 4 Allen bolts securing the caliper housings together. Tighten the bolt to the torque specification listed in **Table 2**. If you cannot achieve the torque value with the caliper on the bench, do a

14

final tightening after the caliper is mounted on the fork leg.

32. Install the brake pads, then install the caliper assembly as described in this chapter.

BLEEDING THE SYSTEM

Bleeding the brake system is the same as on previous models with the exception of the location of the bleed valves and that the front fork is no longer equipped with an anti-dive unit.

Refer to the following illustrations for bleed valve locations:

- a. Front caliper bleed valve (ZX-10): **Figure 47**.
- b. Front caliper bleed valve (ZX-11): **Figure 48**.
- c. Rear caliper bleed valves (ZX-10, ZX-11 C1-4): **Figure 49**.
- d. Rear caliper bleed valve (ZX-11 D1-9): **Figure 50**.

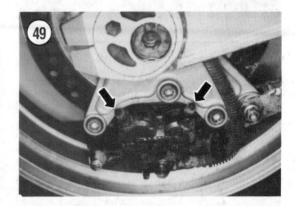

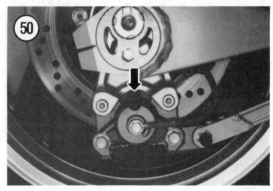

Table 1 BRAKE SPECIFICATIONS

Item	Standard mm (in.)	Wear limit mm (in.)
Brake pad thickness		
ZX1000 (front and rear)	4.5 (0.177)	1.0 (0.039)
ZX1100 C1-4		
Front	4.0 (0.157)	1.0 (0.039)
Rear	4.5 (0.177)	1.0 (0.039)
ZX1100 D1-9 (front and rear)	4.0 (0.157)	1.0 (0.039)
Brake disc thickness		
Front	4.8-5.1 (0.189-0.200)	4.5 (0.177)
Rear	5.8-6.1 (0.228-0.240)	5.0 (0.197)
(continued)		

Table 1 BRAKE SPECIFICATIONS (continued)

Item	Standard mm (in.)	Wear limit mm (in.)
Disc runout	—	0.3 (0.012)

Table 2 BRAKE TIGHTENING TORQUES

Item	N•m	ft.-lb.
Brake hose banjo bolt	25	18
Bleed screw	7.8	69 in.-lb.
Front caliper mounting bolts	34	25
Front caliper housing Allen bolts (ZX1100 D1-9)	21	15
Rear torque link bolts and nuts	25	18

CHAPTER THIRTEEN

FAIRING

This chapter contains removal and installation procedures for the fairing assembly.

NOTE
This chapter covers all procedures unique to the Kawasaki ZX1000 (ZX-10) and ZX1100 (ZX-11) from 1988-on. If a specific procedure is not included in this chapter, unless otherwise specified refer to ZX1000 models in Chapter Thirteen at the front of this manual for service procedures.

FAIRING
(ZX-10)

Lower Fairing
Removal/Installation

Refer to **Figure 1** for this procedure.
1. Place the bike on the centerstand.
2. Remove the lower fairing mounting bolts (A, **Figure 2**) and nylon washers and lower the fairing away from the bike. Don't lose the collar on each lower rear bolt (B, **Figure 2**).
3. Installation is the reverse of these steps. Tighten the bolts securely.

Side Fairing
Removal/Installation

Refer to **Figure 1** for this procedure.
1. Remove the lower fairing as described in this chapter.
2. Remove the side fairing mounting bolts (A, **Figure 3**) and nylon washers and remove the side fairing from the bike. Don't lose the collar on each lower rear bolt (B, **Figure 3**).
3. Installation is the reverse of these steps. Tighten the bolts securely.

Upper Fairing
Removal/Installation

Refer to **Figure 4** for this procedure.
1. Remove the lower and side fairings as described in this chapter.
2. Remove the screws, nylon washers and well nuts securing the windshield and remove the windshield (**Figure 5**).
3. Remove the screws securing the front inner cover (A, **Figure 6**) and remove the cover. Don't forget the single front screw (**Figure 7**).
4. Remove the right- and left-hand caps on the rear inner cover.

14

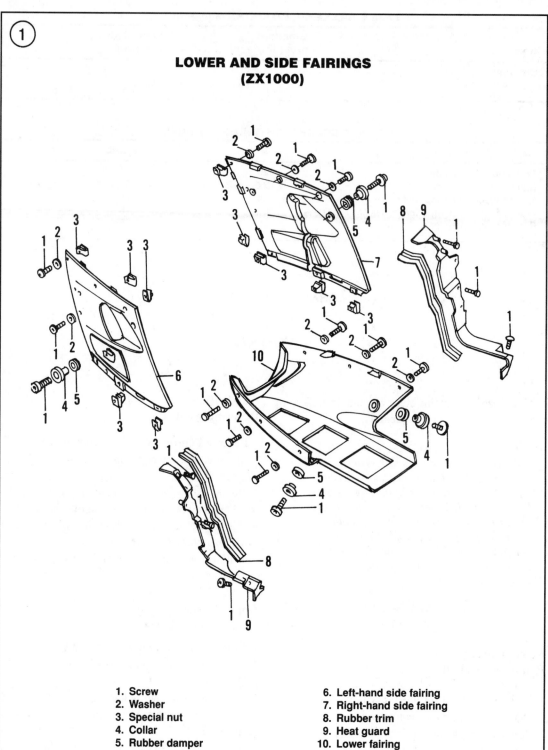

LOWER AND SIDE FAIRINGS
(ZX1000)

1. Screw
2. Washer
3. Special nut
4. Collar
5. Rubber damper
6. Left-hand side fairing
7. Right-hand side fairing
8. Rubber trim
9. Heat guard
10. Lower fairing

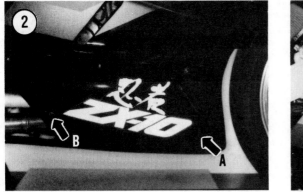

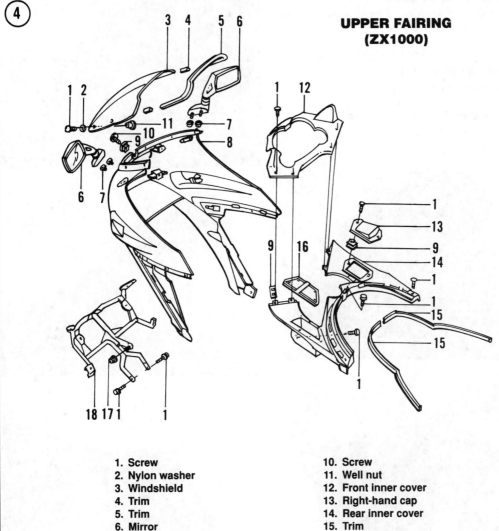

UPPER FAIRING
(ZX1000)

1. Screw
2. Nylon washer
3. Windshield
4. Trim
5. Trim
6. Mirror
7. Nut
8. Upper fairing
9. Special nut
10. Screw
11. Well nut
12. Front inner cover
13. Right-hand cap
14. Rear inner cover
15. Trim
16. Left-hand cap
17. Nut
18. Mounting bracket

14

5. Disconnect the multi-pin electrical connector (**Figure 8**) for the front turn signals and headlight.

6. Remove the nuts (A, **Figure 9**) securing the rear view mirror on each side and remove both mirrors (B, **Figure 9**).

7. Remove the seat as described in this chapter.

8. Remove the fuel tank (**Figure 10**) as described in Chapter Seven in this section of the manual.

9. Remove the screws securing the rear inner cover (B, **Figure 6**) and remove the cover.

10. Remove the screws and nylon washers securing the upper fairing to the mounting bracket and remove the upper fairing. The headlight assembly will come off with the upper fairing.

11. Installation is the reverse of these steps. Tighten the screws securely.

**Side Cover and Rear Cowl
Removal/Installation**

Refer to **Figure 11** for this procedure.

1. Place the bike on the centerstand.

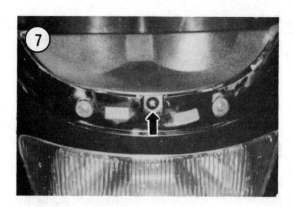

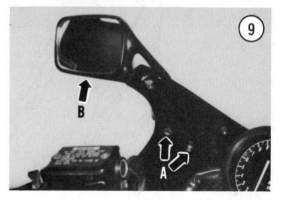

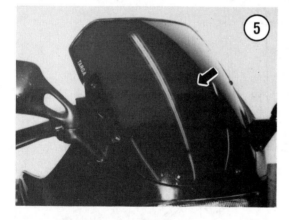

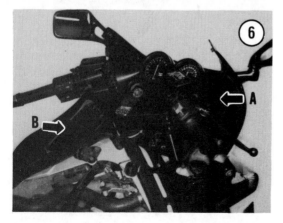

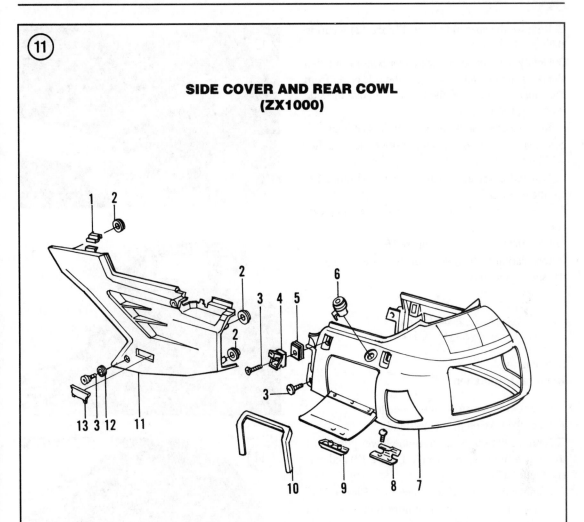

**SIDE COVER AND REAR COWL
(ZX1000)**

1. Clip
2. Rubber damper
3. Screw
4. Hook
5. Damper
6. Tool box lock
7. Rear cowl
8. Hook cover
9. Grip
10. Trim
11. Side cover
12. Rubber damper
13. Trim

2. Remove the special bolt (A, **Figure 12**) securing the side cover.

3. Gently pull out on the side cover bottom and then the front and rear and disengage the side cover from the rubber dampers on the frame. Remove the side cover (B, **Figure 12**).

4. Remove the seat as described in this chapter.

5. Open the tool box lid and remove the 2 screws within the tool box.

6. Disconnect the electrical connectors (**Figure 13**) for the rear lights.

7. Remove the rear screws (**Figure 14**) and side screws (A, **Figure 15**) securing the rear cowl and remove the rear cowl (B, **Figure 15**).

8. Installation is the reverse of these steps. Tighten the screws securely.

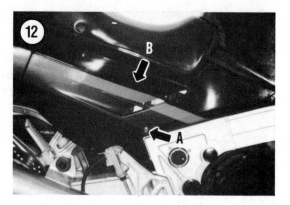

FAIRING
(ZX-11 C1-4)

Side Fairing
Removal/Installation

Refer to **Figure 16** for this procedure.

1. Place the bike on the centerstand.

2. Remove the screw securing the lower portion of the side fairings at the front (A, **Figure 17**) and rear (B, **Figure 17**).

3. Remove the side reflex reflector (C, **Figure 17**).

4. Remove the side fairing mounting bolts and nylon washers and remove the fairing (D, **Figure 17**) from the side of the bike. Don't lose the collar on each lower rear bolt (B, **Figure 17**).

5. Installation is the reverse of these steps. Tighten the screws and bolts securely.

Upper Fairing
Removal/Installation

Refer to **Figure 18** for this procedure.

1. Remove both side fairings as described in this chapter.

2. Remove the screws and nylon washers securing the windshield and remove the windshield (**Figure 19**).

3. Remove the screws securing the front inner cover (**Figure 20**) and remove the cover.

4. Remove the fuel tank (A, **Figure 21**) as described in Chapter Seven in this section of the manual.

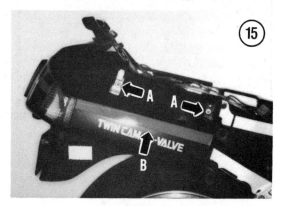

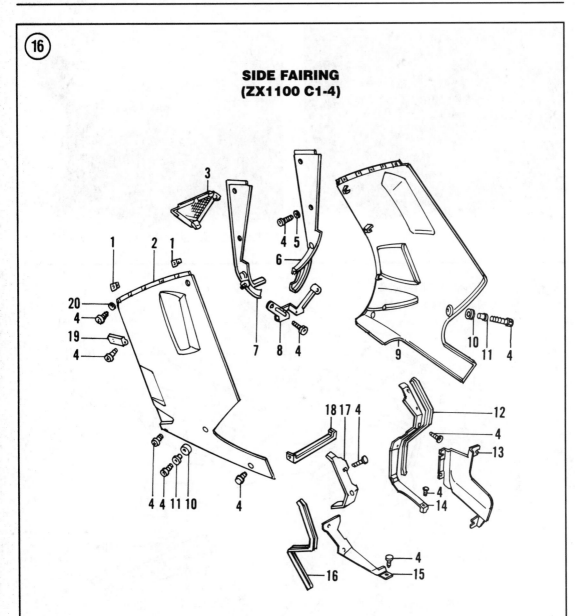

**SIDE FAIRING
(ZX1100 C1-4)**

1. Special nut
2. Left-hand side fairing
3. Screen
4. Screw
5. Nylon washer
6. Right-hand front cowling
7. Left-hand front cowling
8. Front bracket
9. Right-hand side fairing
10. Rubber damper

11. Collar
12. Rubber trim
13. Heat guard
14. Heat guard
15. Heat guard
16. Rubber trim
17. Heat guard
18. Lower bracket
19. Trim
20. Nylon washer

14

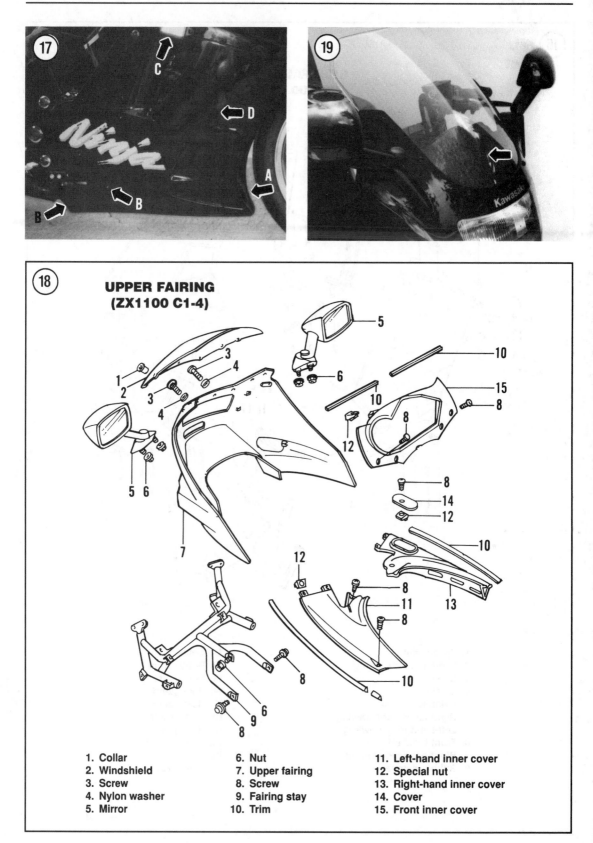

UPPER FAIRING
(ZX1100 C1-4)

1. Collar
2. Windshield
3. Screw
4. Nylon washer
5. Mirror
6. Nut
7. Upper fairing
8. Screw
9. Fairing stay
10. Trim
11. Left-hand inner cover
12. Special nut
13. Right-hand inner cover
14. Cover
15. Front inner cover

5. Remove the screws securing each side inner cover and remove both inner covers (B, **Figure 21**).

6. Remove the nuts securing the rear view mirror on each side and remove both mirrors (**Figure 22**).

7. Disconnect the electrical connector for the front turn signals.

8. Remove the screws and nylon washers securing the upper fairing to the mounting bracket and remove the upper fairing.

9. Installation is the reverse of these steps. Tighten the screws and nuts securely.

Side Cover and Taillight Cover Removal/Installation

Refer to **Figure 23** for this procedure.
1. Place the bike on the centerstand.
2. Remove the seat.

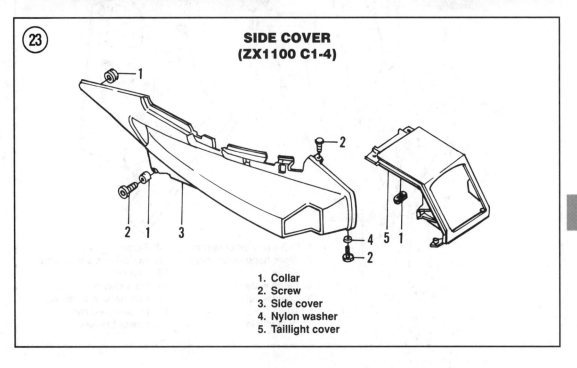

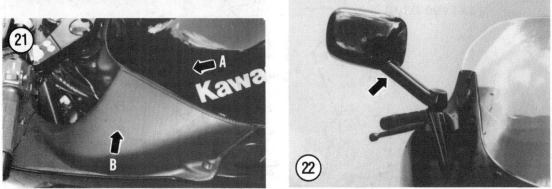

SIDE COVER
(ZX1100 C1-4)

1. Collar
2. Screw
3. Side cover
4. Nylon washer
5. Taillight cover

14

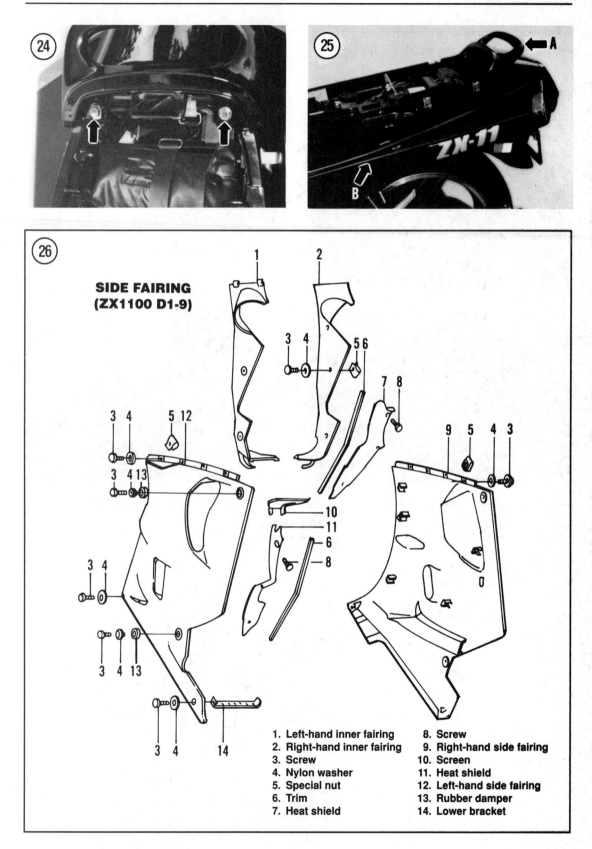

**SIDE FAIRING
(ZX1100 D1-9)**

1. Left-hand inner fairing
2. Right-hand inner fairing
3. Screw
4. Nylon washer
5. Special nut
6. Trim
7. Heat shield
8. Screw
9. Right-hand side fairing
10. Screen
11. Heat shield
12. Left-hand side fairing
13. Rubber damper
14. Lower bracket

3. Remove the bolts (**Figure 24**) securing the passenger grab rail and remove the grab rail (A, **Figure 25**).

4. Remove the screws securing the taillight cover and remove the cover.

5. Disconnect the electrical connector for the rear lights.

6. Remove the screws and nylon washers securing the side cover and remove the side cover (B, **Figure 25**) from each side.

7. Installation is the reverse of these steps. Tighten the screws securely.

FAIRING
(ZX-11 D1-9)

Side Fairing
Removal/Installation

Refer to **Figure 26** for this procedure.

1. Place the bike on the centerstand.

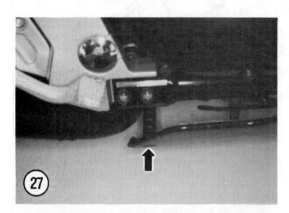

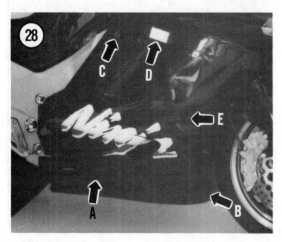

2. Remove the screw securing the lower portion of the side fairings at the rear. Refer to **Figure 27** and A, **Figure 28**.

3. Remove the screw securing the lower portion of the side fairings at the front (B, **Figure 28**).

4. Remove the screw securing the upper portion of the side fairings at the rear (C, **Figure 28**).

5. Remove the side reflex reflector (D, **Figure 28**).

6. Remove the side fairing mounting bolts and nylon washers and remove the fairing (E, **Figure 28**) from the side of the bike.

7. Installation is the reverse of these steps. Tighten the screws and bolts securely.

Upper Fairing
Removal/Installation

Refer to **Figure 29** for this procedure.

1. Remove both side fairings as described in this chapter.

2. Remove the screws and nylon washers securing the windshield and remove the windshield (A, **Figure 30**).

3. Remove the screws and nylon washers securing the front inner cover (A, **Figure 31**) and remove the cover.

4. Remove the fuel tank (A, **Figure 32**) as described in Chapter Seven in this section of the manual.

5. Remove the front screws (B, **Figure 32**) and Allen bolt securing the inner cover and remove the inner cover (B, **Figure 31**).

6. Remove the nuts securing the rear view mirror on each side and remove both mirrors (B, **Figure 30**).

NOTE
Both air ducts and the headlight remain attached to the upper fairing and are removed as one assembly.

7. Loosen the air duct clamp bolts and slide the air inlet rubber tubes off both air ducts. Disconnect the small hoses from the air ducts.

8. Disconnect the electrical connector for the front turn signals and headlight.

9. Remove the screws and nylon washers securing the upper fairing to the mounting bracket and remove the upper fairing assembly.

10. Installation is the reverse of these steps. Tighten the screws and nuts securely.

14

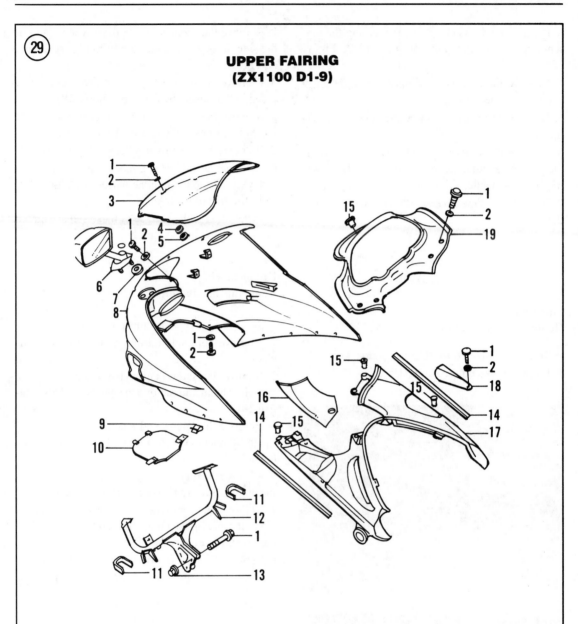

29

UPPER FAIRING
(ZX1100 D1-9)

1. Screw
2. Nylon washer
3. Windshield
4. Washer
5. Nut
6. Mirror
7. Washer
8. Upper fairing
9. Special nut
10. Filler panel
11. Clip
12. Fairing stay
13. Nut
14. Trim
15. Screw
16. Left-hand trim panel
17. Inner cover
18. Right-hand trim panel
19. Front inner cover

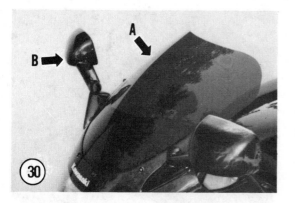

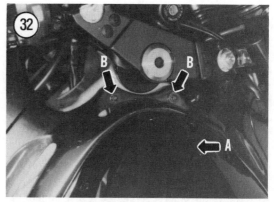

Side Cover and Taillight Cover Removal/Installation

Refer to **Figure 33** for this procedure.

1. Place the bike on the centerstand.

2. Remove the seat.

3. Remove the bolts (**Figure 34**) securing the passenger grab rail and remove the grab rail (A, **Figure 35**).

4. Disconnect the electrical connector for the rear lights.

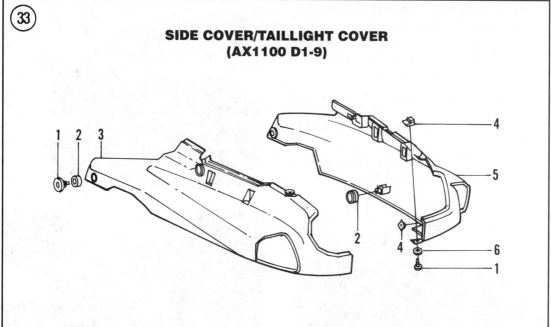

SIDE COVER/TAILLIGHT COVER
(AX1100 D1-9)

1. Screw
2. Rubber damper
3. Left-hand side cover/taillight cover
4. Special nut
5. Right-hand side cover/taillight cover
6. Nylon washer

14

5. Remove the screws and nylon washers securing the side cover on the side (**Figure 36**) and at the rear (B, **Figure 35**). Unhook the right- from the left-hand side covers at the rear and remove the side cover (C, **Figure 35**) from each side.

6. Installation is the reverse of these steps. Tighten the screws securely.

WINDSHIELD

Remove the screws and nylon washers (and well nuts on models so equipped) securing the windshield and remove the windshield (**Figure 37**).

Tighten the screws securely.

REAR FENDER
(ALL MODELS)

Removal/Installation

1. Remove the seat.

2. Remove the side covers and rear cowl as described in this chapter.

3. Remove the bolts securing the rear section of the rear fender and remove it.

4. Remove the battery, ignition igniter and starter relay from the side of the rear fender.

5. Remove the rear brake master cylinder reservoir from the rear fender and move it out of the way. Do not disconnect the brake hose from the reservoir.

6. Remove the junction box from the top of the rear fender.

7. Remove the bolt(s) securing the rear fender to the frame.

8. Make sure all components have been removed from the rear fender and remove it.

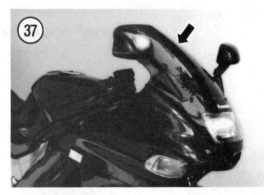

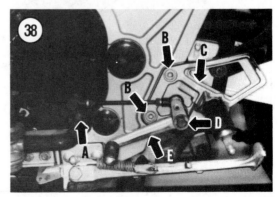

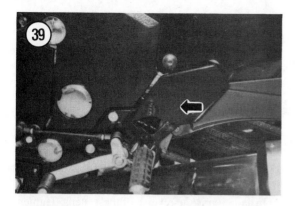

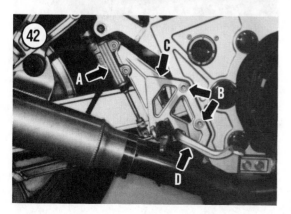

9. Installation is the reverse of these steps. Tighten the bolts securely.

FOOTPEG BRACKETS

**Front Left-hand
Footpeg Bracket
Removal/Installation**

1. Remove the left-hand side cover.

2. Loosen the clamping bolt and disconnect the shift linkage from the shift shaft (A, **Figure 38**).

3. Remove the left-hand footpeg bracket bolts (B, **Figure 38**) and remove the bracket with the shift lever attached. Refer to C, **Figure 38** for ZX-10 models, **Figure 39** for ZX-11 C1-4 or **Figure 40** for ZX-11 D1-9 models.

4. If necessary, remove the circlip and outer washer (D, **Figure 38**) and remove the shift shaft pedal (E, **Figure 38**) from the footpeg bracket. Don't lose the inner washer on the pivot shaft.

5. Installation is the reverse of these steps. Tighten the bolts securely.

**Front Right-hand
Footpeg Bracket
Removal/Installation**

1. Remove the right-hand side cover.

2. Disconnect the rear brake light switch electrical connector.

3. Remove the cotter pin and disconnect the pivot pin (**Figure 41**) from the brake pedal and master cylinder pushrod.

4. Remove the rear brake master cylinder bolts and remove the master cylinder (A, **Figure 42**) from the footpeg bracket.

5. Remove the right-hand footpeg bracket bolts (B, **Figure 42**) and remove the bracket with the rear brake pedal attached. Refer to C, **Figure 42** for ZX-10 models, Figure 43 for ZX-11 C1-4 or **Figure 44** for ZX-11 D1-9 models.

6. If necessary, unhook the pedal return spring, then outer washer and bolt and remove the brake pedal (D, **Figure 42**), bushing and inner washer from the pivot shaft.

7. Installation is the reverse of these steps. Tighten the bolts securely.

14

8. If the brake hose was disconnected, bleed the rear brake as described under *Bleeding The System* in Chapter Twelve in the front section of this manual.

9. Make sure the rear brake works properly. If not, the brake light switch may need adjustment. See Chapter Eight in the front section of this manual.

Rear Footpeg Bracket
Removal/Installation

The right- and left-hand rear footpeg bracket removal is identical.

1. Remove the right- or left-hand side cover (A, **Figure 45**).

2. Remove the cap nut and cup washer (A, **Figure 46**) securing the muffler to the footpeg bracket. Remove the bolt from the backside of the footpeg bracket.

3. Remove the footpeg bracket bolts (B, **Figure 46**) and remove the bracket. Refer to C, **Figure 46** for ZX-10 models or B, **Figure 45** for ZX-11 models. Don't lose the muffler mounting bolt hole rubber bushings.

4. Installation is the reverse of these steps. Tighten the bolts securely.

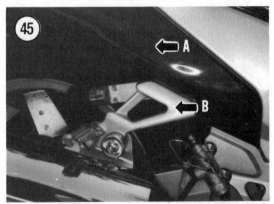

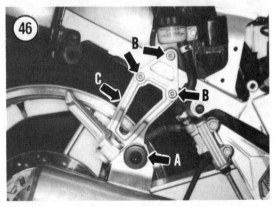

INDEX

15

15

15

1984-1985 KAWASAKI ZX900 A1, A2 (U.S. AND CANADA)

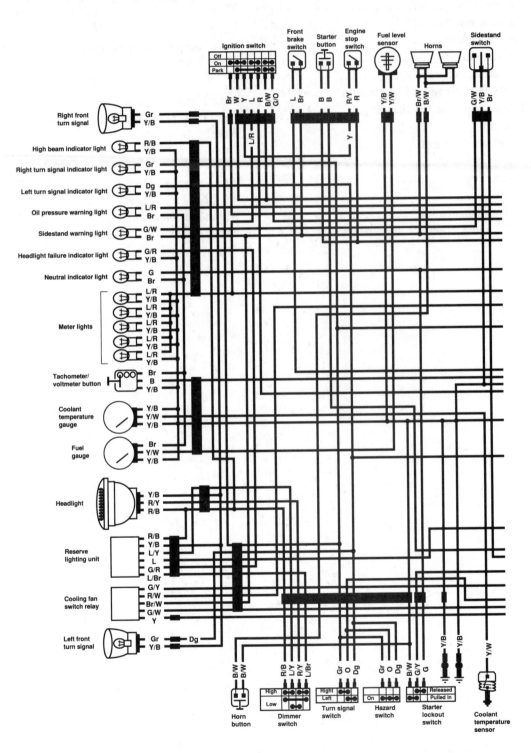

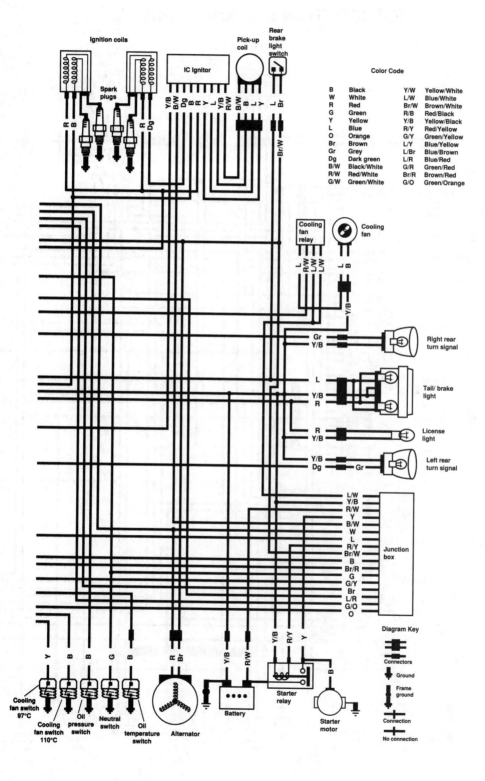

1984-1985 KAWASAKI ZX900 A1, A2
(OTHER THAN U.S. AND CANADA)

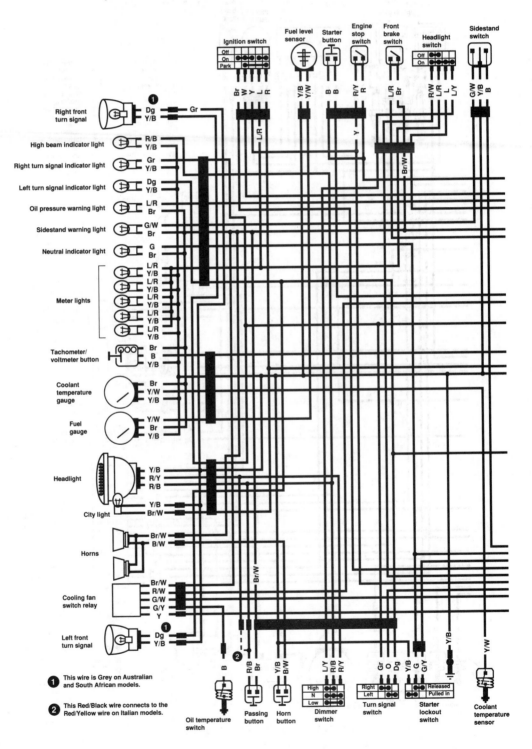

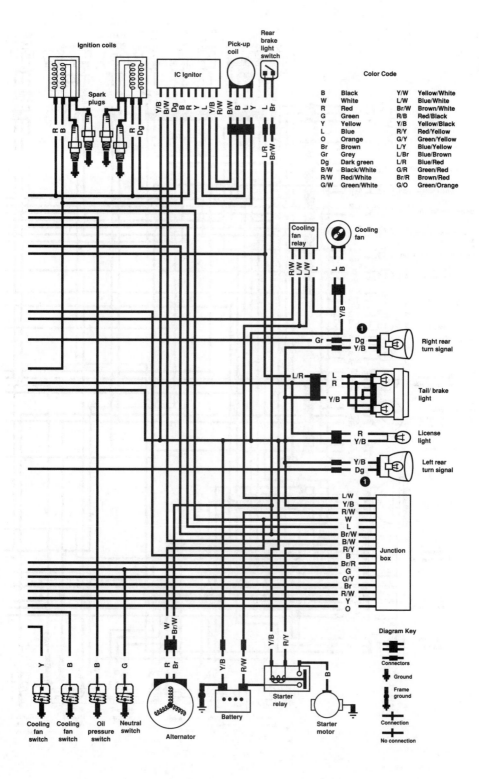

1986 KAWASAKI ZX900 A3 (U.S. AND CANADA)

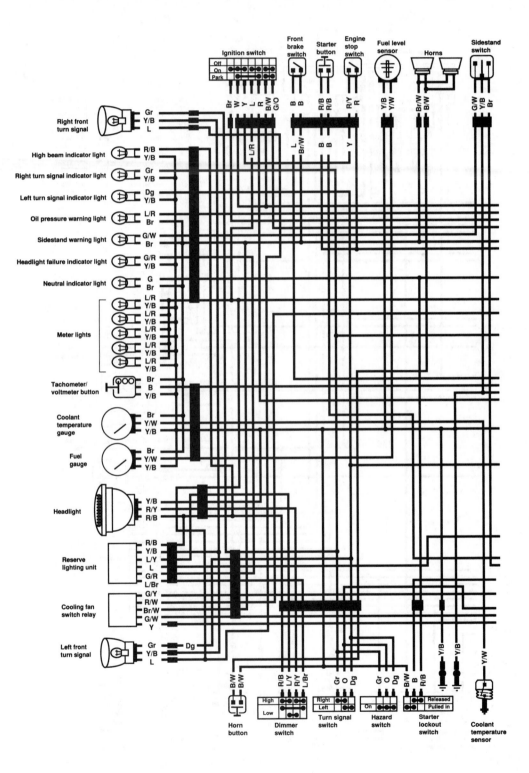

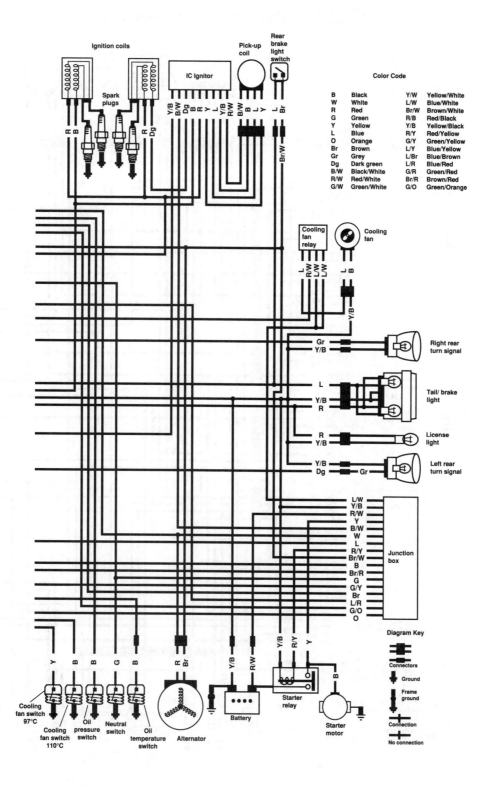

1986 KAWASAKI ZX900 A3
(OTHER THAN U.S. AND CANADA)

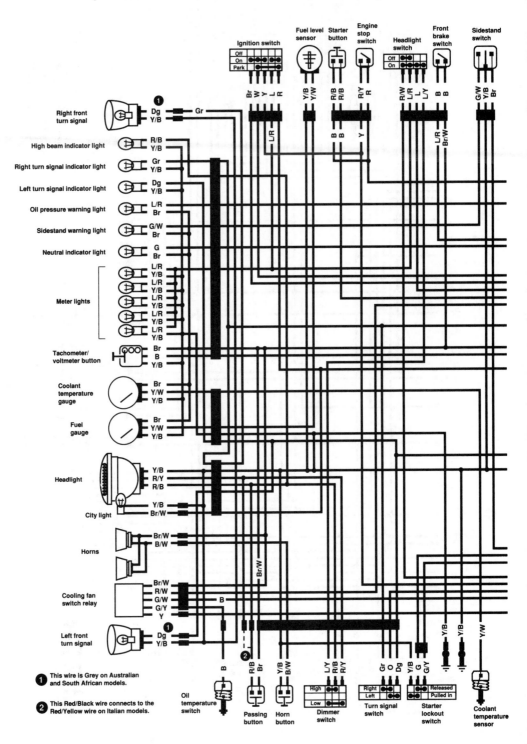

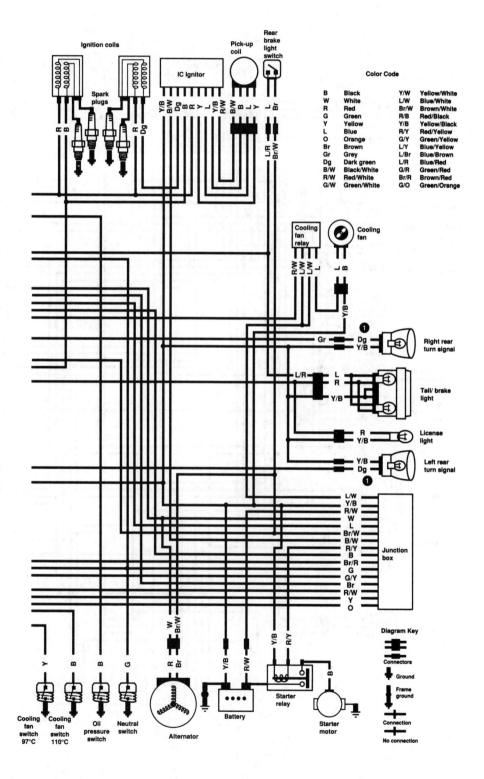

1986-1987 KAWASAKI ZX1000 A1, A2 (U.S. AND CANADA)

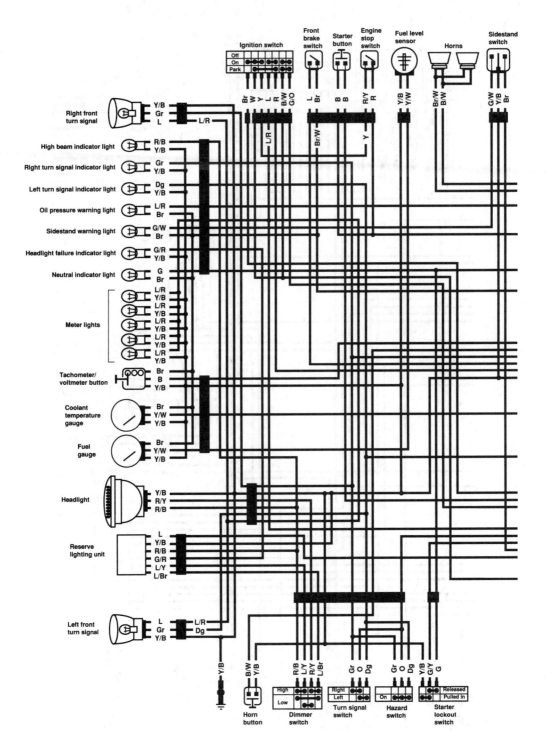

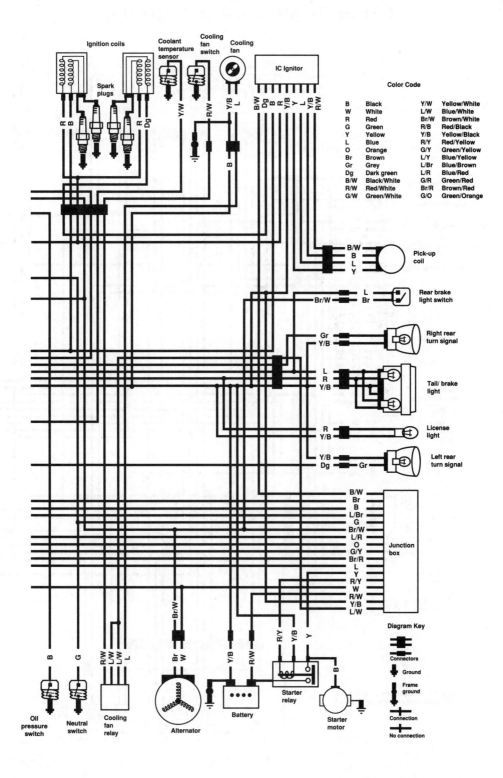

Color Code

B	Black	Y/W	Yellow/White
W	White	L/W	Blue/White
R	Red	Br/W	Brown/White
G	Green	R/B	Red/Black
Y	Yellow	Y/B	Yellow/Black
L	Blue	R/Y	Red/Yellow
O	Orange	G/Y	Green/Yellow
Br	Brown	L/Y	Blue/Yellow
Gr	Grey	L/Br	Blue/Brown
Dg	Dark green	L/R	Blue/Red
B/W	Black/White	G/R	Green/Red
R/W	Red/White	Br/R	Brown/Red
G/W	Green/White	G/O	Green/Orange

Ignition coils

Spark plugs

Coolant temperature sensor

Cooling fan switch

Cooling fan

IC Ignitor

Pick-up coil

Rear brake light switch

Right rear turn signal

Tail/ brake light

License light

Left rear turn signal

Junction box

Oil pressure switch

Neutral switch

Cooling fan relay

Alternator

Battery

Starter relay

Starter motor

Diagram Key

Connectors

Ground

Frame ground

Connection

No connection

16

1986-1987 KAWASAKI ZX1000 A1, A2
(OTHER THAN U.S. AND CANADA)

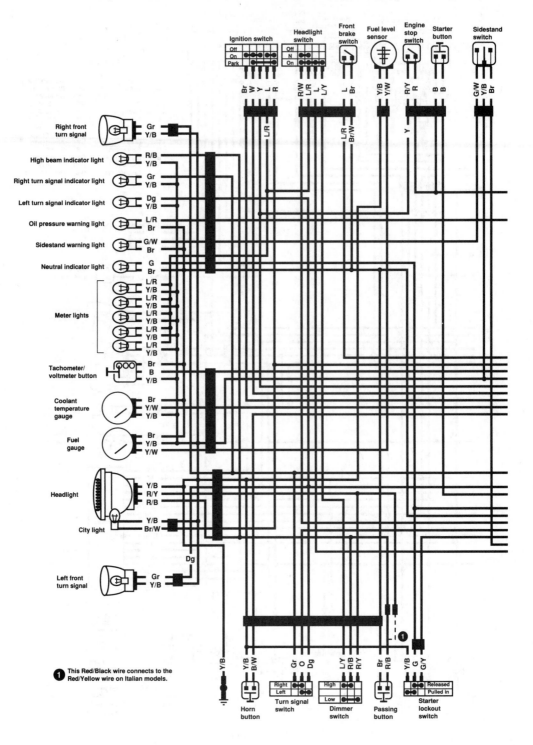

This Red/Black wire connects to the Red/Yellow wire on Italian models.

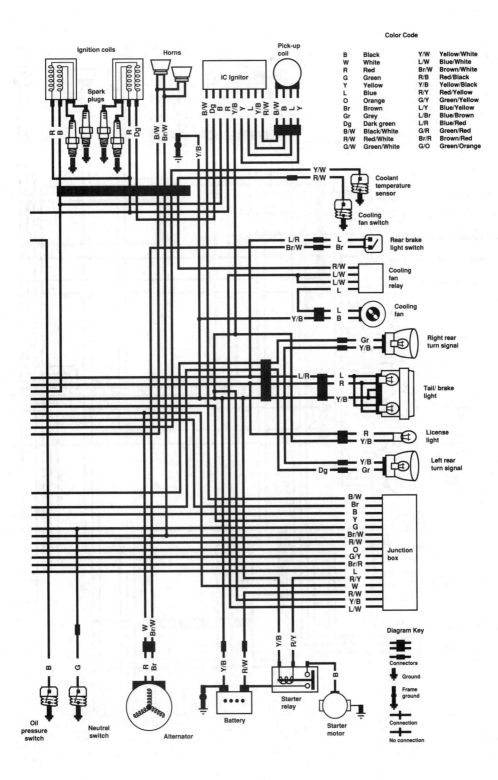

Color Code

B	Black	Y/W	Yellow/White
W	White	L/W	Blue/White
R	Red	Br/W	Brown/White
G	Green	R/B	Red/Black
Y	Yellow	Y/B	Yellow/Black
L	Blue	R/Y	Red/Yellow
O	Orange	G/Y	Green/Yellow
Br	Brown	L/Y	Blue/Yellow
Gr	Grey	L/Br	Blue/Brown
Dg	Dark green	L/R	Blue/Red
B/W	Black/White	G/R	Green/Red
R/W	Red/White	Br/R	Brown/Red
G/W	Green/White	G/O	Green/Orange

Ignition coils

Horns

Pick-up coil

IC Ignitor

Spark plugs

Coolant temperature sensor

Cooling fan switch

Rear brake light switch

Cooling fan relay

Cooling fan

Right rear turn signal

Tail/ brake light

License light

Left rear turn signal

Junction box

Diagram Key

Connectors

Ground

Frame ground

Connection

No connection

Oil pressure switch

Neutral switch

Alternator

Battery

Starter relay

Starter motor

1988-1990 KAWASAKI ZX1000 B1, B2, B3 (U.S. AND CANADA)

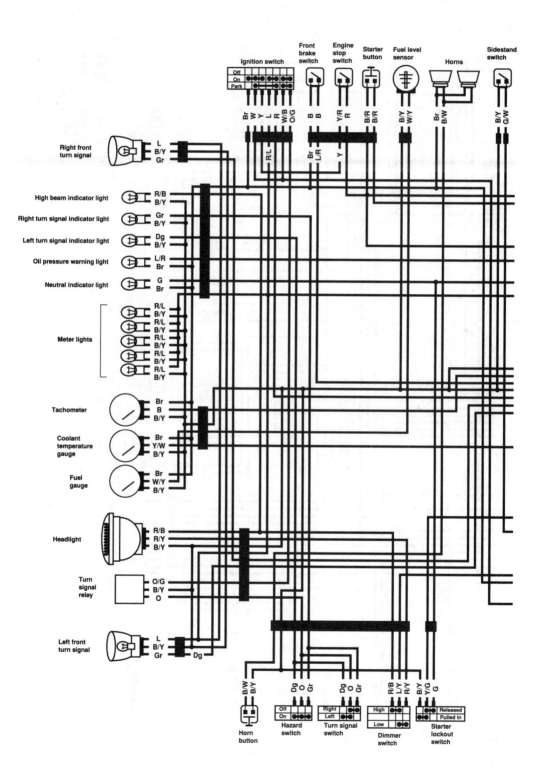

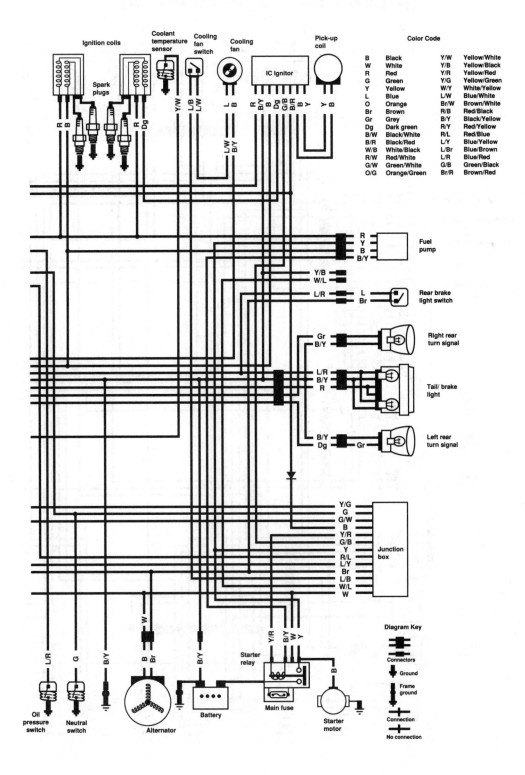

1988-1990 KAWASAKI ZX1000 B1, B2, B3 (OTHER THAN U.S. AND CANADA)

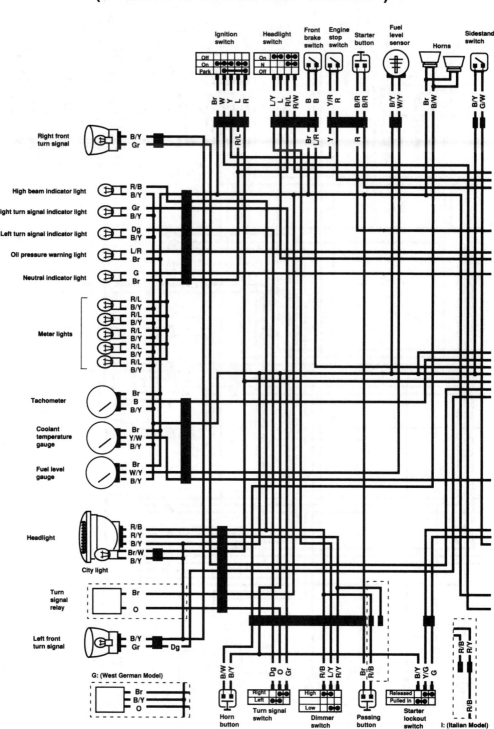

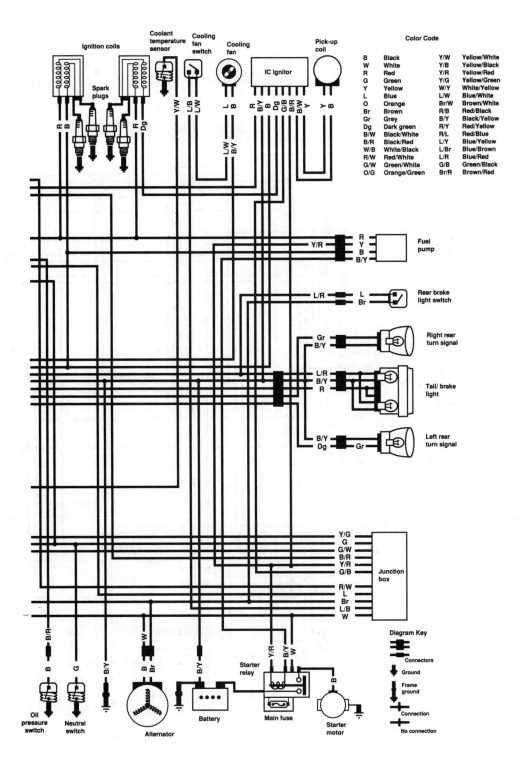

1990-1993 KAWASAKI ZX1100 C1, C2, C3, C4 (U.S. AND CANADA)

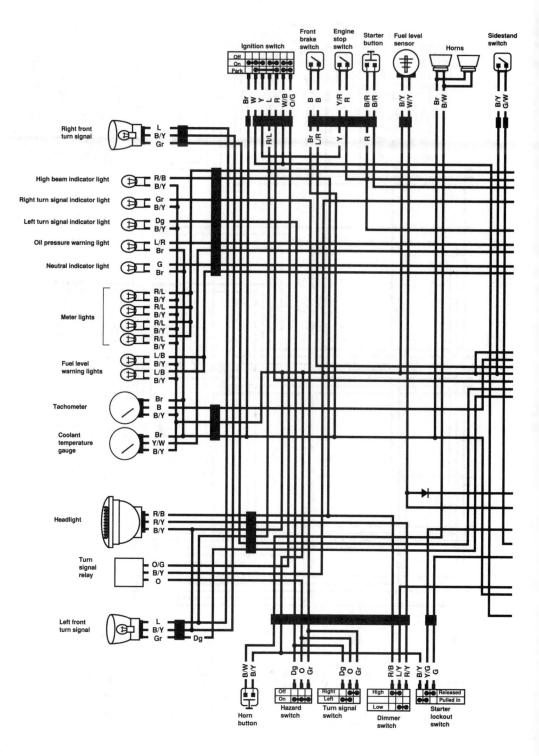

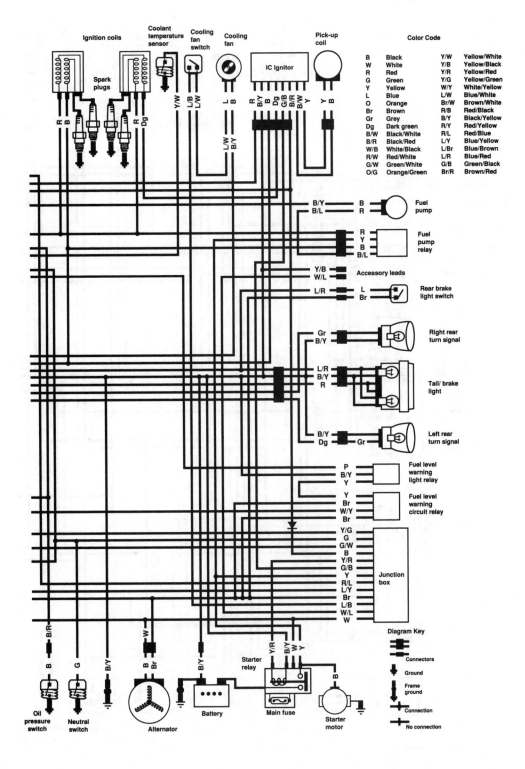

1990-1993 KAWASAKI ZX1100 C1, C2, C3, C4
(OTHER THAN U.S. AND CANADA)

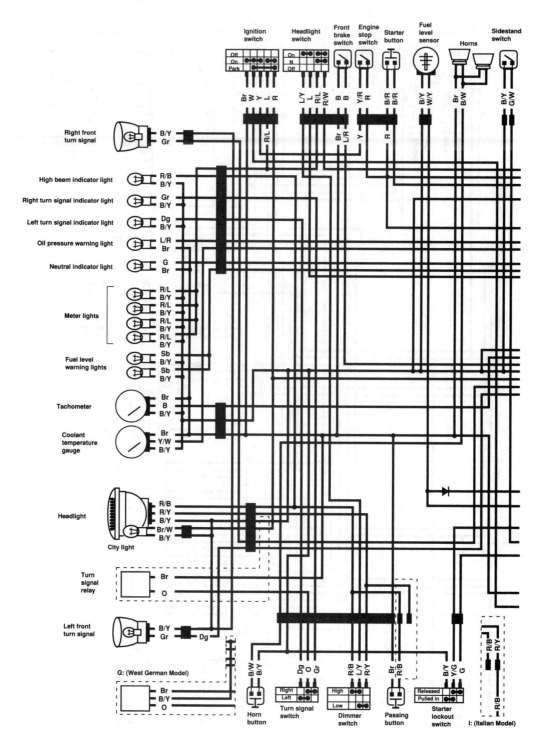

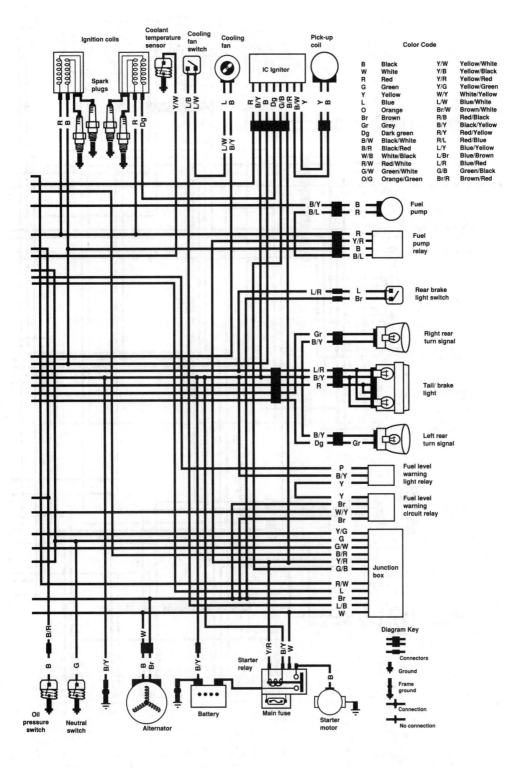

1992 KAWASAKI ZX1100 C3 (AUSTRALIA)

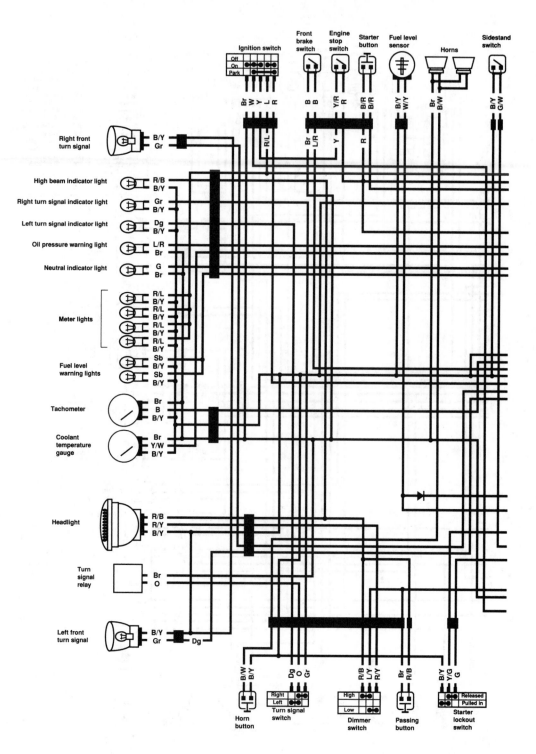

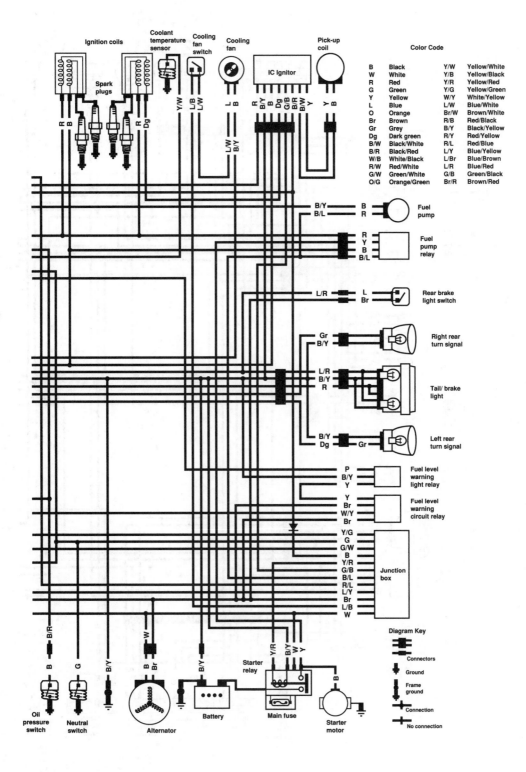

16

1993-1994 KAWASAKI ZX1100 D1-2 (U.S. AND CANADA)

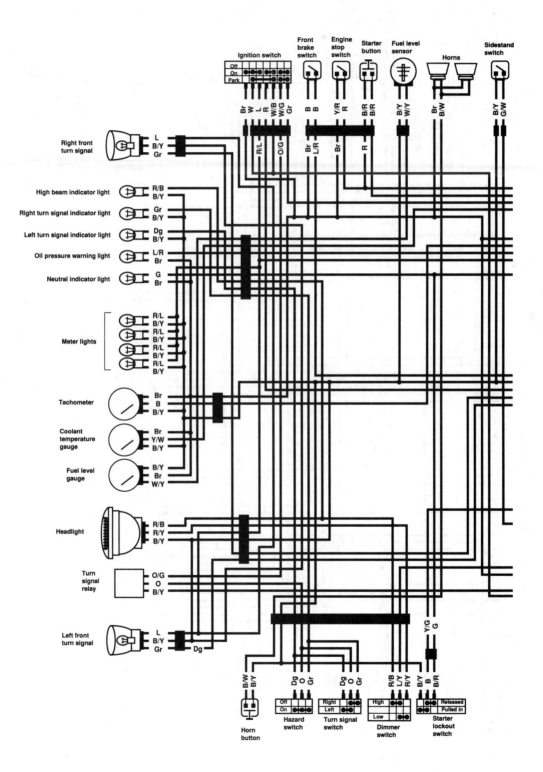

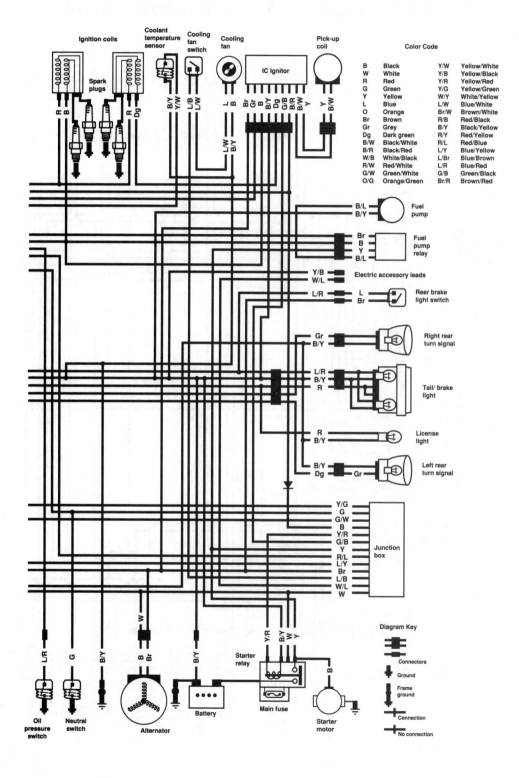

1993-1994 KAWASAKI ZX1100 D1-2
(OTHER THAN U.S., CANADA AND AUSTRALIA)

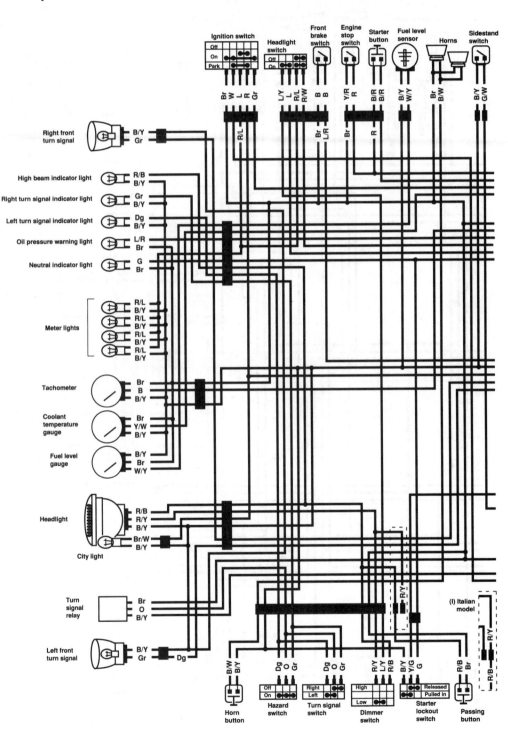

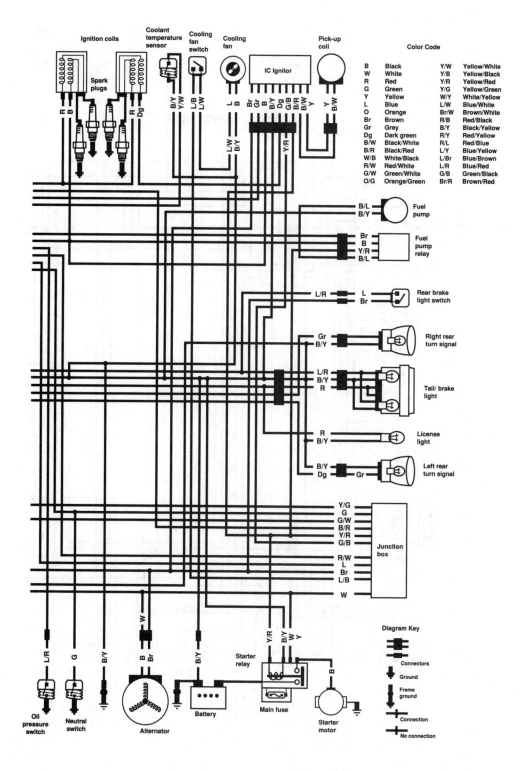

Color Code

B	Black	Y/W	Yellow/White
W	White	Y/B	Yellow/Black
R	Red	Y/R	Yellow/Red
G	Green	Y/G	Yellow/Green
Y	Yellow	W/Y	White/Yellow
L	Blue	L/W	Blue/White
O	Orange	Br/W	Brown/White
Br	Brown	R/B	Red/Black
Gr	Grey	B/Y	Black/Yellow
Dg	Dark green	R/Y	Red/Yellow
B/W	Black/White	R/L	Red/Blue
B/R	Black/Red	L/Y	Blue/Yellow
W/B	White/Black	L/Br	Blue/Brown
R/W	Red/White	L/R	Blue/Red
G/W	Green/White	G/B	Green/Black
O/G	Orange/Green	Br/R	Brown/Red

16

1993-1994 KAWASAKI ZX1100 D1-2 (AUSTRALIA)

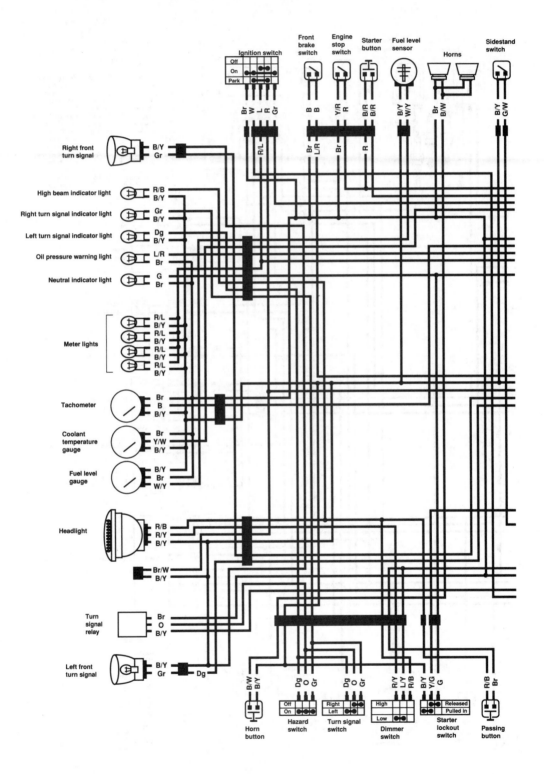

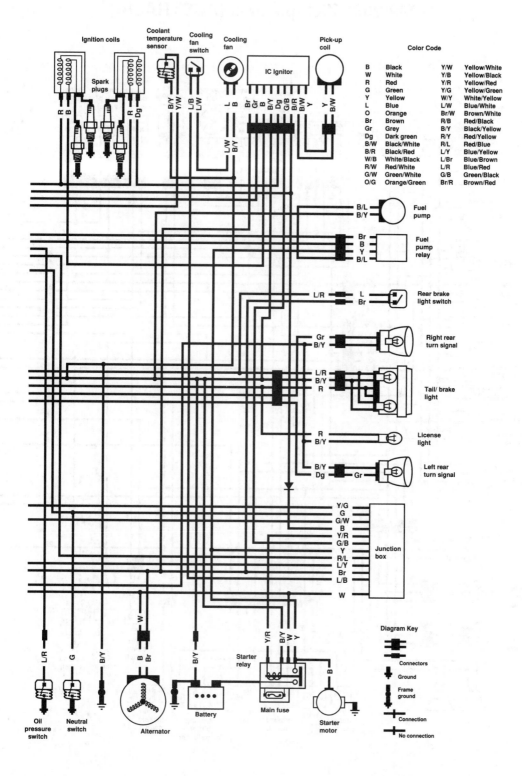

16

1995-2001 ZX1100 D3-9 (U.S. & CANADA)
1999-2001 ZX1100 D7-9 (AUSTRALIA)

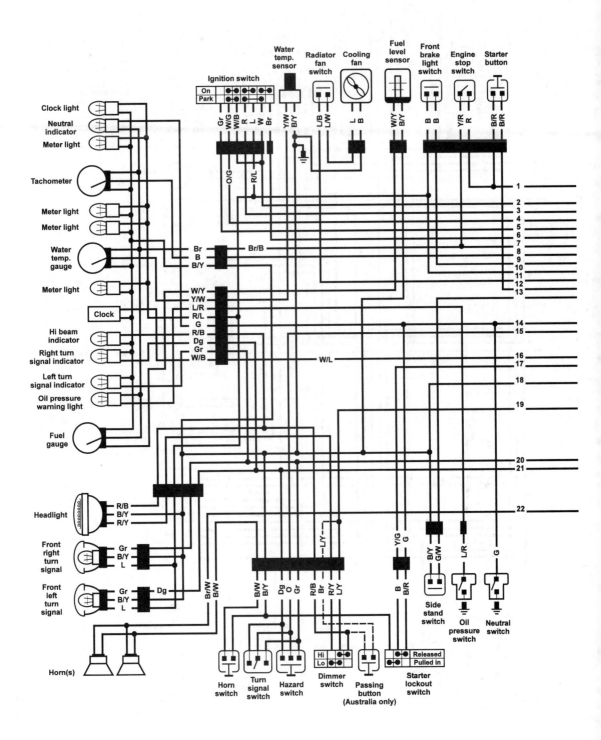

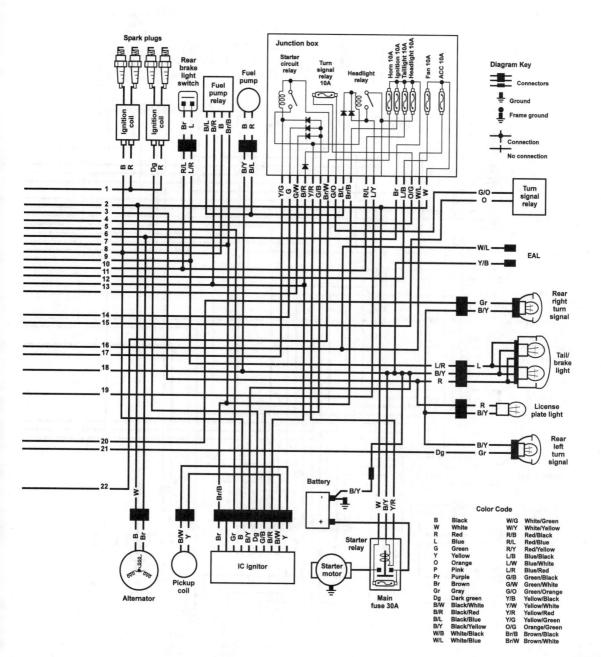

1995-2001 ZX1100 D3-9
(OTHER THAN U.S., CANADA AND AUSTRALIA)

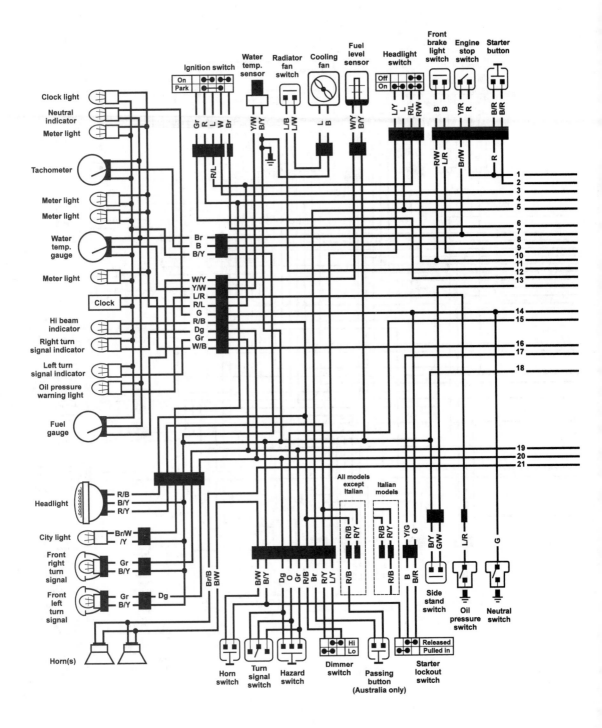

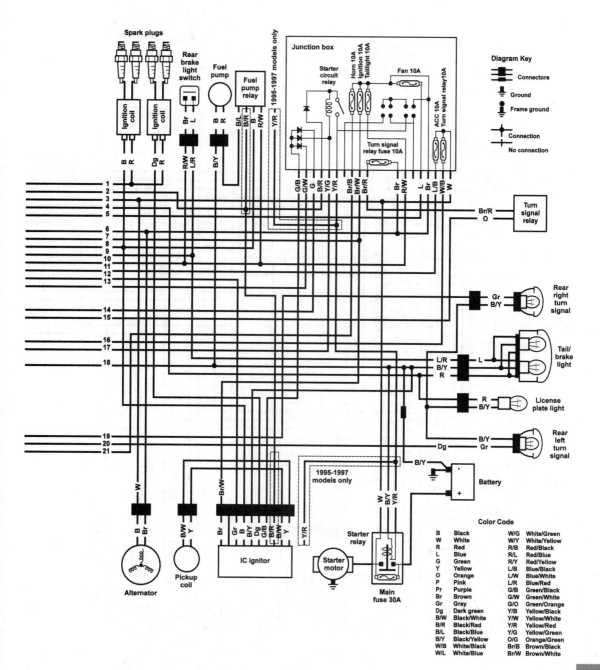

1995-1998 D3-6 ZX1100 (AUSTRALIA)

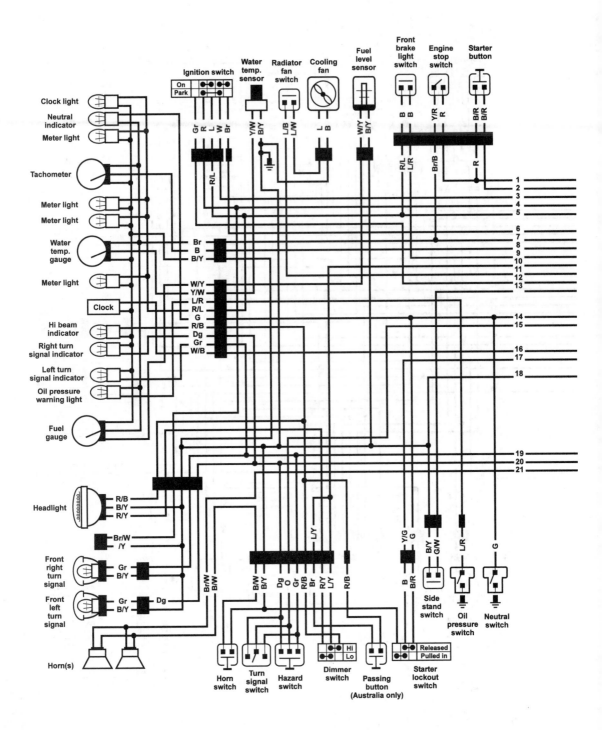

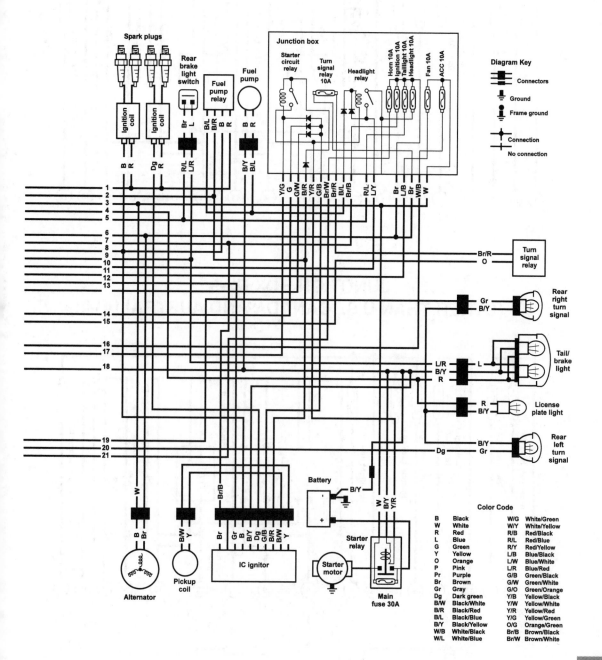

JUNCTION BOX D3-9 (U.S., CANADA AND AUSTRALIA)

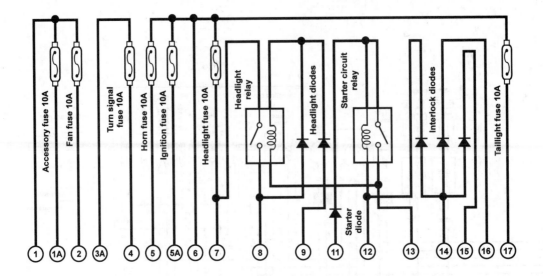

JUNCTION BOX D3-9
(OTHER THAN U.S., CANADA AND AUSTRALIA)

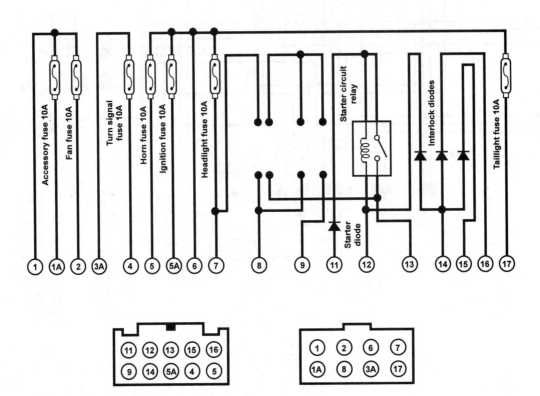